D1195870

THE OXFORD HANDBOOK OF

FREEDOM

THE OXFORD HANDBOOK OF

FREEDOM

Edited by

DAVID SCHMIDTZ

and

CARMEN E. PAVEL

OXFORD
UNIVERSITY PRESS

OXFORD
UNIVERSITY PRESS

Oxford University Press is a department of the University of Oxford. It furthers
the University's objective of excellence in research, scholarship, and education
by publishing worldwide. Oxford is a registered trade mark of Oxford University
Press in the UK and certain other countries.

Published in the United States of America by Oxford University Press
198 Madison Avenue, New York, NY 10016, United States of America.

CIP data is on file at the Library of Congress
ISBN 978–0–19–998942–3

1 3 5 7 9 8 6 4 2
Printed by Sheridan Books, Inc., United States of America

Contents

PART III. INSTITUTIONAL PREREQUISITES OF FREEDOM

PART IV. CULTURE, DIVERSITY, EXPECTATIONS

Contributors

Elizabeth Anderson is Arthur F. Thurnau Professor and John Dewey Distinguished University Professor of Philosophy and Women's Studies at the University of Michigan, Ann Arbor.

Richard J. Arneson is Distinguished Professor of Philosophy at the University of California, San Diego.

Ralf M. Bader is a Fellow of Merton College and an Associate Professor in the Department of Philosophy at the University of Oxford.

David Boonin is Professor of Philosophy and Director of the Center for Values and Social Policy at the University of Colorado, Boulder.

Jason Brennan is the Robert J and Elizabeth Flanagan Family Chair of Strategy, Economics, Ethics, and Public Policy at the McDonough School of Business, Georgetown University.

Piper L. Bringhurst is a PhD Student in Philosophy at the University of Arizona.

Allen Buchanan is James B. Duke Professor of Philosophy and Professor of Law at Duke University.

Mark Bryant Budolfson is Assistant Professor of Philosophy at the University of Vermont.

Kyla Ebels-Duggan is Associate Professor of Philosophy at Northwestern University.

Edward Feser is Associate Professor of Philosophy at Pasadena City College.

Gerald Gaus is the James E. Rogers Professor of Philosophy at the University of Arizona, and Director of the program in Philosophy, Politics, Economics, and Law.

Ryan Patrick Hanley is Mellon Distinguished Professor of Political Science at Marquette University.

Michael Huemer is a Professor of Philosophy at the University of Colorado, Boulder.

David Keyt is Emeritus Professor of Philosophy at the University of Washington and Research Professor at the University of Arizona.

Frank Lovett is Associate Professor of Political Science, and Director of Legal Studies at Washington University in St. Louis.

Fred D. Miller Jr. is Emeritus Professor of Philosophy and Executive Director of the Social Philosophy and Policy Center at Bowling Green State University.

Elijah Millgram is E. E. Ericksen Professor of Philosophy at the University of Utah.

Eddy Nahmias is Professor of Philosophy and Associate Faculty at the Neuroscience Institute at Georgia State University.

Serena Olsaretti is ICREA Research Professor in the Law Department at the Universitat Pompeu Fabra, Barcelona, Spain.

James R. Otteson is Thomas W. Smith Presidential Chair in Business Ethics and Professor of Economics at Wake Forest University.

Orlando Patterson is John Cowles Chair in Sociology at Harvard University.

Carmen E. Pavel is Lecturer in International Politics, King's College, London, author of *Divided Sovereignty: International Institutions and the Limits of State Authority* (Oxford University Press, 2015), and Associate Editor of *Social Philosophy & Policy*.

Mark Pennington is Professor of Political Economy and Public Policy at King's College London, UK.

Daniel C. Russell is Professor of Philosophy at the University of Arizona.

David Schmidtz is Kendrick Professor of Philosophy, Eller Chair of Service-Dominant Logic, editor-in-chief of *Social Philosophy & Policy*, and founding Head of the Department of Political Economy and Moral Science at the University of Arizona.

David Sobel is Irwin and Marjorie Guttag Professor of Ethics and Political Philosophy at Syracuse University.

Hillel Steiner is Emeritus Professor of Political Philosophy at the University of Manchester, UK, and Fellow of the British Academy.

Virgil Henry Storr Research Associate Professor of Economics and Director of Graduate Student Programs in the Mercatus Center at George Mason University.

Steven Wall is Professor of Philosophy at the University of Arizona.

Matt Zwolinski is Professor of Philosophy and Director of the Center for Ethics, Economics, and Public Policy at the University of San Diego.

INTRODUCTION

DAVID SCHMIDTZ AND CARMEN E. PAVEL

NEARLY everyone would say freedom is a good thing, but not everyone who says that would mean the same thing, partly because terms like "freedom" or "liberty" have so many time-honored uses.

We talk of being at liberty to speak our minds, go to college, and open a bank account. Are these the same? We speak of being cancer-free, debt-free, and worry-free. We speak of being free from doubt, free from pressure, and free from prison. Different threats lead us to focus on different meanings. This volume reflects on freedom's various dimensions: legal, cultural, religious, economic, political, and psychological.[1]

We cover current theoretical developments and key historical trends, but not with any particular checklist in mind. Rather, we found interesting authors and turned them loose to do what it was in their veins to do. Fred Miller and David Keyt proposed to write on freedom in the ancient world. Orlando Patterson wanted to reflect on freedom from the remarkable and relatively unknown perspective of renaissance Florence. Elizabeth Anderson wanted to recast the tension between freedom and equality. Eddy Nahmias wanted to discuss free will as a psychological accomplishment.

In many ways, the volume represents the culmination of long histories of asking questions about the nature of freedom. The questions themselves are not free floating, but come out of lived experiences in which individual and groups have been denied freedom in its many forms. Answering questions about freedom appropriately is not merely an academic exercise, but a way of ensuring people's lives go better.

Debates about freedom have traditionally focused on a few central themes. The chapters of this volume continue those debates and sometimes transcend them. One of the main questions scholars of liberty have asked is whether liberty is best thought of as one thing or as several. Is there more than one kind of freedom worth having? Isaiah Berlin's essay "Two Concepts of Liberty" (1958) is well known for valorizing negative freedom, namely the freedom to do as one pleases without interference as a political ideal, and not positive freedom, understood as self-mastery,. Negative freedom involves removing obstacles from people's pursuit of their goals, including obstacles created by government action. Positive freedom involves enabling the capacities that allow people to develop and execute plans of life and exercise self-government individually and collectively. Different strands of liberal thought have taken one or the other as the freedom worthiest of protection in our political life. Several authors in this volume, including Piper Bringhurst, Jerry Gaus, and Ryan Hanley, caution that different ideals of freedom illuminate various features of our relationships to self and others. We misconstrue the complexity of those relationships if we suppose that freedom has only one true nature.

A second set of themes revolve around the trade-off between freedom and other values such as equality. On some conceptions of freedom and equality, such as Ronald Dworkin's, there are no trade-offs because we can define conceptions of freedom and equality that render their combination frictionless. Of course, the point of philosophical analysis is not to define concepts in such a way as to render real tensions invisible, so the real question inevitably remains: are there ideals of freedom, genuinely worth having, that conflict with ideals of equality also genuinely worth having? For example, it is easy to imagine believing in ideals of equal opportunity while also believing that people should be allowed to give their fortunes to their own children if that is what they want to do. But don't widely held ideals of equality and freedom cut against each other in practice? That the answer might be no is intriguing, and Elizabeth Anderson and Hillel Steiner do indeed defend this answer.

A third theme in debates about freedom is how to make freedom institutionally secure, namely how to make sure that all (or enough of) the machinery of modern states is directed at protecting and preserving freedom rather than undermining it. The experience of the last few centuries has taught us important lessons about the cultural and institutional conditions needed to support freedom. Failed socialist experiments, dictatorships, racial and ethnic discrimination, and radical social engineering have exposed faults in our thinking about freedom and its enabling conditions. We have learned that constitutionally defined restraints on government authority are important, as is an ethos among individual citizens committed to fairness and equality for all. We have learned that material wealth can give individuals both the independence and the capacity necessary to resist encroachments into their private lives, while a culture of equality and freedom can sustain a commitment to nondiscriminatory laws and policies and to welfare-enhancing measures for the least fortunate.

One of the last frontiers of research on the institutional conditions of freedom is the recognition that public policy involves trade-offs. Measures to increase freedom along some dimensions can undermine it along others. Sometimes public policies attempt to correct a problem only to create a larger one by introducing new incentives and compliance problems. For example, mandating certain fuel efficiency standards for cars on roads makes them less environmentally damaging but more expensive and thus less accessible to those on the lower ranks of the economic ladder. Subsidizing certain food crops such as corn can create overproduction and waste. Governments and legislatures are not always in a good position to anticipate or find solutions for these new problems. This means that evaluating public policy solutions to common problems of market or government failures involves competencies that cross disciplinary boundaries and combine the best that philosophy, politics, and economics can offer.

Fourth and finally, research has focused on freedom of the will as a precondition for acting freely. How do we reconcile the apparent fact that we live in a world where every event has a cause with the apparent fact that there are agents—beings who have options and who can *will* themselves to act in one way rather than another? In what way can we conceive of ourselves as self-directed?

To be sure, when we treat the paradigm of an event as the transfer of momentum that occurs between billiard balls, free will seems mysterious, even miraculous. Skepticism today is less of a worry about choice being inexplicable in terms of physics, and more of a worry about evidence from psychology to the effect that we are not as autonomous as we think. Even if we set aside metaphysical skepticism, this latter worry remains.

The free will problem today is being reconceived as a problem of twenty-first-century psychology rather than nineteenth-century physics. The issue today is not so much whether there is a level of the material universe that is deterministic but whether we can ever know ourselves well enough to be truly autonomous.

Indeed, insofar as the first key to being self-*directed* is to have a self, it is particularly interesting that recent psychological research suggests that having a self is harder than it looks. Evolutionary psychology suggests that minds are not thoroughly unified things, but rather collections of subroutines that evolved somewhat independently, as responses to specific problems, and that exist as outcomes of separate selection processes. The mind as a whole was not selected for, and exists only in the sense in which societies exist. In other words, there obviously is something to which the term "mind" refers in the same way in which there is something to which the term "society" refers, but that something is not a substance. There is a certain unity to either concept, yet each refers less to a thing we observe than to a chosen way of understanding what we observe.

Neither are minds as transparent as we once thought. We have suspected ever since Freud, and now we have ample reason to believe, that some of what goes on in our minds is hidden from us. Jonathan Haidt likens the human mind to a rider sitting on an elephant. The "rider" is our conscious mind. We think the rider is in charge, but often the elephant has a goal of its own. Moreover, the rider is always constructing a narrative to justify the path he thinks he has chosen. The rider is unaware that the elephant often makes the decisions that matter, and the rider's story is often just a story.

We take it for granted that there are events—let us call them *choices*—that we control in a way that we don't control other events. Moreover, our choices make a difference. Things can go better or worse for us, and how well things go depends partly on what we choose to do. In turn, our ability to *care* about how things go implies that we can have a *reason* for choosing one way rather than another. So do we (ever) control ourselves well enough to do what we have reason to do? Cutting even closer to the philosophical bone, do we control ourselves well enough to believe what we have reason to believe? Suppose not. Suppose our very beliefs are mere events that simply happen to us. Suppose the felt experience of weighing evidence and then deciding what to believe is a delusion.

We take it to be as well confirmed as an empirical fact can be that people (including the psychologists who produced the research we discuss) make choices—including choices about how to weigh experimental evidence—more or less freely. (If we do not choose, more or less freely, whether to view evidence against free will as empirically confirmed, then we have no reason to take our view seriously.) But we say "more or less" for a reason. Schmidtz and Brennan's conjecture, in their *Brief History of Liberty*, is as follows:

(a) Freedom of the will is not an on/off switch, something you either have or not. Instead, real-world freedom of the will is an ongoing achievement.
(b) Freedom of the will is achieved in degrees, and not everyone achieves it to the same degree.
(c) Moreover, not only are some wills more free than others, but any given individual's will is more free in some circumstances than in others.
(d) It is because our culture and system of government affect people's inclination and ability to make up their own minds that the most fascinating and important versions of the free will problem today have more to do with psychology and politics than with metaphysics.

None of the findings emerging from recent decades of experimental psychology underwrites metaphysical skepticism about the general idea of free will, but the results considered together do suggest an alternative (and politically portentous) psychological basis for a measure of skepticism, implying that threats to the autonomy of our wills are various, serious, and real.

1. Conceptual Frames

In contemporary political thought, at least since Isaiah Berlin's famous essay "Two Concepts of Liberty," positive and negative freedom have been defended as competing accounts. Piper Bringhurst and Jerry Gaus believe that this is a mistake. Both have their place in a social world where a person can be free in one way but not in another. Without multiple concepts of freedom, we cannot make sense of the complexity of interpersonal relations, or of the place of related but separate commitments to non-interference, moral responsibility, and moral agency. In this spirit, Bringhurst and Gaus defend an interpretation of positive freedom as reasoned control, then treat this as a necessary condition for the exercise of moral responsibility. They ask whether freedom so conceived is compatible with the general will defined as regulation by a common moral law. Drawing on contemporary accounts of moral and cognitive diversity, they reconsider in a new light Rousseau's old question of whether we can be subjects of the moral law yet remain free.

Elizabeth Anderson likewise takes a hard look at old myths about conceptual conflicts: in her case, freedom and equality. Given that freedom and equality have been used to refer to so many ideas, it cannot be true that the basic concepts necessarily are opposed. Do particular freedoms oppose particular egalitarian ideals in particular times and places? Obviously, freedom and equality can be interpreted in such a way as to manufacture a spurious opposition between them. We might imagine some sort of Nietzschean caricature—freedom to be a blonde beast—that would oppose equality quite generally. Just as easily, we might conceive of forms of equality, such as Kurt Vonnegut's caricature of leveling egalitarianism in *Harrison Bergeron*, that are antithetical to any ideal of freedom that anyone takes seriously. But setting aside caricatures, the question is whether particular freedoms, genuinely worth wanting, are systematically opposed to particular equalities that likewise are genuinely worth wanting.

Perhaps not. Or, if the answer is yes, then the further question would be whether such opposition is necessary or contingent. If the opposition is contingent, then a further question is whether we have it in our power to resolve the opposition, and whether one way of resolving the opposition (if there be more than one) is better than the alternatives. So, for example, we might be able to formulate a conception of freedom along the lines of Herbert Spencer (subsequently embraced by Mill, Rawls, Hart, Feinberg, Steiner, Rawls, and many others): that is, we might formulate an ideal of freedom as involving the maximum liberty compatible with equal liberty for all. Fleshing out that thought without begging the question is notoriously hard work, but the underlying intuition is nonetheless attractive. Interestingly, this extreme commitment to liberty, which defines—and was once a driving force behind—liberalism as a tradition, is at the same time a commitment to a kind of equality: equality as citizens. This was equality before the law.

To pursue this line of thought, we need to tease apart several related distinctions. A freedom to work could be purely *formal* in the sense that there is no law that makes it illegal to work, notwithstanding the fact that such freedom has no material significance unless the work that one is able to do has sufficient value to move an employer to offer one a job. Equality before the law has been attacked as a purely formal notion, but a purely formal notion is not what defenders have defended. No one regards our right to legal representation as adequately respected by the bare fact of there being no law to stop us from hiring a lawyer.

Or a freedom to work could be purely *negative* in the sense that one is at liberty to take a job if one is offered: one has no positive entitlement to be given a job, yet one remains free to work in the sense that there is no duty to avoid competing for jobs with members of a more favored class.

The idea of having a right to say no was a notion of negative freedom, but what liberals demanded in the nineteenth century was a right to say no in a robust, substantive way that would make a tangible difference to life on the ground. The assertion that women have a right to say no to the advances of men without being at risk of being thrown in the "Clink," or that women have a right not to be stopped from opening up a bank account, starting a business, or registering a patent in their own name—these were assertions of negative, but not merely formal, freedom.

Finally, a freedom to work could be a *moral* ideal insofar as an economy is judged by how closely it approximates a state of full employment such that everyone who wants a job has one. This moral ideal is compatible with, but distinct from, a *political* ideal of there being no arbitrary obstacles that prevent would-be employers and employees from arranging to exchange services in whatever way they find mutually agreeable.

The bottom line is that freedom and equality were not conceived as opposing values in the nineteenth century, and the case for seeing them as opposed today should not be accepted uncritically. Anderson's own view is that moderate egalitarianism is compatible with commitments to various core liberties that are well worth wanting.

Hillel Steiner agrees with the general idea that there is no conflict between liberty and equality. Indeed, given his Law of Conservation of Liberty, liberty cannot conflict with anything at all, since the sum total of liberty is a constant.[2] Steiner claims that those who object to egalitarian redistribution on the grounds that it reduces liberty would have to show that net reductions in liberty are real—meaning that the curtailment of liberty for some is greater than the increase in liberty for others. Since the metric for making this calculation is not available, the "net reduction of liberty" argument is a non-starter in Steiner's view. Of course, this is not to deny that various scholars focus instead on what is in fact at stake, and on what can in fact be lost in the course of egalitarian redistribution. If real worries cannot be expressed in terms of what Steiner calls liberty, that does not make real worries go away.

So, for example, consider Hayek's worry about the "road to serfdom." Hayek would have agreed with Anderson (and perhaps with Steiner too) that conceptual conflict (or impossibility thereof, for that matter) is not worth discussing. He had no problem with equality per se. What he deplored is what actually happens when we create institutions to try to guarantee that society unfolds along egalitarian lines. Are those institutions used for the purpose that their creators had in mind? Hayek's observation is that in practice such institutions are used to further the purposes of whichever candidate wants power badly enough to do whatever it takes to win the battle to acquire it.

What opposes liberty—that is, the liberty that is very much at stake in the empirical world—is not equality so much as concentrated power that we create *in the name* of equality. This is the real worry. Acknowledging this reality does not settle what to do. It does not clinch the case for a minimal state. It does not end the conversation or make further debate unnecessary. Still, we do well to acknowledge that the relentlessly predictable corruption of power—what political philosophy now seems largely to ignore—is the real worry.

Freedom from interference can be compared and contrasted to freedom from domination. Frank Lovett defends the republican account of freedom and shows why freedom as non-domination can contribute to a distinctive understanding of political freedom. Domination is an ability to act, and there is a special wrong in dominating as opposed to mere interfering. A benevolent despot who does not interfere with his subjects nonetheless still makes them unfree, Lovett claims. By contrast, a democratic government may interfere with subjects' choices without making them unfree. The difference is that subjects can determine the manner and extent of interference in the second case, but cannot in the first. Political freedom must consist in being able to limit the (corruptible) power of some to frustrate and dominate the choices of others.

Debates concerning freedom do not always distinguish between moralized and non-moralized conceptions of freedom. Is freedom merely a descriptive concept, such that any restriction counts as interference and is thus prima facie problematic? Or should we distinguish liberty from license, moralizing liberty by definition, so that we can say that only wrongful restrictions limit true freedom? Ralf Bader defends a rights-based moralized conception of freedom to determine which courses of action an agent can be free to perform, and which obstacles count as constraints. To Bader, this is the only way to connect our normative concerns to a conception of freedom; normative significance has to be built into freedom by definition; the connection cannot be an empirical discovery.

Liberalism was once a revolutionary idea: the idea that kings don't own their subjects. Subjects own themselves. It took further revolutionary moments to establish that men cannot own other men, and that men cannot own their wives. It takes even further moments for people to realize that, among fellow citizens, owning *oneself* means being treated as an equal before the law.

So, Dan Russell says, if you have a right to interfere with your neighbor, then your neighbor has that same right to interfere with you. That assumption of symmetry is another assumption at the heart of liberal equality construed as equality before the law. Society does not divide into classes when it comes to the rights that go with being a fellow citizen. The idea also implicitly captures the point of modesty when it comes to asserting rights. Dan Russell likewise is careful to avoid even a whiff of the "atomism" that liberalism's critics sometimes are too eager to see as one of liberalism's core features.

If we speak of people as if they were pieces of property owned by themselves, are we showing respect for them or disrespect? One place to start is to point out that respect for persons begins with acknowledging a right to say no. Having a right to say no to proposals to use one's body or mind in a particular way marks a person as a self-owner. Indeed, this right to say no arguably is precisely what marks a person as a person. Someone has a right to decide what kind of life one's self should be living. The right to say no to other people's will locates that right in oneself rather than in someone else, and is the political foundation of anything like the liberal commitment to letting people live lives of their own. To be sure, those who attack what they call self-ownership may have—must have—something else in mind. In any case, the right to say no construed in this way is fundamental. Many other topics are worth talking about, but this understanding of self-ownership underlies concepts of ownership in general, freedom in general, individual rights in general, and liberalism in general.

Ownership is related to jurisdiction. It is the right to make the call—to decide whether the answer is yes or no. So, there is something odd in asserting that the *world* owns, say, mineral rights. People say such things without specifying who will make the actual decisions. The idea is not really about ownership per se so much as fiduciary responsibility. When theorists say that the world owns the minerals, they are saying that those who are responsible for managing the minerals ought to manage them in the best interest of the world. That makes sense. Or at least, that is the least controversial interpretation of what they are saying. But there will, after all, be a decision maker who makes the call, and effective jurisdiction resides in that person (or body of persons).

People will have different views as well about what justifies treating a resource management question as falling within one person's jurisdiction rather than another's. Is the idea that the right to say no should be understood in whatever way is to the greatest advantage of the least advantaged? If so, then seeing which way of assigning rights best tracks that idea will be a complex question whose answer will not be timeless. In a given time and place, are people more concerned about water pollution or water shortage? Are they concerned with whether their descendants will be able to collect royalties two hundred years from now, or will be held liable for damages two hundred years from now? Does it matter whether the right to post a *No Trespassing* sign extends to the heavens? What happens when it suddenly matters a great deal, after not having mattered for thousands of years?

Our mutual understandings of jurisdiction are, in the real world, sensitive to questions about what our understanding needs to be in order for us to be good neighbors. Over the course of centuries, the contours of that understanding will change. It will matter whether our nearest neighbor lives five miles away, or five meters. Still, the point is for us to be able to form mutual expectations: we need to know what to expect from each other. Yet we need freedom to do the unexpected too.

Analogously, in the realm of collective decision-making, we need to be able to make democratic decisions, but we also need to be able to count on making those decisions within a constitutional framework. We are not a constitutional democracy unless some things are off the table; for example, we do not get to vote on whether to deprive a particular minority of the right to vote. The constitutional part of constitutional democracy turns democracy into something that a community of free citizens, responsible for themselves and accountable to each other, can afford. By virtue of the constitutional part of constitutional democracy, citizens can count on their status as citizens not being up for grabs every time someone is in a position to bring a motion to a vote.

When people speak of civil liberties or call themselves civil libertarians, they usually have particular rights in mind: rights of privacy, of free speech, of assembly, of lifestyle choice, of control over sexual conduct, voting rights, or legal rights such as the right to a fair trial. Some elements of the rule of law are preconditions of civil liberty, and there will never be a once-and-for-all victory for the rule of law. Even today, civil liberties remain precarious for many. We still have a long way to go; perhaps we always will. Honestly determining where we are and where we still need to go requires not only that we acknowledge real problems, but also that we recognize real solutions and real progress already made.

We might offer an analogy that illustrates central points of several of these essays; namely, claiming that one has jurisdiction is like claiming that one has a green light, which goes hand in hand with claiming that others have a red light. To assert rights is thus to declare oneself willing to impose a cost on fellow citizens. If everyone takes their turn facing red and green lights, that is a profoundly egalitarian institution even though there will never be a snapshot in which everyone has a green light at the same time, and therefore there will never be a snapshot in which people *look* equal. But an institutional framework where everyone gets a turn is not only an egalitarian but also a liberal institution—so long as we are careful to install traffic lights only where their net effect is to put everyone in a better position to pursue destinations of their own choosing while staying out of each other's way. The traffic metaphor is a way of illustrating a way of living together that always looks like a zero-sum game in the snapshot, but nevertheless tends to be mutually advantageous when we look at the dynamics.

It is understood that people living ordinary lives in close proximity are bound to be somewhat of a nuisance to each other. We need boundaries, but we also need to understand that boundaries cannot solve all of our problems. We also need to understand ways in which being a good neighbor requires more than a good fence. Our jurisdictions as self-owners must be respected, but that respect cannot be properly understood apart from a conception of what it means for neighbors to be considerate. Thus, whether you can take my kidney is squarely within my jurisdiction, but whether you can exhale (thereby releasing greenhouse gases into the atmosphere that we share) is not. David Sobel believes questions such as these, at the edge of the concept of self-ownership, reveal some of its limits. The concept of self-ownership does not yield fine-grained distinctions between my neighbor taking my kidney without permission versus my neighbor reading my newspaper without permission. Sobel invites us to think about whether there are answers to these questions that preserve the strong deontological and morally plausible features of self-ownership while dispensing with its implausible implications.

If there is no theoretical solution, however, that may be because there is no theoretical problem. I have a right to forbid your driving by my house at a hundred miles per hour, but no right to forbid your driving by my house at twenty miles per hour. Yet such lines are never drawn by a philosophical principle. I find out what I have a right to do by checking facts about the street on which I live, not by coming up with a philosophical argument. To determine the nature and limits of my jurisdiction, I need to track lines drawn by historically situated decision makers specifying the details of what citizens have a right to expect from each other in particular communities. Communities need to draw lines. Philosophy can tell them that much. Philosophy also can indicate rough parameters. Is taking organs without permission out of bounds? Yes, because neighbors can't afford neighbors having that right. Is exhaling in bounds? Yes, because neighbors can't afford *not* having that right. Such sensibility is the rough guidance that a community's decision makers need in order to have parameters within which to draw a line. The line they draw becomes the line that neighbors have a right to forbid each other to cross. What makes the line more precise over time is not more precise arguments but rather the history of conflict resolution. Neighbors take neighbors to court so that they can ask a judge to rule on whether certain kinds of nuisance count as crossing the line. Judges rule, the line becomes sharper, and typically that settles the matter. Philosophy identifies broad limits of what it is reasonable to expect from neighbors. And that, in turn, is the limit of what it is reasonable to expect from philosophy.

2. HISTORICAL FRAMES

Philosophers tend to know the history of ideas better than they know history as such, yet the latter can be more illuminating. So, for example, if you wonder why Adam Smith, an advocate of free trade, also favored public education, the answer could lie more in Smith's situated historical experience than in his philosophy. There is a freshness and sometimes a deeper truth in thinking a little less about the texts and a little more about the times that produce the texts.

To be sure, the history of freedom precedes the history of ideas about freedom.[3] It was around forty thousand years ago that *Homo sapiens* became the wisest of primates, when we learned to make deals with strangers. Many steps we've made in our social evolution involved expanding the spheres of mutually advantageous commerce. Paradoxically, we are inclined, perhaps even biologically programmed, to see commerce as a zero-sum game: that is, we see people who profit by selling us food or tools as getting rich at our expense. Eons ago, though, brave souls began to imagine what human beings could do, and saw that the key to a better life was trade. Thus began our liberation from the brutality of life as cave-dwellers.

As we spread, our closest cousins, the Neanderthals, went extinct. Why? Recent research speculates that the ascent of *H. sapiens* was driven by something relatively mundane: an evolving propensity to truck and barter.[4] Thus Horan, Bulte, and Shogren's explanation of why Neanderthals disappeared and modern humans flourished is that the former were not entrepreneurs. Cultural cross-fertilization did not occur. By contrast, modern humans evidently practiced some rudimentary division of labor almost from the start, engaging in both intra- and inter-group trade (Horan, Bulte, and Shogren, 2005: 5). They were innovators, pushing the boundaries of their negative liberty in ways that ended up raising the ceiling of the positive liberty for all.

Our authors take up the history of freedom from the ancient world onward, starting with essays on Platonic and Aristotelian freedom, respectively, by noted ancient philosophers Fred Miller and David Keyt. Miller traces the development of the concept of political freedom in Plato's thought, and argues that despite limitations, Platonic ideas of freedom have contributed to many innovations in our political vocabulary and practice. For example, Keyt shows that Aristotle builds on the Platonic notion of "aristocratic freedom" as an ideal of individual freedom according to which reason rules desire. Individual freedom is thus for Aristotle both a psychological and an intellectual accomplishment. Orlando Patterson has contributed substantially to our understanding of freedom in both ancient and modern worlds. For this volume, he chose to write on the understudied topic of slavery in the Florentine Renaissance. Patterson shows that the fact that Florence was a fountain of freedom in Renaissance Italy was a product both of elite discourse and of the practical struggles against the use and abuse of power by ordinary people. Covering everything in between would be, of course, a thankless and impossible task, but Ed Feser helps to bridge the gap with a wide-ranging essay on freedom in the Scholastic era. He shows that although philosophical ideas of freedom in Scholastic thought occupy somewhat of a middle ground between classical liberal and authoritarian positions, the Scholastics were more friendly to freedom-preserving institutions such as democracy, the rule of law, and the market economy than it is commonly appreciated.

Ryan Hanley chose to continue a theme from the first part of the handbook and write on the ways in which for Enlightenment thinkers such as Smith, Rousseau, and Kant, positive and negative liberty were complementary rather than contradictory. For these thinkers, freedom did not rest solely on political institutions, but on the cultivation of virtues of personal responsibility enabling individuals to exercise and support political freedom. Hanley shows that Smith, Rousseau, and Kant saw moral freedom as indispensable to political freedom. Jim Otteson wrote on how Adam Smith treated the line between justice and beneficence and how Smith thought that drawing it in one place rather than another would bear on rationales for coercion. Otteson argues that Adam Smith developed his own version of "libertarian paternalism" in trying to defend people's freedom of choice on the one hand but help them make better choices on the other. Indeed, Otteson claims that by learning from Smith, we can avoid problems that plague more recent defenses of libertarian paternalism by Richard H. Thaler and Cass R. Sunstein (Sunstein and Thaler, 2009).

3. INSTITUTIONAL PREREQUISITES OF FREEDOM

Progress in our understanding of freedom is possible, and nowhere is progress better demonstrated than in the great strides various societies have made in creating the institutional conditions that protect freedom. The fact that two recent institutional artefacts, the rule of law and constitutional restraints on majority rule, contribute to political regimes where freedom receives, on balance, better protection, is now part of conventional wisdom. This conventional wisdom is also supported empirically. Countries in transition to democratic regimes are more likely to revert to authoritarianism without constitutional separation of powers and effective accountability of political officials through law (Collier, 2007: 65–75).

Against this background, few doubt that constitutions can carry the weight they are expected to, and critics of constitutional restraints complain that they work too well at restricting democratic decision-making (Levinson, 2008). But Michael Huemer, breaking ranks with both the critics and conventional wisdom, argues that constitutions in fact work much less well than we think. Huemer believes that the case of the United States, often celebrated as one of the early and successful adopters of a constitution, shows just how much the constitution has failed to restrain government expansion beyond areas explicitly approved in the constitutional text. He estimates that most of the activities of the U.S. government are not constitutional. The intention behind this criticism is not to damn the project of building constitutional constraints as such. Indeed, the constitution has been successful in some areas and failure is not inevitable. Therefore, Huemer proposes various measures to counteract the weaknesses of existing constitutional restraints.

The evolution of the rule of law provided the essential foundation for the explosive economic progress of recent centuries that liberated the West from extreme poverty. Institutions facilitate coordination. Liberal institutions are those that aspire to (literally as well as metaphorically) manage traffic without assuming that everyone ought to have a common destination. As Steve Wall frames the issue, liberal institutions regard citizens as planners, and aim to put people in a position to make and pursue plans, and to adjust to each other's plans in such a way as to minimize conflict and take advantage of potential synergy.

The insight about the conditions of success for constitutional restraints feeds well into an instrumental justification of the rule of law. According to Wall, the core idea of the rule of law is that holders of political and legal office should be constrained to exercise power in ways that are efficacious, nonarbitrary, and predictable. Effective legal constraints on political power are important because they create the conditions in which individuals can plan their lives. Wall draws a close connection between freedom and autonomy, understood as the capacity to reflect on and choose personal projects and commitments that one reflectively endorses as one's own. Planning agency is necessary for autonomy, and planning agency is fostered and enhanced by an environment in which the rules are predictable and enforced evenly and effectively. If constitutions, as part of the bigger arsenal of rule-of-law protections, do not work well, Wall provides additional reasons for worrying about their failures.

Institutions can be better or worse at protecting freedom. Jason Brennan asks where we should place democracies on the continuum from best to worst. There are strong empirical correlations between democracy as a mode of decision-making and civil, political, and economic liberties. But this is where, in Brennan's view, the correlation ends. There is no additional increment of freedom—understood as autonomy or non-domination—simply by virtue of participating in democratic processes as such. Collective decision-making adds neither to our capacity to express ourselves, nor to our ability to protect ourselves from those who wish to control us.

Yet there may be value in understanding democratic decision-making as an important kind of freedom when the alternative is the imposition of rules from the outside. Proponents of the "all affected interests" principle raise the spectrum of precisely this kind of threat when they argue that political decisions should be made by those most likely to be affected by them. This would entail in many instances that decisions are made by groups much larger than existing political communities, when it is likely that such groups would be affected by the decisions taken within traditional political communities. On some proposals all decisions should be made by a global demos. Carmen Pavel argues that the principle of "all affected interests" is not fit for assigning rights of political participation. We are better advised to think in terms of ideals of democratic self-rule and individual rights, which have been a force both for improving the condition of many historically marginalized groups, and for resisting encroachments on the political autonomy of groups from outside.

Freedom can be enhanced or thwarted not only by the most general forms of decision-making but also by granular policy decisions made by various public agencies in the normal course of providing public goods and avoiding public bads. The two remaining essays in this section shed light on another important insight of recent scholarship: the complexity of public policy processes means that goals will not always translate into results. Mark Pennington and Mark Budolfson explain that understanding when this is likely to happen, and evaluating different alternatives of public and private regulation and the incentives and compliance problems they generate, places governments and legislatures in a better position to recognize when regulation protects or undermines freedom. If both market failures and government failures are real problems that we try to avoid, more regulation is not always better. Solving social dilemmas such as tragedy-of-the-commons problems often involves a mix of private and private regulation, but importantly, the mix will vary depending on the particular features of commons and the group trying to solve it. This has been one of the great insights of Elinor Ostrom (Ostrom, 1990). Pennington and Budolfson incorporate it into ongoing debates about the nature of freedom-preserving public policies.

The phrase "market failure" describes outcomes where not all potential gains from trade have been realized. Institutional economists such as Harold Demsetz have developed tools for measuring market success by looking at what comparative institutional frames do to minimize the sum of external costs plus transaction costs. Some institutions are matters of informal custom; others are explicit formal creations, often funded by taxation and thus imposing their own packages of external and transaction costs, and thus the ultimate practical questions about institutions tend to involve comparative institutional analysis rather than theoretical comparison to models of perfect competition.

4. CULTURE, DIVERSITY, EXPECTATIONS

Voluntary cooperation is important not just for solving social dilemmas and distributing gains from trade, but also for facilitating the expression of important kinds of freedoms such as freedom of association and freedom of conscience. Freedoms of this type create additional puzzles about the proper relationship of voluntary intermediate groups and the state, and Richard Arneson focuses on a few. Arneson unravels the puzzle of whether "religious liberty is special," in the sense of both deserving special protection from the law and in justifying special exemptions from otherwise generally applicable laws. In his view, all attempts to argue that religion is special either fail to distinguish in what way it is unique, or if it is unique, what is valuable about it being so that merits special protection.

Freedom means letting individuals, especially adults, live as they see fit, but what does educating for freedom entail for less than fully grown individuals? Can educational practices be designed such that their freedom is preserved rather than subverted by the imposition of a particular conception of the good? Kyla Ebels-Duggan argues that educating children for freedom and teaching them to embrace a particular conception of the good are virtually indistinguishable. There is a stage when the task is developmental: not simply to respect a child's autonomy but to help make sure there is something there to be respected.

If we cannot harm individuals *before* they take shape, by predisposing them toward a particular view about the good life, what about harming them after they die? David Boonin provides an original defense of the posthumous harm principle, the idea that it is possible to act to harm a person even if the act takes place after the person has died. Boonin gives us good reasons to think that, if the posthumous harm thesis is true, then it implies that many acts that otherwise appear harmless may prove harmful.

5. Economies and Normative Trade-offs

As trade emerges, there emerges with it a new way of being self-sufficient: in a market society, people can produce enough to meet their own needs by producing enough to meet other people's needs. Freedom of commerce under the rule of law empowers people to cooperate on a massive scale, liberating each other from poverty.

But is there a dark side to a free society? Can an opportunity that enhances our freedom harm us in other ways? Matt Zwolinski situates himself between classical Marxists, who claim that markets are rife with exploitation, and classical liberals, who see opportunities for exploitation in the exercise of power by modern states. The danger comes both from people's private market relations and from their relations with the state, Zwolinski says. The state can take unfair advantage by engaging in predatory, parasitic behavior to favor some people at the expense of others. Licensing monopolies is one such example. This is why preventing exploitation is not straightforward: reducing one kind of exploitation could facilitate another.

One way to assess the problematic nature of exploitation is to assess the nature of the consent that leads to the emergence of an exploitative situation. Consent manifests itself in various ways. We consent to offers under financial pressure that we would not accept if the alternatives were not grim. Is that the kind of consent that we hold sacred? Which variations on the theme of a "right to say no" are conducive to people retaining respect for themselves and a kind of wholeness?

Exploitation is closely related to consent that in some crucial way is not as voluntary as it should be. Serena Olsaretti argues we should think of a choice as forced when the alternative is unacceptable. An account of voluntariness is not just important for understanding exploitation, but integral to understanding self-ownership. Voluntariness pushes self-ownership away from a rights-based account and toward an account of voluntary or unforced choice.

Given the potential for involuntary, exploitative choice, we are tempted to conclude that the market represents in the end a system that encourages vice and discourages virtue. This is indeed a prevalent view among critics and even some supporters of markets. But Virgil Storr claims that, far from rewarding vices such as greed and selfishness, the market actually punishes them. Drawing on an account of morality inspired by Adam Smith's impartial spectator, Storr argues that as market relations expand to include larger groups of people, our sphere of sympathy and concern also expands. We are changed, just as the critics claim, but for the better, not worse.

6. Body and Mind

The preceding chapters discussed humanity's halting progress in removing external impediments to our freedom. This progress has diminished one external impediment after another; but the end result is not so much, or not only, that all impediments have disappeared; rather, we are now in the best position we have ever been to see that there are impediments other than the obvious ones. The most perfect success at removing external impediments to our positive freedom would leave us still needing to confront the last frontier: internal obstacles.

Markets change us in many ways, some positive, some negative. They may make it harder for us to think for ourselves; at least, this is the worry that Elijah Millgram raises. The division of labor induces hyper-specialization, which means that an increasing number of people have skill sets that enable them to produce more, innovate more, and be of service to a larger customer base, all the while becoming more interdependent. But it is a consequence of this dynamic of increasing specialization and division of labor, and arguably an essential and in some ways desirable consequence, that as people become ever more specialized and smaller components of ever larger productive processes, they do so without understanding the competence of those on whom they depend, and without being able to evaluate each other's performance. The consequence of specialization is that we think for ourselves in smaller and smaller niches of social and economic life, and thus autonomy as thinking for ourselves is irreversibly undermined. (Compare this to Jason Brennan's worry about the corrosion of democratic deliberation as voters become ever more unable to evaluate elected representatives or even to have more than the vaguest idea of what good performance in public office would look like.)

More optimistically, Eddy Nahmias holds that free will is within our reach as a psychological accomplishment. We have free will when we can exercise complex capacities in making decisions and directing our lives according to them. We become more free by cultivating and exercising our capacities of imagination, decision-making, and self-control. Science, far from showing that we lack free will due to the way our actions are determined by physical laws, can help us better understand and expand our capacities and make more effective use of them in driving our behavior and actions to match our goals.

As noted earlier, freedom of the will need not be seen as resembling an on/off switch, something you either have or not. Instead, real-world freedom of the will is an ongoing achievement that comes in degrees, and not to everyone to the same degree. Moreover, our wills can be more free in some circumstances than in others. Because our cultures and systems of government affect people's inclination and ability to make up their own minds, the most intriguing versions of the free will problem today are personal, social, and political, not metaphysical.

In the final chapter, Allen Buchanan emphasizes an important but often overlooked dimension of freedom as thinking for yourself. We are free not only to the extent that we think for ourselves and act on the beliefs we form, but also to the extent that those beliefs are true. Mistaken beliefs can undermine our freedom to the extent that we fail to act in ways that are competently self-directed.

These and other theoretical challenges raised in this volume are at the cutting edge of research about freedom. We have recruited an outstanding team of contributors who went where their curiosity led them, traveling at times through alien territory and at times through well-trodden terrain. We intended this volume to be an exercise in freedom as much as it is a study of freedom. We are grateful to our authors for caring about this project and for having the courage and confidence to pursue visions of their own. The sign of good parents is a child who does not need them. Perhaps that is a sign of good editorship too.

Acknowledgments

This project is supported by a grant from the John Templeton Foundation. Opinions expressed here are those of the authors and do not necessarily reflect the views of the Templeton Foundation. Thanks also to the Georgetown Institute for the Study of Markets and Ethics and Georgetown's McDonough School of Business for generously supporting Schmidtz's research in the fall of 2016.

Notes

1. Ian Carter, Matt Kramer, and Hillel Steiner have compiled an excellent anthology of previously published material from Machiavelli to the present. Our Handbook complements theirs more than competes with it. A scholar who reads both volumes will know the lay of the land.

2. To borrow Steiner's example, "if we all acquire the freedom to brew beer in our basements, bottle it, and put it in our refrigerators, then as fast as I can put beer in my refrigerator, thereby acquiring a freedom to fetch it from my refrigerator, my neighbor also comes to have unfreedoms to fetch that same beer." In Steiner's own words, "our technologically enhanced repertoire of act-types also increases out inventories of act-tokens which we're

prevented by others from doing." See Schmidtz (1996), paraphrasing Steiner, as quoted at 286.

3. This paragraph and the three that follow are from chapter 1 of Schmidtz and Brennan (2011).

4. As chapter 1 of Schmidtz and Brennan's *Brief History of Liberty* goes on to elaborate, there is no evidence of major technological progress in Neanderthal societies. Neither is there evidence of trade between groups. Neanderthals did not experiment much, nor did they learn from each other's experiments. Neither their technology nor their social organiza-tion changed much over hundreds of thousands of years. Five hundred thousand years ago, Neanderthals formed hierarchical hunter-gatherer groups of about two dozen. Forty thousand years ago, Neanderthals were still living in isolated groups of two dozen hunter-gatherers. It is hard to imagine a human society remaining so static for 460 years, let alone 460,000.

References

Collier, Paul, 2007. *The bottom billion: why the poorest countries are failing and what can be done about it*. 1st ed. Oxford: Oxford University Press.

Horan, R., Bulte, E., and Shogren, J., 2005. How trade saved humanity from biological exclu-sion: an economic theory of Neanderthal extinction. *Journal of Economic Behavior and Organization*, 58, pp.1–29.

Levinson, Sanford, 2008. *Our undemocratic constitution: where the constitution goes wrong*. 1st ed. Oxford and New York: Oxford University Press.

Ostrom, Elinor, 1990. *Governing the commons: the evolution of institutions for collective action*. Cambridge, UK: Cambridge University Press.

Schmidtz, David, 1996. Critical notice: Steiner's essay on rights. *Canadian Journal of Philosophy*, 26, pp.283–302.

Schmidtz, David, and Brennan, Jason, 2011. *A brief history of liberty*. New York: Wiley Blackwell.

Sunstein, Cass R., and Thaler, Richard H., 2009. *Nudge: improving decisions about health, wealth and happiness*. London: Penguin.

PART I

CONCEPTUAL FRAMES

CHAPTER 1

SELF-OWNERSHIP AS A FORM OF OWNERSHIP

DANIEL C. RUSSELL

1. WHAT SELF-OWNERSHIP IS FOR

1.1. The challenge of coexistence

Whenever human beings prosper together in peace, it is a profound accomplishment. Coexistence presents a constant challenge: everybody needs the freedom to live a life of his own without unwelcome interference from others, and yet living a life of one's own creates inevitable spillover effects. If A can forbid B to create any spillover effects, then B will not be free to live a life of his own; but since B can then likewise forbid A, the zeal with which A insists on freedom from interference diminishes the zeal with which A can insist on freedom to live a life of his own. Merely by sharing an environment, we each face a trade-off between freedom to act and freedom from interference. Coexisting is costly. That is why its success an accomplishment.

Of course, *not* coexisting is costly too. Freedom to live a life of one's own has a point when it is freedom to live in peace with others, and to enjoy the prosperity humans create only in multitudes.[1] So the challenge of coexistence is to discover patterns of interacting that optimize the trade-off between freedom to live one's life and freedom from interference. Groups that prosper together in peace are the groups that make that discovery, converting mere coexistence into mutual association for reciprocal benefit. That is what makes the accomplishment profound.

These patterns of interacting—customs, practices, and institutions—shape *expectations* on which people plan their futures. To optimize the trade-off inherent in coexistence, a practice or institution must create in each person an expectation of protection of his freedom from interference, in ways that he can *afford* to be protected as the beneficiary of his freedom to act.

Ownership is an institution that has emerged in response to precisely this challenge. The thesis of this chapter is that *self-ownership is a form of ownership*, an institution for optimizing the trade-off between freedom to go about one's life and freedom from the interference of others, in a world in which going about one's life almost always interferes with someone else's.

1.2. Reciprocal benefits

Ownership may seem more like a *cause* of the trade-off of freedoms than a response to it. It is easy to see the way in which ownership rights are zero-sum: A's right to exclude is B's prospect of being excluded. That is the *point* of an ownership right, like a traffic light that not only turns green in one direction but also turns red in the other. What is easy to overlook, though, is that the *institution* of ownership rights can be positive-sum, like a *system* of traffic lights (Schmidtz, 2010: 85). What does it take for an institution in which interactions are zero-sum *in vacuo* to create reciprocal benefits in the greater scheme of things?

Anglo-American property law has evolved in response to just that question, as Baron Bramwell observed in his landmark opinion in *Bamford v. Turnley* (1862). The defendant had been baking bricks in a kiln on his property; his neighbor complained of noxious fumes from the kiln. Their dispute was over the precise location of a boundary, not between two properties but between two freedoms: the plaintiff's freedom to go about his life without nuisance from the defendant, and the defendant's freedom to go about his life even if it annoyed the plaintiff. Bramwell made the crucial observation that in protecting people from nuisance, there is risk of *over-protecting* them—protecting them to *their own detriment*—by subjecting the one protected from everyday nuisances today to a prohibition against creating everyday nuisances tomorrow.

> There must be, then, some principle on which such cases must be excepted. It seems to me that that principle may be deduced from the character of these cases, and is this, viz., that those acts necessary for the common and ordinary use and occupation of land and houses may be done, if conveniently done, without submitting those who do them to an action. . . . *It is as much for the advantage of one owner as of another;* for the very nuisance the one complains of, as the result of the ordinary use of his neighbour's land, he himself will create in the ordinary use of his own, and the reciprocal nuisances are of a comparatively trifling character. The convenience of such a rule may be indicated by calling it a rule of give and take, live and let live. (*Bamford,* 1862: 33, emphasis added)

Bramwell's insight was that A should be permitted to do things that create nuisance for B when the permission is not just for the benefit of A *but for the overall benefit of B as well.* This principle of "reciprocal benefits" (Epstein, 1979) makes ownership an institution for turning zero-sum disputes into positive-sum outcomes of even greater significance.

Bramwell's simple rationale for this principle, one might say, is that because freedoms are mutual, *turnabout is fair play*; therefore, protecting A's freedom to do everyday things even if those things annoy B benefits not just A but even B, because it equally protects B's freedom to go about *his* daily life as well. Finding for B against A today, then, would be more than even B could afford in the greater scheme of things. Likewise, one reason to find against the defendant in *Bamford* is that permitting him to undermine his neighbors' hope of escaping a quasi-industrial area for a residential area would have permitted them to undermine the very same hope of his. Such protection one day would have been more than the defendant could afford the next.

But there is also a second, much deeper rationale for the principle of reciprocal benefits. Taking the plaintiff and defendant as proxies for all neighbors, to overprotect either of them would undermine the broader benefits of coexistence *that even that party enjoys*. People have different preferences: the odd defendant may not mind turnabout on the part of his neighbors; the odd plaintiff may have no use for freedom to create the sorts of nuisances his neighbors do (Mack, 2015: 204–207). But even that defendant and even that plaintiff enjoy the disproportionate benefits made possible only through the cooperation of multitudes. First, though, there must *be* a multitude, and therefore a multitude that just about everybody can afford to belong to (Schmidtz, 2010: 86, 96–97).

With this second rationale, the principle of reciprocal benefits becomes also a principle for *distinguishing* protection from overprotection. For instance, in commerce the presence of a competitor is a nuisance, and every such rivalry is zero-sum. But even the one who loses in competition with a rival is still better off in the larger scheme of things when people are vulnerable to just such losses. One reason for this is economic: even the one who loses in competition still owes as high a standard of living as he has to the prosperity made possible by the institution of competitive commerce—an institution that is positive-sum, *provided* it is fueled not only by the hope of profit but also by the risk of loss (Boudreaux and Roberts, 2008). But there is also a moral reason, since there can be no legitimate claim on grounds of justice that one be promised protection from interference in ways that one also wants to be promised that others will not be protected. The principle of reciprocal benefits is a Pareto principle—an assurance that at least some will advance and none retreat—but only at the high level of what systems, what institutions, and what expectations make mutual association an attractive prospect for everybody.

This second rationale for the principle of reciprocal benefits is evident in decisions such as that in *Hinman v. Pacific Air Transport* (1936), in which the court ruled that even though land rights extend "to the heavens" (the traditional *ad coelum* doctrine), this does not empower landowners to forbid airlines to fly overhead. As Richard Epstein (1979: 82) observes about restrictions of *ad coelum*,

> The reciprocal benefits are evident over a broader universe of discourse, as all landowners in their capacity as citizens can gain through increased air transportation. The widespread benefits of traveling by air and using goods shipped by air are thus properly brought into the case. While an occasional individual might suffer some psychological wrench from the forced loss of air rights, virtually all persons are better off because of the universal overflight easement.

Although this second rationale appeals to what benefits just about everybody, the point is not that benefits for the aggregate outweigh costs for the unprotected owner. Rather, by preserving expectations that make coexistence a better proposition for just about everybody, the principle of reciprocal benefits preserves the cooperation of multitudes, which in turn preserves freedom to live one's life, *for both parties to the dispute*. Both parties thus walk away whole from a zero-sum interaction, because each has received exactly the protection from interference that he can afford "over a broader universe of discourse." The force of an ownership right is not that one must prevail, but that one must be made whole. The judge in *Hinman* succeeded not by identifying whose rights should be sacrificed for whose benefit, but by identifying what the ownership rights had to be *in order for the owners* to be better off in the greater scheme of things. "His verdict," therefore, "left us with a system of rights that we could *afford* to take seriously" (Schmidtz, 2010: 96).

As powerful as the principle of reciprocal benefits is, though, it would be a mistake to suppose that it is tidy. Creating reciprocal benefits requires protecting owners as they can afford to be protected in the greater scheme of things, but it is not always obvious what protection meets that standard. The cooperation of multitudes made possible by air travel benefits everybody, but it is also true that not everybody lives near the airfield. On the one hand, compensation may be able to redress such unequal nuisances; but on the other hand, it takes not just an airfield but people living near it for air traffic to create a nuisance, and explicit compensation could incentivize housing choices that create more nuisance rather than less (cf. Coase, 1960: 32–33, 41–42; Epstein, 1979: 78; Mack, 2015: 218). The test of the principle of reciprocal benefits, as with every principle for managing social life, is not whether it makes hard problems artificially easy, but whether it really does help make social life more manageable.

We can summarize the principle of reciprocal benefits as the following general principle:

> *Freedom from interference entitles one to be made whole in those ways that one can afford to be made whole in the greater scheme of things, as one who also has the freedom to live his own life.*

And the same, one can maintain, is true of self-ownership: as a form of ownership, self-ownership is an institution for creating reciprocal benefits between free persons.

1.3. Is self-ownership a form of ownership?

Treating self-ownership as a form of ownership is not the common practice of philosophers, though. The guiding idea in recent decades has been G. A. Cohen's treatment of self-ownership as "the fullest right a person (logically) can have over herself provided that each other person also has just such a right" (1995: 213). Although Cohen rejected the belief that persons own themselves, proponents like Peter Vallentyne, Hillel

Steiner, and Michael Otsuka have followed Cohen's approach to the content of self-ownership: "full self-ownership is the logically strongest set of ownership rights that one can have over one's person that is compatible with someone else having the same kind of ownership rights over everything else in the world" (2005: 205).

In a word, the dominant approach to self-ownership in recent years is one that diverts self-ownership from any institutional goal of creating reciprocal benefits. If A's self-ownership means that A is protected by rights that "fully" constrain B—constrain B as far as logic allows—then B is similarly protected from A. So if A owns his skin, say, then B is forbidden to do anything that might cause dust to fall on A's skin without A's permission, and whatever B is forbidden to do A will also be forbidden to do. Since A and B are proxies for everyone, nothing is permitted that may cause dust to fall on anyone. A's protection from B is a disaster for both.

Noticing the costliness of absolute prohibition, David Sobel (2012) argues that since A cannot accept such an infinitesimal contraction of permitted actions, A must "back away" from full self-ownership (cf. Railton, 1985: 89, 103, 119; Wall, 2009: 402, 404). But in that case, Sobel (2013) argues, self-ownership must be constrained by independent concerns; in particular, A must accept attenuations of his rights when these would create more "social good" in the aggregate. At best, the self-ownership we can live with offers much less freedom from interference than we thought.

One cannot help but notice how, on both sides of this debate, things said about owning oneself are things no one would say about owning anything else. To say that A owns a car is not to say that A is entitled to protection from any action of B's that might cause unwanted dust to fall on A's car. Taken as an absolute ban on interference, self-ownership could do nothing to lower the cost of coexistence—on the contrary, it would make coexistence *prohibitively* costly. The challenge of coexistence is one of balancing freedoms, but one does not balance freedom from interference with freedom to live by driving the latter out with the former. And so if ownership is an institution for meeting that challenge, then "the fullest right a person logically can have" is not well understood as a form of ownership. Making an owner whole has costs, including costs *for that very owner*—and an owner's right therefore *includes* the right against its unlimited protection. It is one thing for ownership to be real, and another for it to be protected though the heavens fall (cf. Schmidtz, 2010: 82–84; Epstein, 2011: 68).

But neither are the heavens kept in place by eliminating ownership when doing so creates enough aggregate "social good." Ownership is more than just a weight on an owner's side of the scale; it must be a right to be made whole, or else it will be too costly to belong to the multitude. If self-ownership is anything less, then it is again not well understood as a form of ownership. But people avoid overprotection not by "backing away" from ownership but by keeping the institution of ownership on task. That was Bramwell's point.

Neither side sees self-ownership as a form of ownership, then, since neither side sees self-ownership as responding to the problems of shared life to which the institution of ownership has emerged as a response. Surprisingly, the thought that self-ownership is a form of ownership turns out to be contentious.

How has philosophical discussion of self-ownership become so far removed from ownership? It is worth noting that Cohen's approach, as he himself explains (1995, 213), was driven by the idea that the belief that persons own themselves must reflect a particular political ideology, on pains of lacking any determinate political implications. This is not entirely surprising, because for decades ostensible debates over self-ownership have in fact been a front. The real debate beneath the surface has been an ideological debate over government-enforced redistribution of wealth, income, and property. Hence the belief that if self-ownership carries any weight at all, the weight it carries must be deeply ideological.

It is of course true that belief in self-ownership should have determinate political implications. The mistake is the thought that it should have such implications *all at once*. Whatever implications self-ownership may prove to have will ultimately depend both on *moral considerations* about what goods mutual association must make it possible for us to enjoy, and on *empirical considerations* about what specific institutions it takes for the enjoyment of those goods to be possible in the world as we find it.

This chapter proposes to make a fresh start, leaving questions of ideology—and of ownership of wealth, income, and property in the physical environment—for another time. Instead, it will begin with the proposition *that self-ownership is indeed a form of ownership*, considering first the goods that the institution of self-ownership must cultivate (Part 2), and then making some general observations about what it takes for that institution to cultivate those goods (Part 3).

2. What Self-Ownership Is

2.1. The right of self-ownership

The institution of ownership exists to help people optimize trade-offs between freedom from interference from others and freedom to live one's life, in a world in which living one's life regularly interferes with someone or other. It follows that an ownership right could only be a conjunction of these two freedoms. More precisely, ownership conjoins what Wesley Hohfeld (1917) called a *liberty right* to act and a *claim right* that others refrain from certain acts. The liberty right is freedom from any obligation to refrain from such actions as using and enjoying what one owns, making it available to other people, and so on. In the case of self-ownership, the liberty right is the freedom to do the things that constitute living a life of one's own. The claim right is the obligation against all others that they not act as if they themselves had those liberties regarding what one owns.

Like all forms of ownership, self-ownership requires this *conjunction* of rights. Without claim rights—the rights of *exclusive* use—one's rights of use are *mere* liberties

(Schmidtz, 2010: 80). And without liberty rights over what one owns, one is exposed to the potentially abusive power of others to veto acts of living one's life (cf. Epstein, 2011: 78–79). To have the liberty right alone, then, is to be unfree to make *exclusive* use of one's person, labor, and freedom; to have the claim right alone is to be unfree to make *any* use of one's person, labor, and freedom at all. Ownership includes both rights because nobody could afford it to be otherwise.

Ownership is therefore a freedom to engage in exclusive use of whatever lies within the owner's boundary—to be free to act within that boundary without interference. This "boundary" is a boundary between the freedom of the owner and the freedom of everybody else, and its frontier is defined by the claims that the owner has against all others with respect to his liberties. Questions of ownership are therefore questions of who, if anyone, has what rights against whom, and transfers of ownership are in fact transfers of such rights (Demsetz, 1967: 347). Ownership is therefore not a relation between an owner and a thing, but between an owner and all other persons. Ownership comprises claims and liberties that define *social* relations; it is not a relation in which a Robinson Crusoe could stand. It is only because we live together that ownership is part of human life.

Being a form of ownership, self-ownership is also a relation between persons, a right of exclusive use against others with respect *to oneself*. In the simplest possible terms, ownership is a right to tell other people no, and self-ownership is a right to tell other people no when it comes to oneself. It is important to be clear on this point. One barrier to appreciating self-ownership as a literal form of ownership is the thought that ownership is a relation between a person and a thing owned, since of course it is inapt to think of oneself as a mere *thing* (e.g., Brenkert, 1998: 48–52; Kekes, 2010: 2). From that perspective, self-ownership could no more be a form of ownership than false pregnancy is a form of pregnancy. But because ownership is a relation between persons with respect to what is owned, there is nothing remotely mysterious about the idea of owning oneself. As a form of ownership, self-ownership is a relation between each person and the rest of the world. Each person may dispose of his own person without the permission of others in ways that no one else may dispose of that person without his permission.

Self-ownership is not just any relation, though. It is a fundamental moral relation, a relation by which persons are honored *as* persons. In the modern world, the issue of self-ownership originated in the attempt to understand who has *authority* or *jurisdiction* over whom. During the Spanish colonization of the Americas in the sixteenth century, controversy arose as to whether the American Indians had the right to refuse enslavement or the forced baptism of their children. The Dominican theologian Francisco de Vitoria saw this controversy as coming down to one question: who had jurisdiction over the Indians—that is, who had *dominium* over them, the right of a master and owner (*dominus*)? Vitoria's answer was that because the Indians had moral standing as persons, each of them had the right of *dominium sui*—jurisdiction over himself. In the English tradition this right was treated as *self-ownership*, most famously in John Locke's *Second Treatise of Government* (see Tomasi and Zwolinski, 2015: ch. 2).

Vitoria perceived that to say that the Indians had no moral entitlement to freedom to live their own lives without interference would have been to say that the Indians were in the commons. In asserting each Indian's entitlement to that freedom, Vitoria affirmed that the Indians were not available for use or appropriation by others. Vitoria's insight was that ours is a world of claims, of obligations—it is a world of *owners*, in which every person is already beyond the liberties of every other person. Each person possesses a jurisdiction that is proper (*proprius*) to that person alone—a jurisdiction that is that person's property (*proprietas*)—and within the jurisdiction of each person is *that person himself*. Owning oneself does not reduce a person to a mere thing. On the contrary, it is not owning oneself—being in the commons—that does that.

Notice also that understanding self-ownership as an institution, as a social practice, is not rival to understanding it as a natural right. Self-ownership is an institution to which persons in society naturally—just in virtue of being persons—have a right (cf. Mack, 2010).

2.2. The institution of self-ownership

As a form of ownership, self-ownership is an institution, so the justification of self-ownership is its justification *as* an institution. Justifying the institution of ownership is different from justifying what a given person owns. It is easy to conclude, correctly, that the world would be a better place if something of A's had belonged to B instead. To justify the *institution* of ownership, though, is to show that the expectations it shapes make coexistence a better proposition. Institutions that do so have moral weight. What A happens to own has moral weight in virtue of being permitted within an institution that has moral weight (Schmidtz, 1994: 49–50).

Likewise, there is often little to recommend what someone is able to do or keep away from others in virtue of owning himself. Reallocating A's spare kidney to B who will die without a transplant may make the world a better place than would letting A decide what to do with it (Sobel, 2012: 33). Putting A's labor into fighting obesity may make the world a better place than letting A put his labor into advertising sugary drinks. And denying A the freedom to live as he sees fit may even leave A better off, if A sees fit to live by the prognostications of astrologers. But even when there is little to recommend what A might do within the boundary that protects his body, his labor, or his freedom, there can be everything to recommend the *institution* within which that boundary lies where it does.

But how can that be? Critics sometimes complain that self-ownership does not guarantee that freedoms will always be allocated where they will do the most "social good" (Sobel, 2012; Sobel, 2013). Those critics are correct, but the absence of that guarantee is actually one of the institution's greatest virtues. The problem with guaranteeing that rights will belong to those who will use them for the greatest good at every point in time, given the background circumstances at that time, is that that very guarantee worsens those background circumstances over time. An institution of optimizing every point is an institution in which it is impossible to plan one's life, beyond appreciating how very costly it can be to appear in public with any good or talent of value to one's neighbors. A multitude like that is a multitude that nobody can afford to belong to. So the absence of the guarantee is precisely the point.

Like all forms of ownership, self-ownership is an institution for cultivating the conditions of peace and prosperity (§§ 1.1–1.2). However, self-ownership is *basic* in a way that other forms of ownership are not: it is because persons have rights to pursue lives of their own without interference from others that they have the *moral standing* to acquire other sorts of ownership rights. So the *conditions of peace* cultivated by the institution of self-ownership are not merely the absence of conflict but the rich relations through which persons mutually recognize the moral standing of persons. It is the peace of a world of persons sacred within their jurisdictions.

The institution of self-ownership helps neighbors live in *that* sort of peace by assuring them of a boundary within which each can expect to plan his future. Severing the connection between one's labor and one's future is a profound affront against another person, because it substitutes one's own judgment as to whose future his labor is in fact to serve, as if that labor were in the commons. By contrast, the institution of self-ownership creates reciprocity between neighbors, each A recognizing the authority of every B to obligate him not to act as if he too had liberty rights over B. There is a saying that "good fences make good neighbors." Good fences give neighbors a chance to engage in productive acts, and a chance to live their lives free of each other's gaze. But having good fences is also a form of neighborliness itself. Fences face both ways: a good fence is one that entitles A to dispose of his person, labor, and freedoms as he sees fit, *and is also* a fence by which A honors B's mutual entitlement to do the same.

The institution of self-ownership must also cultivate *conditions of prosperity* worthy of persons with equal moral standing to pursue their own lives. When B owns himself, A does not have the luxury of simply letting the effects of his actions spill over onto B at no cost to himself, as he would if B's right to live his life free of interference were merely a liberty. Such unwelcome spillover effects arise when the benefits of an activity can be concentrated on some while the costs of the activity are dispersed across others. Pollution, resource depletion, and nuisances are all clear examples of such unwelcome spillovers, or what economists call *negative externalities*: the unwelcome effects of A's activities that get passed on to B at no cost to A. But negative externalities also include taking what belongs to others without having to internalize the (full) cost of the taking—and not just the taking of *things*. A's conscription of B's labor—or what comes to the same thing, the taking of the value of B's labor—concentrates benefits for A and spills the cost over onto B (Demsetz, 1967: 348–349), as if B lacked the moral standing to remove himself from the commons. By recognizing B's authority to say no to A, A may proceed only if he makes B whole. The institution of ownership thus concentrates both the benefits *and* the costs of A's activity in A's hands, so that A will go forward only when the benefits of A's activity exceed the costs of that activity, *including* the costs of doing what it takes for A to recognize the moral standing of B within his jurisdiction.

The institution of self-ownership cultivates conditions of prosperity by protecting people from the extraction of their contributions to their neighbors, as if they were in the commons. Instead, the institution moves people to contribute by giving them a reason to contribute voluntarily. When A might offer B a trade for the use of B's talents, *and B is free to decline the offer*, B has reason to develop talents that A will hopefully find valuable. When A is also free to say no to the deal, neither A nor B will agree to trade unless he places more value on what he gets out of the trade than on what he gives up. The institution of self-ownership therefore gives each a reason to be useful to others, creating surplus value above what he himself is able to capture. The institution does this through the assurance that the one who makes himself useful to his neighbors will be able to recover the costs of his investment by controlling access to his usefulness. When each is entitled to basic respect of his personhood by others, he is liberated to pursue a life of his own in a way that also makes life better for his neighbors.

The cultivation of conditions for peace and prosperity is the currency in which institutions are measured as "costly" or "beneficial," as "affordable" or "prohibitive," for those whose expectations are shaped by them. In the specific case of self-ownership, though, the ultimate benefit is to live together on terms that accord each other the basic respect due to persons with their own lives to live, and the ultimate cost is to accept anything less.

2.3. Self-ownership and reciprocal benefits

Self-ownership entitles one to protection from the interference of others, but when does one person interfere with another? Because ownership is a boundary between the freedoms of persons, interference is causally symmetrical. (A *causal* symmetry may be *morally* asymmetrical; more on this in § 3.1.) The symmetry of interference in the case of property ownership is illustrated in *Sturges v. Bridgman* (1879). The defendant operated noisy machinery in the making of confections; the physician next door complained that the noise kept him from examining patients. If we think of interference as a physical phenomenon—exciting the air with sound waves, say—then the case is clearly asymmetrical (Epstein, 1979: 72–73). But in terms of the *liberty right* to go about one's business, the case is perfectly symmetrical: if A prevails, then B must go about his business in the midst of noise, and if B prevails, then A must go about his business in the midst of silence. When going about one's business creates noise, enforced silence is as truly an imposition as enforced noise is for someone else. The right to work in silence was a factor of production for the physician, but the right to create noise was a factor of production for the confectioner (Coase, 1960: 44).

As a sheer description of the world we live in, interference is symmetrical. But for that reason it is *morally* crucial that freedom from interference be *mutual*; otherwise, disputes that are zero-sum *in vacuo* remain zero-sum in the greater scheme of things. A desires free use of B's talent. Causally speaking, A's use of B's talent without B's consent would interfere with B; *and* causally speaking, B's withholding that talent would also interfere with A (for B, that is the point!). If A has the right of freedom to live without interference, *but B does not*, then B lacks standing to obligate A to internalize the cost of using that talent, and freedom from interference thus entitles A to create a negative externality for B. Coexistence is now zero-sum: the As are free to interfere with the Bs because Bs are not free to interfere with As. Actually, zero-sum is wildly optimistic, since Bs have reason to withdraw if they can, and they certainly have less reason to make themselves useful to As.

The mutuality of freedoms is therefore crucial for turning mere coexistence into mutual association. When A complains of B's interference with A's free use of B's talent, *and B is free to complain against A*, then it is not merely the case that B cannot afford for A to prevail. Not even *A* can afford for A to prevail, in the greater scheme of things. When freedom to live one's life without interference is mutual, the institution of self-ownership forbids people to create costs they don't internalize, and liberates them to be a truly welcome presence to each other.

Consequently, in a mutual association of self-owners people have reason to bear only those rights, and only those protections of those rights, that they can afford—afford in terms of the conditions of peace and prosperity—in the greater scheme of things in which rights are mutual. The *mutuality* of self-ownership, therefore, means that the principle of reciprocal benefits applies in the case of self-ownership exactly as it does in the case of owning property. In any dispute between self-owners, the *in-vacuo* winner can afford only those victories that make even the *in-vacuo* loser better off in the greater scheme of things.[2]

2.4. What self-owners own

Self-ownership entitles one to protection from the interference of others, but their interference with what, exactly? Just what things fall within the boundary of self-ownership? As with all forms of ownership, the answer is, whatever things *have* to fall within that boundary in order for the institution to respond effectively to the challenge of coexistence, creating benefits of shared existence that are worth what it costs to create them.

In our world, ownership has responded so effectively to that challenge that it is all too easy to forget that that is what ownership is for. Ownership is not costless, however; it costs something to establish boundaries, enforce boundaries, negotiate with owners of boundaries, adjudicate disputes over boundaries, and so on. So in general, as Harold Demsetz observed (1967), within the physical environment the commons is historically the default situation, giving way to an institution of ownership only as the costs of leaving resources in the commons come to exceed the costs of establishing ownership rights.

In the case of self-ownership, though, the costs of leaving ourselves in the commons are *always* too high (§ 2.1). In the case of persons, then, there is a presumption of self-ownership instead of a presumption of a commons. But this is not actually a contrast: in both cases, the single principle is that an institution of ownership should exist wherever a commons would be too costly.

That same principle also affords a way of understanding more precisely what self-owners need to keep within their jurisdiction, on the grounds that the costs of leaving those things in the commons would be too high for everybody. Such an understanding makes it clear why traditionally self-ownership has extended to one's person, one's labor, and to such basic freedoms as freedom of movement and freedom of conscience. An association in which one has no right to say no to invasions of his body, to conscriptions of his labor, or to destruction of his freedoms is an association that is too costly for just about anybody to belong to.

But we must be more precise than that. Just what freedoms the right to say no extends to, and the sort of protection to which it entitles one where it does extend, can be determined in any given case by following the principle of reciprocal benefits to clarify just what self-ownership *must* protect when a boundary is in dispute.

3. WHAT SELF-OWNERSHIP PROTECTS

When freedoms are mutual, in the greater scheme of things what is good for A in a dispute of A vs. B is also what would be good for A in a dispute of B vs. A. That is the *reciprocity* of the principle of reciprocal benefits. The principle is thus a cousin of the Golden Rule: protect yourself from others as you would have others protect themselves from you. That is how the principle turns zero-sum disputes into positive-sum coexistence.

As with all forms of ownership, so too self-ownership helps cultivate conditions of peace and prosperity according to its own version of the general principle of reciprocal benefits:

> *The institution of self-ownership entitles the bearer of a claim right to protection from interference with his person, labor, and freedom, in ways that that person can afford to be protected in the greater scheme of things as the bearer of a liberty right to live a life of his own.*

Disputes over boundaries always raise two questions (Calabresi and Melamed, 1972). The first is a question of *ownership*: is the object of the dispute to lie within the complainant's boundary? If so, then the second question concerns the *protection* of ownership: exactly how is that boundary to be protected with respect to the object of the dispute? It is important to distinguish an owner's *right* from the *protection* of that right. When a boundary is transgressed, the owner's right entitles him to be made whole by the transgressor. The question of protecting that right is a question of what counts as making the owner whole. The principle of reciprocal benefits serves as a reminder that, in a world of mutual freedoms from interference (§ 2.3), the protection of that freedom in a given dispute has costs in the greater scheme of things for the one protected. Self-owners therefore must also have the right to be protected against *over*protection.

3.1. When does self-ownership protect?

Self-owners are entitled to reciprocal benefits in the resolution of the first question, of *what exactly is to fall within their boundaries*. There is a strong presumption of owning one's person, labor, and basic freedoms, since being left in the commons is prohibitively costly (§ 2.4). To create reciprocal benefits, though, the right to protection must also be a right against overprotection. A has the right to be free from bumping and jostling by other people; A is not in the commons, free for others to use as they might. But if A were to have a claim against B not to be bumped even in the everyday ways that are unavoidable in public places, then B would have the same claim against A; and since A and B are proxies for everybody, the transaction costs involved in securing all the necessary permissions would make sharing public places impossible. Nobody can afford to forgo the prospects for living a life of his own that the cooperation of multitudes makes available, *and therefore not even A* could afford any claim that would undermine that cooperation. As the beneficiary of a liberty right, what A is actually entitled to is to be *denied* the authority to be made whole here.

Hence a first corollary to the principle of reciprocal benefits:

> *There is no protection one is owed when there is no protection that one can afford to be owed in the greater scheme of things.*

The principle of reciprocal benefits therefore guides in disputes over what is to be protected in the first place, for self-ownership as for other forms of ownership. In a dispute over A's use of B's kidney or talents, even A cannot afford, in the greater scheme of things, that those things be *anywhere but* within B's boundary. Thus such interferences between A and B, although *causally* symmetrical (§ 2.3), cannot be *morally* symmetrical: leaving such things in the commons would be so destructive that it simply cannot be an option. The same reasoning applies to basic freedoms: if A finds B's way of life distasteful, that distaste entitles A to precisely nothing—not just because B cannot afford it to be otherwise, but because even *A* cannot afford it. On the contrary, A has a claim *against* being given jurisdiction here.

3.2. Property-rule protections

Self-owners are also entitled to reciprocal benefits in the resolution of the second question, of *how they are to be protected* against boundary crossings. When B's interference would cross A's boundary, how is it appropriate for A to be protected? When A has a right to be made whole, what should count as making A whole? An owner retains the highest degree of control over a boundary when it is protected with a *property rule*, which forbids crossing a boundary without paying the owner his price.[3] (His price may be zero, as with gifts, and it may be infinite, as with injunction.) A property-rule protection contrasts with *liability-rule protections*, which permit boundary crossings provided one pays the owner an independently determined price, and with *inalienability protections*, which forbid boundary crossings outright (Calabresi and Melamed, 1972). (I shall set aside inalienability protections in what follows.)

It should be clear that the reasons for ownership of one's kidney, talent, or freedom of conscience in the first place are also reasons for protecting that ownership with a property rule. Particularly when it comes to one's person, labor, and freedom, the cost of anything less than a property-rule protection quickly becomes prohibitive for the owner. Liability-rule protections often do make owners whole, but the prospect is always dangerous. When the terms on which A may cross B's boundary are determined by public functionaries, any errors in valuating that crossing will be borne not by those functionaries but by B, as if he were an innocent bystander to his own fate (cf. Schmidtz, 2010: 81). Nor does the danger end there, since the discretionary power vested in those functionaries creates opportunities for abuse and political rent-seeking (see Epstein, 2011: ch. 7; Somin, 2015). But even without error and corruption, there is something horrifying about the prospect of an institution that allowed even those of one's attributes that have a market price to be the subject of public valuations—of allowing A to take liberties with B on the presumption of buying the permission at a price set by a third party C. And even when A can compensate B for the *harm*, it may be impossible for anyone to compensate B for the *wrong* (cf. Epstein, 1979: 78; Wall, 2009: 407; Mack, 2015: 201–204). There certainly could be no *presumption* of liability-rule protections (pace Nozick, 1974: ch. 4; see Mack, 2014: § 2.4).

Because property-rule protections put the control of boundaries into the hands of those who have the most to lose, self-owners benefit most from a presumption of property-rule protections (cf. Epstein, 1979: 77, 88; Schmidtz, 2010: 81). Anything less than that presumption would be prohibitively costly. That is in fact why invasions of one's person, labor, or freedoms are generally forbidden and punished with criminal sanctions (Calabresi and Melamed, 1972: 1124–1127; Schmidtz, 2010: 92). Hence a second corollary:

> An owner is owed a level of protection no less than he can afford to be owed in the greater scheme of things.

But while coexistence with no presumption of property-rule protection for self-owners would be horrifying, life with *only* property-rule protections would scarcely be an improvement. A is protected by a property rule from B's attempts to break A's leg, but not when B does something that increases the risk that A's leg will be broken, such as driving a car in A's vicinity (Calabresi and Melamed, 1972: 1126–1127). If it could be known in advance that it is A's leg that B specifically puts at risk, it would be better to protect A with a property rule and allow A to determine whether to allow B to proceed and (if so) on what terms. But if B's driving raises the risk only that someone or other will be injured, then the transaction costs entailed by protecting every potential victim A with a property rule would keep every potential driver B from driving at all. Since even A benefits in the greater scheme of things from the endeavors made possible by vehicular travel, A couldn't afford a property-rule protection against B. As the bearer of a claim right, A has a presumption of property-rule protection. But as the bearer of a liberty right, A often benefits from *not* being able to say no outright (cf. Coase, 1960: 35; Epstein, 1979: 101).

There must be a presumption of property-rule protection in the case of self-ownership. But there must also be *other* ways of protecting claim rights against interference when property rules are too costly for the owner. That is why there are liability-rule protections.

3.3. Liability-rule protections: extraordinary nuisance

As Bramwell stated in *Bamford*, nobody can afford mutual protection by the law from the nuisances of everyday life. The law therefore recognizes a distinction between *ordinary* and *extraordinary* nuisances, and confines legal action to the latter.[4] When it can be known in advance who will extraordinarily annoy whom, and it is feasible for those parties to negotiate, it is best to let them negotiate, because this assures each party of no less protection of his right than he can afford (§ 3.2). Otherwise, it may be possible for a third party to award an exchange of rights, in order to approximate an arrangement the parties would have reached by voluntary negotiation if that had been feasible (Coase, 1960). So, whereas property-rule protections forbid crossing a boundary without paying the owner the *owner's* price, liability-rule protections forbid crossing without paying the owner an *independently determined* price.

Liability rules typically apply after a crossing has already occurred (and the cost of transacting the permission is therefore infinite), and whenever transaction costs would block a mutually beneficial exchange of rights. So although A's risk of injury is increased by B's driving, A's optimal level of risk is not zero, because zero risk would mean no drivers, and thus much less of the general prosperity that accounts for much of what A is able to do in living a life of his own. Since drivers typically do not know in advance whom (if anyone) they might injure, and since requiring them to negotiate in advance with everyone they might injure would also mean no drivers, it is better to protect those injured in traffic accidents with liability rules. Hence one last corollary of the general principle of reciprocal benefits:

> An owner is owed a level of protection no greater than he can afford to be owed in the greater scheme of things.

Property rules and liability rules give the owner of a boundary very different levels of control over that boundary. Note, though, that the choice of protections has nothing to do with whether the owner is a "full" owner of that boundary—whether, say, A is a "full" owner of his leg. Self-ownership, as a form of ownership, is not an instantiation of a concept but a response to the challenge of coexistence. That response is a balancing of the owner's claim right and liberty right that most benefits the owner through the creation of reciprocal benefits for everybody, himself included, in the greater scheme of things. To be sure, liability-rule protections of A from B's interference put A at some risk. But here too, zero risk itself is something A can have a right to be protected from.

3.4. Liability-rule protections: ordinary nuisance

The reason that ordinary nuisances should not be legally actionable is that freedom to go about everyday business has benefits in the greater scheme of things even for the one annoyed on a given day. B cannot afford to be protected from the dust that falls on him as A passes by because B cannot afford that A be similarly protected from B. More generally, since A and B are proxies for everybody, no bearer of a liberty right could afford the shutdown of mutual association that such a protection of his claim right against interference would entail.

It would be a mistake, however, to conclude that owners are completely unprotected from ordinary nuisance. To be sure, they are not protected *by the law*, either with property rules or with liability rules entitling them to explicit compensation.[5] But besides explicit compensation there is *implicit* compensation (Epstein, 1979: 78–80), and on the principle of reciprocal benefits implicit compensation takes two forms.

For one, the very institution of not overprotecting owners from ordinary nuisance implicitly compensates the neighbor who is annoyed today with the freedom to do things even if those things annoy his neighbors tomorrow, because turnabout is fair play (Epstein, 1979: 77–78, 84). But even more than that, by keeping mutual association safe for those things people do to prosper together in peace, the very institution implicitly compensates owners for everyday nuisances that arise along the way. When the law does nothing about ordinary nuisance, it protects self-owners by no more than they can afford. And that itself is a most crucial benefit, and again, one to which self-owners are entitled.

The other, deeper form of implicit compensation is also a simple one: it is courtesy, good manners, and neighborliness on the part of the transgressor. If A steps on B's toe— above ordinary public-space bumping (no boundary crossing), but not as far as battery (boundary crossing with criminal sanction)—then it is best not just for A but also for B that the law not get involved. And yet A *has* interfered with B; the best evidence of this is our social understanding that A *does owe* something to B. Here, making B whole requires no more than A's apology: since freedom from interference is mutual, any greater compensation would be more than even B could afford the authority to demand in the greater scheme of things. Making B whole requires no less than A's apology, though. B's freedom from being stepped on by A is after all a claim that B has against A and not merely a liberty. Apologizing to B is not magnanimity but fairness on A's part—it is what A owes B.[6] Actually, even ordinary nuisances become legally actionable when they are so unneighborly as to be malicious.[7] Through shows of neighborliness, the transgressor implicitly compensates the owner for an everyday nuisance, creating reciprocal benefits by keeping it worthwhile to have neighbors in the first place (cf. Epstein, 1979: 84).

The principle of reciprocal benefits therefore explains why extraordinary but not ordinary nuisance should be actionable. In fact, that principle explains the very distinction between ordinary and extraordinary nuisance, as those for which implicit compensation is the most that owners can afford and those for which formal protection is the least that owners can afford.

Speaking of neighborliness, the principle of reciprocal benefits also explains why some acts of deliberate interference with another person actually cross no boundary at all (as in § 3.1). B steps unwittingly toward a rotten bridge; A pushes him away because there is no time to warn him (Wall, 2009). There is no question but that A interferes with B—that is precisely what A *means* to do. But B's boundary does not extend to where A's interference would cross that boundary, because by crossing B's boundary A would incur *some* sort of debt to B, and that B cannot afford. Of course, the odd B may prefer to take his chances even with a rotten bridge or a speeding bus to being interfered with *at all*.[8] But even the odd B benefits enormously from being free to live a life of his own in an association where nobody ever has to shrink from being a good neighbor. By the same token, not everything A might do for B's sake would be neighborly. An institution allowing A to push B out of the way of a speeding bus creates reciprocal benefits. An institution allowing A to push B out of the way of a prognosticating astrologer does not.

4. CONCLUSION

The aim of this chapter has been to elucidate a conception of self-ownership that results from taking it seriously as a form of ownership, a social institution with the mission of making mutual association possible. We have not even attempted to settle *exactly* what such an institution would have to be in order to accomplish that mission, much less what it might entail for ownership of wealth, income, or property. Does that mean that the protections to which self-owners are entitled depend on empirical factors, and not only on moral principles? Of course it does. That is just to say that justice is whatever it has to be for us to prosper together in peace in the world as we find it. What has here been proposed is that whatever else justice must do, it must make shared coexistence a good proposition for persons who own themselves.[9]

NOTES

1. See Aristotle, *Politics* I.2, 9; *Nicomachean Ethics* V.6; Adam Smith, *An Inquiry into the Nature and Causes of the Wealth of Nations* I.3.
2. What is mutual between persons is their *standing* as self-owners. Not all self-owners have the same rights at a very fine-grained level: A who loves noise and B who loves quiet cannot both control the sound level in the same space; it is best that only one of them obtain

that right. The point of mutuality is not that each must be the same but that each must be made whole.

3. Despite the overlapping terminology, not everything we call "property" is to be protected with a property rule.

4. Of course, what counts as an ordinary nuisance—or Bramwell's "trifling nuisance"—varies with both place and time (Coase, 1960: 20–21; Epstein, 1979: 85, 87–89).

5. Alternatively, one may interpret liability-rule protections more broadly than is done here, to include protections by extralegal practices and sanctions.

6. By contrast, Mack (2015) views ordinary nuisance as no boundary crossing at all. Mack and I therefore disagree either as to whether A owes any debt to B, or as to whether any such debt can be (fully) explained without any appeal to a boundary crossing.

7. So Bramwell (*Bamford*, 1862): many things "which would be [actionable] nuisances if done wantonly or maliciously, nevertheless may be lawfully done."

8. Things are more complicated when B *wittingly* steps toward a rotting bridge or speeding bus, as A's action becomes a different sort of paternalism.

9. I thank the John Templeton Foundation for support during the period of writing this chapter. I also thank Gerald Gaus, Carmen Pavel, David Schmidtz, Mario Villareal, Steve Wall, and two anonymous referees for their comments on an earlier draft; Carmen Pavel, Jeremy Reid, and Stephen Stich for editorial assistance; and David Schmidtz for the opportunity to contribute.

References

Bamford v. Turnley, 122 Eng. Rep. (1862), 27–34.

Boudreaux, D., and Roberts, R., 2008. Boudreaux on globalization and trade deficits. 21 January 2008. http://www.econtalk.org/archives/2008/01/don_boudreaux_0.html.

Brenkert, G., 1998. Self-ownership, freedom, and autonomy. *Journal of Ethics*, 2, pp.27–55.

Calabresi, G., and Melamed, A. D., 1972. Property rules, liability rules, and inalienability: one view of the cathedral. *Harvard Law Review*, 85, pp.1089–1128.

Coase, R., 1960. The problem of social cost. *Journal of Law and Economics*, 3, pp.1–44.

Cohen, G. A., 1995. *Self-ownership, freedom, and equality*. Cambridge, UK: Cambridge University Press.

Demsetz, H., 1967. Toward a theory of property rights. *American Economic Review*, 57, pp.347–359.

Epstein, R., 1979. Nuisance law: corrective justice and its utilitarian constraints. *Journal of Legal Studies*, 8, pp.49–102.

Epstein, R., 2011. *Design for liberty: private property, public administration, and the rule of law*. Cambridge, MA: Harvard University Press.

Hinman v. Pacific Air Transport, 84 F.2d 755 (9th Cir. 1936).

Hohfeld, W. N., 1917. Fundamental legal conceptions as applied in judicial reasoning. *Yale Law Journal*, 26, pp.710–770.

Kekes, J., 2010. The right to private property: a justification. *Social Philosophy and Policy*, 27, pp.1–20.

Mack, E., 2010. The natural right of property. *Social Philosophy and Policy*, 27, pp.53–78.

Mack, E., 2014. Robert Nozick's political philosophy. *Stanford encyclopedia of philosophy*. http://plato.stanford.edu/entries/nozick-political/.

Mack, E., 2015. Elbow room for rights. In: D. Sobel, P. Vallentyne, and S. Wall, eds. *Oxford studies in political philosophy*, 1. Oxford: Oxford University Press. pp.194–221.

Nozick, R., 1974. *Anarchy, state, and utopia*. New York: Basic Books.

Railton, P., 1985. Locke, stock, and peril: natural property rights, pollution, and risk. In: M. Gibson, ed. *To breathe freely*. Totawa, NJ: Rowman & Allanheld. pp.89–123.

Schmidtz, D., 1994. The institution of property. *Social philosophy and policy*, 11, pp.42–62.

Schmidtz, D., 2010. Property and justice. *Social Philosophy and Policy*, 27, pp.79–100.

Sobel, D., 2012. Backing away from libertarian self-ownership. *Ethics*, 123, pp.32–60.

Sobel, D., 2013. Self-ownership and the conflation problem. In: M. Timmons, ed. *Oxford studies in normative ethics*. Oxford: Oxford University Press. pp.98–122.

Somin, I., 2015. *The grasping hand: Kelo v. the City of New London and the limits of eminent domain*. Chicago: University of Chicago Press.

Sturges v. Bridgman, 11 Ch. D. 852, 865 (1879).

Tomasi, J., and Zwolinski, M., 2015. *A brief history of libertarianism*. Princeton, NJ: Princeton University Press.

Vallentyne, P., Steiner, H., and Otsuka, M., 2005. Why left-libertarianism is not incoherent, indeterminate, or irrelevant: a reply to Fried. *Philosophy and Public Affairs*, 33, pp.201–215.

Wall, S., 2009. Self-ownership and paternalism. *The Journal of Political Philosophy*, 17, pp.399–417.

CHAPTER 2

POSITIVE FREEDOM AND THE GENERAL WILL

PIPER L. BRINGHURST AND GERALD GAUS

1. CONCEPTS AND CONTEXTS OF FREEDOM[1]

AMONG the first essays one reads as a student of political philosophy is apt to be Isaiah Berlin's (1969) classic, "Two Concepts of Liberty." Despite its elegance and rhetorical power, the effects of this paper have been somewhat unfortunate: Berlin's thesis that negative and positive liberty are competing conceptions, and that a fundamental task of a political theory is to defend *a* conception of liberty against competitors, continues to influence theorists of freedom. Berlin famously defends negative liberty as a truer and more humane ideal than positive liberty, as it recognizes that "human goals are many," and no one can make a choice that is right for all people (Berlin, 1969: 171).[2] Not surprisingly, this claim elicited counter-criticisms that negative liberty was the truly flawed ideal (see, e.g., Pettit, 1997, especially chapters 1 and 2; Taylor, 1979). Behind this tendency to defend a specific concept of freedom as foundational, or generally correct, is an understandable philosophic impulse for a general theory of freedom, which would provide a unified and elegant understanding of free action and the various senses in which a person might be said to be free.[3] Even Gerald MacCallum (1972), who sought to transcend the debate between negative and positive liberty, endeavored to do so by providing a single coherent scheme that encompassed both.

An alternative understanding of a "theory of freedom" is one that, within a coherent normative framework, distinguishes different contexts, and tries to show why, say, the "negative conception" is especially important in contexts of interpersonal claims about freedom, while positive accounts make much more sense when talking about free agency, or what it means to lead a free life.[4] Such an approach is not simply eclectic, drawing on different conceptions willy-nilly, but seeks to understand the complexity of our commitment to freedom, and how in some contexts a person can be free in one way and not in another; the aim is to show how a reasonable view of humans and their relations can make room for, and explain, these complexities and tensions. This, indeed, is in the spirit of T. H. Green, who explicitly introduced the idea of positive liberty into our political discourse. Green did not seek to supplant negative liberty as a false or "atomistic" doctrine; rather he acknowledged that "it must be of course admitted that every usage of the term [i.e., freedom] to express anything but a social and political relation of one man to other involves a metaphor.... It always implies ... some exemption from compulsion by another" (1986: 229). While acknowledging this, Green explored an extension of this usage employing the positive conception—one that centers on the idea of free agency and decision-making, rather than the quintessential question of freedom of action in relation to interference by others.

The aim of this chapter, then, is not to defend the concept of positive liberty "against" negative or republican liberty. Nor does it present a comprehensive account of freedom that relates different contexts, and the different understandings of freedom appropriate to each. The aim here is modest, examining but one context of freedom: relations of moral responsibility. We seek to show how one understanding of positive liberty—what we call *freedom as reasoned control*—is presupposed by our relations of moral responsibility. We argue that what may seem simply Rousseau's quixotic goal—of insuring that all subjects of the moral law remain morally free—is necessary to the maintenance of responsibility relations within a moral community. Unless all are free in the sense of exercising reasoned control in accepting moral demands—that is, their acceptance of these demands expresses their status as reasoning persons—they cannot be held responsible for their failure to comply. This then leads us to the second concern of the chapter: whether the concept of the general will can reconcile positive freedom and moral responsibility with regulation by a common moral law. In section three we briefly look at two classic accounts of the general will—those of Rousseau and Bosanquet—while section four turns to contemporary proposals that seek to understand how a general will might arise in a diverse society.

2. FREE REASONED MORAL AGENCY

2.1. The practice of responsibility and reasoned control

As Peter Strawson (1962) famously showed us, our moral practices are inescapably about our reactions to what we perceive to be the good or ill will of those with whom we interact. We make demands on them, and they on us; and we hold them (and ourselves) responsible for failure to meet these demands. The reactive attitudes are fundamental to these relations of responsibility; we experience resentment at those whose failure to meet our demands manifests an ill will toward us, and indignation when, as a third party, we view others as the objects of such will. As Strawson stressed, we do not really have the option of deciding whether or not we should care about the attitudes of others toward us in these practices. "The human commitment to participation in ordinary inter-personal relationships is, I think, too thoroughgoing and deeply rooted for us to take seriously the thought that a general theoretical conviction might so change our world that, in it, there were no longer any such things as inter-personal relationships as we normally understand them" (Strawson, 1962: 197). Because we are so deeply committed to this interpersonal responsibility perspective, when we reflect on our practices we must be concerned about the conditions that are necessary to sustain this perspective—the conditions that make oneself and others fit to be held responsible. "The fact that fitness to be held responsible becomes salient to anyone involved in that practice, and that it represents what we think of as freedom in the agent," Philip Pettit observes, "means that the concept of free agency is intimately woven into the tapestry of inescapable human sentiments and responses" (2001: 20).

Following Strawson, our social morality can be understood as such a practice of responsibility (1962: 199ff; see also Strawson, 1961). Thus understood, our interpersonal morality is not simply about objective judgments of the rightness or wrongness of the actions of others (and ourselves): it is a system embedded in our attitudes toward others, and our judgments of their intentions and attitudes toward us. When I hold another responsible I do not simply judge his action against some standard; I react to his ill will, his lack of respect or consideration. We deeply care about maintaining this web of personal relations. As a result, we must care about the conditions that render individuals fit for moral responsibility and, as Strawson, Pettit, and many others have stressed, a fundamental condition is freedom (see, e.g., Hayek, 1960: ch. 5)—and not simply as regards only one "concept" of freedom. In any given responsibility context, negative freedom of a certain sort is certainly necessary for a person to be fit for responsibility. If one is threatened and coerced to perform a wrongful act such that, we say, one had no choice, it will generally not be an action for which one is responsible (Strawson, 1962: 189–190). The act is not a manifestation of one's will, but the ill will of the coercer (see further Hayek, 1960: ch. 9).

A type of positive freedom is also necessary, for we must see the person to be held responsible as, in some sense, in reasoned control of her actions. A clear example of a person lacking such control is one in the grips of an obsessional neurosis. Consider the case of a nineteen-year-old girl with obsessional sleep ceremonies, which needed to be performed nightly. Clocks had to be stopped or removed from the room, including her small wristwatch; flower pots and vases needed to be collected and put on a writing table; the door between her room and that of her parents must be half-open; "[t]he pillow at the top end of the bed must not touch the wooden back of the bedstead. . . . The eiderdown . . . had to be shaken before being laid on the bed so that its bottom became very thick; afterwards, however, she never failed to even out this accumulation of feathers by pressing them apart" (Freud, 1973: 305).[5] According to Freud, those in the grips of such obsessions have difficulty adjusting their actions to their settled aims and their intrusive thoughts make it very difficult for them to carry on with their lives. "All these things combine," Freud concluded, "to bring about an ever-increasing indecisiveness, loss of energy, and curtailment of freedom" (1973: 299). This type of unfreedom is very much what Green had in mind. A person who is subject to some impulse that he cannot control is, Green said, "in the condition of a bondsman who is carrying out the will of another, not his own" (1986: 228). For both Freud and Green, in these cases the person has lost reasoned control of his or her activity, and is in this sense unfree.

Suppose one demands from our nineteen-year-old obsessive that she conforms to the demand "Give your parents privacy at night; let them close their door!" And let us suppose that there is a good reason for her to see this as a bona fide moral requirement. Because she cannot exercise reasoned control over her actions, she cannot comply with the directive, which appeals to her reason—it gives her reasons to act. Consequently, it would seem that her failure to comply cannot be taken as an indication that she bears ill will toward her parents because she has set aside, ignored, or otherwise chosen not to comply with the directive; instead, the impulse subverts her ability to control her behavior via such directives. "When we see someone in such a light as this, all our reactive attitudes tend to be profoundly modified" (Strawson, 1962: 194).

Now consider a second case, where you address a moral directive "ϕ!" to a twenty-year-old undergraduate, but the directive to ϕ is one that you know is beyond his ken to appreciate as based on reasons. Suppose, for example, that the reason that ϕ-ing is morally required can only be understood given a complicated argument from an exceedingly complex original position setup, an especially demanding transcendental deduction, or an intricate formal proof in first-order predicate calculus. Here by directing the undergraduate to ϕ you are directing him to *ignore* his reasoned control, for if he reasons as well as he can or as well as we expect of him, he just cannot see why he ought to ϕ. In the case of the compulsive she may well know that she has reason to give her parents privacy, and so perhaps an especially rigorous person might still say "she really did know better than to do what she did, though she just could not help herself." She lacks the ability to control her will through reasoned deliberation (or, as Green would say, she is not controlled by her rational will). It is not unintelligible for our rigorous critic to claim that the nineteen-year-old obsessive does manifest a sort of ill will, albeit it one she cannot control. Imagine that her compulsive behavior was a murderous rage; then one might quite intelligibly say that she had an ill will that was outside of her reasoned control. In contrast, in our second case the undergraduate's actions are subject to reasoned control, but he simply cannot see how complying with that directive is consistent with such control. Here no ill will or lack of consideration can intelligibly be inferred: given the exercise of his rational control, you admit that he simply cannot see what is wrong with not ϕ-ing. This does not imply that it is false that he ought to ϕ; it does mean that the practice of responsibility will, again, be profoundly modified in such cases.[6]

Quintessentially, to rationally hold a person morally responsible for failing at time t to obey a directive D to ϕ one must hold (i) she has reasoned control over her actions—more specifically, at time t such that if she concluded at t that she had sufficient reason to conform to D, she could have ϕ-ed at t and (ii) under some conditions C, the exercise of her reasoning to a certain level l would lead to the conclusion that ϕ-ing was morally required at t. Of course both these conditions are subject to diverse specifications: long-standing disputes about moral responsibility have often centered on disagreements about these specifications. Regarding (i), for example, different accounts have sharp

conflicts as to what "*could* have ϕ-ed at *t*" means, as well as what sort of psychic pathologies render a person incapable of such control. And regarding (*ii*), in specifying *C*, varying theories of moral responsibility greatly differ in specifying from what impairments
(drugs, emotional distress, psychological pressure, and so on) the agent must be free.[7]
And they disagree about what level of reasoning (*l*) about *D* our practice of responsibility
specifies such that, if the person did engage in *l* under *C*, she would conclude that ϕ-ing
was morally required at *t*. Must she be ideally rational, or simply adequately reflective?[8]
These questions have been answered in widely different ways and many of the answers
may be contextual, generating different and complex accounts of moral responsibility.
Debates about these specifications are, of course, terribly important, but they do not
obviate the claim that some versions of (*i*) and (*ii*) must be met to sustain our practice of
responsibility. For you to be fit for moral responsibility for conformity to directive *D*, you
must have been able to grasp the moral reasons for it, and you must have had the capacity
to act on them. These are conditions of free reasoned moral agency.

2.2. Pettit's objection to rational control

Pettit provides a detailed analysis of "freedom as rational control," but ultimately rejects
it as an inadequate understanding of the sort of freedom presupposed by attributions
of responsibility. Think again of our twenty-year-old undergraduate; we evaluate ϕ as
the moral thing to do on the basis of a difficult derivation, and direct him to do it. So, we
have seen that, on our account,

> rational control is quite consistent with the agent's not having any beliefs to the effect,
> say, that this or that is what they ought to do and that they can be rightly held respon-
> sible for whether or not they conform to that evaluation. Thus it is quite consistent
> with the agent being unfit to be held responsible for what they have done. There may
> be no standards acknowledged or embraced by the agent and no standards to which
> they may be expected to answer.
>
>   . . .
>
> This line of thought shows that if an agent is fit to be held responsible then not
> only must their beliefs and desires constitute rational control over what they do; the
> agent must also have evaluative beliefs to the effect that this or that is what is required
> of them, whether in rationality or prudence or in morality, and they must have the
> desires to live up to such evaluations. Only agents who are capable of recognizing
> and responding to standards in this way can be held responsible for what they do and
> can count as free or unfree. (Pettit, 2001: 40)

Our understanding of "reasoned control" is not precisely equivalent to an obvious
interpretation of "rational control." Consider unreflective Ursula, whose actions always
manifest rational control insofar as she has the capacity to, and actually does, base her
actions on her current beliefs and desires, but she is cognitively unable to reflect on

them. If she does not presently endorse D, she cannot reason herself to endorsing it, because she is unable to reason to level l (on any account where level l requires any significant reflection on her current beliefs). In this case Ursula would exercise "rational" but not "reasoned" control.

In the context of fitness for moral responsibility and the reactive attitudes, reasoned control makes much more sense than mere rational control. Suppose one more case: your neighbor currently possesses beliefs and desires such that, given them, he sees no reason to refrain from dumping waste in your yard. However, if he reflected (under C to level l) on the reasons not to dump his waste in your yard he would accept the moral directive to stop, but he never bothers to think about the matter that deeply. If, because he failed to reason about his dumping and its effects, he goes ahead and dumps, this would by no means undermine your reactive attitudes toward him and his act. That he acted wrongly because he failed to take the time and effort to think things through hardly absolves him of ill will. He possesses reasoned control, in contrast to unreflective Ursula, who simply cannot think things through. One such as the thoughtless neighbor, who cares that little about the impact of his actions on others, does not show them consideration, but rather a sort of contempt.

In the above passage Pettit stresses that rational control does not guarantee fitness for responsibility, and for him this is its core problem: he is searching for a concept of freedom F such that if a person possesses F, she is inherently fit for moral responsibility. Thus he quite rightly points out that freedom as reasoned control does not meet this condition—our undergraduate manifests freedom as reasoned control, but he is "unfit to be held responsible" for not ϕ-ing because, given the use of his reason (under C to level l), he does not "have evaluative beliefs to the effect that" ϕ-ing is required of him. However, on our account, freedom as reasoned control is a necessary, not a sufficient, condition for being fit for moral responsibility. No account of positive liberty alone could provide sufficient conditions. Even if one possesses perfect freedom as reasoned control and even if one does hold the relevant evaluative beliefs, if one is a chattel slave subject to constant coercion and threats—one is almost entirely deprived of negative freedom—one will not be fit to be held responsible.

This leads to the fundamental difference in our analyses. Pettit seeks to develop a concept of freedom-as-control such that it is a conceptual truth that those who are free in this sense are also fit for attributions of moral responsibility. The status of being free entails the status of being a moral agent—a member of our moral community who is fit to be held responsible. Now certainly we would like to *show* that under an acceptable morality, the set of persons whose actions are controlled by their reasoning is very close to the set of moral agents fit to be held responsible, and so subject to the practice of responsibility. But this, as it were, is what we must seek to demonstrate, not by an analysis of the concept of freedom, but by an account of the nature and substance of morality. We ask: how can there be a morality such that, if not all, almost all, free (qua reason-controlled) agents are participants in the practice of responsibility?

2.3. Rousseau's "quixotic" quest

Recall Rousseau's fundamental problem: "*to find a form of association*" in which each, while uniting himself with all, "nevertheless obeys only himself, and remains as free as before. Such is the fundamental problem to which the social contract furnishes the solution" (Rousseau, 1988: 92 (Bk. I, ch. 6), emphasis supplied). Note that for Rousseau, the aim is not to find a *concept of liberty* that reconciles individual freedom with moral responsibility to others, but a form of *social life* in which these are reconciled. Many in the analytic tradition have found this quixotic or woolly-headed: how can one be subject to a common law and responsible to others for compliance and yet obey only oneself? This, it is often thought, is simply nonsense. So far from being nonsense, however, some approximate solution to Rousseau's problem is needed to achieve a community that sustains the relations that make moral responsibility possible. We might rephrase Rousseau's problem: "to find a form of moral community in which each free person is fit to be held responsible."[9] As Rousseau was well aware, many moral communities fail to solve the problem: in many communities individuals possessing reasoned control are not fit to be held responsible, as the exercise of their reason does not lead them to endorse the oppressive or sectarian morality of their society. Like our undergraduate, they possess reasoned control (the capacity-to-control condition is met), but simply cannot reason themselves to the community's morality (they fail to satisfy the reasoning condition). Freedom and responsibility are thus driven apart. Rousseau appreciated that they cannot be brought together through conceptual analysis, but only through moral reform. Thus the fundamental link between positive freedom and the general will is revealed, for Rousseau believed that only a society whose rules were an expression of the general will could unite positive freedom and responsibility.

3. The General Will: Two Classic Accounts

3.1. Rousseau's limited diversity account

On Rousseau's view, because no person has natural authority over another, and because mere force could never legitimate authority, society must be founded upon agreement among its members (1988: 88 (Bk. I, ch. 4)). The form of society or moral community advocated by Rousseau is one of direct democracy, in which each citizen participates in government by voting for or against general laws that are presented as impartial and aimed at the common good. When citizens vote on such general laws with their common survival and well-being in mind, the outcome of the vote reveals the general will of the community.

There are well-known difficulties in interpreting Rousseau's theory of the general will (see Gaus, 1997). However, on perhaps the most plausible reading, it points to a rather precarious combination of (*i*) a shared idea of the common good and (*ii*) a diversity of views about how individuals' other private interests relate to that common good. The general will is supposed to direct the community's forces in accordance with the common good, as it is "the agreement of [private interests that] has made [society] possible. It is what these different interests hold in common that forms the social bond" (Rousseau, 1988: 98 (Bk. II, ch. 1)). Thus the general will arises out of the agreement or similarity between individual interests. Complete unanimity or homogeneity among the interests of all members of society is not required;[10] rather, the general will takes the *somewhat disparate* contributions of individuals and identifies through them the best collective decision about the common good. Without some measure of differences in the interests of society's members, according to Rousseau, a procedure aimed at discovering or revealing the common interest would be unnecessary: "everything would proceed on its own, and politics would cease to be an art" (Rousseau, 1988: 100, n. 9 (Bk. II, ch. 3)). While citizens have moderately divergent private interests, these are not completely detached from the common interest, and in a well-ordered society, the benefits each individual gains from promoting the common interest outweigh any share of misfortunes that result from divergences between his private interest and what the common interest requires (1988: 149 (Bk. IV, ch. 1)). In this way, individuals reflectively endorse the laws selected by the general will as being consistent with their good. They thus freely conform to the general will because (*i*) they have reasoned control over their actions, and (*ii*) their reasoning, focusing on their own good, leads them to the conclusion that following the law is morally required.

Citizens support impartial laws aimed at promoting the common interest because considerations of their own private interest direct them to do so. However, private interest and common interest will only sufficiently align for all individuals when their situations are largely comparable. To see this, consider a society, perhaps much like our own, in which there is a vast diversity of cultures and traditions, a variety of careers and ways of living, and significant stratification between social and economic classes. In such a society, because of the diversity of positions we occupy and circumstances in which we find ourselves, it is most unlikely that laws will affect us equally, and thus, that we will be able to see them as arising from the essential identity of our individual interests. Such concerns demonstrate that, on Rousseau's account, although total homogeneity of interests among citizens is not required, *deep diversity* among citizens' interests and viewpoints jeopardizes the general will: "The more harmony reigns in the assemblies, that is, the closer opinions come to being unanimous, the more dominant, therefore, is the general will, *but long debates, dissentions, and tumult* proclaim the ascendancy of private interests and the decline of the state" (1988: 150 (Bk. IV, ch. 4), emphasis added).[11] This gives us reason to be skeptical that Rousseau's account of the general will can provide a mechanism for our own diverse society by which we might unite freedom and moral responsibility. Because Rousseau's solution to our fundamental problem—to ensure that each free person is fit to be held responsible (or, to put it differently, to ensure that complying with moral demands is an exercise of positive freedom)—is a form of moral community that forbids, or simply cannot tolerate, deep diversity among citizens' viewpoints, it looks much less attractive as a solution for deeply diverse societies (see Chapman, 1956: chs. 6–7).

3.2. Bosanquet's diversity account

As the history of political thought is taught—at least in philosophy departments—even advanced students (and, indeed, scholars!) could be excused for thinking that Rousseau was the only theorist of the general will. In fact, other important political philosophers developed their own very different interpretations of the idea, including the British idealists, who, it should be stressed, were especially interested in relating positive freedom to the general will.[12] In sharp contrast to Rousseau, Bernard Bosanquet emphasized the *need* for a deep diversity of views and ways of life as the foundation for the general will. For Bosanquet, the private wills of individuals—which are based on personal interests and moral beliefs, an individual's own knowledge and history, and his dispositions and traits—are diverse.[13] It is these diverse individual wills interacting with each other in complex ways that allow the general will to arise—here the general will is more of a correlated system of ideas than a core shared interest. Thus, for Bosanquet the division of labor in a free society expresses the general will; each person takes account of the will and abilities of others, and seeks to adjust his own will and activity to theirs. "Each unit of the social organism has to embody his relations with the whole in his own particular work and will" (Bosanquet, 2011a: 344–345): private wills, on Bosanquet's view, presuppose the existence of communal life, and thus, must support and be supported by the individual wills of others in the moral community (see further Gaus, 2001). "The man's plans and principles all depend upon the support of other wills, and, apart from such agreement, there is no feature of his life which he could possibly hope to realise" (Bosanquet, 2011b: 307–308). Nonetheless, each private will "stops at a certain point": no single individual grasps the entire system of moral relations—the general will (Bosanquet, 2011b: 308). The complex interaction that takes place between individual members of the moral community, however, helps the individual to see possibilities for what is truly good and just, of which she could not conceive on her own. Thus, on this view, a system of deep diversity gives rise to the general will, and the possibility for uniting freedom and responsibility within a diverse society appears anew.[14]

4. THE GENERAL WILL AND DIVERSITY: TWO CONTEMPORARY PROJECTS

4.1. Spontaneous rules in a publicly justified order

Although Bosanquet explores the possibility of a general will under conditions of deep diversity, his proposal relies on absolute idealism, which posited that the interrelated moral views of individuals are ultimately all part of a harmonious system of reality—the absolute (see further Gaus, 1994). Thus, in place of Rousseau's deliberative account, Bosanquet's general will proffers something of an invisible-hand analysis. Because the general will is a system of moral relations that cannot be grasped by any single mind, it arises without design from diverse wills. A contemporary account along these lines, shorn of its idealist foundations, would require (*i*) a plausible account of a system of morality as a spontaneous order, arising essentially unplanned out of the complex inter-actions of heterogeneous agents and, (*ii*) a claim that the reasoned control of each agent endorses this emergent morality. Now the first claim certainly has been defended with-out resort to the absolute. Hayek, for one, has presented an evolutionary analysis of morality as a system of evolved rules to order complex and diverse societies (see Hayek, 1973). That the interaction of diverse agents gives rise to moral rules to structure their interactions is by no means beyond credibility. Indeed, contemporary analyses of the emergence of social norms present detailed models of how this might occur (see, e.g., Bicchieri, 2006: ch. 6; Brennan et al., 2013: Pt. II).

The pressing problem would seem to be claim (*ii*), that the reasoned control of each endorses this spontaneous order. Hayek himself was deeply skeptical that explicit justi-fication of these rules is to be had (Hayek, 1988, esp. chs. 1 and 2). It is not clear, though, that such pessimism is warranted. As contemporary theorists of social morality and social norms stress, basic normative rules to structure the interactions of heteroge-neous agents, especially those that help them escape social dilemmas with Prisoner's Dilemma–like structures, are critical to their successful agency; without such rules each does far worse than under universal conformity to them. As in Rousseau's account, agents—even very heterogeneous ones—surely share private interests in escaping from the traps of destructive social dilemmas. Moreover, recent evidence indicates that con-formity to such rules is not only endorsed by the private interests of each individual, but by evolved commitments to fairness.[15] If so, we have at least the outlines of how a con-temporary Bosanquet-inspired theory of the general will might proceed: if a system of rules and norms arises out of the interactions of diverse agents, which help them escape from social dilemmas, and if these rules correspond to their normative commitments concerning fairness, then given the interests and normative commitments of each, each may reason themselves to endorsing these shared rules of order.

To see this better, suppose we have a diverse group of agents *G*, who are caught in social dilemmas in which, if each acts as she thinks best, each will be worse off than if all cooperated—but if all the others cooperate, each does best by defecting. Respect for bodily integrity and property, and sustainable resource use, are a few of the critical social dilemmas all societies face. In *G* rule *R* may have evolved such that, given the diverse interests of the members of *G* and their diverse judgments about the fair way to resolve social dilemmas, each does better by her own lights when conforming to *R* than she would do if there were no rule, or widespread violation of *R*. Because the character of *R* is such that compliance furthers their interests and is consistent with their values and commitments regarding fairness, when they exercise their reason to level *l* members of *G* would conclude that they have sufficient reason to conform to *R*'s directives. And if this is so, then diverse agents living under *R*, exercising their freedom as reasoned control, will be fit for responsibility. As with Bosanquet's account, it is not required that they all, collectively, perceive this; what is critical is that all are fit to be held responsible for violations of these rules of cooperative order, which advance the interests of all. Should the presently evolved system not be so endorsable, we could inquire whether explicit revisions could make it so. This, of course, is not to say the project can be carried through, but it certainly does not seem a will-o'-the-wisp.

4.2. Diverse agents solving moral problems

The rules and order project sketched above is something of a compromise between Rousseau's and Bosanquet's visions of the general will. Like Rousseau, it sees the general will as focusing on rules for advancing the interests of each; like Bosanquet, it sees these rules as arising out of the diverse interactions of heterogeneous agents rather than a "shared point of view."[16] Some contemporary lines of analysis indicate that we might even move closer to Bosanquet's vision of a general will in which, as heterogeneous moral agents, when one agent's insight into the general will "stops," another picks up. This idea nicely captures an interpretation of the philosophical import of recent work by Lu Hong and Scott E. Page about the necessity of diversity for solving our problems (Page, 2007a) and, we propose, this includes our moral problems.

The starting point of Hong and Page's analysis is a group of cognitively diverse agents: people who look at the same problem in different ways.[17] In their terms, our heterogeneous group has diverse *perspectives*—different ways of representing a given problem and solutions. Suppose we take a problem that might confront a moral community, say choosing the most fair taxation system.[18] Perspectives are diverse if the set of what is feasible is mentally represented in different ways. So, for example, suppose a group is thinking about the problem, and in the end (though not necessarily at the outset) all can recognize that they can choose from five possible tax reforms (a–e); their question is how well each of these proposals does in solving their problem of achieving the most fair system. Each perspective represents the underlying structure of the options in different ways. Alf's might represent the set of possible tax reforms based on the number of votes each proposal is likely to receive in the Senate, Betty's might arrange them based on their simplicity, while Charlie's perspective might organize them based on how much they are likely to cut taxes for the middle class. The way in which a person organizes the set of possible solutions determines which options are similar to others and which are very different; since a perspective determines how one structures the options, it also structures how one thinks of alternatives and locates new solutions.[19] For simplicity's sake, let us suppose that each of our three individuals can, after reflection, decide how well each member of the set solves their fairness problem, though at the outset each simply considers a few options that their perspective makes salient. Alf, for example, might start off with the option most likely to pass the Senate, Betty seeks the simplest alteration of the tax code, and Charlie looks at the proposal that is best for the middle class. Suppose, then, that if all the options were presented to them they would be ranked as $\{a > b > c > d > e\}$; call this the objective fairness ordering. Because they have different perspectives on the problem, they do not immediately see all the possibilities. Suppose we have the three perspectives:[20]

Alf: $e-c-d-b-a$
Betty: $d-c-b-e-a$
Charlie: $e-d-c-b-a$

Suppose that Alf deliberates about the fairest policy, using the simple method (what Hong and Page call a *heuristic*: a strategy for locating solutions within a perspective (Page, 2007a: ch. 2))[21] of taking the first option in his perspective, and then searching for a better answer until he gets to the point where the next thing he thinks of is worse; at that point he stops his search. In more formal terms, this would be a "local optimum" for Alf; given the way he understands the problem, he has arrived at the best answer he can see—the next step is worse. Employing this idea, Alf might start with e (the most likely proposal to pass the Senate), but he then sees whether he can find a better policy by searching his perspective. So he next considers c, which is indeed an improvement. Having found this improvement Alf is excited and keeps on searching; however, the next proposal that his perspective suggests is d, which is worse than c. Disappointed, he stops. But Betty can, as Bosanquet indicated, pick up from there; she locates c on her perspective and finds that, using the same heuristic as Alf, she can arrive at a better solution, b. She, however, gets stuck at b, for it is surrounded on both sides by worse options (c and e). Charlie then thinks about his middle-class tax perspective and where b is on it; he sees that, again, using the same heuristic, he can improve on b, and can move to a, the "global optimum." They thus arrive at the most fair option.

This toy account shows why the reasoned control of each would support a—on each of their views it is the best and, interestingly, none would have arrived at it on their own. Thus the general will, as Bosanquet argues, augments the reasoning of each; by each reasoning to, say, level l (correctly employing our simple heuristic given their perspective, for example), they can collectively arrive at a result that is better than anyone could have arrived at by alone employing l. Although none of our agents can arrive at a, *the objectively best answer*, by exercising their reasoned control alone, if they reason together, picking up in the process where others left off, by the end of their collective problem-solving enterprise, they can each see how the exercise of their reason leads them to endorse a. The idea, as we saw above with Bosanquet, is that people can build on the solutions of others to produce moral improvement.[22] Of course there is a critical difference: in the end all of our perspectives do fully grasp the general will (the global optimum); unlike in the rules-and-order version (§4.1), the general will arises from an explicit search.

To better appreciate the power the Hong-Page analysis, let us imagine a community containing members of unequal individual ability—from the very good to the mediocre. Now divide the community into two groups: one homogenous group composed only of the best reasoners, in which the individual members each possess approximately the same perspective, and another group that contains a diverse group of competent reasoners, but not the best. Under certain conditions,[23] the diverse group will outperform the better, but homogeneous, group (this is the Hong-Page "Diversity Trumps Ability Theorem") (Page, 2007a: 158–165). The key to the result is that the best problem solvers tend to have similar tools and solve problems in similar ways, so that a group of the best problem solvers tends not to perform much better than any single member of the group. On the other hand, a group of relatively good, but diverse, problem solvers can perform collectively better than the group of homogenous experts (Page, 2007a: 137). Indeed, when the relevant conditions are satisfied, a group of diverse problem solvers must outperform the best individual problem solver. This does not show that ability does not matter, but rather, once individuals meet a certain ability threshold, diversity matters even more than does ability for solving difficult problems (see Page, 2007b: 11).[24]

On this account, diversity generates a type of "superadditivity" (Page, 2007a: 339–340): "When a collection of people work together to solve a problem, and one person makes an improvement, the others can often improve on this new solution even further. Problem solving is not the realization of a state but a process of innovation in which improvements build on improvements" (Page, 2007b: 13–14). Bosanquet believed that the general will arises through a complex interaction of individual viewpoints, and this, it turns out, is the case with problem solving through diversity. To realize the benefits of diversity, however, the members of our diverse community must interact so that they can build upon the work of each other and spot solutions where others have gotten stuck or "stopped."[25] It will also be necessary to describe with some specificity the particular moral problems our diverse agents are working to solve.[26] It is implausible to think of our agents as trying to divine the general will in terms of the "entire system of moral relations." Rather, we can think of them as trying to solve the discrete moral problems with which they are confronted. This might include concrete questions surrounding the distribution of burdens and benefits within a political order, the morality of physician-assisted suicide, the death penalty, certain interrogation techniques, and abortion, difficulties involving the ethical treatment of nonhuman animals, and so forth. By solving these discrete problems (and so many other distinct moral problems to which we have already engineered more settled solutions), the general will in terms of the "entire system of moral relations" can emerge, even though no one is attempting to discern the whole scheme.

We do not wish to suggest that the Hong-Page theorem and its approach to diversity are unproblematic. As we saw in our toy example, the approach supposes that while each perspective disagrees about how each option is related to the others, there is consensus about the value of each option as a solution to the collective problem. We certainly might query the stability of this combination of diversity in how the options are understood with consensus about the value of each. The theorem also supposes that each perspective, while viewing the options very differently, nevertheless successfully communicates its findings to individuals with other perspectives. These are real problems.[27] However, the point is not that the Hong-Page approach to diversity is without difficulties, but that it demonstrates, in a sophisticated and thoughtful way, how the very diversity that seems to militate against the formation of a general will might, instead, be the engine of its discovery.

5. POSITIVE FREEDOM AND MORAL RESPONSIBILITY IN A DIVERSE SOCIETY

As we have argued, to sensibly hold another morally responsible we must suppose that the person has reasoned control over his actions and that, exercising that control, he would be capable of acting on the relevant moral directive. From this thesis one might proceed in two ways. One might suppose that moral responsibility is unproblematic—*of course* we can be held morally responsible. Given this, the preferred conception of freedom simply will be one that shows us to be fit for moral responsibility. We might say this this approach reasons *from* our acknowledged responsibility *to* a conception of freedom that supports it (this, we suspect, is along the lines of Pettit's analysis). The other tack, which we have followed here, is to first analyze the concept of freedom as reasoned control, and then *inquire*: are agents with such freedom fit for responsibility, given the character of their morality? This allows that in certain social orders agents with positive freedom may not be fit for responsibility, because they could not use their reasoned control to comply with it. On this second view we need to ask under what conditions free agents will be fit for responsibility.

Taking this second route, we have argued, ties positive freedom to the general will: how could a morality be such that each person's positive liberty is congruent with the demands of a shared morality, and so each is fit to be held responsible? Rousseau's own solution, we have suggested, does not seem appropriate for a diverse society—it cannot show how members of a diverse society are all fit to be held responsible for violating the moral rules that structure their lives. However, Rousseau's account does not exhaust theorizing about the general will. Picking up on some clues from Bosanquet, we have very briefly sketched two analyses according to which a highly diverse society can share a general will. Our aim was not to establish these accounts, but to show that Rousseau's project—of showing how each can be free yet obey the moral laws—is alive and important today.

NOTES

1. Our thanks to the participants in the 2014 Tucson workshop on freedom for their questions and comments; our special thanks to Dave Schmidtz, Carmen Pavel, and two anonymous readers.
2. For a sophisticated defense of a negative liberty view, see Kramer 2003.
3. Philip Pettit (2001) explicitly argues this; for another such example, see Swanton 1992.
4. This is the sense in which S. I. Benn (1988) offers a "theory of freedom" (see also Benn and Weinstein, 1971). From a very different perspective, this is Amartya Sen's (2002) approach.
5. "She found out the central meaning of her ceremonial one day when she suddenly understood the meaning of the rule that the pillow must not touch the back of the bedstead. The pillow, she said, had always been a woman to her and the upright wooden back a man. Thus

she wanted—by magic, we must interpolate—to keep man and woman apart—that is, to separate her parents from each other, and not allow them to have sexual intercourse. . . . If a pillow was a woman, then the shaking of the eiderdown till all the feathers were at the bottom and caused a swelling there had a sense as well. It meant making the woman pregnant; but she never failed to smooth away the pregnancy again, for she had been for years afraid that her parents' intercourse would result in another child" (Freud, 1973: 307–308, paragraph break deleted).

6. But perhaps the teacher should be considered as a moral expert. Suppose the undergraduate was directed by a doctor to administer some medicine to his ailing mother who is in his care. Although he may be unable to understand the biochemical molecular interactions that are responsible for making this particular medicine an effective treatment for his mother's condition, we would nonetheless hold him morally responsible for disregarding the doctor's expert counsel. In other words, although he may not be able to appreciate the reason why the medicine will cure his mother's condition, he nonetheless has a reason (i.e., the direction of an expert) to administer the medication. Perhaps we should think that the undergraduate has similar reason with respect to the demanding transcendental deduction or intricate formal proof. This matter brings to light difficult problems of the epistemic warrant of expert testimony. Even if the undergraduate does not understand the science behind the expert medical advice, presumably he does have understandable evidence that the doctor is an expert—if there is no such sufficient evidence then he is not responsible for ignoring the medical advice. And here lies the rub: does the undergraduate have evidence that this instructor is an expert on *morality* (as opposed to proofs, or the literature in moral philosophy)? There are many reasons to answer in the negative. On simply epistemic grounds, if the body of purported experts disagree among themselves, then there is apt to be insufficient evidence as to who is the expert. More generally, an ideal of moral autonomy may entail that free moral agents cannot morally follow expert authorities without full understanding—such action would have no moral worth. Thus it is reasonable to suppose that the undergraduate need not defer to the doctor's conclusion that *morality requires* the undergraduate to administer the medicine to his mother, only to the doctor's judgment that *this medicine* is the one he should administer. In any case, if our undergraduate is truly unable to appreciate the reasons why he should administer some kind of aid to his ailing mother, while his lack of appreciation does not make that demand false, it does suggest that our practice of holding him responsible will be profoundly modified (much as it is with young children whose understanding of moral requirements often fails, but whom we might expect to defer to a parent during the learning process). Our thanks to a reader for Oxford University Press for bringing this matter to our attention.

7. Benn (1988: 155–164) argues that the person must be free from three classes of defects—epistemic, of practical rationality, and of psychic continuity. See also Joel Feinberg's analysis of voluntary action in *Harm to Self* (1986: 115).

8. Compare, for example, Michael Smith's view (1994: 151ff) with that of Gerald Gaus (2011: §13).

9. There is evidence that Rousseau, at least on occasion, saw the problem in the way we have rephrased it. In arguing against unlimited forms of government with "absolute authority" and requiring "unlimited obedience," Rousseau writes that "Such a renunciation [of one's liberty] is incompatible with man's nature, and *to strip him of all freedom of will is to strip his actions of all morality*" (1988: 89 (Bk. I, ch. 4), emphasis supplied). For Rousseau, then, any form of moral community that strips people of their positive freedom will also rob them of moral responsibility because such freedom is a necessary condition for responsibility.

10. This holds except with respect to the initial formation of the state, which must be accomplished via the unanimous vote of those who will become citizens (see Rousseau, 1988: 151 (Bk. IV, ch. 2)).

11. See also, e.g., Rousseau 1988, p. 112 (Bk. II, chap. 9): "The same laws cannot be appropriate for so many diverse provinces, which have different moral habits as well as contrasting climates and cannot all tolerate the same form of government."

12. For an excellent analysis of different accounts of the general will, see Chapman, 1956: ch. 10.

13. Unlike Rousseau, who thought that vast differences in circumstances would make it difficult or impossible for individuals to be governed under a single state (see note 11, above), Bosanquet thought such vast diversity of circumstance could be accommodated within a general will (see Bosanquet, 2011b: 309: "It is even possible, and obviously usual, to support by our private will different arrangements in different localities, adapted to different conditions; and, in fact, this principle runs throughout our whole social and political life.").

14. Bosanquet also stressed that for these diverse minds to form a coherent system they must be organized by common psychological structures (see his fascinating 2011c).

15. Bowles and Gintis (2011), Bicchieri (2006: chs. 1 and 3), and Gaus (2011: ch. 3) each offer examples of how normative rules that prevent us from succumbing to social dilemmas are endorsed by our evolved fairness commitments. This distinguishes these accounts from the traditional contractarian project, as exemplified by David Gauthier's *Morals by Agreement* (1986).

16. According to Rawls, Rousseau's idea of the general will requires a shared "point of view" (2007: 229ff).

17. Note that what is required here is *cognitive* diversity—different cognitive tools that individuals can bring to bear on the problem. This is distinct from identity diversity, involving gender, race, ethnicity, culture, age, and so on. Still, identity diversity will often correlate with or drive cognitive diversity because people's cognitive tools are shaped by their life experiences, as well as by learning routines, rules, and scripts from other contexts. And these things, in turn, are often shaped by our cultures, values, and identities. Nonetheless, the benefits of identity diversity and its correlation with cognitive diversity vary by context (see Page, 2007b: 19: "As life experiences often frame how people see social issues, for public policy problems identity differences can translate directly into diverse perspectives. On more scientific and technical problems, the linkages are less direct.").

18. There are many such communal problems, of different levels, from responses to terrorist acts to places for dumping trash (see Page, 2007a: ch. 1, esp. pp. 30–33).

19. Not all perspectives will be useful ones. If we are trying to determine the best places to dump trash, a perspective that considers only nearness to the individual's current location will probably not be as useful as, for example, one that organizes solutions based on long-term viability (see Page, 2007a: 35).

20. For a somewhat similar example, see Landemore, 2013: 102.

21. In this example, we consider only one simple heuristic. However, agents may employ more than one heuristic, and different agents may employ diverse heuristics, which, when combined with each other or paired with different perspectives, allow agents to locate solutions that might not be found otherwise.

22. Two other important cognitive tools also contribute to diversity: interpretations and predictive models. *Interpretations* classify or sort parts of the world; they provide mappings of features of the world into mental categories (Page, 2007a: ch: 3, esp. pp. 79–81). For example, we might sort that place called "Rocco's Little Chicago" into the category of

pizza restaurants, or classify that cold, brown, creamy ball as a kind of chocolate dessert. *Predictive models* then use these interpretations, which have sorted features of the world into categories, to tell us what might happen (Page, 2007: ch. 4, esp. pp. 92–94). For example, I might predict that I'll like that dessert because I like creamy, chocolate things. These interpretations and models make regular appearances in our everyday thinking, from predicting whether one will like a dessert, to predicting which policy will effectively deter violent crime, or which area of specialty in philosophy will be most sought-after on the job market.

23. They are: (*i*) the problem is difficult enough that no single individual always locates the best solution; (*ii*) the problem solvers are smart, and have relevant cognitive tools—that is, they are each capable of composing a list of their local optima; (*iii*) the problem solvers are diverse—for any proposed solution other than the global optimum, there is at least one individual problem solver who can locate an improvement; (*iv*) the problem-solving group must be at least reasonably sized and drawn from a relatively large population so that the collection of problem solvers is sufficiently diverse (Page, 2007a: 159–162). For a formal proof of the theorem, see Hong and Page (2004).

24. We have only considered here the "Diversity Trumps Ability" theorem, which has strong conclusions, but also requires a set of conditions to be met. Page also develops the "Diversity Beats Homogeneity Theorem," which is less demanding, and shows that more diverse groups of problem solvers will on average beat their more homogenous equals (2007a: 153–157).

25. Strictly speaking, diverse members of the community cannot realize the benefits of diversity just by interacting with one another; they must do so with a positive outlook toward the advantages that diversity can generate: "If people do not believe in the value of diversity, then when part of a diverse team they're not as likely to produce good outcomes" (Page, 2007b: 7; see also Page, 2008; Page, 2007a: xiv–xviii).

26. Our thanks again to a reader for Oxford University Press for encouraging us to clarify this point.

27. These worries are developed in Gaus and Hankins, 2017.

References

Benn, S. I., 1988. *A theory of freedom.* Cambridge, UK: Cambridge University Press.

Benn, S. I., and Weinstein, W. L., 1971. "Being free to act, and being a free man." *Mind,* new series, 80 (Apr.), pp.194–211.

Berlin, I., 1969. "Two concepts of liberty." In: *Four essays on liberty.* Oxford: Oxford University Press. pp.118–172.

Bicchieri, C., 2006. *The grammar of society.* Cambridge, UK: Cambridge University Press.

Bosanquet, B., 2011a. "The antithesis between individualism and socialism philosophically considered." In: G. F. Gaus and W. Sweet, eds. *The philosophical theory of the state and related essays.* South Bend, IN: St. Augustine's Press. pp.324–346.

Bosanquet, B., 2011b. "The notion of a general will." In: G. F. Gaus and W. Sweet, eds. *The philosophical theory of the state and related essays.* South Bend, IN: St. Augustine's Press. pp.305–311.

Bosanquet, B., 2011c. "Psychological illustration of the idea of a real or general will." In: G. F. Gaus and W. Sweet, eds. *The philosophical theory of the state and related essays.* South Bend, IN: St. Augustine's Press. pp.160–176.

Bowles, S., and Gintis, H., 2011. *A cooperative species*. Princeton, NJ: Princeton University Press.

Brennan, G., Eriksson, L., Goodin, R. E., and Southwood, N., 2013. *Explaining norms*. Oxford: Oxford University Press.

Chapman, J. W., 1956. *Rousseau—totalitarian or liberal?* New York: Columbia University Press.

Feinberg, J., 1986. *Harm to self*. Oxford: Oxford University Press.

Freud, S., 1973. *Introductory lectures on psychoanalysis*. Translated by J. Strachey. Harmondsworth, UK: Penguin Books.

Gaus, G., 1994. "Green, Bosanquet and the philosophy of coherence." In: S. G. Shanker and G. H. R. Parkinson, gen. eds. *The Routledge history of philosophy*, vol. 7, C. L. Ten, ed., *The nineteenth century*. London: Routledge. pp.408–436.

Gaus, G., 1997. "Does democracy reveal the will of the people? Four takes on Rousseau." *Australasian Journal of Philosophy*, 75 (June), pp.141–162.

Gaus, G., 2001. "Bernard Bosanquet's communitarian defense of economic individualism." In: D. Weinstein and A. Simhony, eds. *The new liberalism: reconciling liberty and community*. Cambridge, UK: Cambridge University Press. pp.136–158.

Gaus, G., 2011. *The order of public reason*. Cambridge, UK: Cambridge University Press.

Gaus, G., and Hankins, K., 2017. "Searching for the ideal: the fundamental diversity dilemma." In: M. Weber and K. Vallier, eds. *Political utopias*. Oxford: Oxford University Press.

Gauthier, D., 1986. *Morals by agreement*. Oxford: Oxford University Press.

Green, T. H., 1986. "On the different senses of 'freedom' as applied to the will and the moral progress of man." In: T. H. Green, *Lectures on the principles of political obligation and other writings*, edited by P. Harris and J. Morrow. Cambridge, UK: Cambridge University Press. pp.228–249.

Hayek, F. A., 1960. *The constitution of liberty*. London: Routledge & Kegan Paul.

Hayek, F. A., 1973. *Rules and order*. London: Routledge.

Hayek, F. A., 1988. *The fatal conceit*. Edited by W. W. Bartley III. Chicago: University of Chicago Press.

Hong, L., and Page, S. E., 2004. "Groups of diverse problem solvers can outperform groups of high-ability problem solvers." *Proceedings of the National Academy of Sciences*, 101(46), pp.16385–16389.

Kramer, M. H., 2003. *The quality of freedom*. Oxford: Oxford University Press.

Landemore, H., 2013. *Democratic reason*. Princeton, NJ: Princeton University Press.

MacCallum, G., 1972. "Negative and positive freedom." In: P. Laslett, W. G. Runciman, and Q. Skinner, eds. *Philosophy, politics and society*. 4th ser. Oxford: Basil Blackwell. pp.174–193.

Page, S. E., 2007a. *The difference: how the power of diversity creates better groups, firms, schools and societies*. Princeton, NJ: Princeton University Press.

Page, S. E. 2007b. "Making the difference: applying a logic of diversity." *Academy of Management Perspectives*, 21(4), pp.6–20.

Page, S. E., 2008. "The power of diversity." *The School Administrator*, 65(9), pp.35–41.

Pettit, P., 1997. *Republicanism: a theory of freedom and government*. Oxford: Oxford University Press.

Pettit, P., 2001. *A theory of freedom: from the psychology to the politics of agency*. Oxford: Polity.

Rawls, J., 2007. *Lectures on the history of political philosophy*. Edited by S. Freeman. Cambridge, MA: Harvard University Press.

Rousseau, J. J., 1988. The social contract. In: A. Ritter and J. C. Bondanella. *Rousseau's political writings*. Translated by J. C. Bondanella. New York: Norton.

Sen, A., 2002. "Arrow lectures." In: *Rationality and freedom*. Cambridge, MA: Harvard University Press. pp.581–712.

Smith, M., 1994. *The moral problem*. Oxford: Blackwell.

Strawson, P., 1961. "Social morality and individual ideal." *Philosophy*, 36 (January), pp.1–17.

Strawson, P., 1962. "Freedom and resentment." *Proceedings of the British Academy*, 48, pp.188–211.

Swanton, C., 1992. *Freedom: a coherence view*. Indianapolis: Hackett.

Taylor, C., 1979. "What's wrong with negative liberty." In: A. Ryan, ed. *The idea of freedom*. Oxford: Clarendon Press. pp.175–194.

CHAPTER 3

··

MORALIZED CONCEPTIONS
OF LIBERTY

··

RALF M. BADER

1. INTRODUCTION

ONE of the key questions regarding liberty[1] is the question whether liberty is a descriptive/value-neutral concept or one that is essentially normative/moralized. Are descriptive facts sufficient for determining whether x is free to ϕ, or is it necessary to also bring in moral facts for understanding and applying the concept of liberty?[2] This question is of central importance because it determines whether liberty has intrinsic normative significance, thereby determining what role liberty can play in moral and political theorizing.[3]

Value-neutral theories consider liberty to be a purely descriptive concept. This kind of approach does not presuppose any moral judgments, but it cannot underwrite them either. This is because the resulting concept will not have intrinsic normative significance and will be too thin to do any justificatory work by itself. It will merely be a "flat description that carries, in itself, no suggestion of endorsement or complaint" (Dworkin, 2000: 125). This should be clear insofar as assigning intrinsic significance to freedom (where this is construed in a non-moralized manner) amounts to considering being free to ϕ as mattering in itself, such that any constraint on ϕ-ing would thereby be pro tanto problematic, no matter what ϕ-ing consists in. If no restrictions are placed on ϕ-ing, such that, say, the freedom to torture, to rape, and to murder are classified as genuine freedoms, it is evident that considerations of freedom do not as such constitute pro tanto reasons. There will be some freedoms that are not to be infringed, whereas others are to be restricted, which implies that freedom will not have intrinsic normative significance, i.e., freedom as such will not be of significance.

A moralized notion, by contrast, builds morality into the very concept of liberty, thereby ensuring that it is intrinsically normatively significant and that it can, consequently, play a central justificatory role in moral and political theorizing. Liberty then matters in its own right and its significance is not to be reduced to the value of the actions that one is free to do. Accordingly, constraints on freedom are problematic as such and there is a pro tanto reason not to restrict liberty, which allows us to underwrite the "presumption that humans should not obstruct one another's activity" (Miller, 1983: 69).[4]

This chapter will be concerned with rights-based conceptions of liberty.[5] Section 2 will elucidate how exactly rights-based accounts moralize liberty, identifying two ways in which rights enter into the analysis of freedom, namely (i) by determining which courses of action an agent can be free or unfree to perform, and (ii) by determining which obstacles classify as constraints on freedom. Section 3 distinguishes moralized negative conceptions of liberty from positive conceptions of liberty, thereby showing that moralizing liberty is not tantamount to adopting a positive conception. Section 4 contrasts rights-based conceptions with the moral responsibility view, showing that the latter does not constitute a viable alternative and that a rights-based approach is the only acceptable way in which liberty can be moralized.

2. MORALIZING LIBERTY

Negative conceptions of freedom, which consider freedom to consist in the absence of constraints, are primarily divided with respect to the question as to which obstacles or interferences classify as constraints on freedom and which ones are not freedom-infringing. Rights-based conceptions provide a distinctive answer to this question by considering only rights-violating interferences as infringements of liberty. A rights-violating interference is an interference with an action that (i) an agent has a right to perform and that (ii) violates this right. This implies that rights-based accounts involve moralized characterizations of both the y- and the z-parameter in MacCallum's triadic schema, giving rise to restrictions with respect to the type of action that is being interfered with, as well as with respect to the source of the obstacle.

According to MacCallum, any freedom claim takes the form: agent x is free from constraints y to do/be/become z (cf. MacCallum, 1967). Differing conceptions of freedom disagree about the specification of the domains of these parameters, i.e., to which subjects freedom is to be attributed (= x), which obstacles classify as constraints on freedom (= y), and which actions an agent can be free or unfree to perform (= z). Using this schema, we can distinguish between an agent being free, unfree, and not free to ϕ.[6] In particular, an agent x is free to ϕ iff ϕ is in z and nothing in y is preventing x from ϕ-ing. By contrast, x is unfree to ϕ iff ϕ is in z and something in y is preventing x from ϕ-ing. Finally, x is not free to ϕ iff ϕ is not in z. This means that there are two ways in which x can be prevented from ϕ-ing without this being inimical to x's freedom, namely insofar as (i) though x is prevented from ϕ-ing, the action in question is not in z, in which case x was not free to ϕ in the first place, and (ii) though x is prevented from ϕ-ing, what is doing the preventing is not in y, in which case x is unable to ϕ yet still free to ϕ.

The restriction to rights-violating interferences gives rise to both of these possibilities. On the one hand, the agent in question can fail to have a right to ϕ, such that preventing the agent from ϕ-ing does not classify as a rights-violating interference and hence does not infringe liberty. This amounts to moralizing the z-parameter by restricting its domain to normatively possible courses of action, i.e., permissible actions that the agent has a right to perform, thereby excluding certain obstacles from classifying as infringements of liberty, namely those that prevent actions that are merely part of license and not of liberty. On the other hand, the agent can be prevented from ϕ-ing without the agent's right to ϕ being violated, thereby failing to be inimical to liberty. This moralization of the y-parameter appeals to the notion of a rights-violating interference in fixing the precise conditions that an obstacle must satisfy, in particular the kind of causal origin that it must have, in order to classify as a constraint that restricts liberty. (Discussions in the literature have so far exclusively focused on the rights-based moralization of the z-parameter, i.e., the contrast between liberty and license, and have not considered the moralization of the y-parameter.)

2.1. Liberty vs. license

The domain of the z-parameter specifies the possible actions that an agent can be free or unfree to perform. Any action that is not in this domain is not in the relevant sense a possible action in the first place and is hence not one to which freedom is applicable, which ensures that an agent can neither be free nor unfree to perform such an action. The distinction between freedom and unfreedom is only applicable within the domain of the z-parameter, i.e., among "possible" actions, where the notion of possibility could be, for instance, that of logical, nomological, technological, or moral possibility.

This means that anything that defines the domain of possible actions and that is constitutive of the relevant type of possibility cannot classify as a constraint on freedom, even if it renders certain actions impossible with respect to a more encompassing notion of possibility. This is because to be a constraint is to be something that renders a possible course of action (i.e., one that is in the domain of the z-parameter) physically impossible for the agent in question (or, possibly, merely ineligible). For instance, the laws of nature make it the case that certain types of actions are nomologically impossible, without in any way being detrimental to freedom (given that the relevant modality is not broader than that of nomological possibility). Likewise, anything that renders something impossible that is not in the relevant sense possible is also not a constraint. For instance, if the relevant type of possibility is that of normative possibility, then something that renders an action physically impossible is not a constraint on freedom if the action in question is not normatively possible. Given that the action is not a member of the domain of possible actions, it cannot be one with respect to which an agent can be rendered unfree.

Rights-based conceptions draw an important distinction between liberty and license when it comes to characterizing the domain of the z-parameter (cf. Locke, 1689: §6). In particular, according to such moralizations this domain only consists of legitimate courses of actions, i.e., one is only free to do things one has a right to do. That is, the relevant notion of possibility that specifies which actions an agent can be free or unfree to perform is that of normative possibility. Actions that are not normatively possible, i.e., impermissible actions, are not ones that one is free to perform (where one is not unfree to perform them either, but where one is rather neither free nor unfree to perform such actions). As such, they are not in the domain of the z-parameter and are not part of liberty, but instead belong to mere license.

The restriction to normatively possible courses of actions has the effect that certain obstacles do not restrict liberty. In particular, any obstacle that renders a normatively impossible action physically impossible (or ineligible) will not be a constraint on freedom. This is because actions that are not normatively possible are ones to which freedom is not applicable and hence ones which one cannot be rendered unfree to perform. Put differently, if the agent is prevented from doing something that he is not free to do in the first place, due to not having a right to do that thing, then the agent's freedom has not been restricted. Accordingly, only rights-violating interferences infringe liberty, whereas preventing someone from doing something that person does not have a right to do does not restrict freedom. Instead of these kinds of interferences infringing liberty, they merely restrict license.

The restriction of the domain of the z-parameter that is due to the contrast between liberty and license thus explains why only some interferences classify as constraints, insofar as it implies that only rights-violating interferences restrict liberty, whereas those that do not violate rights are not inimical to freedom but are only inimical to license.

2.2. Rights-violating interferences

Once the domain of possible actions is fixed, the next step is to determine which obstacles and interferences infringe an agent's liberty and render an agent unfree to perform an action, and which obstacles simply make a possible course of action less desirable or constitute cases of mere inability, without being detrimental to the agent's liberty. This issue splits into two questions.

On the one hand, there is the question as to the strength of the constraint. Here the question is whether the obstacle has to render the action (physically) impossible or whether it suffices to render it ineligible. Whereas a pure negative conception, such as the one espoused by Steiner (1994), will consider actions that are ineligible as a result of an interference (such as a threat) as merely being rendered undesirable but still ones that the agent is free to perform, other theories will consider this ineligibility to amount to unfreedom. Rights-based conceptions as such are neutral with respect to this question and can be combined both with an impossibility view as well as with an ineligibility view.[7]

On the other hand, there is the question of the source of the constraint. Various restrictions can be imposed that specify the kind of causal origin that an obstacle or interference has to have in order for it to be a constraint that restricts liberty. Given that one is concerned with freedom insofar as it features in political philosophy and as such regards social and political relations among agents, it is plausible to require obstacles to involve human agency.[8] That is, constraints on freedom have to be due to or at least removable by human agency. This means that constraints that are due to nature and not alterable by human agency can be set aside, i.e., such obstacles do not restrict freedom but merely make it the case that the agent is unable to perform the action in question.

The restriction that the obstacle has to be attributable to human agency still leaves open a number of possible restrictions on sources of constraints. One might, for instance, restrict freedom-infringing interferences to those for which someone is causally responsible, those that are intentionally brought about, those that are the result of actions rather than omissions, those the eventuation of which is foreseen or foreseeable, or those for which someone can be held morally responsible.

Purely descriptive approaches face the problem of being either too broad or too narrow, both with respect to our intuitive judgments concerning freedom and with respect to generating a notion of freedom that can have a plausible claim to being normatively significant.[9] Moralized accounts, by contrast, allow us to address the source question in a satisfactory manner, by providing a distinctive understanding of the y-parameter.

On a moralized account, freedom is restricted by rights violations that render actions impossible (or ineligible). This means that, in the context of a rights-based account, the specification of the relevant restriction simply becomes a question as to what kinds of interferences with an agent's possible actions classify as rights violations. By determining what constitutes a rights violation, one determines which obstacles that render possible courses of action impossible (or ineligible) are ones that restrict liberty. For instance, in order to determine whether a particular obstacle, such as an obstacle that is due to a negligent (in)action, infringes liberty, one has to determine whether this (in)action classifies as a rights violation. If negligently bringing about an obstacle amounts to a rights violation, then it is an unjustified form of interference that constrains liberty.

The fact that the y-parameter is restricted in this manner means that it is possible that ϕ-ing is impossible/ineligible for x (as a result of someone else's agency) without x's freedom being infringed, even in cases where x has a right to ϕ. The analysis of infringements of liberty thus cannot be decomposed into two separate conditions, such that x's freedom to ϕ is infringed iff (i) ϕ-ing is impossible/ineligible and (ii) x has a right to ϕ. The fact that a right is violated (and hence that liberty is infringed) does not just amount to ϕ-ing being rendered impossible/ineligible together with the agent having a right to ϕ, i.e., an infringement of liberty is not just an interference with an action that an agent has a right to perform. That is, the moralized account does not simply supplement the value-neutral analysis by adding the condition that x has a right to ϕ, but instead identifies distinctive conditions that interferences have to satisfy to classify as constraints. The impossibility/ineligibility needs to involve a rights violation, i.e., that which renders the action impossible/ineligible must amount to a rights violation in order for it to constitute an infringement of liberty.

A theory specifying what rights we have determines the contrast between liberty and license, whereas a theory specifying the conditions under which these rights are violated will allow us to determine what causal origins an obstacle must have in order to classify as an infringement of liberty. The y-parameter is thus morally determined, insofar as the precise delimitation and explanation as to which interferences are classified as constraints is understood in terms of moral notions, in particular in terms of the notion of a rights-violating interference.

3. MORALIZED VS. POSITIVE LIBERTY

Theories of positive liberty identify freedom with self-realization, self-mastery, self-determination, or self-perfection, i.e., with acting/being/becoming a certain way, whereby that the doing, being, or becoming of which liberty is taken to consist in is specified in moral terms. Freedom is thus seen to amount to behaving morally or achieving a certain telos, and the domain of the z-parameter, accordingly, consists of rational, virtuous, or authentic actions.[10] As such, these theories also consider liberty to be essentially normative/moralized, rather than merely being a purely descriptive concept.

The fact that positive conceptions of liberty are moralized in this way has led some to consider a rights-based conception to be tantamount to a positive conception of liberty. Waldron, for instance, claims that the moralized account "transforms our conception of freedom into a moralized definition of positive liberty (so that the only freedom that is relevant is the freedom to do what is right)" (Waldron, 1991: 308). This he thinks is ironic given that "[i]t was precisely the identification of freedom with virtue (and the inference that a restriction on vice was no restriction at all) that most troubled liberals about theories of positive liberty" (Waldron, 1991: 307). The moralization involved in a rights-based conception of negative liberty is, however, to be sharply distinguished from the type of moralization involved in a positive conception of liberty.

According to positive conceptions of liberty, the concept of liberty is not an opportunity concept but an exercise concept (cf. Taylor, 1979). This means that liberty does not merely consist in having certain opportunities that can be left unrealized without liberty being in any way reduced, such that all that matters is that the relevant obstacles are absent. Rather, liberty consists in acting/being/becoming a certain way, i.e., the relevant opportunities do not just have to be available but actually need to be exercised. That is, to be free is to act/be/become a certain way and not merely to have the opportunity of so acting/being/becoming. Positive freedom is thus specified not in terms of a class of possible actions that one is free to do, but in terms of a class of actions that are required by the telos and that need to be performed in order to be free, i.e., actions the doing of which is that which freedom consists in.[11]

Anything that prevents the actual realization of the elements in the domain of the z-parameter, accordingly, classifies as an obstacle. The absence of obstacles hence implies the actual realization and not merely the opportunity of realizing the elements in z. That is, insofar as anything that is incompatible with the realization of the z-parameter is understood as a constraint, the absence of constraints necessitates the realization of

the z-parameter (whereas the absence of constraints merely makes possible its realization in the case of negative conceptions). In this way, the opportunity is only present if it is in fact realized. Were the opportunity to be present without being realized,
then there would be something preventing its realization and this would accordingly
also classify as an obstacle, ensuring that the opportunity was actually not present after
all.[12] This holds independently of whether the relevant obstacles are internal or external,
which explains why positive conceptions problematize the relation between freedom
and desires, as well as independently of whether the obstacles are due to human agency
or due to nature, which explains why positive conceptions problematize the relation
between freedom and abilities.

The key issue dividing negative and positive conceptions of liberty is thus that,
whereas opportunity concepts provide an independent specification of the y-parameter
by identifying which obstacles classify as constraints and consider freedom as consisting in the relevant constraints being absent, i.e., x is free to ϕ iff ϕ is in z and one is not
prevented from ϕ-ing by the constraints in y, exercise concepts understand freedom as
consisting in the z-parameter being realized, whereby they specify the z-parameter by
identifying the telos that is to be achieved, and then derivatively specify the y-parameter,
i.e., constraints are simply understood as all those things that interfere with the realization of the z-parameter.[13]

Given that the moralized notion of liberty only requires non-interference with permissible courses of action in order for one to be free, rather than requiring that one
realize one's telos or the rational wants of a higher self, it clearly classifies as an opportunity concept and, accordingly, belongs to the family of negative conceptions of liberty.
The moralized notion does not require the performance of particular actions and does
not require that one's freedom be exercised in any particular way. As a result, rights-
based accounts are not concerned with internal obstacles, such as impulses and addic-
tions, and do not problematize the relation between desires and freedom (for instance
by imposing requirements of authenticity).[14] Likewise, inabilities need not amount to
unfreedom on the moralized account, unlike in the case of positive theories which consider them to be detrimental to liberty.

Instead of requiring the performance of particular actions, merely having the relevant
opportunities as a result of rights-violating interferences being absent is sufficient for
freedom, independently of whether these opportunities are realized or not, as well as
independently of whether the agent has the ability to realize them. All that is required for
the agent to be free is that constraints are absent, such that it is possible for him to perform the actions that are in the domain of the z-parameter (where this need not imply
that the agent is able to perform them). What is peculiar about the moralized account
is simply that the opportunities that one must have if one is to be free are restricted to
permissible opportunities and do not include those actions that are part of mere license.

The fact that the moralized conception involves an opportunity concept can be
brought out by considering what happens if an agent fails to realize the opportunities
that open up as a result of the absence of the relevant constraints. While someone who,
for instance, acts irrationally will be unfree according to a positive conception, someone

who is not constrained but acts impermissibly will be free according to a moralized negative conception. Acting impermissibly, i.e., doing something that one is not free to do, does not result in unfreedom. In other words, there is no need to realize the z-parameter in order to be free, i.e., no need to take a legitimate course of action. All that is required to be free is the absence of the constraints specified by the y-parameter, which in this case is restricted to the absence of rights-violating interferences.

Moralizing freedom simply has the consequence that restricting people from acting impermissibly will not count as an infringement of their liberty, but it does not require them to act permissibly if they are to be free. The difference between the accounts is thus that performing an action that is not in the domain of the z-parameter amounts to doing something that one is not free to do on the moralized negative conception, whereas it amounts to doing something the doing of which makes one unfree on the positive conception.

It is true that moralized conceptions have the consequence that restrictions on vice will not count as infringements of liberty.[15] Yet, contrary to Waldron, this does not seem to be what "most troubled liberals about theories of positive liberty." What was troubling them was that positive conceptions allow that one can be restricted in the name of freedom, that one can be made free by coercion. This, however, is not possible on the rights-based conceptions. One cannot force people to be free in the name of moralized negative liberty.[16] Rather than allowing for the possibility of being forced to be free, these conceptions allow for the possibility that one is free despite being forced. People can be restricted from doing certain things, namely from doing what they do not have a right to do, without undermining their freedom. It is, however, not possible to force people to be free by making them do something that is viewed as the realization of their telos.

4. RIGHTS VS. MORAL RESPONSIBILITY

In addition to rights-based conceptions that understand constraints as those interferences that violate rights, it is usually held that there is a different type of moralization that is concerned not with rights but with moral responsibility. More precisely, the moral responsibility view considers an interference to be an infringement of liberty iff there is someone who is morally responsible for the obstacle in question,[17] whereas obstacles that are not due to human agency or for whom no one is morally responsible do not classify as constraints on freedom.

The moral responsibility view likewise renders claims about liberty dependent on the background moral theory. In the same way that one needs to specify what rights people have and under what conditions they are violated in order to determine what people are free to do and which interferences restrict liberty, one needs to specify what moral responsibility consists in so that one can determine for which obstacles someone can be morally responsible.[18]

Rights-based and responsibility-based approaches differ in two respects. On the one hand, they would seem to disagree as to which obstacles classify as infringements of liberty that render an agent unfree rather than merely unable to perform a course of action. On the other, they characterize the domain of the z-parameter differently insofar as the moral responsibility view, unlike the rights-based approach, does not moralize the z-parameter by drawing a contrast between liberty and license.[19]

4.1. Constraints and rights violations

The two types of theory would seem to differ in terms of how they understand the y-parameter. According to the moral responsibility view, an obstacle classifies as a constraint on freedom iff someone is morally responsible for the obtaining of the obstacle, whereas the rights-based approach considers constraints to be all those obstacles the obtaining of which classifies as a rights violation.

Whether these criteria diverge and lead to different classifications and, if so, which of them is more plausible depends on the particular account of moral responsibility/rights that is under consideration. Only once the details of the respective accounts are fixed can one evaluate whether someone is morally responsible for an obstacle iff the obtaining of this obstacle classifies as a rights violation. Accordingly, it might appear that not much can be said in the abstract.

However, we can see that rights-based views are preferable over responsibility-based accounts, on the grounds that the notion of moral responsibility by itself risks being too broad, ensuring that any plausible moral responsibility account will have to be restricted in such a way that it collapses into a rights-based theory. In particular, in order to provide a plausible characterization of the y-parameter, a moral responsibility view needs to impose a number of restrictions.

1. ASYMMETRY

One can be morally responsible both for what is praiseworthy and for what is blameworthy. For instance, it is equally possible to be morally responsible for offers as for threats. Moreover, both of them can render actions ineligible by changing the relative desirability of the available options, such that certain options no longer constitute reasonable alternatives. Yet threats and offers differ in terms of whether they infringe liberty and hence need to be treated asymmetrically. This can be achieved by being concerned with moral responsibility only insofar as it involves the violation rather than fulfillment of a duty, i.e., one only considers those cases in which questions of blame but not of praise are applicable, thereby ensuring that constraints are essentially problematic (in at least some respect) and that we have (at least pro tanto) reason to avoid them.

2. DIRECTEDNESS

In order for the duty that explains the agent's moral responsibility to be connected in a suitable manner to the person whose freedom is infringed, one has to restrict the relevant cases to those involving directed duties that are owed to particular individuals, rather than undirected duties that are not owed to anyone. That is, the agent who is morally responsible for the obstacle affecting the person in question must be accountable to that particular person on the basis of owing a duty to that person, i.e., it is that person to whom he needs to address himself in providing the justification for putting in place or failing to remove the obstacle. Otherwise, the account will misclassify cases in which there are indirect effects. For instance, if x has a duty towards y, though not towards z, to remove a certain obstacle but negligently fails to do so, then x is morally responsible for this obstacle. However, x only owes a justification to y but not z, and the obstacle only classifies as a constraint with respect to the former and not the latter.

3. ENFORCEABILITY

Intuitively, liberty can be defended and upheld, such that one can use force to prevent or remove constraints on freedom (at least those that are unjustified). In order for freedom claims to have the requisite normative strength, the duties need to be in principle enforceable, i.e., they need to be strict/perfect duties rather than wide/imperfect duties for which agents are also morally responsible.

Obstacles that classify as constraints on an agent's freedom thus need to involve (i) the violation of a duty, whereby (ii) this duty is directed towards the agent in question, and (iii) is a perfect duty that is in principle enforceable. This amounts to nothing other than the violation of a duty that is correlative to a right. Accordingly, one can explain why an obstacle that is due to x's (in)action restricts y's freedom in terms of x's (in)action violating y's right to ϕ by rendering ϕ-ing impossible or ineligible. Such a rights-based account underwrites the asymmetry between threats and offers, since threats involve rights violations whereas offers do not. Moreover, rights are held against particular people, which ensures that an obstacle facing y is a constraint on y's freedom if it involves a violation of y's rights, such that if x puts in place an obstacle that prevents both y and z from ϕ-ing, whereby only y but not z has a right to ϕ, then x only infringes y's but not z's freedom. Finally, it is plausible to hold that all rights are in principle enforceable, in that one can use force to prevent unjustified infringements of rights.

The y-parameter is thus fundamentally to be characterized in terms of rights-violating obstacles. Infringements of liberty are restricted to violations of enforceable obligations that are owed to individuals, i.e., to violations of perfect obligations that are the correlates of rights. Facts about rights violations rather than about moral responsibility are thus ultimately doing the work, and concerns about moral responsibility can be seen to drop out from an account of constraints in terms of rights violations. This is because y's right to ϕ is violated by x iff x is morally responsible for the existence of an obstacle that makes the exercise of y's right to ϕ impossible or ineligible. Moral responsibility accounts thus collapse into rights-based conceptions as far as the y-parameter is concerned.[20]

4.2. Prisoners, license, and the presumption of liberty

The moral responsibility view is usually differentiated from rights-based conceptions on the grounds that only the former view is able to distinguish unfreedom from unjustified unfreedom (cf. Miller, 1983: 72 n 10), and that it is consequently not susceptible to the standard objection to rights-based conceptions, namely that they have the seemingly unpalatable implication that the freedom of a justly imprisoned prisoner is not infringed (cf. Cohen, 1995: 60).

This is taken to be the case because the moral responsibility view implies that all constraints are such that a justification needs to be given, without implying that this demand cannot be met. "To be responsible for something is to be answerable for it; it is not necessarily to be blamable. . . . Responsibility, one might say, opens the door to questions of praise and blame without deciding them. In the same way, showing that an obstacle is a constraint on someone's freedom raises the question of its justifiability but does not resolve it" (Miller, 1985: 313). By contrast, a rights-based view is seen to connect constraints with culpability.[21]

However, pace Miller et al., being able to distinguish unfreedom from unjustified unfreedom is not sufficent for distinguishing an account of freedom from a rights-based conception. According to such a conception, the fact that an obstacle involves a rights violation implies that the agent's liberty is infringed, but it does not necessarily imply that the rights violation is unjustified. This means that the claim that constraints on freedom imply wrongness does not apply to rights-based conceptions as such. More precisely, this only holds for theories that consider all rights violations to be wrongful, but it does not hold in the case of theories that accept that rights can be justifiably infringed.

Although moralized accounts are sometimes understood as distinguishing between justified and unjustified interferences, only classifying the latter as infringements of liberty (in which case constraints on freedom would indeed be connected with culpability), one should rather distinguish between those interferences that involve rights violations and those that do not. Given that one countenances the possibility of justified rights violations, there is then room for interferences that violate rights and hence restrict liberty but that do so in a justified manner. In this way, a rights-based account can countenance the possibility of justified infringements of liberty, i.e., of unjustified unfreedom. Defenders of rights-based conceptions are, accordingly, likewise able to distinguish between unfreedom and unjustified unfreedom, as long as they do not consider all rights violations to be unjustified.

Moreover, being able to draw a distinction between unfreedom and unjustified unfreedom is not by itself sufficient for rendering a conception of freedom immune from the prisoner objection. This is because it is possible for a view to allow there to be justified unfreedom, without making room for cases in which no rights are violated but in which the agent is nonetheless unfree, thereby underwriting the judgment that the liberty of a justly imprisoned prisoner, none of whose rights are violated, is not infringed. This should be readily apparent, given that standard rights-based conceptions can make this distinction if they allow for justified infringements of rights but are nonetheless still susceptible to the prisoner objection because of their moralization of the z-parameter.[22]

In fact, the prisoner problem would seem to apply equally to the moral responsibility view. This is because it would seem to not only be the case that the jailer is not blameworthy for putting someone into prison (who is justly imprisoned), but also that he does not even have a (pro tanto) obligation not to do so (cf. Kristjánsson, 1996: 72). Yet, for Miller at least, moral responsibility presupposes moral obligation (cf. Miller, 1983: 86). The jailer is, accordingly, not morally responsible for the obstacles facing the prisoner, which implies that the prisoner's freedom is not constrained. As a result, Miller's version of the moral responsibility view would seem to imply that the prisoner is merely unable to leave the prison rather than being unfree to do so.

Kristjánsson tries to solve this problem by requiring, not the existence of a moral obligation for suppressing the obstacle, but merely the existence of an "objective *reason*, satisfying a minimal criterion of plausibility, why . . . a normal, reasonable person could have been expected (morally or factually) to suppress [the obstacle]" (Kristjánsson, 1996: 74). However, even if there should be such a reason as to why the jailer can be expected not to imprison the convicted prisoner, a closely related variant of the prisoner problem arises. This is because physically preventing someone from performing a highly repugnant action that he has every reason not to perform will not be classified as a constraint, despite the fact that this kind of situation, like imprisonment, would seem to constitute a paradigm case of unfreedom.

Moreover, as Shnayderman has pointed out, Kristjánsson's account has the bizarre implication that, while physically preventing someone from performing such an action does not classify as a constraint, threatening someone with imprisonment for engaging in this sort of behavior does restrict liberty, since the various threatened consequences might well be such that there is some reason why one might be expected to suppress them (cf. Shnayderman, 2013: 729).

Thus, unless one is willing to posit various obligations or reasons not to prevent people from performing repugnant and impermissible actions, physically preventing people from engaging in such behavior will not be classified as a restriction of liberty, thereby ensuring that the moral responsibility account has analogous implications as the rights-based account and is likewise subject to (some variant of) the prisoner objection.

In order to circumvent these problems, Shnayderman includes praise along with blame when specifying the conditions of moral responsibility. "Someone is morally responsible for an obstacle when she is appropriately considered susceptible to either blame or praise for creating it or for not preventing its creation or for not removing it" (Shnayderman, 2013: 730). This criterion avoids the prisoner objection and classifies restrictions of repugnant behavior as constraints.

However, this proposal satisfies neither the asymmetry nor the enforceability condition and overgenerates cases in which freedom is infringed, for instance misclassifying offers. There will be cases where it will be good to restrict liberty, where this is not simply a situation in which doing so is good all-things-considered, i.e., where the constraint is justified and the presumption of liberty is overridden, but where the constraint is good qua being a constraint on the freedom in question, i.e., the freedom to ϕ is itself bad, thereby making it good and praiseworthy to constrain it. In this way, the account is not able to preserve the intrinsic normative significance of freedom and there will not be a pro tanto reason not to constrain liberty, which implies that the presumption of liberty is lost.

More generally, we can see that in order to ensure that liberty has intrinsic normative significance, certain interferences cannot be classified as constraints. This is because intrinsic normative significance implies (at a minimum) that there is a pro tanto reason not to restrict liberty. Yet certain objectionable and impermissible actions are such that there is no reason whatsoever not to restrict them, i.e., there is no presumption in favor of letting people engage in such behavior. In fact, quite the opposite is true, in that there are plenty of reasons to prevent people from performing these actions. Interferences with such actions thus cannot constitute constraints on freedom. This, however, ensures that (some variant of) the prisoner objection will be applicable, insofar as there will be situations in which a person is prevented from performing such actions without thereby being rendered unfree. In short, an account of liberty can accord intrinsic normative significance to freedom and can underwrite the presumption of liberty iff it is subject to the prisoner objection.

In order to defend the presumption of liberty, one thus needs to ensure that certain interferences do not classify as constraints on freedom. As we saw above, this can be achieved in two different ways, namely by restricting the y-parameter such that only obstacles originating from certain sources classify as constraints, or by means of a restriction of the domain of the z-parameter.

A moral responsibility view that eschews the contrast between liberty and license will have to adopt the y-parameter option and classify such cases as involving mere inability. This, however, is rather counterintuitive since these obstacles seem to have all the requisite source features to classify as constraints, i.e., they are clearly attributable to human agency and are intentionally brought about by means of actions rather than omissions in order to prevent the agent in question from engaging in morally objectionable and impermissible behavior.

Moreover, establishing that restricting such behavior does not infringe liberty is not enough. In particular, there is the problem that considering such freedoms to be genuine freedoms conflicts with attributing intrinsic normative significance to freedom, since this would imply that they are worth protecting. Rather than claiming, as the moral responsibility theorist does, that such restrictions give rise to mere inability and that the agent is still free to perform such actions, one should favor the approach of the rights-based theorist who claims that the person is neither free nor unfree to perform these actions. This means that one needs to restrict the domain of the z-parameter, such that it does not include mere license. Doing so allows one to explain why these interferences do not infringe liberty, despite being deliberately imposed by human agents, on the basis that the agent is not free to perform the action in the first place. The presumption of liberty thus turns out to be defensible only if liberty is distinguished from license.

Furthermore, the distinction between liberty and license enables one to address the prisoner objection. Although many have taken the prisoner problem to constitute a decisive objection to moralized conceptions of liberty, this problem can be solved once one distinguishes the range of action types as well as action tokens that a person is free to do, i.e., the size of the domain of the agent's z-parameter, from the question to what extent a person's freedom is infringed, i.e., the extent to which an agent is prevented from doing things that he has a right to do. This is because one can then explain how a prisoner is less free in the sense that he is free to do fewer things, without his liberty being infringed (cf. Bader, forthcoming). This explanation presupposes that the domain of the z-parameter is identified with liberty as opposed to license, since it explains the way in which the prisoner is rendered less free (rather than unfree) in terms of the size of the z-parameter, i.e., in terms of the number of action types/tokens that the prisoner is free to perform in the sense of having a right to perform them (rather than in terms of a change in ability).

The moral responsibility approach thus faces a dilemma. Either it will be subject to the prisoner objection (without having the requisite resources to address this objection) and will effectively collapse into a rights-based conception with respect to the y-parameter, or it will imply an account of constraints that is too broad and that ensures that the notion of liberty lacks intrinsic normative significance and is hence unable to underwrite the presumption of liberty. Accordingly, it would appear that the only viable moralized approach is a rights-based conception and that the moral responsibility approach does not constitute a plausible alternative.

5. Conclusion

Thus, we have seen (i) that rights-based conceptions distinguish liberty from license, characterizing the domain of the z-parameter in terms of legitimate courses of action, thereby ensuring that restrictions of illegitimate courses of actions do not infringe liberty; (ii) that the source of constraints is to be understood in terms of the notion of a rights-violating interference and that obstacles that do not involve rights violations do not classify as constraints, even when they prevent an agent from ϕ-ing who has a right to ϕ; (iii) that moralized conceptions consider liberty to be an opportunity concept and, as such, are to be sharply distinguished from positive conceptions of liberty that treat it as an exercise concept; and (iv) that moral responsibility views do not constitute a viable alternative since, on the one hand, the characterization of the y-parameter collapses into a rights-based view, and, on the other, one needs to distinguish between liberty and license if one is to assign intrinsic normative significance to freedom and defend the presumption of liberty.[23]

Notes

1. "Liberty" and "freedom" will be treated as synonyms.
2. Whether x is free to ϕ will ultimately be fixed by descriptive facts. This follows from the supervenience of the normative on the descriptive and is not denied by the proponent of a moralized account, who rather argues that which descriptive facts are relevant is something

that is determined by normative principles. Liberty thus classifies as a normative concept, according to moralized accounts, because they consider it to be necessary to bring in normative notions to explain why the descriptive facts in virtue of which x is (un)free to ϕ make it the case that this is so.

Analogous questions arise when it comes to analyzing other notions, such as harm, coercion, and voluntariness. In the case of the concept of harm, for instance, one needs to specify the baseline with respect to which the actual outcome is to be compared to determine whether an agent has been harmed or benefited. Can this baseline be characterized in descriptive terms, for instance via counterfactual, statistical, temporal, or normalcy baselines? Or is the baseline essentially normative, specified for instance in terms of rights, interests, or reasonable expectations?

3. In addition, it is important to be clear on this issue since much theorizing proceeds on the basis of implicit moralizations, which is problematic for two reasons. First, it leads to a situation in which people are prone to talk past each other. In particular, different implicit moralizations ensure that the concept of freedom is used in different ways, where disagreement is due not to the analysis of freedom, but due to differing underlying moralizations. Second, an implicit moralization brings with it the risk of question-begging arguments, whereby one argues that p is the case on the basis of a moralized concept c, but where c ultimately relies on p being the case, rendering such an argument dialectically ineffective. Nozick's Wilt Chamberlain argument is probably the most famous instance of this problem, insofar as the conflict between (moralized) liberty and patterned theories of justice that he identifies simply seems to presuppose the capitalist property rights that he is trying to establish (cf. Ryan, 1977).

4. Cf. "If one regards coercion as a neutral concept, like 'speaking' or 'walking', it is something of a mystery why there should be a *presumption* against coercion, as many philosophers have insisted. The link with individual rights shows how this presumption (like the presumption against theft) is, as it were, built into the concept itself" (Ryan, 1980: 494–495).

The flip side of the moralization is that the concept does not really add anything. In particular, there is no fundamental justificatory work that it can perform, given that everything can be said in terms of the more fundamental moral notions in terms of which the concept is understood. The moralized notion then turns out to be nothing but a convenient shorthand that allows us to describe things in a perspicuous manner, but that is not capable of performing any substantive work of its own and is in that sense dispensable. We thus seem to be faced with the dilemma that the concept is either too thick (if it is moralized), or too thin (if it is merely descriptive). For arguments to the effect that this dilemma is to be resolved in favor of a moralized notion, cf. Bader, forthcoming.

5. This kind of moralization is espoused by Locke, 1689; Kant, 1797; Nozick, 1974; and Dworkin, 2000, among others.

6. An agent being free simpliciter can be understood in terms of being free to ϕ for all ϕ in z.

7. There is a distinctive way in which moralized accounts can address the impact of threats, though not via a distinctive characterization of the y-parameter but rather of the z-parameter, which allows for the possibility of considering threats to be inimical to freedom while retaining an impossibility view regarding the strength of constraints (cf. Bader, manuscript).

8. It is this restriction that gives rise to a distinction between freedom and ability, ensuring that not all cases of inability classify as cases of unfreedom but only those that are (in the relevant way) attributable to human agency.

9. Miller has put forward a number of convincing cases that suggest that fine-grained restrictions are necessary and has argued that value-neutral accounts will misconstrue the y-parameter (cf. Miller, 1983; Miller, 1985; also cf. Shnayderman, 2013: sections 1–3).

10. Frequently, this goes together with the x-parameter being a morally characterized entity/subject, such as a higher or true self.

11. This ensures that whereas negative theories are primarily divided with respect to the interpretation of the y-parameter, positive theorists disagree most fundamentally as to how one is to understand the z-parameter.

12. It is worth noting that the telos can be disjunctive, such that the agent can choose as to which disjunct is to be realized. In that case, being free still consists in the disjunction being realized, and the availability of a plurality of options between which one can choose is entirely incidental and freedom would not be reduced in any way if only one of them were available.

13. The fact that they are to be distinguished in terms of which of the parameters is prior and independently specified is precisely what Nelson's critique is missing (cf. Nelson, 2005).

14. Relatedly, the subjects to whom freedom is attributed are ordinary individuals (and possibly also groups and nations), rather than some sort of higher, true, or rational self.

15. It is important to note that restrictions on vice only fail to count as infringements of liberty if vice is understood as the violation of an enforceable duty. Put differently, restricting someone from violating a non-enforceable duty, such as a duty of beneficence, will be an unjustified restriction of liberty and will accordingly classify as an infringement of freedom even on the moralized account. Being free to ϕ thus has to be understood in the sense of ϕ-ing being a permissible course of action, not in the sense of the agent being blameless for ϕ-ing.

16. The only way in which force can be used in the name of freedom is when it comes to restricting people from interfering with the freedom of others. However, one cannot be forced in the name of one's own freedom.

17. It is worth noting that one can be responsible for intentionally as well as negligently putting in place an obstacle, letting it come into existence, failing to remove it, or preventing it from going out of existence.

18. This has the implication that on either approach debates about freedom cannot be settled independently of debates about rights/moral responsibility. On the one hand, this ensures that the real issue of contention will not be about freedom but will be located elsewhere. On the other hand, it ensures that normative significance is built into freedom and that a presumption of freedom follows straightforwardly.

19. This, at any rate, holds for extant moral responsibility accounts, all of which try to distance themselves from the rights-based specification of the z-parameter. (There is nothing in principle that precludes characterizing the y-parameter in terms of moral responsibility while accepting a rights-based distinction between liberty and license.)

20. It is worth noting that the case-based motivations for adopting a responsibility-based view are subsumable by a rights-based view. For instance, the cases that Miller takes to motivate the moral responsibility view (cf. Miller, 1983) can be explained by means of a rights-based conception.

21. Cf. "A moralised account (such as Nozick's) links constraints on freedom with moral wrongness or culpability" (Kristjánsson, 1996: 32; also cf. p. 20).

22. Once one allows for justified infringements, one could claim that the prisoner has a right to, say, move about freely but that this right can be justifiably infringed such that

imprisonment is justified while nevertheless violating rights and infringing liberty, rather than classifying this as a situation in which the prisoner forfeits this right and hence is no longer free to move about (or rather than saying that the right is conditional in nature, e.g., a right to move about freely unless justly imprisoned, and hence not infringed by imprisonment).

23. For helpful comments, I would like to thank Dan Waxman, as well as participants of workshops in Tucson and Prague.

References

Bader, R. M., forthcoming. *Moralising liberty*. Oxford Studies in Political Philosophy.

Bader, R. M., manuscript. Liberty, threats, and ineligibility.

Cohen, G. A., 1995. *Self-ownership, freedom and equality*. Cambridge: Cambridge University Press.

Dworkin, R., 2000. *Sovereign virtue: the theory and practice of equality*. Cambridge: Harvard University Press.

Kant, I., 1797. *Metaphysische Anfangsgründe der Rechtslehre*. Königsberg: Friedrich Nicolovius.

Kristjánsson, K., 1996. *Social freedom: the responsibility view*. Cambridge: Cambridge University Press.

Locke, J., 1689. *Second treatise of government*. London: Awnsham Churchill.

MacCallum, G., 1967. Negative and positive freedom. *The Philosophical Review*, 76(3), pp.312–334.

Miller, D., 1983. Constraints on freedom. *Ethics*, 94(1), pp.66–86.

Miller, D., 1985. Reply to Oppenheim. *Ethics*, 95(2), pp.310–314.

Nelson, E., 2005. Liberty: one concept too many? *Political Theory*, 33(1), pp.58–78.

Nozick, R., 1974. *Anarchy, state, and utopia*. New York: Basic Books.

Ryan, C. C., 1977. Yours, mine, and ours: property rights and individual liberty. *Ethics*, 87(2), pp.126–141.

Ryan, C. C., 1980. The normative concept of coercion. *Mind*, 89(356), pp.481–498.

Shnayderman, R., 2013. Social freedom, moral responsibility, actions and omissions. *Philosophical Quarterly*, 63(253), pp.716–739.

Steiner, H., 1994. *An essay on rights*. Oxford: Blackwell Publishers.

Taylor, C., 1979. What's wrong with negative liberty. In: A. Ryan, ed. *The idea of freedom: essays in honour of Isaiah Berlin*. Oxford: Oxford University Press. pp.175–193.

Waldron, J., 1991. Homelessness and the issue of freedom. *UCLA Law Review*, 39, pp.295–324.

CHAPTER 4

ON THE CONFLICT BETWEEN LIBERTY AND EQUALITY

HILLEL STEINER

1. Introduction

WHEN my son, Sam, was only one and a half years old, his sole term of condemnation was the phrase "not nice." Knee-scraping falls, unkindnesses, disagreeable foods, and even disappointing gifts were all *not nice*. It was not long, however, before he began to acquire a more nuanced vocabulary of disapproval and predictably came into possession of that one concept that is, for virtually all young persons, the strongest and most indispensable term of condemnation in their lexicon: *unfair*. And although it has to be said that Sam's grasp of the many complex dimensions of unfairness remained at a largely pretheoretical stage for some while longer, it was clearly developing such that, by the time he reached adolescence, his beliefs certainly reflected a more than embryonic understanding of what most of us would take to be among the most salient of those dimensions.

Earliest and foremost among these beliefs was the conviction that an unequal division, of good and bad things among people, is unfair. Somewhat later came the qualifying thought that, if someone's getting an inferior share of those things is the result of choices she has made, then perhaps that inequality is *not* unfair. And, still later, there emerged the counter-qualifying idea that some of those inferior share choices can be choices which have to be made in circumstances which are themselves—in a sense that Sam had yet to formulate—unfair. When he did come to formulate it, it consisted in the thought that such circumstances are unfair insofar as they have been relevantly shaped in certain unequal ways, not by that person's own choices but, rather, by the choices of others.

It seems, then, that Sam had thereby grasped the rudiments of a view which many persons share: namely, that a fair division of things has to reflect the demands of both equality and responsibility. An equal division of things that takes no account of the choices people make is unfair and so, too, is an unequal one that takes no account of the circumstances in which those choices have to be made. At this level of abstraction, the metaphor of a *level playing field*—of players being *initially* equally equipped for the game—seems readily to capture what he would regard as necessary, and perhaps also sufficient, for the final score to be fair. So it requires no great stretch to infer that, for Sam, a fair distribution will have the properties of being *ambition-sensitive* and *endowment-insensitive*. *Any* distribution is fair if it is one resulting from a situation in which people are unprevented from variously deploying the resources or opportunities they each successively derive from their own respective sets of initially equal resources or opportunities.

Of course, and as we know from Ronald Dworkin's elaboration of this view, the theoretical and practical complexities attending its translation into a structure of distributive rights are formidable (Dworkin, 2000; see also Burley, 2004). The aim of this chapter is to explore one aspect of those theoretical complexities and, on that basis, to suggest that what Dworkin has identified, and rebutted, as a significant possible objection to his egalitarian view of distributive fairness is not a valid objection at all. But the reasons for its not being so are different from—and opposed to—the reasons he himself offers for its lack of validity. Dworkin famously derives that egalitarian view from a foundational claim that each person has a right to equal concern and respect. It is from these rights that all our myriad other moral entitlements flow. The significant objection proposed here is the claim that equality and liberty conflict: that, indeed, *any* set of egalitarian distributive entitlements curtails personal liberty and, conversely, that such rights cannot be sustained if persons are to enjoy maximal personal liberty. In what follows, it will be argued that the case for this claim is unproven, inasmuch as *any curtailment of a person's liberty implies a concomitant increase in that of others.*

2. RIGHTS

What is the role that liberty should play in our conception of distributively fair rights? Should it play any significant role at all? On the face of it, one might imagine that the answer to this latter question would be uncontroversially affirmative. For consider: if all of us always and everywhere agreed on what would be the best thing to do in any particular situation, it looks pretty undeniable that rights would rapidly disappear from our moral language. If you and I and everyone else all agreed on the most appropriate destination for my latest salary increment—whether it be a particular charity or the Internal Revenue Service or my bank account—any talk about who has what rights with respect to that increment would be utterly superfluous. It is the brute fact that we often morally disagree about such matters, and that some of us are better placed than others to implement our contested views, that occasions the very presence of rights in that language.

For what a set of rights does is to assign protected spheres of discretion to individuals. The various claims, powers, liberties, and immunities which it allocates to them serve to demarcate domains within which those persons should not be prevented, by others, from having their dispositive choices implemented. As such, rights are readily conceived as *normative allocations of liberty*. They reserve parts of the world to their owners' discretion and imply that, within those domains, such changes (or continuities) in the state of the world as those owners wish to occur must not be obstructed by others. Those others bear duties to refrain from such obstruction and disabilities to waive those duties (Steiner, 1998: 236–239). Compliance with those duties does not, of course, signify their bearers' agreement with right-holders' choices. Nor do right-holders' entitlements to that protected dispositive discretion imply that their exercise of it is invariably well advised or even morally permissible: people can exercise their moral rights foolishly and even wrongly.[1] All that is thereby implied is that it would be even *more wrong* forcibly to interfere with such exercises.[2] And it is in that respect that liberty—as the absence of forcible interference—seems quite central to our understanding of rights.

The third chapter of Dworkin's *Sovereign Virtue* is entitled "The Place of Liberty," and the opening of its first substantive section, "A Famous Conflict," poses the following set of questions:

> Do liberty and equality often conflict, as is widely supposed? Must an egalitarian society cheat the liberty of its citizens? Or can the two virtues be recon ciled, so that we can have all we should anyway want of each? If so, is this reconciliation a happy and perhaps temporary accident? Or are the two virtues tied together in some more conceptual way, so that compromising one necessarily violates the other? (Dworkin, 2000: 123)

Now, if, as suggested above, rights—regardless of their myriad contents—simply *are* assignments of liberty, we might well wonder how there could ever be a widespread supposition that liberty and equality conflict at all, let alone often. If we suppose that people's rights simply do vest them with certain kinds of liberty, it seems difficult even to make sense of the idea that the demands of such rights—equal or otherwise—in some way trench upon the demand that persons be possessed of liberty. True, the duties correlative to rights are presumed to be enforcible ones, and enforcement certainly does curtail liberty. But since breaches of those duties—violations of the rights they entail—also curtail liberty, it is fundamentally puzzling how a set of equal (or, indeed, unequal) rights can be thought to *conflict* with liberty. That thought seems to be something approaching what used to be called a "category mistake."

We will presently consider several possible moves that might be made to dissolve this puzzle, and to exhibit what seems to be meant by the suggestion that there can be such a conflict. In order to do that, however, we need first to turn our attention to some aspects of value conflict in general.

3. VALUE CONFLICTS

Can values conflict? The answer to this question is, perhaps, one of the least elusive objects of philosophical enquiry. Of course they can. The compassionate art critic, asked by the timorous aspiring artist for her frank opinion of his (distinctly unpromising) work, is trapped between the moral demands of honesty and those of kindness. To be sure, the particular facts of the case may sometimes be such that the conflict is more apparent than real: this might be an instance where the critic needs to be cruel in order to be kind. But, equally, it might not: that critic's adverse judgement might be the one thing that could deprive this artist of an optimism which would otherwise sustain him through a long (and likely) succession of subsequent disappointments.

That easily answered question of whether values can conflict does, however, point us in the direction of a set of other questions which are less easily answered and which continue to engage considerable philosophical attention. For instance: Are such conflicts ineliminable? That is, do they reflect some conceptual, rather than contingent, fact? One example, which Dworkin draws from Isaiah Berlin, is that of a person who is at once attracted to the idea of a life given over to spontaneity *and* one responsive to the demands of prudence: that is, the demands of a life committed to forethought. As Dworkin rightly observes, "The[se] two values cannot be combined because they are, in the nature of the case, at war with each other" (Dworkin, 2001: 78–79).

Other troubling questions quickly arise. Whether values are at war with each other necessarily or only contingently, does this signify some deficiency in our understanding of morality itself? Is non-univocality in moral codes an endemic feature of the human condition? Or were Aquinas, Kant, and Bentham, despite their considerable differences, correct to deny this?[3] And if at least some values that are at war with each other are so only contingently, how are we to conceive of the structure that would make peace among them? Can our art critic hope to find some feature shared by kind acts and honest acts (and other types of valued act) that is either intrinsic to them or to their likely consequences, and that endows them with the value they have? If so, can the presence of this feature be quantified in particular instances of those act types, and thereby assist her in determining which is the right thing to do in any given situation of choice? Or, even if they possess no such commensurating feature, can she nonetheless hope to discover a uniquely plausible ranking of valued act types—one that, by means of a lexical ordering or weighting or thresholding of these values, promises authoritatively to resolve such conflicts? (Steiner, 1996: 235–236).

These are all ancient questions and we might well suppose that it is their very longevity that helped to confirm Berlin in his somber conviction that, as Dworkin reports, "the ideal of harmony [among our values] is not just unobtainable but 'incoherent' because securing or protecting one value necessarily involves abandoning or compromising another" (Dworkin, 2001: 78). Should we, then, join Berlin in this belief?

It seems that to do so would be somewhat hasty. It is surely not true, for example, that *every act* of securing or protecting one value necessarily involves abandoning or compromising another. The fact that, under certain circumstances, the art critic's honest response to the unpromising artist would also be the kind response—because, say, it might shunt him onto a vastly more satisfying career path—indicates that value conflicts need not invariably pervade our moral choices. But it must be admitted that the possibility of such happy coincidences is unlikely to have been the target of Berlin's somber conviction, and would give neither him nor us much cause to revise it. What *would* warrant its revision, however, might be some reason to suppose that at least some of our values can indeed be reconciled with each other in a systematic and non-fortuitous way. Are there any such values?

One thing that is true about values—indeed, true about most things—is that instances of them each come in varying sizes. There are big kindnesses and small ones; gross injustices and trivial ones; lies which are whoppers and lies which are white. What is also true about values is that, ceteris paribus, more of a value is better than less of it. This ceteris paribus caveat encompasses the usual suspects. That is, we all have some sense of what it means to say that one can have, or do, too much of a good thing. Acts of kindness that exceed certain magnitudes risk creating dependency in, or eroding the autonomy of, or even inflicting humiliation upon, their recipients. Courage untempered by prudence can endanger the well-being of others as well as oneself. Excessive prudence is a familiar fetter on creativity. And so forth. We do not need to be believers in the Aristotelian *golden mean*—much less in the mathematical representability of the equilibrium it adumbrates—to appreciate that the reason why some amount of a value may be excessive in some circumstances is that it is encroaching too much on another value. That said, it remains true of any value that, in the absence of any such encroachment, more of it is better than less of it. So it seems safe, if also seriously uninformative, to say that a world in which each of our values is maximally realized is better than one in which this is not the case.

Precisely what this aggregate magnitude would be, in the case of any particular value, is probably impossible to specify. But what we do know is that the aggregate magnitude of *anything* is either constant or variable. (Energy, for example, is of constant magnitude since, as the First Law of Thermodynamics tells us, the total energy of a thermodynamic system remains constant although it may be transformed from one form to another.) And there is no reason to suppose the case to be otherwise with respect to values. So let us call those values whose aggregate magnitude is constant *CAM* values or simply *CAMs*, and their variable counterparts *VAMs*.

Now it is certainly true that most values are *VAMs*. Happiness, trust, friendship, honesty, and kindness are each items of which there can plainly be more or less for individuals, whether those persons are taken disjunctively or conjunctively. I can now be less happy than I was half an hour ago. And my being less happy does not entail that someone else has become more happy. Despite occasional gloomy suspicions to the contrary, we do not generally consider the universal quest for happiness to be a zero-sum game. The same is true of most other values. One feature of our art critic's choice is that it is a choice about whether to increase the aggregate amount of honesty in the world. That is, we have no reason to imagine that, were she to do so, there would be some decline in honesty elsewhere.

Of course, there can be circumstances where, due to the presence of a complex causal nexus, a decrement in one value sits somewhere in a causal chain that terminates in some increment of the same value. When it comes to the value of physical well-being, for instance, some painful medical treatments are an obvious case in point. And among the more familiar examples discussed by moral philosophers in this regard, we would certainly want to include Bernard Williams' "Jim and the Indians" story, the Trolley Problem, and the various dilemmas posed by Innocent Shields and Innocent Threats. But the possibility of such circumstances is insufficient reason to withhold *VAM* status from the values involved in these cases because, being reliant on the presence of that causal nexus, the association of increments with decrements in them is a purely contingent relation: had previous conditions gone differently, or had some persons made choices different from some of the ones they actually did make, that causal nexus would have been absent.[4] For a value to be a *CAM*, that association between increments and decrements has to be a necessary, and not merely contingent, one.

What would it take to *prove* that the aggregate magnitude of something is constant? A short answer is "More reasons than I currently have in hand." Perhaps that answer is a bit too short. What such a proof would evidently require is (a) a comprehensive metric for ascertaining the respective magnitudes of particular instances of the thing in question, and (b) the presence of parity between the respective magnitudes of each set of its increments and each set of its decrements that are located on the same causal chain. Lacking (a), one would certainly be in no position to supply reasons for (b).

Nevertheless and even without these essential conditions of proof, it is possible to make some headway toward establishing that a value may be a *CAM*. For, clearly, it is undeniably not a *CAM* if there can conceivably be increments of it which are accompanied by *no* decrement whatsoever, and vice versa. Condition (b) implies, trivially, that any increment, whatever its magnitude, must be accompanied by *some* decrement (and vice versa). That requirement, I believe, is satisfied by one conception of liberty that has deep roots in our ordinary usage.

4. LIBERTY

By way of a prologue to the vindication of this claim, and in order to indicate that its basis is not an entirely novel one, the following quotations are offered:

> As against the coercion applicable by individual to individual, no liberty can be given to one man but in proportion as it is taken away from another. (Bentham, 1843: 57)

> But does not freedom of the press exist in the land of censorship? . . . True, in the land of censorship the state has no freedom of the press, but one organ of the state has it, viz. the *government*. . . . Does not the censor exercise daily an unconditional freedom of the press, if not directly, then indirectly? (Marx, 1975: 155)[5]

> Nozick, though he too views the distribution of freedom as regulated by social institutions, thinks of freedom itself as a nonconventional good. The options of the various individuals are located within a pre-existing space. They are, in the first instance,

options with respect to chunks of space-time, physical objects, and persons. There are, in addition, second-order options, that is, options to make certain changes in the distribution of first-order options (for example, gaining an option or depriving another of one), as well as third-order options, and so on up. While ground rules bring into being new kinds of relations between persons and options—persons can now have options *legitimately*, can be entitled to them—they do not alter the space of possible options or the possible options themselves. Therefore, seeing that a given universe of space-time, objects, and persons fixes the space of possible options, Nozick tends to think of freedom as a constant-sum good. (Pogge, 1989: 51)

Freedom for the pike is death for the minnows; the liberty of some must depend on the restraint of others. (Berlin, 1969: 124; see also Tawney, 1931: 238)

Let me immediately hasten to add that the evidence that these thinkers would themselves endorse the claim that liberty is a *CAM* is, at most, inconclusive. Berlin, for example, much more characteristically observes, in a nearby passage, that

> If the liberty of myself or my class or nation depends on the misery of a number of other human beings, the system which promotes this is unjust and immoral. But if I curtail or lose my freedom, in order to lessen the shame of such inequality, and do not thereby materially increase the individual liberty of others, *an absolute loss of liberty occurs.* (Berlin, 1969: 125)

And Nozick's familiar view, that patterned and end-state distributions can be maintained only at the cost of personal liberty, seems equally resistant to the conception of liberty as a *CAM*.

What these counter-indications unsurprisingly suggest is that each of these writers (and others too) is in fact deploying several quite different conceptions of liberty, rather than investing it with univocal meaning throughout their respective accounts. However, it must be acknowledged that, in so doing, one offense of which they cannot reasonably be accused is straying from ordinary usage. For the plain fact is that ordinary usage's treatment of liberty is notoriously promiscuous: it grants no monopoly to any one conception of liberty, and stubbornly persists in licensing the numerous inconsistencies to which such non-univocality readily lends itself. This, indeed, is the starting point of Berlin's argument in his seminal essay, *Two Concepts of Liberty*.[6] So what are we to say, in the face of these constantly shifting goal posts?

In a paper of over forty years ago, the idea that liberty might be conceived as a *CAM* was suggested as entailing what I rather grandiosely labeled the *Law of Conservation of Liberty* (hereafter, *LCL*) (Steiner, 1975, reprinted in Miller, 1991; see also Steiner, 1994: 52–54). The core of this inference is expressed in the claim that the magnitude of my overall liberty is inversely related to that of others. And this is taken to imply that liberty, so conceived, is such that it makes no sense to speak of it as being aggregately increased or diminished—much less maximized or minimized—but only as being interpersonally dispersed or concentrated to some particular extent.

What will definitely not be attempted here is to mount a full defence of *LCL*, since, as one might imagine, it has met with far too many diverse objections to allow for the accomplishment of such a large project in a single paper.[7] Nor in any case, and as was suggested previously, are we in possession of the sort of metric that a full such defense would require.[8] So, instead, the most that can presently be offered is a series of examples and arguments which, though certainly insufficient to vindicate *LCL*, do lend support to the following claim: namely, that there is a perfectly ordinary conception of liberty, the properties of which are such that any increment of it is accompanied by some decrement of it, and vice versa. Accordingly, we might call this the *weak version* of *LCL*.

The conception set forth here is the one which Dworkin attributes to Berlin and which he has described as the "flat" conception of liberty:

> Liberty, [Berlin] says, is freedom from the interference of others in doing whatever it is that you might wish to do. (Dworkin, 2001: 84)

> [It] carries, in itself, no suggestion of endorsement or complaint. . . . We use "liberty" in its flat sense simply to indicate the absence of constraint. (Dworkin, 2000: 125)

It is liberty in this sense that Berlin holds to be in conflict with equality, and Dworkin concurs in that view. For it is this conception of liberty, he suggests, that is the one being invoked when objections to redistributive taxation and minimum-wage legislation characterize such measures as invasions of liberty (Dworkin, 1998: 39–42; Dworkin, 2000: 125 ff.; Dworkin, 2001: passim).

It is not certain that this suggestion is correct. It *would* be correct if those issuing such condemnations were thereby claiming that these egalitarian measures bring about a net reduction in everyone's flat liberty or, at least, in the overall amount of flat liberty in society. And there can be little doubt that, for the most part, this is indeed what those objectors wish to be understood as claiming. But, if so, their claim is far from being transparently true. It is far from being transparently true, because it presupposes that flat liberty is a *VAM* and not a *CAM*.

An alternative view of their claim—one that *would* make it very probably true—is that such measures reduce the flat liberty of (only) wealthy taxpayers and employers. But, of course, this sort of complaint seems unlikely to be the one that those objectors have in mind.

Yet another view of their claim that would make it a candidate for being true is that the conception of liberty they are deploying is not, in fact, the flat one at all, but rather one of a type which Dworkin himself favors, when he tells us that

> [L]iberty isn't the freedom to do whatever you might want to do; it's freedom to do whatever you like so long as you respect the moral rights, properly understood, of others. It's freedom to spend your own rightful resources or deal with your own rightful property in whatever way seems best to you. (Dworkin, 2001: 84)

Two responses to this claim of Dworkin's seem immediately warranted. The first is simply that this *moralized* conception of liberty is logically superfluous when deployed as the grounds for proposing (or opposing) any particular measure whose merits (or demerits) are not already implied by the proponents' (or opponents') view of what counts as "moral rights properly understood" or "your own rightful resources/property." It is simply circular reasoning to argue that a measure, which protects (or violates) moral rights, is morally desirable (or objectionable) because it protects (or curtails) liberty. Indeed, in practice, what often lies behind the deployment of such a conception of liberty is a conflation of *legal* property rights with moral ones, whereby the former are mistaken for the latter.[9]

The second comment is this. In the quotation above, Dworkin relies upon a distinction between liberty and freedom. Now, there can be little doubt that ordinary usage does frequently sustain that distinction, whereby our set of liberties intersects with—but is not identical to—our set of freedoms, and the term *liberty* is reserved for something akin to its Hohfeldian normative sense as a synonym of "permission" or absence of a forbearance duty. On this view of the matter, while I might well have the freedom to commit a murder—might well be unprevented by others from doing so—I would (typically) lack the liberty to do so.

Suffice it here to say that Berlin was *not* using liberty in that normative sense and that, if he had been, there is every good reason to believe that he would have been entirely receptive to Dworkin's claim that there is indeed no conflict between liberty and equality. For under that semantic rubric, Berlin would simply have reformulated his account of what he considered to be a—perhaps *the*—paradigmatic value conflict, and instead labeled it as the tragic conflict between *freedom* and equality. In short, Berlin used the two terms interchangeably and that is how they are being used in this chapter (Kramer, 2003: 60–75; Kramer, 2002).

The claim here is thus a twofold one: (a) that Dworkin is right to reject Berlin's insistence on there being a conflict between liberty and equality, and (b) that the rejection of that view can safely rely upon the flat, non-moralized conception of liberty. It can rely upon that flat Berlinian conception because there are good reasons to suppose that flat liberty is a *CAM* and, hence, that measures which advance equality do not diminish liberty but, rather, merely redistribute it.[10] What are those reasons? Here the series of examples and arguments are offered that were previously described as insufficiently rigorously to vindicate the original strong version of *LCL*, but probably sufficient to justify its weak version: namely, the claim that any increment of flat liberty is accompanied by some decrement of it, and vice versa.

Consider a legal rule giving ramblers enforcible rights of way over agricultural land. Such a rule certainly increases the freedom of ramblers. But it also reduces the liberty of farmers, by mandating the legal prevention of many actions which they might otherwise do involving their use of the land over which ramblers enjoy rights of way. Similarly, a law abolishing slavery may confer a great deal of liberty on the emancipated slaves, as well as on others who are thereby no longer legally prevented from entering into various kinds of relation with those emancipated. But such a measure also considerably reduces some persons' freedom: namely, that of slave owners. For prior to emancipation, slave owners are not legally prevented from forcing persons who are their slaves to do anything. After it, they are. A minimum wage law reduces both employers' liberty to dispose of their capital as they might wish and of other persons to accept sub-minimum wages. And, depending on prevailing economic conditions, it may also reduce the freedom of others to gain employment. But it also increases the liberty of those who are employed, by removing barriers to their doing many things which could not be done with their previous smaller wage packets. When a railroad is nationalized, a vast set of freedom-conferring claims, powers, immunities, and (Hohfeldian) liberties is transferred from its previous private owners to—at least—some state bureaucrats. And while it is certainly true that this measure may not achieve any significant egalitarian result, it is also true that there is no obvious reason to suppose that those bureaucrats thereby acquire any less freedom than what the private owners had previously enjoyed.

More prosaically, consider what happens when you lock me up in an inescapable closet for three hours. One thing that does is to close down the possibility of my participating in a particular political demonstration occurring at that time. But locking me up in that closet opens up some action possibilities for others (including, perhaps, yourself)—possibilities that would otherwise have been closed. Had I not been locked up there, I would have gone to the cinema. As it is, someone else is now, and thereby, unprevented from occupying the cinema seat that I would have occupied. Her flat freedom to occupy it has been purchased at the cost of my flat unfreedom. More generally, it is sometimes suggested that the Hobbesian state of nature, being devoid of any enforcible obligations, is a condition of maximal flat liberty. But residents of that state, though clearly possessed of Hohfeldian liberty—i.e., *permission*—to do whatever they might wish to do, are not thereby free to do so, for they are extensively prevented from doing so by one another. And the creation of a legal system, though it may redistribute the flat liberty they have, does not thereby increase (or diminish) it in aggregate. Commercial options are opened up, while homicidal ones are closed down. Property and other rights are created and their enforcement confers some gains in flat liberty on their owners but, and for the very same reason, that forcible exclusion of others from those portions of property imposes some flat liberty losses on them.

Why is all this so? The reason is not all that elusive. Flat liberty, as Dworkin says, is simply the absence of constraint: it is the non-interference of others in doing whatever it is that you might wish to do. We can formulate the condition of flat liberty thus:

> A person is free to do an action if, and only if, were she to attempt to do that action, her doing it would not be rendered impossible by the action of another. And, conversely, she is unfree to do an action if, and only if, were she to attempt to do that action, her doing it would be rendered impossible by the action of another. (Steiner, 1994: 8).

There are many probing questions that can be asked about this definition, but we shall here take it as read that this adequately captures the flat conception of liberty that Dworkin attributes to Berlin.

As such, our judgments about whether one person deprives another of the flat liberty to do a certain action turn essentially on questions of physical interaction. I can make you unfree to go to a particular cinema at a particular time by incarcerating you in a closet, or by blocking the cinema entrance, or by immobilizing the means of transportation that you need to get there, or by crippling your legs, or by forcibly brainwashing you so that you are incapable of approaching the cinema, and so forth. In so doing, I reduce the set of possible actions open to you. And, as my preceding prosaic example suggests, I thereby increase the set of possible actions open to persons other than you.

Indeed—and putting this thought in its most general form—to engage in any of those preventive actions, I must deploy my body, and perhaps other objects, in such a way that they cease to occupy the spatio-temporal location that they would occupy, were I not to engage in any of those actions. In vacating that location, I make it available to others who thereby cease to be prevented from doing some possible actions which require the occupation of that location, and access to which would be denied them were I instead to remain in it. And in preventing you from doing the particular action that you otherwise would have done, I make its location available to persons other than you, including possibly myself. In short, any action we engage in obstructs some persons and liberates others: *anything* we do both removes and installs preventions of some conceivable actions of others. Whether those others would actually exploit these possibilities, whether these actions are ones which they have any interest in doing, has no bearing at all on whether they have been made free or unfree to do them, in the flat liberty sense.

For flat liberty is all about access to the physical means of acting. To constrain a person from performing a particular action—to make her unfree to do it—it is necessary and sufficient to deny her that access. Successful denials of access confer that access on someone else. Accordingly, decrements of flat liberty are accompanied by increments of it. And that being so, we have a necessary—if also insufficient—reason to believe that flat liberty is a *CAM*, and thus a necessary, though insufficient, reason to think that strong *LCL* is true. To have a sufficient reason would require, as I previously suggested, *both* that we be in possession of a liberty metric capable of measuring those mutually accompanying increments and decrements *and* that their respective magnitudes be equal. Lacking that metric, we lack the means for demonstrating that parity.

5. Conclusion

Briefly, then, it looks as though we are entitled to at least the following conclusion. Since decrements of flat liberty are invariably accompanied by increments of it, opponents of egalitarian redistributive policies confront a serious difficulty in straightforwardly sustaining their objection to such policies on grounds of net liberty reduction. For, in order to sustain that objection on *those* grounds, they would have to be able to show that the flat liberty decrements, which are undeniably engendered by such policies, are of a greater magnitude than the flat liberty increments that invariably accompany them. Such a demonstration would, however, require the sort of metric that is currently lacking.

In its absence, net liberty reduction is a nonstarter, and the only alternative grounds for rejecting egalitarian redistribution must lie in a claim that those decrements, though not demonstrably *larger* than their accompanying increments, are nevertheless *more valuable* than them. Now it is certainly true that claims of this latter sort are very far from being unintelligible: indeed, we make them all the time. What is unclear, however, is just how far such *greater worth claims* can be pressed, in the face of both the value pluralism described earlier, and any avowed neutrality with regard to rival conceptions of the good life. And what *is* clear is that, even if those obstacles can be overcome, objections to redistributive policies would thereby signify the presence of a conflict *not* between equality and liberty, but rather between equality and whatever value was being invoked to prove the greater worth of those flat liberty decrements. In short, there is no good reason to suppose that liberty, understood as Berlin understood it, conflicts with equality at all.[11]

Notes

1. "Wrongly," by virtue of that exercise being one that breaches the demands of moral values other than those of moral rights.
2. Strictly, this "more wrong" judgement is implied by the premise that moral rights—the demands of justice—enjoy the status of lexical primacy (Rawls) or side-constraints (Nozick) or trumps (Dworkin) or peremptory reasons (Raz) in moral argument. Arguments for this premise are to be found in Steiner, 1994: 188–207, and in Steiner, 2013: 232–237, where it is called the *Moral Primacy Thesis*.
3. Cf. Hilpinen, 1971: 16: "The principles of deontic logic determine conditions of consistency for normative systems. By a 'normative system' we understand here simply any set of deontic sentences closed under deduction. When is a set of deontic sentences consistent? It seems natural to require that at least the following 'minimal condition' should be satisfied: . . . [that] all obligations in this set can be simultaneously fulfilled, and that [an act] is permitted only if it can be realized without violating any of one's obligations."
4. I here set aside very pertinent questions concerning agency, blameworthiness, negative causation, and so on.
5. I am grateful to Jerry Cohen for drawing this passage to my attention.
6. A good indication of the vast range of conceptions of liberty rooted in aspects of ordinary usage is offered in Carter, Kramer and Steiner, 2007.
7. Included among such objections are: that liberty is *not* a bivalent concept (i.e., that it is not true that, with respect to every particular action, we are either free or unfree to do it); that threats against doing a particular action do curtail the liberty to do it; that the set of actions to which liberty judgments apply consists of *only* the subset of actually desired actions and *not* the full set of conceivably desired ones; that each person's overall liberty is a function of *only* the particular liberties—and *not* the particular absences of liberty—that pertain to him or her; that technological advances increase the magnitude of overall liberty; that the amount of overall liberty in human society is *not* the simple sum of all individuals' amounts of overall liberty; and that the magnitude of any liberty must reflect its value as well as its empirical properties. One thing that this plethora of objections confirms is, indeed, the vast plurality of conceptions of liberty on offer. For there are no necessary connections between most pairs of these objections: they are not all coming from the *same place* and their respective proponents consequently would, and do, equally disagree with one another in their respective inferences concerning whether someone has or lacks the liberty to do some particular action.

8. For an unsuccessful attempt to devise a formula that would generate a liberty metric, see Steiner, 1983. Considerably more sophisticated refinements of this formula are to be found in Carter, 1999: ch. 7, and Kramer, 2003: ch. 5, though differences among us, over several properties of the concept of liberty, preclude their acceptance of *LCL*.

9. Robert Nozick similarly deploys a moralized conception of liberty, but is not guilty of conflating legal with moral property rights (Nozick, 1974: 167–174). Criticism of Nozick's use of a moralized conception of liberty is advanced in: Scanlon, 1976: 13–14; Cohen, 1988: 252, 256, 295; Steiner, 1994: 12, 14; Carter, 1999: 68–74; and Olsaretti, 2004: ch. 5.

10. Note that, even under the flat conception of liberty, whereby it is synonymous with freedom, liberty remains a *value*, inasmuch as individuals desire it for themselves and others and may therefore seek to acquire more of it. The fact that, as is suggested here, they can succeed in doing so only at the cost of diminishing the liberty of others, does not detract from its status as a value per se.

11. This chapter has benefited considerably from comments received from Ralf Bader, Brian Barry, Daniel Butt, Ian Carter, Richard Child, G. A. Cohen, Ronald Dworkin, Leslie Green, Alan Hamlin, Ross Harrison, Matthew Kramer, Brian Leiter, Martin O'Neill, Michael Otsuka, Geraint Parry, David Schmidtz, George Sher, Zofia Stemplowska, Steven Wall, Jonathan Wolff, three anonymous reviewers for this volume, and participants in philosophy seminars held at the CEVRO Institute Prague and the following universities: Bristol, Cambridge, Haifa, Halle, Manchester, Oxford, Rice, Stockholm, Texas, University College London, and Uppsala.

References

Bentham, Jeremy, 1843. Anarchical fallacies. Reprinted in Jeremy Waldron, ed. 1987. *Nonsense upon Stilts*. London: Methuen. pp.46–69.

Berlin, Isaiah, 1969. *Four essays on liberty*. Oxford: Oxford University Press.

Burley, Justine, ed., 2004. *Dworkin and his critics*. Oxford and Malden, MA: Blackwell.

Carter, Ian, 1999. *A measure of freedom*. Oxford: Oxford University Press.

Carter, Ian, Kramer, Matthew, and Steiner, Hillel, eds., 2007. *Freedom: a philosophical anthology*. Oxford and Malden, MA: Blackwell.

Cohen, G. A., 1988. *History, labour and freedom*. Oxford: Oxford University Press.

Dworkin, Ronald, 1998. Do liberty and equality conflict? In: P. Barker, ed. *Living as equals*. Oxford: Oxford University Press. pp.39–57.

Dworkin, Ronald, 2000. *Sovereign virtue: the theory and practice of equality*. Cambridge, MA: Harvard University Press.

Dworkin, Ronald, 2001. Do liberal values conflict? In: M. Lilla, R. Dworkin, and R. B. Silvers, eds. *The legacy of Isaiah Berlin*. New York: NYREV. pp.73–90.

Hilpinen, Risto, ed., 1971. *Deontic logic: introductory and systematic readings*. Dordrecht: D. Reidel.

Kramer, Matthew, 2002. Freedom as a normative condition, freedom as a physical fact. *Current Legal Problems*, 55, pp.43–63.

Kramer, Matthew, 2003. *The quality of freedom*. Oxford: Oxford University Press.

Marx, Karl, 1975. Debates on freedom of the press, 1842. In *Karl Marx/Friedrich Engels collected works*, vol. 1. London: Lawrence & Wishart. pp.40–41.

Miller, David, ed., 1991. *Liberty*. Oxford: Oxford University Press.

Nozick, Robert, 1974. *Anarchy, state, and utopia*. Oxford: Blackwell.

Olsaretti, Serena, 2004. *Liberty, desert and the market*. Cambridge, UK: Cambridge University Press.

Pogge, Thomas, 1989. *Realizing Rawls*. Ithaca, NY: Cornell University Press.

Scanlon, Thomas, 1976. Nozick on rights, liberty and property. *Philosophy and Public Affairs*, 6, pp.3–25.

Steiner, Hillel, 1983. How free? Computing personal liberty. In A. P. Griffiths, ed. *Of liberty: Royal Institute of Philosophy lectures*. Cambridge, UK: Cambridge University Press. pp.73–89.

Steiner, Hillel, 1975. Individual liberty. *Aristotelian Society Proceedings*, 75, pp.35–50. Reprinted in D. Miller, ed., 1991, *Liberty* (Oxford: Oxford University Press), pp.123–140.

Steiner, Hillel, 1994. *An essay on rights*. Oxford: Blackwell.

Steiner, Hillel, 1996. Duty-free zones. *Aristotelian Society Proceedings*, 96, pp.231–244.

Steiner, Hillel, 1998. Working rights. In: Matthew Kramer, Nigel Simmonds, and Hillel Steiner, eds. *A debate over rights: philosophical enquiries*. Oxford: Oxford University Press. pp.233–301.

Steiner, Hillel, 2013. Directed duties and inalienable rights. *Ethics*, 123, pp.230–244.

Tawney, R. H., 1931. *Equality*. London: George Allen & Unwin.

CHAPTER 5

FREEDOM AND EQUALITY

ELIZABETH ANDERSON

FREEDOM and equality are typically presented as opposing values. In the quick version of the argument, economic liberty—the freedom to make contracts, acquire property, and exchange goods—upsets substantive economic equality (Nozick, 2013: 160–164). Suppose some people sail to an uninhabited island and divide its territory and the provisions they brought into shares of equal value. If they are free to produce, trade, and accumulate property, some would rapidly get richer than others due to good luck and good choices, while others would become poor due to bad luck and bad choices. Any attempt to enforce strict material equality across large populations under modern economic conditions would require a totalitarian state. Gracchus Babeuf, a radical of the French Revolution, and the first modern advocate of strict material equality under state communism, understood this perfectly. He saw that the only way to ensure strict material equality was for the state to run society like an army—to control all property and production, assign everyone to their jobs, and control everyone's thoughts (lest some get the ideas that they deserve more than others, or that they should be free to choose their own way of life) (Babeuf, 1967; Buonarroti, 1836). He thought such equality was worth the sacrifice of freedom. Few who have actually lived under communism agree.

While the quick argument is true and of great historical importance, it does not address moderate types of egalitarianism. Virtually no one today advocates strict material equality. Social democrats, particularly in northern Europe, embraced private property and extensive markets well before the collapse of communism. Friedrich Hayek (1944) argued that social democratic experiments would lead societies down the slippery slope to totalitarianism. His prediction failed: moderate egalitarianism of the social democratic type has proved compatible with democracy, extensive civil liberties, and substantial if constrained market freedoms.

To make progress on the question of normative trade-offs between freedom and equality within the range of options for political economy credibly on the table, we must clarify our concepts. There are at least three conceptions of freedom—negative, positive, and republican—and three conceptions of equality—of standing, esteem, and authority. Republican freedom requires extensive authority egalitarianism. To block arguments that freedom requires substantial material equality, libertarians typically argue that rights to negative liberty override or constrain claims to positive liberty. This chapter will argue that, to the extent that libertarians want to support private property rights in terms of the importance of *freedom* to individuals, this strategy fails, because the freedom-based defense of private property rights depends on giving priority to positive or republican over negative freedom. Next, it is argued that the core rationale for inalienable rights depends on considerations of republican freedom. A regime of full contractual alienability of rights—on the priority of negative over republican freedom—is an unstable basis for a free society. It tends to shrink the domains in which individuals interact as free and independent persons, and expand the domains in which they interact on terms of domination and subordination. To sustain a free society over time, we should accept the priority of republican over negative liberty. This is to endorse a kind of authority egalitarianism. The chapter concludes with some reflections on how the values of freedom and equality bear on the definition of property rights. The result will be a qualified defense of some core features of social democratic orders.

1. Conceptions of Freedom and Equality

Let us distinguish three conceptions of freedom: negative freedom (noninterference), positive freedom (opportunities), and republican freedom (nondomination). Sarah has negative freedom if no one interferes with her actions. She has positive freedom if she has a rich set of opportunities effectively accessible to her. She has republican freedom if she is not dominated by another person—not subject to another's arbitrary and unaccountable will.

These three conceptions of freedom are logically distinct. They are also somewhat causally independent: one can enjoy high degrees of any two of these freedoms at substantial cost to the third. Lakshmi could have perfect negative and republican freedom on an island in which she is the only inhabitant. No one else would be interfering with her actions or dominating her. She would have little positive freedom, however, since most opportunities are generated in society with others. Maria could have high degrees of negative and positive freedom while lacking republican freedom. She could be the favorite of an indulgent king, who showers her with wealth and privileges, and permits her to say and do what she likes—but who could throw her in his dungeon at his whim. Finally, Sven could have high degrees of positive and republican freedom while being subject to many constraints on his negative liberty. He could reside in an advanced social democratic state such as Norway, where interpersonal authority is constrained by the rule of law (so he is not subject to anyone's *arbitrary* will), and a rich set of opportunities is available to all, at the cost of substantial negative liberty constraints through high levels of taxation and economic regulation.

Traditionally, most discussions of freedom focused on the contrast between negative and positive freedom. The recent revival of the republican conception of freedom
as nondomination adds an important dimension to thinking about the lived experience
of unfreedom and the social conditions of freedom. Pettit (1997: 22–25) stresses the contrast between negative and republican freedom in the case where a dominator could but
chooses not to interfere with subordinates. He argues that such vulnerability to interference can make subordinates submissive, self-censoring, and sycophantic toward their
superiors. It is also important to consider some differences between negative liberty constraints imposed by a dominating power and those imposed in accordance with the rule of
law by a liberal democratic authority. Domination is often personal: think of the husband
under the law of coverture or the violent husband today, the slaveholder, the bullying,
micromanaging boss. Rule-of-law constraints are impersonal and of general applicability. This arm's-length character of the rule of law often relieves people of the humiliation
of submission to domination, since they know "it's not about me." Dominating interference can arrive unannounced. Rule-of-law constraints must be publicized in advance, giving people time to figure out how to pursue their projects in ways that avoid interference.
Dominating interference does not have to justify itself. Rule-of-law constraints in a liberal
democratic order must appeal to public reasons, which limits the constraints that can be
imposed. Dominating interference is unaccountable. Applied rule-of-law constraints in
a democracy are subject to appeal before an impartial adjudicator, and those who enact
them can be removed from power by those to whom the constraints apply.

These remarks apply to ideal types only. Actually existing formally liberal democratic
regimes have devised innumerable ways to exercise domination under the guise of the
rule of law. It is possible to devise a set of impersonal, generally applicable, publicized laws
that regulate conduct so minutely that almost anyone innocently going about their business could be found to have run afoul of one of them. Such is the case with traffic laws in
the United States. If enforcement action on the trivial infringements were limited to mere
warnings or token fines, as in police stops to warn drivers that their tail lights are broken,
they could be a service to the drivers and others on the road. Often, however, such traffic
stops are a mere pretext for police exercise of arbitrary power to harass, intimidate, invade
privacy, and seize people's property without due process of law.[1] In other cases, impersonal
rule-of-law regulations impose constraints so out of touch with local conditions, with such
draconian penalties for noncompliance, that enforcement amounts to domination. Such
is the case with the high-stakes testing regime imposed by the federal government under
No Child Left Behind, with uniform arbitrary progress goals foisted on local school dis-
tricts without any empirical research demonstrating that these goals were feasible. In some
cases, the NCLB regime has created a culture of intimidation and cheating (Aviv, 2014).
This is a centralized planning regime akin to the five-year plans of communist states. In
both cases, the imposition of goals plucked out of thin air in combination with severe sanctions is premised on the assumption that lack of sufficient will is the primary obstacle to
progress—an assumption that rationalizes domination of those required to meet the goals.

We should be skeptical of attempts to operationalize the conditions for nondomination in formal terms. Powerful agents are constantly devising ways to skirt around

formal constraints to dominate others. Republican freedom is a sociologically complex condition not easily encapsulated in any simple set of necessary and sufficient conditions, nor easily realized through any particular set of laws.

Turn now to equality. In other work, I have argued that the conceptions of equality relevant for political purposes are relational: they characterize the types of social relations in which members of society stand to one another (Anderson, 2012b; Anderson, 2012a). Relational equality is opposed to social hierarchy. Three types of hierarchy—of standing, esteem, and authority—are particularly important. In hierarchies of standing, agents (including the state) count the interests of superiors highly, and the interests of inferiors for little or nothing. In hierarchies of esteem, some groups monopolize esteem and stigmatize their inferiors. In hierarchies of authority, dominant agents issue arbitrary and unaccountable commands to subordinates, who must obey on pain of sanctions. Egalitarians oppose such hierarchies and aim to replace them with institutions in which persons relate to one another as equals. For example, they want members of society to be treated as equals by the state and in institutions of civil society (standing); to be recognized as bearing equal dignity and respect (esteem); to have equal votes and access to political participation in democratic states (authority). Each of these conceptions of relational equality is complex and implicates numerous features of the social setting.

These three types of hierarchy usually reinforce each other. Groups that exercise power over others tend to enjoy higher esteem, and often use their power to exact special solicitude for their interests from others. Sometimes they come apart. Upper-class married women under the law of coverture enjoyed high esteem and standing, but had little authority and were subordinate to their husbands and to men generally. Some ethnic minorities, such as Chinese Malaysians, enjoy high standing and authority through their ownership and control of most businesses in Malaysia, but are racially stigmatized in Malaysian society.

Given this array of distinct conceptions of freedom and equality, it is harder to argue that freedom and equality are structurally opposed. There is a deep affinity between republican freedom as nondomination and authority egalitarianism. These are not conceptually identical. Domination can be realized in an isolated, transient interpersonal case (consider a kidnapper and his victim). Authoritarian hierarchy is institutionalized, enduring, and group-based. Yet authority hierarchies cause the most important infringements of republican freedom. Historically, the radical republican tradition, from the Levellers to the radical wing of the Republican party through Reconstruction, saw the two causes of freedom and equality as united: to be free was to not be subject to the arbitrary will of others. This required elimination of the authoritarian powers of dominant classes, whether of the king, feudal landlords, or slaveholders. Republican freedom for all is incompatible with authoritarian hierarchy and hence requires some form of authority egalitarianism.

Authority egalitarianism so dominates public discourse in contemporary liberal democracies that few people openly reject it. However, conservatives have traditionally supported authority hierarchy, and continue to do so today, while often publicizing their views in other terms. For example, conservatives tend to defend expansive discretionary powers of police over suspects and employers over workers, as well as policies that reinforce race, class, and gender hierarchies, such as restrictions on voting, reproductive freedom, and access to the courts.

The connections between relational equality and conventional ideas of equality in terms of the distribution of income and wealth are mainly causal. Esteem egalitarians worry that great economic inequality will cause the poor to be stigmatized and the rich glorified simply for their wealth. Authority egalitarians worry that too much wealth inequality empowers the rich to turn the state into a plutocracy. This radical republican objection to wealth inequality is distinct from contemporary notions of distributive justice, which focus on the ideas that unequal distributions are unfair, and that redistribution can enhance the consumption opportunities of the less well off.[2] The latter notions are the concern of standing egalitarianism. Concern for distributive justice—specifically, how the rules that determine the fair division of gains from social cooperation should be designed—can be cast in terms of the question: what rules would free people of equal standing choose, with an eye to also sustaining their equal social relations? The concern to choose principles that sustain relations of equal standing is partly causal and partly constitutive. In a contractualist framework, principles of distributive justice for economic goods constrain the choice of regulative rules of property, contract, the system of money and banking, and so forth, and do not directly determine outcomes (Rawls, 1999: 47–49, 73–76). From this point of view, certain principles, such as equality of rights to own property and make contracts, are constitutive of equal standing.

Absent from this list of conceptions of equality is any notion of equality considered as a bare pattern in the distribution of goods, independent of how those goods were brought about, the social relations through which they came to be possessed, or the social relations they tend to cause. Some people think that it is a bad thing if one person is worse off than another due to sheer luck (Arneson, 2000; Temkin, 2003). I do not share this intuition. Suppose a temperamentally happy baby is born, and then another is born that is even happier. The first is now worse off than the second, through sheer luck. This fact is no injustice and harms no one's interests. Nor does it make the world a worse place. Even if it did, it would still be irrelevant in a liberal political order, as concern for the value of the world apart from any connection to human welfare, interests, or freedom fails even the most lax standard of liberal neutrality.

2. A Freedom-based Justification of Property Must Favor Positive or Republican over Negative Freedom

The conventional debate about freedom and distributive equality is cast in terms of the relative priority of negative and positive freedom. If negative liberty, as embodied in property rights, trumps positive freedom, then taxation for purposes of redistribution of income and wealth is unjust (Nozick, 2013: 30–34, 172–173; Mack, 2009).

One way to motivate the priority of negative freedom is to stress the normative difference between constraints against infringing others' liberties, which do not require anyone to *do* anything (merely to refrain from acting in certain ways), and positive requirements to supply others with goods, which carry the taint of forced labor. This argument applies at most to taxation of labor income. Nozick (2013: 169) tacitly acknowledged this point in claiming that "Taxation of earnings *from labor* is on a par with forced labor" (emphasis added). People receive passive income (such as interest, mineral royalties, capital gains, land rents, and bequests) without lifting a finger, so taxation of or limitations on such income does not amount to forcing them to work for others. Such taxation is the traditional left-libertarian strategy for pursuing distributive equality consistent with negative liberty constraints. Land and natural resource taxes can be justified in Lockean terms, as respecting the property rights in the commons of those who lost access to privately appropriated land. Paine's classic version of this argument (1796) claims that Lockean property rights should be unbundled: just appropriation entitles owners to use the land and exclude others, but not to 100 percent of the income from land rents. Citizens generally retain rights to part of that income stream. This grounds a moderate egalitarianism without resort to the extravagant premises needed to support a more demanding distributive equality in libertarian terms, as for instance in Otsuka (1998).

Arguments for the priority of negative over positive freedom with respect to property rights run into more fundamental difficulties. A regime of perfect negative freedom with respect to property is one of Hohfeldian privileges only, not of rights.[3] A negative liberty is a privilege to act in some way without state interference or liability for damages to another for the way one acts. The correlate to A's privilege is that others lack any right to demand state assistance in constraining A's liberty to act in that way. There is nothing conceptually incoherent in a situation where multiple persons have a privilege with respect to the same rival good: consider the rules of basketball, which permit members of either team to compete for possession of the ball, and even to "steal" the ball from opponents. If the other team exercises its liberty to steal the ball, the original possessor cannot appeal to the referee to get it back.

No sound argument for a regime of property *rights* can rely on considerations of negative liberty alone. Rights entail that others have correlative duties. To have a property right to something is to have a claim against others, enforceable by the state, that they not act in particular ways with respect to that thing. Property rights, by definition, are massive *constraints* on negative liberty: to secure the right of a single individual owner to some property, the negative liberty of everyone else—billions of people—must be constrained. Judged by a metric of negative liberty alone, recognition of property rights inherently amounts to a massive net loss of total negative freedom. The argument applies equally well to rights in one's person, showing again the inability of considerations of negative liberty alone to ground rights. "It is impossible to create rights, to impose obligations, to protect the person, life, reputation, property, subsistence, or liberty itself, but at the expense of liberty" (Bentham, 1838–1843: I.1, 301).

What could justify this gigantic net loss of negative liberty? If we want to defend this loss as a net gain in overall freedom, we must do so by appealing to one of the other conceptions of freedom—positive freedom, or republican freedom. Excellent arguments can be provided to defend private property rights in terms of positive freedom. Someone who has invested their labor in some external good with the aim of creating something worth more than the original raw materials has a vital interest in assurance that they will have effective access to this good in the future. Such assurance requires the state's assistance in securing that good against others' negative liberty interest in taking possession of it. To have a claim to the state's assistance in securing effective access to a good, against others' negative liberty interests in it, is to have a right to *positive freedom*.

Considerations of republican freedom also supply excellent arguments for private property. In a system of privileges alone, contests over possession of external objects would be settled in the interests of the stronger parties. Because individuals need access to external goods to survive, the stronger could then condition others' access on their subjection to the possessors' arbitrary will. Only a system of private property *rights* can protect the weaker from domination by the stronger. The republican argument for rights in one's own body follows even more immediately from such considerations, since to be an object of others' possession is per se to be dominated by them.

Thus, there are impeccable freedom-based arguments for individual property rights. But they depend on treating individuals' interests in either positive or republican freedom as overriding others' negative liberty interests. Against this, libertarians such as Nozick could argue that the proper conception of negative liberty is a *moralized* one, such that interference with others' negative freedom does not count as an infringement of liberty unless it is *unjust*. Such a moralized view of liberty is implicit in Nozick's moralized accounts of coercion and voluntariness (1969: 450; 2013: 262–263). Hence, no genuine sacrifice of others' negative liberty is involved in establishing a just system of property rights.

In response, we must consider what could justify claims to negative liberty *rights* in property. The problem arises with special clarity once we consider the pervasiveness of prima facie conflicts of property rights, as in cases of externalities settled by tort law or land use regulation. Whenever prima facie negative liberty *rights* conflict, we must decide between them either by weighing their value in terms of non-liberty considerations, or in terms of some other conception of freedom—positive or republican. If we appeal to considerations other than freedom, we treat freedom as subordinate to other values. For example, desert-based arguments for property rights, which point to the fact that the individual created the object of property, or added value to it through their labor—treat freedom as subordinate to the social goal of rewarding people according to their just deserts. Similarly, Nozick's resolution of conflicting claims in terms of a moralized notion of negative liberty covertly imports utilitarian considerations to do the needed normative work (Fried, 2011). To base the justification of property rights on considerations of freedom itself, we must regard freedom as a value or interest and not immediately as a right. That is, we must regard freedom as a nonmoralized consideration. Otherwise we have no basis in *freedom* for justifying property rights or resolving property disputes when uses of property conflict.

A contractualist framework can offer a freedom-based justification of private property rights that departs from libertarian premises. In this picture, the principles of right are whatever principles persons would rationally choose (or could not reasonably reject) to govern their interpersonal claims, given that they are, and understand themselves to be, free and equal in relation to one another. If they chose a regime of privileges only, this would amount to anarchist communism, in which the world is an unregulated commons. Such a regime would lead to depleted commons—razed forests, extinct game, destroyed fisheries. It would also give everyone a greater incentive to take what others produced than to produce themselves. Few would invest their labor in external things, everyone would be poor, and meaningful opportunities would be rare. By contrast, adoption of an institutional scheme of extensive private property rights, including broad freedoms of exchange and contract, would create vastly richer opportunities for peaceful and cooperative production on terms of mutual freedom and equality. All have an overwhelming common interest in sustaining an institutional infrastructure of private property rights that generates more *positive freedom*—better opportunities—for all.

This argument justifies rights to negative freedom with respect to external property in terms of positive freedom. It does not suppose, as libertarian arguments do, that the liberty interests of the individual *override* the common interest. Rather, it claims that people have a common interest in sustaining a regime of individual rights to property. On this view, individual rights are not justified by the weight of the individual interest they protect, but by the fact that everyone has a common interest in relating to each other through a shared infrastructure of individual rights (Raz, 1994). The infrastructure of private property rights is a public good, justified by its promotion of opportunities—of positive freedom—for all. A well-designed infrastructure provides a framework within which individuals can relate to one another as free and equal persons.

So far, the argument is one of evaluative priority only. It has been argued that if one wants to justify private property rights in terms of freedom, one must grant evaluative priority to positive or republican over negative freedom. Discussion of the implications of this argument for the *content* of a just scheme of private property rights—to whether a just scheme would look more libertarian, or more egalitarian—will be postponed to the last section of this chapter.

3. REPUBLICAN FREEDOM AND THE JUSTIFICATION OF INALIENABLE RIGHTS

If negative freedom were the only conception of freedom, it would be difficult to offer a freedom-based justification of inalienable rights. If Sarah's right is inalienable, then she is immune from anyone changing her right. This could look attractive, except that it entails that she is disabled from changing her own right—that she lacks the power to waive others' correlative duties to respect that right (Hohfeld, 1913–1914: 44–45, 55). This is a constraint on her higher-order negative liberty. This liberty is higher-order because it concerns not the liberty to exercise the right, but the liberty over the right itself.

Inalienable rights might also leave the individual with an inferior set of positive freedoms than if her rights are alienable. Contracts involve an exchange of rights. There is a general presumption that voluntary and informed contracts produce gains for both sides. To make Sarah's right inalienable prevents her from exchanging it for rights she values more, and thereby reduces her opportunities or positive freedom.

However, there are strategic contexts in which individuals can get much better opportunities if some of their rights are inalienable (Dworkin, 1982: 55–56). In urgent situations, when one party cannot hold out for better terms, the other can exploit that fact and offer terms that are much worse than what they would otherwise be willing to offer. Peter, seeing Michelle drowning, might condition his tossing her a life ring on her agreeing to become his slave, if her rights in herself were fully alienable. But if she had an inalienable right to self-ownership, Peter could not exploit her desperation to subject her to slavery, but would offer her better terms.

Such considerations leave libertarians torn between accepting and rejecting the validity of voluntary contracts into slavery.[4] Those tempted by the negative liberty case in favor of full alienability of rights should recall the antislavery arguments of the Republican Party before the Civil War. Republicans objected to slavery because it enabled slaveholders to subordinate even free men to their dominion. The Slave Power—politically organized proslavery interests—undermined the republican character of government. It suppressed the right to petition Congress (via the gag rule against hearing antislavery petitions), censored the mail (against antislavery literature), and forced free men, against their conscience, to join posses to hunt down alleged fugitive slaves. It violated equal citizenship by effectively granting additional representation to slaveowners for their property in slaves (via the three-fifths rule for apportioning representatives). By insisting on the right to hold slaves in the territories, the Slave Power threatened the prospects of free men to secure their independence by staking out individual homesteads. Slave plantations would acquire vast territories, crowding out opportunities for independent family farms. Chattel slavery of blacks threatened to reduce whites to wage slaves, subordinate to their employers for their entire working lives (Foner, 1995).

The Republican antislavery argument is similar to the positive liberty argument above: it stresses how the constitution of a scheme of liberty rights provides the public infrastructure for a society of free and equal persons. The critical point is to institute a scheme of individual rights that can sustain relations of freedom and equality—understood as personal independence and nondomination—among persons. While the Republican Party limited its arguments to securing relations of nondomination among men, feminist abolitionists extended their arguments to married women, who, like slaves, lacked the rights to own property, make contracts, sue and be sued in court, keep their earned income, and move freely without getting permission from their masters (husbands) (Sklar, 2000). Like the positive liberty argument for individual rights, it recognizes how individuals have a vital stake in *other people's liberty rights* being secure against invasion *or appropriation* by others. The stability of this public infrastructure of freedom depends on individual rights being *inalienable*.

It is to no avail to reply that a libertarian scheme of fully alienable rights that permits voluntary slavery would reject the forced slavery of the antebellum South, along with the violations of free speech and republican government needed to secure the institution of slavery against state "interference." For the Republicans' antislavery argument was about the stability of certain rights configurations under realistic conditions. It was that a society that enforces rights to total domination of one person over another will not be able to sustain itself as a free society of equals over time. How the dominators acquired those rights, whether by force or contract, is irrelevant to this argument. Slaveholders, in the name of protection of their private property rights, used the immense economic power they gained from slavery to seize the state apparatus and crush republican liberties. This is a version of the classical republican antiplutocratic argument against extreme wealth inequality. But it was also directed toward the threat that slavery posed to economic independence of free men—to their prospects for self-employment, for freedom from subjection to an employer.

Debra Satz (2010: 180, 232n40), citing Genicot (2002), offers a similar argument against debt bondage, adapted to contemporary conditions. Two dynamics threaten the ability of workers to maintain their freedom if they have the power to alienate their right to quit to their creditor/employer. First, the availability of debt bondage may restrict opportunities to obtain credit without bondage. Bondage functions as a guarantee against destitute debtors' default: they put up their own labor as collateral. However, the institution of debt bondage makes it more difficult to establish formalized credit and labor markets by which alternative methods of promoting loan repayment (such as credit ratings and garnishing wages) make credit available without bondage.

Second, living under conditions of bondage makes people servile, humble, and psychologically dependent—psychological dispositions that they are likely to transmit to their children. Servile people lack a vivid conception of themselves as rights-bearers and lack the assertiveness needed to vindicate their rights. Moreover, the poor are unlikely to hang on to their freedom for long, given their strategic vulnerability when others are already giving up their alienable rights under hard bargaining. A system of fully alienable libertarian rights is thus liable to degenerate into a society of lords and bondsmen, unable to reproduce the self-understandings that ground libertarian rights. A free society cannot be sustained by people trained to servility and locked into strategic games where some individuals' alienation of their liberty rights puts others' liberties at risk (Satz, 2010: 173–180).

This argument generalizes. Workers may have a permanent interest in retaining other rights besides the formal right to quit, so as to prevent the authority relations constitutive of employment from conversion into relations of domination. For example, they have a permanent interest against sexual and other forms of discriminatory harassment. Under U.S. law, workers have inalienable rights against such degrading treatment. In addition, since lower-level workers have minimal freedom at work, but spend their workdays following others' orders, they have a vital interest in secure access to a limited length of the working day—in having some hours in which they act under their own direction. This is the purpose of maximum hours laws, which forbid employers from conditioning a job offer on having to work too many hours per week. The logic in both cases is strategic: once employers are free to make such unwelcome "offers" (or rather, threats), the decision of some to accept removes better offers from other workers' choice sets, and thereby deprives them of both positive and republican freedom.

As in the case of contractual slavery, libertarians are divided over this type of argument. Mill (1965: XI, §12) supported maximum hours laws as an exception to laissez faire, on strategic grounds. The early Nozick would probably have accepted laws against sexual harassment, because conditioning a job on putting up with a hostile atmosphere or compliance with the boss's sexual demands makes workers worse off relative to a normative baseline of not being subject to unwelcome sexual affronts, and hence counts as coercive.[5] However, the Nozick of *Anarchy, State, and Utopia* would have rejected such laws as interfering with freedom of contract, given that he accepted contractual slavery. Eric Mack (1981) also upholds an absolute principle of freedom of contract, and so would be committed to the alienability of rights against sexual harassment and even assault in labor contracts.

Mack recognizes that it is disingenuous to claim that restraints on freedom of contract that improve workers' choice sets violate their freedom of contract. Hence minimum wage laws, if they only raise wages and do not increase unemployment, do not violate workers' rights. His complaint is that such restraints violate employers' rights, coercing them into offering better terms to workers than they wanted to make. They treat employers as mere resources to be used by others in pursuit of goals the employer does not share (Mack, 1981: 6–8). This argument, if applied to laws against sexual harassment and similar forms of personal domination, is bizarre. One would have thought that employers who threaten their workers with job loss if they do not put up with sexual subordination are treating *them* as mere resources to be used by the employer in pursuit of goals the *workers* do not share.

Mack contrasts a morality of "social goals" with one of deontological side constraints, claiming that the former treats people as mere means and the latter treats people as ends in themselves. A deontology of complete alienability of rights in one's person, however, leads to a society in which some are made others' partial or total property, reduced to instruments of the others' arbitrary wills, and deprived of all three kinds of freedom. That they entered such a state by choice does not undermine the conclusion. Rather, it proves that liberty does not only upset equality—it also upsets liberty. To be more precise: *negative* liberty upsets liberty.

Suppose our "social goal" is to sustain a society in which individuals relate to each other as free persons—which is to say, as equal and independent, not subject to the arbitrary will of others? That would seem to be not merely unobjectionable to a libertarian, but the very point of a libertarian view. The scheme of rights required to realize such a society cannot be devised without tending to the likely consequences of choices made within it. The infrastructure of rights needed to sustain a society in which individuals relate to each other as free persons requires that the rights most fundamental to the ability to exercise independent agency be inalienable, so that no one becomes subject to another's domination. Thus, the fundamental freedom-based rationale for inalienable rights is based on considerations of republican freedom. It entails that a free society requires substantial authority egalitarianism.

4. FREEDOM, EQUALITY, AND THE DEFINITION OF PROPERTY RIGHTS

I conclude with some remarks on the definition of property rights. Much libertarian writing supposes that as soon as an argument is given to justify a right to private property in something, this justifies all the classical incidents of property—including rights to exclude, use, alter, and destroy it, to give, barter, or sell all or any parts of it or any rights to it, to rent, loan, or lease it for income, all with unlimited duration (Honoré, 1961). Why is a separate argument not required for each of these incidents? Shouldn't the nature and function of the property in question play a role in determining which rights are attached to it, and for how long? For example, while the right to destroy is easily granted to most chattels, the positive liberty of future generations provides compelling reasons to deny it to property in land and water resources. Such interests also justify limits on dividing property into parcels or rights bundles too small to use (Heller, 1998). It is also questionable how any case for intellectual property *rights* can be grounded in considerations of negative liberty, given that a regime of universal *privilege* with respect to ideas does not interfere with the liberties of authors and inventors to create and use their works. A freedom-based case for intellectual property can only be made on positive liberty grounds, and then only justify limited terms for copyrights and patents, given the role of the intellectual commons in expanding cultural and technological opportunities.

A just system of legal rules of property, contract, banking, employment, and so forth constitutes a public infrastructure that can sustain a free society of equals over time. Since, in a well-ordered society, members sustain this infrastructure by paying taxes and complying with its rules, each member has a legitimate claim that the rules secure their access to opportunities generated by that infrastructure. The case is no different from the system of public roads. Fair distributions of access to opportunity matter here, too. A system of roads that accommodates only cars, with no pedestrian sidewalks, crosswalks, and stop lights, denies adequate opportunities for freedom of movement to those without cars. It would be absurd for drivers to object to pedestrian infrastructure because it interferes with their negative liberty. They have no claim that the publicly supported infrastructure be tailored to their interests alone.

Arguments over the rules defining private property rights are comparable. Since everyone needs effective access to private property to secure their liberty interests, property rules should ensure such access to all. Such distributive concerns might be partially secured, for example, by way of estate taxes, the revenues of which are distributed to all in the form of social insurance. As Paine (1796) argued, such taxes do not infringe private property rights, but rather constitute a partial unbundling of property rights to secure the legitimate property rights of others. That one of the incidents of property (protecting wealth interests) partially expires upon the death of the owner is no more a violation of property rights than the fact that patents expire after twenty years: such rules simply define the scope of the right in the first instance.

Three features of the public infrastructure of economic rights in social democratic orders promote, and arguably are needed to secure, decent opportunities for all to live on terms of republican freedom and hence authority egalitarianism with respect to everyone else. First, as argued above, individuals need a robust set of market inalienable rights, to avoid domination by their employers. Second, as Paine argued, they need a universal system of social insurance to secure their independence in cases of inability to work or to find work (Anderson, 2008). Third, under modern conditions, they need free, universal education, to avoid domination by parents and others, and to secure a self-conception as someone with rights of personal independence. Each of these can be understood as individual property rights, secured via partial unbundling of classical private property rights. None require state ownership or management of productive enterprises, or bureaucratic administration of individuals' lives. They merely constitute an alternative type of private property regime. It is superior to a libertarian one *on grounds of freedom*, because it better secures positive and republican freedom for all. Since any credible freedom-based argument for private property rights must already recognize the normative priority of positive and republican freedom over negative freedom, it is hard to run credible freedom-based arguments against these core institutions of social democracy at the level of abstraction at which these arguments proceed in political philosophy. Of course, the details of any particular implementation of these institutions may have many objectionable features, as is also true of private employment relations. Because the conditions of republican and positive freedom are sociologically complex, we cannot expect arguments at a high level of abstraction to settle disputes over the details of a property regime suitable for a free society of equals. The current chapter demonstrates that the ideal of a free society of equals is not an oxymoron: not only is relational equality not fundamentally opposed to freedom, in certain senses equality is needed for freedom. Inequality upsets liberty.

NOTES

1. Ferguson, Missouri, the site of protests triggered by the police homicide of a black man stopped for jaywalking, illustrates this phenomenon. With a declining tax base, Ferguson turned to police to raise revenue by incessantly harassing mostly black citizens with traffic citations. They turned citations into the second-highest source of city revenue by issuing an average of three warrants and $321 in fines *per household*. Poor individuals who cannot pay the fines and fail to appear in court to explain why are often arrested and thrown into jail for weeks (Tabarrok, 2014). By comparison to such gross violations of republican freedom, the negative liberty constraints of a regular tax raising the same total revenue are trivial.

2. Rawls clearly distinguished the republican concern that extreme wealth inequality leads to plutocracy from the egalitarian interest in the fair division of income and wealth as such. This is why he grounded progressive inheritance taxes in the principle of equal basic *liberties* (including the fair value of political liberties—an antiplutocratic principle), rather than the difference principle, which takes the fair distribution of income and wealth as its direct object (Rawls, 1999: 245, 70).

3. For the classic distinction between privileges and rights, see Hohfeld, 1913–1914: 30–44.

4. For libertarians who oppose contractual slavery, see Mill (1859: 184) and Rothbard (1998: 40–41). For those who think slave contracts should be enforceable, see Nozick (2013: 331), Alexander (2010), and Block (2003). Locke, an inspiration to libertarians, rejected contractual slavery; see Locke, 1824b: §23 and more aptly Locke, 1824a: §42. However, both his arguments rely on non-libertarian premises: in the *Second Treatise*, against a right to suicide; in the *First Treatise*, asserting a positive right to charity.

5. Nozick (1969) argues that a proposal can count as a threat, and hence be coercive, even if the proposer has a legal right to carry out the negative consequence for the recipient (452), and that such cases of coercion can include employer threats to fire workers if they fail to comply with the employer's wishes (for example, by voting to be represented by a union) (453). Hence, in his early view, employers can coerce workers even if workers have exit rights and employers have the right to fire them at will. See also Flanigan (2012), arguing that sexual harassment at work constitutes wrongful coercion if the empirical expectation for the job does not include sex work. This allows employers to get off the sexual harassment hook simply by listing sexual harassment in boilerplate contractual language for all employees, even for jobs such as cashier and carpenter that have nothing to do with performing sexual services. Still, it reflects some appreciation by a libertarian, however ambivalent, of the reality of workplace coercion.

References

Alexander, Larry, 2010. Voluntary enslavement. San Diego Legal Studies Paper No. 10–042. http://ssrn.com/abstract=1694662.

Anderson, Elizabeth, 2008. How should egalitarians cope with market risks? *Theoretical Inquiries in Law*, 9, pp.61–92.

Anderson, Elizabeth, 2012a. Equality. In: David Estlund, ed. *The Oxford Handbook of Political Philosophy*. New York: Oxford University Press. pp.40–57.

Anderson, Elizabeth, 2012b. The fundamental disagreement between luck egalitarians and relational egalitarians. *Canadian Journal of Philosophy*, S36, pp.1–23.

Arneson, Richard, 2000. Luck egalitarianism and prioritarianism. *Ethics*, 110, pp.339–349.

Aviv, Rachel, 2014. Wrong answer. *The New Yorker*, 21 July. http://www.newyorker.com/magazine/2014/07/21/wrong-answer.

Babeuf, Gracchus, 1967. *The defense of Gracchus Babeuf before the High Court of Vendôme*. John Anthony Scott, ed. and trans. Amherst: University of Massachusetts Press.

Bentham, Jeremy, 1838–43. Principles of the civil code. In: John Bowring, ed. *The works of Jeremy Bentham, published under the superintendence of his executor, John Bowring*. Vol. 1. Edinburgh: William Tate. pp.297–364.

Block, Walter, 2003. Toward a libertarian theory of inalienability: a critique of Rothbard, Barnett, Smith, Kinsella, Gordon, and Epstein. *Journal of Libertarian Studies*, 17(2), pp.39–85.

Buonarroti, Philippe, 1836. *Buonarroti's history of Babeuf's conspiracy for equality*. Bronterre [pseud.]. London: H. Hetherington.

Dworkin, Gerald, 1982. Is more choice better than less? *Midwest Studies in Philosophy*, 7, pp.47–61.

Flanigan, Jessica, 2012. Workplace coercion. http://bleedingheartlibertarians.com/2012/03/workplace-coercion/. Posted on 12 March 2012; Accessed on: 29 July 2014.

Foner, Eric, 1995. *Free soil, free labor, free men: the ideology of the Republican Party before the Civil War*. New York: Oxford University Press.

Fried, Barbara, 2011. Does Nozick have a theory of property rights? In: Ralf Bader and John Meadowcraft, eds. *The Cambridge companion to Nozick's* Anarchy, state and utopia. New York and Cambridge, UK: Cambridge University Press. Http://ssrn.com/abstract=1782031.

Genicot, Garance, 2002. Bonded labor and serfdom: a paradox of voluntary choice. *Journal of Development Economics*, 67(1), pp.101–127.

Hayek, Friedrich A., 1944. *The road to serfdom*. Chicago: University of Chicago Press.

Heller, Michael, 1998. The tragedy of the anticommons: property in the transition from Marx to markets. *Harvard Law Review*, 111, pp.621–688.

Hohfeld, Wesley, 1913–1914. Some fundamental legal conceptions as applied in judicial reasoning. *Yale Law Journal*, 23, pp.16–59.

Honoré, Anthony, 1961. Ownership. In: Anthony G. Guest, ed. *Oxford essays in jurisprudence*. Oxford: Clarendon Press. pp.107–147.

Locke, John, 1824a. First treatise of government. In: *The works of John Locke in nine volumes*. vol. 4. 12th ed. London: Rivington. pp.212–337.

Locke, John, 1824b. Second treatise of government. In: *The works of John Locke in nine volumes*, vol. 4. 12th ed. London: Rivington. pp.338–485.

Mack, Eric, 1981. In defense of "unbridled" freedom of contract. *American Journal of Economics and Sociology*, 40(1), pp.1–15.

Mack, Eric, 2009. Individualism and libertarian rights. In: Thomas Christiano and John Christman, eds. *Contemporary debates in political philosophy*. Malden, MA: Wiley-Blackwell. pp.119–136.

Mill, John Stuart, 1859. *On liberty*. London: J. W. Parker and Son.

Mill, John Stuart, 1965. *Principles of political economy*. Vol. 3 of *Collected works of John Stuart Mill*, edited by J. M. Robson. Toronto: University of Toronto Press.

Nozick, Robert, 1969. Coercion. In: Sydney Morganbesser, Patrick Suppes, and Morton White, eds. *Philosophy, science, and method: essays in honor of Ernest Nagel*. New York: St. Martin's Press. pp.440–472.

Nozick, Robert, 2013. *Anarchy, state, and utopia*. New York: Basic Books.

Otsuka, Michael, 1998. Self-ownership and equality: a Lockean reconciliation. *Philosophy and Public Affairs*, 27(1), pp.65–92.

Paine, Thomas, 1796. Agrarian justice. http://www.ssa.gov/history/paine4.html. Accessed on 27 July 2012.

Pettit, Philip, 1997. *Republicanism: a theory of freedom and government*. New York: Oxford University Press.

Rawls, John, 1999. *A theory of justice*. Rev. ed. Cambridge, MA: Harvard University Press.

Raz, Joseph, 1994. Rights and individual well-being. In: *Ethics in the public domain*. Oxford: Clarendon. pp.44–59.

Rothbard, Murray, 1998. *The ethics of liberty*. Rev. ed. New York: New York University Press.

Satz, Debra, 2010. *Why some things should not be for sale: the moral limits of markets*. Oxford and New York: Oxford University Press.

Sklar, Kathryn Kish, 2000. *Women's rights emerges within the anti-slavery movement, 1830–1870: a brief history with documents*. Boston: Bedford/St. Martin's.

Tabarrok, Alex, 2014. Ferguson and the modern debtor's prison. http://marginalrevolution.com/marginalrevolution/2014/08/ferguson-and-the-debtors-prison.html. Posted on 21 August 2014; Accessed on 22 August 2014.

Temkin, Larry, 2003. Egalitarianism defended. *Ethics*, 113, pp.764–782.

CHAPTER 6

NON-DOMINATION

FRANK LOVETT

How should we characterize freedom as a political ideal? Generally speaking, we take freedom to be something a well-ordered society should honor and promote. It follows that this question—which has proved among the most contentious in political theory and philosophy—is best understood in substantive rather than conceptual terms. In other words, we ought to be interested less in the *meaning* of freedom per se than in *what sort* of freedom a well-ordered society should honor and promote. To serve in its role as a public ideal one might say that a conception of freedom should have broad appeal in a diverse society, be practically demanding without being infeasible, and capture most of our stronger prior intuitions about what living in a free society would be like.

Consider, for example, the well-worn debate between what have aptly been described as *exercise* conceptions of freedom on the one hand, and *opportunity* conceptions on the other (Taylor, 1979). On the former view, roughly speaking, a person enjoys freedom in some choice or other to the extent that she exercises management over that choice effective enough to achieve her genuine or fundamental aims: the addicted gambler, for example, is free whenever she actually succeeds in overcoming her addiction. On the latter view, by contrast, a person enjoys freedom in some choice or other simply to the extent that no external obstacle stands the way of whatever opportunities the choice presents: the addicted gambler, for example, is free provided no one actually hinders her leaving the casino. The contrast between these differing characterizations of freedom has, under various descriptions, been the subject of many discussions, perhaps none more famous than Isaiah Berlin's 1958 lecture on "Two Concepts of Liberty" (published in Berlin, 1969). That lecture attacks exercise conceptions of freedom, and defends an opportunity conception. His argument is not primarily conceptual, however: there is nothing, in his view, inherently confused or incoherent about exercise conceptions of freedom as such. Rather, the difficulty lies in what the public promotion of freedom, so understood, would entail. For which aims are genuine and fundamental to human beings, and thus worth achieving? In societies characterized by reasonable pluralism there exist fundamental disagreements concerning the proper ends of human life it would be unjust to override or suppress. It follows that freedom in the politically relevant sense is best characterized as an opportunity conception: our public aim should be to remove the obstacles to choice, so individuals can decide for themselves what ends to pursue.

Not everyone is fully persuaded by Berlin's argument, but for present purposes let us grant that a well-ordered society should promote opportunity rather than exercise freedom. How encompassing is this portfolio? Should the removal of any possible obstacle to choice count as freedom enhancing? Probably not. The social ideal of freedom ought at least be limited to the removal of those hindrances having some causal connection—however distant or remote—to human agency.[1] Most accounts go even further, for neither must we count every possible such hindrance as freedom reducing. Here we will explore one such account, commonly called "republican" or sometimes "neo-Roman," which concentrates on those hindrances presented by relationships of domination. On the view of republican authors such as Quentin Skinner, Philip Pettit, and others, the specific sort of freedom a well-ordered society ought to promote first and foremost is freedom from domination.[2]

Recently, a number of new challenges to this view have been raised. The most important of these are, first, that republicans have failed to develop a conception of freedom distinct in any meaningful sense from the well-known non-interference conception; and second, that in concentrating on relationships of domination, republicans have inappropriately narrowed the scope of freedom. In response, this chapter will argue that when we carefully attend to the role in which a conception of freedom ought to serve—namely, as a central public ideal for well-ordered societies—these particular challenges can be seen to fail. Some other challenges remain, however, as we shall see. The first section introduces the republican account in terms of a non-domination condition. Section two responds to the complaint that non-domination is not relevantly distinct from non-interference. Section three clarifies some technical aspects of the non-domination condition. Finally, the fourth and fifth sections respectively discuss the republican claim that non-domination is *necessary* for political freedom, and then whether it should also be regarded as *sufficient*.

1. THE NON-DOMINATION CONDITION

The republican account of freedom is most easily explained in relation to another competing opportunity conception, freedom as non-interference. As it happens, the latter is the view favored by Berlin: in his words, freedom should be understood as "the area within which . . . a person or group . . . is or should be left to do or be what he is able to do or be, without interference by other persons" (1969: 121–122). Obviously, the term "interference" here must be given a precise meaning, and this has not proved entirely easy to do.

Roughly speaking, we might say that to interfere with a choice is to more or less intentionally frustrate that choice in some reasonably direct manner. Two clear and undisputed examples of interference are physical restraint and coercive threat. Somewhat less obvious examples might include deceiving someone with the aim of influencing their choice, and deliberately undermining a choice by depriving someone of resources needed to carry it out. As most commonly understood, however, not every possible hindrance properly counts as an interference. Suppose, for instance, I cannot view New York harbor from atop the Statue of Liberty because I am too poor to pay the admission charge, or because I am confined to a wheelchair and there are no elevators. Of course neither poverty nor disability are mere natural obstacles unconnected to human agency altogether, for I might have afforded the admission charge under an alternative economic dispensation, and elevators might have been installed if sufficient public resources were devoted to that purpose. Certainly, therefore, both count as hindrances. But we generally experience such indirect resourcing failures differently than we do interferences, for in the former case we do not usually feel the operation of a specific human will intentionally opposed to our own—or at any rate, not in the absence of some elaborate social theory.[3] To distinguish these two distinct experiences, then, we might designate unintentional resourcing failures *vitiations* (following Pettit, 2012: 37–40).[4] Exactly where to draw the line between vitiation and interference is a difficult question which need not be resolved for present purposes, provided the contrast is not dismissed altogether (but see Hayek, 1960: 135–137; Berlin, 1969: 122–123; Miller, 1983).

Whatever their views about the effect of vitiation on freedom in the politically relevant sense, all advocates of freedom as non-interference subscribe at least to the following *non-interference* condition:

F_1: A is not free to ϕ if some B intentionally frustrates A's ϕ-ing.

On this view, when we say that a well-ordered society ought to honor and promote freedom, what we mean is that it ought to provide for a wide sphere of individual choice unhindered by interferences, at least so far as doing so is reasonably practicable and consistent with other worthy public aims. This view is often referred to as the "liberal" conception of freedom on the grounds that many liberal authors have subscribed to some version of the non-interference condition, including among others Jeremy Bentham, William Paley, Benjamin Constant, J. S. Mill, Herbert Spencer, and Henry Sidgwick in the nineteenth century; Isaiah Berlin, John Gray, and Joel Feinberg in the twentieth. Against this, however, it might be pointed out that some liberals such as John Rawls held more ambiguous views, and that others such as John Locke clearly rejected the non-interference condition (see Larmore, 2001).[5] Following Berlin's terminology, freedom as non-interference is also often referred to as "negative freedom" on the grounds that it characterizes freedom as the mere negation or absence of a hindrance. Against this, however, it might be pointed out that every opportunity conception is similarly negative, and indeed a wide variety of quite distinct views have claimed that title. To avoid such complications, we will simply refer to "freedom as non-interference."

Freedom as non-interference is a comparatively modern view, having no real advocate prior to Thomas Hobbes. The republican account of freedom as non-domination, by contrast, is a much older view. Indeed, it has a good claim to being the standard view of freedom from ancient times down until the late eighteenth century. Before Bentham and his fellow travelers popularized freedom as non-interference, it was more or less universally held that to be free, in the politically relevant sense, is simply to have no master: it is to be a "free man" rather than a slave or other dependent person (Patterson, 1991). Mastery or domination refers not to any actual interference, but rather to the *ability* to interfere when that ability is not suitably controlled. Traditionally, an uncontrolled ability to frustrate the choices of another was termed "arbitrary power," and until recently contemporary republican authors commonly used this expression; unfortunately, its inherent ambiguity generated much confusion and misguided criticism. For example, to say that power is "arbitrary" might mean that it is unpredictable, or that it is discretionary, or that it is unjustified—each of which would, in different ways, be problematic for an account of freedom (Lovett, 2012). Fortunately, republicans never intended "arbitrary" to mean any of these things. Rather, they just meant "insufficiently controlled," and they might as well say so directly (Pettit, 2012: 58).

We will subsequently consider in more detail what sort of control is sufficient, but roughly speaking the ability of the police to issue coercive threats is controlled by the judicial system, whereas the ability of criminal gangs is not: thus the existence of criminal gangs, but not of the police, detracts from our republican freedom. More precisely, all republicans subscribe to the following *non-domination* freedom condition:

> F_2: A is not free to ϕ if some B has the uncontrolled ability to intentionally frustrate A's ϕ-ing.

On this view, when we say that a well-ordered society ought to honor and promote freedom, what we mean is that it ought to provide for a wide sphere of individual choice unhindered by domination, at least so far as doing so is reasonably practicable and consistent with other worthy public aims. This is referred to as the "republican" account of freedom not because the classical republican authors—Machiavelli, Milton, Harrington, Sidney, Montesquieu, Price, Madison, and so forth—alone endorsed a version of the non-domination condition. Indeed, as noted above, so did nearly everyone prior to Bentham, including Locke for instance.[6] Rather it is because the classical republicans enthusiastically extolled freedom, so understood, as a central political and social ideal. Were they right to do so? That is what we shall consider subsequently.

2. Are Domination and Interference Distinguishable?

Before assessing the merits and demerits of the republican account of freedom, however, we must first satisfy ourselves that it constitutes a coherent alternative view. Against this possibility, some authors have recently suggested that interference and domination are in fact not relevantly distinct (Carter, 2008; Kramer, 2008). If this were so, then the republican account of freedom as non-domination would add nothing to the more familiar non-interference account. Offhand, however, it is not obvious why this should be. Interference is an action, whereas domination is an ability to act: they are no more the same than walking is the same as the ability to walk. Why might we believe the difference between them irrelevant with respect to freedom?

To take a paradigmatic instance of interference, suppose that B is a gangster who intercepts A on her journey to town: "Your money or your life!" he demands at point of gun. On any plausible view, A's freedom to journey to town unmolested has been interfered with. Strictly speaking, however, this is not because she has lost either the ability to keep her money, or the ability to reach town alive. Rather, what she has lost is the conjunctive opportunity to keep her money *and* to reach town alive. Now suppose that B is the sort of gangster who prides himself on robbing only those who to his own mind deserve such treatment: provided travelers are suitably polite and deferential, he will generally let them pass. In this second scenario, A's freedom to journey to town is on any plausible view dominated by B's uncontrolled ability to frustrate that journey. Here again, however, it is not strictly the case that she has lost the ability to reach town alive, money in hand. Rather, what she has lost is the conjunctive opportunity to reach town alive, money in hand, *and* to do this without acting deferentially towards B along the way. What have we learned from these examples? We have learned that both interference and domination can similarly be analyzed as reductions in a person's conjunctively exercisable opportunities.

This discovery is bound to lead to the thought that freedom might best be characterized not as the absence of interference only, nor the absence of domination only, but rather as the absence of any factor that might reduce our conjunctively exercisable opportunities—or, at any rate, any factor somehow connected to human agency.[7] Interestingly, interference and domination are not alone in reducing our conjunctively exercisable opportunities: vitiating resource failures do as well. Thus it may be that the poor man does not, strictly speaking, lack funds to pay the admission charge at the Statue of Liberty, but rather funds sufficient to pay the admission charge *and* to purchase his next meal. Indeed, the scope of freedom so characterized would extend further still, to any possible hindrance of choice. Thus it should be clear, on reflection, that "factors reducing our conjunctively exercisable opportunities" is simply a technically sophisticated way of articulating what we mean by a hindrance in the first place.

Recall, however, that the relevant issue is not what we *mean* by freedom, but rather *what sort* of freedom a well-ordered society should honor and promote. To define freedom as here suggested thus begs the question—namely, *which* hindrances, specifically, should it be our public concern to remove? Interferences only? Domination instead? Either or both, together with vitiations, or not? And so forth. One certainly might claim that the best answer is *all of the above*, but if so that has to be argued for substantively, hindrance by hindrance. And at least one possible objection must be considered against such a view. Characterizing freedom in the politically relevant sense as the removal of any factor that would reduce our conjunctively exercisable opportunities conveys the distinct impression that all such factors are easily commensurable. It would follow that between the elimination of x units of interference and x units of domination (or of vitiation) we ought properly to stand indifferent: degrees of freedom are degrees of freedom, regardless of their form. But this does not seem right. In the waning days of the Roman republic, violent civil wars interfered with people's lives in a multitude of ways until Augustus finally imposed personal dominion over the empire. No one at the time would have said they merely traded one sort of freedom for another just as good: on the contrary, the tragedy was precisely that Rome was in the end forced to sacrifice freedom for peace. Whether that sacrifice was worth it might be debated, of course, but it is hard even to articulate the dilemma on the view that all hindrances count against freedom indifferently (Harbour, 2012).

Let us therefore return to the central comparison with which we began, that between on the one hand a characterization of political freedom concentrating on interferences, and on the other a characterization concentrating on relationships of domination. In one significant respect the two views are similar—namely, both constitute opportunity rather than exercise conceptions of freedom. On neither view must a person successfully manage some range of choices in order to enjoy freedom: it is sufficient that she merely have some range of choices unhindered by either interference or domination.

Apart from this similarity, however, the two views are decidedly distinct. This is most easily seen in those cases where the non-interference condition and the non-domination condition would score freedom differently. Consider first cases of domination without interference. An example might be benevolent autocrats like Augustus who generally refrain from interfering with their subjects, though their *ability* to do so is in no way suitably controlled. The non-domination condition would score those subject to a benevolent autocrat as unfree. Not so the non-interference condition, as Berlin makes perfectly clear: freedom as non-interference "is not incompatible with some kinds of autocracy," he observes.

> Just as a democracy may, in fact, deprive the individual citizen of a great many liberties which he might have in some other form of society, so it is perfectly conceivable that a liberal-minded despot would allow his subjects a large measure of personal freedom. (1969: 129)

This was indeed one of the main attractions of the non-interference view to its originator, Thomas Hobbes, for he was very keen to argue against the republicans of his day that "whether a commonwealth be monarchical, or popular, the freedom is still the same" (1651: 143).

Second, consider cases of interference without domination. The laws and policies of a suitably controlled democratic government might be an example. All laws and policies in some degree frustrate whatever choices they aim to regulate. Thus Berlin observes that "every law seems to me to curtail some liberty, although it may be a means to increasing another" (1969: xlix). Similarly, since "the only freedom which deserves the name is that of pursuing our own good in our own way," it must follow, according to

J. S. Mill, that "all restraint, *qua* restraint, is an evil" (1859: 12). The non-domination condition, however, scores such cases differently. Provided the government issuing those laws or policies is suitably controlled, it will not subject its citizens to domination, and thus not detract from their freedom. On the contrary, the rule of law is a necessary condition for our enjoying freedom in the first place. In the proverbial state of nature, even if people generally let one another alone there will always be individuals or groups strong enough to interfere with my choices should they so desire: there is thus no "natural" freedom from domination at all. The only genuine freedom from domination we enjoy is that specifically constituted by public institutions designed to control the ability of others to interfere in at least some of our choices. "Where there is no law, there is no freedom," says William Blackstone, for "laws, when prudently framed, are by no means subversive but rather introductive of liberty" (1765: 122).

3. NON-DOMINATION: FURTHER CLARIFICATIONS

On the republican account, one is not free in some choice so long as others have the uncontrolled ability to frustrate that choice—so long as, in other words, one is subject to domination. Some criticize this account of domination as too narrow. It requires, first, that there be a *agent* of domination; and second, that said agent have the ability to frustrate choices *intentionally*. These critics point out, however, that many of the problems and challenges disadvantaged persons presently experience do not have this character. Consider, for instance, poor minorities in the United States. While existing civil rights legislation no doubt sometimes fails to protect specific individuals from uncontrolled interference in specific instances, such failures are no longer the primary cause of the persistent disadvantages faced by poor minorities as a whole. These disadvantages stem rather from systemic factors, such as residential housing patterns which divorce poor minorities from good schools and good jobs. Surely, one is tempted to say, poor minorities are *dominated* by these circumstances, even if they are merely the unintended consequence of various structural features of American society.

Before addressing this objection, two clarifications might be in order. The first is that we need not suppose an agent of domination must be an individual human being. Quite the contrary, provided we are willing to grant the reality of group agents, there is no reason to suppose that people cannot experience domination at the hands of a group. Autocratic regimes, for example, clearly dominate their subject populations, much as successful criminal gangs dominate their neighborhoods. In both cases, the individuals composing the regime or the gang are able to do so precisely because they act as a group agent. The second is that we need not suppose a given agent of domination either wanted or deliberately sought to obtain an uncontrolled ability to frustrate the choices of other people. Under traditional Western family law and custom, for example, all husbands and fathers possessed considerable uncontrolled abilities to intentionally frustrate the choices of their wives and children. This was equally true of those husbands and fathers who detested having such power as it was of those who relished having it. Confusion on these points may lead some to imagine the account of domination as uncontrolled interference narrower than it really is.

These clarifications aside, let us return to the case of unintended structural disadvantage. Should such disadvantage count as domination? The best answer is no. To the extent that unintended structural disadvantages hinder our choices they will count as what were earlier termed vitiating resource failures. The real issue is thus not whether domination has properly been defined, but rather whether we should adopt the following *non-vitiation* condition in place of—or in addition to—the non-domination condition:

F_3: A is not free to ϕ unless she commands resources sufficient to ϕ.

Now of course we could redefine the term "domination" to mean *either* uncontrolled interference *or* vitiation. But since uncontrolled interference and vitiation are two different sorts of choice-hindering experiences, we would then stand in need of a new term to designate the former as contrasted with the latter. The argument would thus not advance in the slightest. It is better to leave terms as they are, and pose the real substantive issue as the following: should the best account of freedom in the politically relevant sense include a non-vitiation condition? This issue will be addressed in a subsequent section.

Before moving on, however, one important aspect of the non-domination condition stands in need of further clarification—namely, the meaning of "control." In what sense must the ability of some person or group to frustrate another's choices be controlled if that ability is not to count as domination? In other words, what sort of control does republican freedom require? The republican authors are not entirely agreed on this point. Roughly speaking, there are two different views.

On the first view, which we may term "procedural," an ability to frustrate the choices of another will be suitably controlled provided it is reliably constrained by effective rules, procedures, or goals that are common knowledge to all persons or groups concerned (Lovett, 2012). Rules are *effective*, let us say, provided the probability p that they will actually constrain a given agent's ability is reasonably high. Robust social norms might meet this criterion, for instance, but not unenforced laws or merely aspirational ethical standards. Effective rules are *reliable* provided that p remains reasonably high across a wide range of nearby possible worlds: thus, relatively small changes in local circumstance should not undermine the effectiveness of a rule. Controls on police conduct, for instance, might be not be reliable if the judges who are supposed to enforce them are readily susceptible to bribes. Roughly speaking, the procedural view equates republican freedom with the traditional idea of the rule of law, provided we are willing to extend the latter idea considerably (List, 2006).

On the second view, which we may term "democratic," an ability to frustrate the choices of another will be suitably controlled provided it is governed by the directed influence of those persons whose choices they are. In other words, if B has the ability to frustrate A's choices, that ability is suitably controlled if A can not only *influence* when and where B will interfere, but further guide those interferences in the *direction* she desires. In an example offered by Pettit (2012: 57–58), suppose that A has given the keys to her alcohol cupboard to B, with strict instructions that no matter how much she pleads he is not to return them except at twenty-four hours' notice. Further suppose that B is sufficiently bound to follow those instructions such that, in effect, he acts as her servant in this regard. In this case it would seem strange to say that A lacks freedom when B frustrates her subsequent efforts to drink. On the democratic view she remains free because B's ability to frustrate that choice is governed by her directed influence. Directed influence can also be jointly exercised by the members of a group, but in that case each member must have roughly an equal share in the control.[8] The control exercised by a properly constituted democratic people over their government might exemplify the latter. It is true, of course, that even in a democracy the government may sometimes frustrate a person's choices in ways she does not endorse. Nevertheless, she need not regard such frustrations as the imposition of an uncontrolled alien will provided the government remains suitably controlled through a process of directed influence in which she has an equal part: from her point of view, it is merely "tough luck" that not every decision will go her way (Pettit, 2012: 152–153).[9]

Which view is better? Most contemporary republicans prefer some version of the second, democratic view. The most compelling reason for this preference is given by the problem of unjust rules. Consider the apartheid regime in South Africa. While not strictly true in historical fact, we might imagine the ability of white South Africans to frustrate the choices of blacks was rigorously controlled by law and policy: ergo, on the procedural view, we would apparently have to say that the latter enjoyed freedom from domination. Obviously, this is counterintuitive. Why not stipulate that rules must be substantively just in order to count as domination reducing? Unfortunately, doing so would "moralize" our conception of freedom, effectively smuggling into that conception an account of justice. Freedom would then no longer carry independent weight as an ideal, but merely serve as a rhetorical tag to whatever we have already identified as just on other grounds (Larmore, 2001: 239–242; Carter, 2008: 64–66). The alternative is to adopt the democratic view. On the one hand, since criteria for democratic control can be specified in a manner agnostic with respect to substantive accounts of justice, we avoid the moralization problem; on the other, since people usually exercise democratic control so as to protect themselves from injustice, we mostly avoid the problem of unjust rules.

Unfortunately, the democratic view has disadvantages of its own. For one thing, it apparently excludes the possibility that constraints generated by robust social norms, stable market equilibria, or rules of common law could operate so as to impose suitable control. In such cases, the constraints in question lack a democratic pedigree, and so presumably cannot count as domination reducing.[10] Indeed, most of the constraints we ordinary depend upon for protecting our freedoms are at best indirectly democratic. Consider, for instance, the ability our fellow citizens might have to invade our property: our freedom of ownership is secured only because that ability is suitably controlled. But it is not controlled by us directly, as in the case of the alcohol cupboard, but rather by the rules of property law enforced by police; the ability of the police to disregard those rules, in turn, is again not controlled by us directly, but rather by judges; and so on. The whole institutional complex may in some sense be answerable to us in our collective capacity as democratic citizens, and perhaps on those grounds we enjoy freedom of ownership. Notice, however, that all our freedoms will thus depend on our living in a properly constituted democratic society. On the democratic view, apparently, the subjects of a monarchy would enjoy no more freedom were their monarch to introduce the rule of law than before. This sets the bar rather high.

It is also problematic in cases where, for various reasons, democratic control is not realistically feasible. The United States, for instance, has considerable abilities to frustrate the choices of people living in other countries. On the democratic view, alas, the freedom prospects for those individuals are rather dim, for it would apparently not be enough that international law and custom effectively and reliably constrain the conduct of the United States: until those constraints have a democratic pedigree, the domination experienced by non-Americans remains undiminished. There are plenty of domestic cases as well: children, for instance, or the mentally disabled simply cannot exercise democratic control. Does it follow they cannot enjoy freedom from domination? On this issue, in short, consensus continues to elude contemporary republicans.

4. Is Non-domination Necessary for Freedom?

To assess the republican account of freedom, we must first ask whether non-domination is indeed necessary to enjoy freedom in the politically relevant sense. If our answer is yes, then the best conception of political freedom must include a non-domination condition, whatever else it may or may not include. The main argument supporting a non-domination condition—what might be termed the "kindly master" argument—is perhaps the signature argument of both classical and contemporary republicanism. It runs as follows.

Suppose the contrary, that it is possible for A to enjoy freedom in some range of choices ϕ even though some B has the uncontrolled ability to intentionally frustrate A's ϕ-ing. What might be a plausible example? The most likely scenario is when B is favorably or benevolently disposed towards A, and thus in practice not inclined to frustrate her choices, or inclined to do so only when it is for her benefit. For example, traditional Western family law granted husbands and fathers the uncontrolled ability to frustrate their wives and children across a considerable range of choices: nevertheless, many husbands and fathers were sufficiently loving and good-natured so as not to exercise that ability, or to exercise it only for benevolent purposes. If it were possible anywhere to enjoy freedom even when subject to domination, it would be possible here. But is it? Many have asserted that the wives and children of even benevolent and good-natured husbands and fathers in the nineteenth century did not enjoy freedom. This is because, although the former were often in practice left to choose for themselves, they did so only by permission, as it were. Since a husband or father might at any time change his mind about this or that permission, those subject to his control are bound to feel constrained to choose in ways that will not upset the status quo. This cannot be genuine freedom.

The classical republicans were especially fond of highlighting the kindly-master scenario. One of the most emphatic statements comes from the seventeenth-century English commonwealth advocate Algernon Sidney:

> The weight of chains, number of stripes, hardness of labour, and other effects of a master's cruelty, may make one servitude more miserable than another: but he is a slave who serves the best and gentlest man in the world, as well as he who serves the worst. . . . For this reason the poet ingeniously flattering a good emperor, said, that liberty was not more desirable than to serve a gentle master; but still acknowledged that it was a service, distinct from, and contrary to liberty. (Sidney, 1698: 441)

This is of course less argument than rhetoric—albeit powerful rhetoric. Fortunately, contemporary republicans have added at least two further lines of argument in support of the non-domination condition.

First, note that a plausible account of freedom ought to be appropriately "contoured"—it should, in other words, accurately track the comparative degrees of freedom in different scenarios. Now suppose that some slave through long practice and experience gains considerable insight into his master's psychology, and is thus able to cultivate increasingly benevolent dispositions in the latter. Absent the non-domination condition, it would appear the slave is thus correspondingly enjoying increasing freedom. This, however, does not seem correct. Next suppose that political reforms lead to the abolition of slavery, emancipating both the slaves of benevolent masters and the slaves of malevolent ones. Absent the non-domination condition, it would appear that only the freedom of the latter is thereby increased, or at any rate that it is increased more than that of the former. Again, this does not seem correct. Thus something like the non-domination condition is needed to capture these reasonable comparative judgments about freedom and appropriately guide the public policy of a well-ordered society.

So much for the first line of argument. The second proceeds as follows. Suppose B decisively frustrates A's ϕ-ing. As in the fable of sour grapes, A might say to herself, "That's quite all right since I didn't want to ϕ anyway: my freedom consists in my being able to do what I want to do; it is irrelevant whether or not I am able to do what I don't want to do." When expressed so baldly, this line of reasoning is apt to strike us as absurd. Surely we cannot make ourselves free simply by adapting our desires to our opportunities! Further, to adopt such a view as a guide to public policy would be disastrous, for it would entail that the citizens of even the most despotic regime might count as perfectly free provided they are willing to tailor their wants to their opportunities (Berlin,

1969: 135–141; Pettit, 2012: 30–33). Now by parallel, suppose B has the uncontrolled ability to frustrate A's ϕ-ing. Analogously, A might say to herself, "That's quite all right since if I want to ϕ, I need only cultivate B's good graces until he permits my ϕ-ing; it is irrelevant the means by which I might secure the opportunity to ϕ, provided I can do so." This line of reasoning is apt to strike us as just as absurd as the previous. Surely we cannot make ourselves free simply by ingratiating ourselves to the whims of others (Pettit, 2012: 64–67)!

Are these arguments decisive? Must the best account of freedom in the politically relevant sense include a non-domination condition? Republicans have generally faced two recurring objections. The first, interestingly enough, is that freedom from domination is too radical to serve as a public ideal. Thus, referring to the republican view, William Paley argued that

> those definitions of liberty ought to be rejected, which, by making that essential to civil freedom which is unattainable in experience, inflame expectations that can never be gratified, and disturb the public content with complaints, which no wisdom or benevolence of government can remove. (1785: 315)

The classical republican authors, it must be admitted, were no less parochial in their outlook than most of their contemporaries: women and children, un-propertied laborers and servants, ethnic minorities, and so on simply did not figure into their political calculus. Thus when they extolled the value of freedom from domination, it was the freedom of a propertied male elite they had in mind. All this began to change in the late eighteenth and early nineteenth centuries, when a powerful constellation of cultural, social, and economic pressures began to upset traditional hierarchies and widen the scope of public concern to include those previously excluded. Viewed in light of these transformations, freedom from domination was bound to appear radical indeed, for taking it seriously would mean granting independence from mastery to women, to servants, and all the rest. Not surprisingly, many early socialists and feminists explicitly drew on the traditional republican language, castigating the wage slavery of the factory worker, and the slavish bondage suffered by women under traditional family law and custom.

The radical implications of the non-domination condition may have contributed to the eclipse of the republican conception of freedom in the nineteenth century (see Pettit, 1997: 41–50), but are less likely to register as a serious objection today. Not so a second objection, first raised by Bentham and Paley and reiterated by many critics ever since. Perhaps the most familiar contemporary variant of the objection is the so-called "gentle giant" case (Kramer, 2008: 41–50). Suppose there lives in some bucolic valley a powerful giant. This giant has the wide-ranging ability to interfere in the lives of the valley dwellers should he so desire, and the valley dwellers for their part do not have the strength to control him. Fortunately, he just happens to be a gentle giant. Indeed, so deeply rooted is his mild disposition that little the valley dwellers might say or do would actually move him to exercise his considerable powers: he is content to let them go about their business, regarding their hustle and bustle with bemused indifference. Now how much freedom do the valley dwellers enjoy? According to the non-domination condition, apparently, hardly any at all. This is because the giant has the uncontrolled ability to frustrate just about anything any one of them might happen to want to do, even if it is extremely unlikely that he ever will. This does not seem quite right. Suppose next that an evil wizard passes through the valley, and along the way magically transforms the giant's gentle disposition into a mean one: the giant is now inclined to interfere with the valley dwellers in all sorts of devious ways. Surely, the latter have now lost a great deal of the freedom they previously enjoyed, yet the non-domination condition denies this on the grounds that they never had any to lose!

The gentle giant case is designed to reveal that the non-domination condition confuses freedom as such with the security of that freedom. Intuitively, as we have said, the servant of a kind master lacks freedom even though her choices are not intentionally frustrated—even though she does not experience actual interference. But perhaps we have this intuition simply because her freedom from interference lacks security. To the extent that her master's ability to intentionally frustrate her choices is not suitably controlled, there is some probability he might find reason to interfere with her in the future. Ordinarily, it is true, the most practical way to reduce the expected probability of interference is to impose external controls, but it is a mistake to confuse those controls with freedom itself. The gentle giant case illustrates this point by artificially suppressing the expected probability of interference in the absence of external controls. If we agree that the valley dwellers initially enjoyed freedom and then lost it, then freedom cannot hinge on non-domination.

But should we agree? Here we must recall once more that our aim is to establish not the *meaning* of freedom, but rather *what sort* of freedom a well-ordered society should honor and promote. Suppose lessening the probability of interference were our public aim (Goodin and Jackson, 2007). One problem is that this approach seems to ignore the specific harm of uncertainty itself (Skinner, 2008: 97–99). From a strictly expected-interference point of view, we should be indifferent between experiencing a relatively minor interference for certain on the one hand, and an even chance of experiencing an interference twice as burdensome on the other. Thus we might apparently enhance our freedom, on this approach, by granting tax-collecting authorities wide discretion to set individual tax burdens on a case-by-case basis, provided the average level of taxes collected overall is somewhat lower. But this is problematic: surely the value of freedom, at least in part, consists in our being able to plan our lives according to our own designs, with a certain and clear knowledge of the parameters society will impose (Wall, 2003).

Of course the advocate for non-interference might evade this difficulty by proposing that we instead set as our aim not reducing expected interference, but rather reducing interference uncertainty. This concedes much to the republicans, but the even deeper problem with the whole security-of-non-interference outlook is that it suggests we ought to be indifferent as to the *means* by which that security might be achieved (Pettit, 1997: 73–74). In an autocratic state, we might reduce the probability that the ruler will interfere with his subjects either by trying to introduce institutional controls on his authority, or—as in the classic "mirror-for-princes" literature—by trying to make him a better and more virtuous ruler. Other things equal, the security-of-non-interference approach would not favor one strategy over the other. Analogously, the probability that husbands will interfere with their wives under the traditional family law regime might be reduced either by trying to reduce the dependency of wives on their husbands, or by trying to educate husbands to be gentler with their spouses. Again, other things equal, the security-of-non-interference approach would not favor one strategy over the other. This seems wrong. Our public aim should be to purge relationships of domination from society, not merely to ameliorate their effects. For our ideals to properly align with our aims, freedom in the politically relevant sense must include non-domination.

5. Is Non-domination Sufficient for Freedom?

Suppose we agree with the republicans that non-domination is necessary for the enjoyment of freedom in the politically relevant sense. Is non-domination sufficient? Many different things, as we have seen, can act as hindrances to choice. Now we must ask which of these, if any, should count (together with non-domination) as freedom reducing.[11]

Before proceeding, it is worth reiterating what was said in the introduction—namely, that our discussion here is limited to opportunity conceptions of freedom. We will not therefore consider accounts of political freedom that attempt to supplement or replace the non-domination condition with demands for either personal or collective autonomy. The reason for this restriction is pragmatic: however appealing they might be as accounts of what it *means* to enjoy freedom in the fullest or richest sense, such exercise conceptions are poor candidates for the political ideal of a well-ordered society. Generally speaking, state policies designed to enhance the autonomous capacities of its citizens will be ineffective, oppressive, or both (Berlin, 1969; Wall, 2003: 308; Pettit, 2012: 48–49). Restricting our view to opportunity conceptions of freedom alone, then, should any hindrances to choice besides domination also count as freedom-reducing? The two most obvious candidates that come to mind are none other than vitiation and interference. Either or both the non-vitiation condition and the non-interference condition might plausibly be combined with the non-domination condition in an overall account of political freedom. Arguments for and against each will be examined in turn.

Let us consider vitiations first. Should vitiating resource failures also count as detracting from our political freedom? That is to say, should a well-ordered society aim to reduce and remove both vitiation and domination in its efforts to honor and promote the freedom of its citizens? At first pass it might seem obvious that it should. Can we in all fairness say that a person is free to do something she manifestly lacks the wherewithal to do? Does it not seem ungenerous, to put it mildly, to assert that the poor as well as the rich are free to live in mansions, or that the disabled as well as the fully able are free to run marathons? Some have argued along these lines that the republican account of freedom as non-domination is insufficiently attentive to freedom-reducing vitiations (e.g., Krause, 2013).

In defense of the republicans, however, two observations are in order. The first is that there is no logical obstacle to combining non-domination and non-vitiation conditions into a single account of political freedom like this:

F_4: A is not free to ϕ unless:

(a) A commands resources sufficient to ϕ, and

(b) no B has the uncontrolled ability to intentionally frustrate A's ϕ-ing.

While one might argue against doing so, nothing in republican doctrine as such prohibits such a move. The second is that, even if we decline to include a non-vitiation condition in our conception of freedom, the non-domination condition itself necessarily entails some concern for adequate resourcing. This is because severe resourcing failures can render people to vulnerable to domination. For instance, when faced with starvation people might accept employment on extremely disadvantageous terms. The advocate of non-domination is thus committed to ensuring at least some threshold level of resourcing (Lovett, 2009).[12]

What, if anything, might be said against including a non-vitiation condition in our account of political freedom? Perhaps the most vigorous objection is given by Friedrich Hayek (1960: 16–19), and adapted to present purposes would run roughly as follows. If we adopted an account of political freedom including both non-vitiation and non-domination conditions, then it would follow that reducing vitiation and reducing domination commensurably contribute to freedom. But this cannot be correct. Imagine a society in which extensive social planning has more or less eliminated resourcing failures, but only by subjecting everyone to the absolutely unfettered power of a caretaker state. In nearly every choice we might make, the state has the uncontrolled ability to frustrate that choice, though when it does not we have at our command all the resources we might wish for whatever we might then choose to do. Would such a society be desirable? That can be debated. But it would not be a society characterized by extensive freedom. When we exchange non-domination for better resourcing we are not exchanging like for like, but rather one good for another, competing good. To subsume both under the heading of "freedom" merely obscures the difficult problem of balancing their respective values.[13] What is worse, it lends spurious plausibility to totalitarian states that claim they advance freedom even as they oppress their citizens.

Next we may consider interferences. Should a well-ordered society aim to reduce and remove interference as well as domination in its effort to honor and promote the freedom of its citizens? Perhaps the most compelling reason for thinking that it should is illustrated by the case of the justly imprisoned felon (Carter, 2008: 65). Suppose that A lives in a well-ordered democratic society that respects the rule of law; unfortunately, however, she has been convicted of grand larceny and sentenced to prison. How much freedom does A enjoy? It seems obvious the answer must be *hardly any at all*—surely the person confined to prison must count as unfree if anyone does! But the non-domination condition would apparently suggest otherwise, for the ability of the state to imprison her is per assumption suitably controlled. This consequence might be avoided if we combine non-interference and non-domination conditions like this:

F_5: A is not free to ϕ unless:

(a) no B intentionally frustrates A's ϕ-ing, and

(b) no B has the uncontrolled ability to intentionally frustrate A's ϕ-ing.

Many authors find something like this combined account of political freedom attractive—including both some republicans (Skinner, 1998; Viroli, 2002) and others (Wall, 2003). What considerations are there against it?

The main argument against this move is that it might undermine the traditional republican claim that law potentially constitutes rather than reduces freedom (Pettit, 2002: 344–346). Recall the alcohol cupboard example discussed earlier: provided B's conduct is indeed suitably controlled by A, it does not seem that her freedom is compromised in the event that he interferes with her ability to drink. Perhaps by analogy the legitimate constraints imposed by a well-ordered democratic society interfere without compromising the freedom of its citizens. But it seems this can only be true if the non-interference condition at least sometimes does not hold.[14] In order to reduce the force of the justly imprisoned felon example we might insist that while she is obviously not free in the broadest sense of the term, she remains free in the politically relevant sense: there is nothing further we must do as a matter of public policy to honor and promote her freedom. Republicans remain divided as to whether this position has more to recommend it than the former.

6. CONCLUSION

In this chapter, we have examined the republican account of freedom, characterizing it in terms of a non-domination condition: contemporary civic republicans are committed to the idea that we cannot enjoy freedom in the politically relevant sense to the extent that other persons or groups have the uncontrolled ability to frustrate our choices. This freedom from domination, it was argued, represents a genuinely distinct and potentially attractive opportunity conception of political freedom contrasting with freedom from interference. Some important questions remain, however. First, republicans are not entirely agreed on how to specify the sort of control necessary to secure freedom. Second, the various possibilities for combining a non-domination condition with other conditions in an overall account of political freedom have so far only been explored in a preliminary manner.

NOTES

1. Thus, for instance, we tend to say that people lack not the freedom to live on the moon, but rather the ability. This point has been made many times, for example by Hayek, 1960: 12–13; Berlin, 1969: 122; Miller 1983: 68–70.

2. For some of the leading contemporary republican accounts of freedom see Pettit, 1997, 2002, 2012; Skinner, 1998, 2008; and Viroli, 2002.

3. Marxists of a conspiratorial bent might in every economic disadvantage see the deliberate effort of the capitalist class to undermine our freedom, for instance. As it happens, Berlin is prepared to accept as an interference economic hardship when inflicted through deliberate human agency.

4. Unintentional in the sense that no human agent intends to frustrate the choice of a person or group through that vitiation. Of course vitiations might be intentional under a different description—e.g., elevators might not have been installed with the intention of saving public funds.

5. As Locke says, "that ill deserves the name of confinement which hedges us in only from bogs and precipices" (1690: 32).

6. "Freedom then is not . . . a liberty for every one to do what he lists," but rather "to have a standing rule to live by, common to every one," and "not to be subject to the inconstant, uncertain, unknown, arbitrary will of another man" (Locke, 1690: 17).

7. Often referred to as the "pure negative liberty" view, this account of freedom is built on a reading of Hobbes advanced by Hillel Steiner, Matthew Kramer, and Ian Carter among others.

8. Here I will leave aside complicated issues of aggregation and coordination whose resolution would be necessary to make sense of group control.

9. Note that this condition fails if she turns out to be the member of a persistent political minority: such situations do not satisfy the equal shares in control requirement (Pettit, 2012: 211–213).

10. For his part, Pettit avoids this consequence by suggesting that such constraints can remove the ability to frustrate choices itself, thus obviating the need for controls (2014: 49–52). This move renders his account more or less equivalent to the procedural view in practice, while remaining semantically democratic.

11. Note that the following discussion concerns what hindrances should be seen as reducing freedom as such. Set aside are various attempts to show that certain hindrances, without *reducing* freedom proper, nevertheless *condition* it in the sense of undermining either its effectiveness or its value.

12. The advocate of non-interference is not similarly committed: while deprivation increases the *ability* of others to interfere, it need not increase the *likelihood* that they will do so.

13. Giving extra weight to domination over vitiation in F_4 above would of course make it very unlikely that the most extensive freedom could be secured by a caretaker state, but the problem of obscuring difficult choices persists.

14. Or at any rate, not unless we take the proverbial state of nature as our baseline for comparison. In a state of nature, no one would enjoy any freedom because every choice is vulnerable to domination. Many of our choices remain unfree (on interference grounds) after the introduction of law: what we gain is freedom in those choices which the law protects from domination. This approach reconciles F_5 with the traditional republican claim that law constitutes rather than reduces freedom.

References

Berlin, Isaiah, 1969. *Four essays on liberty*. Oxford: Oxford University Press.

Blackstone, William, [1765] 1979. *Commentaries on the laws of England*. 4 vols. Chicago: University of Chicago Press.

Carter, Ian, 2008. How are power and unfreedom related. In: Cécile Laborde and John Maynor, eds. *Republicanism and political theory*. Malden: Blackwell Publishing. pp.58–82.

Goodin, Robert E., and Jackson, Frank, 2007. Freedom from fear. *Philosophy and Public Affairs*, 35(3), pp.249–265.

Harbour, David Michael, 2012. Non-domination and pure negative liberty. *Politics, Philosophy, and Economics*, 11(2), pp.186–205.

Hayek, Friedrich A., 1960. *The constitution of liberty*. Chicago: University of Chicago Press.

Hobbes, Thomas, [1651] 1998. *Leviathan*. Edited by J. C. A. Gaskin. Oxford: Oxford University Press.

Kramer, Matthew H., 2008. Liberty and domination. In: Cécile Laborde and John Maynor, eds. *Republicanism and political theory*. Malden: Blackwell Publishing. pp.31–57.

Krause, Sharon R., 2013. Beyond non-domination: agency, inequality, and the meaning of freedom. *Philosophy and Social Criticism*, 39(2), pp.1–22.

Larmore, Charles, 2001. A critique of Philip Pettit's republicanism. *Philosophical Issues*, 11(1), pp.229–243.

List, Christian, 2006. Republican freedom and the rule of law. *Politics, Philosophy, and Economics*, 5(2), pp.201–220.

Locke, John, [1690] 1980. *Second treatise of government*. Edited by C. B. Macpherson. Indianapolis: Hackett Publishing.

Lovett, Frank, 2009. Domination and distributive justice. *Journal of Politics*, 71(3), pp.817–830.

Lovett, Frank, 2012. What counts as arbitrary power? *Journal of Political Power*, 5(1), pp.137–152.

Mill, John Stuart, [1859] 1979. *On liberty*. Edited by Elizabeth Rapaport. Indianapolis: Hackett Publishing.

Miller, David, 1983. Constraints on freedom. *Ethics*, 94:1, pp.66–86.

Paley, William, [1785] 2002. *The principles of moral and political philosophy*. Indianapolis: Liberty Fund.

Patterson, Orlando, 1991. *Freedom in the making of western culture*. New York: Basic Books.

Pettit, Philip, 1997. *Republicanism: a theory of freedom and government*. Oxford: Clarendon Press.

Pettit, Philip, 2002. Keeping republican liberty simple: on a difference with Quentin Skinner. *Political Theory*, 30(3), pp.339–356.

Pettit, Philip, 2012. *On the people's terms: a republican theory and model of democracy*. Cambridge: Cambridge University Press.

Pettit, Philip, 2014. *Just freedom: a moral compass for a complex world*. New York: W. W. Norton.

Sidney, Algernon, [1698] 1996. *Discourses concerning government*. Edited by Thomas G. West. Indianapolis: Liberty Fund.

Skinner, Quentin, 1998. *Liberty before liberalism*. Cambridge: Cambridge University Press.

Skinner, Quentin, 2008. Freedom as the absence of arbitrary power. In: Cécile Laborde and John Maynor, eds. *Republicanism and political theory*. Malden: Blackwell Publishing. pp.83–101.

Taylor, Charles, 1979. What's wrong with negative liberty. In: Alan Ryan, ed. *The ideal of freedom*. Oxford: Oxford University Press. pp.175–193.

Viroli, Maurizio, 2002. *Republicanism*. Translated by Antony Shugaar. New York: Hill and Wang.

Wall, Steven, 2003. Freedom as a political ideal. *Social Philosophy and Policy*, 20:2, pp.307–334.

CHAPTER 7

....

THE POINT
OF SELF-OWNERSHIP

....

DAVID SOBEL

THE Self-Ownership Tradition addressed in this chapter is committed to powerful rights of the individual against the (enforceable) claims of group benefit, and views with great suspicion involuntary impositions on individuals except in self-defense.[1] This tradition maintains that such rights are not merely indirectly justified from their general usefulness at promoting aggregate benefit, but offer a sharp contrast to any variant of consequentialism by championing the inviolability of the individual. This tradition draws inspiration from Locke, who maintained that "every man has a property in his own person: this no body has any right to but himself" (Locke, 1980), and received its most searching exploration in Nozick's *Anarchy, State, and Utopia* (Nozick, 1974).

It maintains that one initially owns, and thus has property rights over, one's body and may use it to acquire property rights in previously unowned natural resources. More recently there has been very interesting work on "left-libertarianism" that keeps many aspects of this tradition in place but attempts to secure a more egalitarian distribution of world-ownership than is ensured by the older versions of the view. Such differences between these variants of the tradition will not concern us here. Rather we will be concerned with some quite broad-brush problems for all views in this neighborhood and broad-brush attempts at solutions.

The picture in which people have forceful property-like claims over their person that may not be infringed merely for the sake of others nicely captures an important strand in our moral thought. You may not take my "spare" kidney simply because you need it more than I. I own it and so have a say over what may happen to it that your greater desire or need rarely, if ever, can outweigh. You may not stop me from engaging in consensual sexual relations with competent adults who also own themselves because in doing so you would be treating as your own something that does not belong to you. Further, the Self-Ownership Tradition's relentless championing of voluntary ways of people living together over involuntary ones has obvious moral attractions. Finally, consider how seemingly morally unproblematically I make a host of daily decisions that involve what will happen to my body, including decisions about what to wear, which beer to drink, and whether to go for a run or not. This broad range of apparent moral powers I have for legitimately making such decisions needs explanation. The Self-Ownership Tradition seems to provide the most straightforward and intuitive explanation. That I own something intuitively provides me a wide range of rights over a thing even when others could benefit more if they had it or controlled it. This shows that the Self-Ownership Tradition fits well with some powerful aspects of our thinking about morality.

But, like other moral theories, the self-ownership tradition fits uneasily with other strands of our ethical thinking and runs into cases that it handles much less convincingly. Here we will be investigating a few ways in which it does not fit our ethical thinking as well as might be hoped, and exploring ways in which the view might evolve to improve this fit.

1. THE PROBLEM

The self-ownership explanation for why you may not bar me from selling my own kidney, tax me to pay for health care for orphans, or prohibit me from engaging in homosexual relations with competent adults is that such actions infringe upon my very powerful property rights to my body or my extra-personal possessions. But this explanation, on its own, feels quite inadequate to the varied moral landscape we face. I own lots of things, including this scrap piece of paper I have been meaning to throw away. Why is it so much more serious if you damage my body than if you damage that piece of paper? I own both things. In both cases you are interfering with something I own without my permission. Any moral theory that cannot adequately distinguish the moral seriousness of these different sorts of actions and that cannot vindicate the thought that interfering with the latter is much easier to justify than the former will be gravely flawed. Similar thoughts might be pressed about the vast moral difference between taking my kidney and taking a strand of hair, or about putting a tiny amount of not very toxic pollution in the air and poisoning my only water supply.

Self-ownership would seem to need to be supplemented with some story about the various significances of things that can be owned, and this story will have to go beyond an account of ownership. A picture in which any interference with anything I legitimately own is as morally impermissible as any other possible such interference will radically conflate the seriousness of quite morally different types of action. Common sense does not approve of the view that you may not take a single strand of my hair if doing so will prevent a murder, nor that flying a plane over my head is impermissible because you involuntarily inflict upon my body minor noise and trivial risk.[2]

We have so far considered what has elsewhere been called Self-Ownership's "Conflation Problem"—the conflating of the moral significance of very different types of infringements upon a person's property (Sobel, 2013). When the Conflation Problem is combined with the traditional stringency of property rights insisted upon by the

Self-Ownership Tradition, we get the "Problem of Trivial Infringements." That is, the view seems forced to treat trivial infringements, such as nearly harmless pollution, as a morally very significant infringement such that just about any pollution (kicking up dust, etc.) would seem impermissible.

2. One Solution and its Cost

So how might the Self-Ownership Tradition respond to this difficulty so as to make the view less counterintuitive? One way of doing so was offered in Sobel, 2012 and Sobel, 2013. The proposal was a bit off-hand but perhaps it suggests directions worth exploring. It does show how we might capture some otherwise difficult-to-capture intuitions within a recognizably Self-Ownership Libertarian framework. The Self-Ownership Libertarian can find a way to acknowledge the distinction between more and less morally serious infringements by treating as morally relevant the size of the costs and benefits of different infringing acts. Noticing the Problem with Trivial Infringements seemed a good opportunity to add to the traditional framework by trying to solve the more general Conflation Problem. It was proposed to treat harmful infringements as harder to justify than trivial infringements. For example, one might say that an infringement that causes N amount of the relevant kind of cost is only permissible if it is required to produce at least 25 N of compensating benefit for society. The relevant benefits and costs could include utility, freedom, autonomy, and the like. The view would make permissible the intuitively permissible, socially useful small infringements, such as minimally toxic pollution caused by an industry that is crucial to a great number of people living a good life. This structure solved that problem, remained deontological, vindicated the thought that because something is mine I have say over what may be done with it well beyond the extent to which I can create the most good with it, kept in place the thought that ownership of even small and trivial things gives the owner some small claim over them (even against accidental damage)—avoiding the suggestion that there is a magic cutoff for infringement cost, below which it matters not at all and above which it is as bad as any infringement can be—and justified the common-sense view that, for example, I may borrow your tennis racket without your permission if I need it to ward off a deadly attacker, but I cannot take it without permission just because I am interested in trying it out. The view could also justify some soft paternalism, such as pushing someone out of the way of a bus without his or her consent (Wall, 2009). So, on this picture, the Conflation Problem and the Problem of Trivial Infringements are overcome and the heart of the intuitive attractions of the view seems to be maintained.

But some characteristic aspects of the traditional view, such as the idea that agents are in some important sense inviolable, were lost. It permits some infringements on one individual simply because they produced enough of the relevant sort of value for others, whereas views that capture the inviolability intuition would rule out such trade-offs or permit them only in quite extreme cases. While it is true that Nozick contemplated tolerating some infringements to avoid "catastrophic moral horrors," the view proposed here does so at such a low price (relative to what the tradition has tolerated) that it is best to be honest and accept that it cannot capture the sort of moral inviolability of the individual for the sake of group benefits that the view has traditionally championed.

3. Mack's Solution: The Point of Self-ownership

Another way for the tradition to respond to the general Problem of Trivial Infringements would be to offer a compelling story about the point of self-ownership, or of rights generally, which would allow us to shape the underlying property rights so as to serve that point. Such a picture might explain why an understanding of rights according to which trivial intrusions count as infringements does not serve the underlying point of rights well, and so should be amended so that such intrusions—what Eric Mack calls "boundary crossings"—do not count as infringements at all. Such a story would seem an independently desirable feature for the tradition to offer. It could help to reveal the deeper moral attractions of the view that animate its sometimes counterintuitive particular conclusions. A persistent worry about the view is that we are simply finding in self-ownership whatever rights we are independently attracted to and lack a principled way of explicating what the rights of self-ownership are when we get past the simplest cases (Fried, 2012). Articulating an underlying rationale for self-ownership could provide a powerful response to such concerns.

Further, some have wondered if the attractions of self-ownership hinge on contingent features of owning oneself that apply locally but not across all the cases that we want to morally assess (Lippert-Rasmussen, 2008). Self-ownership, the suggestion here is, might provide morally desirable outcomes in worlds like this one but does not do so in imaginable cases that ought to be tested in order to establish full moral adequacy. Again, articulating the underlying point of self-ownership rights might allow a convincing response. It might be conceded that such property rights only secure the underlying point of such rights in some possible worlds and not others, so that different rights might apply in wildly different empirical circumstances.

What might well be needed, then, is an understanding of the point of such rights, which will help to show why very minor boundary crossings, or small risks of such, are permitted by the theory, yet the traditional stringency and inviolability of the view would be kept otherwise intact.

Such a story is exactly what Eric Mack thinks is needed and tries to provide (Mack, 2015).[3] Mack tries to deal with the Problem of Trivial Infringements by championing an

"elbow room for rights" explanation for the permissibility of minor intrusions. The key idea is that, when one thinks about how to articulate or delineate the character or the boundaries of the rights one ascribes to persons, one crucial guide is the moral elbow room postulate. According to this postulate, a reasonable delineation of basic moral rights must be such that the claim-rights that are ascribed to individuals do not systematically preclude people from exercising the liberty-rights that the claim-rights are supposed to protect. . . . The elbow room postulate tells us that, since the impermissibility of minor intrusions would be hog-tying, a reasonable delineation of rights does not construe minor intrusions as boundary crossings. . . . The permissibility of minor intrusions is explained on the basis of a refinement in the location of boundaries rather than a general attenuation of rights. (p. 6)

The elbow room postulate is itself derived from a better understanding of the general "underlying rationale for ascribing moral rights to individuals" (p. 7). Mack claims that

> The rationale for the deployment of the postulate in the delineation of people's basic rights emerges from the rationale for ascribing people rights in the first place. . . . As I view it, the most basic organizing principle for Self-Ownership Libertarian rights theory is the moral principle that each individual is to be allowed to live his own life in his own chosen way. Each abstract moral right provides individuals with moral protection against one of the diverse ways in which they can be prevented (by others) from living their own lives in their own chosen ways. For example, people can be prevented from living their own lives in their own chosen ways by being deprived of discretionary control over their own bodies and faculties. For this reason, the abstract right of self-ownership is a crucial and salient dimension of the proper codification of the primordial libertarian principle. (p. 7)

Mack's picture of the point of property rights in a Self-Ownership Libertarian system does not appear idiosyncratic. Recall that Nozick offers a somewhat similar picture of the foundation of the rights he champions. He claims that the basis of those moral constraints was largely "the moral importance of this additional ability to form a picture of one's whole life (or at least of a significant chunk of it) and to act in terms of some overall conception of the life one wishes to lead." Nozick adds that "a person's shaping his life in accordance with some overall plan is his way of giving meaning to his life; only a being with the capacity to so shape his life can have or strive for meaningful life" (Nozick, 1974: 50). When Nozick explains why we should opt for a strongly deontological conception of our moral claims, he argues first that we should not sacrifice one person for the sake of others because "there are distinct individuals each with his own life to lead" (Nozick, 1974: 33). Finally, when Nozick explains why paternalist interference is unjustified he stresses the fact that "there are distinct individuals, each with his own life *to lead*" (Nozick, 1974: 34). Strong deontological constraints, Nozick claims, respect the individual's unique life and allow that person to live her own life in a way which makes it possible for her life to have meaning. The point of such rights, Nozick seems to be saying, is that they recognize and respond to the morally crucial claim individuals have to live their own lives by their own lights.[4]

Locke, too, thought it important to ensure that each person enjoys a "Liberty to dispose, and order as he lists, his Person, Actions, Possessions, and his whole Property. . . . For who could be free, when every other Man's humour might domineer over him?" (Locke, 1980: §57).

One qualification must be stated. Mack seems to be saying that the point of rights is to provide protection not only from other people forcibly preventing me from living my life by my lights, but also from a system of rights that would morally prohibit me from doing so. After all, Mack uses this thought as if it told against a system of strict property rights. His thought seems to be that a system of rights that morally precludes one from being able to kick up a bit of dust violates one's claim to not be precluded from living one's own life as he or she sees fit. Mack can therefore be interpreted as saying that the point of rights is to enhance our ability to live our own lives by our own lights, unprevented by others *or by the moral force of other people's rights.* This addition is significant, since now my moral right to control my body looks as though it threatens to impede your ability to live your own life by your own lights.

4. TWO CASES

In order to assess Mack's attempt to make small or trivial boundary crossings count as no infringement at all due to a more careful understanding of the point of rights, we will need to think hard about what it means for a person "to be allowed to live his own life in his own chosen way. Each abstract moral right provides individuals with moral protection against one of the diverse ways in which they can be prevented (by others) from living their own lives in their own chosen ways." How should we understand this idea? It is somewhat skeletal so far, from the theoretical standpoint. But we do learn more about it in action, so to speak, when Mack generates some abstract rights from the proposal.

Two different moments in Mack's deployment of this idea in deriving rights are to be noted. These two moments suggest two different models for developing Mack's, or the generic, proposal that the problem of trivial boundary crossings for self-ownership views can be addressed by explicating more carefully the point of rights, in such a way that these trivial cases can be seen to be no infringement at all, while still maintaining the traditional severity of the inviolability of property rights. The issues raised by these two different ways of pursuing the Mackian strategy will be examined via two case studies.

The first case involves what may be the most beautiful result of Mack's proposal. This argument is designed to thread a very narrow needle and show us why some intentional minor boundary crossings are impermissible, while other similar unintended but foreseen boundary crossings remain permissible. There is a general issue, noted by Peter Railton, in understanding why it is more impermissible for an agent to *intend* to φ, rather than merely foreseeing that particular φ: this issue lies in the difference in degree of intentionality (Railton, 2003). For it would seem that before intending to φ can be awful or impermissible, there must independently be something awful or impermissible about φ itself. If there were nothing wrong with φ-ing, what would be bad about doing so intentionally? And so a difficulty in a Self-Ownership theorist's claim that we have rights against others intentionally φ-ing in ways that cross our boundaries, but not against their foreseeably doing so, is that this seems to make intending what is not an infringement into an infringement. Yet it would seem that the Self-Ownership Libertarians must rely on the distinction between intending and not intending, since surely they want to justify some very minor involuntary intrusions, such as minor pollution cases, yet they also want to retain the idea that "stealing a penny or a pin" from me is something my property rights give me some claim against (Nozick, 1974). And surely the Self-Ownership Libertarian must also grant us some protections against more serious unintended but foreseen harms. You cannot blow up a building next to me, foreseeing the harm that will come to me, and claim that because the harm was no part of your plan, I have no moral protection against it. So seemingly the Self-Ownership Libertarian must distinguish between intentional and unintentional boundary crossings, permit trivial unintentional ones, forbid intentional ones, and forbid more seriously harmful ones whether intended or merely foreseen, all without claiming that intending something that itself is no infringement is the source of the claim against being permitted to do it.

Mack offers an elegant solution. The rationale for distinguishing between intentionally crossing a boundary and foreseeably doing so is not to be found in the greater viciousness or greater impact upon the victims of the former infringement, but rather in the fact that we only need to permit foreseeable very minor infringements in order to unimpede the rights holders. The person who is forbidden from intentionally crossing boundaries in trivial ways is not precluded from living a life of her choosing, whereas the person forbidden from foreseeably crossing boundaries in trivial ways is. There are many options that we may permissibly choose without intentionally crossing other people's boundaries, but almost no options for how to live that would avoid unintentionally crossing boundaries. For us to be able to live a life of our choosing, we need to be permitted to unintentionally cross boundaries. The central difference between intentional minor boundary crossings and foreseen ones is not to be found in the stronger claim we have against the former being perpetrated against us, but in our greater need to perpetrate the latter if we are to avoid being immobilized ("hog-tied," to use Mack's expression). Here, according to Mack, we see the appropriate structure for rights to take by seeing what structure would best enable people to live lives of their own choosing. There is no need here to prioritize some sorts of potentially chosen lives over others, or to antecedently distinguish the morally acceptable potentially chosen lives from the others. The case for restricting intentional trivial boundary crossings, but not unintentional ones, hangs on the former restriction being sufficient to create moral free space in which agents can shape their own lives in a wide variety of attractive ways. We would have very few options if we could not unintentionally cross anyone else's boundaries. Indeed, that is the essence of the Problem of Trivial Infringements.[5]

In our second case study, Mack asks if "an individual who needs a kidney [is] disallowed from living her own life in her own chosen way by another individual declining to supply her with his spare kidney or by his evading her attempts to extract that needed kidney" (p. 8). As mentioned above, we need to add here to the list of potentially limiting conditions on a person living her own life in her own way, on Mack's behalf, the moral force of other people having rights to their possessions.

His answer to the kidney case is that

> The organizing principle for Self-Ownership Libertarian rights answers these questions in the negative. Agents who are not enabled to live as they choose because another party declines to supply one of his kidneys or declines to participate in desired sexual interactions are not thereby made unable—or precluded from—living their own lives in their own chosen way. . . . Absent this understanding, ordinary exercises of rights by one party will regularly also count as ordinary violations of the other parties' rights and the moral claims of individuals to live their own lives in their own chosen ways will systematically conflict. Any resolution of that conflict would require the demotion of rights into moral commodities that are to be traded off against one another. (p. 8)

5. Moralized and Non-moralized Conceptions of the Point of Rights

Mack's discussion of the point of rights suggests two fundamentally different models for how the proposal is supposed to work.

First we must briefly mark a distinction that will be relevant to this discussion. The distinction is between moralized and non-moralized conceptions of the point of rights. For Mack's conception to be moralized in the sense intended here would be for the point of rights to be to avoid preventing people from living lives of their own choosing so long as those lives pass some moral test. In contrast, he would be using a non-moralized conception if he maintained that the point of rights was to avoid preventing people from living lives of their own choosing whether or not those lives pass some moral test. The following discussion will claim that neither a moralized nor a non-moralized understanding of the point of rights vindicates Mack's proposal.

Let us return to the two cases discussed above. In the kidney case it seems clear what is animating Mack. He wants to say that the person who needs another person's kidney to live has no claim at all on that kidney, not even a claim that is outweighed by the stronger claim of the person whose kidney it is. Mack surprisingly suggests that if we allow that the person who needs a kidney counts as prevented from living a life of his own choosing if she were not permitted to take it, we thereby would have to say that the rights of the person who needs the kidney were infringed and thus rights must be demoted to commodities. This seems not to be the case. We can say that a specification of rights according to which one has no claim to another person's kidney does to some degree (morally) prevent that person from living the life of her choosing without saying that thereby her rights are infringed. After all, rights are what emerge from this story when we see what system would best expand people's ability to live their lives as they choose. Rather we might say the person who needs the kidney has a pro tanto right-making claim to be unprevented from taking another person's kidney but that that claim is outweighed by the greater overall ability people would have to live their own lives if that type of claim were denied. But, as Mack sees, this picture does involve systematic conflicts between people's pro tanto right-making claims. Rights need not be turned into mere commodities on such a view, for rights are what emerge only after the pro tanto right-making claims have been weighed against each other. But the pro tanto right-making claim to live one's own life unprevented by others has been turned into a commodity that must be traded off against other people's ability to do so.

Inviolability of our "rights" would seem less impressive if we regularly diminished one person's holdings with respect to the point of rights so as to increase other people's ability to live their lives by their own lights. But any non-moralized conception of the point of rights seems sure to have to adjudicate and tolerate such trade-offs. This is what seems to be driving Mack towards a moralized conception of what it is to live a life of one's own choosing unprevented by others. Intuitively, the person who needs a kidney and would like to take the one in my body but is thwarted from doing so by the existence of rights I have against her doing so, or by others defending themselves against my actions, has been prevented from living a life of her own choosing. For that not to be the case, Mack must mean that we have a pro tanto right-making claim to live our life as we choose, unprevented by others or by moral requirements that we not do so, provided that chosen life does not violate other people's rights or is in other ways morally unacceptable. This is what it would be to moralize the point of rights. It seems to be something we might be driven to if we want to avoid allowing that there are persistent trade-offs between a scheme that does not prevent X from living a life of her own choosing and a scheme that does not prevent Y and X from doing so. For if there are such persistent trade-offs, then the fear is that the only good sense to be made of a system that well serves the point of rights that Mack imagines would have to be a system that served that point aggregatively. And if that is the case, then it is hard to see that anything like inviolability remains. This is the danger that seems to lead Mack towards a moralized conception of the point of rights. Non-moralized conceptions of what it is for a person to be unprevented from living a life of her own choosing look as though they have to give up inviolability and serve this point aggregatively.

Let us consider two of the more obvious ways this threat to non-moralized conceptions might be overcome; two ways, that is, that someone might resist the claim that the only good sense to be made of a system that well serves the non-moralized point of rights Mack champions is aggregative. The first hope would be if there were a Pareto-optimal way to promote the underlying point of rights. Pareto-optimal solutions have a strong claim to not sacrificing the one for the sake of the group. The problem is that pareto-optimality only provides guidance against a baseline or against a well-defined comparison class and it is not clear what either would be supposed to be in this case.

This problem would be greatly alleviated if there were a default rationale for starting from strict property rights and allowing only Pareto-optimal changes from that baseline. Then, since generally allowing non-intentional minor boundary crossings plausibly provides a Pareto improvement, but allowing more major (or more intentional) ones may not, we might get to where Mack wants to end up. However, the framework he offers does not seem to fit well with the idea that strict property rights provide a privileged baseline (at least on the non-moralized conception of the point of rights that we are currently exploring). If the point of rights is to keep people from being prevented (by agents or other people's rights) from living a life of their own choosing, then strict property rights are just a poor first stab at providing such protections. That baseline privileges, without explanation, our claims against some ways in which we are prevented from living a life of our choosing and downgrades other claims of that same type. And without a privileged baseline, Pareto-optimality is much less likely to provide much guidance. If Mack is deprived of strict property rights as a Pareto baseline, then seemingly he must argue only for rights specifications that provide a Pareto-optimal distribution of claims against being prevented from living one's life by one's own lights when compared to any other possible distribution of rights. This is not plausible.

Second, perhaps a case could be made that the package of rights Mack ends up with (permission to perpetrate minor unintentional boundary crossings, lack of permission to perpetrate minor intentional boundary crossings, etc.) provides each and every person a maximally large space in which to live their own lives unprevented by others or by morality. Or, at least, this is so if we assume that everyone must get the same set of rights. Again, if this were so, we need not trade off the point of rights for the one for the sake of the greater point of rights for the many.

To make such a case we would need to understand what would make a package of rights provide a larger or smaller space free to live as one likes unprevented by others or by morality. A first point to make here is that, if we are dealing with a non-moralized conception, the largeness of such a set will not be one that dominates other sets—that is, it will not be one that includes all the other freedoms that other sets provide and more still. This is because, on a non-moralized conception, some possible sets will increase our ability to live as we like by greatly harming others. If such a set is smaller than Mack's set, it is not because Mack's set offers all the freedoms such a set offers and then some.

So what will make one set of freedoms to live as we like larger in the relevant sense here? We might try to simply count the ways one can act without being prevented from doing so with one set of rights in place and compare that to the number we get when we imagine another set of rights in place. Or we might think that the ability to grate off the skin on one's forearm a less significant option than being able to worship one's God, and so weigh more heavily sets of rights that give us the latter option rather than the former. And we might think this either because people in fact have no interest in such an option, or we might think it because they ought not have interest in such an option. More generally, we might think that the relevant weighty options might be agent-relative and depend on what sort of lives a particular person cares about or might care about. On this picture, if there were someone who only cared about living lives in which they intentionally cross other people's boundaries harmfully, and found that having permission to do so was worth paying the price of others doing the same to her, then Mack could not offer such a person a conception of their rights that gave that person at least as large a set of cared-for options as any other possible set (where everyone gets the same set). Or we might think that some types of lives are good for people, or worth choosing, regardless of their opinion on the matter, and weigh those options more heavily. But the more we filter in this way the set of relevant sorts of lives that one should not be unprevented from choosing, the less it seems as if we are clearly promoting the agent's autonomy by doing so.

However we sort out these tricky issues about what makes a set of options that one is unprevented from living larger in the relevant way, it seems certain that some people will want to choose lives that are ruled out by the set of rights Mack ends up with. After all, on any sane conception of what the moral rules are, some people surely choose to break those rules. Mack presumably must argue, following this path, that even though that is so, still literally no agents, regardless of what their aims and what their lights suggest about how they ought to live, will find that any other set of rights (universally applied) would protect their ability to be unprevented from others, or by morality as well, from living their life by their own lights. The most likely thought here would be that even though these people would want to infringe on rights as Mack has them, they would in fact do less well in being unprevented in a world in which all were given the right to cross boundaries as they propose to do. The structure of the argument under consideration is perhaps a bit reminiscent of Kant's first formulation of the categorical imperative, in which we imagine a world in which all have the rights that we propose for ourselves and we learn to our surprise that in such a world we are unable to advance the goals we had that motivated us to advance the claim that we had those rights. Yet while Kant aspired to show that his argument generated the results he sought regardless of what sort of agent we imagined, this seems (even more) unlikely in Mack's case.

Mack's picture of how to determine what set of rights we have is to see what is needed to allow people to live their own lives without being prevented from doing so by others (or by the rights themselves). Different sorts of rational agents, or agents with unusual goals, might need different sets of rights to accomplish this. Creatures like us need to be able to literally kick up a bit of dust to have any chance at autonomous lives. We can imagine rational agents capable of autonomous action that are different from us in this respect. These other creatures are incapable of movement or breathing, are nourished by the sun, and are mainly interested in trying out chess openings in their heads. For such creatures, gaining the permission to kick up a bit of dust would not enhance their ability to live their own life according to their choosing. Yet they are slightly negatively affected by trivial boundary crossings such as pollution. In such a case, I presume, Mack would allow that for such creatures there is no rationale to diminish the strictness of their property rights in order to create elbow room. On Mack's view, broad empirical features of a creature that are relevant to what it would take to fail to prevent it from living a life of its choosing are highly relevant to the proper specification of such a creature's rights.[6]

Now suppose that we share a planet with such creatures and that they are negatively affected in minor ways by our kicking up some dust. The point of positing such creatures is that we can no longer make a case that their tolerating some dust being kicked up is more than compensated for by their increased ability to not be prevented from living as they want. In a system of rights where we get to kick up dust, they suffer the minor harms the rest of us do but do not get freedom-compensating benefits. In a system of rights where we do not get to kick up dust, we are hog-tied. Is there a privileged starting point, perhaps strict property rights, such that only freedom Pareto-improvements are permissible from it? It is hard to see why that should be, on Mack's picture. But if that were the case, then we would be hog-tied in worlds that we have to share with Those that Need Only Non-Interference to be Unprevented from Living as They Like. If not, then in cases like this, where curtailing A's strict property rights is needed to un-hog-tie B but will trivially cost A some and will not benefit A any, then Pareto-optimality will be of little help. As usual, Paretian criteria need a privileged starting point to provide much guidance.

One thing Mack's own view tries to preserve from the traditional Self-Ownership Libertarian views is "inviolability." He would surely claim that the view outlined here does not preserve that thought, and this is probably true. A case can be made that a view like Mack's, at least on its non-moralized interpretation, cannot both preserve inviolability and ensure that we are not hog-tied.

What inviolability amounts to, on Mack's view, is to not have one's claim on others (or a system of rights) to not prevent me from living my life as I see fit compromised for the sake of others. Inviolability amounts to it being wrong to sacrifice the one in the relevant way for the sake of the group. But, as the above example shows, this aspect of the view may not be sustainable. A moral view like Mack's must admit that when quite different sorts of rational agents are living together, his view must either diminish the property rights of some without compensating gains for them in terms of the point of property rights, or it must not diminish the unusual creatures' property rights, in which case we will be hog-tied. Mack has not shown us how a moral theory can, with full generality, uphold inviolability and avoid hog-tying agents.

It might seem sufficient to show that in relevant or local scenarios we can combine inviolability with avoiding hog-tying anyone. This is not the case. If we think that it is a fundamental moral truth that agents are inviolable, we must explain how that would work in merely possible scenarios. It seems that there are possible scenarios in which either the point of property rights as Mack understands them must radically give way, such that many are severely prevented from living autonomously, or we must allow that inviolability is not a fundamental requirement of morality. If this is correct, it would make it more plausible that my proposal discussed above, in giving up on the traditional Self-Ownership Libertarian notion of inviolability, is rejecting an aspect of the Self-Ownership Libertarian picture that cannot be sustained.

Or, more realistically, suppose that, for different people, different trade-offs between strict property rights and elbow room are better for allowing them to not be prohibited from living their life as they see fit. It is possible that all actual humans gain in freedom in the switch away from strict rights and towards some elbow-room attenuation of the strictness of such rights.[7] But the fact that all would see a Pareto improvement in freedom in such a transition does not imply that we could get to any particular attenuation without going beyond the freedom-Pareto criterion. Each different possible attenuation of rights away from strict property rights will, to different degrees, prohibit each agent from living according to her own lights. The asthmatic and the industrialist might both agree that they need some elbow room but quite disagree about what look like attractive ways of attenuating strict property rights so as to attain that elbow room. Perhaps there is a particular contaminant that some asthmatics are especially vulnerable to but which also is difficult to avoid without quite costly pollution scrubbing. It seems insufficient to say to whoever loses such cases that they are nonetheless better off freedom-wise than they would have been with no attenuation. It is possible that being involuntarily enslaved in an attenuated property regime would still be freedom-superior to life in a strict property regime. We will have to move beyond the freedom-Pareto criterion in settling on a particular favored trade-off between attenuating our property rights and providing elbow room. In settling on a particular trade-off we are seemingly forced to accept a situation that is freedom-worse for some, on the grounds that it is freedom-better for many. And Mack's sensible claim that these trade-offs need not be determined by the philosopher but can be determined culturally by a judicial system seems to me irrelevant to the broader point that the system we are envisaging will sacrifice the freedom of some for the greater freedom of others. Again, this appears to leave inviolability behind.[8]

6. The Moralized Conception of the Point of Rights

How must we understand a moralized conception of the point of rights so that it might explicate the point of rights assignments? Seemingly we must not understand it to be tacitly assumed that the point of rights is to be unprevented from doing that which we have a right to do. For this will throw us back onto the project of understanding what those presupposed rights are, and will not help to explicate what their point is or to understand why they are not infringed when others cross our boundaries in trivial ways. The point of rights could not be to protect our rights. There must be some priority to the point for it to count as potentially an informative and helpful account of the point of rights.

So we must understand the notion of being unprevented by others from living a life of one's choosing as not already restricting the range of lives one might choose to those that are permissible by some background assumed assignment of rights.[9] Specifically we presumably must not presuppose what people are entitled to do if others do not prevent them. So we would have to understand the things that we must be unprevented from doing and the things we are to be free to choose for ourselves as not respecting other people's antecedent rights or presupposing a demarcation of mine and thine, since protecting such a sphere is meant to provide the point for demarcations of mine and thine. Such a starting point might appear clearly hopeless as a normatively attractive point of rights assignments, but G. A. Cohen (1995) provides a model for how such a picture might work without presupposing that the background freedoms which provide the point of rights are themselves shaped by antecedently understood property rights.

Perhaps the hope for the moralized conception, at least when it comes to explicating the point of rights, would be to contrast the type of normative facts we are presupposing in shaping the sort of lives that we must be unprevented from choosing from the sort of normative facts we aspire to vindicate. Scanlon (2014), for example, offers a non-reductionist, fully normativized conception of an agent's reasons, and hopes to build some moral facts out of those. There seems nothing problematic in principle with starting with some moral facts and using them to explicate the (non-instrumental) point of rights. But these moral facts would have to be more specific than just that it is morally good when we are unprevented by others from living lives of our choosing. The moral facts here would have to tell us which sort of lives it is morally good that we are unprevented by others from choosing. And there will have to be sufficient distance between those moral facts and the rights we hope to vindicate such that the former might explicate the point of the latter, rather than just be a restatement of them.

Consider, as a possible model, a consequentialist view that moralizes welfare. Such a view would claim that the sort of welfare we want to maximize is welfare that passes a moral test. Most obviously, apparent benefits that flow from enjoying another person's undeserved misery might be judged not to pass this test. Much will hinge on exactly how this test is understood. But the point for the moment is that this moralizing test for welfare need not render the resulting consequentialist proposal entirely vacuous. It would still be contentious, and interesting if true, if the point of morality were to further morally permissible happiness, rather than serving up deontological constraints against sacrificing one person's morally permissible happiness for the sake of the morally permissible happiness of the many.

So it does not immediately follow that if Mack moralizes the relevant kind of cases, in which we have a claim that others not prevent us from living a life of our own choosing, the resulting picture could not capture illuminatingly the point of rights. But to do so Mack would have to back away more clearly from the suggestion that the way he is moralizing the relevant kind of cases is with a background conception according to which we are entitled to a privileged say over how some items may be used because they are ours. Such a conception looks too close to the resulting picture of rights to be vindicated to stand behind them and serve as an illumination of this point of rights. If Mack offers a moralized conception of the point of rights, he will have to explicate more clearly what moralized conception he is working with, and persuade us that there is enough distance between that conception and the notion of rights he aspires to vindicate for the former to illuminate the point of the latter. Until we have this background normative picture in place, his story will not genuinely illuminate the point of rights.

7. Conclusion

If Mack opts for a non-moralized conception of the point of rights he is not entitled to what he says about the kidney case. This is because his handling of that case supposes that what does and does not count as preventing a person from living a life of her choosing already involves an understanding of what she is and is not entitled to—she is not entitled to other people's bodies, for example, and that is why her being denied access to other people's bodies does not count as being denied the ability to live her own life by her own lights. Further, the non-moralized conception seems inevitably to have to live with the thought that we must persistently trade off your ability to live your life as you see fit against other people's ability to live their lives as they see fit. Such trade-offs make it difficult to see how to recapture a normatively serious sense in which agents are inviolable in the way that the self-ownership tradition has maintained they are.

But if he offers a moralized conception, then he must allow that his understanding of the point of rights is to protect our antecedent moral status—a moral status which the story he has so far given us about the point of rights does not help explicate, but rather simply needs to presuppose. Only by understanding and vindicating that background normative status could we vindicate a particular picture of what does and does not count as preventing people from living lives of their choosing in the moralized sense. Mack's story does not help with that task.

Notes

1. This chapter continues a thread of argumentation from two earlier papers of mine, Sobel 2012 and Sobel 2013. In order to minimize overlap with these earlier papers, some of the setup and motivation for the problems with the self-ownership tradition explored here are not repeated. The discussion here is meant to be motivated and intelligible independently of those discussions, but in some cases additional arguments relevant to a full assessment of the view are offered in those other papers. Thanks for help with this chapter are gratefully given to David Schmidtz, Steve Wall, the audience at the Tucson Freedom Center Conference for this volume, the audience at NOISE 2013, and helpful referees for this volume.

2. Nozick seems to have taken these concerns very seriously and significantly adjusted his view to deal with such cases. Nozick is discussed at length on these matters in Sobel 2012 and Sobel 2013. Railton (2003) searchingly explores such worries.

3. Mack, 2015 was not yet in print at the time this book went to press. Page numbers in the text refer to the manuscript.

4. We will mention, and then ignore, what seem to be two large unresolved issues for views of this kind. The first is why morality should be thought to focus on failing to prevent people from being autonomous, rather than helping people to be autonomous. The second is why, even with that focus, we should think that morality has a deontological rather than a consequentialist structure. We might think that if it is so important that people not be prevented

from living lives of their own choosing, then perhaps we ought to prevent one person from living such a live if in doing so we could keep 5 others from being prevented from living a life of their own choosing.

5. A natural way to interpret Mack's view, at least roughly, is that any act that unintentionally produces below a certain threshold of harm or expected harm is permissible. But this interpretation will probably not suffice, as it would put a lot of pressure on act individuation and permit quite harmful sequences simply because they can be broken up into a series of small acts. If I restart the generator each half-hour, can I put out the same amount of pollution that would have been impermissible had it been the result of a single act? Better, probably, would be to have a yearly amount of (unintended) harm one may impose. We might be tempted to require that this yearly amount can only be spent in very small increments, so that no boundary-crossing act that produces above a low threshold of harm will be permissible. But this will produce the same problem of small transgressions building up to harmful sequences. Further, we might be tempted to somehow require that the harms of an individual's actions and of the group's actions not fall too disproportionately on a narrow range of people.

6. Recall that not only does Nozick clearly think such wild counterfactuals relevant to assessing a moral theory, as in his Utility Monster example, but he takes seriously the possibility that our inviolability might only obtain when we are dealing with creatures such as ourselves and might not make sense were we to interact with quite different (in his case, higher and better) sorts of beings.

7. This must be thought to justify the claim not only that therefore all would be rational to approve such a transition, but also that we may attenuate people's strict rights without their permission. For the former thought alone will not, for our Self-Ownership Libertarian, justify treating people in ways that they would have been rational to agree to but do not in fact agree to.

8. Perhaps maxi-min for freedom might be appropriate in such cases. That is, we could compare the different attenuating trade-offs for which leaves the person in that system worst off in terms of freedom and choose that attenuation in which the freedom-worst-off person is least badly off in terms of freedom. Perhaps that returns a notion of inviolability that is sustainable in cases where inevitably each particular trade off is freedom-better for some than others. Maxi-min perhaps allows us to say that no one must accept less freedom simply so that others may have more. At least we can then say that we are not preventably allowing some to have less freedom simply so that others may have more. However, this rationale may have the feel of a thought that is too much from behind the Veil for Mack's purposes.

9. Perhaps we could understand the point of X type of rights as being in terms of Y type of rights? Even so, Mack's story would then not tell us much useful about the more fundamental sort of rights.

References

Cohen, G. A., 1995. Self-Ownership: Delineating the Concept, In: *Self-Ownership, Freedom, and Equality*. Cambridge: Cambridge University Press, 1995. p.213.

Fried, Barbara, 2012. Does Nozick have a theory of property rights? In: Ralf Bader and John Meadowcroft, eds. *The Cambridge companion to Nozick's* Anarchy, State, and Utopia. Cambridge. pp.230–254.

Lippert-Rasmussen, Kasper, 2008. Against self-ownership. *Philosophy and Public Affairs*, 36, pp.86–118.

Locke, John, 1980. *Second treatise on government*. Hackett. Indianapolis.

Mack, Eric, 2015. Elbow room for rights. In: David Sobel, Peter Vallentyne, and Steven Wall, eds. *Oxford studies in political philosophy*. Vol. 1.

Nozick, Robert, 1974. *Anarchy, state, and utopia*. Basic Books, New York City.

Railton, Peter, 2003. Locke, stock, and peril: natural property rights, pollution, and risk. In *Facts, values, and norms*. Cambridge University Press.

Scanlon, T. M., 2014. *Being Realistic About Reasons*, Oxford University Press.

Sobel, David, 2012. Backing away from self-ownership libertarianism. *Ethics*, 123(Oct.), pp.32–60.

Sobel, David, 2013. Self-ownership and the conflation problem. *Oxford Studies in Normative Ethics*, 3, pp.98–122.

Wall, Steven, 2009. Self-ownership and paternalism. *Journal of Political Philosophy*, 17(4), pp.399–417.

PART II

HISTORICAL VIEWS

CHAPTER 8

PLATONIC FREEDOM

FRED D. MILLER, JR.

1. INTRODUCTION

THOUGH freedom and its opposite, slavery, are attested in writings as ancient as the code of Hammurabi, the transference of the concepts to the political realm apparently occurred for the first time in world history in ancient Greece. In *The Discovery of Freedom in Ancient Greece,* Kurt Raaflaub traces the evolution of the political use of freedom from its emergence during the Persian Wars at the beginning of the fifth century BCE to its full differentiation in content and function by the end of the Peloponnesian War in 404 BCE. Three important stages in this evolution are the development of a concept of ethnic freedom during the struggle of the Greeks to avoid conquest and enslavement by the Persians in 480 BCE, of a concept of polis freedom in reaction to Athenian hegemony following the Persian Wars, and of a concept of democratic freedom with the rise of Athenian democracy. Although Raaflaub's study yields valuable insights, it is his explicit aim "to take the Greek concept of freedom seriously as a phenomenon, not primarily of the history of philosophy and ideas, but of social and political history" (2004: 4). This leaves open the question of whether freedom played a role in the thought of ancient Greek philosophers such as Plato and Aristotle. The question receives a skeptical answer from Morgens Herman Hansen, who maintains that "Plato and Aristotle seem to have had no problem rejecting democratic freedom as a mistaken ideal without developing an alternative understanding of political freedom" (2013: 96). Others, such as Karl Popper, go further and represent Plato in particular as the consummate enemy of freedom and "the open society" (1963: 94 *et passim*). Whether Plato made any positive contribution to the evolution of the concept of political freedom is thus a matter of controversy. The aim of this chapter is to offer an accurate interpretation of Plato's conception of freedom and to show how it is grounded in his moral and political philosophy. No attempt is made to defend or criticize his understanding of freedom; that would require a much more extensive treatment than is possible here.[1]

"Free," "freedom," and so forth are the standard English translations of *eleutheros, eleutheria*, and other Greek words with the stem *eleuther-*. The first question is how closely the Greek and English terms correspond, but to answer it requires an understanding of the modern concept of freedom. An especially illuminating analysis has been advanced by Gerald MacCallum, who understands freedom as a *triadic relation* among (i) an agent, (ii) an impediment, and (iii) a goal: agent *a* is free of impediment *i* to pursue goal *g* (1967: 314). Often the triadic character of freedom is not made explicit because either the impediment or the goal is taken for granted. According to MacCallum, whenever an agent is free he enjoys both negative and positive freedom. Negative freedom is being free *of* an impediment; positive freedom is being free *to* pursue a goal. For example, the slave who is "free at last" is a human being who is free *of* bondage and free *to* make his own way in life.

MacCallum's triadic analysis fits ancient Greek rather well, as illustrated in the following passage from Plato's *Lysis*: "in these matters we shall do what we wish, and no one will willingly impede (*empodiei*) us," Socrates says, "but we shall be free (*eleutheroi*) ourselves in these matters" (210b3–4). Note that Socrates mentions all three terms of the triadic relation of freedom: *we* shall be *unimpeded* by others *in doing* what we wish.

Different *domains* of freedom can be distinguished on the basis of the three terms of the triadic relation. For example, personal freedom is the freedom *of* a person *from* impediments *to* pursue his own goals. (The prepositions "of," "from," and "to" signal agent, impediment, and goal respectively.) Legal freedom is the freedom *of* a person *from* legally imposed servitude *to* pursue his goals. Psychological (or psychic) freedom, on one account at least, is the freedom *of* the rational part of the psyche *from* the sway of its irrational parts *to* direct the entire psyche. Political freedom, an important topic of this chapter, has two subspecies: internal civic freedom is the freedom *of* a citizen *from* impediments *to* his personal freedom imposed by the political system under which he lives; and external polis freedom (i.e., self-government or self-determination) is the freedom *of* a polis *from* impediments *to* its autonomy.[2]

It is the contention of this chapter that Plato, vehemently opposed to a democratic *conception* of personal freedom, but unwilling to concede the ideal of personal freedom to his ideological opponents, advances a *conception* of his own. These rival conceptions are easily understood as falling under a common *concept* but involving different views about the end, or goal, of personal freedom. According to the characterization of democracy offered by Plato, the goal of democratic personal freedom is to live as one wishes, which in his view is simply the license to live wantonly.[3] The proper goal of personal freedom in his view is to live a virtuous life, that is to say, a life of moral and intellectual excellence. Taking our cue from remarks in the *Republic* (IV.445d6, VIII.544e7) and the *Laws* (III.701a2), we shall dub this rival conception "aristocratic" freedom. This, needless to say, is the freedom of what Plato deems a "true" (i.e., ideal) aristocracy rather than any historical aristocracy such as Sparta. One important difference between the two conceptions is that the one, democratic freedom, is firmly rooted in the ideology and historical institutions of democratic Athens, whereas the other, aristocratic freedom, is a development and idealization of an ancient contrast between the qualities characteristic of a free man and those characteristic of a slave, marked in Greek by the adjective *eleutherios*, on the one hand, and by the adjective *doulios*, on the other:

> In the sixth century or earlier, the slave and the free man were sharply contrasted in terms of physical appearance, character, and behavior. Everything that was straight, beautiful, good, and noble was defined by the free man; all that was crooked, ugly, bad, and base was to be expected in and from a slave. As with the word *doulios* (belonging to a slave, slavish), which appears already in the *Iliad*, the word *eleutherios* was created to describe the typological characteristics and claims of the *eleutheros*, the free man. (Raaflaub 1983: 533)

To set the stage for discussion of Plato's positive views on freedom, we shall first show how he understands the legal distinction between free and slave, and then consider how aristocratic freedom is conceived of as a moralized idealization of the distinction between free man and slave by Socrates in the *Memorabilia* of Xenophon. We shall then examine how Plato articulates and applies a similar conception of freedom focusing primarily on two major dialogues: the *Republic*, in which Socrates describes an ideally just and beautiful city ("Kallipolis," *Rep.* VII.527c2), and the *Laws*, in which the Athenian Stranger lays down a constitution for the imaginary colony of Magnesia in Crete.

2. FREE AND SLAVE

Plato does not formally define "free" and "slave," but he describes the distinction in legal terms in the *Laws*. A slave is a human being owned as property by a master who is a free man (*Laws* VI.777b) and can be bought and sold under the laws of Magnesia (XI.916a). Slaves should be ruled over by their masters, just as sheep by their shepherds and children by their tutors (VII.808d). This might suggest that some humans are naturally suited to be slaves, but Plato does not say so (unlike Aristotle, who argues that there are natural slaves in *Politics* I.4–7), and he allows that it would be correct for the polis to make a slave free and pay his master the price of manumission (XI.914a; cf. Aristotle *Politics* VII.10.1330a32–33). In any case, the Athenian Stranger observes that "it is clear that the human creature is troublesome, and in regard to the necessary distinction in deed between a slave and a free man and a master, it appears that he is in no way willing to be or become useful but is a difficult possession" (VI.777b).

We get a vivid picture of what Plato has in mind in his thought experiment at *Republic* 9.578d10–579e8. In dialogue with Glaucon, Socrates observes that those wealthy private citizens who own many slaves feel secure and do not fear them:

> "What do they have to fear, anyway?"
>   "Nothing," I said, "but do you know the reason?"
>   "Yes, because the whole polis is ready to defend each private person."

"Correct. But what if some god were to lift one these men, who has fifty or more slaves, out of the polis, and put him down—with his wife, his children, his servants, and his other property—in a deserted place, where no free men would be able to defend him? What do you think is the sort and amount of fear he would feel that he and his children and wife would be killed by his servants?"

"It would be huge," he said, "if you ask me."

These descriptions convey the notion of a slave as a human being who is subject to the rule of someone else but typically unwilling to be in this condition. This implies that a free man is someone who is unimpeded by the rule of anyone else from doing what he wants.

3. SOCRATIC FREEDOM

The source for Plato's conception of freedom may well have been Socrates, who is depicted offering a similar account in Xenophon's *Memorabilia* (IV.5):[4]

[Socrates] also tried to make his companions more fitted for action, as I will now discuss. For because he thought that self-control (*egkrateia*) is good for whoever intends to perform a noble act, he first of all made it clear to his companions that he himself had practiced it more than any other human being, and then in conversation with them he exhorted them to self-control above all.

So he continually recalled the things useful for virtue and reminded his companions of all of them. I remember the following conversation he once had with Euthydemus about self-control.

"Tell me, Euthydemus," he said, "do you think that freedom (*eleutheria*) is a noble and great possession for a man (*anēr*) and a polis?"

"Yes, it is the noblest and greatest," he said.

"Then, do you think that the person who is ruled by the pleasures of the body and who is because of them incapable of doing the best things is free?"

"Least of all," he said.

"For, surely, it appears to you that doing the best things is characteristic of a free person, and consequently having those who prevent you from doing these is characteristic of an unfree person."

"Absolutely," he said.

"Do you absolutely believe, therefore, that persons lacking self-control (*akrateis*) are also unfree?"

"Yes, by Zeus, for sure."

"And do you believe that persons lacking self-control are merely prevented from doing the most noble things, or are they also compelled to do the most shameful?"

"I believe," he said, "that the latter persons are compelled no less than are those who are prevented from doing the former acts."

"What sort of masters do you think are those who prevent the best (*ta arista*) and compel the worst (*ta kakista*)?"

"The worst possible, by Zeus," he said.
"And what sort of slavery do you think is the worst?"
"I think it is slavery to the worst masters."
"Therefore, is the worst slavery that by which persons lacking self-control are
    enslaved?"
"I believe so," he said.

This interchange between Socrates and Euthydemus provides all the elements needed for a triadic analysis of the personal freedom they are discussing. They agree that freedom is a noble and great possession for a man and a polis. Thus, the agent of personal freedom is a man. His goal is to do the best things. The bodily pleasures, which are said to prevent the man from achieving his goal, are the impediment. Socrates and Euthydemus agree that the man who lacks self-control and is a slave of his passions is unfree, while the man who has self-control is free. This amounts to defining the free man as the one who can do the best things unimpeded by the bodily pleasures. Because Socratic freedom enables one to do the best things (*ta arista*), his freedom is aristocratic in the literal sense of "rule by the best." As we shall see, Plato develops a conception of aristocratic freedom which is similar to (though not the same as) that of Xenophon's Socrates. We shall now consider how Plato's conception unfolds in his dialogues.

4. FREEDOM IN THE *PHAEDRUS* AND THE *REPUBLIC*

4.1. Psychological freedom

Plato's conception of aristocratic freedom is based on his tripartite psychology, as illustrated by some striking images in the *Phaedrus* and *Republic*. First, in the Great Myth of the *Phaedrus* (244a–257b) Socrates imagines a charioteer holding the reins of two horses yoked to his chariot, an undisciplined black horse, who responds only to the whip and the goad, and a docile white horse, who responds to verbal commands alone and aids the charioteer in his struggle with the black horse. The complex of charioteer and two horses symbolizes the human psyche: the charioteer symbolizes reason; the black horse symbolizes sexual desire, or *epithumia* (for the word, see 255e2 and 264a3); and the white horse—a lover of honor (253d6)—presumably symbolizes spirit, or *thumos* (though the word does not occur in the dialogue). Using this symbolism and the language of freedom and slavery Socrates describes the souls of a lover and his beloved—a man and a boy—whose sexual desire for each other is held in check by reason: "they live a life of blessedness and concord here on earth, self-controlled (*egkrateis*) and orderly, having enslaved (*doulōsamenoi*) that [part] by which vice was brought into the soul and having freed (*eleutherōsantes*) that [part] by which virtue was brought in" (256a8–b3). If we apply the triadic analysis of freedom, the agent is the soul; the goal is happiness; and sexual desire is the impediment. The soul is able to reach its goal when reason is able, with the aid of spirit, to restrain its sexual appetites, just as, in the myth, the charioteer is able to guide his chariot to its destination by exerting control over the undisciplined black horse by enlisting the aid of the docile white horse. In applying the triadic analysis we assume that Socrates means to claim that the whole soul is free when its principal part is free, even though this goes beyond what he actually says. This reticence is made good in the *Republic*, where he explicitly infers that the soul is enslaved when its better parts are enslaved to its worst part (IX.577d1–8). By implication and parity of reasoning the soul is free when its principal part is free. But note that in both the *Phaedrus* and the *Republic* "free" and "unfree" (or "enslaved") are predicated of a soul (*psychē*), not, as in the passage from the *Memorabilia*, of a man (*anēr*). In the *Phaedrus* and the *Republic* a man is an ensouled body.

The simile of the Multiform Creature in the *Republic* (IX.588b) provides a straightforward parallel with the simile of the Charioteer in the *Phaedrus* and an easy transition from the latter dialogue to the former. In this simile Socrates compares an embodied soul to a creature composed of three parts—a many-headed beast, a lion, and a man—wearing a costume shaped like a man. The costume symbolizes the human body; the multiform creature wearing the costume symbolizes the soul; and the beast, lion, and man symbolize the three parts of the soul—appetite, spirit, and reason respectively. The use of the free–slave opposition is not as vivid in this simile as it is in the other, but it can be ferreted out nonetheless. At 589d2–3 Socrates speaks of the shamefulness of the tame parts of the soul being enslaved (*douloumena*) to the wild, and at 591b2–3 of the bestial element of the soul being calmed and tamed, and the gentle part being set free (*eleutheroutai*). (He does not, however, speak here of the bestial part being enslaved, as he does at *Phaedrus* 256b2.)

What brings freedom to the soul are the cardinal virtues, especially temperance, which in the *Republic* is characterized as "a sort of order," consisting in "the self-control (*egkrateia*) over certain sorts of pleasures and appetites" (IV.430e3–7) and defined as the friendship and concord of the three elements of the soul "when the one that rules and the two that are ruled believe in common that the rational element ought to rule and do not engage in faction against it" (*Republic* IV.442c10–d1). (The association of temperance with psychic order and self-control, it should be noted, links the discussion of freedom in the *Republic* with that in the *Memorabilia* and the *Phaedrus*.) Since psychic freedom is dependent upon the virtues, we would expect the virtues to be associated with freedom, and unfreedom to be associated with the vices. This is, indeed, what we find. Socrates associates freedom with bravery, temperance, and piety (III.395c4–5), and unfreedom with hubris and madness (III.400b2), with badness and intemperance (III.401b4–5), with stripping the corpse of an enemy warrior (V.469d6), with pettiness (VI.486a4–5), and with cowardice, love of money, and pretentiousness (486b3, 6–8). The waning of the bodily appetites that comes with old age provides a similar sort of psychic freedom, as Cephalus notes when he relates Sophocles' remark about his welcome escape in old age from the slavery of sexual desire (I.329a1–d6, especially 329c6–7). Achilles in the grip of inner turmoil is an example of psychic bondage, or unfreedom (III.391b7–c6).

4.2. Political freedom

We turn now to the evidence in the *Republic* for freedom in the political domain—freedom as predicated of a polis. What we called "polis" freedom—the freedom of a polis from foreign domination or conquest—is mentioned twice. In his interchange with Thrasymachus in Book I Socrates speaks of enslaving poleis (I.351b1–3), and later he describes the guardians (i.e., auxiliaries, or warriors) of his ideal polis as "craftsmen of the freedom of the polis" (III.395c1). In both instances it is the external freedom of the polis that is at issue. The following passage describes a polis lacking internal freedom:

> "First, then," I said, "speaking of a polis, would you call the one ruled by a tyrant free or enslaved?"
>
> "As enslaved," he said, "as it is possible to be."
>
> "Yet you see in it masters and free men."
>
> "I see," he said, "a small group like that at any rate; but virtually the whole [population], and the most respectable part of it, is shamefully and wretchedly enslaved." (IX.577c5–10)

The polis referred to in this passage is said to be "enslaved" because most of its citizen body (including the best) is enslaved, which would seem to imply that a polis is internally, or civically, free if most of its citizen body (including the best) is free (sc. to live according to virtue). This is as close as we get to a concept of civic freedom in the *Republic*.

Though the concept may lack explicit expression, the following passage would seem to be describing an instance of it:

> "[I]t is better for all to be ruled by what is divine and wise, especially if one possesses it as his own within himself, but, if not, it is imposed from outside, so that we may all be as similar and friendly as possible, because we are governed by the same thing."
>
> "That's also right," he said.
>
> "And it is clear also that this is the aim of the law, which is the ally of everyone in the polis, and of the rule over children, not allowing them to be free until we have established a constitution in them as in a polis, and we have taken care of their best part [i.e., their reason] with the similar one in ourselves and established in our place a similar guardian and ruler. Only then do we set them free." (IX.590d3–591a3)

The freedom in question is psychic freedom: the constitution that the parent wishes to establish in the child's soul is one in which reason rules and is willingly obeyed by spirit and appetite. The impediment to the child's freedom is its own unruly passions, an impediment that the parent wishes to remove by means of such a constitution. The child is living under an institution—presumably the communal family of the guardians in Plato's ideal polis—that fosters psychic freedom, and enjoys aristocratic civic freedom when it has been educated by its parents.

The fact that Plato endorses a conception of political freedom in the *Republic* is easily missed,[5] since it is overshadowed by his sustained account and criticism of democratic freedom (not to mention his hair-raising illiberal proposals for his ideal polis such as censorship of poetry, communism of families and property, and a rigged lottery for arranging sexual coupling). Plato pairs an account of democratic personal freedom— "each person would arrange his own life privately in the polis in whatever way pleases him" (VIII.557b8–10)—with a thumbnail sketch of democratic institutions: "the poor share equally in the constitution and the ruling offices, and the majority of offices in it are assigned by lot" (557a2–5). Since these institutions were devised to foster, to protect, and to preserve democratic personal freedom, it is natural to say that any polis enjoying such institutions is civically free in the democratic sense.

The following passage, in which Socrates explains the transition from democracy to tyranny, implicitly marks democratic freedom off from other sorts: "For too much freedom (*agan eleutheria*) does not seem to change into anything other than too much slavery (*agan douleian*), in both a private individual and a polis. . . . Tyranny, then, is probably established out of no other constitution than democracy—from extreme freedom (*akrotatēs eleutherias*), I suppose, the heaviest and fiercest slavery" (VIII.564a3–8). The story Plato tells is this (VIII.562b9–566d4). In democracy the citizens have an insatiable desire for unlimited freedom, which leads eventually to disregard of the laws "in order that they may have no master at all" (563d7–e1). In this state of anarchy a popular leader, a champion of the people, arises by promising a redistribution of wealth from the rich to the poor. When the rich resist and begin plotting against the people's champion, the popular leader asks for and gets a bodyguard consisting of many freed slaves. With such an armed force at his command he is now a strongman, or tyrant, and the rest of the population is at his mercy. Thus, by fleeing the "smoke of slavery to free men" the democratic citizens plunge into the "fire of mastery by slaves" (569b8–c2).[6]

The quotation above indicates how Plato can reject one sort of freedom while championing another. The adverb *agan* ('too much') and the superlative *akrotatē* ('extreme') indicate that freedom comes in degrees—an idea developed in the *Laws*. Democratic freedom is excessive because, in Plato's view, it does not recognize the restrictions of law; aristocratic freedom, which acknowledges such restrictions, is not excessive.

We cannot leave the *Republic* without mentioning that the centerpiece of the dialogue, the allegory of the Cave (VII.514a ff.), is a symbol of moral and intellectual liberation. The allegory begins in a cave that is a prison (*desmōtērion*) in which prisoners (*desmōtoi*) are forced by fetters (*desma*) around their necks and legs to sit in the same place, looking forward at shadows cast onto a wall before them by a fire behind them that they cannot see, and describes the removal of the fetters from one of the prisoners and his ascent out of the cave into the light of the sun. Even though the words for "free" and "slave" never occur in the allegory, the three words on the stem *desm-* indicate that the ascent out of the cave is a journey from the bondage of prison to freedom. As Plato explains (VII.517a8–c5, 532a6–d1), the physical journey of the prisoner out of the cave symbolizes a moral and intellectual journey of the psyche from moral and intellectual benightedness to moral and intellectual knowledge. (For the moral dimension of the journey see 518c4–519b5.) The attainment of physical freedom can thus be taken to symbolize the attainment of psychic freedom. We can go one step further: since the ideal polis of the *Republic* has educational institutions designed to produce just such psychic freedom, it can be regarded as a paradigm of aristocratic civic freedom.

But who among the citizenry of Kallipolis enjoys such freedom? Does the allegory of the Cave imply that aristocratic freedom is confined to the philosophical ruling class, while the rest of the citizens remain in bondage? Commentators are divided over this difficult question. R. F. Stalley defends the interpretation that only philosophers are free, because "[i]n Plato's view one is free in so far as one responds to reason and is free from the bonds of irrational necessity" (1997–1998: 157). This implies that in Plato's ideal state the working class is in a condition of "idealized slavery" under the benevolent philosopher-rulers.[7] If we assume, by analogy, that a polis is free insofar as (by virtue of its rulers) it is guided by reason, we are led to a paradoxical result: Kallipolis is free only if most of its citizens are unfree! This interpretation is rejected by Malcolm Schofield, who contends that "Socrates never suggests that those in the economic class are generally weak in reason (even if it is not what rules their souls), still less that they cannot control their appetites. Certainly they do not have the status of slaves" (2006: 274). At issue is a passage at *Republic* IX.590c2–d6, which states that a manual laborer's "best part [i.e., reason] is naturally weak and thus unable to rule the creatures [i.e., desires] within," so that "he ought to be the slave of the best man who possesses the divine ruler within himself." Schofield questions whether this description applies to the lower classes of Kallipolis. It could be argued that as a result of their education and supervision by the guardians they are ruled by reason to some extent[8] and are thus in a sense free. This agrees with another passage which describes the actions of the timocratic rulers *after* the overthrow of the ideal constitution: "They distribute the land and houses to themselves, enslave and hold as serfs and servants those whom they formerly guarded as free friends (*eleutherous philous*) and providers of upkeep" (VIII.547b7–c4.). This implies that the citizens of the previous ideal state were "free" in some sense even if not in the full aristocratic sense. We must turn to Plato's *Laws* for a fuller picture of aristocratic freedom.

5. Freedom in the *Laws* and the *Theaetetus*

5.1. Psychological and personal freedom

The Athenian Stranger, Plato's spokesman in the dialogue, mentions freedom early on in his conversation with Kleinias and Megillus, his Cretan and Spartan interlocutors, preliminary to his description of an imaginary constitution for a Cretan colony, which will be presented as an attainable, second-best approximation of the ideal (V.739a–b). Those who are incapable of enduring pleasures, he remarks, "will have a soul that is partly slave and partly free (*eleutheran*), and will not be worthy to be called brave and free men[9] (*eleutherioi*) without qualification" (I.635d4–6). Those of whom the Athenian Stranger speaks are citizens (635c6) (i.e., persons). Having souls that are only partly free, these citizens, who are of course legally free, are said not to be free without qualification. In other words, a person who is legally free but in psychological bondage is not free without qualification. The Athenian Stranger is thus implicitly marking two distinctions. In the passage quoted, the bearer of the English word "free" in its first occurrence is a soul, and in its second, persons. The Greek is clearer: the first occurrence is the feminine singular *eleutheran* and the second the masculine plural *eleutherioi*. Thus one implicit distinction is between psychic freedom and personal freedom. The other is between legal freedom and a stricter, higher, and truer freedom—what we have called "aristocratic" freedom. The passage also implies that to be a free man without qualification is to have a soul that is wholly free—not partly slave and partly free. This conflicts with the language of the Charioteer simile where the appetitive part of a soul that is self-controlled is said to be enslaved (*Phaedrus* 256a8–b3), though it fits the language of the Multiform Creature simile where punishing a miscreant is said to calm and tame, rather than enslave, the bestial element of his soul (*Republic* IX.591b2–3).

The counterpart in the *Laws* of the Charioteer and the Multiform Creature is the graphic Puppet of the Gods (I.644d–645c). In this metaphor each of us is a divine puppet pulled in one direction by cords of iron and in an opposite direction by one "soft and golden cord." The "hard and iron cords" symbolize appetitive desires and spirited emotions (see IX.863e6–8), whereas the "soft and golden cord" symbolizes reasoning and the common law of the polis (645a1–2). These cords, unlike those of ordinary puppets, are not totally controlled by the puppet master; their motion can be affected by us. The golden cord, being "gentle rather than violent," needs our assistance if it is to prevail over the iron cords. When it does prevail, a man is superior to himself (645b2), or self-controlled (*egkratēs*) (645e8), not a slave to his appetitive desires and his spirited emotions. The reference here to self-control (*egkrateia*), which, as we saw, is identified with freedom in the conversation between Socrates and Euthydemus in the *Memorabilia*, makes it reasonable to regard the Puppet of the Gods passage as a representation of psychic freedom.

In the *Laws* Plato develops the idea first advanced in the *Republic* that freedom and slavery both for a person and for a political system form a continuum with total slavery (*pasa douleia*) at one extreme and total freedom (*pasa eleutheria*) at the other (III.699e3–4). One point on this continuum is right; all others are wrong. The correct point is the one that displays "the measure (*to metron*)." The measure, in the sense of *due* measure or moderation, is a basic evaluative notion throughout the *Laws* (see especially III.691c1–692c7, 694a3–5, 698a9–b2, 701e1–8; XI.918c9–d8). With respect to value Plato is of course the arch absolutist, steadfastly opposed to Protagorean relativism (for which see *Theaetetus* 151e8–152a4 *et passim*): god, not man, is the measure (*metron*) of all things (*Laws* IV.716c4–6).

On the personal level literal, or legal, slavery is one end of the continuum; unrestrained freedom—doing what one wishes—is the other. Aristocratic freedom is the due measure of freedom and slavery. (For the use of the term "aristocracy" in this connection see III.701a2.) When freedom and slavery are duly balanced, a person is, "in a way, willingly enslaved to the laws" (*tina hekōn edouleue tois nomois*) (700a4–5). The Athenian Stranger marks the stages in the collapse of due measure, or aristocratic freedom, into lawlessness and total freedom: (i) lack of respect for one's betters, (ii) unwillingness to be enslaved to the rulers, (iii) unwillingness to be enslaved to parents and elders, (iv) disrespect for the law, and finally (v) contempt for oaths, promises, and religion (701a7–c4). At each stage in this collapse an impediment to total freedom is removed. If we reverse these stages, restore the impediments one at a time, and progress along the continuum from total freedom to the due measure of freedom and slavery, Plato counts the willing acceptance of each impediment as an increasing degree of willing enslavement. Plato says nothing directly about the progression along the continuum from due measure to total slavery, but presumably willing subjection to the law and to authority is replaced by coerced subjection (as suggested by his description of Persia's descent into despotism at 694c–698a).

Plato's notion of being willingly enslaved to the law provides a transition from personal freedom to political freedom. To understand this idea we need to note two points. First, Plato is speaking of correct law (*orthos nomos*) (II.674b7, IV.715b3).[10] Correct, or ideal, laws "make those who practice them happy" by providing the divine goods of wisdom (*phronēsis*), temperance, justice, and bravery and the human goods of health, beauty, strength, and wealth (I.631b3–d2). Secondly, such laws are inculcated by persuasion, not by coercion. A correct law should not only state what must and must not be done and specify a penalty for violation but, by explaining its purpose, dispose people to follow it (IV.719c1–723d4)—to recognize it, indeed, as law they impose upon themselves (for which see V.733e1). The Athenian Stranger says that the legislator should be like the free doctor treating free men, who learns from his patient, teaches him about his sickness, and persuades him of the wisdom of a course of treatment, not like the slave doctor treating slaves, who simply makes a diagnosis and issues commands "wilfully like a tyrant" (720a2–e2). Taking the two points together we can understand why Plato conceives of the inculcation of correct law as moral education (IX.857b9–e1).

The doctor analogy leads Plato to an important innovation. A complete statement of a law must include two parts: the law (in the narrow sense) and a preamble which precedes it. By means of the preamble "he who receives the law stated by the legislator shall receive the command—that is, the law—favorably and as a result of this favorable attitude be more capable of learning" (IV.722e4–723b2, cf. c1–4).[11] An illustration of a simple statement of a law is "A man is to marry when he is between the ages of thirty and thirty-five; and if he does not, he is to be punished with fines and dishonors." The preamble includes the observation that the human race has a natural share of immortality and that everyone naturally desires immortality in any way. By leaving behind children, the individual contributes to the immortality of the species, and it is impious to deprive oneself of this role (721b–d; cf. *Symposium* 207d–208b). This places the marriage law within a wider metaphysical and moral context, in much the way that the preamble to the United States Constitution articulates its higher purposes.[12] The main point underlying the analogy is that free men should obey the law voluntarily rather than under compulsion as far as possible.

In the personal domain, the aristocratically free man has little free time. Indeed, he lacks leisure for any activities beyond those of his station in life, that is to say, those of a head of a household and an active citizen of his polis. There "should be regulation of how all the free men spend all their time" (VII.807d6–7), including their hours of sleep. "For while a person is sleeping he is worth nothing—no more than one who isn't living. But whoever among us cares for living and thinking to a special degree stays awake as long as possible" (808b5–c1). To loll in bed is "shameful and unbefitting of a free man" (808a2). Among other things the free man will need to keep himself in shape physically, mentally, and morally (VII.807c1–d5). But he will not spend time chasing money (I.644a2–5, V.747b7–8,), engaging in trade (XI.919d3–e5), or practicing a banausic or vulgar art (V.741e4–5).

5.2. Political freedom

Turning now to the political domain, we find Plato again speaking of a spectrum of freedom and slavery now applied to both cities (III.693b3–4) and constitutions (701e1–2) in both a positive and a superlative degree. The freest (*eleutherikōtatēn*) constitution, represented for the Athenian Stranger by the extreme democracy of the Athens in which he resides, enjoys "total freedom from all rule" (698a9–b2). At the other end of the freeslave continuum the most despotic (*despotikōtatēn*) constitution, represented this time by the Persian empire under Xerxes, suffers from a total lack of freedom (697c5–698a7). Anarchy at one end of the continuum is matched by slavery at the other. Here again, the ideal point on the continuum is the one with a due measure (*metron*) of freedom and despotism. The Athenian Stranger claims that the imagined constitution "constructed in speech" (702d1–2) in *Laws* IV–XII has due measure (VI.758d10, VII.807c1, VIII.846c8) and that the historical constitutions of Sparta and Crete and ancient Athens (i.e., the Athens that fought the Persian Wars) approach due measure (III.693e5–694a1). There are two factors involved in moving along the continuum: moving from the freedom pole toward due measure midway, the factor involved is the increasing respect for, or enslavement to, the law; moving from the slavery pole toward the center, the factor is the increasing check on unbridled power. Plato's great and enduring contribution to the philosophy of freedom is his thought that this midpoint of due measure, which is political freedom correctly understood, can be achieved through mixing and balancing the various elements of a constitution.[13]

The Athenian Stranger claims that "the lawgiver ought to aim at three things in laying down his laws, namely that the polis for which he legislates be free (*eleuthera*), that it be a friend to itself, and that it possess intelligence" (III.701d8–9; see also 693b4, c7–8, d8–e1, and 694b6). Given that freedom is here stated to be one of the three goals of correct law, its importance in the *Laws* should not be minimized. But what does the Athenian Stranger mean when he speaks of a polis being free? Most obviously he means that the polis is not enslaved to, or under the domination of, another polis. Thus, he says that the Persians under Cyrus "first became free [of the Medes], and then became depots over many" (694a4–5; see also 687a7–8). This external freedom is what we have called "polis" freedom. But the internal freedom of a polis is at least as important as its external freedom, and it is this sort of freedom that the Athenian Stranger focuses on. How does he understand it?

The answer to this question turns upon the distinction in the *Laws* between a constitution (*politeia*) and a factional state (*stasiōteia*). By a factional state Plato means a regime established when one faction (*stasis*) defeats its rivals and succeeds in gaining control of a polis. The rulers in a factional state rule in their own, rather than the common, interest (IV.715b2–6). As a consequence, the polis divides into two factions—rulers and subjects—the latter obeying the former unwillingly under the threat of force (VIII.832c2–5). In a passage parallel to the one at I.635d4–6 on psychic freedom discussed above, the Athenian Stranger characterizes the relation of subjects to rulers in such a polis as enslavement. He explains to the Cretan Kleinias and the Spartan Megillus that the reason neither is able to say whether his polis is a democracy, an aristocracy, a tyranny, or a monarchy is that they "belong to constitutions [i.e., the mixed constitutions of Crete and Sparta]. The other ones we just named [i.e., democracy, aristocracy, etc.] are not constitutions, but cities under occupation [i.e., 'factional states'] which are under the sway of despots and enslaved to some parts of themselves. Each takes its name from the authority that is the despot" (IV.712e9–713a2; see also 715a8–b6). Under the mixed constitution of the imaginary Cretan city, in contrast to these factional states, (i) the citizens are ruled in "the common interest of the whole polis" (715b4), not the private interest of their rulers only (IX.875a5–b1), (ii) obey willingly (VIII.832c3–5), and (iii) are "free from one another" (*eleutheros ap' allēlōn*) (832d2) rather than enslaved to those in power. Though these three conditions may be logically independent, from the standpoint of human motivation they are tightly tied together and satisfied simultaneously. This is internal political freedom, what we have dubbed "civic freedom." Thus, when the Athenian Stranger speaks of the polis being free, he means it is free both internally and externally. These are the two dimensions of political freedom.

The end, or goal, of correct law is expressed in two different ways in the *Laws*. At the very beginning of the dialogue, as we have already noted in our discussion of aristocratic personal freedom, the end is said to be happiness, where happiness is understood as the possession of all good things but primarily as the possession of the cardinal virtues (I.631b3–d2). In our discussion of aristocratic civic freedom we saw that it is also said to be the triplet freedom, friendship, and wisdom.[14] We can understand how these two notions of the goal of correct law are related if we recall that civic freedom fosters and preserves personal freedom. The imaginary Cretan polis, the exemplar of a free city, is ruled in the common interest, where the common interest is taken to be the happiness of its citizens rather than the city's greatness or its wealth or the multitudes ruled by it "by land and sea" (V.742d2–e1). Thus, for a polis to enjoy aristocratic civic freedom it must be ruled in the common interest. This means that among its citizens the cardinal virtues must be fostered and preserved. But that is simply to foster and to preserve aristocratic personal freedom. To be sure, Plato's vision of civic freedom is a far cry from modern liberalism. Though the more radical trappings of the *Republic* have been discarded, the regime of the *Laws* remains highly authoritarian: the citizens' personal conduct is strictly regulated; atheists are imprisoned and in some cases executed; and supreme power is vested in a hermetic Nocturnal Council.

The digression on the philosopher and the orator at *Theaetetus* 172c–177c provides a fitting capstone of our discussion of Plato. In this passage Socrates remarks on how reasonable it is that those who spend their lives studying philosophy should be laughable when they appear as litigants in law courts. The upbringing of litigious men stands, he says, to that of the philosophically minded as the upbringing of household slaves stands to that of free men (*eleutherous*). This is because the philosopher has plenty of time for discussion and has the freedom (173b6) to change the subject if he wishes, whereas the speech of the litigious man is limited by the water clock and to the lawsuit at hand. His speech, moreover, "concerns a fellow slave and is addressed to a master [i.e., the jurors in a popular law court]" (172e5). In sum, the philosopher is brought up in freedom (*eleutheria(i)*) and leisure (175e1), whereas the litigious man lacks the grace of a free man (175e7).

This passage is notable in several respects. First of all, the litigious man is not only a legally free man but presumably an Athenian citizen[15] possessing democratic freedom. Since he does not enjoy the freedom attributed to the philosopher, the philosopher's freedom must be of a higher grade than his: it can only be what we have called "aristocratic" freedom. Secondly, the philosopher's leisure to pursue his philosophical discussion wherever it leads is the counterpoint to the highly structured life of the aristocratically free man outlined at *Laws* 807d6–7. Thirdly and finally, the fact that the philosopher is said to be free in this higher sense of the word confirms our interpretation of the journey out of the Cave as a journey from bondage to aristocratic freedom.

6. CONCLUSION

It is proper to render Plato's term *eleutheria* as "freedom" because the Greek term signifies the same triadic relation as the English term—freedom *of* an agent *from* impediments *to* a given end, or goal. Depending on the specification of these three factors, freedom has different domains: personal, psychological, and political. We saw that Plato rejects the democratic idea of personal freedom on the ground of its consistency with psychological bondage and offers in its place an alternative, "aristocratic," conception of freedom, originating in the moral psychology of Socrates and in the popular conception of the qualities that are polar opposites of those characteristic of a slave. In the *Republic* Plato gives an account of aristocratic freedom consisting in the rule of reason over the soul unimpeded by desires, in both the psychological and political domains. In the *Laws* he offers a fuller account of aristocratic freedom in the personal and political domains with the idea of a due measure between extreme slavery and extreme freedom, which is achieved by means of "willing enslavement to the laws." Despite ominous Orwellian overtones,[16] Plato's conception led him to important innovations, for example, that legal codes should include persuasive preambles, and that political constitutions should be "mixed" in order to attain a proper balance of individual freedom with the rule of law. Plato's ideal of aristocratic freedom was embraced and more fully developed by his student Aristotle, which is the subject of another chapter.

NOTES

1. This chapter is the outcome of close collaboration with David Keyt, author of the chapter on "Aristotelian Freedom." I am, however, responsible for the final statement and for all translations of Plato and Xenophon. Both of us are greatly indebted to Jeremy Reid for assistance, suggestions, and criticisms. In addition, Allan Silverman and anonymous referees provided valuable comments.

2. The Greek term *polis*, pl. *poleis* (often translated "city," "state," or "city-state"), is transliterated in this chapter.

3. The proponents of democratic freedom are not named, but they are presumably the demagogues alluded to in *Republic* VIII.564b–c, *Sophist* 268b, and *Laws* X.908b.

4. Both Plato (427–347 BCE) and Xenophon (c. 430–c. 354 BCE) were pupils of Socrates (469–399 BCE), who is a major character in their dialogues. Despite important disagreements, there are striking similarities in their depiction of Socrates, including his view of freedom.

5. Not everyone has missed it. David Reeve finds what he calls "critical freedom" in the *Republic* (1988: 233), and Malcolm Schofield finds "rational freedom" (2006: 84–88). See also M. Pohlenz (1955: 89–112), D. Nestle (1967: 89–112), R. Muller (1997), R. F. Stalley (1997–1998), C. Griswold (1999), and D. Cürsgen (2007: 121–124). On the contrary, according to Johnson and Smith (2001), Plato holds that "political freedom is not valuable even to the truly free."

6. Not surprisingly, the proponents of Athenian democracy (Samaras 2002) take a different view. For example, Aeschines (c. 397–c. 322) contends, "Tyrants and oligarchs are governed at the whim of rulers, but democratic states are governed by the established law" (*Against Timarchus*, 1.4). See Hansen 1991: 74–78 for a sympathetic interpretation of the democratic conception of freedom.

7. Stalley here follows Vlastos (1977: 27; 1995: 92). For similar interpretations see Irwin (1977: 329; 1995: 351), Reeve (1988: 48 together with 285 n. 3), and Taylor (1999 [1986]: 295). See Vlastos (1973) on the question of whether there is literal slavery in the ideal city of the *Republic*.

8. Kraut (1972: 216–222) defends an interpretation along these lines.

9. I.e., possessors of the qualities characteristic of brave and free men.

10. See Miller (2012) for an interpretation of Plato's conception of correct law in terms of the rule of reason.

11. It is reiterated several times that the purpose of preambles is to teach those subject to the law (IV.720b5, d6; IX.857d7, e4–5; X.885d2, 888a2).

12. See Schofield (2006: 85–86, 320–321), who agrees with Bobonich (1991; 2002: 97–119) that the preambles are intended to provide *rational* persuasion. In contrast, however, Stalley (1983: 43) views them as "exhortations rather than arguments"; cf. Stalley (1994: 171–172) and Morrow (1960: 553–558).

13. This doctrine is invoked in a letter attributed to Plato (though possibly by one of his followers) which is addressed to two opposing factions in Sicily: one desiring democracy and the other seeking restoration of tyranny. The letter advises them to seek the due measure (*to meson*) between the extremes of freedom and slavery in the form of "responsible kingly rule where the laws exercise mastery over citizens and kings alike" (*Letter VII*.344c2–355e3; see Nestle (1967: 91–97)).

14. Laks (2007: 135–137) notes that although freedom leads the triplet at 693b4, it is replaced by temperance (*sōphrosunē*) at 693c2, and takes this replacement to signal "the beginning of freedom's disappearance" from the Athenian Stranger's agenda. But the replacement need not imply the elimination of freedom. For as was noted above, freedom is equated with self-control in Xenophon's *Memorabilia* and temperance with self-control in the *Republic*. The fact that freedom and temperance are spoken of interchangeably within a few lines would not be surprising if they turn out to be equivalent.

15. Meletus (referred to at *Theaetetus* 210d3), who brought an indictment against Socrates, springs to mind.

16. Modern echoes include Jean-Jacques Rousseau ("[W]hoever refuses to obey the general will be compelled to do so by the whole body. This means nothing less than that he will be forced to be free"; in *Social Contract* I.7.8) and Maximilian Robespierre ("The government of the Revolution is the despotism of liberty against tyranny"; in "To the National Convention," *Moniteur universal* 19 Pluviôse, l'an 2, p. 562). See Laks (2000: 279).

REFERENCES

Bobonich, C., 1991. Persuasion, compulsion and freedom in Plato's Laws. *The Classical Quarterly*, 41(2), pp. 365–388.

Bobonich, C., 2002. *Plato's utopia recast*. Oxford: Oxford University Press.

Cürsgen, D., 2007. Freiheit/Notwendigkeit (*anankē*). In: C. Schäfer, ed. *Platon-Lexicon: Begriffswörterbuch zu Platon und der platonischen Tradition*. Darmstadt: Wissenschaftliche Buchgesellschaft. pp. 121–124.

Griswold, C., 1999. Platonic liberalism: self-perfection as a foundation of political theory. In: J. M. Van Ophuijsen, ed. *Plato and Platonism*. Washington, DC: Catholic University of America Press. pp. 103–134.

Hansen, M. H., 1991. *The Athenian democracy in the age of Demosthenes*. Oxford: Blackwell.

Hansen, M. H., 2013. Democratic freedom and the concept of freedom in Plato and Aristotle. In: *Reflections on Aristotle's Politics*. Reprint from *Greek, Roman, and Byzantine Studies*, 50 (2010), pp. 1–27. Copenhagen: Museum Tusculanum Press. pp. 71–96.

Irwin, T. H., 1977. *Plato's moral theory*. Oxford: Oxford University Press.

Irwin, T. H., 1995. *Plato's ethics*. Oxford: Oxford University Press.

Johnson, C., and Smith, N. D., 2001. What is liberty for? Plato and Aristotle on political freedom. *Skepsis* 12, pp. 78–84.

Kraut, R., 1972. Reason and justice in Plato's *Republic*. In: E. N. Lee, A. P. Mourelatos, and R. M. Rorty, eds. *Exegesis and argument*. Assen: Van Gorcum. pp. 207–224.

Laks, A., 2000. The *Laws*. In: C. J. Rowe and M. Schofield, eds. *The Cambridge history of Greek and Roman political thought*. Cambridge: Cambridge University Press. pp. 258–292.

Laks, A., 2007. Freedom, liberality, and liberty in Plato's Laws. *Social Philosophy and Policy*, 24(2), pp. 130–152.

MacCallum, G., 1967. Negative and positive freedom. *The Philosophical Review*, 76(3), pp. 312–334.

Miller, F. D., 2012 The rule of reason in Plato's *Laws*. In: J. Jacobs, ed. *Reason, religion, and natural law*. Oxford: Oxford University Press. pp. 31–56.

Morrow, G. R., 1960; repr. 1993. *Plato's Cretan city*. Princeton: Princeton University Press.

Muller, R., 1997. *La doctrine platonicienne de la liberté*. Paris: J. Vrin.

Nestle, D., 1967. *Eleutheria: Studien zum Wesen der Freiheit bei den Griechen und im Neuen Testament, vol. 1, Die Griechen*. Tübingen: J. C. B. Mohr.

Pohlenz, M., 1955. *Griechische Freiheit: Wesen und Werden eines Lebensideals*. Heidelberg: Quelle & Meyer.

Popper, K., 1963. *The open society and its enemies, vol. 1, The spell of Plato*. 4th ed. New York: Harper & Row.

Raaflaub, K., 1983. Democracy, oligarchy, and the concept of the "free citizen" in late fifth-century Athens. *Political Theory*, 11(4), pp. 517–544.

Raaflaub, K., 2004. *The discovery of freedom in ancient Greece*. Chicago: University of Chicago Press.

Reeve, C. D. C., 1988. *Philosopher-kings*. Princeton: Princeton University Press.

Samaras, T., 2002. *Plato on democracy*. New York: Peter Lang.

Schofield, M., 2006. *Plato: political philosophy*. Oxford: Oxford University Press.

Stalley, R. F., 1983. *An introduction to Plato's Laws*. Oxford: Blackwell.

Stalley, R. F., 1994. Persuasion in Plato's Laws. *History of Political Thought*, 15(12), pp. 157–177.

Stalley, R. F., 1997–1998. Plato's doctrine of freedom. *Proceedings of the Aristotelian Society*, 98, pp. 145–158.

Taylor, C. C. W., 1999. Plato's totalitarianism. In: G. Fine, ed. *Plato 2: ethics, politics, religion, and the soul*. Oxford: Oxford University Press. pp. 280–296.

Vlastos, G., 1973. Does slavery exist in Plato's *Republic*? In: *Platonic Studies*. Princeton: Princeton University Press. pp. 140–146.

Vlastos, G. 1977. The theory of social justice in the polis in Plato's *Republic*. In: H. North, ed. *Interpretations of Plato*. Leiden: E.J. Brill, pp. 1–40.

Vlastos, G. 1995. *Studies in Greek philosophy. vol. 2, Socrates, Plato, and their tradition*. Princeton: Princeton University Press.

CHAPTER 9

ARISTOTELIAN FREEDOM

DAVID KEYT

1. INTRODUCTION

AN ancient Greek democracy awarded citizenship to any native within its borders who was not a slave. Such a native was called "free," and the quality signified by the term in this context is usually dubbed "democratic" freedom in modern discourse about ancient democracy. Aristotle, just like Plato, is a severe critic of such freedom, and his description of it tracks Plato's sardonic sketch of Greek democracy in the *Republic*. In its detail, systematization, and explicitness, however, Aristotle's description of democratic freedom goes well beyond anything in Plato. Aristotle claims that the exponents of democracy define freedom badly, which implies that a good definition would define a conception of freedom different from the democratic conception. We search in vain in Aristotle's works for such a definition. But a survey of his use of the term "free" and its cognates in the *Politics* and elsewhere reveals that he, again like Plato, champions a conception of freedom that is richer and more refined than democratic freedom. What emerges from this survey is an account of an "aristocratic" freedom that is markedly similar to the account that seems to capture Plato's best thoughts about freedom in the *Laws*.[1]

2. THE CONCEPT OF FREEDOM

Aristotle gives us little help in sorting his various uses of "free," which is unfortunate since freedom turns out to be a surprisingly complex concept. Recent philosophy fortunately comes to our aid. One analysis that is particularly enlightening is that of Gerald MacCallum (1967). MacCallum's key insight is that freedom is a triadic, rather than a dyadic, relation among (i) an agent, (ii) an impediment, and (iii) a goal: agent *a* is free of impediment *i* to pursue goal *g* (1967: 314). Sometimes the triadic character of freedom is not apparent because the impediment or the goal is unspecified. There are two sorts of impediments. For example, if I am driving down a road on a Sunday and come to a broad river across which cars are ferried to the road on the other side every day except Sunday, the impediments to my further progress are the *presence* of the river and the *absence* of an operating ferry. The presence of the river may be called an "obstructing" impediment, and the absence of an operating ferry a "disabling" impediment. One of MacCallum's important insights is that ostensible disagreements over the meaning of freedom often mask what are in fact conflicting interpretations of one or more of the three terms of the triadic relation, especially over what is to count as an impediment (1967: 322). Whether the nonexistence of something (such as an operating ferry) should count as an impediment will be disputed by some.

MacCallum's analysis provides a useful tool in classifying the various uses of "free" and its cognates (i.e., the words on the stem *eleuther-*) in Aristotle's *Politics*. Every occurrence of every word in the treatise signifying freedom can be found by searching the relevant portion of that vast digitized database of Greek literature, the *Thesaurus Linguae Graecae*, and the sense of each of these words at each of its occurrences can be characterized by determining in each instance the three terms of the triadic relation. It will be argued that all the various kinds of freedom that we now proceed to define are mentioned in the *Politics*. (The prepositions "of," "from," and "to" signal agent, impediment, and goal respectively.) Legal freedom is the freedom *of* a human being *from* legally imposed servitude *to* pursue unspecified goals. Personal freedom is the freedom *of* a person *from* unspecified impediments *to* pursue his own goals. Aristotle believes that each person's ultimate goal is happiness and that people conceive happiness differently (*EN* I.5). This leads to different conceptions of personal freedom and in particular to democratic and aristocratic conceptions of personal freedom. Political freedom divides into two subspecies: polis freedom and civic freedom. Polis freedom is the freedom *of* a polis *from* impediments *to* its autonomy, or self-government, imposed by another polis or nation, whereas civic freedom is the freedom *of* a citizen *from* impediments *to* his personal freedom imposed by the political system under which he lives.

3. DEMOCRATIC FREEDOM

Here is Aristotle's description of democratic freedom:

> A fundamental principle of the democratic constitution is freedom. (For this is what people are accustomed to say, on the ground that only in this constitution do they have a share of freedom—which is what they declare every democracy aims at.) One mark of freedom is ruling and being ruled in turn. For democratic justice is having an equal share on the basis of number, not worth. When this is what is just, the mass is necessarily supreme; and whatever seems right to the majority—this is the end (*telos*), and this is what is just. For they say that each of the citizens ought to have an

equal share, so that in democracies it comes about that the needy are more sovereign than the prosperous. For they are a majority, and the opinion of the majority is supreme. This, then, is one sign of freedom, which all democrats take as a mark of the constitution. Another is to live as one wishes. For this they say is the function of freedom, if indeed it is a feature of one who is enslaved not to live as he wishes. This, then, is the second mark of democracy; and from it has come the call not to be ruled, preferably not by anyone, or failing that, [to rule and be ruled] in turn. And in this way the second mark contributes to the freedom based on equality. (VI.2.1317a40–b17)[2]

The connection of the two marks of democratic freedom is not immediately obvious (see, for example, Barnes [2005: 191–193]), but the triadic analysis provides a clue. Take the second mark first. The agents under this analysis are all those counted as free adult male natives under the constitution of a given democracy; the end, or goal, is living as one wishes; and the impediment to this goal is presumably the interference of others. In the passage before us it is said that democrats say that living as one wishes is the function, or *ergon*, of freedom. This fits our analysis perfectly, since for Aristotle the *ergon* of a thing *is* its end, or goal (*De Caelo* II.3.286a8–9, *Metaphysics* III.2.996b7, *Eudemian Ethics* II.1.1219a8). By the triadic analysis, then, the second mark yields a definition of what we may call "democratic personal freedom": a free adult male native under the constitution of a given democracy enjoys democratic personal freedom to the extent that he can live as he wishes without interference from others.

The penultimate sentence of the passage before us explains the connection of the second mark of freedom with the first. From the second mark, Aristotle says, "has come the call not to be ruled, preferably not by anyone, or failing that, [to rule and be ruled] in turn. And in this way the second mark contributes to the freedom based on equality." In Aristotle's view democrats are anarchists at heart; but their heart's desire is tempered by a desire to live with others in a political community, even though this will restrict their freedom of action. What they especially fear is having their personal freedom restricted by fellow citizens acting in the name, and with the coercive power, of the political community. They respond to this fear by introducing the political institution of ruling and being ruled in turn—the first mark of democratic freedom. The two institutions of ruling in rotation and majority rule are said to follow from democratic justice, understood as having an equal share of political power and authority. Ruling in rotation is best taken as an instance of synecdoche—using a part to stand for the whole. As such, it represents the many clever devices used by Greek democrats to equalize political power and authority. In the passage immediately following the one before us Aristotle specifies what these were: sortition, short terms of office, strict limits on the repeated tenure of the same office, pay for services, no qualification for full citizenship other than free status (among adult male natives), election by all from all when an office, especially a military office, requires experience or technical skill (1317b17–1318a3).

The two "marks" of freedom are actually two sorts of freedom, and Aristotle indicates as much when he calls the first mark "the freedom based on equality (*kata ison*)" and says that the second mark contributes (*sumballetai*) to it. What the second mark contributes to the first is a rationale. The second mark explains why democrats seek an equal distribution of political power and authority. They regard the interference of others, particularly that of political officials, as preventing them from living as they like, as making them akin to slaves.[3] They would eliminate such interference altogether if a political community could exist without it. Since this is not possible, they attempt to minimize such interference by distributing it equally among the citizen body, their idea being that if no citizen is a master of other citizens to a greater degree than any other, then no citizen is either a master or a slave of any other. This is to be "civically" free. In the triadic relation of freedom (a) the citizens of a given democracy (g) wish to live as free men, not as virtual slaves, (i) unimpeded by domineering rulers. Thus, by Aristotle's account of the two marks of democratic freedom, a citizen of a Greek democracy regards himself as civically free if, through the equal distribution of political authority and power, no one vested with political authority is his virtual master.

Aristotle is a critic of democracy, and his criticism focuses on the democratic definition of freedom:

> In democracies—those that are held to be especially democratic—the opposite of what is advantageous has come about. The reason for this is that people define freedom badly. For there are two things by which democracy is thought to be defined: the supremacy of the majority, and freedom. For it is held that the just is equality, that equality is the supremacy of whatever seems right to the mass, and that freedom . . . is doing whatever one wishes. Thus in such democracies each man lives as he wishes, and "For what he happens to crave," as Euripides says. But this is bad. For one should not think it slavery to live in harmony with the constitution, but safety. (V.9.1310a25–36)

In this passage it is democracy, rather than freedom, that is said to be defined by two things, namely, majority rule and freedom. What is here called "freedom" is precisely what was counted as the second mark of freedom in the passage quoted earlier. Majority rule was part of the first mark of freedom in that passage, but is here connected not with freedom but with equality. Thus, when Aristotle says people define freedom badly, it is the democratic conception of personal freedom, "doing whatever one wishes," that he has in mind. His objections to such freedom are both moral and political. The moral objection is given later in the *Politics*: "For the license (*exousia*) to do whatever one wants has no power to keep guard over the evil in each man" (VI.4.1318b39–1319a1). The political objection implied by the passage before us is that the exponents of such freedom "think it slavery to live in harmony with the constitution." Why should they think this? Well, to live in harmony with a constitution is to abide by its laws and to support its political institutions. This means that a man will not do anything illegal or insurrectional even if he wishes to: his personal freedom, like that of a slave, will be restricted. The political objection thus takes democratic freedom to be actively, not just at heart, anarchic. This, we should note, is inconsistent with Aristotle's comments on democratic freedom in the passage from VI.2 quoted above: "This [i.e., democratic personal freedom], then, is the second mark of democracy; and from it has come the call not to be ruled, [i] preferably not by anyone, or [ii] failing that, [to rule and be ruled] in turn" (1317b13–16). Aristotle's objection highlights the first disjunct and ignores the second.

We expect Aristotle to say that it is not slavery to live in harmony with the constitution, but freedom. What he says instead is that it is safety (*sōtēria*). This reflects the high value he puts on safety in legal and constitutional matters. He says in one place that "the safety of a polis resides in its laws" (*Rhetoric* I.4.1360a20) and in another that "the safety of the community is the function of its citizens, and the community is the constitution" (III.4.1276b28–29). In any case, what Aristotle refrains from asserting the Greek democrat declares. For the elaborate devices for equalizing political power and authority that constitute the first mark of democratic freedom are designed to protect democratic personal freedom. Contrary to what Aristotle implies, the Greek democrat believes that it is not slavery to live in harmony with a democratic constitution but freedom.

We need to understand democratic freedom for two reasons. First of all, it allows us to understand what Aristotelian aristocratic freedom is reacting to. Secondly, the two components of democratic freedom suggest a template for a description of aristocratic freedom. We need such a template since Aristotle provides no systematic account of aristocratic freedom comparable to his account of democratic freedom. We must search among the remarks favorable to freedom scattered about in his works for intimations of two marks of aristocratic freedom, one defining aristocratic personal freedom and the other specifying the civic institutions designed to foster it.

4. NATURAL FREEDOM

Aristotle says that "he who, being human, is by nature not his own but another's is by nature a slave" (I.4.1254a14–15). Who in Aristotle's view are these people who are by nature not their own but another's? They include anyone whose psyche completely lacks the deliberative part (I.13.1260a12) and who "shares in reason to the extent of apprehending it but without possessing it" (I.5.1254b22–23). Aristotle thinks that such people, lacking foresight, will perish without someone to look out for them. Now, given that they wish to survive, that the impediment to their survival is their lack of a deliberative capacity, and that the only way to remove this impediment is to enslave themselves to someone with that capacity, then slavery for such people is safety (I.2.1252a30–34)—indeed, it is a sort of freedom! Except for the very last step, a step implied but never taken, this line of reasoning accurately portrays Aristotle's train of thought: he thinks "there is a certain mutual benefit and mutual friendship" between natural master and natural slave and that natural slavery, unlike legal slavery, does not, or at least should not, rest on force (I.6.1255b12–15).

Aristotle explains that "a person is another's who, being human, is an article of property; and an article of property is a tool for action and separable from its owner" (I.4.1254a15–17). Several comments are in order. First of all, the notion that one person can be the property, or possession, of another *by nature* assumes, controversially, that some of a man's possessions may belong to him by nature (and not just by law or convention). This is indeed Aristotle's view. Natural slavery is just one instance of a general type of natural property (I.8.1256b7–26). Secondly, to conceive of a natural slave as a tool for action (*praxis*) rather than production (*poiēsis*) (1254a5–8) is to conceive of him as a body servant rather than as a craftsman's assistant. His place is in the household, not in the shop or factory. This perhaps explains why Aristotle never considers any way of dealing with a person who lacks a capacity for deliberation other than enslavement. He was apparently unable to conceive of a household that consisted of anyone beyond family and slaves (I.3.1253b4–7). A final point, which will become important later, is that the slave, as a piece of property, serves the interest of its owner: mastership (*despoteia*), Aristotle says, "rules in the interest of the master . . . and only incidentally in that of the slave (for it is not possible for the mastership to be preserved if the slave is destroyed)" (III.6.1278b34–37). The opposite of the person who is a slave by nature is the person who is free by nature (I.5.1255a1–2, b5, 7). Such a person possesses what the natural slave lacks, a capacity to deliberate.

The notions of natural slavery and natural freedom are the root of Aristotle's distinction between rule of a master (of slaves) and political rule (of naturally free men)—between *despotikē archē* and *politikē archē* (I.7.1255b16–18). This distinction between different kinds of rule, which Aristotle was the first to mark (I.1.1252a7–13), will play a leading role in our analysis below.[4]

5. ARISTOCRATIC PERSONAL FREEDOM

We get an intimation of Aristotle's conception of personal freedom by conjoining two passages in the *Politics*. At the very end of the treatise Aristotle distinguishes two sorts of audience at a musical festival, "one free (*eleutheros*) and educated, the other coarse and composed of artisans, laborers, and other such," and goes on to characterize the souls, or psyches, of the latter as "warped from their natural state" (VIII.7.1342a18–23). At the beginning of the treatise he says that what is natural and beneficial is for the affective, or desiring, part of the psyche to be ruled by the part that has reason (I.5.1254b6–9). We can infer from these two passages together that a man who enjoys the sort of freedom that Aristotle favors has a psyche in which reason rules desire.[5] Such freedom, it should be noted, is predicated of the man, not of his psyche. This point reflects the fact that Aristotle treats the soul as a form, or complex capacity, of a human being, and attributes actions not to the soul but to the human being by means of the soul: "It would be better perhaps not to say that the soul pities or learns or thinks, but that the human being (*anthrōpon*) does so by means of the soul" (*De Anima* I.4.408b13–15).

Aristotle's conception of personal freedom is appropriately labeled "aristocratic." The free audience mentioned above is educated and listens to more refined music than the audience of artisans, laborers, and others of the same ilk (VIII.7.1342a18–28). Since music is provided for these artisans and laborers as well as for the free and would not be provided for slaves, we may infer that these artisans and laborers are legally free even though they do not qualify as citizens of Aristotle's ideal polis (see VII.9.1328b39–40). But even if they were citizens of the polis they inhabit, which would have to be a broad-based democracy to include them among the citizenry (VI.4.1319a24–30), they would not be "free" in the sense in which the educated audience is free. Thus, Aristotle is attributing to the free audience a freedom that goes beyond and is superior to both legal and democratic freedom.

In a similar vein Aristotle distinguishes tasks (*erga*) that are free from those that are unfree, the unfree being those that "make the body or the mind of free men useless for the practices and activities of virtue" (VIII.2.1337b5–11). Think of metallurgy and the smith. Aristotle also distinguishes the useful and the necessary from the noble, or the fine (*to kalon*) (VII.1.1323b12, 14.1333a32–33, 36, b1–3; VIII.3.1338a31–32), and associates the latter with the free and the former with the unfree. Thus, Aristotle says that "there is a kind of education in which sons must be educated not because it is useful or necessary but because it is suitable for a free man (*eleutherion*[6]) and noble" (VIII.3.1338a30–32), and that "to search everywhere for the useful is least suited to men who are great souled and free (*eleutherois*[7])" (1338b2–4). In all of these passages Aristotle is advancing a view of freedom that is much more robust than legal or democratic freedom.

Aristotle gives us an idea of what the life of a free man (*ho bios tou eleutherou*) (VII.3.1325a19–20, 24) will be like under his more robust conception of freedom when he discusses the end, or goal, of his ideal city in *Politics* VII.1–3. "It is evident," he says, "that the best constitution is necessarily that order under which anyone whatsoever could act best and live blessedly" (2.1324a23–25). However, there is disagreement over what form the best life takes: is it the political life or the philosophical life (1324a25–35)? Aristotle's discussion takes the form of a debate between proponents of the two lives with Aristotle himself as the judge. Each side argues that the opposing way of life is inimical to virtue and happiness. "Some reject political offices as unsuitable because they take the life of the free man to be different from the political life and most choiceworthy of all, others think that the latter is best; for it is impossible for the inactive man to act well, but acting well and happiness are the same" (3.1325a18–23). Aristotle's verdict is that what each of them says is partly right and partly wrong. He considers first the case presented by the opponents of the political life (1325a23–31). They are right, on the one hand, to affirm that "the life of a free man is better than that of a master [of slaves]." "This is true," Aristotle says, "for there is nothing especially dignified in using a slave as a slave; for the giving of orders about necessities has no share of the noble" (1325a24–27). Aristotle accepts here that the life of a free man involves the performance of noble actions (see VIII.2.1337b19–20). We were told earlier that "[i]t is impossible for those who do not do noble things (*ta kala*) to act nobly (*kalōs*); and no deed, either of a man or a polis, without virtue and practical wisdom is noble (*kalon*)" (VII.1.1323b31–33). This implies in turn that the life of a free man is the life of virtuous activity. The opponents of the political life are wrong, on the other hand, "to believe that every kind of rule is rule by a master; for the rule over free men is no less removed from the rule over slaves than being free by nature [is removed] from being a slave by nature" (VII.3.1325a27–30).[8] Ruling over free men, unlike ruling over slaves, is a noble activity. Aristotle offers a similar assessment of the case against the philosophical life (1325a31–b29). The opponents of the philosophical life contend that such a life is inactive whereas happiness is acting well (1325a21–23). Aristotle accepts the point about happiness but denies that the philosophical life is inactive: "it is not necessary for an active life to involve others, as some think, nor for those thoughts alone to be active that are pursued for the sake of what issues from the acting; but much more so are the contemplations and thoughts that are ends in themselves and for their own sake" (1325b16–21). Although Aristotle does not draw an explicit conclusion, his remark that each side is partly right and partly wrong points to the conclusion that the best life is the life of a free man, that the life of a free man is the life of virtuous activity, and that the life of virtuous activity is specifically the life of politics and philosophy (I.7.1255b35–37; VII.2.1324a29–32, 15.1334a22–34).[9]

The concept of leisure (scholē) is closely associated with freedom. For instance, Aristotle approves of the traditional view that music is a leisurely pastime of free men (VIII.3.1338a21–24). Leisurely activity (scholazein) involves pleasure, happiness, and blessed living, and is done for its own sake (1338a1–6). Unleisurely activity (ascholia), often translated as 'occupation' or 'business', is carried out for the sake of something one does not yet possess; it includes working at a craft and work done for wages, which, Aristotle maintains, debase the mind of free men and deprive it of leisure (2.1337b8–15). Though closely related, leisure and freedom are distinct: leisurely activity is unimpeded noble activity, whereas freedom in the aristocratic sense is the ability and the opportunity to engage in leisurely activity.

Even though leisure (scholē) goes along with aristocratic freedom (VIII.3.1338a21–24), the free man leads a highly structured life: "[I]n a household the free men have the least opportunity to act haphazardly, but all things or most things have been ordained for them, whereas the slaves and the animals pay little heed to the common interest, and for the most part do act haphazardly" (Metaphysics XII.10.1075a19–22).

The agents of aristocratic personal freedom are adult males who are free by nature; their goal is a life of politics and philosophy; and the impediments blocking this goal are lack of natural aptitude, education, wealth, and opportunity. In Aristotle's view a man enjoys aristocratic personal freedom to the extent that he is able to devote himself to politics and philosophy in virtue of his natural aptitudes, education, wealth, and opportunity.

6. Aristocratic Civic Freedom

This leads directly to the question whether Aristotle has a corresponding conception of civic freedom. Some have thought not. The distinguished Danish scholar Mogens Herman Hansen claims that in the Politics Aristotle betrays no serious interest in the concept of political (i.e., civic) freedom (Hansen 2013: 79)—that he seems "to have had no problem rejecting democratic freedom as a mistaken ideal without developing an alternative understanding of political freedom" (2013: 96). It will be argued that, contrary to Hansen, one can find passages in the *Politics* where Aristotle, in developing his own ideas, transfers the free–slave opposition into the political realm, unmistakably uses "free" (*eleutheros*) to signify civic freedom, and develops an elaborate account of such freedom.

The concept of civic freedom makes its first appearance in *Politics* III.6 in connection with Aristotle's division of constitutions into "correct" and "deviant." Aristotle prepares the ground for this division by discussing once more[10] the relation of a head of a household to his wife, children, and slaves (1278b30–1279a8). This time[11] he distinguishes mastership (*despoteia*), which deals with slaves, from household management (*oikonomikē*), which deals with wife and children, and makes the point that rule over slaves is primarily for the advantage of the master and only incidentally for that of the slave, whereas rule over wife and children is primarily for the advantage of wife and children and only incidentally for that of the husband and father. He then transfers this distinction to the political realm (1279a8–21), and distinguishes "correct" from "deviant" constitutions according to whether rule under them seeks the common advantage or solely the advantage of the rulers. The reason deviant constitutions are so called, Aristotle explains, is that "they are despotic (*despotikai*), whereas the polis is a community of the free (*tōn eleutherōn*)" (1279a21). It is my contention that the free spoken of here are not just those with free status but those who are civically free. This, of course, requires argument.

We can begin by recalling Aristotle's distinction between despotic rule (*despotikē archē*) and political rule (*politikē archē*). Originally the former was defined as rule over natural slaves, the latter as rule over the naturally free (I.7.1255b16–18). Thus, when Aristotle says that deviant constitutions are *despotikai*, he must be speaking metaphorically.[12] The citizens under every constitution, even a deviant one, are legally free (and presumably free by nature), and do not have masters (*despotai*) literally. But if the rulers under a deviant constitution are metaphorically masters of their subjects, their subjects are metaphorically slaves.

We find this metaphorical language of master and slave in two notable passages. In the first Aristotle describes the relation between those citizens of a polis who are favored by fortune and those who are not. He claims that the fortunate become arrogant, and, though they know how to rule, never learn how to be ruled, whereas those upon whom fortune frowns become submissive and, though they know how to be ruled, never learn how to rule. The result, he says, is "a polis of masters and slaves, not of free men (*eleutherōn*)" (IV.11.1295b13–23; see also II.9.1274a17–18). In the second passage Aristotle describes a tyrant's suppression of his subjects through intimidation, humiliation, and expropriation: "It is characteristic of a tyrant to delight in no man who is dignified or free (*eleutherō(i)*). For the tyrant thinks he alone is worthy to be a person of that sort; and the man who matches his dignity, or acts like a free man (*eleutheriazōn*), takes away the superiority and the mastery (*despotikon*) of his tyranny" (V.11.1314a5–10).

Let us now return to Aristotle's statement that deviant constitutions "are despotic (*despotikai*), whereas the polis is a community of the free (*tōn eleutherōn*)" (1279a21). Who are the free of whom Aristotle speaks? They are the opposite of metaphorical slaves. This does not mean that they are free metaphorically. For a metaphorical slave is not literally, or properly (*kuriōs*), a slave; but the opposite of such a slave *is* literally free. The opposite of a metaphorical slave is a man who is superlatively, or truly, free—a man whose freedom exceeds legal freedom and free status. (As we have already remarked, all citizens under all constitutions, whether correct or deviant, enjoy free status.) The appropriate rule over such men, the opposite of the rule by metaphorical slave masters, is true political rule. Aristotle usually avoids using "political rule" in this narrow sense, preferring the expression "rule over the (truly) free" (III.4.1277b15–16, 17.1288a11; VII.14.1333b27–29); but in one passage at least (VII.2.1324a35–38) he does contrast "politically" (*politikōs*) with "despotically" (*despotikōs*) while using the latter adverb metaphorically, thus giving the former adverb the narrow sense.

One interpretative problem remains. When Aristotle says that deviant constitutions "are despotic, whereas the polis is a community of the free," he implicitly denies that a polis with a despotic constitution *is* a polis. How can that be? The answer is that the implicit denial brings with it an implicit qualification of "polis." It must be Aristotle's view that a polis with a despotic constitution is only a so-called polis, not a polis "truly so called" (for which see III.9.1280b7–8).

Since the true freedom of which we have been speaking is the freedom of a citizen with respect to the political system under which he lives, it seems appropriate to call it "civic" freedom.

The next question concerns Aristotle's characterization of civic freedom. We can begin by considering his notion of the rule of a master of slaves. Such rule has three primary features. First of all, it is rule with a view to the advantage of the master and only incidentally with a view to the advantage of the slave (III.6.1278b32–37). Secondly, if it is rule over legal, as distinct from natural, slaves, it is based on force (I.3.1253b20–23, 6.1255b12–15). Finally, though Aristotle finds this point too obvious to note, it is continuous rather than alternating rule: master and slave never trade places. Rule over the free—political rule—is just the opposite. First of all, it is rule that seeks the common advantage, rather than the advantage of the rulers (III.61279a17–19; VII.14.1333a3–6). Secondly, such rule is willingly accepted. This feature is stressed when Aristotle distinguishes kingship from tyranny (III.14.1285a25–29, b8, b21–22; V.10.1313a5–6). Thirdly and finally, such rule is alternating, rather than continuous, whenever rulers and ruled are equals in the appropriate respect (II.2.1261a30–b5; VII.3.1325b7–8, 14.1332b25–27): "it is impossible," Aristotle remarks, "for those who are able to use force and to resist to endure being ruled continuously" (VII.9.1329a9–11).

Given that political rule has these three features, which of them defines civic freedom? It is interesting that each of them has found a champion among modern scholars. According to W. L. Newman, "Aristotle's view is that the governed are free when the government is exercised for their benefit" (1887: I, 246). Similarly, R. G. Mulgan, appealing to I.12.1259a39–40 and VII.14.1333a3–6, contends that Aristotle defines freedom "in terms of rule in the interest of the ruled" (1970: 98). In opposition to this interpretation Hansen claims that in distinguishing political rule from despotic rule,

Aristotle means only to distinguish rule over free men, meaning "citizens," from rule over slaves (2013: 88). But this seems wrong. "Rule over free men" cannot here amount simply to "rule over citizens," because Aristotle also maintains that deviant constitutions involve despotic rule of one or more citizens over other citizens (see III.6.1279a20–21). The second feature is championed by Roderick Long, who maintains that Aristotle at V.9.1310a30–36 rejects the democratic conception of freedom as living as one wishes as base and equates freedom instead with willing subjection to the constitution (1996: 795). In opposition to this way of reading the passage Hansen points out that it states that "one should not deem it slavery, but rather preservation (*sōtēria*) [*not* freedom], to live according to the constitution." So Aristotle cannot be intending here to offer a definition of freedom (Hansen 2013: 89). Hansen's point is well taken, but Long's passage is more apposite when combined with the passages cited above that use willing subjection as the mark that distinguishes kingship from tyranny, rule over the free from rule over virtual slaves. With respect to the third feature Peter Liddel argues that Aristotle's conception of political freedom consists in the principle of ruling and being ruled in turn, and that his conception has this much in common with the democratic conception (2007: 325–331; see also Kraut [2002: 452 n. 35]). Hansen rejects this view on the grounds that in his critique of democratic freedom Aristotle rejects rotation in office because it depends on the democratic principle of arithmetical equality (VI.2.1317b3–10, 16–17) (2013: 90). However, Hansen does not mention the passages cited at the end of the last paragraph, in particular VII.14.1332b25–27, which applies to Aristotle's own ideal constitution: "it is evident that for many reasons it is necessary for all to share alike in ruling and being ruled by turns."

This diversity of interpretation illustrates Aristotle's adage that everyone has a part of truth, but no one the whole (*Metaphysics* II.1.993a30–b5). Each interpretation captures a part, but only one part, of Aristotle's conception of civic freedom. This is evident from the fact that the three features are not independent. For rule to be willingly accepted it must be in the common interest and (among equals) alternating rather than continuous. Thus, Aristotle says that the rule of a monarch who rules "for his own advantage, not that of the ruled . . . is borne unwillingly, since none of the free willingly endures such rule" (IV.10.1295a19–23).[13]

So far this characterization of civic freedom is perfectly general. Nothing in it need be rejected by a democrat. Whether the civic freedom so characterized is democratic or aristocratic depends upon how (i) equality and (ii) the common advantage (*to koinon sumpheron*) are specified. The common advantage will presumably include or involve the fostering of personal freedom, specified as either democratic or aristocratic, among the citizenry. Equality can also be specified in either of two ways—arithmetically or proportionally (V.1.1301b29–35). Democrats distribute political rights on the basis of arithmetical equality, counting every man of free status equal to every other, whereas aristocrats distribute them on the basis of proportional equality, evaluating each man according to his moral worth. It is important to note, however, that democratic civic freedom so specified will be enjoyed only in an egalitarian, not a proletarian, democracy. A "proletarian" democracy is a democracy in which the poor use their superior numbers and the principle of majority rule to virtually disenfranchise the rich—in which, as

Aristotle says, "the needy are more sovereign than the prosperous" (VI.2.1317b8–9). Aristotle regards such a democracy as deviant (III.7.1279b4–10) and hence despotic. An "egalitarian" democracy—"what is held to be most of all a democracy" (VI.2.1318a5–6)—is a democracy in which the despotic majority of a proletarian democracy is replaced by fluctuating majorities of rich and poor, the majority that rules on one issue being different from the majority that rules on another (see IV.4.1291b30–38, VI.2.1318a3–10).

The aristocratic understanding of equality and the common advantage is totally different from the democratic. Consider first the common advantage. In Aristotle's view "the best life, both separately for each individual and collectively for poleis, is the life of virtue sufficiently equipped to partake of virtuous actions" (VII.1.1323b40–1324a2). Thus, a constitution promotes the common advantage in Aristotle's view if it promotes the best life for each and every citizen, and in order to do so it must secure the external goods such as education and property for each and all. This strong requirement is supported by the following passage: "A polis is excellent by reason of the citizens who share in the constitution being excellent; and for us all the citizens share in the constitution. This, then, we must investigate, how a man becomes excellent. For even if it is possible for all the citizens to be excellent, without each being so individually, the latter is more choiceworthy; for 'all' follows from 'each'" (VII.13.1332a32–38). Here Aristotle distinguishes two states of affairs: one in which the citizens are "all" (collectively) virtuous even though some of them are not; and one in which each and every citizen is virtuous. And he regards the latter as superior. This argument sets the stage for his discussion of the education appropriate for a free man (VIII.2.1337b4–15), and the clear implication is that such an education should be provided for all of the citizens. He makes a similar argument that property should belong to the citizens who are described as "craftsmen of virtue" (VII.9.1329a17–26). These arguments all proceed from his basic assumption about the end of the ideal constitution: "For happiness necessarily belongs with virtue, and we must call a polis happy looking not to a particular part of it but looking to all the citizens" (1329a22–24).

A polis will be civically free in the aristocratic sense, then, to the extent that its institutions remove the impediments to a life devoted to politics and philosophy for each and every citizen and allow for equal political participation by equally virtuous citizens where the impediments that need to be removed are unfavorable political institutions, lack of moral and intellectual education, and insufficient material resources.

7. POLIS FREEDOM

The comments in the *Politics* about polis freedom, the freedom of a polis from external domination, are sparse and easily missed. Given the threat to polis freedom posed by the rise of Macedon during the period in which the treatise was written—the assassination of Philip II, the father of Alexander the Great, is mentioned at V.10.1311b1–3—it is surprising that Aristotle has so little to say on the subject. We find only one passage in the *Politics* in which a word on the root *eleuther-* is used in connection with the external freedom of a political community. Aristotle says that Codrus, a legendary king of Athens, and Cyrus the Great, the founder of the Persian Empire, became kings by conferring benefits on their cities or nations: Codrus "by preventing their enslavement in war," Cyrus "by setting them free (*eleutherōsantes*) [of the Medes]" (V.10.1310b36–38). Though Aristotle mentions polis freedom explicitly just this once, there can be no doubt that he regards it as a prime goal of every polis. He gives bravery in battle pride of place in his catalogue of moral virtues, assumes that every polis needs an armed force (IV.4.1291a6–9, VII.8.1328b7 10), and discusses the advisability of building fortified walls for defense (VII.11.1330b32–1331a18). Rather than speaking of polis freedom he speaks of avoiding its opposite, polis enslavement. We gain some understanding of Aristotle's conception of polis freedom from the following passage, heavily laden with mention of enslavement, on the three aims of war. Like most of the *Politics*, it is addressed to those wielding power, rather than to those subject to it. "One should pay attention to military training," Aristotle says, "not for the sake of this—in order that men may enslave (*katadoulōsōntai*) those who do not deserve it—but, first, in order that they themselves will not be enslaved (*douleusōsin*) to others; then so that they may seek hegemony (*hēgemonian*) for the benefit of the ruled, but not for the sake of mastery (*despoteias*) over all; and, third, to be master (*despozein*) over those who deserve to be enslaved (*douleuein*)" (VII.14.1333b38–1334a2; see also 6.1327a40–b6). The third aim refers to the capture of natural slaves (I.8.1256b23–26), and the first to the use of military power to prevent enslavement, or, what comes to the same thing, to preserve polis freedom. The second speaks of hegemony, the military and political dominance of one polis over others. Athens and Sparta were hegemons (leaders) of rival hegemonies during the Peloponnesian War. Consonant with his distinction between correct and deviant constitutions, Aristotle distinguishes a hegemony for the benefit of the ruled from a hegemony for the sake of mastery, and makes it clear in other places in the *Politics* that he thinks the Athenian and Spartan hegemonies were of the latter sort (IV.11.1296a32–36, V.7.1307b22–24). The former sort are apparently as rare as poleis with correct constitutions. What is significant for our purposes is the implication that in Aristotle's view one polis can be a hegemon, or leader, of other poleis without exercising mastery over them, that is to say, without enslaving them and destroying their freedom.

8. CONCLUSION

In discussing and deploying the concept of freedom Aristotle for the most part follows and builds upon what he finds in Plato. He shares Plato's dim view of democratic freedom—though his analysis of such freedom is more detailed and systematic than anything in Plato—and along with Plato speaks of a freedom that is more demanding than democratic freedom. His description of this "aristocratic" freedom, both personal and civic, is also congruent with Plato's. The life of the aristocratically free man, by both accounts, is a highly structured life of virtuous activity. And the characterization of aristocratic civic freedom that can be gleaned from the *Politics* mirrors the one that can be similarly gleaned from Plato's *Laws*. For Aristotle citizens enjoy true civic freedom if they live under rule that (i) seeks the common advantage, (ii) is willingly accepted, and (iii) is alternating, rather than continuous, whereas in the *Laws* citizens enjoy such freedom when they (i) are ruled in the common interest of the whole polis, (ii) obey willingly, and (iii) are free from enslavement to those in power. Aristotle goes beyond Plato, however, in sharply distinguishing political rule—the rule over the truly free— from despotic rule—the rule over virtual slaves.

Due to their radically different psychological theories the two philosophers are fur thest apart on the subject of psychological freedom. Plato conceives of the soul and its parts as agents which in their relations to each other can be master or slave, free or bound. When in the *Laws* he implicitly distinguishes personal freedom—freedom of an incarnate soul—from psychological freedom—freedom of the soul in itself—he opens conceptual space between the two notions. Psychological freedom would seem to be a necessary, but not a sufficient, condition of personal freedom: a man who is psychologically free in the Platonic sense might be in chains or enslaved. Aristotle, for his part, treats the soul as a suite of capacities of a human being and attributes actions to the human by means of the soul, thus leaving no conceptual room for a psychological freedom distinct and separate from personal freedom.

Returning finally to democratic freedom, we can use MacCallum's triadic analysis of freedom in combination with the distinction between obstructing and disabling impediments to see how democratic freedom differs basically from aristocratic freedom. Democratic freedom focuses only on obstructing impediments, namely, the interference of others, whereas aristocratic freedom focuses on both obstructing and disabling impediments, the latter being the lack of material resources and of a moral and intellectual education.[14]

NOTES

1. The discussion of democratic freedom in this chapter draws heavily from Keyt (1999). The rest of the chapter is the fruit of close collaboration with Fred D. Miller, Jr. All translations of Aristotle are my own.
2. Unless otherwise indicated all references are to the *Politics*.
3. In the *Metaphysics* Aristotle says that "the man is free . . . who exists for the sake of himself and not of another" (I.2.982b26), and in the *Rhetoric* he says that "it is the mark of a free man not to live by reference to another" (I.9.1367a32–33).
4. For a critical analysis of Aristotle's doctrine of natural slavery see Keyt (2006: 406–407).
5. This is much more than natural freedom. Natural freedom is the mere *capacity* to deliberate, whereas freedom as understood here is this capacity in a *developed* state. Aristotle makes a similar distinction in the *De Anima* between two senses in which somebody is a "knower": in the first, he is the sort of being (namely, a human) capable of acquiring knowledge; in the second, he "is capable of exercising knowledge whenever he wishes if nothing external prevents him" (II.5.417a24–28). This distinction seems to be overlooked by Walsh, who takes Aristotle "to hold that only the wealthy, free from material necessity, could be *eleutheroi phusei*" (1997: 506).

6. The term *eleutherios* ("suitable for a free person") is derived from *eleutheros* ("free") by paronymy (see *Categories* 1.1a13–16). The close connection between the two terms is obscured by those translators who render *eleutheros* as "free" and *eleutherios* as "liberal."

7. The reading of all the manuscripts. Ross, unnecessarily, accepts Susemihl's emendation *eleutheriois*.

8. See the final paragraph of the preceding section.

9. Aristotle never mentions the *life* of a free man in his ethical treatises. But in connection with the virtue of ready wit he does speak of the (aristocratically) free man (*ho eleutherios*: sometimes rendered as "the well-bred man") (*Nicomachean Ethics* IV.8.1128a20; see also 1128a18, 26, 32), and he counts freehandedness (*eleutheriotēs*: often translated as "liberality") as one of the moral virtues (IV.1). Freehandedness is a virtue concerned with the getting and the giving of wealth, especially the latter, and is the mean between the two vices of prodigality and tightfistedness (*aneleutheria*: literally "unfreedom"). The free(handed) man (*ho eleutherios*), in pursuit of the noble, gives the right amount to the right person at the right time (1120a24–27), whereas the tightfisted man (*ho aneleutheros*: literally "the unfree man") is either unscrupulous in getting or niggardly in giving or both (1121b12–1122a16). The tightfisted man is well known to readers of Theophrastus's *Characters*: four of its thirty character sketches (VI, X, XXII, XXX), including one entitled Tightfistedness (XXII), are devoted to him.

   The use of the words on the root *eleuther-* in *Nicomachean Ethics* IV.1 and IV.4 shows that their sense is highly sensitive to context. Aristotle's definition of *eleutherios* in IV.1 does not fit the occurrences of the term in IV.4 let alone those in the *Politics*. His description of the freehanded man can at best be taken as a miniature portrait, or cameo, of the aristocratically free man. The impediments to freehandedness are lack of material resources and lack of moral education.

10. Discussed earlier in *Politics* I.3, 7, 12.

11. Previously mastership was counted as a part of household management (I.3.1253b1–4, 12.1259a37–39).

12. Metaphor is discussed at length in *Poetics* 21. The metaphor in question is what Aristotle calls a metaphor by analogy. When *A* is to *B* as *C* is to *D*, then one can put *A* in place of *C* or *C* in place of *A* (1457b16–19). Thus, since old age is to life as evening is to day, one can speak of old age as the evening of life or evening as the old age of day (1457b22–25). In the case in point, since the rule of a master over slaves stands to the domestic realm as the self-aggrandizing rule of officials stands to the political realm, one can speak of the latter as despotic rule.

13. This passage suggests a connection between being free (*eleutheros*) and acting willingly (*hekōn*). The notion of the willing (or voluntary) is discussed in *Nicomachean Ethics* III.1–5 and *Eudemian Ethics* II.6–11, which have inspired a prodigious secondary literature. On this topic, which is beyond the purview of this chapter, see Bobzien (2014) and Meyer (2006) for recent overviews.

14. I am indebted to my wife, Christine Keyt, for carefully reading and critiquing the penultimate draft of this chapter and to Jeremy Reid for lively discussion of many of the issues related to democratic and aristocratic freedom with Fred Miller and me in the seminar on Platonic and Aristotelian freedom that led to this chapter and the preceding one on Platonic freedom.

References

Barnes, J., 2005. Aristotle and political liberty. In: R. Kraut and S. Skultety, eds. *Aristotle's Politics: critical essays*. Lanham, MD: Rowman & Littlefield. pp.185–202.

Bobzien, S., 2014. Choice and moral responsibility (NE III.1-5). In: R. Polansky, ed. *The Cambridge companion to Aristotle's Nicomachean Ethics*. Cambridge: Cambridge University Press. pp.81–109.

Hansen, M. H., 2013. Democratic freedom and the concept of freedom in Plato and Aristotle. In: *Reflections on Aristotle's Politics*. Copenhagen: Museum Tusculanum Press. pp.71–96.

Keyt, D., 1999. *Aristotle: Politics: Books V and VI*. Oxford: Oxford University Press.

Keyt, D., 2006. Aristotle's political philosophy. In: M. L. Gill and P. Pellegrin, eds. *A companion to ancient philosophy*. Oxford: Blackwell Publishing. pp.393–412.

Kraut, R., 2002. *Aristotle: political philosophy*. Oxford: Oxford University Press.

Liddel, P., 2007. *Civic obligation and individual liberty in ancient Athens*. Oxford: Oxford University Press.

Long, R. T., 1996. Aristotle's conception of freedom. *Review of Metaphysics*, 49(4), pp.775–802.

MacCallum, G., 1967. Negative and positive freedom. *The Philosophical Review*, 76(3), pp.312–334.

Meyer, S. S., 2006. Aristotle on the voluntary. In: R. Kraut, ed. *The Blackwell guide to Aristotle's Nicomachean Ethics*. Oxford: Blackwell. pp.137–157.

Mulgan, R. G., 1970. Aristotle and the democratic conception of freedom. In: B. F. Harris, ed. *Auckland classical essays presented to E. M. Blailock*. Auckland: Auckland University Press. pp.95–111.

Newman, W. L., 1887–1905. *The Politics of Aristotle*. 4 vols. Oxford: Clarendon Press.

Walsh, M. M., 1997. Aristotle's conception of freedom. *Journal of the History of Philosophy*, 35(4), pp.495–507.

CHAPTER 10

FREEDOM IN THE SCHOLASTIC TRADITION

EDWARD FESER

THERE are two broad notions of freedom which have been of special interest to philosophers: freedom of the will; and freedom in the political sense that is related to questions about rights, justice, market exchanges, and the like. Scholastic thinkers have commented on both notions, and what they have said about the former is highly relevant to what they say about the latter.

Scholasticism is that tradition of thought whose most illustrious representative is Thomas Aquinas (c. 1225–1274) and whose other luminaries include John Duns Scotus (c. 1266–1308), William of Ockham (c. 1287–1347), and Francisco Suárez (1548–1617), to name only some of the most famous. By no means only a medieval or premodern phenomenon, the Scholastic tradition was carried forward in the twentieth century by Neo-Scholastics like Reginald Garrigou-Lagrange (1877–1964) and Neo-Thomists such as Jacques Maritain (1882–1973) and Etienne Gilson (1884–1978). In contemporary analytic philosophy it finds sympathizers among writers sometimes identified as "analytical Thomists" (Haldane, 2002a; Paterson and Pugh, 2006). The philosophical core of the mainstream of the Scholastic tradition is Aristotelian, with key insights drawn from Neoplatonism but suitably Aristotelianized. Into this philosophical matrix, Scholastic thought embedded Christian theology as it had been shaped by, above all, Augustine. But the focus in this chapter will be on Scholastic philosophical ideas and arguments (as opposed to theological ones) relevant to the topic of freedom.

These ideas are of obvious historical interest, and the renewed attention Aristotelian ethics has received in recent decades indicates that they should be of contemporary interest as well. But since the ideas are not well known, the emphasis in this chapter will be on exposition of the key claims and arguments of the tradition, rather than on novel variations. Still, Thomist sympathies will be evident, and the chapter will indicate the main lines of response a Scholastic might offer to queries and objections likely to be raised by contemporary philosophers.

The approach will be thematic rather than historical, though questions about the historical development of certain ideas will arise in the course of the discussion. The next section will briefly sketch the natural law approach to ethics which provides the moral and metaphysical background to Scholastic discussions of freedom. The subsequent section will present two main conceptions of freedom of the will developed within Scholasticism, associated with Aquinas and Ockham respectively. These different conceptions are associated in turn with two conceptions of natural rights, and the section that follows will, accordingly, discuss how the idea of natural rights enters into Scholastic moral and political thought. The final section will discuss the attitudes that thinkers in the Scholastic tradition have taken toward liberal democracy and the market economy. We will see that, particularly in its Thomist version, the Scholastic tradition developed a conception of political and economic freedom which in some respects represents a middle-ground position between classical liberalism or libertarianism on the one hand, and egalitarian liberalism on the other.[1]

1. Natural Law

For a Scholastic thinker like Aquinas, ethics is grounded in human nature, where "nature" is understood in a broadly Aristotelian way. In particular, Aquinas's natural law theory has its foundation in a metaphysics of *essentialism* which affirms the reality of immanent or built-in *teleology* or *final causality*. The jargon might seem forbidding, but the basic idea is clear and can be illustrated using simple examples. Consider a tree and its characteristic attributes and activities—sinking roots into the ground, drawing in water and nutrients through them, growing leaves which carry out photosynthesis, and so forth. These are ends or outcomes *toward which* the tree tends, what it will do unless somehow prevented (because of damage, disease, or some other defect). They are, accordingly, instances of teleology or finality—directedness toward an end or goal. And these tendencies toward the ends or outcomes in question are not something imposed on the tree from outside, the way a time-telling function is imposed from outside by a watchmaker on the bits of metal that make up a watch. Rather, the tendencies are *inherent in* or *immanent to* the tree, just by virtue of being a tree. That is to say, they flow from the *essence* or *nature* of the tree.

What is true of trees is also true of animals. A lion, for example, will, given its nature, tend to develop traits like sharp teeth and claws, powerful muscles, a thick mane, and so forth; and it will tend toward certain characteristic activities like hunting down prey and (in the case of a lioness) nurturing cubs, and so on. These are the ends or outcomes toward which a lion is directed given its essence.

Now the ends toward which a thing tends given its nature entail an objective standard of goodness or badness. A tree which, due to damage or disease, fails to sink deep roots or grow healthy leaves, is to that extent a bad tree; while a tree which realizes these ends is to that extent good. A lion which, due to disease, injury, or genetic defect, fails to develop strong muscles or to hunt prey or nourish its cubs will to that extent be a bad lion, while a lion which realizes these ends will to that extent be a good lion. So far we are, of course, not talking about *moral* goodness and badness; the claim is not that the sickly tree or lazy lion is wicked or blameworthy. The sense of "good" and "bad" operative here is rather the one that is operative when we speak of a good or bad specimen, a good or bad instance of a kind of thing. It has to do with a thing's success or failure in living up to the standard inherent in the kind of thing it is (cf. Philippa Foot's [2001] notion of "natural goodness").

Moral goodness or badness enters the picture with creatures capable of *freely choosing* whether or not to act in a way that either facilitates or frustrates the ends toward which their nature or essence directs them, and which thereby either promotes or frustrates the realization of what is objectively good for them. Human beings are *rational* animals and for that reason capable of such free action. Moral goodness or badness in human beings involves deliberate choice either to act in a way that facilitates the ends inherent in human nature or to act in a way that frustrates these ends.

What are the ends which define what is good for us? A complete answer would require a systematic study of human nature, but a rudimentary understanding can in principle be had by any human being. Aquinas speaks in this context of the good for us being that toward which we have a *natural inclination*, and which we can know precisely because of the existence of such inclinations (*Summa Theologiae* I-II.94.2). He gives as examples goods common to all things (such as self-preservation), goods common to all animals (such as sexual intercourse and child-rearing), and goods unique to human beings (such as knowing God and living together in society). We know these as goods to be pursued precisely insofar as we are naturally inclined to pursue them—just as a tree tends naturally to grow roots and a lion tends naturally to seek out prey, albeit they do not rationally apprehend these ends as goods the way we do.

It is important to emphasize, though, that a mere deep-seated conscious desire for something does not constitute a "natural inclination" in Aquinas's sense. A sickly tree might grow deformed roots, and a genetically defective lioness might have a tendency to eat rather than nurture her cubs. However deeply ingrained, these are not natural tendencies in the relevant sense, but rather defects or deviations from natural tendencies. Similarly, human beings might as a result of psychological conditioning or genetic defect exhibit inclinations—a predisposition for alcoholism, say—that are not "natural" in the relevant sense, but on the contrary are at odds with the ends that nature has set for us. Alcoholism obviously frustrates the use of reason—our highest and most distinctive attribute—as well as damages bodily health.

How do we know when some tendency really *is* "natural" in the relevant sense, rather than an aberration? There are general principles that can guide us. For example, if a certain tendency is very widespread in living things of a certain kind and is absent only in cases where the thing is damaged and/or where the absence is associated with what on independent grounds we can judge to be dysfunction, then we have good reason to judge that the tendency is natural to things of that kind. Similarly, if a certain tendency is *rare* in things of a certain kind but is also associated with damage and/or with what on independent grounds we can judge to be dysfunction (again, alcoholism would be an example), then we have grounds to count the tendency as a deformity or defect rather than natural in the relevant sense. Thus we are not reduced to the circular reasoning of saying that such-and-such really are natural inclinations because normal members of the kind have them, and those members of the kind are the normal ones because they have such-and-such natural inclinations. For example, it would be ridiculous to allege that only circular reasoning could lead us to say that seeing is a natural tendency of human beings. For not only are working eyeballs almost universal to human beings, but human beings who lack them are severely impaired in their various basic activities, and this lack is also typically the result of fairly easily specifiable damage of a physical or genetic sort. Still, judgments about which inclinations are truly "natural" are fallible, cannot be settled from the armchair, and may require much empirical investigation for their justification (a fact which—contrary to a common caricature—is acknowledged by Scholastic philosophers).[2]

Now the basic imperative that nature has put into us is to pursue good and avoid evil, in the very thin sense that we naturally only ever pursue what we *take to be* in *some* sense good and avoid what we *take to be* in some way bad. Aquinas calls this the "first precept" of the natural law (*Summa Theologiae* I-II.94.2). Even someone who pursues what he believes to be morally bad obeys this precept insofar as he takes the object of his action to be good in some other way. For instance, the drug addict who is ashamed of his addiction but nevertheless buys and uses drugs believes that it would be good to satisfy the craving that he has at that moment.[3]

Practical reasoning, then, has for a natural law theorist like Aquinas the following general structure: (1) *Good is to be pursued and evil to be avoided*; (2) *X is good and Y is evil*; therefore (3) *X is to be pursued and Y avoided*. Aquinas takes (1), the first precept of natural law, to be self-evident (again, given the very thin sense of "good" and "evil" operative in the principle). The values of *X* and *Y* in premise (2), at least for the most fundamental goods and evils, are revealed to us by our natural inclinations (again, in Aquinas's sense of "natural inclination"). For example, our natural inclinations tell us that truth is good and error bad, and given the general structure of moral reasoning it follows that we should pursue truth and avoid error. Of course, many moral questions are much more complicated than that, and even the application of a seemingly straightforward principle like *Pursue truth and avoid error* raises many questions. Natural law ethics as a body of moral theory is the enterprise of working out the complex ramifications of these basic principles in a systematic way.[4]

No doubt the greatest misgiving contemporary philosophers will have about this approach to ethics concerns the ambitious and highly controversial metaphysics it presupposes. Can Aristotelian essentialism and teleology really be defended today, in a way consistent with modern science? Obviously this is not an issue that can be dealt with in any detail here, so the following three points will have to suffice. First, contemporary Thomistic natural law theorists are aware that the metaphysical presuppositions in question require defense, and have tried to provide it.[5] Second, recent years have seen, even among analytic philosophers with no Thomist or natural law ax to grind, a revival of interest in Aristotelian metaphysics.[6] Third, as the examples of Philippa Foot (2001) and Rosalind Hursthouse (1999) indicate, one need not "go the whole hog" metaphysically in order to take a neo-Aristotelian position in ethics. One could, arguably, take on board just *enough* of the Aristotelian conceptual apparatus to do the needed metaethical work, but situate it in the context of a broadly naturalistic metaphysics of the sort which most contemporary philosophers embrace.[7]

2. THE WILL

As this discussion of natural law indicates, for Aquinas, the will is not neutral as to its ends, but rather is naturally directed toward what the intellect apprehends to be good. Since this makes the will in an obvious sense subordinate to the intellect, Aquinas's position is often described as "intellectualist" (as contrasted with the "voluntarist" view that the intellect is subordinate to the will). The intellect, in turn, is naturally directed toward knowing truth. That is *its* end or final cause.

This is associated by Aquinas with a conception of freedom that Servais Pinckaers has characterized as "freedom for excellence" (1995: ch. 15).[8] We are, on this view, freer to the extent that we find it easy to pursue the ends toward which our intellects and wills are naturally directed: the true and the good. Virtues like courage and temperance thus increase our freedom, since they enable us to resist impulses that might lead us into error and vice and thus away from the true and the good. Thus for Aquinas, for someone to be as likely to choose evil as to choose good is not a mark of his will being more free. Indeed, Aquinas makes it clear in the *Summa Theologiae* that in his view, to be as likely to choose evil as to choose good is a mark of *imperfect* freedom, so that "the angels, who cannot sin, enjoy greater freedom of choice than do we, who can."[9]

Compare once again the examples of a tree and a lion. A sapling which is bound with rope or wire, or which is very closely surrounded by debris, will likely exhibit distorted growth patterns. We would naturally say that such a tree is not growing *freely*, precisely because it is being prevented from manifesting the growth pattern toward which it is *naturally* directed. We would also naturally think of a lion kept even in a large cage as not free, whereas we would not necessarily think of a spider kept in the same cage as less than free. The reason is that the lion cannot in such a situation carry out the activities to which it is naturally directed (hunting, etc.) whereas a spider can even in that situation carry out the activities toward which it is naturally directed (catching insects in its web, etc.). Similarly, for Aquinas, human beings are free to the extent that they can pursue the ends toward which they are naturally directed—the true and the good—and restricted in their freedom to the extent they cannot. Vice and ignorance are in this way like fetters or cages.[10]

Now, Ockham's conception of free will is very different, and the difference reflects his very different metaphysical assumptions. Aquinas was a realist vis-à-vis universals. For him, human beings share the same nature, and thus the same natural ends. Hence what is good for one human being is, fundamentally, the same as what is good for every other. For example, if it is good for us by nature (rather than just as a matter of contingent circumstance) to love God and be faithful to our spouses, then this will be true for every human being as such. Combine this thesis with Aquinas's intellectualism, and it follows that even God, whose will reflects what his intellect knows to be good for us, could not command us to hate him or to commit adultery consistent with willing what is good for us.

Ockham, however, is a voluntarist, for whom the will—including the divine will—is prior to the intellect. This led him to resist the idea that there is anything that might put limits on what God could command, which in turn motivated his famous anti-realism about universals, variously interpreted as either nominalist (an outright denial that universals exist) or conceptualist (treating universals as mere constructs of the mind). For if we really did instantiate a universal essence or nature, this would, in the way just described, imply limits on what even God could command us to do, consistent with willing what is good for us. But for Ockham, God *could* in principle command us to do things like committing adultery or even hating him, and if he did so then these things really would be good for us. Hence Aquinas's realism about universals must be rejected.

Morality for Ockham is therefore not a matter of following the natural inclinations that are in us by virtue of our instantiating a universal essence. It is rather a matter of obeying arbitrary divine commands, a system of laws laid down by fiat. Nor, given voluntarism, is the will inherently directed toward the good as grasped by the intellect. *Inherently* the will is directed neither toward good nor toward evil, but is indifferent to both. Contrary to Aquinas, for whom we are freer to the extent that we are oriented to the good, for Ockham our will's freedom manifests itself precisely in being inherently oriented toward neither of any two contraries. Thus, argues Pinckaers, was Aquinas's "freedom for excellence" replaced by Ockham with a "freedom of indifference" (1995: ch. 14). For Ockham that did not mean that morality has no hold on us, but again, this is not because the will is naturally directed toward the good, toward what will fulfill our nature. Morality is rather simply a matter of our will's submitting itself to the dictates of a more powerful, indeed infinite, will.

To Ockham's "freedom of indifference" Pinckaers traces the modern tendencies to divorce morality from human nature and to isolate individual actions from the context of a whole human life and evaluate their moral character in terms of conformity to law rather than conduciveness to virtuous or vicious habits. He also associates with it the modern celebration of "being arbitrary for the sheer pleasure of it" and the "passion for self-affirmation" (1995: 339). We might also see in it the origins of the Hobbesian conception of the state of nature as a war of conflicting wills, and of good and evil as products of the fiat of the sovereign who imposes order on the state of nature—Ockham's voluntarist and nominalist God made mortal.[11]

3. NATURAL RIGHTS

Among writers sympathetic to Aquinas's conception of natural law and the freedom of the will, there has been controversy over the notion of natural rights, precisely because the very idea has been alleged by some of these sympathizers—though by no means all of them—to reflect Ockham's nominalism and voluntarism. Some stage-setting is required in order to understand this controversy.

A key distinction drawn in these disputes is that between *objective right* and *subjective right*. Right in the objective sense is the *object* or aim of justice, and it has to do with the way we ought to act with respect to one another. For objective right to be achieved is for the right thing or the just thing to be done, so that individuals in a society stand in just relationships to one another—as, for example, when an employer pays his employee the wages due him for the services he has rendered. Objective right is a theme of Aristotle's *Nicomachean Ethics*, and it is, uncontroversially, to be found in Aquinas as well (cf. Brett, 1997: ch. 3). Right in the subjective sense is something inhering in the individual *subject*, by which he might demand something from others—for instance, a demand to the effect that others ought to allow one to carry out actions of a certain sort, if one so desires. Subjective right is what we have in mind when we speak of a person "having a right to" such-and-such.[12]

Legal theorist Wesley N. Hohfeld (1946) influentially distinguished four senses in which a person might be said to have a right in the subjective sense:[13]

(i) Person A might have a right in the sense of a *claim* against another person B that B do action X, insofar as B has a duty to A to do X. For example, an employee who has done the work his employer hired him to do for a certain wage has a claim (and thus a "right") against his employer that the employer pay him the wage.[14]

(ii) Person A might have a right in the sense of a *liberty*, vis-à-vis another person B, to do action X, insofar as A does not have a duty to B not to do X. For example, if someone for whom you have never before worked offers you a certain job but you would rather go on vacation than accept this offer of employment, you have a liberty (and thus a "right") to do so.

(iii) Person A might have a right in the sense of a *power*, vis-à-vis another person B, to bring about an obligation in B by virtue of doing an action X. For example, if a father decrees that his child must do his homework before supper, then by virtue of the father's power to make such decrees (to which the father thus has a "right") the child has an obligation to do his homework before supper.

(iv) Person A might have a right in the sense of an *immunity* against B's doing action X insofar as B does not have the power, vis-à-vis A, to do X. For example, if a child decrees that his father allow him to watch television rather than do his homework, the father has an immunity from such decrees (and thus a "right" to ignore them) given that the child has no power to make them.

These four kinds of right might be combined in various ways. For example, your having a property right in a certain object might involve having a *claim* against others that they not take it from you, a *liberty* to do with it what you like, a *power* to allow others to use it only in certain ways, and an *immunity* against others putting limits on how you might use it.

Several prominent writers have claimed that there is a deep incompatibility between objective rights and subjective rights, one which reflects the difference between classical natural law theory as understood by thinkers like Aristotle and Aquinas and modern state of nature theory as articulated by thinkers like Hobbes and Locke. Hence Leo Strauss spoke of a "fundamental change from an orientation by natural *duties* to an orientation by natural *rights*" (1953: 182, emphasis added). Alasdair MacIntyre, in the course of defending an Aristotelian position in ethics, says of subjective rights that "there are no such rights, and belief in them is one with belief in witches and in unicorns" (1984: 69).

Several writers, most prominently Michel Villey, have argued that the notion of subjective rights traces to Ockham's voluntarism and nominalism, and for that reason cannot be reconciled with Thomistic natural law. The idea is that if nominalism is true, then there are no natural relations between individuals of the sort needed to ground objective right. There are just the individuals themselves, with wills inherently "indifferent" to all ends and bound only by whatever law a superior will happens to have imposed by fiat. Subjective rights, on this view, are just the potentially unlimited liberties of action afforded the Ockhamite subject in those areas where a superior will happens not to have imposed a law against such action.[15]

However, as Brian Tierney has argued in an influential critique, Villey's "Manichean" pitting of objective right against subjective rights is simplistic (2001: 30). In fact, according to Tierney, it is not clear that there really is any connection between Ockham's voluntarism and nominalism and his affirmation of subjective rights, and one finds even in Ockham elements of the notion of objective right. Moreover, one finds the notion of subjective rights in thinkers who rejected voluntarism and nominalism. Tierney argues that it can be found in medieval canon law prior to Ockham. The sixteenth-century Thomistic Scholastic writers Francisco de Vitoria and Bartoloméo de Las Casas are commonly interpreted as having developed a doctrine of natural rights in arguing for limits to Spanish power over colonized peoples and in calling for just treatment of the American Indians (Tierney, 2001: ch. 11; cf. Brett, 1997).

Nor, contrary to what followers of Villey suppose, is there any reason to attribute this late Scholastic interest in subjective rights to voluntarist and nominalist corruption of the authentic Thomist tradition. Though Aquinas himself did not have a notion of subjective rights, modern Thomists have plausibly argued that the idea follows from his understanding of natural law, and that subjective rights can be understood precisely as safeguards of "freedom for excellence" rather than "freedom of indifference."[16]

This modern Thomist argument for natural rights goes as follows. We are rationally obliged to pursue what is good for us and to avoid what is bad, where "good" and "bad" are to be understood in terms of the essentialist and teleological metaphysics underlying Scholastic natural law theory. For example, we are obliged to pursue truth and avoid error, to sustain our lives and our health and to avoid what is damaging to them, and so on (ignoring for present purposes the complications and qualifications a fully developed natural law theory would spell out). The force and content of these obligations derive from our nature as human beings.

Now, it is part of that nature that we are *social* animals. We tend naturally to live in communities with other human beings and we depend on them in various ways, both negative (insofar as we need not to be harmed by others) and positive (insofar as we need various kinds of assistance from others). Most obviously, we are related to others by virtue of being parents, children, siblings, grandparents, grandchildren, cousins, and so on. Within the larger societies that collections of families give rise to, other kinds of relationships form, such as that of being a friend, an employee or an employer, a citizen, and so forth. To the extent that some of these relationships are natural to us, their flourishing is part of what is naturally good for us. Hence it is bad for us to fail to do what is necessary for these relationships to flourish.

For example, as Philippa Foot writes, "like lionesses, human parents are defective if they do not teach their young the skills that they need to survive" (2001: 15). For it is part of our nature to become parents, and part of our nature that while we are children we depend on our parents. Thus, it is good for us—not just good for our children, but (since being parents is an end toward which our nature directs us) for *us*—to be good parents and bad for us to be bad parents.[17] And it is good for children to be taken care of by their parents and bad for them to be neglected. (The satisfaction good parents often feel and the sense of failure bad parents feel reflect these facts, but it is important to reiterate that natural law theory does not regard the fluctuating feelings and desires of individuals to be what is most fundamental to an analysis of what is good for them. The commonness of such feelings and desires *reflects* our natural inclination to be good parents—in Aquinas's understanding of a "natural inclination" as our inherent directedness toward a certain end—but it does not *constitute* that inclination.)

Now if it is good for a parent to provide for his or her children, then given that we are obliged to do what is good for us, it follows that a parent has an obligation to provide for them. Similarly, since given their need for instruction, discipline, and the like, it is good for children to obey and respect their parents, it follows that they have an obligation to obey and respect them. But an obligation on the part of a person A to another person B entails a Hohfeldian claim-right on the part of B against A.[18] It follows in turn, then, that children have a Hohfeldian claim-right to be provided for by their parents, and parents have a Hohfeldian claim-right to be obeyed and respected by their children. Since the instruction and discipline of children entail making certain demands of them, parents also have certain Hohfeldian power-rights against their children. Since children are obliged to obey and respect their parents, parents also have certain Hohfeldian immunity-rights and liberty-rights against their children. Of course, various qualifications would need to be made in a more complete treatment of the rights and duties of parents and children. For example, parents have no right to abuse their children; children need a certain degree of liberty of action in order to flourish; a parent might forfeit his rights over his children either voluntarily (by giving a child up for adoption) or involuntarily (by being so abusive that it is in the best interests of the child to be taken from the parent); and so forth. But the basic idea should be clear enough.

Since the obligations that generate the rights in question are obligations under *natural* law (rather than positive law) it follows that they are *natural* rights, grounded not in convention but in human nature. Other obligations we have under natural law toward various other people will similarly generate various other natural rights. At the most general level, we are all obliged to refrain from interfering with others' attempts to fulfill the moral obligations placed on them by natural law. For as Austin Fagothey puts it, "man cannot have such obligations unless he has a right to fulfill them, and a consequent right to prevent others from interfering with his fulfillment of them" (1959: 250). The most *basic* natural right is the right to do what we are obligated to do by the natural law. Hence everyone necessarily has a natural Hohfeldian immunity-right not to be coerced into doing evil. There are also many things that are naturally good for us even if we are not strictly obligated to pursue them, such as having children. This particular example is, according to natural law theory, the basis for the natural Hohfeldian liberty-right to marry. And of course we cannot pursue any good or fulfill any obligation at all if our very lives could be taken from us by others as they saw fit, so that the natural law entails that every human being (or at least every innocent human being) has a natural Hohfeldian immunity-right not to be killed.

If natural law entails the existence of natural rights, it also entails that there are limits on those rights. To be sure, a right to a significant measure of personal liberty seems to be implied by human nature. For given the many inevitable differences between individuals vis-à-vis their interests, talents, upbringing, and other personal circumstances, there are myriad ways in which human beings might concretely realize the capacities and potentials inherent in their common nature, and each person will need to be free to discover for himself which way is best for him. But for the natural law theorist, this freedom cannot be absolute, for while there is much that the natural law permits, there is also much that it forbids as absolutely contrary to the human good, and rights only exist to allow us to fulfill the human good. Thus, as one natural law theorist has put it, "the rights of all men are limited by the *end* for which the rights were given" (Bittle, 1950: 293, emphasis added); and therefore, to cite another, "there can never be a right to that which is immoral. For the moral law cannot grant that which is destructive of itself" (Higgins, 1958: 231). Natural rights have a *teleological* foundation, and cannot exist except where they further the purposes they serve.

However, it is important to emphasize that this does not entail the institution of a totalitarian "morality police." For Aquinas, "human law does not prohibit everything that is forbidden by the natural law," and there are many cases where it would be counterproductive for it to do so (*Summa Theologiae* I-II.96.2). But the limits on the state's power to curb vice have largely to do with considerations of prudence rather than justice. It is not necessarily the case with *all* private vices that it would be strictly unjust to forbid them, since no one has a natural right to indulge in them. For the natural law theorist, the idea of a "right to do wrong" is an oxymoron (cf. Oderberg, 2000a). The main consideration is rather that enforcing such prohibitions may be practically impossible, or may inadvertently do more harm than good.[19]

4. DEMOCRACY AND THE MARKET

Needless to say, the Thomistic approach to natural rights differs from the libertarian natural rights theories of thinkers like Robert Nozick (1974) and Murray Rothbard (1998).[20] Still, the Thomist position is far from authoritarian, and not merely because it does not require that all vice be suppressed by force of law. For one thing, natural rights put absolute limits on what the state may require of its citizens. Though he does not use the language of rights, Aquinas argues that laws that are contrary to the human good are unjust and not binding (*Summa Theologiae* I-II.96.4).

A second consideration is the *principle of subsidiarity*, which modern Thomists have taken to be a concomitant of respect for natural rights. The principle holds that:

> [N]o higher organization should take over work that a lower organization can do satisfactorily. The higher does not exist to absorb or extinguish the lower but to supplement and extend it. Otherwise the rights given by nature to the individual and to the family, and man's freedom to organize for lesser pursuits within the state, are rendered meaningless. (Fagothey, 1959: 394)

The idea is not unrelated to F. A. Hayek's influential thesis that the knowledge relevant to making social decisions is largely dispersed, so that such decisions are best made, where possible, at the level of individuals and private organizations rather than by centralized governmental authorities.[21]

A third element in the Scholastic tradition which runs counter to authoritarianism is the notion that governmental authority derives in part from the consent of the governed, as developed by Scholastic writers like Robert Bellarmine in his *De Laicis* (On the Laity) and Suárez in his *De Legibus* (On Laws). Now, Bellarmine and Suárez hold that we are by nature social, and obliged under natural law to come together in a political order. They also hold that political authority derives ultimately from God. Hence they would reject the view of thinkers like Hobbes, Locke, and Rousseau that society is artificial and that authority derives *entirely* from the consent of the governed. However, Bellarmine and Suárez draw a distinction between (a) the *authority* associated with governmental power and (b) the decision about which specific *form* governmental power should take and *which persons* should hold offices in government. The former derives from God but the latter, Bellarmine and Suárez hold, rests with the governed.[22]

These various strands of thought led the Scholastic tradition to an approach to political philosophy which, though not classical liberal or libertarian, was not absolutist or statist either, but rather a middle position. If liberal democracy was not insisted on in principle, neither was it ruled out, and by the twentieth century was commonly accepted in practice (in some cases, such as that of Maritain, with enthusiasm).[23] Following Michael Novak (1989), we can distinguish between liberal *philosophy* and liberal *institutions*, such as democracy, the rule of law, and the market economy. Modern Scholastic thinkers have tended to reject the former, but not necessarily the latter, and indeed, some have held that the latter can be given a better intellectual foundation within a Thomistic framework.

In the case of the market economy, this is facilitated by the theory of private property developed within the Thomistic tradition. Though there is in Aquinas's thought no notion of a subjective natural *right* to private property, he does argue that the institution of property has several benefits: first, people are more inclined to work when what they produce is their own than they are when it is held in common; second, social affairs are more orderly when each person is responsible for his own goods; and third, people are more likely to be at peace with one another when each has something of his own (*Summa Theologiae* II-II.66.1–2).

Now among medieval Scholastics, Franciscans tended sharply to distinguish the legitimate *use* of goods from *ownership* of those goods, and while affirming the legitimacy of private use resisted affirming any natural right of private ownership. But the Dominican tendency was precisely to regard legitimate use as linked to ownership, and this led to the development of the notion of a natural right to private property. The Dominican theologian John of Paris (d. 1306) argued on Thomistic grounds that human beings actualize their distinctive potentials through the use of property. Anticipating Locke, he regarded the individual's labor as key to the acquisition of a right to private ownership (cf. Coleman, 2000: 126–130). The trend in Scholastic thinking toward recognition of a natural right to private property was cemented when Pope John XXII, who canonized Aquinas a saint, decided in favor of the Dominican position over the Franciscan.[24]

Some modern Scholastic writers, like classical liberal ones, have linked private property with liberty.[25] However, even the fully developed Thomistic position did not make private property rights absolute. Aquinas held that "with regard to . . . their use . . . man ought to possess external things, not as his own, but as common, so that, to wit, he is ready to communicate them to others in their need" (*Summa Theologiae* II-II.66.2). Later Thomists would incorporate this principle into the theory of the natural right to private ownership by means of the principle that rights have a teleological foundation. The institution of private property is necessary both for our bare survival and for the exercise of our world-interactive natural capacities. In order for property to serve these ends, ownership rights must be robust, but if they were *so* robust that those with insufficient property who are in extreme distress had no claim to assistance from those with surplus property, then the very point of the institution (which is to allow *all* human beings to flourish) would be undermined.[26]

Given their affirmation of private property and the principle of subsidiarity, modern Thomists have naturally tended to be highly critical of socialism and communism. And already in the sixteenth and seventeenth centuries, Late Scholastic thinkers of the School of Salamanca had anticipated free market ideas concerning the unintended consequences of price controls, and the subjective theory of economic value (Chafuen, 2003).

However, just as modern Scholastic writers have resisted classical liberalism and libertarianism in political philosophy, so too have they declined to endorse a thoroughgoing laissez-faire position in economics. Some have favored the "distributism" of G. K. Chesterton and Hilaire Belloc, with its agrarianism and nostalgia for the medieval guild system. But more common is the sober acceptance of capitalism, in some "mixed economy" version. As a once widely used textbook of Thomistic ethics sums up what is probably the standard view:

> We cannot turn back the clock of history and get people to give up the comforts of modern living for the simple life. Nor was this life wholly desirable. One can romanticize the past by overlooking its disagreeable features, which for the mass of mankind were far worse than anything we have today . . .
>
> Capitalism is not the only possible economic alternative to communism and socialism, but some form of it is the only practical alternative in an advanced society in our times. (Fagothey, 1959: 525, 536)

The qualified language—"*some* form of [capitalism]"—is significant. Some libertarians have distinguished sharply between *principled* approaches to political philosophy (those which deduce political conclusions from abstract moral principle) and *pragmatic* approaches (those which argue from practical considerations derived from economics and other social sciences), and they tend to emphasize one approach or the other (cf. Kukathas and Pettit, 1990: 75–76). Modern Scholastic writers insist on combining both. Some general, non-negotiable conclusions can in their view be derived from abstract principle. In particular, socialism at the one extreme and rigid adherence to laissez-faire at the other are generally taken to be ruled out absolutely by the natural law account of property rights defended by modern Thomists. Given the principle of subsidiarity, there is also a strong presumption in favor of private solutions over governmental solutions, and, where governmental solutions are in order, for localized government over centralized government. But this presumption can be overridden, and determining exactly when and how requires going beyond abstract principle and applying the (inevitably much less tidy) considerations to be drawn from economics and other social sciences, not to mention concrete political reality and historical circumstances.[27]

Notes

1. An omission in what follows (and admittedly, not a small one) is any discussion of the topic of religious freedom, about which Scholastic thinkers have had much to say—negative for much of the history of the tradition, though more positive in the years before and since Vatican II. The reason for this omission is that distinctively Catholic theological issues (as opposed to purely philosophical issues) have dominated the debate in the very large literature on this subject, putting it beyond the scope of this article. For an important recent discussion, see the exchange between Thomas Pink and John Finnis in Keown and George (2013).
2. For recent Thomistic discussion of the issue of which of a thing's attributes truly flow from its nature or essence, see Oderberg, 2007: 156–166; Oderberg, 2011; and Feser, 2014a: 230–235.
3. For a Thomistic response to David Velleman's (2000) well-known criticisms of the claim that the ends of action are always chosen under the guise of the good, see Feser 2014b.

4. For further exposition and defense of Aquinas's natural law theory, see Feser, 2009: ch. 5; Lisska, 1996; and McInerny, 1997.

5. For recent "analytical Thomist" defenses of Aristotelian metaphysics, see Haldane, 2002b; Stump, 2003: chs. 1 and 2; Oderberg, 2007; Oderberg, 2010; and Feser, 2014a.

6. Recent anthologies of representative work include Tahko, 2012; Groff and Greco, 2013; Feser, 2013; and Novotný and Novák, 2014.

7. To be sure, a critic might object that such a position is unstable—in particular, that it must either collapse into a metaphysical naturalism of the standard sort, yielding notions of essence and teleology too "thin" to do the needed metaethical work; or that, to ensure sufficiently "thick" notions of essence and teleology, it will, after all, have to take on board the whole traditional Aristotelian metaphysical apparatus and abandon metaphysical naturalism. However, the objection is controversial, and what matters for present purposes is that a less ambitious metaphysical position is at least *arguably* open to someone sympathetic to a broadly Aristotelian approach to ethics.

8. John Lamont characterizes it as "teleological liberty" (2009: 178).

9. *Summa Theologiae* Ia, q 62 a 8, ad 3, quoted in Pinckaers, 1995: 388–389. Cf. II *Sent.*, dist. 25, q 1, a 1, ad 2, quoted in Pinckaers, 1995: 388.

10. As is indicated by the fact that Aquinas regards the angels as freer than we are precisely because they cannot sin, Aquinas does not think that free will entails the ability to have done otherwise. Hence he would reject at least some libertarian accounts of free will. (Naturally, "libertarianism" is here meant in the metaphysical sense rather than the political sense.) However, Aquinas would also deny that free will is compatible with causal determinism. Hence he is not a compatibilist either. In general, it is not easy to locate Aquinas's position on the map of the contemporary debate over free will, because the background metaphysical assumptions he brings to bear on the subject are so different from those taken for granted by most contemporary philosophers. But since the focus of this chapter is on the moral and political implications of Scholastic views about free will, pursuing these metaphysical issues is beyond its scope. For detailed discussion of them, see Stump, 2003: chs. 9 and 13.

11. Cf. Gillespie, 2008: ch. 7. There are several respects in which nominalism and voluntarism lend themselves to a Hobbesian picture of moral and social life. If, as nominalism entails, there is no universal human nature, then (contrary to Aristotle and Aquinas) human beings are not by nature directed toward the end of forming society. Nor, if there is no universal human nature, are there ends of any other sort toward which the will is naturally directed. There is only what different individuals contingently happen to will. Thus is the Hobbesian state of nature a state of individuals with no natural obligations to one another and no common natural end by reference to which their conflicting wills might be harmonized. Nor can the sovereign to whom they decide to submit themselves (so as to escape the inevitable chaos of the state of nature) appeal to some universal human nature to guide him in determining the content of law. Like the God of voluntarism, he must determine this by fiat.

12. Note that this has nothing to do with "subjectivity" in any of the various senses in which that term is commonly used in other philosophical contexts (e.g., in subjectivist theories of moral value, or in discussions of the subjectivity of conscious experience).

13. Hohfeld himself was not addressing the question of natural rights specifically nor framing the issue in terms of the language of objective right versus subjective right, but his analysis is nevertheless applicable to any account of rights as inhering in the individual (whether they be thought of as natural or conventional).

14. There is of course an element of "objective right" in this scenario, insofar as when the wage is paid for work done, employer and employee stand in a just relationship to one another. But that does not preclude there also being an element of "subjective right," insofar as the employee's claim to the wage is something inhering in the employee. That the notions of objective right and subjective right are *different* notions does not by itself entail that they are incompatible notions.

15. See, e.g., Villey 1964 and 2003, and Bastit, 1990. Cf. Lamont, 2009 for a sympathetic account of Villey's views, and Tierney, 2001: ch. 1, for a critical account.

16. Cf. Cronin, 1939a: ch. 20; Fagothey, 1959: ch. 15, Feser, 2011; Higgins, 1958: chs. 15 and 16; Maritain, 1951: ch. 4; Oderberg, 2000b: 53–85; Oderberg, 2013.

17. It does not follow that, for the natural law theorist, it is intrinsically immoral not to become a parent. Someone may legitimately forgo having children for the sake of some yet higher calling—the priesthood would be a stock example. Or someone may simply be unable to find a suitable mate. However, there is given human nature a *presumption* in favor of family and children as part of a fully flourishing human life. And if one does become a parent, one is obliged to follow through and be as good a parent as one can be. In any event, the natural law ethics of the family is a large topic that would require a separate treatment.

18. It might be objected that a distinction can be drawn between having an obligation *toward* a person and having an obligation *to* a person, and that only the latter generates a Hohfeldian claim right. For example, if I promise to you to take care of your children while you are traveling, I have an obligation *toward* your children insofar as I am obliged to house and feed them while you are away, etc., but it is you *to* whom I have an obligation of the sort that generates a claim right, insofar as you (rather than the children) are the one to whom I made the promise. This is true, but obligations *to* and obligations *toward* don't always come apart in this way. For example, if I promised you I would take care of *you*, then it would be one and the same person *to* whom and *toward* whom I have an obligation. And the natural law theorist's claim is that in the case of our own children, we have obligations both to them and toward them.

    It might also be objected that the situation may be as follows: We have an obligation to take care of our children, but the obligation is *to* God rather than to our children, so that it is God rather than they who have a claim right. There are two things to be said in response to this. First, it is not clear why we need to bring God into the picture. While it is true that Thomistic natural law theorists tend to be theists, appeal to God is *not* (contrary to a common caricature!) the natural law theorist's way of resolving most moral issues. For the Thomist, essentialism and teleology suffice to ground the particular moral claims so far discussed, and essentialism and teleology can be defended independently of theism. Second, even if we do bring God into the picture, it wouldn't follow that our obligations are only to God and not to our children. For it is not as if we cannot have obligations to both. (Suppose I promise you that I'll take care of your children while you are traveling, and suppose I *also* promise *your children* that I will do so. Then I am obliged *to* you and also *to* them, so that both you and they have a claim right against me.)

19. It might be objected that *A* might lack a right to do *X*, while still having a claim right against *B* that *B* not forcibly prevent *A* from doing *X*. This is true, but it depends on the details concerning what *X* is and who *A* and *B* are. Anyway, the natural law theorist is not claiming that it is *always* merely a matter of prudence rather than justice whether the state refrains from preventing some vice, but only that it sometimes is.

20. Though it is worth noting that the medieval theologian Henry of Ghent, who represents the rival, voluntarist tendency in Scholasticism, appears to have anticipated the notion of self-ownership, which plays such a large role in the thought of Locke, Nozick, and Rothbard (cf. Tierney, 2001: 83–89). It is also worth noting that some libertarian natural rights theorists regard the Scholastic natural law approach to rights theory as a precursor to their own (cf. Rothbard, 1998: ch. 1; Palmer, 2001). And yet other libertarian natural rights theorists have argued for their position on broadly Aristotelian grounds (cf. Rasmussen and Den Uyl, 1991; Machan, 1989; Miller, 2011).

21. It may be objected that the Scholastic principle is making a point about justice, whereas Hayek is making a point about feasibility. But for the Scholastic, these considerations cannot be neatly separated. If the very *nature* of human social life is such that decisions are more competently made by lower-level authorities—a judgment Hayek's point reinforces—then it is *unjust*, and not merely unfeasible, for higher-level authorities to take over responsibility for those decisions.

22. See Bellarmine, *De Laicis*, Book III, Chapter 6; and Suárez, *De Legibus*, Book III, Chapter 2. The former work is available in English translation in Bellarmine, 1928.

23. Maritain held that the different approaches to moral theory on offer under modern conditions of pluralism could converge on a common doctrine of natural rights (Maritain, 1951; cf. McInerny, 1988), a thesis similar to John Rawls's notion of an "overlapping consensus" (Rawls, 1993).

24. For discussion of the dispute between Franciscans and Dominicans over property, see Coleman, 2000: 78–80, 119–124, and Tierney, 2001: ch. 6.

25. Pope Leo XIII reflected this view when he defended private property against socialism in the name of "every wage-earner[s'] . . . liberty of disposing of his wages" and "every man[s' having] by nature the right to possess property as his own" (*Rerum Novarum*, paragraphs 5–6).

26. For exposition and defense of the modern Thomistic approach to property, see Cronin, 1939b: chs. 4 and 12; Fagothey, 1959: chs. 28 and 29; Feser, 2010; and Higgins 1958: chs. 17 and 18.

27. For very helpful comments on an earlier version of this chapter, I thank David Schmidtz, Carmen Pavel, and two anonymous referees.

References

Bastit, Michel, 1990. *Naissance de la loi moderne: la pensée de la loi de saint Thomas à Suárez.* Paris: Presses universitaires de France.

Bellarmine, Robert, 1928. *De laicis or The treatise on civil government.* Translated by Kathleen E. Murphy. New York: Fordham University Press.

Bittle, Celestine N., 1950. *Man and morals.* Milwaukee: Bruce Publishing Company.

Brett, Annabel S., 1997. *Liberty, right and nature: individual rights in later scholastic thought.* Cambridge: Cambridge University Press.

Chafuen, Alejandro A., 2003. *Faith and liberty: the economic thought of the late scholastics.* Lanham, MD: Lexington Books.

Coleman, Janet, 2000. *A history of political thought: from the Middle Ages to the Renaissance.* Oxford: Blackwell.

Cronin, Michael, 1939a. *The science of ethics, Volume 1: general ethics*. Dublin: M. H. Gill and Son, Ltd.

Cronin, Michael, 1939b. *The science of ethics, Volume 2: special ethics*. Dublin: M. H. Gill and Son, Ltd.

Fagothey, Austin, 1959. *Right and reason*. 2nd ed. St. Louis: The C. V. Mosby Company.

Feser, Edward, 2009. *Aquinas*. Oxford: Oneworld Publications.

Feser, Edward, 2010. Classical natural law theory, property rights, and taxation. *Social Philosophy and Policy*, 27, pp.21–52.

Feser, Edward, 2011. The metaphysical foundations of natural rights. In: Thomas Cushman, ed. *The Routledge international handbook of human rights*. London: Routledge. pp.23–34.

Feser, Edward, ed., 2013. *Aristotle on method and metaphysics*. Basingstoke: Palgrave Macmillan.

Feser, Edward, 2014a. *Scholastic metaphysics: a contemporary introduction*. Heusenstamm: Editiones Scholasticae/Transaction Books.

Feser, Edward, 2014b. Being, the good, and the guise of the good. In: Daniel D. Novotny and Lukas Novak, eds. *Neo-Aristotelian perspectives in metaphysics*. London: Routledge. pp.84–103.

Foot, Philippa, 2001. *Natural goodness*. Oxford: Clarendon Press.

Gillespie, Michael Allen, 2008. *The theological origins of modernity*. Chicago: University of Chicago Press.

Groff, Ruth, and Greco, John, eds., 2013. *Powers and capacities in philosophy: the new Aristotelianism*. London: Routledge.

Haldane, John J., ed., 2002a. *Mind, metaphysics, and value in the Thomistic and analytical traditions*. Notre Dame, IN: University of Notre Dame Press.

Haldane, John J., 2002b. A Thomist metaphysics. In: Richard M. Gale, ed. *The Blackwell guide to metaphysics*. Oxford: Blackwell. pp.87–109.

Higgins, Thomas J., 1958. *Man as man: the science and art of ethics*. Rev. ed. Milwaukee: Bruce Publishing Company.

Hohfeld, W. N., 1946. *Fundamental legal conceptions as applied in judicial reasoning*. New Haven, CT: Yale University Press.

Hursthouse, Rosalind, 1999. *On virtue ethics*. Oxford: Clarendon Press.

Keown, John, and George, Robert P., eds., 2013. *Reason, morality, and law: the philosophy of John Finnis*. Oxford: Oxford University Press.

Kukathas, Chandran, and Pettit, Philip, 1990. *Rawls: a theory of justice and its critics*. Stanford: Stanford University Press.

Lamont, John R. T., 2009. Conscience, freedom, rights: idols of the enlightenment religion. *The Thomist*, 73(2), pp.169–239.

Lisska, Anthony J., 1996. *Aquinas's theory of natural law: an analytic reconstruction*. Oxford: Clarendon Press.

Machan, Tibor, 1989. *Individuals and their rights*. LaSalle, IL: Open Court.

MacIntyre, Alasdair, 1984. *After virtue*. 2nd ed. Notre Dame, IN: University of Notre Dame Press.

Maritain, Jacques, 1951. *Man and the state*. Washington, DC: Catholic University of America Press.

McInerny, Ralph, 1988. Maritain and natural rights. In: *Art and prudence: studies in the thought of Jacques Maritain*. Notre Dame: University of Notre Dame Press. pp.123–136.

McInerny, Ralph, 1997. *Ethica thomistica: the moral philosophy of Thomas Aquinas.* Rev. ed. Washington, DC: Catholic University of America Press.

Miller, Fred D., Jr., 2011. Neo-Aristotelian theories of natural rights. In: Douglas B. Rasmussen, Aeon J. Skoble, and Douglas J. Den Uyl, eds. *Reality, reason, and rights.* Lanham: Lexington Books. pp.133–153.

Novak, Michael, 1989. *Catholic social thought and liberal institutions: freedom with justice.* 2nd ed. New Brunswick, NJ: Transaction Publishers.

Novotný, Daniel D., and Novák, Lukáš, eds., 2014. *Neo-Aristotelian perspectives in metaphysics.* London: Routledge.

Nozick, Robert, 1974. *Anarchy, state, and utopia.* New York: Basic Books.

Oderberg, David S., 2000a. Is there a right to be wrong? *Philosophy,* 75(4), pp.517–537.

Oderberg, David S., 2000b. *Moral theory: a non-consequentialist approach.* Oxford: Blackwell.

Oderberg, David S., 2007. *Real essentialism.* London: Routledge.

Oderberg, David S., 2010. The metaphysical foundations of natural law. In: H. Zaborowski, ed. *Natural moral law in contemporary society.* Washington, DC: Catholic University of America Press. pp.44–75.

Oderberg, David S., 2011. Essence and properties. *Erkenntnis,* 75(1), pp.85–111.

Oderberg, David S., 2013. Natural law and rights theory. In: G. Gaus and F. D'Agostino, eds. *The Routledge companion to social and political philosophy.* London: Routledge. pp.375–386.

Palmer, Tom G., 2001. Saving rights theory from its friends. In: Tibor R. Machan, ed. *Individual rights reconsidered.* Stanford: Hoover Institution Press. pp.35–85.

Paterson, Craig, and Pugh, Matthew S., eds., 2006. *Analytical Thomism: traditions in dialogue.* Aldershot: Ashgate.

Pinckaers, Servais, 1995. *The sources of Christian ethics.* Washington, DC: Catholic University of America Press.

Rasmussen, Douglas B., and Den Uyl, Douglas J., 1991. *Liberty and nature: an Aristotelian defense of liberal order.* Chicago, IL: Open Court.

Rawls, John, 1993. *Political liberalism.* New York: Columbia University Press.

Rothbard, Murray, 1998. *The ethics of liberty.* New York: New York University Press.

Strauss, Leo, 1953. *Natural right and history.* Chicago: University of Chicago Press.

Stump, Eleonore, 2003. *Aquinas.* London: Routledge.

Tahko, Tuomas E., ed., 2012. *Contemporary Aristotelian metaphysics.* Cambridge: Cambridge University Press.

Thomas Aquinas, 1948. *Summa theologica.* Translated by the Fathers of the English Dominican Province. New York: Benziger Brothers.

Tierney, Brian, 2001. *The idea of natural rights.* Grand Rapids: Eerdmans.

Velleman, J. David, 2000. The guise of the good. In: *The possibility of practical reason.* Oxford: Oxford University Press. pp.99–122.

Villey, Michel, 1964. La genèse du droit subjectif chez Guillaume d'Occam. *Archives de philosophie du droit,* 9, pp.97–127.

Villey, Michel, 2003. *La formation de la pensée juridique moderne.* Paris: Quadrige/PUF.

....

CHAPTER 11

FREEDOM, SLAVERY, AND IDENTITY IN RENAISSANCE FLORENCE

The Faces of Leon Battista Alberti

....

ORLANDO PATTERSON

1. INTRODUCTION

IN this chapter I propose to take an outsider's look at a critical phase of Western culture—the fifteenth-century Florentine Renaissance—focusing on an important, though neglected, aspect of the history of freedom during this period. Let me state from the start that I am an outsider in not one but at least three senses. First, I am not a Renaissance scholar but a historical sociologist of culture with special interest in the problems of slavery and freedom. Second, my approach is with the history of freedom over the course of Western civilization (Braudel, 1979: ch. 1), rather than with the life-long exploration of a specific period and its problems, as is typical of most Renaissance scholars. Third, my focus is primarily on the dialectic between ideas and social context, and especially on the ways in which dominant ideas, including though not restricted to those of great interest to elite thinkers, are generated and refashioned through social interactions and conflicts encompassing the bottom end of societies. I make no apologies for this "invasioni di campo," as the Italian writer Primo Levi called it, since, like him, I find that such incursions into other people's intellectual territory can be quite productive (Ross, 2010: 75).

The socially constructed nature of freedom evolved, in the Western world, in two related lines of action, thought and values—the discursive, produced usually by the elite and prescriptivist thinkers of each age whose reactive, normative practices and judgments attempt to define the true, worthy, or proper freedom, and the existential tradition of freedom that emerges from the engagement with power in ordinary life, informed by the peculiar centrality of slavery and its derivatives in Western society and culture. The two lines are linked in complex ways: philosophers, political theorists, moralists, and other elite thinkers, like prescriptive linguists, must ultimately get their ideas from the real world of existential cultural productions, sometimes directly, more often from other more or less grounded prescriptivists. Ultimately, as I and others have attempted to show, the distinctive construction of freedom *as a central value*, institutionally grounded in some form of democracy, originated in the city-states of fifth-century Greece, during which emerged the historically unprecedented civilizational dependence on large-scale slavery (Finley, 1960; Pohlenz, 1966; Raaflaub, 1983; Raaflaub, 2004; Patterson, 1991). No sooner had the first democratic institutions, and the accompanying full flowering of freedom consciousness, emerged in ancient Athens than elite thinkers—most notably Plato (Plato, 1914, 1955, 1980; Patterson, 1991)—began to appropriate and reinterpret it in their own, prescriptivist terms. Ancient Greek political theory, Cynthia Farrar has persuasively argued, emerged in direct response to the radical democracy generated from the long post-Solonic struggles of the Athenian demos (Farrar, 1993). This interaction between the existential (usually bottom up, pragmatic, and/or resistant) and discursive (usually elite and appropriative) has persisted throughout the Western history of freedom, the Italian Renaissance period being an especially striking instance.

The period between the waning years of the fourteenth century and the first part of the fifteenth in Italy marked another great moment in the long history of freedom in which political upheaval, in the struggle for and against power, elicited among elite thinkers and their patrons both the increased salience of freedom as value and reformulations of what freedom truly meant or should mean (Baron, 1966). A sustained, although ultimately losing, struggle against external and internal tyranny, compounded by plague and tremendous economic changes,[1] formed the background to the maturing social thought of this period. The most important intellectual achievement of elite thinkers of the period was not only a renewed invigoration of the central Western commitment to the value of freedom, but a reconstruction of the ideal in terms of what Pocock has called a "new vocabulary of citizenship" focused on the notion of republican liberty and virtue. We may interpret the period, he argues, in terms of a "sociology of liberty" which set the tone of, and provided the impulse for, one of the dominant themes of the modern history of freedom (Pocock, 1975: esp. ch. 4). An exploration of the unheralded, darker side of this sociology of liberty will be the object of this chapter.

In Renaissance Italy, indeed, in all of early modern Europe up to the period of pamphleteering frenzy during the English civil war, Florence remained unique in the extraordinary degree of freedom-worship among its elite and broader patrician citizenry. Two brief experiences with despotic rule in the first half of the fourteenth century had intensified Florentine commitment to traditional republican conceptions of liberty. Florentine elite writers and statesmen never tired of praising Florence's love of freedom. Florence was celebrated variously as "a fountain head of freedom," and having thrown out the duke of Athens in 1343 after his year's reign of tyranny, a model speech sang that "God has granted you, citizens, to recover sacred liberty, a gift to be desired above everything else" (Pocock, 1975: 21). Describing the Florentine constitution in the 1430s, Leonardo Bruni wrote that "One of the democratic characteristics of our constitution is that we worship freedom more than anything else, as the end and goal of our commonwealth" (Rubinstein, 1952: 22). Nearly half a century later Rinuccini has one of his characters observing, with respect to "the native Florentine love of liberty," that "there is no city that has so energetically and enduringly championed the cause of liberty. Nor is there any place where it has flourished in so pure and ample a form" (Rinuccini, 1978: 195). One could give numerous other instances of such songs of praise to freedom.

Where did this extraordinary elite commitment to the value of freedom come from, and why at that time? Partly it was a continuation of the great tradition of late medieval republican freedom, itself part of the broader history of freedom during the Middle Ages,[2] all the more vocally expressed precisely because it was already a thing of the past, yet close enough to be remembered. Yet the intensity of the commitment to the ideal of freedom cannot be explained in terms of continuity alone for the simple reason that other Italian republics had such continuities without the obsessive ringing of the liberty bell. Continuities with the late medieval republican past were perhaps greatest in Venice, given its social conservatism. But the striking thing about Venice was that while it preserved the tradition of liberty, it did not make a fetish of it. One would hardly call it the supreme value of the Venetian state.

Hans Baron has argued strongly in favor of a direct relationship between the sophisticated political thought of the day and the political turmoil that prompted it (Baron, 1966). This has been criticized by Bucker, who interprets the intellectual changes as reflecting a shift from the earlier corporatist system to a more politically durable, though elitist, *reggimento*, one strengthened by an enlarged bureaucracy, concentrated magistracies, and the deliberate cultivation of civic pride.[3] (Brucker, 1977, 248–318). There may not be any real conflict here: the cultural resources of the late medieval past were used to make sense of the economic and political shocks of the late fourteenth century, and in the process something new emerged.

The subterranean, existential experience and expression of freedom running beneath its elite expressions is usually not easily discerned, since it is rarely found in the written records produced by elite thinkers and must typically be inferred from actions and indirect, symbolic gestures.[4] On rare occasions, however, one comes across an individual who experiences and expresses both levels of freedom. In the ancient world, Epictetus, the manumitted Roman *verna* (a houseborn slave) who became one of the greatest Stoic philosophers, was the classic example (Oldfather, 1979; Millar, 1965; Patterson, 1991). In the Middle Ages, Marguerite Porete, the upper-class French mystic burnt at the stake in 1310 for her free-spirit heresies, was another;[5] in the nineteenth century in the United States, there was Frederick Douglass, the former slave who powerfully expressed in his autobiographies what it was like to yearn for freedom as a slave, but who also rose to the elite ranks of the abolitionist movement and represented his nation as its ambassador, in which capacities he spoke of freedom in prescriptive, discursive terms;[6] and, in the twentieth century, Primo Levi, the eminent Jewish Italian writer and Auschwitz survivor who found and was sustained by primal, existential freedom in the face of genocidal defilement, but also wrote discursively on the affinity between freedom, work, and responsibility.[7] In Renaissance Italy we find just such a figure in one of the most celebrated of quattrocento humanists, Leon Battista Alberti, who moved in the highest circles of cultural and social life and was singled out by Burckhardt as the quintessential Renaissance man, the representative universal genius of his age, who wrote more eloquently than most on freedom in discursive terms for his elite audience but who, as we will see, had much to say on freedom existentially experienced in the humiliation of his indelible status as a bastard and outsider and in his contemplation of slavery. In probing this side of Alberti, we will move from the grandeur of the Medici court and the Vatican to the unwashed linen of private life; from the formal male world of the civic culture, the *virilia officia*, with its self-consciously discursive view of freedom, to the terrain of the *famiglia*, the world of women, servants, wet nurses, and, beneath all, slaves. In short, without in any way slighting the elitist aura that embraces the traditional accounts of freedom in Euro-American Renaissance historiography, I propose to explore the bottom end of those "ideas born of the Florentine crisis," as Baron rightly called them, that same dialectic of thought and action, tyranny and freedom that is the foundation of the West's most protean value.

2. ELITE DISCURSIVE FREEDOM IN RENAISSANCE ITALY

Before delving into this lesser-known terrain of Renaissance freedom, however, and in order to highlight the differences between the two dimensions of freedom, it will be useful first to summarize the much better-known dominant, discursive views on the subject, views that Alberti, on one of his many levels of intellectual interaction and agonistic self-definition with his world, also espoused (Grafton, 2000: 25). What exactly did republican freedom mean? One common meaning was simply political independence. During a period of rising tyrannies, this meaning acquired special importance; indeed, it was given greater force by the independent republics in the face of its loss all around them.

Institutionally, freedom meant, first and foremost, the rule of law. It is this which guarantees the other aspects of freedom and prevents tyranny. In Book 4 of his *History of Florence*, Bruni has Giano della Bella saying in a speech in 1292: "The liberty of the people consists in two things: the laws and the judges . . . when some people scorn the laws and the judges with impunity, then it is fair to say that liberty is gone."[8] Rinuccini reflects the socially conservative side of these essentially elitist thinkers in his observation that freedom is constrained not only by law but by custom and convention (Baron, 1959–60).

The rejection of external subordination was closely tied to the second meaning of the term "liberty": some form of self-government by the citizens who mattered, namely those with wealth and power: "It was directed not to a single end from above, by a prince, but by a body of citizens, who somehow represented the community and its interests, and who were related to one another by a principle very different from that of hierarchy"

(Bouwsma, 1968: 11). Now as Bouwsma and others have made clear, this never meant adult suffrage in the sense in which we now know it. But it did partake of a good part of what we mean by democracy today: namely, a mixed government with representative bodies, which ruled with the consent, however passive, of the populace. At its broadest, it meant participation by all taxpayers. The principle of no taxation without representation is explicit in Rinuccini: "It is considered best for liberty and justice if all those who aid the republic privately by payment of taxes are also given a chance to participate in its rewards and advantages" (Rinuccini, 1978: 206). This, as McLean has recently documented, entailed a "relationship to the state that was both adversarial and participatory" with important consequences for broader political developments (McLean, 2007: 190).

In this innovative commercial society, security of one's property, especially from rapacious princes waging unneeded wars, was considered as important a prerequisite of personal freedom in fifteenth-century Florence and Venice as it was in late eighteenth-century America. Wealth secured independence, and is to that extent desirable even though avarice was condemned in theory. Nowhere is the discursive Renaissance view of freedom and property more clearly expressed than in Alberti's *Della Famiglia*:

> The body must not be formed in idleness and indulgence; our only use for wealth must be to make us free. It is perhaps, a kind of slavery to be forced to plead and beg from other men to satisfy our necessity. That is why we do not scorn riches, but learn to govern ourselves and to subdue our desires while we live free and happy in the midst of affluence and abundance. (Alberti, 1969: 148)

The similarity between the humanists' view of wealth and those of the Calvinist entrepreneur has, of course, been frequently commented on.[9] One does not have to choose between Weber, who locates the source of the capitalist spirit much later, in Calvinism, and Sombart, who traces it back to the commercial capitalism of Renaissance Italy. Both are right in that both the Reformation and the Renaissance reflected, and in part generated, an ethic of personal freedom in relation to property that was conducive to entrepreneurial activity. The important recent work of John Padgett on the commercial revolution in Renaissance Florence leaves us in little doubt about this (Padgett and Powell, 2013: ch. 7).

The most distinctive aspect of the Renaissance construction of freedom was its association with the idea of virtue. The two terms were sometimes used synonymously; more frequently, freedom was seen as the expression of virtue. Only the virtuous person, and the virtuous republic, were truly free. But what precisely was virtue? There can be no doubt that the notion was lifted straight from the classics, especially from the Ciceronian conception of the late republican era. As such, it reflects the same reinterpretation of ancient Roman elite conceptions of the person in the light of Stoic conceptions of the good and wise individual. As in ancient Rome, the idea is a fluid one, verging always on tautology: Virtue is the good, which only is free, which is the essence of virtue.

Poggio Bracciolini has left us perhaps the most extreme expression of the sanctification of virtue. In his dialogue, *On Nobility*, the rich Florentine Niccolo Niccoli tells a skeptical Lorenzo de' Medici: "We must cherish virtue, Lorenzo, for it not only makes us noble, but blessed and immortal to the memory of men. From virtue, nobility; from virtue, glory; from virtue, our conduct should derive; from virtue comes all right conduct and the willingness to strive" (Bracciolini, 1978: 147). Lorenzo both correctly identifies the source of this passion for virtue, and expresses the skepticism of most bourgeois and elite Florentines when he observes: "Your stoic virtue, Niccolo, is too naked, needy, and almost disagreeable to come into our cities and seems to stand rather forsaken and solitary. It has been often praised, that's true, but few can be found who really desire it" (Bracciolini, 1978: 144). Basically, most humanists held the ancient notion of inner and outer liberty and virtue. Inner virtue is a state of mind, that condition in which the emotions are controlled by reason, a state of utter tranquility; this is equated with true freedom. However, virtue also refers to the outer actions of the person. For the more scholarly and retiring, such as Niccolo, it is the person "who lives prudently and wisely" (Bracciolini, 1978: 143), and the same is true of Rinuccini's Eleutherius, who equates freedom and virtue with privacy and pastoral bliss. This, however, is definitely the minority view. For most, virtue is expressed in noble, meritorious action that promotes the good of the community. The free and virtuous person is the one who actively participates in the civic culture of his republic, and the free republic is most virtuous when it encourages the widest and most glorious display of virtuous behavior by its citizens. The counterpart to the negative freedom, which is the fortitude to disobey unjust commands, is the positive capacity to exercise one's will in relations with others. It is, as Alitheus says, the "power to live." Further: "Both the free and the strong man reveals himself most clearly in action. We praise a man's strength, however, when he with reason exposes himself to bodily danger, while we admire his freedom when he is speaking and giving counsel. Frank and noble spirits must possess both virtues. . . . In states where liberty exists, these qualities are most useful, for there the citizens speak without subterfuge and give advice to the Republic based on their real conviction" (Rinuccini, 1978: 202–203).

As in the ancient world, such outward virtuous action often means the domination of other individuals, and other states, for their own good. What Watkins said of Bruni would be true of most elite and bourgeois Florentines, that "to be truly free a state must know how to subjugate her neighbors," and in personal relations within the state, "Liberty—in the sense of autonomy—rests on self-control, voluntary sacrifice, and power over certain others. The price of liberty—it turns out—is repression" (Watkins, 1978: 12–13). In other words, what I have called elsewhere sovereignal freedom (Patterson, 1991: ch. 1) was of the essence of republican virtue, and it was expressed not only in power over lesser individuals but, collectively, in Florence's growing powers over its expanding territory and its "use of the language of empire to justify them," the ancient imperial Roman word *dominium* becoming the favored term (Brown, 2000). This is in no way inconsistent with the emphasis on civic freedom or participation, since it was generally understood that such participation was restricted to the taxpaying bourgeoisie and elite. The Florentine polity, according to Bruni, was one which "while mixed of democracy and aristocracy, had an oligarchical slant" (Rubinstein, 1979: 99–100). At the same time, it was a fairly open political elite, even by the standards of nineteenth-century England, allowing for the participation of between 2,500 and 3,000 eligible citizens out of a total male population of approximately 20,000 (Rubinstein, 1979: 107).

A man's outer goodness, freedom, and virtue is expressed in his "name and general fame," the dignity with which he bears himself, and the degree to which he "serve[s] the public eye" by freely participating in, and contributing to, the civic culture, says Adovardo in the *Famiglia*. Furthermore, such public virtue redounds to the individual's private virtue and gain, "for it is our task to please the public if we hope to draw an abundance of friends to ourselves, whom we shall choose from the public" (Alberti, 1969: 274). This theme of public virtue serving private gain was to grow and overwhelm all other meanings during the late fifteenth century, so that by the time we get to Machiavelli, virtue simply means that which best serves the interest of the all-powerful, sovereignally free prince.

In concluding this section we may ask, to what degree did this elite discourse conform to the sociological realities of Renaissance Florence? Later twentieth-century scholarship has strongly contested the Burckhardtian claim that the period marked the birth of modern individualism (Caferro, 2010: ch. 2). On the one hand, medievalists have strongly argued that the discourse on individualism and the idea of freedom as virtue were well established in the Middle Ages (Caferro, 2010: ch. 1). On the other hand, and more to the point, it has been forcefully argued that actual social life bore little resemblance to the celebration of freedom in this elite discourse. Brucker states flatly that "The social freedom of the Renaissance man postulated by Burckhardt and elaborated by his followers is, in fifteenth century Florence, at least, a myth" (Brucker, 1969: 101), a position largely supported by more recent scholarship. According to Connell, "Florentine individualism has by now been discarded as a serious theory" (Connell, 2002: 6). But this may have overstated the case. Everyone, including the most powerful, may have been "enmeshed in a network of obligations and commitments, which limited and controlled his freedom of action"(McLean, 2007: 33) but, as Paul McLean has recently argued, agency and the culture of networks operate interactively in the individual's "desire to choose the optimal strategy—and in the ability to detach practice instrumentally from intentions," through standardized modes of evasion, manipulation, and rule-breaking, resulting "probably for the first time since antiquity, [in] a flexible, context-specific form of 'interdependent self' " (McLean, 2007: 198). Nowhere is this more explicitly exhibited than in Alberti's *Famiglia*, which has been read recently as a parody of Renaissance patriarchy, revealing its "shaky foundations" (Najemy, 2002: ch. 2).

3. The Culture of Slavery in Renaissance Italy

There is one aspect of the period during which the elite intensification of freedom-worship in Florence took place that is of special interest in light of the earlier history of freedom. This is the seemingly paradoxical reemergence of urban-domestic slavery in Florence during the fourteenth and fifteenth centuries.[10] Consistent with similar trends in the rest of Western Europe, there had been a major decline in slavery during the tenth and eleventh centuries in Italy. However, from the twelfth century onward, Italian merchants began trading in slaves once again, in spite of papal prohibitions.[11] By the end of the twelfth century Genoa had become a thriving slave trading center, its merchants replacing the Venetians who had previously dominated the traffic of humans, taken mainly from the Black Sea area and from Muslim Spain and North Africa. By the last decades of the thirteenth century they had spread out to dominate other slave marts, especially Caffa on the northern Black Sea. From then on, most of the slaves traded came from the Black Sea area, the main ethnic groups traded being Tartars, Greeks, Bulgarians, Turks, Circassians, and Russians.[12]

What all this points to is the fact that a significant part of the commercial revolution of the major Italian city-states during the fourteenth century was based on the trade in human beings, including Europeans. As is true of all slave trading groups, there was a spillover effect, with numbers of slaves being used by the Italians themselves. Even so, the numbers were very small during the 1300s. Slavery helped to support the rise of the major Italian republics largely in external trade. With an abundance of cheap native Italian labor, there was little need for foreign slaves.

All this was to change with the coming of the Black Death, which hit northern Italy especially hard, places like rural Pistoia losing over two-thirds of their population, the cities on average over a half (Herlihy, 1969: 80). In the commercial city-states of Italy, the plague meant not only higher wages, but a crisis in domestic service, as native Italians were reluctant to work in the households of the middle and upper classes at any wage. To solve this problem, the Italians turned to imported slave labor, and nowhere more so than in Genoa and Florence.[13] In 1363 Florence removed all restrictions on the importation of slaves, except the stipulation that they should all have been non-Christians. Venice also did the same and the presence of slaves among its servant class, including blacks, was striking (Lowe, 2013). Once Florence resumed the practice it rapidly spread all over Tuscany. Hence it is precisely in those parts of Renaissance Italy most committed to the preservation and celebration of republican freedom that we find this significant revival of domestic slavery, and, as Origo comments, it is "startling" that this development should have taken place "in the middle of the fourteenth century—at the time of the finest flowering of Tuscan civilization" (Origo, 1955: 324).

Slaves were of little significance in the productive economy of the city, being marginal, and subject to market forces, even in the labor-intensive construction industry of the city (Goldthwaite, 1980: 120–121). But by the mid-fourteenth century they had become an important sociocultural element in the domestic service, and in the familial and sexual life of Florence: "Every prosperous noble or merchant had at least two or three of them; many had more. Even a notary's wife, or a small shopkeeper's, would have at least one, and it was far from uncommon to find one among the possessions of a priest or nun" (Goldthwaite, 1980: 321). With what Herlihy and Klapisch-Zuber describe as the "fantastic growth" of the servant population during the latter half of the fifteenth century we find another surge in the domestic slave population, slaves and former slaves making up 15 percent of the servant class during this period. Leaving aside Palermo, where the share (12 percent) was high by any standard, the spillover population in

Genoa between 1360 and 1460 (Alberti was born and spent his childhood there, 1404–1416, before leaving to study in Padua) was up to 5 percent, which suggests that every elite and even middle-class family likely had one or more. The fear of them, as well as the numerous provisions in its laws relating to them, "show just how embedded slaves were in the general context of Genoese life" (Epstein, 2001: 98). Of equal significance was the cultural and psychological presence of slaves all over Italy, including cities where the numbers were not as great as Genoa. "Slavery," Epstein notes, "remained a vivid issue in the Italian consciousness, through the periods when there was a fair amount of slavery down to when there was hardly any" and "the language of slavery remained a lively discourse, keeping alive ways of thinking that would stay relevant long after people thought (or hoped) that the institution had died out" (Epstein, 2001: 41, 61).

Like their ancient counterparts, too, Renaissance Florentine slaves were sexually exploited in every manner conceivable (McKee, 2008: 318–319). Kuehn found that "Servants and slaves were considered devoid of scruples or moral principles and thus fair game for the males of the household, their relatives and guests, even total strangers." Sex with them "expressed the prepotent prerogative of the elite" (Kuehn, 2002: 137). The typical elite adolescent no doubt gained his first sexual experience in a slave's embrace. Men of all classes used them as concubines, often right under their wives' noses in their household, the matron being obliged to put up with this behavior. Some of the children born of these unions were brought up in the household, used as servants, and freed eventually. Others were ruthlessly exposed or sent to the foundling hospitals (Trexler, 1973: 266–268).

In light of what we have to say later, it is significant that most of these illegitimate children were born to the wealthiest families in Florence. Of the twenty children fathered by Paolo Niccolini, three were sons by his slaves, all brought up in his household (Klapisch-Zuber, 1986: 69–70). At least one member of the Medici clan, Alessandro de' Medici (1511–1537) who ruled Florence from 1530–1537, was clearly of African ancestry (Figures 11.1 and 11.2). Nicknamed 'Il Moro (the Moor) he was allegedly the illegitimate son of Lorenzo de' Medici, Duke of Urbino, but rumored to be actually the son of Giulio (later Pope Clement VII) by Simonetta, a black slave in the Medici household (Fletcher, 2016). One scholar has suggested that elite Florentine males "sired entire satellite families," the Medici clan being typical; however, by their nature these families left little trace in the records (Kuehn, 2002: 138). At the same time, there was no denying their slaveness: unlike the native household servants, these were "for almost all real purposes, socially dead and simply things" (Epstein, 2001: 99), legal non-persons, completely without honor—they could not only be whipped, but sold, and they had no custodial rights in their children. What is more, they were often feared with a loathing intensified by sexual jealousy, their angry and demanding mistresses referring to them as "*femmine bestiali*" (Klapisch-Zuber, 1986: 101).

The effect on social attitude toward freedom was similar to that which we have seen in the ancient world and on modern New World plantations. Within the household of the wealthy and bourgeois, the experience of being brought up by or with slaves, semi-slaves, and servants who, as Klapisch-Zuber notes, were assimilated to the status of slaves, would have generated that same sense of superiority, that same identification of freedom with absolute personal power, which we find in other slaveholding societies.[14] This would have been the household and individual counterpart to the growing sense of *dominium* or powers over other states and regions in Florence's mini-imperial expansion, mentioned earlier. At the same time, there was the classic use of manumission as a means of motivation which we find in all urban slave societies; manumission rates, as Origo shows, were extremely high. Thus the love of negative personal freedom on the part of the exploited slave would have been very much a part of life in the household. And the young Renaissance child-master, Alberti almost certainly being one, would have come both to value the raw negative freedom which he sensed from the bosom of his maid—the deep, existential yearning to be free of her social death—and at the same time to view it with contempt when compared with the superior freedom which he enjoyed in his power over her: crude, basic practice in the exercise of sovereignal freedom which he

FIGURE 11.1 Public domain image of Annibale Carracci, attrib., portrait of an African Slave Woman, ca. 1580s

FIGURE 11.2 Public domain image of Duke Alessandro de' Medici by Jacopo Pontormo

would later exercise in the public household. The primal dialectics of slave and master, already long institutionalized in the republican tradition of the late medieval culture he inherited, was regenerated at the very same time as the rediscovery of the classical studies that had recently come to dominate the formal education of the Renaissance child.

4. THE OTHER SIDE OF ALBERTI: ILLEGITIMACY, SLAVERY, AND EXISTENTIAL FREEDOM

The most remarkable, and from a sociohistorical point of view the most revealing, of the extraordinary group of humanists who lived in fifteenth-century Florence was Leon

Battista Alberti. In a celebrated, though highly contested, passage, Burckhardt singles him out as one of the giants of the Renaissance, its ideal type, the very embodiment of the "universal man," whose "iron will pervaded and sustained his whole personality," the living proof that, in Alberti's own words, "Men can do all things they will" (Burkhardt, 1904: 136–138). His greatness rests on the extraordinary range of his works, and the originality and scholarship he brought to all he surveyed: from dialogues, poems, fables, and letters to normative and descriptive sociologies; from pathbreaking treatises on the theory of perspective and the art of painting to the monumental foundational works on architecture.[15] This is the Alberti of the high Renaissance, the Alberti with which the *Vita Anonyma*—the main source on Alberti's life, very likely authored by Alberti himself[16]—would seem to harmonize perfectly. It was, however, a self-aggrandizing portrait: by Alberti in the first place, in keeping with similar life-writings of the times, further compounded by Burckhardt's highly selective reading of the *Vita*.[17]

There is, however, another Alberti, one which recent scholarship is increasingly showing to have been, not so much the real man behind the elite mask, since the elite persona was real enough, but another no less real. Far from being the aesthetic superman of Burckhardt's imagination, this Alberti was a profoundly alienated person, one who went through life with a chronic sense of unease, of being on the outside, suffering many debilitating physical ailments and a deep existential angst resulting in at least one mental breakdown, all of which colored his works and explain the bitterness, melancholy, pessimism, political disillusionment, and persistent misogyny (somewhat restrained in *Della Famiglia*) of his literary works. Far from being an integral part of the great company of quattrocento humanists, as traditionally conceived, this Alberti, as Michel was the first to see clearly, was "isolated from his age," and although his works were on one level "very quattrocento" and he "remains Florentine in our heart and in our memory," nonetheless he was someone who was "born and died in exile."[18] True, he had many friends from among the highest circles of Florentine society, and indeed he made friendship and belonging, the central theme of the great fourth book of *Della Famiglia*, into the greatest of virtue. But as Grafton notes: "The great dilettante who tried to shape his own character as a seal imprints a form on hot wax oscillated throughout his life between creative hyper-activity and paralyzing depression" (Grafton, 2000: 20).

It is to this Alberti that we now turn, for it is he who wrote the most penetrating exploration of the slavery-into-freedom dialectic of any modern Western writer. His ideas on the subject surpass, in every way, the bookish cleverness and rationalistic gamesmanship of Hegel, writing on this theme three and a half centuries later. One reason they do is that Hegel knew nothing about real slavery, while Alberti had not only observed it firsthand as well as reading about it in the classics, but had empathized with the condition to the point where the perspective of the slave yearning for freedom can be said to inform much of his thinking about society and liberty.

Alberto was first and foremost an illegitimate child in a city and time where, in general, "bastards were dishonorable creatures, scarcely better than beasts" (Kuehn, 1985: 164). True, he was among the most fortunate of bastards, one of the *naturales* as opposed to the unfortunate *nati ex damnato coitu*, most of whom were abandoned or killed in infancy, especially if female (Kuehn, 1985: 166). His father was a wealthy merchant who acknowledged and apparently cared for him, but this should in no way lead us to underestimate how devastating a blow this was to the pride and identity of any child, especially in a highly honorific society, much more so one as sensitive and ambitious as Alberti. Indeed, the fact that his father was from the mercantile elite and made genuine efforts to provide for him, and encouraged his natural relatives and elite peers to accept him, merely worsened his identity problems. He developed an acute sense of just how much he had lost by his very proximity to it. There may be some truth to the claim, going back to Burckhardt, that the outsider status of the high-born bastard promoted intellectual and artistic originality—Petrarch, Boccaccio, Filippino Lippi, and da Vinci were all illegitimate—but, as Kuehn notes, even those children raised by benevolent fathers and later granted legitimacy remained *legitimatus* (legalized), never *legitimus* (born legal). And Alberti, though cared for by his father, was never legitimized by him, even though he had no children by the woman he later married, which must have been a special additional source of grief.

Not only was Alberti illegitimate, he was the bastard of a man who had been exiled from Florence, for many years with a bounty on his head.[19] Born in Genoa in 1404, Battista grew up in northern Italy and studied at Padua and Bologna. In fact, he went back "home" to Florence only when he was about twenty-four, after the exile of the Albertis had been lifted by Cosimo, and stayed only a short time, being at first deeply disillusioned by the city. It was not until he was about thirty that he went back to, and settled for a while in, Florence. Although he found the city far more congenial on this second return, for Alberti Florence was very much the home to which he could not really return again, for he eventually left again and spent most of his adult life outside of the city.

For a person who felt himself to be a member of the elite, and was pathetically proud of his "family name," there was only one thing worse than being the illegitimate son of an exiled banker: that was to be an orphan. Alas, that fate also befell Alberti. He lost his mother at a tender age and only infrequently alludes to her. "The absent mother," writes Sydie, "is the shadow in his autobiography" (Sydie, 1997: 313). One strongly suspects that, in spite of her patrician background and previous marriage, indeed because of it, he was deeply ashamed of her disgraceful concubinage with his father. In any case, at the age of seventeen he lost the two persons who had shielded him from legal isolation and complete familial isolation: first his father, followed a few months later by his paternal uncle. Thus he became an "'outsider' to his family, lineage and city. Overwhelmed by his marginality, Alberti prayed sarcastically to the gods that in future they show no compassion to such a "pitiable" youth who had suffered such "unjust fortune."[20] His natural relatives added injury to his shame by cheating him out of his inheritance. He lived on the edge of poverty through college. Later, outraged by Alberti's alleged attacks on them in his *Famiglia*, his relatives apparently tried to assassinate him.[21]

Illegitimate, exiled, orphaned, impoverished, rejected by those closest to him, and with his life in constant danger: this is about as close as a free person could come to the condition of natal alienation that is one defining element of human slavery (Patterson,

1982: chs. 1–2). Lionardo's cry of anguish over the state of exile goes beyond any such lament—a near-hackneyed theme among Renaissance humanists—from ordinary political exiles. In such a condition:

> Nothing is more wearisome than living. Happy are they who have not felt our miseries and have not wandered like us in foreign cities, without dignity or authority, dispersed, away from relatives, friends and loved ones. Happy are they who have not been scorned, despised, spurned and hated. . . . We have been exiled without cause, persecuted without reason, scorned and hated without pity. (Alberti, 1969: Bk. 1, p. 60)

Given his father's status and wealth, the young Alberti would almost certainly have been brought up in a household attended by servants and slaves. As we noted earlier, it was customary for children with mothers who were alive and well to be left to the care of slaves. He may even have been nursed by one, for although free women were greatly preferred as wet nurses, they were not only hard to get, but were extremely picky about their employers, and very much at the top of the fifteenth-century "labor aristocracy," as Klapisch-Zuber has demonstrated (Klapisch-Zuber, 1984). It was not snobbishness alone that made these women so selective, but also the fact that if they were to maintain their reputation and relatively high incomes, they had to avoid all taint of scandal. The disgraced concubine of an exile with a bounty on his head would have a hard time securing the employment of any free nursemaid worth having, so it is a reasonable guess that the Alberti household would have settled for a slave. It is perhaps not insignificant that Adovardo goes on at interminable length about the problems and dangers—the "torment and sorrow"—of finding a suitable wet nurse (Alberti, 1969: Bk. 1, pp. 56–57). Further, having lost his mother early, it is a reasonable assumption that he would have been mothered by a slave woman.

More than any other Renaissance writer, Alberti used classical as well as earlier humanist literary models to express his deepest feelings about his own life and the world around him from which he felt increasingly alienated; as David Marsh notes, his writings "often dramatize his personal aspirations and frustrations" (Marsh, 1987: 2). Jarzombek has gone much further. "Personal experiences are drawn on as raw material," he argues, "but they are instantly typified, depersonalized, and transformed into generalizing postulates" (Jarzombek, 1989: 3). He finds in the Albertian experience an endless dialectic of author, text, and context in which Alberti uses a large group of semi-autobiographical characters as so many "allegorical tropes" to explore the life of the honest, isolated writer determined "to rid society of the 'spirit of death' " (Jarzombek, 1989: 12, 80).

I find it significant, then, that Alberti's first work, written at the age of twenty, was a Latin prose comedy, *Philodoxus*, largely inspired by the Roman comedies of Plautus and Terence. Although the *Philodoxus* is an allegorical love story set among mythological figures,[22] Alberti was in all likelihood drawn to the playwrights themselves as well as their vividly portrayed slave characters. There is the same complex relationship between the Roman playwrights, their texts, and their own marginal social condition as one finds in Alberti and his world, and the similarities could not have been missed by the latter. Terence, of course, had been a slave from North Africa, and Plautus, although reputedly from Umbria, was very familiar with them. Both classical dramatists had done with Greek middle comedy exactly what Alberti chose to do with their own works: adapted them to their own society and personal experiences. What E. F. Watling writes of Plautus could almost exactly apply to Alberti: "It is difficult to resist seeing some connexion between this fact—the slavery of the actors and Plautus's close association with their class—and the brilliantly vivacious portrayal of the slave characters in his comedies" (Watling, 1964: 9). Indeed, so successful were Alberti's plautinized adaptations of Plautus that for many years the fictitious Latin author he had invented as his pseudonym, Lepidus, was thought by contemporary scholars to have been a genuine classical writer. The degree of identification with the characters in the play is best revealed by Alberti's motivation for writing it: in the *Vita* he tells us that it was to console himself after learning, at age twenty, how vicious and inhuman his relatives were.

However, it is in another early work, *De Felicitate*, that Alberti reveals fully the extraordinary extent to which he empathized with the slaves he had known, and first demonstrated how deeply he saw and employed the dialectics of slavery as an exemplar of the human condition, a condition that, for Alberti, (as for Camus five hundred years later) was inherently paradoxical, an absurdity latent with meaning (cf. Camus, 1956: ch. 1).

How does one write an essay on the theme of human happiness? For Alberti there was only one way: by writing a dialogue about the reaction to their tragic condition by a group of recently bought slaves. The essay, one of his *Intercenales* or *Dinner Pieces*, is typical in the way it draws on classical sources (he would have learned a great deal from Plautus and Terence about the slave condition), on recent Italian histories (the dialogue is set at a time only a few years before Alberti's birth, and is taken from the work of his contemporary Poggio Bracciolini), and, of course, from his own experience. But in every other respect it stands apart. Renee Neu Watkins has observed that "it is by centuries the first work of fiction in which an author imaginatively identifies with slaves."[23] It would remain so for several centuries more. (I exclude Shakespeare's Caliban and Defoe's Friday, who, though slave-like, were really prototypical colonials, as West Indian literary critics and writers remind us all too often.)

Glad to have returned home safely with their cargo of slaves, the Italian slavemongers hold a feast, which they offer to share with the dejected slaves in an effort to cheer them up. When the slave merchant urges the slaves to "drink till you are drunk, drink and then sing," one cannot help recalling native American slaves being deliberately snared, then hooked on alcohol by their Spanish captors, or dejected Africans on slave ships and plantations being forced to sing and dance. However, what makes me very nearly certain that Alberti was describing something he must have seen is the statement: "First an amazing silence fell upon them."[24] The silence. That is the near-universal observation of all acute, firsthand observers of recently bought slaves. As I have shown elsewhere, for many new slaves it was a silence unto death. Scores of newly bought Africans in eighteenth-century Jamaica simply fell into an utterly impenetrable silence which was broken only by the final thud of their expired bodies (Patterson, 1967: ch. 6). Alberti would not have learned this from either Plautus or Terence since, to the best of my knowledge, there is no such depiction in any of the comedies, or in any description of slaves from the ancient sources. And it is not something one could have made up. He saw it himself, which is highly probable since, as noted earlier, he spent his childhood in Genoa, which had a thriving and very visible slave trade, the largest in Italy at the time. Furthermore, on moving to Padua to study he would have been only twenty-six miles from nearby Venice, where vessels carrying hundreds of slaves turned up so frequently that they were "Noticeable to the public at large"; Petrarch, for example, described a scene of slaves arriving in Venice which he witnessed on his visit there in the 1360s (McKee, 2008: 315–316).

The silence was broken by their lamentations, after which an old slave, then a middle-aged one, followed by an adolescent, and finally a mother of the infant slaves said, in turn, what it was that most grieved them about their condition. Each considered the condition of their group worse than the others. However, what is remarkable about all the laments is the thing they mourned in common: the rupture from ties of family and community, on the one hand, and from bonds of memory and history on the other. Here Alberti is describing the condition of slavery perfectly; he is also just as surely reflecting on his own personal condition: in describing what was most lost, Alberti was doubtless emphasizing what was most important to him. As Kuehn notes, a common theme running through the *Famiglia* is "the meaning of kinship" (Kuehn, 1985: 168). The elderly mourn their "poor abandoned family whom we governed and protected with our cautions and advice"; those in the prime of life mourned that they will never be able to do what men should do at their age: "earn merit through deeds or arms and council, to rise to honor and authority, to begin to enjoy the pleasures of our children"; the adolescents lament that "instead of wives and spouses we shall have salt sacks and jars of metal to fill . . . blows and beatings instead of games . . . [torn] away from the sweetest union of companions"; the mothers cry that their infants have "been born to perpetual sorrow," deprived of parental protection. (Alberti, we should note, not only had no legitimate family of orientation, and was literally an orphan when still young; he also had no family or procreation, remaining a celibate cleric throughout his life. Like the quintessential slave, he was a genealogical isolate (Patterson, 1982: intro).)

An interesting difference of views then follows: all the others tell the weeping mothers that the children are best off, for "they have no memory of lost joys to make them grieve, and any change of fortune can only bring betterment for them." This is a commonly held view in all slave societies; and here it must be admitted that Alberti might have picked it up from his classical sources, since it was a commonplace that the *verna,* the houseborn or reared slave, suffered less pain and had a higher chance of manumission. Every humanist knew about Marcus Tullius Tiro, Cicero's beloved and adoring freedman manager and research assistant.[25] Even so, he would also have observed the same thing himself in the domestic slavery of Genoa and Florence. But note that Alberti was not deluded by this piece of conventional wisdom about slavery, since he had the mothers stating clearly what was a universal and perhaps the most grievous feature of slavery: that parents had no custodial rights in their children. Of course, this is the aspect of slavery with which Alberti would most easily and bitterly empathize: the illegitimate child had no binding custodial claims. That is what illegitimacy means in law. His cousins had, and in fact cruelly asserted, full legal claims to his natural father's patrimony, leaving him impoverished.

What does a reflection on slavery have to do with happiness and freedom? The answer to the first is already given. Happiness is the enjoyment of all the things that the slaves spelled out as the most important losses: full integration in one's family, community and history, in short, identity (or, more properly, identities) and belonging; civic participation; the achievement of honors; the companionship of loved ones and friends; and the passing down to posterity of what one, through one's achievements, has added to the heritage of one's homeland. The civic ideal of the humanist emerges in existential contradistinction from the degradation of the slave.

For Alberti, like most of his fellow humanists, the capacity to engage in this civic culture was the essence of true freedom. However, Alberti also saw clearly how slavery was a powerful source for both the generation and the intense valorization of this real freedom. The really remarkable thing about this dialogue is that it is an attempt to portray the primal moment of the discovery of freedom as value. The experiences whose loss the slaves lament had been things previously cherished, but they had not been known or valorized as freedom. The existential crisis of its loss, like the crisis of Alberti's own personal loss of natality, generates at once both the desire to be removed from the power of the master and the primal need for release to those things they held most dear. Alberti remains true to his era in his refusal to separate the negative from the positive, and to make a value only of this negation. Valorizing negation is only the beginning of the construction of freedom—an important beginning, to be sure, and a beginning that is something new. Thus, Alberti has the prime slaves ending their lament on a note that is at once completely natural, yet profoundly philosophical: "Nothing remains for us but to be permitted to die," they say, but then they add, as if confounded by their own insight, confused because the insight is generated by their situation rather than their conscious reasoning: "And what then? What would we gain from such an untimely and bitter death, except to despair of our freedom and to die as wretches in slavery?" This is the closest any medieval or modern author has ever, and would ever, come to the primal moment in the discovery of freedom. To escape slavery, as Camus saw centuries later in his discourse on freedom (Camus 1956: ch. 1), the slave must say no. In this primal "no" he sets a limit, and within the bounds of that limit, he defines and creates what is most profoundly important in the human condition. Alberti saw that already, a half a millennium before Albert. But he saw something else: that the slave says no not only to slavery, but also to death, for this is his other choice. It is however, a shameful choice, a surrender of will. So the creation of freedom is really then not simply a matter of setting limits, it is a matter of choosing life. Freedom, in essence, is the startling discovery that one can *choose* life in the face of social death and dishonor. This is an awesome realization. It is what separates the humanistic person from the mere person. The mere person takes life, and his participation in it, for granted; it is something given, by God, by parents, whatever. To the pre-humanistic person the very idea of choosing life must seem to be either an absurdity or a blasphemy. For Alberti, freedom comes with the realization that the life one lives one has chosen and one must make.

But what does one make of it? That too is inherent in the slave condition: in slavery one comes to see what is most fundamental in the making of the life one has chosen, first at the cost of dishonor, then in the rebirth of redemption. And that is the experience of belonging; integration in, and participation in, one's natal community. The civic ideal is merely a refinement of this most basic truth. Of course, Alberti was not suggesting that one could only come to this realization through empathy with the slave condition. He implicitly suggested that this might have been the way it originally came about; but that discovery had been institutionalized in the ancient city-state, was deeply buried in the defining Christian doctrine of redemption (Latin: *redemptio*, being bought out of slavery into freedom by Christ's salvific crucifixion, which Alberti, as a cleric, obviously understood, the secularism of his writings notwithstanding), and had found its best late medieval and early modern secular exemplification in the free Italian republics. Reflecting on the modern slave condition, however, becomes a powerful surrogate means of reliving the primal moment in the discovery of freedom, of separating the wood from the trees, of focusing our attention on what is most essential for the free, rational person. The rational person, he suggests, will be able to arrive at the same conclusion through reasonable reflection. This is the meaning of the seemingly anticlimactic and pedestrian last sentence of the dialogue: "Do you see from the various laments of these people how all that human reason judges of happiness and unhappiness merely accords with common opinion?" (Cf. Camus, 1956: 106).

Needless to say, there is a broader purpose to all this, for the piece is a dazzling example of the humanistic integration of themes and the use of seemingly innocuous studies for veiled political criticism. In addition, we find Alberti also expressing impatience with many of the cherished clichés of his fellow humanists. Take the humanist concern with the cruelties of fortune. The slave merchant tells the slaves that "it was not we who brought adversity upon you but the power of fortune." Alberti would have little patience for this superficial view of the matter, so reminiscent of what he no doubt heard all too frequently in his interactions. The role of fortune, or chance, is one that preoccupied Alberti; he uses the term 204 times in the *Famiglia*, and as McLean notes, developed a "complicated multivocal strategy for dealing with it" (McLean, n.d.). Indeed, by so starkly showing up its absurdity as uttered by the slavemonger, he is implicitly criticizing all the self-serving cant about *fortuna*.[26]

But there is also some criticism of the most cherished philosophical refuge of his fellow humanists: the superficial retreat to stoicism. For the same slavemonger shortly thereafter attempts to console the slaves with this piece of stoic rhetoric: "Take the lot that fate awards you and be of strong and untroubled spirit." It was this speech that the slaves met with their strange, deathly silence. Indeed, in another dialogue on slavery, Alberti even more scathingly satirizes the more superficial Stoic view of freedom. After a long discourse with a Stoic philosopher, one slave said sarcastically that he began "to doubt whether it is not better for me to be a slave than a master, unless I am lured by the golden name of freedom" (Alberti, 1987b: 91–97). In a final passage, Alberti criticizes both slaves and the slave condition, as only someone who had known slaves well could have done: "a dull slave is no help to his owner, but an honest slave, while rare, is defiant in serving you." The real object of his sarcasm may have been the elaborate, faction-ridden patronage system of quattrocento Florence, focused on the Medici court, copiously expressed in the fawning "ritualized prostrations" of elite letter writers whose reputation, sociopolitical survival, and relational identities depended on their connection to the court and other superiors.[27] This critical stance is supported by a unique feature of Alberti's life and work: as noted by Sydie, his relationship with painters, sculptors, and architects was not clientelistic but collegial (Sydie, 1997: 313). Indeed, his great achievement in regard to these arts was not only to write foundational modern works on them, but to elevate them, for the first time in modern Western history, from their lowly status as artisanal and mechanical crafts to the humanistic heights of poetry, music, and philosophy. To be sure, in doing so Alberti attracted the patronage of powerful persons such as Pope Nicholas V and a position, however precarious, in elite society. But we are led to believe that he did so the hard, uncorrupt, and truly virtuous way, like the rare honest slave, defiant in service, innovative in his achievements for his master and ultimately, himself.

This proud defiance in the face of fortune is reflected in the two medallion portraits of him bearing his personal emblem and motto (Figure 11.3). The first medallion, believed to be a self-portrait cast in bronze c.1435, shows Alberti robed in a Roman toga and wearing a leonine hairstyle, evocative of his chosen name, "Leone"

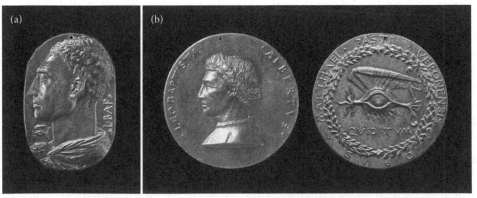

FIGURE 11.3 (a) Alberti's Self- Portrait c.1435. (b) Two sides of Medal of Leon Battista Alberti. C.1454, by Matteo de Pasti

(Latin: Lion). In front of his neck was his personal emblem, the winged eye with rays of light emanating from it. The second, struck ca. 1446–1448, by the sculptor Matteo de' Pasti, shows the emblem on the reverse side of the medallion, with Alberti's personal motto, "Quid Tum." There has been much speculation about their meaning, one influential theory arguing that the winged eye reflects Alberti's view that the painter's gaze more truthfully understands humanity and the world than the discourses of philosophy. (Pearson, 2011: 1–12) However, Alberti himself, as Watkins (1960) showed, indicated that the winged eye signified the all-knowing and all-seeing God, under whose gaze we render praise and "fulfill a flourishing and manly ideal of excellence," but also reminds us "to be awake, all-embracing as far as the power of intelligence allows."(Watkins, 1960: 256–257) The Latin motto, Quid Tum literally means "What next?" Or "What then?" but David Marsh (1996) has pointed out that generations of controversy over its true meaning was likely settled by Guglielmo Gormi who traces it to a passage in Virgil's Eclogues (1916: X:31): "quid tum si fuscus Amyntas?" meaning "What if Amyntas is swarthy?, which indicates that the proper translation of the term is "So What?" "Viewed in this context," Marsh (1996) comments, "the motto makes light of Alberti's illegitimacy." Virgil's dark-skinned Amyntas singing his beauty though black as violet and hyacinth, like the illegitimate Alberti, are ancient and renaissance echoes of a modern black American rapping defiantly, "So what if I am born out of wedlock and black?"

5. The *Tempio Malatestiano*: Womb or Tomb? Christian Freedom or Pagan Humanism?

Alberti was, of course, best known for his theoretical and applied work in architecture and it would have been surprising if his experiences of loss and part-belonging, and the contrasting faces of his identities, did not find some expression there (Figure 11.4). Few men of his times knew better the capacity of mankind for evil and oppression, not only from the experiences of his childhood and youth but from his observation of the men he worked for, most notably one of his most famous patrons and architectural clients, Sigismondo Malatesta, the "Wolf of Rimini" who was condemned by Pius II as one of the wickedest men of all times. Through his architectural work for him, Alberti explored the creative tension between good and evil, between the promises of medieval Christian freedom and pagan humanism; and, implicitly, the dialectical relation between slavery and freedom in the most physically embodied way possible. Orsini (1915: IX) is right that it is the work "which most faithfully mirrors the artistic temperament" of Alberti, and given their interdependence, his identities. The Tempio Malatestiano, or Church of San Francesco,[28] is literally a

(a)

(b)

FIGURE 11.4 (a) The Tempio Malatestiano. (b) Interior of Tempio Malatestiano.

triumphal semi-pagan façade commissioned by a rich tyrant encasing (enslaving?) and seemingly violating the structure and purpose of another, older Gothic Christian structure dedicated to, of all the divines, Francis, a saint who sanctified poverty, and exalted those "poor in temporal things, but rich in virtue." In a letter to Matteo de' Pasti during the rebuilding, Alberti wrote that he found the traditional Gothic proportions of the old church "disturbing" (Tavernor 1999: 59–61). Nonetheless, the elaborate interior architectural changes, which he may have partly designed, and certainly approved, so enhanced the Gothic Christian character of the old medieval nave, focused with singular piety on the exquisite Giotto crucifix pinned to the altar wall, that it remains unclear which is in the service of the other: the encased body of the San Francesco sacrilegiously made to bear the burden of the incomplete neoclassical showpiece (the project was abandoned when Malatesta's fortune declined after his excommunication) with its triumphal Roman arches and Corinthian columns memorializing an ungodly tyrant and his mistress, or the neo-classical revival being no more than an elaborate shell and advertisement for the revered old church, beckoning the faithful, ensuring that its inner salvific meaning—the redemptive freedom of the cross, the triumph of life over death—would be forever preserved. To shift to a Sophoclean metaphor: was the Tempio Malatestiano a desecrating, "all-engulfing" tomb (its sides being literally rows of tombs, a Gothic architectural practice symbolically repurposed with Alberti's large blind arcades evocative of Roman aqueducts), or a protected, temporally generative womb? Or, in the unrelenting ambiguity that defined Alberti, was it both, like Antigone's cave, as interpreted by Segal, "a place of contact between the worlds: between life and death, between Olympian and chthonic divinity, between gods and men"?[29] We cannot know. What we do know, as Grafton has persuasively demonstrated, is that "In practice, Alberti was above all an artist of façades—a creator of exteriors that radically altered the appearance of a building but did not directly express its internal organization as an organic, living synthesis" (Grafton, 2000: 325) and, we have argued, that this was equally true of the man behind the identities he crafted.

6. Conclusion: Freedom and Identities through Sublative Struggle

Only through struggle and resistance, only by means of constant encounter with the oppressive, alienating other, could the existential Alberti ever find a way to define his freedom and his identities. "In our labors," he once insisted, "the spirit is never enslaved but always free." In his encounters with all those persons and powers that would delegitimize him and deny his birhright, Alberti did not simply unmask the forces of evil in a cleansing cultural mission, as Jarzombek insightfully argues, but sublated them, making them the opposite of what they were, and in the process creating healing, though fleeting spaces of freedom, and, we have argued, this was equally true of the identities he crafted. As he wrote in one of the most revealing of his many autobiographical projects, in response to a liar assaulting him with fake facts: "I will easily resist you, since by your lies you make it clear to me that which you are, and who I am" (Alberti, 2004).[30]

Notes

1. There is a vast scholarly literature contesting the traditional Burchhardtian claim that the Renaissance marked a major turning point in Western social, cultural, and intellectual history, on which see the valuable survey by William Caferro (2010); also Bouwsma (1998). The narrower question of whether this was a period of economic hardship, prosperity, or a critical transition to capitalism has also generated heated debate, on which see Brown (1989). A major recent challenge to the revisionist "eclipse" is the work of the historical sociologist John Padgett. See in particular his study of the rise of the partnership system in Renaissance Florence (Padgett and Powell, 2013). See also Padgett and McLean (2011).

2. It cannot be too strongly emphasized that, contrary to the traditional historiographic view, the commitment to freedom persisted throughout the Middle Ages, though in distinctively medieval forms, in both religious and secular life. See Patterson, 2006: 31–66.

3. Brucker, ch. V. Quentin Skinner also criticizes Baron for his neglect of the influence of preexisting intellectual traditions (Skinner, 1978: 71).

4. I attempted to do this in my discussion of medieval freedom in Patterson (2006).

5. Porete (1993); see the suggestive interpretation of *The Mirror of Simple Souls* by Joanne Maguire Robinson (2001).

6. Douglass (1845/1995); on the tension between Douglass' experience and expressions of freedom as a former slave and a black man, and his more universalist and discursive view of freedom that emerged in his later writings, see Martin (1986).

7. Existential freedom lurks everywhere in Levi's classic account, *Survival in Auschwitz* (1996). Freedom is more discursively treated in his largely autobiographical fiction, especially *The Monkey's Wrench*. See Homer (2001).

8. Bruni, 1978: 70. On the complexities and social context of Bruni's view of freedom see Baron (1959–60).

9. The most famous case being Werner Sombart, who in *The Quintessence of Capitalism* (1915: 104) traces the origins of the capitalist ethic to this period, using as his main source Book III of the *Famiglia*, which, as Watkins notes, is "a hymn to *masserizia*—economy, thrift, good management" (13). See also pp. 16–20. Max Weber had a different interpretation of this text, seeing it as an example of precapitalist, aristocratic values in his *Protestant Ethic and the Spirit of Capitalism* (Weber, 2001). Grafton notes that other historians agreed with Weber, but himself is of the view that the work exhibits "lifelong contests between opposed values and concerns" in Alberti and, to an extent, the Florentine elite. See his Grafton 2000: 153–154.

10. Slavery in Italy is surprisingly well studied, as Sally McKee recently pointed out (2008: 306). See also Epstein 2001: 1–15.

11. For what is still among the most authoritative sources on late medieval and Renaissance slavery in Italy, see Verlinden, 1977: vol. 2; see also his collection of essays on the subject (Verlinden, 1970: part 2). On Sicily and Genoa, see Epstein, 2001: 183–191.

12. On the economic and ethnic aspects of Italian slave trading during the late medieval and Renaissance periods, see Epstein, 2001: 183–189. Italian slave traders, especially Genoese and Venetians, continued to play a prominent role in the Mediterranean white slave trade down to the late eighteenth century. See Davis, 2003: part 3.

13. See the classic and still very useful study by Iris Origo (1955). See also Verlinden, 1977; Heers, 1981; Klapisch-Zuber, 1986. Of great value also for the information they offer on the extent of slavery and the sexual exploitation of slaves are Trexler, 1973 and 1980.

14. For the classic account of the effects of slavery on the character and attitudes of the children of slaveholders, see Jefferson, 1995.

15. The classic older studies of Alberti are those of Mancini (1911) and Michel (1930). Of the two, I have drawn primarily on Michel, whose emphasis on disjuncture and exile in Alberti makes far more sense to me. By far the most useful introduction to Alberti for the sociologically oriented reader is Grayson (1957), a work which not only offers an excellent analysis of the two phases of Alberti's life and works, but places his ideas in their social context. I have also drawn heavily on Gadol, 1969; Jarzombek, 1989; and Grafton, 2000. On Alberti's architecture, I have found Franco Borsi's work not only very informative, but also quite suggestive in light of my own peculiar interests, especially his discussion of the Tempio Malatestiano in his *Leon Battista Alberti: The Complete Works* (1977).

16. An accessible paperback German edition is now available (Alberti, 2004). On the problem of authorship, see Watkins, 1957. For a persuasive analysis of this text, which takes it for granted that Alberti is the author, although the work is seen as merely one, partly allegorical, "variation in the autobiographical sub-text" of Alberti, see Jarzombek, 1989.

17. For a useful account of Burckhardt's deliberate misreading, as well as commentary on recent approaches to the Vita, see McLaughlin, 2016.

18. Michel, 1930: 74–75. After Michel, an important work focusing on Alberti's alienation, strongly influenced by emerging German existential thought, was Ruth Lang, *Leon Battista Alberti und die Sancta Masseritia* (1938). The most important recent works in this tradition are by Eugenio Garin (1963) and Mark Jarzombek (1989). Like Lang, Jarzombek emphasizes the medieval continuities in Alberti's thought, which he considers "a startling neo-medieval critique of humanism." Anthony Grafton attempts a more even-handed approach in his *Leon Battista Alberti* (2000), but see Martin McLaughlin's (2016) comments on Grafton.

19. On the harsh consequences of exile persisting in quattrocento Italy, see Brown, 2002: ch. 14.

20. Alberti, 1987a: 16–18. Alberti thinly disguised this short autobiographical comment under the classical guise of Philoponius. See Marsh's (1987) note on p. 226.

21. There are numerous veiled references to the brutal treatment Alberti received from his own family in *Della Famiglia*. Indeed, the entire first book can be read as a bitter, ironic denunciation of their treatment by showing how the ideal family ought to bring up its children. Sometimes, however, his anger is explicit. See, for example, Alberti, 1971: Book 2, p. 151; Book 3, p. 209.

22. For a summary of the plot and an interpretation which suggests that the play foreshadows all the major themes in Alberti's humanist works, see Jarzombek, 1989: 13–16. Grafton suggests as much in his work (2000: 3–6).

23. Watkins, 1978: 99. I have mainly used Watkins' translation, but have also drawn on David Marsh's in his edition of Alberti's *Intercenales* (Marsh, 1987: 28–33, 231–232).

24. Alberti, 1978: 104. All references, unless otherwise stated, are to this translation. Marsh translates the sentence as: "A strange silence fell upon them all" (Marsh, 1987: 31).
25. According to Bracciolini, Tiro, "who adhered to his master's virtues, was indeed more noble than the son who abandoned his father's integrity" (1978: 146).
26. In Book 1 of the *Famiglia*, Alberti has Adovardo presenting the more conventional Renaissance view of fortune; in the following Book, however, Battista presents his own view that honor can and will save all that is truly important from the ravages of fortune (Alberti, 1969: 89–90, 148–149). Further, as an ordained priest, he would have been fully cognizant of Augustine's classic broadside against ancient notions of fortune, which he replaced with the Christian belief in God's providence.
27. For a valuable discussion of this, see McLean, 2007: ch. 8.
28. See the excellent and richly illustrated discussion by Franco Borsi in his *Leon Battista Alberti: The Complete Works* (1977: ch. 5); also the very stimulating comments on the building in Jarzombek, 1989: 172–174.
29. Segal, 1999: 180. Segal refers to the cave as "sheltering womb or all-engulfing tomb."
30. Cf. one of Frederick Douglass' (1857) most celebrated remarks: "If there is no struggle, there is no progress. Those who profess to favor freedom and yet depreciate agitation are men who want crops without plowing up the ground. They want rain without thunder and lightning. They want the ocean without the awful roar of its many waters." [I have slightly adapted Watkins' translation, more in line with Grafton's (2000) translation of the passage].

References

Alberti, L. B., 1969. *The family in Renaissance Florence (I libri della famiglia)*. Translated by R. N. Watkins. Columbia: University of South Carolina Press.
Alberti, L. B., 1971. *The Albertis of Florence: Leon Battista Alberti's* Della famiglia. Translated by G. A. Guarino. Lewisburg, PA: Bucknell University Press.
Alberti, L. B., 1978. Happiness. In: R. N. Watkins, ed. *Humanism and liberty: Writings on freedom from fifteenth-century Florence*. Columbia: University of South Carolina Press. pp.98–103.
Alberti, L. B., 1987a. The orphan. In: D. Marsh, ed. *Dinner pieces*. Binghamton, NY: Renaissance Society of America. pp.16–18.
Alberti, L. B., 1987b. The slave. In: D. Marsh, ed. *Dinner pieces*. Binghamton, NY: Renaissance Society of America. pp.115–117.
Alberti, L. B., 1989. Vita. In "L.B. Alberti in the Mirror: An Interpretation of the Vita with a New Translation," *Italian Quarterly*, 30, pp.5–30.
Alberti, L. B., 1993. Philodoxus. Edited and translated by J. R. Jones and L. Guzzi, *Celestinesca*, 17(1), pp.87–134.
Alberti, L. B., 2004. *Vita*. Edited and introduced by Christine Tauber. Frankfurt: Stroemfeld/Roter Stern.
Alberti, L. B. 2016. *La vita, l'umanesimo, le opere letterarie*. Florence: Olschki. pp.3–18.
Baron, H., 1959–60. The social background of political liberty in the early Italian Renaissance. *Comparative Studies in Society and History*, 2, pp.440–451.
Baron, H., 1966. *The crisis of the early Italian Renaissance: Civic humanism and republican liberty in an age of classicism and tyranny*. Princeton, NJ: Princeton University Press.

Borsi, F., 1977. *Leon Battista Alberti: The Complete Works.* London: Faber and Faber.

Bouwsma, W., 1998. Eclipse of the Renaissance. *American Historical Review,* 103(1), pp.115–117.

Bouwsma, W., 1968. *Venice and the Defense of Republican Liberty: Renaissance Values in the Age of the Counter Reformation.* Berkeley and Los Angeles, Calif: University of California Press.

Bracciolini, P., 1978. On nobility. In: R. N. Watkins, ed. *Humanism and liberty: Writings on freedom from fifteenth-century Florence.* Columbia: University of South Carolina Press. pp.121–148.

Braudel, F., 1979. *The perspective of the world: Civilization and capitalism, fifteenth–eighteenth century.* Vol. 3. New York: Harper and Row.

Brown, A., 2000. The language of empire. In: W. J. Connell and A. Zorzi, eds. *Florentine Tuscany: Structures and practices of power.* New York: Cambridge University Press. pp.32–47.

Brown, A., 2002. Insiders and outsiders: The changing boundaries of exile. In: W. J. Connell, ed. *Society and individual in Renaissance Florence.* Berkeley: University of California Press. chapter 14, pp.337–383.

Brown, J. C., 1989. Prosperity or hard times in Renaissance Italy? *Renaissance Quarterly,* 42(4), pp.761–780.

Brucker, G. A., 1969. *Renaissance Florence.* Berkeley: University of California Press.

Brucker. G. A., 1977. *The Civic World of Early Renaissance Florence,* ch. V. Princeton: Princeton University Press.

Bruni, L., 1978. The history of Florence, Book 4. In: R. N. Watkins, ed. *Humanism and liberty: Writings on freedom from fifteenth-century Florence.* Columbia: University of South Carolina Press. pp.27–91.

Burckhardt, J., 1904. *The Civilization of the Renaissance in Italy.* Translated by S. G. C. Middlemore. London: Macmillan & Co.

Caferro, W., 2010. *Contesting the Renaissance.* New York: Wiley-Blackwell.

Camus, A., 1956. *The Rebel.* New York: Knopf.

Connell, W. J., 2002. Introduction. In: W. J. Connell, ed. *Society and individual in Renaissance Florence.* Berkeley: University of California Press. pp.1–12.

Davis, R. C., 2003. *Christian slaves, Muslim masters: White slavery in the Mediterranean, the Barbary Coast and Italy, 1500–1800.* New York: Palgrave MacMillan.

Douglass, F., 1845/1995. *Narrative of the life of Frederick Douglass.* New York: Dover.

Epstein, S. A., 2001. *Speaking of slavery: Color, ethnicity, and human bondage in Italy.* Ithaca, NY: Cornell University Press.

Farrar, C., 1993. Ancient Greek political theory as a response to democracy. In: J. Dunn, ed. *Democracy: The unfinished journey, 508 B.C.–A.D. 1993.* New York: Oxford University Press. pp.17–39.

Finley, M. I., 1960. Was Greek civilization based on slave labor? In: *Slavery in classical antiquity.* Cambridge, UK: W. Heifer & Sons. pp.33–72.

Fletcher, C., 2016. The Black Prince of Florence: The Spectacular Life and Treacherous World of Alessandro de' Medici. New York. Oxford University Press.

Gadol, J., 1969. *Leon Battista Alberti: Universal man of the early Renaissance.* Chicago: University of Chicago Press.

Garin, E., 1963. *Portraits from Quattrocento.* New York: Harper and Row.

Goldthwaite, R. A., 1980. *The building of Renaissance Florence.* Baltimore: Johns Hopkins University Press.

Grafton, A., 2000. *Leon Battista Alberti: Master builder of the Italian Renaissance.* New York: Hill and Wang.

Grayson, C., 1957. The humanism of Alberti. *Italian Studies*, 12, pp.37–56.

Heers, J., 1981. *Esclaves et domestiques au Moyen Age dans le monde méditerranéen*. Paris: Fayard.

Herlihy, D., 1969. Population, plague and social change. In: A. Molho, ed. *Social and economic foundations of the Italian Renaissance*. New York: John Wiley. p.80.

Homer, F., 2001. *Primo Levi and the politics of survival*. Columbia: University of Missouri Press.

Jarzombek, M., 1989. *On Leon Baptista Alberti: His literary and aesthetic theories*. Cambridge, MA: MIT Press.

Jefferson, T., 1995. *Notes on the State of Virginia*. New York: Penguin Classics.

Klapisch-Zuber, C., 1984. Parents de sang, parents de lait: La mise en nourrice à Florence (1300–1530). *Annales de démographie historique*, pp.33–64.

Klapisch-Zuber, C., 1986. Women servants in Florence during the fourteenth and fifteenth centuries. In: B. A. Hanawalt, ed. *Women and work in preindustrial Europe*. Bloomington: Indiana University Press. pp.56–80.

Kuehn, T., 1985. Reading between the patrilines: Leon Battista Alberti's *Della famiglia* in light of his illegitimacy. In: *Tatti Studies: Essays in the Renaissance 1*. Chicago: University of Chicago Press. pp.161–187.

Kuehn, T., 2002. *Illegitimacy in Renaissance Florence*. Ann Arbor: University of Michigan Press.

Lang, R., 1938. *Leon Battista Alberti und die Sancta Masseritia*. Saint Gall: Rapperswil.

Levi, P., 1996. *Survival in Auschwitz*. New York: Touchstone.

Lowe, K., 2013. Visible Lives: Black Gondoliers and Other Black Africans in Renaissance Venice. *Renaissance Quarterly*, 66(2), pp.412–452.

Mancini, G., 1911. *Vita di Leon Battista Alberti*. Florence: G. Carnesecchi.

Marsh, D., ed., 1987. *Dinner pieces*. By L. B. Alberti. Binghamton, NY: Renaissance Society of America.

Marsh, D., 1996. So What": Reply to Ingrid D. Rowland. *New York Review of Books*, Jan. 12, 1995.

Martin, W. E., 1986. *The mind of Frederick Douglass*. Chapel Hill: University of North Carolina Press.

McKee, S., 2008. Domestic slavery in Renaissance Italy. *Slavery and Abolition*, 29(3), pp.305–326.

McLaughlin, M., 2016. 'La vita dellAlberti. Dall'autobiografia al ritratto di Burckhardt' in his book, *Leon Battista Alberti. La vita, l'umanesimo, le opere letterarie*. Florence: Olschki. pp.3–18.

McLean, P. D., 2007. *The art of the network: Strategic interaction and patronage in Renaissance Florence*. Durham, NC: Duke University Press.

McLean, P. D., n.d. "Chance in Renaissance Florence." http://www.rci.rutgers.edu/~pmclean/mclean%20ccacc%20paper%20final.htm

Michel, P.-H., 1930. *La pensée de L. B. Alberti*. Paris: Société d'Editions "Les Belles Lettres."

Millar, F., 1965. Epictetus and the imperial court. *Journal of Roman Studies*, 55, pp.141–148.

Najemy, J. M., 2002. Giannozzo and his elders: Alberti's critique of Renaissance patriarchy. In: W. J. Connell, ed. *Society and individual in Renaissance Florence*. Berkeley: University of California Press. pp.51–78.

Oldfather, W. A., 1979. Introduction. *The discourses*, by Epictetus, edited and translated by W. A. Oldfather. Cambridge, MA: Harvard University Press.

Origo, I., 1955. The domestic enemy: The eastern slaves in Tuscany in the fourteenth and fifteenth centuries. *Speculum*, 30(3), pp.321–366.

Orsini, L., 1915. The Malatesta temple; sixtyfour illustrations, and text. Milan. Bonomi. Available online at: https://archive.org/details/malatestatemplesoooorsiiala

Padgett, J., and McLean, P. 2011. Economic credit in Renaissance Florence. *Journal of Modern History*, 83(1), pp.1–47.

Padgett, J., and Powell, W. W., 2013. *The emergence of organizations and markets*. Princeton, NJ: Princeton University Press.

Patterson, O., 1967. *The sociology of slavery: An analysis of the origins, development and structure of Negro slave society in Jamaica*. London: McGibbon & Kee.

Patterson, O., 1982. *Slavery and social death*. Cambridge, MA: Harvard University Press.

Patterson, O., 1991. *Freedom, vol. 1, Freedom in the making of Western culture*. New York: Basic Books.

Patterson, O., 2006. The ancient and medieval origins of modern freedom. In: J. Stouffer and S. Mintz, eds. *The problem of evil*. Amherst, MA: University of Massachusetts Press. pp.31–66.

Pearson, C., 2011. Philosophy Defeated: Truth and Vision in Leon Battista Alberti's Momus. *Oxford Art Journal*, 34(1), pp.1–12.

Plato. 1914. *Plato: Euthyphro. Apology. Crito. Phaedo. Phaedrus* (Loeb Classical Library). Translated by Harold North Fowler; Introduction by W. R. M. Lamb. Cambridge, MA: Harvard University Press.

Plato. 1955. *The republic*. Translated by H. D. P. Lee. Harmondsworth: Penguin.

Plato. 1980. *Phaedo*. Translated by H. Tredennick. Princeton, NJ: Princeton University Press.

Pocock, J. G. A., 1975. *The Machiavellian moment: Florentine political thought and the Atlantic republican tradition*. Princeton, NJ: Princeton University Press.

Pohlenz, M., 1966. *Freedom in Greek life and thought*. Dordrecht: D. Reidel.

Porete, M., 1993. *Mirror of simple souls*. Edited by E. Babinsky. New York: Paulist Press.

Raaflaub, K., 1983. Democracy, oligarchy and the concept of the "free citizen" in late fifth century Athens. *Political Theory*, 11, pp.517–544.

Raaflaub, K, 2004. *The discovery of freedom in Ancient Greece*. Translated by Renate Franciscono. Chicago: University of Chicago Press.

Rinuccini. Liberty. In Watkins, R. N., ed. and trans., 1978. *Humanism and liberty: Writings on freedom from fifteenth-century Florence*. Columbia: University of South Carolina Press.

Robinson, J. M., 2001. *Nobility and annihilation in Marguerite Porete's Mirror of simple souls*. Albany: State University of New York Press.

Ross, C., 2010. *Primo Levi's narratives of embodiment: Containing the human*. New York: Routledge.

Rubinstein, N., 1952. Florence and the despots: Some aspects of Florentine diplomacy in the fourteenth century. In: *Transactions of the Royal Historical Society*, Fifth Series, vol. 221–245.

Rubinstein, N., 1979. Oligarchy and democracy in fifteenth-century Florence. In: *Florence and Venice: Comparisons and relations, vol. 1, Quattrocento*. Harvard Center for Italian Renaissance Studies (Villa i Tatti). Florence: La Nuova Italia Editrice. pp.99–112.

Segal, C., 1999. *Tragedy and civilization: An interpretation of Sophocles*. Norman: University of Oklahoma Press.

Skinner, Q., 1978. *Foundations of modern political thought*. Vol. 1. New York: Cambridge University Press.

Sombart, W., 1915. *The quintessence of capitalism*. New York: E.P.Dutton & Co.

Sydie, R. A., 1997. The phallocentric gaze: Leon Battista Alberti and visual art. *Journal of Historical Sociology*, 10(3), pp.310–341.

Tavernor, R., 1999. On Alberti and the Art of Building. New Haven. Yale University Press.

Trexler, R. C., 1973. The foundlings of Florence, 1395–1455. *History of Childhood Quarterly*, 1(2), pp.259–284.

Trexler, R. C., 1980. La prostitution florentine au 15è siecle. *Annales–Economies–Sociétés–Civilisations*, 36, pp.983–1015.

Verlinden, C., 1970. *The beginnings of modern colonization*. Ithaca, NY: Cornell University Press.

Verlinden, C., 1977. *L'esclavage dans l'Europe médiévale*. Vol. 2. Brugge: De Tempel.

Watkins, R. N., 1957. The authorship of the *Vita anonyma* of Leon Battista Alberti. *Studies in the Renaissance*, 4, pp.101–112.

Watkins, R., 1960. "L.B. Alberti's Emblem, The Winged Eye, and His, Name Leo," Mitteilungen des Kunsthistorischen Institutes in Florenz 9.Bd.,H. ¾: 256–258.

Watkins, R. N., ed. and trans., 1978. *Humanism and liberty: Writings on freedom from fifteenth-century Florence*. Columbia: University of South Carolina Press.

Watling, E. F., trans. 1964. Introduction. In: *Plautus: The rope and other plays*. Harmondsworth: Penguin Books. pp.7–22.

Weber, M., 2001. *The Protestant ethic and the spirit of capitalism*. New York: Routledge.

....

CHAPTER 12

FREEDOM
AND ENLIGHTENMENT

....

RYAN PATRICK HANLEY

OUR understanding of the freedom bequeathed to us by the political thinkers of the Enlightenment has long been dominated by two conceptual categories. Isaiah Berlin's "Two Concepts of Liberty" codified the distinction between "positive liberty"—freedom to exercise or participate in certain types of power—and "negative liberty"—freedom from being subject to certain types of power—and rendered it a staple of how we understand early modern thinking about freedom (Berlin, 2002: 178–179; cf. Schmidtz and Brennan, 2010: 2–3). Yet the positive-negative dichotomy, however appealing and convenient it may be, may have done us more harm than good—and indeed on two fronts.

First, by offering a convenient classificatory scheme that invites categorizing thinkers on one side of the ledger or the other, Berlin's distinction, for all its clarity, can inhibit appreciation of certain core principles that thinkers on both sides of the ledger held in common. Second, in suggesting that negative and positive liberty have in practice grounded two dramatically distinct visions of the best regime, it can obscure appreciation of the ways in which these two concepts of liberty in fact can and often do work together. This chapter seeks to redress this by examining the conception of freedom set forth by three key Enlightenment thinkers: Adam Smith, Rousseau, and Kant. In so doing it argues that what they called "moral" or "inner" freedom suggests an important way in which positive liberty can serve to promote ends traditionally associated with negative liberty.

What follows thus offers a critique of Berlin's dichotomy in "Two Concepts," and particularly its association of positive liberty with authoritarianism. In so doing it follows a train of previous critiques. Some of these have argued that two concepts are too few and fail to account for a third, namely a neo-Roman or republican theory of freedom that privileges non-domination (Skinner, 1998; Pettit, 1999). Others have suggested that two concepts are too many, as much of what falls under the heading of positive liberty in fact reduces to claims characteristic of negative liberty (Nelson, 2005). The critique presented here is different: namely that Berlin's agenda-setting expression of the positive-negative dichotomy in "Two Concepts" gives insufficient attention to the question of how these two concepts might work together (though cf. Cherniss, 2013: 189–220). Thus the value in turning to the conception of freedom developed by Smith, Rousseau, and Kant lies in how it can help us better appreciate how positive liberty and negative liberty are complementary rather than contradictory (see also Gaus, 2011: esp. 31).

Rethinking the relationship of positive liberty to negative liberty via these three Enlightenment thinkers also has a second benefit. Their conception of inner freedom challenges not only common distinctions of positive and negative liberty but also common ways of distinguishing politics and morality. Today we tend to regard freedom, whether positive or negative, as a political concept distinct from ethical concerns about character, virtue, and flourishing that are generally regarded as the province of certain branches of moral philosophy; political freedom is not a matter of virtue, but of institutions and procedures. But the Enlightenment thinkers that are our focus here saw matters differently. So far from thinking that freedom rests solely on institutions, they suggest that the perpetuation of the institutional structures necessary for political freedom itself depends on a cultivation of virtues of personal responsibility enabling individual agents to bear the political freedoms guaranteed by a well-constituted polity. In this sense, they regard moral freedom as inextricable from political freedom insofar as moral freedom enables us to shoulder the burdens of political freedom. Thus the concept of freedom developed by Smith, Rousseau, and Kant offers good reasons not only to question the line of demarcation separating positive from negative freedom, but to regard moral freedom as indispensible to political freedom.

1. ADAM SMITH: FREEDOM AND SELF-COMMAND

Adam Smith's influence on today's debates over freedom likely eclipses that of any other Enlightenment political thinker; immediately familiar to many readers will be the many ways in which Smith's authority continues to be routinely invoked by advocates of market deregulation and by champions of the rights of individuals to pursue their self-interest to maximum extent (for overview, see Kennedy, 2016). In this vein, Smith's notorious invisible hand remains for many the emblem of a free society, defined as one in which individuals, independent of extensive regulation by government, are left to pursue their economic interests as they see fit and yet in a way that will contribute to public well-being. Smith's discussions of the advantages of divided specialized labor, the benefits of free trade, and the limits of government authority are key elements of our debates over political freedom today. Yet there is an irony to Smith's authority on this front. Smith himself speaks relatively rarely of freedom in any direct sense; with the important exceptions of his explication of "our present sense of the word Freedom" (*WN*, 3.3.5), and his invocations of "perfect" or "natural" liberty (e.g., *WN*, 4.9.28 and

WN, 4.9.51), Smith's discussions of freedom are fewer in his work than one might expect given his reputation. And given that one looks almost entirely in vain for substantive references to freedom or liberty in his other great work, *The Theory of Moral Sentiments*, it seems right to say that Smith "did not present readers with a theory of freedom per se" (Schmidtz, 2016: 208).

What ought we to make of this? Clearly it would be wrong to conclude that Smith's reputation as a champion of freedom is undeserved. Instead we might try to rethink exactly how Smith understood freedom—for here is where his contribution as a theorist of freedom lies. Smith helped advance the Enlightenment debate over freedom in two ways. First, as is now well appreciated, Smith set forth a theory of the relationship of markets to freedom founded on the claim that the interdependence characteristic of market societies severs the freedom-inhibiting dependence characteristic of premodern societies (Berry, 1989: 114–118; Rasmussen, 2008: 123–125, 142–150; Hanley, 2009: 19–24; Schmidtz, 2016). But secondly—and less well appreciated—Smith set forth a theory of the character virtues that enable us to enjoy and exercise our freedom in a manner beneficial to both others and ourselves. And central to this theory is Smith's concept of self-command. Attending to the role of self-command in this process can help us not only to better appreciate how Smith understood concepts often associated with positive liberty as indispensible to the protection of negative liberty, but can also help clarify how his theory compares to the theories of freedom developed by Rousseau and Kant.

What then is self-command according to Smith, and what role does it play in his theory of freedom? Smith presents the core of his definition in distinguishing "two different sets of virtues": "the soft, the gentle, the amiable virtues, the virtues of candid condescension and indulgent humanity," and "the great, the awful and respectable, the virtues of self-denial, of self-government" (*TMS*, 1.1.5.1). The self-command Smith so admires—and ultimately lionizes as "not only a chief virtue" but indeed the virtue from which "all the other virtues seem to derive their principal lustre" (*TMS*, 6.3.11)—is clearly a species of this second set of virtues, and takes for its principal task cultivation of austerity to the self and its desires in the name of achieving a mastery of our selfish inclinations and subjective sentiments (see esp. Montes, 2004: 93–96, 105–122). In this sense, Smithean self-command is crucial to the pursuit of self-mastery traditionally associated with positive liberty.

All of this is clear enough from Smith's account. What is less clear is why he finds self-command so admirable and indeed so indispensible for citizens of modern commercial societies—that is, citizens of societies dedicated to protecting negative liberty, rather than those precivilized societies in which self-command was seen as indispensible to the preservation of the sense of honor on which the moral codes of such societies were founded (see, e.g., *TMS*, 5.2.9–16). Commentators have tended in response to emphasize the degree to which he regarded self-command as a means of promoting social cohesion in civilized societies. Self-command, as they have shown, is the product of our natural desire for the sympathy and the approbation of others, and its exercise generates useful moral norms that emerge spontaneously from the ground up rather than being imposed from on high by elites (*TMS*, 1.1.4.7; Otteson, 2002: esp. 107–110).

Self-command thus plays a crucial role in the process of generating beneficial norms through iterated intersubjective exchanges of sympathy. Yet self-command is also important for a second reason—one that has less to do with generating social concord than with securing the conditions freedom requires. Smith's development of this argument begins with the claim that self-command is in our self-interest as it enables us to resist our momentary inclinations for the sake of pursuing our long-term interests and thereby reap greater dividends over a longer horizon (see *TMS*, 4.2.8; Montes, 2004: 84–85; Davis, 2003: 291–299). Self-command is indispensible to the free society insofar as it enables a free agent pursuing his or her self-interest to maximize the returns on such an agent's self-interested pursuits over the long term. A second way in which self-command is indispensible to the free society concerns its role in the preservation of such societies once established. In his *Lectures on Jurisprudence* Smith explains—citing the example of China in particular—that the "disadvantages of a commercial spirit" lie in the fact that in commercial societies courage and martial spirit are vitiated to such a degree that their "conquest is easy" (*LJB*, 332–333; Hanley, 2014). Self-command is thus necessary to guard against the specific existential threats to which he thought commercial societies were especially prone.

Yet for all this, Smith's reasons for regarding self-command as indispensible to both free societies and free individuals goes beyond simple calculations of utility. For in addition to helping us resist the temptations of short-term-gain pursuits and helping us resist the enemies at the gates, in enabling us to overcome or withstand our momentary passions and occasional inclinations, self-command also helps us to realize another fundamental and very different good: tranquility. Smith is clear on the import of tranquility: "Happiness consists in tranquility and enjoyment. Without tranquility there can be no enjoyment" (*TMS*, 3.3.30). Tranquility is indispensable to happiness on Smith's view, and the greatest obstacles to tranquility are the passions, especially those that overwhelm the agent and "seduce him to violate all the rules which he himself, in all his sober and cool hours, approves of" (*TMS*, 6.3.1). It is the task of self-command to overcome this seduction by rendering us the masters of our subjective and momentary inclinations and enabling us to follow the "rules" we give ourselves.

Herein lies the significance of Smith's theory of self-command for his theories of both happiness and freedom. On the former front, self-command serves to secure the goods most indispensable to human happiness. These are, again, partly material. But they are also moral goods insofar as self-command also secures for its possessor the "esteem and approbation" of spectators as well as the self-esteem of one who, in exercising self-command, both "preserves his tranquility" and indeed "approves and applauds himself" (*TMS*, 3.3.24; see also 3.3.27). Insofar as self-command enables us to resist our momentary inclinations and instead follow those rules of right that we set down for ourselves in our cool moments, it not only promotes our happiness but enables us to liberate ourselves from enslavement to our passions.

This view of self-command binds Smith to both Rousseau and Kant in a key way. Smith's claim that self-command frees its possessor from subjection to "his natural, his untaught and undisciplined feelings," enabling him to act in a manner befitting "his sense of honour, his regard to his own dignity," anticipates elements of Rousseau's and Kant's theories in tying self-command to both freedom and dignity (*TMS*, 3.3.28; cf. Montes, 2004: esp. 83n53, 114–122; Otteson, 2002: 239). It also takes a key step beyond what Taylor called the "caricatural" conception of negative liberty toward the vision of freedom associated with "freedom of self-fulfillment, or self-realization according to our own pattern" (Taylor, 1985: 212). But what is especially important is that Smith valued self-command for its capacity to preserve tranquility—a capacity especially necessary for citizens of modern liberal commercial orders principally committed to negative liberty. For insofar as such orders tend to inflame the self-directed passions of the love of gain and love of esteem (see esp. *TMS*, 1.3.3; Hanley, 2009; Schmidtz, 2016), self-command prevents us from becoming slaves to the very passions on which commercial society depends, and thus helps preserve psychological well-being amidst the ubiquitous temptations of the condition of maximum negative liberty.

2. ROUSSEAU ON MORAL FREEDOM

Smith's concept of self-command, it has been argued above, adds an important dimension to our understanding of freedom. Yet Smith never calls self-command "freedom," nor does he go so far as to suggest that positive liberty might open up horizons that rival or transcend those of a political order based on negative liberty. For the explicit association of self-mastery with freedom, and indeed a freedom that cannot be understood as a mere amplification of negative freedom, we need to turn to Rousseau, a thinker Smith directly engaged (see Rasmussen, 2008; Hanley, 2009; Griswold, 2010). To many of his critics—Berlin not least among them—Rousseau represents the champion of positive liberty par excellence (Berlin, 2002: 183–185), and indeed the defender of a positive liberty inimical to negative liberty. But more recently Rousseau's commitments to individual and negative liberty have begun to receive greater attention (e.g., Gaus, 2011: 24–28; Hanley, 2013; Wokler, 2012; Cohen, 2010: 34–40), and in light of this shift, the discussion that follows aims to show how Rousseau's theory of moral freedom might help to resolve part of the tension between these seemingly opposed attractions on Rousseau's part to both positive and negative liberty.

Seeing this requires focusing on a very specific side of Rousseau's conception of freedom. Rousseau of course is famous as a philosopher of freedom, yet his fame on this front is largely the result of his defenses of freedoms very different from the freedom on which we have been focusing. The first of these is the natural freedom of the savage in precivilized society, as presented in the first book of the *Discourse on Inequality*. The second is the freedom of the citizen of a well-constituted state directed by the general will, as presented in the first book of the *Social Contract*. But Rousseau also presents a third concept of freedom, and his defense of this concept reveals what he shares with Kant and Smith, as well as how he envisioned the relationship of positive to negative freedom and the place of virtue and character in the achievement of freedom.

Rousseau gives this freedom the label "moral freedom," and he offers one of his most important articulations of its fundamental principle in *Social Contract* 1.8. Moral freedom, he here explains, is that "which alone makes man truly the master of himself," as "the impulse of appetite alone is slavery, and obedience to the law one has prescribed to oneself is freedom" (*SC*, 4:142; *OC*, 3:365). His distinction between natural appetite and self-given law restates the distinction between inclination and self-approved rules central to Smith's account of self-command, and translates this distinction explicitly into the terms of freedom. Thus Rousseau's insistence that it is precisely at this moment at which "the voice of duty replaces physical impulse and right replaces appetite" that the human being evolves from "a stupid, limited animal into an intelligent being and a man" (*SC*, 4:141; *OC*, 3:364; see esp. Wokler, 2012: 174–175; Cohen, 2010: 12–14; Williams, 2014: 57–60).

Rousseau's substantive definition of moral freedom is thus quite clear: moral freedom consists in the individual's capacity to resist impulses of physical appetite and instead be governed by laws one gives to oneself. Somewhat less obvious are Rousseau's answers to two questions that follow from this definition. First, how is moral freedom cultivated? Second, why is it so important for modern citizens to cultivate moral freedom? Rousseau provides his fullest answers to both questions in *Emile*. Moral freedom is a focal concept throughout *Emile*, but two passages that bookend the text deserve particular attention here. One comes near the end of the work. Here the tutor offers his response to Emile's fondest wish, namely to marry his love Sophie:

> One aspires in vain to liberty under the safeguard of the laws. Laws! Where are there laws, and where are they respected? Everywhere you have seen only individual interest and men's passions reigning under this name. But the eternal laws of nature and order do exist. For the wise man, they take the place of positive law. They are written in the depth of his heart by conscience and reason. It is to these that he ought to enslave himself in order to be free. The only slave is the man who does evil, for he always does it in spite of himself. Freedom is found in no form of government; it is in the heart of the free man. (*E*, 13:666–667; *OC*, 4:857)

Two important claims are being made here. First, Rousseau makes clear the priority of moral freedom over civil freedom; even in the polity ostensibly dedicated to the rule of law, genuine freedom is to be found not in the state but in the heart. Second, the freedom that is found not in government but in the heart consists in our conscious willingness to be bound by reason's laws rather than by the temptations to evil that Rousseau associates with the self-regarding interests and passions. These claims in turn serve to establish the guidelines for the education the tutor seeks to provide. In a second key passage much earlier in the text, Rousseau describes the fundamental aims of education:

> The only one who does his own will is he who, in order to do it, has no need to put another's arms at the end of his own; from which it follows that the first of all goods is not authority but freedom. The truly free man wants only what he can do and does

what he pleases. This is my fundamental maxim. It need only be applied to childhood for all the rules of education to flow from it. (*E*, 13:215; *OC*, 4:309)

Taken together, these two passages reveal the degree to which Rousseau conceived of freedom as the capacity of a free agent to act in accord with a will determined on the basis of a reasoned assessment of the good independent of the influence of the passions, and specifically those passions that orders dedicated to the maximization of negative liberty are prone to inflame. The task of *Emile* is to demonstrate how exactly the education that aims at this specific goal best proceeds in practice.

The education offered by the tutor and described in *Emile* is itself divided into two parts, one "negative" and meant for the child prior to the onset of adolescence, the other "positive" and meant for the young man who has begun to experience the passions that inflame his desires and imagination and take him "outside of himself" (e.g., *E*, 13:371; *OC*, 4:501). But while the conditions and methods of these two stages are quite different, they share the common goal of promoting the development of a capacity for moral freedom in mature individuals destined to live not in any ideal republic but in the modern world as it is. In the early stages of Emile's education, or the negative period, the tutor focuses on teaching him the limits of his capacities and strength, and thus the need to recognize the ways in which the irresistible claims of necessity, together with our natural weakness, must limit our freedom. The tutor's normative injunctions on this point are clear:

> O man, draw your existence up within yourself, and you will no longer be miserable. Remain in the place which nature assigns to you in the chain of being. Nothing will be able to make you leave it. Do not rebel against the hard law of necessity; and do not exhaust your strength by your will to resist that law—strength which heaven gave you not for extending or prolonging your existence but only for preserving it as heaven pleases and for as long as heaven pleases. Your freedom and your power extend only as far as your natural strength, and not beyond. All the rest is only slavery, illusion, and deception. (*E*, 13:214; *OC*, 4:308–309)

Much of the first three books of *Emile* are dedicated to teaching the child this "hard law of necessity" and the need to cultivate his capacity to withstand the discomfort that necessity's occasional impositions must necessarily evoke (see also *E*, 13:223; *OC*, 4:320). This may seem an odd lesson to emphasize in an education that aims at freedom, but there is a method to Rousseau's madness: freedom, insofar as it lies in a capacity to bear the pains and disappointments that life in the world necessarily brings, enables us to preserve tranquility and maximize happiness in the face of our pains and disappointments.

This, at any rate, is the focus of the first or negative stage of education, much of which involves the child learning how to withstand pain and discomfort. Yet for all this, the freedom of the child is, Rousseau bluntly insists, an "imperfect freedom" ultimately unsuitable to "grown men" (*E*, 13:216; *OC*, 4:311). This is because men are subject to passions children cannot know—passions that emerge with force as Emile enters adolescence. And once these have been awakened, a very different sort of freedom is needed. Thus the speech of the adolescent Emile to his tutor:

> O my friend, my protector, my master! Take back all the authority you want to give up at the very moment that it is most important for me that you retain it. You had this authority up to this time only due to my weakness; now you shall have it due to my will, and it shall be all the more sacred to me. Defend me from all the enemies who besiege me, and especially from those whom I carry within myself and who betray me. Watch over your work in order that it remain worthy of you. I want to obey your laws; I want to do so always. This is my steadfast will. If I ever disobey you, it will be in spite of myself. Make me free by protecting me against those of my passions which do violence to me. Prevent me from being their slave; force me to be my own master and to obey not my senses but my reason. (*E*, 13:495; *OC*, 4:652)

Emile's speech is important for several reasons. The first is the way in which it aims to extend one of the fundamental claims of Rousseau's political thought. Among the most notorious claims of the *Social Contract* is that the citizens of the state must be "forced to be free" (*SC*, 4:141; *OC*, 3:364). This has given powerful ammunition to those who see Rousseau as a proto-totalitarian. But for present purposes what is significant is that Emile himself here replicates this disposition of the good citizen, directly imploring his tutor to make him free through force. The freedom that Emile wishes to be forced to realize is, however, different from the force that we associate with totalitarian domination over the will of another (cf. Gauthier, 2006: 37, 41). And herein lies a second key import of this passage. The freedom Emile seeks is that of one who has achieved freedom from the tyranny of his passions and senses via mastery of desires by reason. And here the parallels with Smith become important. Smith could never have argued that individuals ought to be in any way forced to be free. But Smith clearly does believe, as we have seen, that cultivation of the capacity to overcome our inclinations through self-mastery is indispensible to happiness and tranquility. In this sense, for all their clear differences, Smith and Rousseau share a common and central understanding of the value of self-mastery and self-command, as well as a common insistence that the measure of the good regime is its capacity to render its citizens free to follow their own wills, independent of subjection to the will of any other.

Elsewhere in *Emile* Rousseau develops this same idea as a matter of political theology. A centerpiece of *Emile* is the "Creed of the Savoyard Vicar" in Book Four. The "Creed" is today largely known for its conception of natural religion, but for our purposes what is striking is how the Vicar restates Rousseau's basic understanding of freedom: "my will is independent of my senses; I consent or I resist; I succumb or I conquer; and I sense perfectly within myself when I do what I wanted to do or when all I am doing is giving way to my passions" (*E*, 13:441; *OC*, 4:586). Rousseau makes a similar claim in his own name later in the text, again in a theological context. At the start of Book Five, Rousseau insists that in seeking to "do honor to the human species," the "supreme Being" gave man not only "inclinations without limit" but also "the law which regulates them, in order that he may be free and in command of himself," for "while abandoning man to immoderate passions, he joins reason to these passions in order to govern them" (*E*, 13:533; *OC*, 4:695). This connection of freedom to self-command is further developed in what follows. In a line with key implications for recent discussion of the difference between inflamed or bad self-love and good self-love in Rousseau (e.g., Neuhouser, 2008), the tutor explains that "all passions are good when one remains their master; all are bad when one lets oneself be subjected to them . . . all the passions we dominate are legitimate; all those which dominate us are criminal." Self-mastery is thus a crucial virtue, if not the whole of virtue. As the tutor explains:

> Who, then, is the virtuous man? It is he who knows how to conquer his affections; for then he follows his reason and his conscience; he does his duty: he keeps himself in order, and nothing can make him deviate from it. Up to now you were only apparently free. You had only the precarious freedom of a slave to whom nothing has been commanded. Now be really free. Learn to become your own master. Command your heart, Emile, and you will be virtuous. (*E*, 13:633; *OC*, 4:818)

Virtue then is precisely the capacity to bear and enjoy one's freedom, realized via mastery of one's passions and a willingness to be guided by reason.

Rousseau's defense of moral freedom, all told, suggests an affinity for positive liberty. What remains to be appreciated is precisely why Rousseau was so attached to this ideal. On this front, it is important that Rousseau's key accounts of this type of freedom come in *Emile*. Emile is neither a savage living outside of society nor a citizen of an ideal regime, but something else altogether. He is a natural man in civil society—a man who has preserved as much of his nature as living in modern society will allow. And it is this final point that is crucial. Rousseau has been repeatedly taken to task, as we have already had occasion to mention, on the grounds that his positive freedom necessarily culminates in authoritarianism or totalitarianism. But this allegation rests on the assumption that the freedom described in *Emile* is meant to represent the freedom to which the ideal polity of the *Social Contract* is dedicated (though cf. Cohen, 2010: 12–14; and Williams, 2014: 60). *Emile* points in a different direction, however, arguing that Emile must cultivate his capacity for moral freedom not because he will live in the best of all imagined worlds, but precisely because he is being educated to live in the world as it is, with all the limitations that necessity and the competing passions and interests of his fellow citizens will thrust upon him. In this sense, the tutor's aim is to provide his charge with the resources to flourish not in an ideal republic, but rather in the modern world. *Emile* itself has been called by one of Rousseau's most distinguished scholars the "work which more than any other expresses Rousseau's fullest account of negative liberty" (Wokler, 2012: 164). Put slightly differently, Rousseau's account of moral freedom in *Emile* shows how positive liberty can be useful to citizens of regimes founded on negative liberty.

3. Kant on Inner Freedom

Having examined Smith's concept of self-command and Rousseau's concept of moral freedom, we are well positioned to turn to Kant. Kant's theory of freedom, and specifically his concept of "inner freedom," is the Enlightenment's best-known contribution to the theory of freedom with which we are here principally concerned. And Kant's inner freedom itself replicates many of the core claims made by Smith and Rousseau, perhaps owing in part to Kant's well-known direct engagement with the writings of both thinkers (Fleischacker, 1996; Fleischacker, 1991; Velkley, 2002). But leaving the question of historical influence for a separate occasion, our concern is twofold: first, to document those parts of Kant's theory of freedom that parallel elements of the theories developed by Smith and Rousseau; and second, to suggest one way in which Kant's concept of inner freedom contains elements traditionally associated with "positive" conceptions but yet are seen by Kant as promoting ends traditionally associated with "negative" conceptions.

We can begin with the best-known side of Kant's theory of freedom: the discussion of autonomy in the *Groundwork*. Kant famously considers the capacity for autonomy to be the distinguishing characteristic of humanity and the mark of our dignity. Yet his reasons for so thinking, far from owing to concerns idiosyncratic to his system, emerge from concerns also dear to Rousseau and Smith. Kant begins the *Groundwork* with a distinction between man and nature: "everything in nature works in accordance with laws," while "only a rational being has the capacity to act in accordance with the representation of laws, that is, in accordance with principles, or has a will." The will itself, Kant explains, "is a capacity to choose only that which reason independently of inclination cognizes as practically necessary, that is, as good" (*G*, 66; *AA*, 4:412). Here lies the core of Kant's distinction between reason and inclination—a distinction already familiar to us from its invocations by Smith and Rousseau. Also now familiar is Kant's claim that freedom consists in the capacity of a will to be determined by reason rather than by inclination (*G*, 94; *AA*, 4:446). Kant makes this association of freedom and autonomy clear in a key passage that follows. In elucidating the unique status of the human being as coexisting simultaneously in both a world of experience and an intelligible world, he notes,

> As a rational being, and thus as a being belonging to the intelligible world, the human being can never think of the causality of his own will otherwise than under the idea of freedom; for, independence from the determining causes of the world of sense (which reason must always ascribe to itself) is freedom. With the idea of freedom the concept of autonomy is now inseparably combined, and with the concept of autonomy the universal principle of morality, which in ideas is the ground of all actions of rational beings, just as the law of nature is the ground of all appearances. (*G*, 99; *AA*, 4:452–453)

This is an important passage for several reasons, not least of which is because it introduces the notion, later central, that freedom must be assumed or postulated for morality to be intelligible (e.g., *G*, 105; *AA*, 4:459 and *CPrR*, 178; *AA*, 5:48). But for our purposes what is most significant is Kant's suggestion here that genuine freedom is freedom in two senses, each of which follows principles central to Rousseau and Smith: first, freedom from enslavement to the senses; and second, freedom to follow reason.

Seen in this light, Kant's theory may strike us as somewhat less extreme than it is often represented. A familiar objection to Kant's system concerns its ostensible antipathy to sentiment (though see Guyer, 2010). Yet Kant in fact shares much with the sentimentalist perspectives on moral freedom of Rousseau and Smith. One place this emerges is in the *Metaphysics of Morals*, and especially the "Doctrine of Virtue." Here Kant identifies virtue with the free agent's capacity for self-mastery in ways that directly parallel both Smith's claim that self-command is a chief virtue and the source of the excellence of the other virtues, and Rousseau's association of freedom as self-mastery with virtue. Thus Kant's central discussion of inner freedom here:

> Virtue is the strength of a human being's maxims in fulfilling his duty.—Strength of any kind can be recognized only by the obstacles it can overcome and in the case of virtue these obstacles are natural inclinations, which can come into conflict with the human being's moral resolution; and since it is the human being himself who puts these obstacles in the way of his maxims, virtue is not merely a self-constraint (for then one natural inclination could strive to overcome another), but also a self-constraint in accordance with a principle of inner freedom, and so through the mere representation of one's duty in accordance with its formal law. (*MM*, 524–525; *AA*, 6:394)

Or again:

> Since virtue is based on inner freedom it contains a positive command to a human being, namely to bring all his capacities and inclinations under his (reason's) control and so to rule over himself, which goes beyond forbidding him to let himself to be governed by his feelings and inclinations (the duty of apathy); for unless reason holds the reins of government in its own hands his feelings and inclinations play the master over him. (*MM*, 536: *AA*, 6:408)

All of this culminates in the insistence that it is in mastery of the sentiments by the will that genuine freedom consists, a freedom superior to that of the undisciplined freedom of natural man. Like Rousseau, Kant believes that "one cannot say the human being in a state has sacrificed a part of his innate outer freedom for the sake of an end, but rather, he has relinquished entirely his wild, lawless freedom in order to find his freedom as such undiminished, in a dependence upon laws, that is, in a rightful condition, since this dependence arises from his own lawgiving will" (*MM*, 459; *AA*, 6:315–316).

Kant's definition of inner freedom is clear enough and shares much with the ideas of Smith and Rousseau examined above. But now we need to ask of Kant the same questions that we asked of them: how exactly is inner freedom cultivated, and why exactly is it so necessary for citizens of modern liberal polities? Kant's answer to the first question parallels Rousseau's, evident in his account of the satisfaction that students come to experience in learning how to practice inner freedom:

> The heart is freed and relieved of a burden that always secretly presses upon it, when in pure moral resolutions, examples of which are set before him, there is revealed to the human being an inner capacity not otherwise correctly known by himself, the inner freedom to release himself from the impetuous importunity of inclinations so that none of them, not even the dearest, has any influence on a resolution for which we are now to make use of our reason. (*CPrR*, 268; *AA*, 5:160–161)

Kant clearly shares with Smith and Rousseau the insistence that the inner freedom that liberates one from enslavement to inclinations deserves to be regarded as a form of freedom insofar as it renders one free to act in accord with one's resolutions.

What remains to be explained is why Kant thinks that freedom of this sort is especially valuable in modern liberal societies dedicated more to negative freedom than positive freedom. Kant is of course one of the preeminent theorists of negative freedom, and for good reason. In the *Metaphysics of Morals*, he claims that "freedom (independence from being constrained by another's choice), insofar as it can coexist with the freedom of every other in accordance with a universal law, is the only right belonging to every man by virtue of his humanity" (*MM*, 393; *AA*, 6:237). But Kant goes on to argue that this freedom is inextricable from inner freedom insofar as this principle of freedom "already involves the following authorizations, which are not really distinct from it," including especially "innate *equality*, that is, independence from being bound by others to more than one can in turn bind them; hence a human being's quality of being *his own master (sui iuris)*" (*MM*, 393–394; *AA*, 6:237–238). Kant's insistence that the individual's right to freedom from coercion "already involves" in it self-mastery suggests the degree to which he understood these forms of freedom to be inseparable.

But Kant also suggests a second way in which inner freedom is necessary for modern liberal societies. Kant's "Conjectural Beginning of Human History" offers an image of the unsettling conditions of freedom in describing the experience of the first man on eating from the garden's tree:

> He discovered in himself a faculty of choosing for himself a way of living and not being bound to a single one, as other animals are. Yet upon the momentary delight that this marked superiority might have awakened in him, anxiety and fright must have followed right away, concerning how he, who still did not know the hidden properties and remote effects of any thing, should deal with this newly discovered faculty. He stood, as it were, on the brink of an abyss; for instead of the single objects of his desire to which instinct had up to now directed him, there opened up an infinity of them, and he did not know how to relate to the choice between them; and from this estate of freedom, once he had tasted it, it was nevertheless impossible for him to turn back again to that of servitude (under the dominion of instinct). (*CB*, 166; *AA*, 8:112).

Freedom is unsettling, and not only for the first man. His disorientation on first tasting absolute freedom remains present to us who live under the conditions of maximum individual liberty that modern liberalism makes possible. Thus Kant makes clear that freedom is a double-edged sword, one that "does him honor, to be sure, but at the same time is very perilous, since it drives him out of the harmless and safe condition of infant care, out of a garden, as it were, which cared for him without any effort on his part (Genesis 3:23), and thrust him into the wide world, where so much worry, toil, and unknown ills were waiting for him" (*CB*, 166; *AA*, 8:114).

What then to do? Kant's final words on this front are especially important, and for two reasons. First, Kant's account of the psychological disorientation that is consequent to the conditions of maximum individual freedom suggests that we will need to find within ourselves resources to bear well the challenges freedom brings. Put in terms of our present inquiry, the positive freedom described by the concept of inner freedom is especially necessary for individual agents living in conditions of negative freedom, insofar as it enables them to bear these blessings well and indeed to flourish while so doing. Second, Kant's last words on this front explicitly bind him to Rousseau and Smith. Here Kant explains that the "restless reason" that animates such a man in the condition of freedom "drives him on nevertheless to take upon himself patiently the toil that he hates, and run after the bauble he despises, and even to forget death itself which he dreads, on account of all those trivialities he is even more afraid to lose" (*CB*, 166; 8:115). Readers of Smith will recognize Kant's words insofar as they are the very same words Smith used to characterize the condition of the poor man's son who "serves those he hates and is obsequious to those he despises," and who thereby "sacrifices a real tranquility that is at all times in his power" for "trinkets of frivolous utility" (*TMS*, 4.1.8) or "baubles" (*TMS*, 4.1.10). And students of Smith, in turn, know that these words are themselves drawn from Rousseau, and specifically his account of the wretched modern citizen at the end of the second *Discourse*, who "always active, sweats, agitates himself, torments himself incessantly in order to seek still more laborious occupations; he works to death, he even rushes to it in order to get in condition to live, or renounces life in order to acquire immortality," and "pays court to the great whom he hates, and to the rich whom he scorns" (*SD*, 3:66; *OC*, 3:193). The need for emphasis here is not for reasons that have to do with influence or borrowings; these have been well documented. What matters for our present purposes is that Kant's, Smith's, and Rousseau's common recourse to this shared vision of the psychological challenges endemic to the condition of maximum individual liberty suggest the deep degree to which, for all their other normative differences, Kant and Smith and Rousseau each mean to call our attention to the ways in which positive freedom, conceived as inner or moral freedom, enables us to meet the psychological challenges endemic to those conditions of negative freedom that the liberal commercial state aims to secure.

4. CONCLUSION

Isaiah Berlin deserves to be regarded as one of the most penetrating political thinkers and intellectual historians of the last century, yet it is for his discussion of positive and negative liberty that political theorists today largely remember him. Yet his influential discussion in "Two Concepts" suffers from associating positive liberty with totalitarianism. On its account the desire for self-mastery at the heart of positive liberty necessarily culminates in the desire for mastery over others. Hence Berlin's insistence with regard to positive liberty that "its political implications are clear": "those who believed in freedom as rational self-direction were bound, sooner or later, to consider how this was to be applied not merely to a man's inner life, but to his relations with other members of his society" (Berlin, 2002: 185, 191). And "Two Concepts" leaves little doubt where this ends: namely the shift "from an ethical doctrine of individual responsibility as individual self-perfection to an authoritarian State obedient to the directives of an élite of Platonic guardians" (Berlin, 2002: 198; cf. Schmidtz and Brennan, 2010: 17; Gaus, 2011: 33–36).

Berlin of course may be right that, as a matter of history, many who wielded power in the twentieth century applied the rhetoric of positive liberty in the service of forms of governance deeply inimical to negative liberty. But the fault for this lies not in the Enlightenment's conception of freedom but in those who manipulated this conception for purposes very different from the original intentions of its articulators. On these grounds the Enlightenment's conception of freedom can be exonerated of the blame that "Two Concepts" laid at its feet. Hardly sympathetic to would-be Platonic guardians seeking to dominate or manipulate their inferiors—figures that would have been anathema to Smith, Rousseau, and Kant alike—these thinkers instead offer good reasons to think that the cultivation of a capacity for self-mastery makes it possible for free, responsible individuals to live together without need for masters beyond their own selves. In this sense, the concept of moral freedom that they developed and which stands as one of the most important components of the Enlightenment's legacy deserves to be regarded as a useful and even indispensible element of the political order envisioned by all those who think "any freedom worth defending has responsibility as a corollary" (Schmidtz and Brennan, 2010: 14).

ACKNOWLEDGMENTS

For discussions that inspired this chapter I am very grateful to Charles Griswold and Geoffrey Sayre-McCord. I am also grateful to audiences in Tucson in October 2014 and at Georgetown in April 2015—as well as Leonidas Montes, David Schmidtz, Eric Wilson, and two anonymous readers—for many helpful comments.

REFERENCES

Berlin, I., 2002. Two concepts of liberty. In: H. Hardy, ed. *Liberty*. Oxford: Oxford University Press. pp.166–217.

Berry, C., 1989. Adam Smith: commerce, liberty and modernity. In: P. Gilmour, ed. *Philosophers of the Enlightenment*. Edinburgh: Edinburgh University Press. pp.113–133.

Cherniss, J., 2013. *A mind and its time: the development of Isaiah Berlin's thought*. Oxford: Oxford University Press.

Cohen, J., 2010. *Rousseau: a free community of equals*. Oxford: Oxford University Press.

Davis, G., 2003. Philosophical psychology and economic psychology in David Hume and Adam Smith. *History of Political Economy*, 35, pp.269–304.

Fleischacker, S., 1991. Philosophy in moral practice: Kant and Adam Smith. *Kant-Studien*, 82(3), pp.249–269.

Fleischacker, S., 1996. Values behind the market: Kant's response to the *Wealth of Nations*. *History of Political Thought*, 17(3), pp.379–407.

Gaus, G., 2011. *The order of public reason: a theory of freedom and morality in a diverse and bounded world*. Cambridge: Cambridge University Press.

Gauthier, D., 2006. *Rousseau: the sentiment of existence.* Cambridge: Cambridge University Press.

Griswold, C., 2010. Smith and Rousseau in dialogue: sympathy, *pitié*, spectatorship and narrative. In: V. Brown and S. Fleischacker, eds. *The philosophy of Adam Smith.* London: Routledge. pp.59–84.

Guyer, P., 2010. Moral feeling in the *Metaphysics of morals.* In L. Denis, ed. *Kant's Metaphysics of morals: a critical guide.* Cambridge: Cambridge University Press. pp.130–151.

Hanley, R., 2009. *Adam Smith and the character of virtue.* Cambridge: Cambridge University Press.

Hanley, R., 2013. Political economy and individual liberty. In E. Grace and C. Kelly, eds. *The challenge of Rousseau.* Cambridge: Cambridge University Press. pp.34–57.

Hanley, R., 2014. "The wisdom of the state": Adam Smith on China and Tartary. *American Political Science Review*, 108(2), pp.371–382.

Kant, I., 1900-. *Kants gesammelte Schriften (Akademie Ausgabe).* Edited by Royal Prussian Academy of Sciences. 29 vols. Berlin: Walter de Gruyter. [*AA*]

Kant, I., 1999 [1785]. *Groundwork of the metaphysics of morals.* Translated by M. Gregor. Cambridge: Cambridge University Press. [*G*]

Kant, I., 1999 [1788]. *Critique of practical reason.* Translated by M. Gregor. Cambridge: Cambridge University Press. [*CPrR*]

Kant, I., 1999 [1797]. *Metaphysics of morals.* Translated by M. Gregor. Cambridge: Cambridge University Press. [*MM*]

Kant, I., 2007 [1786]. Conjectural beginning of human history. In G. Zöller and R. Louden, eds. *Anthropology, history, and education.* Cambridge: Cambridge University Press. pp.160–175 [*CB*]

Kennedy, G., 2016. Adam Smith: some popular uses and abuses. In R. P. Hanley, ed. *Adam Smith: his life, thought, and legacy.* Princeton: Princeton University Press. pp.461–477.

Montes, L., 2004. *Adam Smith in context: a critical reassessment of some central components of his thought.* London: Palgrave Macmillan.

Nelson, E., 2005. Liberty: one concept too many? *Political Theory*, 33(1), pp.58–78.

Neuhouser, F., 2008. *Rousseau's theodicy of self-love: evil, rationality, and the drive for recognition.* Oxford: Oxford University Press.

Otteson, J., 2002. *Adam Smith's marketplace of life.* Cambridge: Cambridge University Press.

Pettit, P., 1999. *Republicanism: a theory of freedom and government.* Oxford: Oxford University Press.

Rasmussen, D., 2008. *The problems and promise of commercial society: Adam Smith's response to Rousseau.* University Park, PA: Pennsylvania State University Press.

Rousseau, J.-J., 1959–95. *Oeuvres complètes.* Edited by B. Gagnebin and M. Raymond. Paris: Gallimard. [*OC*]

Rousseau, J.-J., 1992 [1755]. *Discourse on the origins of inequality.* Translated by J. Bush and R. Masters. Hanover, NH: University Press of New England. [*SD*]

Rousseau, J.-J., 1994 [1762]. *On the social contract.* Translated by J. Bush and R. Masters. Hanover, NH: University Press of New England. [*SC*]

Rousseau, J.-J., 2010 [1762]. *Emile, or On education.* Translated by A. Bloom. Hanover, NH: University Press of New England. [*E*]

Schmidtz, D., 2016. Adam Smith on freedom. In R. P. Hanley, ed. *Adam Smith: his life, thought, and legacy.* Princeton: Princeton University Press. pp.123–137.

Schmidtz, D., and Brennan, J., 2010. *A brief history of liberty.* Malden, MA: Wiley-Blackwell.

Skinner, Q., 1998. *Liberty before liberalism.* Cambridge: Cambridge University Press.

Smith, A., 1981 [1776]. *An inquiry into the nature and causes of the wealth of nations*. Edited by R. H. Campbell, A. S. Skinner, and W. B. Todd. Indianapolis: Liberty Fund. [*WN*]

Smith, A., 1982 [1759]. *The theory of moral sentiments*. Edited by D. D. Raphael and A. L. Macfie. Indianapolis: Liberty Fund. [*TMS*]

Smith, A., 1982. *Lectures on jurisprudence*. Edited by R. L. Meek, D. D. Raphael, and P. G. Stein. Indianapolis: Liberty Fund. [*LJB* = "Report dated 1766"]

Taylor, C., 1985. What's wrong with negative liberty. In *Philosophy and the human sciences: philosophical papers, vol. 2*. Cambridge: Cambridge University Press. pp.211–229.

Velkley, R., 2002. *Being after Rousseau: philosophy and culture in question*. Chicago: University of Chicago Press.

Williams, D., 2014. *Rousseau's social contract: an introduction*. Cambridge: Cambridge University Press.

Wokler, R., 2012 [1987]. Rousseau's two concepts of liberty. In B. Garsten, ed. *Rousseau, the Age of Enlightenment, and their legacies*. Princeton: Princeton University Press. pp.154–184.

CHAPTER 13

ADAM SMITH'S LIBERTARIAN PATERNALISM

JAMES R. OTTESON

1. INTRODUCTION

IN their influential book *Nudge*, Richard Thaler and Cass Sunstein argue for what they call "libertarian paternalism," which they define as the strategy to devise policy that will "maintain or increase freedom of choice" (the libertarian part) and at the same time will "influence people's behavior in order to make their lives longer, healthier, and better" (the paternalistic part).[1] Their goal is to help people make the decisions they would have made "if they had paid full attention and possessed complete information, unlimited cognitive abilities, and complete self-control" (Thaler and Sunstein, 2009: 5). This seems like a high standard, and as a result some critics have charged them with erring rather on the side of paternalism than on that of libertarianism,[2] but they insist that their intention is only "to influence choices in a way that will make choosers better off, *as judged by themselves*" (ibid.; emphasis in original).

The desires to allow people freedom of choice, on the one hand, and to help them make better choices, on the other, are often in conflict, and striking the right balance between policies designed to encourage the former or the latter has proved difficult in both theory and practice. John Stuart Mill, perhaps the leading classical proponent of the libertarian position, argued that "the sole end for which mankind are warranted, individually or collectively, in interfering with the liberty of action of any of their number is self-protection" (Mill, 1978 [1859]: 9). Yet even Mill felt the necessity of limiting that principle: in addition to children, Mill argued that "we may leave out of consideration those backward states of society in which the race itself may be considered as in its nonage" (Mill, 1978 [1859]: 9–10). Some more recent critics of the Millian libertarian position have built on insights from Thaler and Sunstein to argue that policy should abandon the libertarian aspect altogether and instead embrace a fully paternalistic "choice architect" position.[3]

Where does Adam Smith fall in this debate? Although Smith did not explicitly develop a theory of freedom, nevertheless we can reconstruct a conception of political freedom and a conception of what it means to be a free person by working backward from some of the specific claims he makes about moral agency and from some of his policy recommendations. This chapter will argue that Smith developed his own version of "libertarian paternalism." It differs in important ways from that of Thaler and Sunstein, but it shares with their version an attempt to balance respect for individual autonomy with a desire to help people lead better lives. The chapter will argue that, contrary to some mischaracterizations of Smith's argument that he was a pure libertarian, Smith acknowledged the important role of a kind of paternalism in helping people make better choices. On the other hand, his sensitivity to the importance of individual choice for developing good judgment leads him also to recommend a robust role for autonomy. It will be argued, then, that Smith's position accommodates the importance of both liberty and paternalism in enabling individuals to construct lives worth living, while at the same time Smith's position avoids some of the problems that have beset more recent versions of libertarian paternalism.

2. SELF-COMMAND AND THE IMPARTIAL SPECTATOR

Let us begin by summarizing Smith's position. Smith claims in his 1759 *Theory of Moral Sentiments* that one of his four central virtues is "self-command." In fact, he claims that self-command is what gives the other three central virtues—namely, "prudence, justice, and proper beneficence"—their "principal lustre."[4] But what is required for self-command to be a virtue? It seems to require that one have an ability to separate oneself both from one's own passions and from the influences of others around one, and then to direct one's judgments and actions with both deliberation and conscious intentionality. Now, Smith had argued that the desire for mutual sympathy of sentiments is one of our strongest social desires, indeed the desire that ultimately gives rise to our shared moral sentiments.[5] It is when we discover that others enter into, or "sympathize" with, our own sentiments that we experience the pleasure of mutual sympathy; because the achievement of this sympathy (or "concord" or "harmony") of sentiments is pleasurable to us, that gives us incentive to judge or behave in ways that generate this mutual sympathy. By contrast, when we realize that others do not enter into our sentiments, we experience the displeasure of an "antipathy" of sentiments, which encourages us to revise our judgments or behavior. The result is a mutual drive toward shared expectations about one another's behavior, a process that over time gives rise to a shared set of standards about morality, manners, and etiquette. Self-command is a virtue for Smith because it enables us to constrain our judgments and behaviors so that they accord, not only with what *we* might like, but also with what others expect of us and with what comes to constitute praiseworthy behavior.

Smith's full argument is, however, more complicated than this. In particular, it involves the creation of the perspective of an "impartial spectator," which ultimately becomes for Smith *the* standard of judgment.[6] According to Smith, people are born with no morality whatsoever. A baby knows only its own wants. The baby has no notion of a proper (or improper) thing to ask for, of a proper (or improper) way to ask for it, or of embarrassment for having asked for something it should not have. Hence the baby attempts to have its wants satisfied simply by alarming its caregiver with howls and cries. Yet we do not blame the baby for such self-indulgence: it is not yet capable of considering *propriety* or *others' interests*; besides, Smith says, it is probably encouraged in its self-centeredness by its indulgent parent or nurse.[7]

According to Smith it is not until the baby has grown to a child and begins playing with his mates that the child has the jolting experience of realizing that he is not the center of everyone's life, only of his own.[8] Smith writes that this is the child's introduction into the "great school of self-command" (Smith, 1982: III.3.22): it is on being with others and experiencing them *judging* oneself—even if only implicitly, by, say, not playing with one or simply ignoring one's demands to have one's desires satisfied—that one experiences the displeasure associated with an antipathy of sentiments. After the initial jolt, one casts about to find a way to relieve the displeasure, eventually hitting upon using one's "self-command" to modify one's sentiments and behavior so that they more closely match those of one's playmates. At that point an exquisite new pleasure is experienced, that of the mutual sympathy of sentiments, and a new and enduring desire for that pleasure has been aroused. The experience of being judged thus triggers in the child what Smith calls "an original desire to please, and an original aversion to offend his brethren" (Smith, 1982: III.2.6). From that point on, according to Smith, the child regularly engages in trial-and-error investigation into what behaviors will achieve this sympathy and thus satisfy this desire.

These trial-and-error attempts lead the individual to adopt habits and then rules of behavior and judgment that increase the chance of achieving mutual sympathy. By the time the child has become an adult, he has adopted a wide range of principles of behavior and judgment that he can apply in many different situations. Since everyone else is engaging in precisely the same investigation, all our disparate sentiments tend to gravitate toward mutually acceptable means.[9] This is the invisible-hand mechanism that Smith thinks generates commonly shared standards of behavior and judgment, indeed a commonly shared *system* of morality.

Another aspect of human judgment-making, however, is *self*-judgments: we often approve or disapprove of our own sentiments or actions, we often in retrospect feel pride or shame for what we felt or did, and we often make resolutions to behave in certain ways or to refrain from behaving in certain ways in the future. Smith accounts for this aspect of human morality by reference to the perspective of what he calls the "impartial spectator."

Smith argues that the process of passing judgment on oneself is, despite what one might initially suspect, quite similar to that of passing judgment on others. In the latter case, "We either approve or disapprove of the conduct of another man according as we feel that, when we bring his case home to ourselves, we either can or cannot entirely sympathize with the sentiments and motives which directed it"; similarly, in the former case, "we either approve or disapprove of our own conduct, according as we feel that, when we place ourselves in the situation of another man, and view it, as it were, with his eyes and from his station, we either can or cannot entirely enter into and sympathize with the sentiments and motives which influenced it" (Smith, 1982: III.1.1). In judging oneself, one must divide oneself "as it were, into two persons": the "I" as agent or person principally concerned, and the "I" who is judging the person principally concerned (Smith, 1982: III.1.6). Smith argues that the habit of judging one's own character in this way is what develops into what is often called one's "conscience." This may sound like a cumbersome process, but Smith's argument is that in practice it happens much more readily than it appears. The idea is this: when you are reflecting on your own sentiments, you consider what another person informed of your situation would think. Would an impartial observer approve of your conduct? If so, then you may proceed; if not, then not.

Why should we care what an imaginary observer thinks of our conduct? For two reasons, Smith thinks. First, because your habit of doing so is so deeply ingrained in you already that if you do not heed your conscience you will be unhappy. We can see the importance of this claim by recalling a classic problem in the history of philosophy. In the second book of Plato's *Republic*, Socrates is asked to respond to one of the most difficult and enduring problems in moral philosophy, namely: Why would a person not commit injustice if he could be absolutely certain he could get away with it? The question is prompted by the story of a young shepherd who discovers a ring with the magical power of making its wearer invisible. According to the story, the shepherd uses the ring's power of invisibility to seduce the king's wife, then to conspire with her to surprise and murder the king, and finally to install himself upon the throne. The lesson of this story, according to Glaucon (who tells it), is that "one is never just willingly but only when compelled to be" (Plato, 1992: II.360c). Socrates thereupon commences a lengthy reply to this challenge, arguing ultimately that the life of injustice is not in fact more desirable than the life of justice: "And haven't we found that justice itself is the best thing for the soul itself, and that the soul—whether it has the ring of Gyges or even it together with the cap of Hades—should do just things?" (Plato, 1992: X.612b). Socrates further suggests that the just person will fare better in the afterworld than the unjust person—providing another reason to act justly in this life, even if one could act otherwise with impunity.[10]

The question of why one should be moral has persisted, however, and Smith develops his own answer. According to Smith, man desires not only to be praised, but has a further desire "of being what he himself approves in other men" (Smith, 1982: III.2.7). It appears that for Smith this further desire results from the continued workings of the desire for mutual sympathy of sentiments.[11] Smith says that all of us have at some time been frustrated or chagrined when people disapproved of our conduct because, we believe, they did not fully understand the circumstances involved (Smith, 1982: III.2.31–2). An only partial familiarity with another's situation might well bias or prejudice the judgment one makes, and all of us have experienced the unpleasantness of being on the wrong end of a biased, prejudiced, or partly uninformed (even misinformed) judgment.

Smith argues that unpleasant experiences like these encourage us in such circumstances to repair, not to the judgment of actual observers, but instead to the judgment of an imaginary, informed, disinterested observer. Smith calls this standard an "impartial spectator." Smith believes that this standard comes about naturally, or unintentionally—as a result, on the one hand, of individuals' wanting mutual sympathy of sentiments and, on the other, of their frequent frustration at others' inability or unwillingness to expend the effort necessary to understand another's full situation before passing judgment on his sentiments and actions. When mutual sympathy is not forthcoming from actual, and often partial, spectators, we may find solace in an imagined impartial spectator who, because of his impartiality, would approve of our conduct.[12] Though the perspective of this imagined spectator is constructed through our own experiences and is hence itself liable to various partialities and biases, Smith argues that his judgment will more closely approximate an idealized standard because it will be informed by our realizations that more accurate judgments ensue from fully informed but disinterested observers. Our desire for mutual sympathy of sentiments then expands to include, and can be satisfied by, a sympathy achieved with such an imagined idealized observer. We are thus naturally led to consult this imaginary observer frequently. Over time the practice of doing so becomes habitual, and so we will as often consult this imagined impartial spectator's sentiments as we will the sentiments of actual spectators.

Now we can see Smith's answer to Plato's Ring of Gyges problem. Even if we were guaranteed that no actual person would discover our misconduct, we would still be unable to avoid the damning judgment of our conscience, our imagined impartial spectator. The force of habit means that this impartial spectator's judgment occurs to us even unwittingly, and in such a case it would inform us that our misconduct is such that we ourselves would condemn it in another person. That realization is sufficient to trigger the antipathy, and thus displeasure, of a failure of an imagined mutual sympathy of sentiments. "The man who has broke through all those measures of conduct, which can alone render him agreeable to mankind," Smith writes, when "he looks back upon it, and views it in the light in which the impartial spectator would view it, he finds that he can enter into none of the motives which influenced it. He is abashed and confounded at the thoughts of it, and necessarily feels a very high degree of that shame which he would be exposed to, if his actions should ever come to be generally known" (Smith, 1982: III.2.9). The worse the misconduct, according to Smith, the greater the shame or guilt the person feels. If the misconduct is of the most grievous kinds, there is no escape from the judgment of the impartial spectator:

> These natural pangs of an affrighted conscience are the daemons, the avenging furies, which, in this life, haunt the guilty, which allow them neither quiet nor repose, which often drive them to despair and distraction, from which no assurance of secrecy can protect them, from which no principles of irreligion can entirely deliver them, and from which nothing can free them but the vilest and most abject of all states, a complete insensibility to honour and infamy, to vice and virtue. (Smith, 1982: III.2.9)

For Smith, then, the reasons to follow the rules of morality include: (1) the anticipated pleasure resulting from a mutual sympathy of sentiments of actual spectators who approve of one's actions, and (2) the pleasure resulting from a sympathy of sentiments with an imagined impartial spectator; but also (3) the fear of an anticipated displeasure resulting from the judgment of other actual spectators who know of one's misdeed, and (4) the displeasure resulting from an antipathy of sentiments with an imagined impartial spectator. These conspire to provide a powerful incentive to follow those rules of conduct that one approves in others and not to follow rules of conduct that one disapproves in others.

Thus the first reason Smith believes we should pay attention to what our conscience tells us is to avoid the substantial risk that we otherwise run of feeling unpleasant shame and disgrace at our own misconduct. But the second reason is the other side of this equation: you are, or might be, able to achieve a pleasurable sympathy of sentiments with your imagined spectator. And the more thoroughly this imagined spectator knows the situations of your sentiments and conduct, and still approves, the more exquisite the pleasure you feel from the ensuing mutual sympathy of sentiments. With diligence and application, a person can train himself, Smith thinks, to heed mainly, even perhaps exclusively, the judgment of the impartial spectator, and such a person will as nearly approximate the conduct of a truly virtuous person as a human being can:

> To a real wise man the judicious and well-weighed approbation of a single wise man, gives more heartfelt satisfaction than all the noisy applauses of ten thousand ignorant though enthusiastic admirers. He may say with Parmenides, who, upon reading a philosophical discourse before a public assembly at Athens, and observing, that, except Plato, the whole company had left him, continued, notwithstanding, to read on, and said that Plato alone was audience sufficient for him. (Smith, 1982: VI.iii.31)[13]

Smith is adamant about this point. Unmerited applause brings no real pleasure, he insists, since we are always "secretly conscious"[14] to ourselves that we do not in fact merit the applause. At the same time, the pain we feel from unjust censure can sting more deeply and remain with us far longer than it should: "Unmerited reproach, however, is frequently capable of mortifying very severely even men of more than ordinary constancy. . . . [A]n innocent man, though of more than ordinary constancy, is often, not only shocked, but most severely mortified by the serious, though false, imputation of a crime; especially when that imputation happens unfortunately to be supported by some circumstances which give it an air of probability" (Smith, 1982: III.2.11). Though such a person should repose and take comfort in the knowledge that an impartial spectator would not so condemn him, Smith allows that only people of the firmest "constancy" are capable of that kind of moral discipline.

On Smith's account, then, a morally mature person is one who judges himself, and others, from the perspective of an imagined impartial spectator who is fully aware of his situation but has no personal stake in the outcome. Self-command is the virtue that is necessary to enable the morally mature person to discipline his actions in accordance with the judgment of the impartial spectator, which at times means acting in opposition to what actual spectators expect or approve.

3. Smith's Libertarian Paternalism

Though we can, then, on Smith's account, distance ourselves from others' expectations of us, one thing from which Smith thinks we cannot distance ourselves is the desire for mutual sympathy of sentiments. This may seem like a liability, but it is actually a crucial part of Smith's account. One reason Smith can be optimistic about the development of relatively beneficial decentralized social orders—that is, orders not administrated by central authorities—is precisely because he believes we all feel the pull of the desire for mutual sympathy of sentiments. This is Smith's *libertarian paternalism*.

The self-command Smith extols comprises two main things. The first is a strong and natural pull toward compliance with others' expectations. It is a kind of centripetal social force. This is a good thing: Because a chief component of happiness is loving relations with others—Smith claims that "the chief part of human happiness arises from the consciousness of being beloved" (Smith, 1982: I.ii.5.1)—each of us thus has to figure out how to establish and maintain such relationships. That means that we will have to moderate our behavior so that it falls within what others find to be acceptable parameters.[15] This gives us reason to seek out companionship with others, but more than that it encourages us to coordinate our behaviors, beliefs, even tastes with those others who matter to us. Their expectations become, then, *nudges* for us, and as naturally social creatures we thus face a natural hypothetical imperative: If I want to be happy, I need to accommodate myself to others' expectations. The key is that we apply such nudges to others—rewarding and punishing behaviors, as the case may be—even when others do not understand why we do so, or would prefer to behave differently from the way we are encouraging. When parents give their children guidelines and corrections for behavior, these *paternalistic nudges* are aimed at helping them comply not only with the parents' own expectations but with what parents know will be others' expectations of their children—again, even when children do not understand or do not agree with the nudges. Parents understand, at least at some level, that their children's relative ability to figure out and even anticipate what others will expect of them will be a skill that is necessary (though, of course, not sufficient) for successful relations with others—and, ultimately, one key ingredient for happiness. So the good parent seeks to give his children a leg up on successful social relations by training them in a particular signature of behavioral habits designed to help them adopt behaviors that are likely to achieve mutual sympathy of sentiments, and avoid behaviors likely to achieve an antipathy of sentiments, with others.[16]

What constitutes appropriate accommodations that any of us should make can fall, however, only within reasonable parameters. And, crucially for Smith, we always retain the ability—in some cases, perhaps even the duty, as when the impartial spectator requires it—to break from others' expectations. This is the second part of Smith's conception of self-command. The desire for mutual sympathy of sentiments means that the default becomes to comport with others' expectations, and our ability to exercise self-command indicates our relative ability to do so. Yet as adults we can also choose when *not* to comply with others' expectations. This is Smith's psychological, moral, and, ultimately, political libertarianism. Now, knowing when to comply and when to defect is not easy. It is a function of good judgment, which Smith, following Aristotle, believes is a skill that must be practiced to be effective. But practice alone is not enough. We must also have feedback, and this feedback must actually have some purchase on us. That is precisely the role that the desire for mutual sympathy of sentiments plays. When others do not enter into our sentiments, it generates a displeasure in us—we cannot escape that. But what we can do is select those opportune moments when the displeasure is worth it—when, that is, some other good (perhaps compliance instead with our imagined impartial spectator) outweighs the cost of failing to achieve mutual sympathy of sentiments with actual spectators. Every morally mature person of good judgment deliberately distances himself from potential instances of mutual sympathy of sentiments at various times in his life. It is often difficult to know when we should do so, and we often get it wrong. But we possess the ability to choose to depart from others' expectations, and virtue will require that we do so in many circumstances throughout our lives.

Hence the picture of human freedom that emerges for Smith is one of *libertarian paternalism*, on the individual level as well as—therefore—on the political level. At the individual level: the behavioral principles framed from others' expectations of us are their nudges, and the overt recommendations we make to people to follow those principles are part of the paternalistic aspect of human sociality. Our default of following the nudges is thus a proper response to that paternalistic impulse. Yet those occasions when we demur are instances of our freedom to follow different paths.

According to Smith, this conjunction of liberty and paternalism is part of what makes morality beautiful, and what makes people morally beautiful. In *The Theory of Moral Sentiments*, Part IV, Smith argues that beauty pertains to (1) order and (2) fitness or propriety. So the morally beautiful person is one whose regular course of behavior follows from a relatively small set of foundational principles of character, and yet whose actions in any particular case are the proper ones in those particular circumstances. This incorporates both aspects of libertarian paternalism. The set of default principles are derived from induction on the basis of experience with other people's expectations; the rules we develop inductively are recommended to us paternalistically, as conducive to happiness (or "utility" or "conveniency," in Smith's words[17]). On the other hand, virtue also requires us to depart from those paternalistic recommendations in the appropriate circumstances. The facts (1) that we can do so, and (2) that we exercise our "self-command" when we do so appropriately, are indicative of our moral freedom—the "libertarian" aspect of Smith's conception of human moral agency.

But Smith's libertarian paternalism applies at the political level as well. Smith's survey of historical and empirical evidence leads him to conclude in *The Wealth of Nations* that those societies that allow labor to divide and people to enjoy the rewards, or suffer the defeats (as the case may be), of their activities are the ones in which prosperity increases, in which a "universal opulence" and a "general plenty" ensue.[18] He concludes that government should do only a few things: enforce justice,[19] against both foreign and domestic aggression, and provide those few "publick works" that both provide benefit to the nation as a whole and cannot be provided by private enterprise.[20] Smith's category of "publick works" seems quite small, however: Smith suggests it is only a few things, mainly infrastructure that facilitates commerce, as well as partially subsidized, locally controlled, primary schooling. But what about all the other things that are required for a fully virtuous life? Smith worried in Book V of *The Wealth of Nations*, for example, about the deleterious effects that extreme division of labor could have on the minds of laborers—it could render them as "stupid and ignorant as it is possible for a human creature to become" (Smith, 1976: V.i.f.50)—and he suggests requiring every citizen to learn to read, write, and do basic arithmetic and geometry as a partial remedy.[21] But in *The Theory of Moral Sentiments* Smith speaks at length about the various aspects of "beneficence"—that is, positive, including paternalistic, actions that one should take on others' behalf—that are required to be fully virtuous. If the state takes no cognizance of such matters, how can we be sure people will be able to develop into virtuous creatures?

The Smithian answer is the libertarian paternalism that underlies his conception of the moral marketplace. The state is discharged from superintending the beneficent actions in which people should engage not only because it is incompetent to do so—such matters cannot be determined in the abstract or from afar, so dependent is proper beneficence on local details of particular situations—but also because people's natural desire for mutual sympathy of sentiments will already do the job as well as can be hoped. The patterns of localized moral judgment become like prices: they convey information (about people's expectations, their tolerances, their willingness to go along with novelty, and so on) that are responsive to people's particular circumstances and exploit people's knowledge of those circumstances in a way that no distant third party, however intelligent or well intentioned, could possibly do.

4. Justice and Beneficence

What we are calling Smith's libertarian paternalism parallels, and relies in part on, the sharp distinction Smith draws between what he calls "justice" and what he calls "beneficence."[22] The next step in capturing Smith's position, then, requires an understanding of Smith's conception of those two virtues.

Smith argues that "because the mere want of beneficence tends to do no real positive evil," it follows that (1) beneficence therefore "cannot be extorted by force" and (2) "the mere want of it exposes to no punishment" (Smith, 1982: II.ii.1.3). According to Smith, acting with justice toward you leaves neither you nor anyone else worse off than you already were, though it may not by itself leave you or anyone else better off. For this reason, Smith calls it "a negative virtue" (Smith, 1982: II.ii.1.9), claiming that "We may often fulfil all the rules of justice by sitting still and doing nothing" (ibid.). The person sitting still and doing nothing is not acting with *positive* virtue—in other words, is not generating any improvement—"But," Smith contends, "still he does no positive hurt to anybody. He only does not do that good which in propriety he ought to have done" (Smith, 1982: II.ii.1.3).

So failing in proper *beneficence*—a category that for Smith includes things like charity, compassion, generosity, and "humanity"—might give us reason to disapprove of and be reasonably disappointed by another's behavior, but it does not license coercive punishment like jailing or fines. If I do not do you the good office you hoped or expected I would, you may be disappointed, even justifiably so; but you are no worse off than you were before. Because I have done you no "real positive hurt," meaning I have not worsened your *ex ante* position, you may not take positive action to punish me. By contrast, if I fail to act with justice toward you, that means I did indeed do "real positive hurt" to you. I left you worse off than you were before, and that gives rise to justified resentment, which licenses punishment.

According to Smith, there are only three rules of justice: "the laws which guard the life and person of our neighbor," "those which guard his property and possessions; and last of all come those which guard what are called his personal rights, or what is due to him from the promises of others" (Smith, 1982: II.ii.2.2). We act justly, then, according to Smith, when (1) we do not kill or molest others, (2) we do not steal from or defraud others, and (3) we do not break our voluntary contracts or promises. By contrast with justice, *beneficence* involves making at least one person better off. Assuming, however, that that improvement was not required of me by promise, contract, or other specific obligation, you cannot have had an enforceable expectation of improvement.

This seems a rather thin conception of justice: What about charity, or helping others who need it, especially when we are in a position to help? Smith's position is that beneficence is indeed frequently morally required, but since it is positive, not negative, it is not part of *justice*, and therefore not justifiable for state or other third-party coercion.

Smith offers several reasons for supporting his thin conception of "negative" justice. Here are three, each of which links to an important difference between Smithian libertarian paternalism and Thaler and Sunstein's more recent version.

Smith's first reason supporting his "thin" conception of justice rests on his empirical claim that no society can subsist unless its members respect these rules of conduct. Even a society of "robbers and murderers," Smith says, must at least "abstain from robbing and murdering one another" (Smith, 1982: II.ii.3.3). On the other hand, according to Smith, a society can subsist if its members respect these rules of justice but do not act with beneficence toward each other. Because beneficence "is less essential to the existence of society than justice," Smith concludes that "Society may subsist, though not in the most comfortable state, without beneficence; but the prevalence of injustice must utterly destroy it" (ibid.) Justice, therefore, "is the main pillar that upholds the whole edifice" of society, while beneficence "is the ornament which embellishes, not the foundation which supports the building"; for that reason, Smith argues, it is "sufficient to recommend, but by no means necessary to impose" beneficence (Smith, 1982: II.ii.3.4).

So: justice is both necessary and sufficient for the existence of society, but beneficence is neither necessary nor sufficient. That means that they enjoy a lexical priority—justice first, beneficence only thereafter—and, if we accept the Smithian claim that the state is justified in providing only what is necessary for human society, then it follows that it is justified in providing only justice.

A second reason Smith supports this thin conception of justice is its relative ease of administration: it is relatively easy (1) to capture its essence in simple rules, (2) to detect infractions of it, and (3) to remedy infractions. By contrast, beneficence is far more difficult to describe in rules, far more difficult to detect in its absence, and far more difficult to remedy.[23] Unlike infractions of justice, improper beneficence can be detected and adjudicated only on the basis of detailed, context-specific knowledge of the situation, persons, and matters involved in particular cases. We might all agree, for example, that we should be generous and that generosity is a virtue; nevertheless, it would be very difficult to generate a set of precise rules that will allow us to determine what generosity requires of me, here, now. In practice, we have to rely on practical judgment, which Smith, like Aristotle, believes does not operate by mechanical execution of general rules.

Smith's final reason is because it allows for a proper sensitivity to individual circumstances. What counts as being sufficiently generous depends on the particular circumstances of the case in question: the history and situation of the people involved, their available means and tradeoffs and opportunity costs, and even their goals and ambitions are all material considerations. There is also typically a *range* of behaviors or actions that might qualify as properly beneficent, which means that often no single course of action will be required to satisfy one's obligations. Therefore, beneficence cannot plausibly be incorporated into the definition of justice, which, because it can license coercion, requires predictable application of clear rules. Smith's thin concept of justice restricts it, therefore, to those few areas of conduct that it can plausibly and effectively address, and leaves to localized judgment the determination of what the virtues of positive beneficence require in light of particular circumstances.

5. Smithian Libertarian Paternalism

We can now see how Smith's version of libertarian paternalism contrasts with the "libertarian paternalism" of more recent vintage, namely, that of Thaler and Sunstein. In both cases we have recommendations about what behaviors to engage in or to avoid based on a (kind of) hypothetical imperative: for Smith, it is the hypothetical imperative deriving from the desire of having a happy life, while for Thaler and Sunstein it is more like having a healthy life. And in both cases we see the desire to satisfy the twin goals of enabling individual free choice while also encouraging and enabling people to make better choices.

Yet there are several important differences between the two accounts. First, Smith's argument that justice (as he understands it) is both necessary and sufficient for society to subsist means that whatever paternalistic nudging we think might help people make good decisions must be (1) pursued entirely within the realm of private—i.e., nongovernmental—social relations, (2) tailored to individuals' localized circumstances, and (3) pursued only after observance of the rules of justice. Second, Smith's argument that justice is relatively easy to administrate centrally, while beneficence (here including paternalism) is much more difficult, means that on Smith's account paternalism must be decentralized and local if it is to be effective. Third and finally, Smith's argument that effective beneficence requires extensive knowledge of, and must be adapted to, people's individual circumstances means that beneficence (and paternalism) will fail if it proceeds from centralized and general laws or regulations.

One place where it might seem that there is a difference is in Smith's relatively stronger emphasis on liberty and relatively weaker emphasis on paternalism than that of Thaler and Sunstein. It might seem as though Smith's definition of justice is a principled one, debarring—on principle, as it were—the state from engaging in any beneficent activity (which might include paternalistic nudging). But that is not Smith's position. When he argues for "publick works" that would (1) provide general benefit and (2) be unable to be provided by private enterprise, a latter-day Smithian might conclude that the members of Smith's putative set of public works are very few indeed—perhaps zero. There are, after all, privately provided roads, bridges, and other infrastructure, private schools and educational programs, and so on. Perhaps even security and dispute resolution can be provided by private enterprise. What, then, is left that markets could not provide? Although this might ultimately be an empirical question, the entire range of nudges Thaler and Sunstein suggest are justified precisely as areas in which private enterprise either cannot or at least does not help society meet optimal results. That means they would qualify for consideration even under Smith's otherwise stringent requirements. The analogy between moral community and political community would hold: just as one should follow the impartial spectator's recommendations, even on those occasions when one does not wish to do so, so too there might be times when we should impose nudges on others, even when others, at least at the moment, do not wish to us to nudge them. For Smith, as long as we still allow others the possibility of choosing otherwise, despite our expectations or nudges, we can respect their autonomy and still encourage them to make wise choices even despite themselves.

6. Conclusion: Smithian Libertarianism?

One might wonder whether Smithian libertarian paternalism as it is presented here counts as properly paternalistic at all. Most contemporary accounts of paternalism include some measure of coercion: either directly, by requiring compliance with a set of policies or behaviors regardless of what individuals wish; or indirectly, by imposing benefits on favored, and costs on disfavored, activities or behaviors, again regardless of individual desires. But if Smith has ruled out state action for beneficent purposes, and relegated "nudging" to the realm of private relations and associations among individuals, then to what extent is his position truly paternalistic? Perhaps Smith's position is like Mill's, according to which one may remonstrate, reason, persuade, or entreat another, but not compel or visit another with evil to get him to comply.[24] So perhaps Smith is just a Millian libertarian after all?

Smith's position cannot be reconciled with the paternalism of Conly or Ubel, which argues for an abandonment of a concern for autonomy altogether. Importantly, they argue for paternalism not only via government action but also via private action: they call on businesses, schools, and other social enterprises also to implement a "choice architecture" strategy with the aim of helping their constituents make good, or better, choices. That position is much closer to Smith's. Smith would not object to private persons and private enterprises adopting a deliberate choice-architecture strategy, and indeed he would recommend they do so on the grounds that their localized knowledge, combined with their localized feedback, can be an important part of the process of encouraging their associates to develop both good judgment and good behavior. At the same time, Smith believes that the withholding of mutual sympathy of sentiments is itself the imposition of a cost, since each of us naturally desires this mutual sympathy. If others choose not to approve of my conduct, this counts, then, as a paternalistic punishment because I do in fact desire their approval and experience the lack of it as a displeasure.

Smith would argue, however, that the Thaler and Sunstein program overreaches when it takes the important insight that sometimes others can help us make better decisions for ourselves and transfers that responsibility to governmental agents. For the reasons discussed earlier, Smith thinks doing that would undermine the benefits that paternalism can potentially provide. Because the relative success of nudges is dependent on the details of particular situations, the level at which nudges are applied matters. The Smithian position would thus call for a decentralized federalism: allowing and encouraging the greatest scope of independent paternalism at the most local levels, with less and less paternalism allowed as the level of decision-making ascends from private individuals, groups, or firms, to municipalities, to states, to federal governments.

On Smith's account, proper paternalistic recommendations arise decentrally from the experiences and expectations of people's actual lives and interactions. Like the social planner attempting to set prices or allocate resources centrally, however, Smith would argue that legislators or regulators are not in a position that would allow them to exploit people's localized knowledge of crucial relevant details about their lives—their unique circumstances, associations, relationships, opportunities, schedules of value, hierarchies of purpose—and thus the paternalistic nudges of centralized legislators would, like those of the central economic planner, likely fail to comport with what would actually conduce to people's well-being. Thus Smithian libertarian paternalism—unlike the Thaler and Sunstein version applied to legislators—would exploit people's local knowledge and respond to people's lived experience.

It would also have what Smith believes is the additional considerable benefit of allowing no centralized group of persons to assume the authority of directing the lives of others about whose unique circumstances they know little. In a famous passage, Smith calls a centralized authority undertaking to guide people in proper directions a "man of system," who, according to Smith, overestimates his knowledge of others' situations, and thus overestimates his ability to actually benefit others. Smith writes that the "man of system"

> seems to imagine that he can arrange the different members of a great society with as much ease as the hand arranges the different pieces upon a chess-board. He does not consider that the pieces upon the chess-board have no other principle of motion besides that which the hand impresses upon them; but that, in the great chess-board of human society, every single piece has a principle of motion of its own, altogether different from that which the legislature might chuse to impress upon it. (Smith, 1982: VI.ii.2.17)

It is crucial to see, however, that Smith's criticism here is directed at centralized legislators, not at local fellow citizens—a distinction Smith himself recognizes when he elsewhere allows that a local "civil magistrate" may, after all, "prescribe rules . . . which not only prohibit mutual injuries among fellow-citizens, but command mutual good offices to a certain degree" (Smith, 1982: II.ii.1.8). Smith rails against the "arrogance" of the "most dangerous" prince who believes himself competent to organize all of society according to his "ideal plan of government" (Smith, 1982: VI.ii.2.17–18) and, by extension, competent to excogitate and implement beneficial nudges from his centralized Olympian perch; and yet Smith recognizes the potential for local communities to organize themselves in mutually beneficial ways using even paternalistic means.

Smith's conception of political freedom and human agency thus incorporates a robust notion of political and economic community by giving people strong incentives to associate beneficially with others. At the same time, it allows the generation and application of robust moral communities, complete with moral agents who feel the pull of the desire for mutual sympathy of sentiments but yet retain the ability to make independent decisions. Smith writes, "A moral being is an accountable being" (Smith, 1982: III.i.3.[3]). That means that Smith's moral agents assume both a responsibility for themselves and an accountability to others—which just is his libertarian paternalism.

ACKNOWLEDGMENTS

I thank the Center for the Philosophy of Freedom at the University of Arizona for allowing me space and time to draft the initial ideas that led to this chapter. I would also like to thank Carmen Pavel, David Schmidtz, and two anonymous referees for excellent constructive criticism of an earlier draft of this chapter. Remaining errors are mine alone.

NOTES

1. Thaler and Sunstein, 2009: 5.
2. See, for example, White, 2013.
3. See, for example, Conly, 2013 and Ubel, 2009.
4. Smith, 1982 (1759): VI.iii.11.
5. Smith writes, "But whatever may be the cause of sympathy, or however it may be excited, nothing pleases us more than to observe in other men a fellow-feeling with all the emotions of our own breast" (Smith, 1982: I.i.2.1); similarly, "Nature, when she formed man for society, endowed him with an original desire to please, and an original aversion to offend his brethren" (Smith, 1982: III.2.6). For discussion, see Otteson, 2002: chap. 1.
6. See Raphael, 2007.
7. See Smith, 1982: III.3.22.
8. In order not to beg any questions, I maintain throughout Smith's exclusive use of the masculine pronoun.
9. Smith writes that we "always endeavor to bring down our own passions to that pitch, which the particular company we are in may be expected to go along with" (Smith, 1982: I.i.4.9). Yet he also claims: "though [different people's] sentiments will never be unisons, they may be concords, and this is all that is wanted or required" (Smith, 1982: I.i.4.7).
10. Much of the *Republic* is an extended response to Glaucon's challenge. Socrates's suggestion that the just person will fare better in the afterworld is contained in his myth of Er, which begins at *Republic* X.614b.
11. Other scholars have different views about the nature and origin of this desire. See, for example, Griswold, 1999: chap. 3.
12. Smith writes: "But though man has, in this manner, been rendered the immediate judge of mankind, he has been rendered so only in the first instance; and an appeal lies from his sentence to a much higher tribunal, to the tribunal of their own consciences, to that of the supposed impartial and well-informed spectator, to that of the man within the breast, the great judge and arbiter of their conduct" (Smith, 1982: III.2.32).
13. As the editors of the Glasgow edition of *TMS* note, the story Smith has in mind probably refers to Antimachus, not Parmenides. Parmenides probably died before Plato was born. See Smith, 1982: VI.iii.31 n27.
14. Smith, 1982: III.4.12 and passim.
15. Consider, for example, the small but telling case of joke-telling, one of Smith's favorite examples: knowing what constitutes a proper joke to tell, and how much—indeed whether—we should laugh at a joke, is determined by judgment that has been honed by experience. See Smith, 1982: I.i.2.1, I.i.3.1–2, and III.i.4.
16. Parents no doubt also want to enjoy the pleasure of imagining that others will form positive judgments of them when their children behave well, and avoid the discomfort associated with becoming aware that others might form negative judgments when their children behave badly.
17. See Smith, 1982: IV.1.1–2.
18. Smith, 1976 (1776): I.i.10.
19. More is said about Smith's conception of justice in the next section.
20. See Smith, 1982: II.ii.2.2, Smith, 1976: IV.ix.51, and Smith, 1976: V.i.c.1.
21. See Smith, 1976: V.i.f.54–5.

22. Smith respects the distinction between "beneficence" and "benevolence": by "beneficence" Smith means taking positive action to do good for another; by "benevolence" Smith means wishing another well. His discussion here concerns the difference he sees between justice and beneficence.

23. Smith offers the following analogy to illustrate the differences: "The rules of justice may be compared to the rules of grammar; the rules of the other virtues, to the rules which critics lay down for the attainment of what is sublime and elegant in composition. The one, are precise, accurate, and indispensable. The other, are loose, vague, and indeterminate" (Smith, 1982: III.6.11). Smith claims that although there are "general rules of almost all the virtues," nevertheless, reflecting his theory of the dynamic and social way in which rules of conduct develop, he also claims that "to affect, however, a very strict and literal adherence to them would evidently be the most absurd and ridiculous pedantry" (Smith, 1982: III.6.8).

24. This is a paraphrase from Mill, 1978 (1859): 9.

References

Conly, Sarah, 2013. *Against autonomy: justifying coercive paternalism*. New York: Cambridge University Press.

Griswold, Charles L., Jr., 1999. *Adam Smith and the virtues of enlightenment*. New York: Cambridge University Press.

Mill, John Stuart, 1978 (1859). *On liberty*. Indianapolis: Hackett.

Otteson, James R., 2002. *Adam Smith's marketplace of life*. New York: Cambridge University Press.

Plato, 1992. *Republic*. Translated by G. M. A. Grube and C. D. C. Reeve. Indianapolis: Hackett.

Raphael, D. D., 2007. *The impartial spectator: Adam Smith's moral philosophy*. New York: Oxford University Press.

Smith, Adam, 1976 (1776). *An inquiry into the nature and causes of the wealth of nations*. Edited by R.H. Campbell and A.S. Skinner. Indianapolis: Liberty Fund.

Smith, Adam, 1982 (1759). *The theory of moral sentiments*. Edited by D. D. Raphael and A. L. Macfie. Indianapolis: Liberty Fund.

Thaler, Richard, and Sunstein, Cass, 2009. *Nudge: improving decisions about health, wealth, and happiness*. Rev. and exp. ed. New York: Penguin.

Ubel, Peter, 2009. *Free market madness: why human nature is at odds with economics—and why it matters*. Cambridge: Harvard Business Press.

White, Mark D., 2013. *The manipulation of choice: ethics and libertarian paternalism*. New York: Palgrave Macmillan.

PART III

INSTITUTIONAL PREREQUISITES OF FREEDOM

CHAPTER 14

MARKET FAILURE, THE TRAGEDY OF THE COMMONS, AND DEFAULT LIBERTARIANISM IN CONTEMPORARY ECONOMICS AND POLICY

MARK BRYANT BUDOLFSON

1. DEFAULT LIBERTARIANISM IN CONTEMPORARY ECONOMICS AND POLICY

WHEN Milton Friedman died, Larry Summers offered the following commentary on his importance to policymaking in a *New York Times* editorial entitled "The Great Liberator":

> [A]ny honest Democrat will admit that we are now all Friedmanites. Mr. Friedman, who died last week at 94, never held elected office but he has had more influence on economic policy as it is practiced around the world today than any other modern figure. I grew up in a family of progressive economists [including Ken Arrow and Paul Samuelson], and Milton Friedman was a devil figure. But over time, as I studied economics myself and as the world evolved, I came to have grudging respect and then great admiration for him and for his ideas. No contemporary economist anywhere on the political spectrum combined Mr. Friedman's commitment to clarity of thought and argument, to scientifically examining evidence and to identifying policies that will make societies function better.

At first glance, it may not be clear what Summers means by his claim that "now we are all Friedmanites." For one thing, Summers intends this claim to be consistent with his view that Friedman voted for the wrong candidate in every election, and Summers also intends this claim to be universal in the sense that it would be endorsed by nearly all experts in economics and policy. This means, first, that his claim that now we are all Friedmanites must be interpreted as consistent with the sort of highly redistributive progressivist policies that Summers and many other experts favor, and second, it cannot be interpreted as endorsing Friedman's many specific theoretical views in economics, most of which are highly controversial. What then does Summers mean by his claim that now we are all Friedmanites?

Here is an answer: A large part of what Summers means by "now we are all Friedmanites" is that economists and policy experts at the highest levels now generally agree on a Friedmanian view that might be called *Default Libertarianism*, to coin a useful term that summarizes the policy evolution to which Summers draws attention. On this view there is a strong presumption in favor of laissez-faire policies that let individuals live their lives as they see fit and that let markets operate without interference. In order for this presumption to be overridden, there must be a very clear case for intervention based on positive empirical evidence that intervention would in practice actually make things substantially better, even in light of impressive empirical evidence that intervention has a natural tendency to fail. And when this presumption against intervention *is* overridden, a presumption remains that policy interventions should involve minimalistic, highly market-based policies that leave individuals as free from regulatory interference and as free to choose as possible and that function primarily by incentivizing socially advantageous behavior, competition, experimentation, and innovation by individuals and firms.

The nature of this presumption derives from empirical evidence that is outlined below, which is taken by proponents to show that a Default Libertarian approach to policy is more effective than the more interventionalist default advocated by economists and policy experts until the 1980s. This evidence has had an important impact on policy experts' estimates of the probability of success associated with the spectrum of more or less libertarian policy alternatives, which in turn has been taken to provide good reason for institutionalizing various presumptions against regulation and in favor of decentralized, market-based regulation when regulation is implemented. So, the "default" in Default Libertarianism refers to two types of presumption: both an *epistemic* presumption about the probability that a more libertarian approach is best when faced with social problems, as well as a resulting *procedural* presumption that is institutionalized in the way that policy is made, which is designed to favor adoption of more libertarian policies in the absence of impressive positive evidence that a departure is warranted.

It is important to stress that endorsing this kind of *strong presumption* in favor of libertarian approaches to policy is consistent with rejecting libertarianism[1] as an all-things-considered approach to policy, and instead endorsing progressivist policies that involve high levels of redistribution of wealth, as Summers himself would endorse along with most other Democratic party experts. The crucial point is that progressivists like Summers believe that overriding the presumption requires impressive reasons, and even when it is overridden, redistribution and other forms of intervention should generally be based on straightforward mechanisms such as (at the limit) simple taxes and cash transfers that, again, involve minimalistic, highly market-based policy that leaves individuals as free to choose as possible, and that allow markets to operate freely. The striking fact to which Summers's claim draws attention is that this Default Libertarian approach is now widely taken to be the gold standard among even leading progressivist policymakers, rather than the radical proposal it was in 1962 when Friedman first defended it at length in his classic book *Capitalism and Freedom*.[2]

2. Objections from Political Theorists vs. More Ambitious Arguments for Empirical Libertarianism

In contrast to Summers's celebration of Default Libertarianism, political theorists and social critics often bemoan the fact that candidates from both sides of the aisle now embrace free markets with such enthusiasm. These critics tend to criticize such a market-friendly approach on the basis of what they take to be straightforward objections, where the take-home message is supposed to be that such an approach depends on naive views of both ethics and economics. The economic strand of these objections is particularly important, because it aims to show that such an approach fails by its own lights even if ethics are set aside. These critics see the current near-consensus around market-based policy as the result of regrettable and irrational ideological drift, rather than any sort of genuine intellectual progress.

In what follows, I argue that these critics' objections, far from reflecting a superior understanding of economics, are outdated, and getting up to date on the economics and related research is the key to explaining why there has been such a shift toward Default Libertarianism.

In addition, getting up to date on the contemporary research also helps to explain why many experts endorse an all-things-considered libertarian view that might be called *Empirical Libertarianism*. This view is a contemporary version of the sort of consequentialist libertarian view defended by Milton Friedman and many others, now supported by more detailed arguments, which are often empirical in nature. Whereas Default Libertarianism is *not* a libertarian view because it implies merely that there is an important *presumption* in favor of libertarian policies that leads to policies with a libertarian flavor often being best all-things-considered, Empirical Libertarianism adds the controversial empirical claim that overriding this presumption *almost always* leads to worse outcomes and thus concludes that libertarian policies are almost always best.

The goal here in connection with Default Libertarianism and Empirical Libertarianism is not to argue for either of these views, but merely to explain why these views appear reasonable given contemporary economics, and to argue that if one or both of these views are false, it is for complex empirical reasons, and not for straightforward reasons that should be clear given our current evidence, contrary to what critics so often suggest. More generally, the goal throughout this chapter is to explain *the structure of the arguments* for these views, and in the process to explain why standard objections from political theorists fail to engage with many of the most respected contemporary economic arguments. I set aside the task of evaluating the ultimate *soundness* of the relevant arguments, because as will be clear from the following discussion, evaluating the soundness of these arguments is a task for economics and related disciplines, and it is a task that most experts would agree is ongoing and evolving.

3. The Tragedy of the Commons and the Standard Market Failure Argument Against Libertarianism

With that introduction in hand, let us turn toward articulating the standard economic argument offered by political theorists against libertarianism. Perhaps the simplest way into this argument is to see how it is deployed against the maximally libertarian view of laissez-faire, according to which markets should be allowed to operate with as little interference as possible, except to protect basic rights and enforce contracts.[3]

Laissez-faire is an important view to consider because it is often defended in public discourse on the grounds that any additional governmental interference beyond laissez-faire would violate individual rights, and on the grounds that additional interference would also lead to worse outcomes, primarily by preventing free exchange that "promotes the common good as if by an invisible hand," "adds to the size of the pie," and thereby contributes to "a rising tide that lifts all boats."[4] As such, the main argument for laissez-faire in public discourse combines strands of both ethical and economic reasoning.

The most familiar ethical argument *against* laissez-faire is that it ignores important goals that government is justified in promoting, such as distributive justice, democratic equality, and the like, and that these goals are actually undermined by laissez-faire, thus justifying additional government interference. Such an objection tends to go hand in hand with skepticism about the ethical grounds of property rights,[5] as well as the thought that there are particular markets—such as markets for prostitution—that must be highly regulated because "some things should not be for sale."[6]

In what follows, I set aside these ethical objections, and focus instead on the main economic argument (i.e., the main *consequentialist* argument) against laissez-faire and other libertarian views. This economic argument begins by claiming that the case for laissez-faire ignores the pervasive phenomenon of *market failure*, which arises from the fact that real-world acts and exchanges tend to impose costs and/or benefits on non-consenting third parties (impose *externalities* on third parties), or lead to inefficient outcomes in other ways (for example, as a result of lack of information, or monopoly power within markets), where these costs frequently exceed the benefits to society from allowing the relevant acts and exchanges. Examples of market failure include the predictable undersupply under laissez-faire of public goods, and the harms associated with the predictable oversupply under laissez-faire of public bads (such as pollution). In the worst cases of market failure, free exchange makes society worse off rather than better off, even though no rights or contracts are violated.

Most political theorists take this phenomenon of market failure to show that laissez-faire fails in an obvious and dramatic way on its own terms, even setting aside the question of whether there are additional legitimate objectives of government beyond those endorsed by laissez-faire. Furthermore, the fact that in real-world transactions market failure is the rule rather than the exception is taken to show that government intervention is justified far beyond any limits that could reasonably be called "libertarian." In what follows, it will be argued that this *Standard Market Failure Argument* is invalid, and that the particular way it fails provides a natural segue into the impressive contemporary arguments for Default Libertarianism.

Perhaps the best way into a detailed examination of the Standard Market Failure Argument is via the example of the tragedy of the commons, which is a paradigmatic illustration of market failure. For example, imagine a village that subsists largely on fish, where those fish are harvested from a fishery that is an *unregulated commons* in the sense that anyone can fish as much as they want without violating anyone's rights. Somewhat more technically, this natural kind of fishery is an *unregulated common pool resource* in the sense that its resources (namely, fish) are both *non-exclusionary*—no one has the right to exclude others from harvesting them—and *subtractable/rivalrous*—each act of harvesting reduces the amount available for others and thus reduces the expected value of the next similar act of harvesting.[7] With such a fishery in mind, it does not take sophisticated economic theory to see why laissez-faire could lead to over-harvesting and even catastrophe in connection with such a fishery. The explanation is that each individual fisher might do best by harvesting as much as possible regardless of what the other fishers do, even far beyond the point at which the collective result of all of the fishers' harvesting leads to the collapse of the fishery and a terrible outcome for all.

If the fishers' situation is as just described, then the economic logic of their situation is roughly a *multi-player prisoner's dilemma* where every player can be represented as having a choice between the same two options, OVERHARVEST and SUSTAINABLE HARVEST, where it is common knowledge that every individual does worse if all choose OVERHARVEST than if all choose SUSTAINABLE HARVEST, but where it is also common knowledge that choosing OVERHARVEST is the *dominant strategy* for each player, in the sense that regardless of what choices the others make, each does best for herself by choosing OVERHARVEST:

		Player n	
		Sustainable harvest	Overharvest
Player 1	Sustainable harvest	3,3	−4,5
	Overharvest	5,−4	−1,−1

A tragedy of the commons that is properly modeled as a prisoner's dilemma and in which individuals act in pursuit of self-interest is a classic example of *market failure*: a situation in which free action and free exchange lead to an outcome that is *inefficient (Pareto-inferior)* compared to another possible outcome, in the sense that another outcome that could have been brought about would have made some people better off without making anyone worse off. (For example, if the fishers follow self-interest in the situation described, the outcome that results is as described by the lower right-hand box above, which is Pareto-inferior to the possible outcome described by the upper left-hand box.) Furthermore, such a situation is the most famous example of a *social dilemma*, which is a situation in which the pursuit of self-interest by members of society is *directly collectively self-defeating*, in the sense that it leads to an outcome that is clearly worse from everyone's perspective than if everyone had not pursued self-interest and acted in a more "universalizable" way instead.[8] In social dilemmas, free action threatens to make not just someone but *everyone* worse off.

Social dilemmas are of great practical and theoretical importance because they approximate many real-world situations in which almost all members of society would prefer a different outcome than a free market can seem destined to deliver, including the oversupply of public bads such as pollution and the undersupply of public goods. Because free action and free exchange can seem destined to make everyone worse off in such cases, most political theorists take this type of market failure to provide an uncontroversial demonstration that economic arguments for laissez-faire and other libertarian views fail by their own lights, and that a more robust role for government is therefore justified to ensure better outcomes.

When this argument for more expansive government is understood in a straightforward way, it is an instance of what might be called the *Standard Market Failure Argument Against Libertarianism*:

> *Main Premise*: In a wide range of identifiable real-world cases, acts and transactions that respect rights but are otherwise done out of self-interest would impose externalities on third parties or lead to market failure for other reasons.
>
> *Intermediate Conclusion*: Therefore, market failure will occur in such cases.

Main Conclusion: Therefore, public policy is justified in such cases beyond laissez-faire and beyond anything that could properly be called "libertarian" to remedy these market failures.

For example, here is the philosopher Derek Parfit explaining what he takes to follow from the existence of social dilemmas:

> If each rather than none does what will be better for himself, or his family, or those he loves, this will be worse for everyone. . . . There is then a practical problem. Unless something changes, the actual outcome will be worse for everyone. This problem is one of the chief reasons why we need more than laissez-faire economics—why we need both politics and morality. Parfit, 1984: 62)

4. Why the Standard Market Failure Argument Is Invalid: Cooperative Behavior, Individuals' Superior Knowledge and Incentives, Government Failure

However, there are two independent objections to the Standard Market Failure Argument, each of which shows that it is invalid. First, the argument from the Main Premise to the Intermediate Conclusion presupposes the problematic neoclassical assumption that individuals will always act in their own narrow self-interest. Second, the argument from the Intermediate Conclusion to the Main Conclusion presupposes that public policy can correct market failures, or can at least improve outcomes over laissez-faire, which in many cases is at least as contentious as the neoclassical assumption. As a result, because the conclusion of the Standard Argument does not follow even if all of its premises are true, it is invalid, and the premises that must be added to make it valid are highly controversial and rejected by many leading experts.

Although these problems with the Standard Argument are occasionally acknowledged by political theorists, they are typically dismissed on the grounds that the assumptions of the Standard Argument are *close enough* to being correct about individual behavior and about the efficacy of government intervention to vindicate its Main Conclusion against libertarian views.

However, this is precisely where political theorists' understanding of economics and relevant disciplines is importantly outdated, as in the last several decades evidence has mounted that these assumptions may not be even approximately correct, at least for the spectrum of cases where they were assumed to hold by theorists of an earlier era. In very rough terms, the contemporary arguments that are most relevant here, which have led to several recent Nobel Prizes in economics, are that:

> First, in a wide range of cases including social dilemmas, individuals are actually disposed to act more altruistically and to cooperate to produce outcomes that are much better than what is predicted by standard neoclassical assumptions.[9]
>
> Second, in these and other situations where market failure threatens, the outcomes facilitated by Default Libertarian policies are often roughly *optimal in practice*, in the sense that over the long run they are better than the results of any practically feasible alternatives, and in particular are better than the results of more substantial interference by government to require individuals to act in accord with a plan that is *optimal in theory* according to standard neoclassical models. In other words, a solution that arises "internally" via individual choice, coordination, bargaining, and experimentation is often superior to an "externally imposed" solution devised by government, even when neoclassical theory implies that the internally generated solution is destined to be inefficient. This is especially true when coordination among individuals and experimentation is facilitated by minimalistic government assistance of the sort that advocates of Default Libertarianism endorse, such as government provision of short-term legal, administrative, and financial assistance in getting individuals together to communicate, coordinate, and get their own chosen form of cooperation up and running, which then removes any future need for government involvement or financing.[10]

In other words, the main thread of these contemporary arguments is that individuals are surprisingly good at coping with situations where market failure threatens when conditions are even somewhat favorable, and that the best outcome that is practically possible is often secured by leaving individuals free to coordinate and solve these problems themselves, free from government interference—except (importantly) via minimalistic government measures endorsed by Default Libertarianism that make the relevant background conditions as favorable as possible without prejudging the details of what solution is best.

To illustrate why experts now tend to maintain a Default Libertarian posture even when market failure threatens, it is useful to note one example of the kind of evidence that is taken to support the claims above. As just one such example, Elinor Ostrom describes a fishery in Alanya, Turkey that had become overfished by the 1960s, which caused economic decline and discord in the adjacent community that depended on the fishery for its livelihood. In response to this tragedy of the commons, the community deliberated internally for over a decade, and experimented with a variety of arrangements to cope with the problem, from which ultimately evolved a low-cost system of self-governance that led to sustainable use of the fishery and thus a "libertarian" solution to their commons dilemma. The solution that the fishers ended up coordinating on involved identifying how fishing locations of varying quality could ideally be spaced out and allotted to one fishing boat each to avoid overharvest and unnecessary interference between fishers and thus to yield maximum aggregate profits; then the initial use of each of those locations was allocated via lottery to individual fishers; then, each day the fishers rotated to the next adjacent spot either east to west, or west to east, depending on the fishing season, so that they could share those spots in a way that was perceived to be fair to all.

Once this system evolved, it was a *stable self-governing system* that did not require government interference or privatization of the fishery, contrary to what policy experts in an earlier era generally advocated as necessary features to any solution to such social dilemmas.[11] In describing the day-to-day facts on the ground relevant to the success of this particular solution, Ostrom notes that "fishers can expect that the assigned fisher will be at [their] spot bright and early. Consequently, an effort to cheat on the system by traveling to a good spot on a day when one is assigned to a poor spot has little chance of remaining undetected. . . . The few infractions that have occurred have been handled easily by the fishers at the local coffeehouse."[12]

At a more theoretical level, Ostrom explains why, given the superior knowledge and incentives of individuals compared to government, this self-governing solution was almost certainly better than what would have resulted from a more interventionalist approach on the part of government:

> Central-government officials could not have crafted such a set of rules without assigning a full-time staff to work (actually fish) in the area for an extended period. . . . Mapping this set of fishing sites, such that one boat's activities would not reduce the migration of fish to other locations, would have been a daunting challenge had it not been for the extensive time-and-place information provided by the fishers and their willingness to experiment for a decade with various maps and systems. Alanya provides an example of a self-governed common-property arrangement in which the rules have been devised and modified by the participants themselves and are also monitored and enforced by them. The case of the Alanya inshore fishery is only one empirical example of the many institutional arrangements that have been devised, modified, monitored, and sustained by the users of renewable [common pool resources] to constrain individual behavior that would, if unconstrained, reduce joint returns to the community of users. [Similar] arrangements have been well documented for many farmer-managed irrigation systems, communal forests, inshore fisheries, and grazing and hunting territories. (Ostrom, 1990: 20–21)

Ostrom draws a more general lesson about how this sort of Default Libertarian response to market failure compares favorably to the sort of *government failure* that is frequently the much worse outcome of greater intervention by government in such situations:

> [Advocates of more centrally planned solutions] presume that unified authorities will operate in the field as they have been designed to do in the textbooks—determining the best policies to be adopted based on valid scientific theories and adequate information. Implementation of these policies without error is assumed. Monitoring and sanctioning activities are viewed as routine and unproblematic. . . . Many

policy prescriptions are themselves no more than metaphors. Both [advocates of centrally planned solutions and privatization schemes] frequently advocate over-simplified, idealized institutions—paradoxically, almost 'institution-free' institutions.... Relying on metaphors as the foundation for policy advice can lead to results substantially different from those presumed to be likely. Nationalizing the ownership of forests in Third World countries, for example, has been advocated on the grounds that local villagers cannot sustain forests so as to maintain their productivity and their value in reducing soil erosion. In countries where small villages had owned and regulated their local communal forests for generations, nationalization meant expropriation. In such localities, villagers had earlier exercised considerable restraint over the rate and manner of harvesting forest products. In some of these countries, national agencies issued elaborate regulations concerning the use of forests, but were unable to employ sufficient number of foresters to enforce those regulations. The foresters who were employed were paid such low salaries that accepting bribes became a common means of supplementing their income. The consequence was that nationalization created *open-access resources* where limited-access *common property resources* had previously existed.[13] The disastrous effects of nationalizing formerly communal forests have been well documented for Thailand, Niger, Nepal, and India. Similar problems occurred in regard to inshore fisheries when national agencies presumed they had exclusive jurisdiction over all coastal waters.[14] (Ostrom, 1990: 22–23)

In addition to Ostrom's point that government intervention often makes things worse rather than better even when that intervention is intended to correct inefficiencies, a further point is that many market failures and other social problems that at first glance might appear to be caused by free markets are actually caused by government interference that prevents markets from operating freely. In such cases, it is even clearer why the best solution might be to make markets freer, rather than to add further regulation that could make the problem even worse and create further problems elsewhere.

In some cases, when there is reliable evidence that the sort of ultra-minimalistic response to market failure illustrated here in connection with the Turkey fishery case will not be enough, the remaining Default Libertarian presumption is that incentives should be created by government for individuals to cooperate via a clear and straight-forward market-based measures, such as, for example, a *Pigovian tax*, which levies a fee for actions that impose externalities on others based on the magnitude of those externalities. For an example of such a Pigovian tax, consider a tax on pollution that levies a fee for each ton of a pollutant emitted based on a calculation of the *marginal social cost* of an additional ton of that pollutant—that is, the aggregate cost of an additional ton of that pollutant to all of those in society.[15] Such a tax creates incentives for pollution reductions in a way that incentivizes socially beneficial innovation and technological progress, while interfering in individual choice as little as possible—it leaves individuals free to choose whether to continue with their polluting behavior and pay its true cost, or to adopt less polluting technologies instead, or to change their behavior in some other way that is best from their perspective after the true costs of their actions are "internalized" by the tax into the possible outcomes of their choices, thereby leveraging the generally superior time-and-place knowledge of individuals. Of particular note, such a tax is designed to achieve all of this—and the goal of securing the optimal level of pollution for society at the least cost—without the sort of *command and control* requirements of particular behavior and technologies that are one hallmark of more substantial government interference that was the default in the previous era.[16] In a situation where an ultra-minimalistic response has been tried and has failed, adding such market-based incentives without command and control often suffices to spur individuals to coordinate and innovate in a way that is roughly optimal in practice, without need for further governmental determination of specific actions and outcomes.

Taken together, these empirical results about the superior knowledge and incentives of individuals and the frequent ability of individuals to cope better than government with situations where market failure threatens are among the leading factors in explaining why Default Libertarianism has become the dominant view in contemporary economics and public policy. They also bring into sharp focus what is ultimately the crucial issue for practical purposes, as well as for the evaluation of libertarianism, which is the extent to which market failure should be expected to occur in situations that involve externalities or other social dilemma–like incentive structures, and the comparative benefits of more or less robust governmental intervention into those situations.

5. The Crucial Empirical Issue in Debates about Libertarianism

As the discussion thus far shows, whether any kind of market failure argument against libertarianism can be salvaged depends on the *empirical* question of *the extent to which* market failure should be expected to occur in situations in which it is predicted by neoclassical assumptions, and *to what extent* government intervention should actually be expected to make things better rather than worse in those situations beyond the limits of what could reasonably be called a "libertarian" approach to policy. With the empirical nature of this issue in mind, and with some indication now in hand of some of the reasons why government might not generally be the best solution to these problems, we are now in a good position to reflect on the *Characteristic Claim of Empirical Libertarianism*, which goes well beyond the claims of Default Libertarianism explained above:

> Market failures under laissez-faire are generally not as bad as the outcomes that would result over the long run from attempting to solve those failures with greater government intervention. In the rare cases where policy can make things better, the best feasible outcomes are provided by non-intrusive, market-based regulation incorporating Pigovian taxes, cash transfers, and other measures that are the strong default according to *Default Libertarianism*. In sum, the best overall package of government policies will involve only very modest government interference beyond

laissez-faire, where that interference will tend to be highly market-based and decentralized in its implementation.[17]

This empirical claim is highly controversial but yet not obviously mistaken given contemporary economics, especially in light of the contemporary research outlined above, which will be described in somewhat more detail in subsequent sections. Empirical Libertarianism follows from this empirical claim together with Default Libertarianism, and such a view is similar to Milton Friedman's consequentialist libertarian view, although now supported by a wider range of empirical arguments.

The important point to make here in connection with this all things considered libertarian view is that if it is false, it is false for complex empirical reasons, and not for obvious reasons that follow from the phenomenon of market failure—contrary to what many political theorists assume. At the same time, it is much more controversial than Default Libertarianism, because it adds the more controversial claim that overriding the default against governmental intervention would very seldom lead to a better outcome over the long run.

6. Contemporary Empirical Arguments for Libertarianism vs. Older A Priori Public Choice Arguments

Having now laid out the structure of the dialectic between, on the one hand, the Standard Market Failure Argument against Libertarianism and, on the other hand, Default Libertarianism and the more controversial view Empirical Libertarianism, the next step is to explain why contemporary arguments for Default Libertarianism have been so compelling to experts across the political spectrum. The primary explanation is that these contemporary arguments are based firmly on impressive *empirical evidence* rather than the kind of neoclassical *a priori reasoning* that was the hallmark of older libertarian economic arguments such as early public choice arguments. In other words, contemporary arguments tend to be based directly on real-world experience with how policies play out in practice, rather than derivations of how things ought to work according to a simplistic economic theory.

For example, older economic arguments for libertarianism tend to begin by noting the familiar fact that government intervention can create perverse incentives and can have seriously bad unintended consequences; furthermore, expanding government power creates new opportunities for bureaucrats within government and special interest groups to benefit themselves at the expense of the public. When these kind of facts are conjoined with the neoclassical assumption that individuals will act to enrich themselves, this allows for the derivation of results in public choice theory such as that bureaucrats will act to fleece the public whenever possible to benefit themselves, including by becoming essentially employees of private interests in exchange for government favors, such as by providing government protection of inefficient monopolies.[18]

The great value in these older public choice arguments is in showing that just as inefficiencies due to *market failure* will arise in a wide range of cases given neoclassical assumptions, so too inefficiencies due to this phenomenon of *government failure* will arise in a wide range of cases given neoclassical assumptions. This is in fact the neoclassical economic objection to the Standard Market Failure Argument Against Libertarianism, which provides another way of showing that the Standard Argument is invalid even given neoclassical assumptions.

However, the great limitation of these older economic arguments when used as arguments *for* libertarianism is that just as the threat of market failure does *not* show that government intervention will make outcomes better, so too the threat of government failure does *not* show that government intervention will *not* make outcomes better than a libertarian approach to policy. So, this kind of older public choice argument fails as an argument *for* libertarianism for structurally the same reasons that the Standard Market Failure Argument fails as an argument *against* libertarianism.

Furthermore, even setting that issue aside, these older public choice arguments for libertarianism can seem unconvincing because they are essentially a priori demonstrations of how things ought to work according to neoclassical economic models, which is a form of argument that is often unimpressive to those outside of the discipline of economics. In particular, such arguments may seem to depend on an implausibly cynical view of government insofar as they are taken to support libertarian conclusions, even if one agrees that some amount of cynicism about government is justified. In light of all this, it is reasonable that political theorists and others do not take these older public choice arguments to provide a decisive economic argument for libertarianism or even Default Libertarianism. In contrast, contemporary empirical arguments are based on impressive evidence about how policies play out in practice, and the comparative outcomes that can thus be expected to result from more or less libertarian policies—which is the kind of argument that is actually needed to answer the crucial questions about what policies should actually be expected to work best in particular cases.

7. Contemporary Empirical Arguments for Default Libertarianism in More Detail

The great evolution in contemporary economics that is important for our purposes is what might be called *the empirical and institutional turn* of the past several decades, which leads directly into the relevant contemporary arguments, which marshal impressive empirical evidence about how policies play out in practice, often based directly on real-world experience. In this section, the elements of this contemporary research that are most relevant to social dilemmas will be described in somewhat more detail, but no attempt will be made to go far enough into the details to do justice to these arguments on their own terms, much less to evaluate the soundness of all deployments of these arguments. Such an undertaking would require a multi-volume series of handbooks of its own. Instead, the goal here is merely to provide a high-level explanation that is sufficient to explain in somewhat more detail why these contemporary arguments, in contrast to older, more a priori libertarian economic arguments, have been so influential in moving experts and policymakers toward more libertarian policy.

First and perhaps most importantly, in the last several decades market-based policies have been increasingly implemented despite the protests of non-economists, and have generally experienced success when deployed in the way that Default Libertarian practitioners favor, arguably performing better than more traditional command and control policy approaches insofar as such an assessment is possible, and often performing dramatically better. As just a few leading examples, the success of the SO_2 cap-and-trade system to reduce acid rain the United States is often cited along with many analogous successful market-based solutions to environmental problems elsewhere in the world.[19] More recent examples include many successes under the Obama administration in a diverse range of initiatives, including reducing overfishing in domestic fisheries via property rights creation and market-based trading schemes that involve minimal government prohibitions on individual choice, and leave the details of how individuals will ultimately coordinate to produce a collectively acceptable outcome almost entirely to those individuals to figure out, given their superior knowledge and incentives.[20] Other examples include conditional cash transfer programs to benefit the poor that have been arguably more effective than other less minimalistic policy measures with the same goals,[21] and the trend is now toward further movement toward these policies in the realm of social welfare, and toward even more Default Libertarian implementation of these policies to make them simpler and more economically efficient, based on these repeated successes.

More indirect support for Default Libertarianism across the full spectrum of policy is provided by the successes associated with various procedural presumptions that have been created against regulation in recent decades, such as requiring that regulations pass a cost-benefit analysis test, which is a requirement that has been in place on regulations issued by the federal executive branch in the United States since the Reagan administration. In practice, this requirement has created a Default Libertarian–like presumption against regulation, where the presumption requires positive empirical evidence to override.[22] In the United States, President Obama has expanded this requirement by adding *retrospective* cost-benefit analyses of policies already in place with the aim of eliminating policies that are not empirically shown to be effective in retrospect.[23] Further initiatives include moves to simplify policies and make improvements based on the results of insights from empirical psychology about the behavioral dispositions of people that are highly sensitive to non-financial cues, and thus lead to predictable departures from neoclassical assumptions about behavior. As Cass Sunstein, the czar of regulation in the Obama administration (and widely cited scholar), argues in his book *Simpler: The*

Future of Government, these initiatives are showing success in outcomes while at the same time reducing the burdens of government on firms and individuals compared with approaches to policy that go beyond Default Libertarianism (Sunstein, 2013).

Reflection on the kind of regulation that does pass an empirically adequate cost-benefit analysis illustrates why Default Libertarianism is at the same time consistent with some substantial government regulation based on compelling empirical evidence, such as limits on pollutants in drinking water.[24] As this example illustrates, Default Libertarianism is not the view that we should have *less* regulation—instead, it is exactly the kind of more nuanced view about regulation that is needed, which counsels us to have not merely *more regulation* or merely *less regulation*, but rather the *best regulation* based on sound empirical analysis and elegant design—which now tends to rely heavily on markets, experimentation, and individual innovation and choice. The other side of this coin is that further support for Default Libertarianism is provided by comparing these successes of Default Libertarian policy with the widespread failure, over many decades, of aid and welfare programs that involve government interference and central planning beyond what is endorsed by Default Libertarianism.

In addition to this wide range of experiences with such failures,[25] the research of Nobel Laureates Elinor Ostrom, Vernon Smith, and others has undermined the assumption of standard neoclassical models that individuals are disposed to avoid cooperation in, for example, the wide range of situations commonly modeled as social dilemmas.[26] Ostrom's research program has been particularly influential in policy circles because it involves meticulous study of hundreds of real-world situations in which individuals use common resources, and has led to great progress in identifying the conditions under which cooperative outcomes that are superior in practice to government intervention are likely to emerge when individuals are left more or less free to solve these problems themselves, especially when such solutions are facilitated by minimalistic government assistance of the sort that is prescribed by Default Libertarianism.[27] In addition to the successes with overfishing and other initiatives noted above that were partly guided by this research, this tradition marshals many examples as diverse as communal forests, grazing areas, and traditional water allocation systems across the world, where individuals have achieved results that are roughly optimal in practice even though they are suboptimal according to standard neoclassical models that in an earlier era were taken to justify large governmental takeovers of such systems, which often had disastrous results.[28] One impressive sign of the resulting shift toward Default Libertarianism is that leading resource management policymakers from both the Democratic and the Republican parties, such as Jane Lubchenco and Lynn Scarlett (from the Obama and George W. Bush administrations, respectively), explicitly endorse these lessons from Ostrom as among the most important we have learned in recent decades.[29] A more general reason why this research is so important is that these examples represent the vast range of cases where policy commentators of the previous era, such as Garrett Hardin, mistakenly claimed that a catastrophic tragedy of the commons was unavoidable without large-scale governmental intervention through either regulation or a privatization scheme.[30]

Somewhat relatedly—and illustrated by many of the examples alluded to above—there is also now increased recognition that policy challenges such as market failures must be understood as embedded within the complex system of local, national, and global economies, which also have similarly complex ties to institutions that overlap and interact in incredibly diverse ways that resist simple modeling. As a result, the status quo equilibrium of such a system, which may seem highly inefficient from the perspective of a simple neoclassical model of one policy challenge that arises within that system, may at a deeper level be a highly evolutionarily tuned equilibrium with many desirable stability properties that would be upset by social engineering. Along one dimension, this is merely a sophisticated way of explaining why an outcome that appears highly suboptimal in theory may be nearly optimal in practice. But an important further point is that evolutionarily tuned complex systems can have more subtle properties that explain this optimality in practice, such as becoming more resilient and even generating better outcomes over time as they are exposed to external shocks.[31] In contrast, when such a system is replaced by a socially engineered system, the result can be a system that is optimized for the short run, given an incomplete and flawed model of the underlying complex system, but that as a side effect becomes highly fragile in the face of external shocks. For example, Nassim Taleb argues that by replacing the allegedly "inefficient" banking system of an earlier era (involving many disconnected banks that occasionally failed and occasionally led to panic) with a more-efficient-in-theory central banking system embedded in a highly socially engineered society with far-reaching government influence, the result was a fragile system that could be utterly destroyed by a financial crisis, rather than merely temporarily set back only to grow back stronger as in an earlier era.[32] Although this particular example is controversial, the point it illustrates is the need for modesty about the ability of government to make sustainable improvements in society, in light of the fact that the economy is a complex system in which the gains in stability from decentralization must not be underestimated, and in which the complex interconnections and contributions of institutions to outcomes cannot be overlooked in the way that was characteristic of more interventionalist approaches to policy in the previous era.

Once these basic points are made salient, it is easy to recognize that many historical failures of social engineering are explained by the replacement of finely tuned, evolutionarily adapted systems with more fragile planned systems that quickly fail. James C. Scott and many other scholars have provided a range of examples of this sort, sometimes interrelated, ranging from monoculture in forest and crop management, to city planning (Scott, 1999).[33] Another example is the following from Elinor Ostrom and collaborators, which illustrates recurring problems with planned development efforts:

> The government-owned Chiregad irrigation system . . . was constructed in Nepal to replace five farmer-owned irrigation systems whos e physical infrastructures were [much more primitive]. In planning the Chiregad system, designers focused entirely on constructing modern engineering works and not on learning about the rules and norms that had been used in the five earlier systems. Even though the physical capital

is markedly better than that possessed by the earlier systems, the Chiregad system has never been able to provide water consistently to more than two of the former villages. Agricultural productivity is lower now than it was under farmer management. Not only do the farmers invest heavily in the maintenance of [their systems], they have devised effective rules related to access and the allocation of benefits and costs. They achieve higher productivity than most government-owned systems with modern infrastructure.[34]

Even if one disagrees with the application of this analysis to one or more of these specific examples (such as, perhaps, the recent financial crisis), the more general point remains that when social problems appear at first glance to be caused by free markets, sometimes in actuality they are caused by government interference in markets, where this fundamental cause goes unnoticed by society because it is not perceptible to an untrained observer.

This concludes the outline of why contemporary economic arguments have been so influential in moving leading experts and policymakers to Default Libertarianism. Again, the main reason why these arguments have had such influence is that they are based on impressive empirical evidence rather than the kind of neoclassical a priori reasoning that was the hallmark of older libertarian economic arguments. Much of this impressive empirical evidence is based directly on real-world experience with how policies play out in practice, rather than merely derivations of how things ought to work according to simplistic economic models.

8. Empirical Replies to Ethical Objections to Libertarianism

In response to all of the preceding arguments for Default Libertarianism, some critics may be tempted to fall back on *ethical* objections to that view. However, at this point it is possible to see the structure of an impressive reply to such objections—namely, that whatever additional ethical goals we might have, the best way of achieving them is by the sort of policy mechanisms endorsed by Default Libertarianism.[35] With this in mind, it is possible to agree with egalitarian philosophers such as John Rawls or Peter Singer concerning "ideal theory" questions about what ideals and goals society and policy should pursue, while disagreeing with, for example, Rawls's view that public policy should aim for a social structure more analogous to that of the former Yugoslavia than any other form of government with which we have experience.[36] According to a Default Libertarian line of thought, we should not adopt such a Rawlsian approach to policy, given the actual cause and effect relationships in the real world, because doing so would make society worse rather than better along the ethical dimensions that ultimately matter. Instead, the Default Libertarian progressivist thought is that we should instead agree with equally progressive contemporary experts who favor a more *effective altruism*, in which growing inequality and other social ills are best combatted by the sort of policies recommended by Default Libertarianism given those goals, such as cash transfers and other social welfare measures originally advocated by Milton Friedman as the most effective way of achieving such ethical goals.

Along these lines, it is telling that some influential political theorists are increasingly incorporating some of the insights outlined above, thereby providing a more empirically informed understanding of how societies can flourish, what the best form of deliberative democracy would be,[37] how to promote global justice and design effective and legitimate global governance institutions,[38] and how best to promote other important political values. For example, in a 2013 editorial in the *New York Times* Peter Singer praises the virtues of charities that facilitate unconditional cash transfers to the poor in developing countries, on the grounds that contemporary evidence indicates that this is likely to be the most effective way of helping such people (Singer, 2013). In response to this, it is easy to imagine Milton Friedman, the original defender of a Default Libertarian approach to policy, writing a response to this kind of change in progressivist attitudes to policymaking over the past several decades:

> Although I do not necessarily endorse Mr. Singer's ethical arguments for the dramatic redistribution of wealth, I applaud his wisdom in endorsing the libertarian mechanisms for such proposed redistribution that I outlined in *Capitalism and Freedom* fifty years ago. To theorists like Mr. Singer I say: Welcome aboard!

9. Conclusion

In sum, although many political theorists take the phenomenon of market failure to show that arguments for libertarianism fail in a straightforward way, this chapter has explained why the most common form of this objection depends on invalid reasoning, and why a more sophisticated understanding of the relevant economics has led most contemporary economists and policy experts to the view here called *Default Libertarianism*. According to this view, the strong default for public policy—even in response to market failures—should be toward decentralized, pro-individual freedom policies that involve minimal government intervention in markets. Many experts (but by no means all) also take these considerations to show that even in the face of substantial market failures, libertarian policies are generally best, all things considered. This shift toward more libertarian policy represents an important change from the mid- to late twentieth century, when the default stance involved more substantial government intervention. The focus of this chapter has been on explaining the *structure* of the arguments that have led to this shift, especially in connection with work that has led to many recent Nobel Prizes in economics—but no pretense has been made of evaluating the *soundness* of these arguments, which is an ongoing project for economics and related disciplines.

Acknowledgments

Thanks to two anonymous referees, Will Braynen, Susan Brison, Nicolas Cornell, William Fischel, Gerald Gaus, Keith Hankins, Douglas Irwin, Hugh Lazenby, RJ Leland, Bethany Lobo, Elinor Mason, Russell Muirhead, Carmen Pavel, Mark Pennington, David Peritz, David Plunkett, Timothy Rosenkoetter, Debra Satz, David Schmidtz, Dan Shahar, Liam Shields, David Sobel, Dean Spears, John Thrasher, Molly Thrasher, and audiences at Dartmouth and a conference organized by the University of Arizona Center for the Philosophy of Freedom for helpful discussions.

Notes

1. Here and throughout, for ease of exposition the term "libertarianism" is used to refer to the general family of views that include more specific views sometimes described as "classical liberalism," "right libertarianism," "hard libertarianism," "neoclassical libertarianism," and "bleeding heart libertarianism." Importantly, "left libertarianism" is not included under this heading. For discussion of this family of views, and similar use of the term "libertarianism," see Brennan, 2012, especially pp. 8–12.

2. Notably, this Default Libertarian approach to policy has not wavered even in the wake of the recent financial crisis. For some limited arguments for change, see Stiglitz, 2010. At the same time, it is telling that even Stiglitz, who is perhaps the most distinguished and withering critic of laissez-faire among leading economists, nonetheless appears largely an ally of the Default Libertarian approach to policy discussed here, and in stating the upshot of his work for policymaking, he can be seen as endorsing a version of that approach analogous to that attributed to Summers here. For example, in "Government Failure vs. Market Failure: Principles of Regulation," Stiglitz criticizes advocates of laissez-faire on the grounds that they commonly "take it as a matter of faith that government attempts to correct market failures by and large make things worse." However, in the next sentence he continues, "To be sure, there are examples of badly designed government regulations, but the disasters associated with unfettered markets at least provide a prima facie case for the desirability of *some* regulation" Stiglitz, 2008: 2–3, italics in the original). Note Stiglitz's own emphasis on 'some'. Similarly, Stiglitz writes in his Nobel Prize autobiography that in his opinion the most important contribution of his tenure on the Council of Economic Advisors during the Clinton administration was in "helping define a new economic philosophy, a 'third way,' which recognized the important, but limited, role of government, that unfettered markets often did not work well, but that government was not always able to correct the limitations of markets. The research that I had been conducting over the preceding twenty-five years provided the intellectual foundations for this 'third way'" (Stiglitz, 2001). Note the reference to the "limited" role of government here. For related discussion see also Stiglitz, 1991. As a separate point, there is a sense in which Default Libertarianism might be claimed to be a particular kind of "neoliberalism," which is a term that is used to mean so many different things that it has little determinate content. However, the forms of neoliberalism that are generally discussed and criticized—leading to corporate welfare, lack of concern for values beyond short-run GDP, and so on—are also forms of neoliberalism that would be rejected by defenders of Default Libertarianism. As a result, Default Libertarianism is a superior alternative to the forms of neoliberalism that are discussed in popular discourse, and is not a version of those forms of neoliberalism.

3. For our purposes, laissez-faire might be understood more precisely as the view that government should not interfere with individual acts insofar as those acts do not violate the directives of well-functioning minimalistic background institutions that exist to protect rights and enforce contracts, and, beyond that, perform only functions that *all* citizens *explicitly agree* to have performed by those institutions by means of such directives. In this definition of laissez-faire, the requisite background institutions are not referred to as "governmental institutions" because, as Elinor Ostrom and others have argued, public goods up to and including police protection and dispute settlement regimes are sometimes best supplied in the real world by non-governmental institutions created by inspired individual public entrepreneurs, rather than by government or governmental actors. Ostrom's views are discussed in greater detail below; see also Schmidtz, 1990. Note also that this definition of laissez-faire captures the intentions of actual defenders of that view that individuals can be required to comply with directives that are purely conventional (e.g., pure coordination conventions, such as what side of the road it is permissible to drive on), insofar as those conventional rules are necessary for the relevant institutions to be well-functioning and/ or to solve problems that all citizens agree to have solved by those institutions by means of such directives. In connection with this, in *Capitalism and Freedom* Milton Friedman imagines a society in which all citizens agree that a safety net be provided for the poor via governmental taxation and a voucher scheme. Such a scheme would not violate laissez-faire if all citizens explicitly agreed to it and continued to endorse it over time, and the definition offered here yields that result. Furthermore, any definition of laissez-faire that does not allow for such possibilities is a definition that does not capture the intended notion and the one that is thus of intellectual interest. Contrary to an objection often raised by political theorists, it is also no objection to laissez-faire that such a society has never existed. At a former point in history it was true that no society had ever existed that did not condone human slavery in one form or other, but that did not show that there was any good objection to promoting a society that did not condone human slavery, and it certainly did not show that such a society was impossible in practice. In light of all of these considerations, I disagree with many political theorists who claim that laissez-faire is impossible in practice. For example, Debra Satz (2012) makes the even stronger claim that laissez-faire is "logically impossible."

4. Despite the allusion to Adam Smith in this popular argument, Smith does not endorse this reasoning. For example, in the most relevant passage Smith writes: "by directing that industry in such a manner as its produce may be of the greatest value, [an individual] intends only his own gain, and he is in this, as in many other cases, led by an invisible hand to promote an end which was no part of his intention. Nor is it *always* the worse for the society that it was not part of it. By pursuing his own interest he *frequently* promotes that of the society more effectually than when he really intends to promote it" (Smith, 1776: Book IV, Chapter II, emphasis added). Note that by Smith's explicit use of "always" and "frequently" he implies that acts and exchanges in the pursuit of self-interest do *not* always promote the common good. On the other hand, it is important to note that Smith also anticipates the phenomenon of government failure discussed below, continuing: "I have never known much good done by those who affected to trade for the public good."

5. For consideration of these issues, see for example Gaus, 2012; Murphy and Nagel, 2004.

6. See for example Satz, 2012. For a response, see Schmidtz, 2011; Fleurbaey, 2011; Brennan and Jaworski, 2015.

7. This is a gloss on these economic concepts that is intended to be useful for current purposes. However, unlike the gloss just given, economists draw the excludable/non-excludable distinction based on whether exclusion is *possible* or not (rather than whether there are currently rights to exclude). In connection with these concepts, it is common to distinguish between the following types of goods via a chart like the following:

	Excludable	Non-excludable
Rivalrous	**Private goods** food, clothing, cars, personal electronics	**Common goods** **(Common-pool resources)** fish stocks, timber, coal
Non-rivalrous	**Club goods** cinemas, private parks, satellite television	**Public goods** free-to-air television, air, national defense

For our purposes, it is worth noting that in contrast to a common pool resource, a public good is non-excludable and *non*-rivalrous, which gives rise to *positive* externalities as a result of each act of its *provision*. This gives rise to an argument for the inefficient undersupply of public goods under laissez-faire that is the other side of the coin to the argument for the inefficient overharvesting of common pool resources described in the main text.

8. For the concepts of social dilemma and direct collective self-defeat, see respectively Dawes, 1980 and Parfit, 1984, especially part one. See also van Lange et al., 2013. Not all tragedies of the commons can be represented as prisoner's dilemmas, as Michael Taylor explains in *The Possibility of Cooperation* (1987), chapter 2. However, those that can be so represented provide a particularly clear and useful example of the kind of situation and incentives that lead to a conflict between free action and the promotion of welfare even when no rights are violated.

9. See for example Ostrom and Walker, 2005; Smith, 2003, especially section 3, "Personal Social Exchange"; Bicchieri, 2006; Kagel and Roth, 1997; Kagel and Roth, unpublished; Ostrom, 1998, and the references therein.

10. See for example Ostrom, 1990; Scott, 1999; Dietz et al., 2002; Ostrom et al., 1999, and the references therein. See also Connelly, 2008 for specific discussion of the negative effects of population control policies motivated by analyses such as that of Hardin, 1968.

11. See for example Hardin, 1968.

12. Ostrom, 1990: 20. See the rest of that book, the other references above, and the references therein for a wide variety of other real-world examples.

13. In connection with common pool resources, four main types of property-rights systems might obtain: *open access*, which involves an absence of enforced property rights; *group property*, in which resource rights are held by a group of users who can exclude others; *individual property*, in which resource rights are held by individuals or firms who can exclude others; and *government property*, in which resource rights are held by a government that can regulate or subsidize use.

14. Footnotes have been omitted, in which Ostrom cites numerous other works in support of her claims. See also the references above.

15. For further discussion, including of some important further subtleties, see Metcalf, 2001; for more general discussion, see Stavins, 2012. The locus classicus for Pigovian taxes is

Pigou, 1920; see also Baumol, 1972. Note that Pigou recognized that government failure was a general phenomenon and could often represent a cure worse than the disease of market failure—e.g., his discussions of the issue approximate the Default Libertarian view articulated here: " . . . where there is reason to believe that the free play of self-interest will cause an amount of resources to be invested different from the amount that is required in the best interest of the national dividend, there is a *prima facie* case for public intervention. The case, however, cannot become more than a *prima facie* one, until we have considered the qualifications, which governmental agencies may be expected to possess for intervening advantageously. It is not sufficient to contrast the imperfect adjustments of unfettered private enterprise with the best adjustment that economists in their studies can imagine. For we cannot expect that any public authority will attain, or will even wholeheartedly seek, that ideal. Such authorities are liable a like to ignorance, to sectional pressure, and to personal corruption by private interest" (Pigou, 1920, II, XX, 4).

16. In other words, in avoiding "command and control," such a tax avoids "performance regulations" and "technical regulations" that require respectively specific actions and specific technology. For example, such a tax does not require that any particular individual reduce pollution, and it does not require that any individual implement any particular lower-pollution technology.

17. Note that this last claim goes beyond what progressivist Default Libertarians like Larry Summers would endorse, given that progressivists favor more substantial interference via highly redistributive policies. Compare Friedman, 2002.

18. See for example Buchanan, 1999; Mueller, 2003; Cowen, 1991; Buchanan and Tullock, 1962.

19. See for example Environmental Protection Agency; Environmental Defense Fund. For criticism of the details of this cap-and-trade system (but not of a market-based approach to environmental problems more generally), see Muller and Mendelsohn, 2013.

20. See for example National Oceanic and Atmospheric Administration, 2010.

21. See for example Gertler et al., 2006; Sadoulet et al., 2001; de Mel et al., 2008; Skoufias and De Maro, 2008.

22. The role of cost-benefit analysis (CBA) in executive branch regulation is to introduce a further hurdle that regulation must pass—not to necessitate or even encourage all regulation that would pass CBA. So, the requirement that regulation pass CBA adds a procedural presumption against regulation, and in that sense is a move in the direction of Default Libertarianism.

23. See USA Executive Order 13563.

24. In addition to these straightforward examples, one can also see general advances in other areas as related successes that bolster the case for Default Libertarianism. For example, the move toward open access to government data in machine-readable formats whenever possible, enabling entrepreneurs to create new products packaging that information for citizens in useful formats, thereby adding value and efficiency to the economy and making citizens better informed without government interference; Data.gov.; and advances in property rights engineering aimed at making the economy more efficient, all give some indication of the wide range of areas ripe for further progress, such as in patent reform and other technology sector domains where property rights may need to be simplified or reengineered to promote efficiency. As Friedrich Hayek wrote long ago, we need a legal framework that is continually adjusted as facts about society and technology change. For some important complications and objections, see Heller, 2010, and his discussion throughout of "the tragedy of the anticommons."

25. As just one example, the non-partisan Coalition for Evidence-Based Policy claims: "U.S. social programs, set up to address important problems, often fall short by funding specific models/strategies ('interventions') that are not effective. When evaluated in scientifically-rigorous studies, social interventions in K-12 education, job training, crime prevention, and other areas are frequently found ineffective or marginally effective. Interventions that produce sizable, sustained effects on important life outcomes tend to be the exception. Meanwhile, respected government measures show that the United States has made little progress over the past 40 years in key areas such as reducing poverty and increasing K-12 educational achievement" (Coalition for Evidence-Based Policy, citing DeNavas-Walt, Proctor, and Smith, 2011; U.S. Census Bureau, 2011; Short, 2005; Rampey, Dion, and Donahue, 2009).

26. See for example Smith, 2003; Kagel and Roth, 1997; Kagel and Roth, unpublished; Ostrom, 1998; Ostrom, 2010. For general arguments regarding the importance of institutions for flourishing societies, see Acemoglu and Robinson, 2012; ; compare Deaton, 2013.

27. Ostrom, 2009. See also Ostrom, 1990.

28. For examples, see references in Ostrom et al., 2007 and Scott, 1999.

29. Jane Lubchenco was the administrator of the U.S. National Oceanic and Atmospheric Administration and undersecretary of commerce in the Obama administration, and Lynn Scarlett was the chief operating officer of the U.S. Department of Interior and deputy secretary of the Interior in the George W. Bush administration. For some representative discussion, see Scarlett, 2012; National Oceanic and Atmospheric Administration, 2010.

30. Hardin, 1968. For a concise reply, see Ostrom et al., 1999; and also Ostrom, 1990.

31. Nassim Taleb (2012) calls this property "anti-fragility." See also Page, 2008 for more general discussion, including of complex systems. For criticism of Page's arguments, see Thompson 2014.

32. Taleb, 2012.

33. Scott, 1999, and references therein. See Coffey and Spears for the important ongoing example of sanitation in development economics and policy.

34. Ostrom et al., 1999: 280. See also other examples referenced there, and in Ostrom et al., 2007.

35. At least insofar as these goals are commonly shared by most progressivists, as opposed to idiosyncratic goals among political theorists. With this proviso in mind, I ignore here idiosyncratic views such as that government must perform many functions *itself* even when those functions would be much better performed by non-governmental actors and markets, which is a view defended by some political theorists. The argument for such a view in contemporary political theory is that many functions, such as criminal punishment and social welfare, are mandated "in the name of US citizens," and thus must be performed by government to be legitimate. However, there are number of independent, powerful objections these arguments. First, they arguably show a lack of serious concern for the very people that their proponents claim to care about, namely the less well-off members of society—because, by hypothesis, endorsing such an approach to policy would knowingly make those people worse off than they might well have been without the sort of government involvement at issue. More importantly from a philosophical point of view, it simply does not follow from the fact that mandates are "in our name" that the government must perform the relevant functions itself for legitimacy. For example, the government often mandates "in our name" that various records be kept about the activities of firms and individuals (i.e., tax returns, and many other forms of records). But it does not follow that

government agents must be the ones who keep those records, or even that the government itself must keep those records. A further complication for many other deployments of "in our name" reasoning is that it does not follow from the fact that the government *claims* to be acting in our name that it actually *is* acting in our name, for the same reason that it does not follow that a person who purports to be signing a contract in your name actually is acting in your name if you have not consented or explicitly given him or her permission or power to make a contract with that content in your name.

36. See Gaus, 2010: 257. The implication results from the Rawlsian idea that the fair value of political liberty requires workers to directly control decision making at their firms.

37. See for example Cohen and Sabel, 1997; Sabel and Simon, 2011. I do not mean to imply that these political theorists would agree with Default Libertarianism, merely that they incorporate (having contributed to understanding) some of the considerations outlined here.

38. See for example de Burca, Keohane, and Sabel, 2014.

References

Acemoglu, Daron and Robinson, James, 2012. *Why Nations Fail.* New York: Crown.

Baumol, William, 1972. On taxation and the control of externalities. *American Economic Review*, 62(3), pp.307–322.

Bicchieri, Cristina, 2006. *The grammar of society.* Cambridge, UK: Cambridge University Press.

Brennan, Jason, 2012. *Libertarianism: what everyone needs to know.* Oxford: Oxford University Press.

Brennan, Jason, and Jaworski, Peter, 2015. *Markets without limits.* New York: Routledge.

Buchanan, James, 1999. *Politics without Romance.* In James Buchanan, *Collected works of James Buchanan*, vol. 1. Indianapolis: Liberty Fund. pp.45–59.

Buchanan, James, and Tullock, Gordon, 1962. *The calculus of consent.* Ann Arbor: University of Michigan Press.

Coalition for Evidence-Based Policy. http://evidencebasedprograms.org

Coffey, Diane and Spears, Dean, 2017. *Where India Goes: Abandoned Toilets, Stunted Development, and the Costs of Caste.* Harper Collins.

Cohen, Joshua, and Sabel, Charles, 1997. Directly-deliberative polyarchy. *European Law Journal*, 3(4), pp.313–340.

Connelly, Matthew, 2008. *Fatal Misconception.* Cambridge MA: Harvard University Press.

Cowen, Tyler, ed., 1991. *Public goods and market failures: a critical examination.* New York: Transaction Publishers.

Dawes, Robin, 1980. Social Dilemmas. *Annual Review of Psychology*, 31, pp.169–193.

Deaton, Angus, 2013. *The Great Escape.* Princeton: Princeton University Press.

de Burca, Grainne, Keohane, Robert, and Sabel, Charles, 2014. Global experimentalist governance. *British Journal of Political Science*, 44(3), pp.477–486.

de Mel, Suresh, et al., 2008. Returns to capital in microenterprises: evidence from a field experiment. *Quarterly Journal of Economics*, 123(4), pp.1329–1372.

DeNavas-Walt, Carmen, Proctor, Bernadette D., and Smith, Jessica C., 2011. *Income, poverty, and health insurance coverage in the United States: 2010.* U.S. Census Bureau, current population reports, P60-239. Washington, DC: U.S. Government Printing Office. http://evidence-basedprograms.org

Dietz, Thomas et al. eds., 2002. *The drama of the commons.* Washington DC: National Academies Press.

Environmental Defense Fund. Acid rain pollution solved using economics. https://www.edf.
    org/approach/markets/acid-rain

Environmental Protection Agency. Clean Air Markets. https://www.epa.gov/airmarkets

Fleurbaey, Marc, 2011. Review of Debra Satz, *Why some things should not be for sale: the moral
    limits of markets,*. *OEconomica*, 1(3), pp.467–471.

Friedman, Milton, 2002. *Capitalism and freedom.* 40th anniversary ed. Chicago: University of
    Chicago Press.

Gaus, Gerald, 2010. *The order of public reason.* Cambridge: Cambridge University Press.

Gaus, Gerald, 2012. Property. In: David Estlund, ed. *Oxford handbook of political philosophy.*
    Oxford: Oxford University Press. 93–112.

Gertler, Paul, et al., 2006. *Investing cash transfers to raise long term living standards.* Policy
    Research Working Paper Series 3994. Washington DC: World Bank.

Hardin, Garrett, 1968. The tragedy of the commons. *Science*, 162, pp.1243–1248.

Heller, Michael, 2010. *Gridlock economy.* New York: Basic Books.

Kagel, John, and Roth, Alvin, 1997. *Handbook of experimental economics.* Vol. 1. Princeton,
    NJ: Princeton University Press.

Kagel, John, and Roth, Alvin, unpublished. *Handbook of experimental economics.* Vol. 2.
    Princeton, NJ: Princeton University Press.

Metcalf, Gilbert, 2001. *Market-based environmental policy instruments.* National Bureau of
    Economic Research. http://www.nber.org/reporter/summer01/metcalf.html

Mueller, Dennis, 2003. *Public choice III.* Cambridge, UK: Cambridge University Press.

Muller, Nicholas, and Mendelsohn, Robert, 2013. *Using marginal damages in environmental
    policy.* Cambridge MA: AEI Press.

Murphy, Liam, and Nagel, Thomas, 2004. *The myth of ownership.* Oxford: Oxford University Press.

National Oceanic and Atmospheric Administration, 2010. NOAA policy encourages catch
    shares to end overfishing and rebuild fisheries. November 4. http://www.noaanews.noaa.
    gov/stories2010/20101104_catchshare.html

Ostrom, Elinor, 1990. *Governing the commons.* Cambridge, UK: Cambridge University Press.

Ostrom, Elinor, 1998. A behavioral approach to the rational choice theory of collective
    action: presidential address. *American Political Science Review*, 92(1), pp.1–22.

Ostrom, Elinor et al., 1999. Revisiting the commons. *Science*, 284, pp.278–282.

Ostrom, Elinor, 2010. Beyond markets and states: polycentric governance of complex eco-
    nomic systems. *American Economic Review*, 100(3), pp.641–672.

Ostrom, Elinor, et al., 2007. Going beyond panaceas. *Proceedings of the National Academy of
    Sciences*, 104(39), pp.15176–15178.

Ostrom, Elinor, and Walker, James, 2005. *Trust and reciprocity.* New York: Russell Sage.

Page, Scott, 2008. *The Difference.* Princeton: Princeton University Press.

Parfit, Derek, 1984. *Reasons and persons.* Oxford: Oxford University Press.

Pigou, A. C., 1920. *The economics of welfare.* London: Macmillan.

Rampey, B. D., Dion, G. S., and Donahue, P. L., 2009. *NAEP 2008 trends in academic prog-
    ress. NCES 2009–479.* Washington, DC: National Center for Education Statistics, Institute of
    Education Sciences, U.S. Department of Education. http://evidencebasedprograms.org

Sabel, Charles, and Simon, William, 2011. Minimalism and experimentalism in the administra-
    tive state. *Georgetown Law Review*, 100(53), pp.53–93.

Sadoulet, Elisabeth, et al., 2001. Cash transfer programs with income multipliers: PROCAMPO
    in Mexico. *World Development*, 29(6), pp.1043–1056.

Satz, Debra, 2012. *Why some things should not be for sale: the moral limits of markets.*
    Oxford: Oxford University Press.

Scarlett, Lynn, 2012. Choices, consequences, and cooperative conservation. In Schmidtz and Willott, eds. *Environmental ethics*. 2nd ed. Oxford: Oxford University Press. pp.472–483.

Schmidtz, David, 1990. *The limits of government: an essay on the public goods argument*. Boulder: Westview.

Schmidtz, David, 2011. Review of Debra Satz, *Why some things should not be for sale: the moral limits of markets. Journal of Philosophy*, 108(4), pp.219–223.

Scott, James C. 1999. *Seeing Like a State*. Yale: Yale University Press.

Short, Kathleen, 2005. *Estimating resources for poverty measurement, 1993–2003*. U.S. Census Bureau, HHES Division. http://evidencebasedprograms.org

Singer, Peter, 2013. Good charity, bad charity. *New York Times*, August 10.

Skoufias, Emmanuel, and Di Maro, Vincenzo, 2008. Conditional cash transfers, adult work incentives, and poverty. *Journal of Development Studies*, 44(7), pp.935–960.

Smith, Adam, 1776. *The wealth of nations*. London: Strahan and Cadell.

Smith, Vernon, 2003. Constructivist and ecological rationality in economics. *American Economic Review*, 93(3), pp.465–508.

Stavins, Robert, ed., 2012. *Economics of the environment*. 6th ed. New York: Norton.

Stiglitz, Joseph, 1991. *The invisible hand and modern welfare economics*. National Bureau of Economic Research. http://www.nber.org/papers/w3641

Stiglitz, Joseph, 2001. Joseph E. Stiglitz—Biographical. http://www.nobelprize.org/nobel_prizes/economic-sciences/laureates/2001/stiglitz-bio.html

Stiglitz, Joseph, 2008. Government failure vs. market failure: principles of regulation. http://academiccommons.columbia.edu/download/fedora_content/download/ac:126998/CONTENT/JES.Govt.Failure.pdf

Stiglitz, Joseph, 2010. *Freefall: America, free markets, and the sinking of the world economy*. New York: Norton.

Sunstein, Cass, 2013. *Simpler: the future of government*. New York: Simon & Schuster.

Taleb, Nassim Nicholas, 2012. *Antifragile*. New York: Random House.

Taylor, Michael, 1987. *The possibility of cooperation*. Cambridge, UK: Cambridge University Press.

Thompson, Abigail, 2014. "Does Diversity Trump Ability?", *Notices of the American Mathematical Society*, 61, pp.1024–1030.

U.S. Census Bureau, 2011. Official and National Academy of Sciences (NAS) based poverty rates: 1999 to 2010. http://evidencebasedprograms.org

van Lange, Paul, Balliet, Daniel, Parks, Craig D., and van Vugt, Mark. 2013. *Social dilemmas: the psychology of human cooperation*. Oxford: Oxford University Press.

CHAPTER 15

....

PLANNING, FREEDOM, AND THE RULE OF LAW

....

STEVEN WALL

THE topic of this chapter is the rule of law. The rule of law is an ideal of political moral-ity that is realized to a greater or lesser extent in different legal systems. Although it is an ideal of political morality, the rule of law is not a basic or fundamental one. Its nor-mative significance is explained by its contribution to other, more fundamental, values. The chapter discusses the contribution that the rule of law can make to individual or personal freedom. To explain this contribution, a general account of political freedom is presented, one that connects freedom to our ability as agents to plan our lives. The planning account of freedom, as it is referred to here, is general, but it does not purport to be complete. Planning agency[1] of the sort to be discussed presupposes a background understanding of entitlements that is not derived from, but is sensitive to, planning con-siderations. Yet while not complete, the planning account of freedom is an important component of a full theory of political freedom, and it is the component of such a theory that best accounts for why the rule of law contributes to personal freedom.

1. THE RULE OF LAW AND ITS ELEMENTS

....

The rule of law has been and remains a prominent ideal in both liberal and republican political thought.[2] It is, however, a complex ideal. So something must be said about its nature before discussing its relationship to planning agency and political freedom.

The first thing to say is that the rule of law does not encompass all that can be good about law, such as the protection of human rights or the promotion of the common good. Accordingly, the rule of law can be achieved by, and remains valuable for, even very imperfect legal systems. As presented here, the rule of law largely concerns the form or shape of law. As such, it consists of a number of different elements. The ele-ments cohere around a simple and compelling idea. This idea—call it the core idea—is that those in positions of political and legal authority should be constrained to exercise power in ways that are efficacious, nonarbitrary, and predictable.

Not surprisingly, the philosophical and legal literature on the rule of law presents competing understandings of it. Some writers pack substantive content into the rule of law that goes beyond the core idea. Other writers claim that the rule of law is an essentially contested concept (Fallon 1997, 6).[3] This claim is surely an exaggeration. There is wide agreement on the core idea expressed by the rule of law, much more agreement than we find with other political and moral concepts, such as freedom or justice, that are commonly purported to be, whether accurately or not, essentially contested. Nevertheless, there is no denying that there is something to the exaggeration. Any account of the rule of law plays up some of its elements and downplays others. The characterization of the ideal here is guided by a concern to bring out its relevance to personal freedom.

The rule of law is sometimes identified with rule by law. Though this identification is understandable, it should be resisted. Those who are subject to a legal system are ruled by law, but some legal systems fail to realize the rule of law. This statement is not intended to take sides in an old controversy. Lon Fuller, whose work will be drawn on in articulating the content of the rule of law, famously argued that if a legal system systematically failed to realize the rule of law then it would fail to be a legal system. Like the Nazi regime, it would be a legal system in a Pickwickian sense only. Fuller's argument was based on an insightful analysis of the rule of law. To effectively guide behavior, laws must be general, widely promulgated, prospective, clear, noncontradictory, possible to follow or comply with, relatively constant, and enforced in a manner that is congruent with their content (Fuller, 1964). These elements are central to rule by law. But the rule of law is an ideal. Even if a legal system must satisfy these elements to some minimal extent in order to be a legal system this minimal satisfaction would fall short of the satisfaction required by the ideal. A legal system, we should allow, can be in very bad shape with respect to the rule of law but remain a legal system.

The jurisprudential question raised by Fuller's analysis of the rule of law, at any rate, is not the main concern here. The elements of the rule of law that he identified are instructive, whether or not they are taken to be essential to law. Fuller describes these elements as formal. They can be distinguished from the "substantive aims of the law," (Fuller 1964, 152) which concern the interests or values that the law seeks to protect or further. Moral standards external to the law can be invoked to criticize the substantive aims it serves and to argue for its reform. For example, with respect to personal freedom, we can praise or criticize a legal system by appeal to how well it serves the substantive aims associated with this value. But the point Fuller sought to highlight is that law also can be defective in how it is made and administered. It can be made and administered so that it is difficult or impossible for its subjects to follow it. Speaking generally, law aims to guide and regulate the behavior of those to whom it applies, but if it is difficult or impossible to follow, then it will fail in this aim. As this aim is internal to law itself, there is, Fuller claimed, an internal morality to law.[4]

Since we will follow Fuller in viewing the rule of law as a formal ideal, it needs to be clarified how its formal character relates to its purported morality. (Fuller's claim that there is an internal morality of law will not be fully endorsed, but, as will emerge, there is something to the claim.) Laws that are difficult to follow are defective insofar as they aim to guide the behavior of their subjects. But defects need not be moral defects. A poorly worded instruction manual is defective, but it is not thereby morally defective. In reply, it can be said that laws, unlike instruction manuals, are typically enforced. Those who disobey them are liable to punishment, and it is unjust to subject a person to punishment for breaking a law if it was impossible, or very difficult, for him to follow it. But this reply, even if correct, overlooks the important fact that not all laws are duty-imposing. Many laws are power-conferring.[5] If a law that allows one to make a binding will is hopelessly vague or inconsistent, then it will be a defective law, but it may not be criticizable on the grounds that it unjustly subjects people to sanctions.[6]

A second problem with Fuller's claim about the internal morality of law is also worth mentioning. If a law aims to guide behavior, but the law is substantively unjust, then, while it might be defective if it is hard to follow, this defect might not always be a moral defect. For it might be good (from the standpoint of morality) that the unjust law is difficult to follow. It might be a morally worse law if it were more efficacious in guiding its subjects.

These problems are not unexpected. If the rule of law is a formal ideal, then there is no guarantee that it will serve moral values. However, if we abandon the claim that the rule of law is a moral ideal internal to law, then we do not need to insist on such a guarantee. We still can say that the rule of law is a moral ideal. Consider these claims from Joseph Raz.

> The rule of law is essentially a negative value ... [T]he rule of law is a negative virtue in two senses: conformity to it does not cause good except through avoiding evil and the evil which is avoided is evil which could only have been caused by the law itself. (Raz, 1979: 224)

John Rawls expressed a similar view. Given the normal conditions of human life, law requires a coercive mechanism to ensure adequate compliance with it. But the establishment of a coercive mechanism creates the danger that it will be used to interfere, arbitrarily and unpredictably, in the lives of those subject to it. The rule of law provides protection against this danger. "Knowing what things [the coercive mechanism] penalizes and knowing that these are within their power to do or not to do, citizens can draw up their plans accordingly. One who complies with the announced rules need never fear an infringement of his liberty."[7]

There is much to be said for the view that the rule of law is essentially a negative value. The elements identified by Fuller, if realized substantially, provide important safeguards against the evils and dangers created by the law itself. These protections empower legal subjects to plan their lives so as to avoid the sanctions that the law can visit upon them.

Still, while the rule of law is a negative value, it is also more than a negative value. The establishment of law creates conditions and instruments that enable its subjects to have greater control over their lives. If we focus on duty-imposing rules, and the criminal law in particular, we may overlook this point. We may see only the dangers that law creates. But if we turn our gaze to power-conferring rules—the rules of contract and property law, for example—then we will see how law enlarges our freedom by enabling us to better plan our lives both with others and across time. Law can secure these positive goods, however, only if it is effectively constructed. If the rules of contract law are too unclear or constantly changing, then they will cease to be valuable to those who could use them. In addition, then, to protecting legal subjects from the dangers created by law, the rule of law is necessary to secure the positive goods that the law makes possible.

Following Fuller, this discussion highlights the connection between the rule of law and the effectiveness of law. When the rule of law is compromised, law becomes less efficacious at guiding its subjects. But the rule of law, as we have just seen, is a safeguard against the dangers of arbitrary power. To be sure, it does not eliminate these dangers, but it does check them. When the rule of law is breached, the law easily becomes an instrument of arbitrary power. The elements of the rule of law identified by Fuller do not fully capture its role in checking arbitrary power, however.

Fuller introduced the elements of the rule of law by inviting us to consider the story of a well-intentioned ruler named King Rex. King Rex repeatedly fails to make effective law, but he is not a tyrant. Indeed, Fuller describes King Rex as striving to make reasoned and fair-minded decisions about the law and its application. If King Rex treats his subjects poorly, he does so out of incompetence, not out of a desire to subject them to his capricious will. The lesson one might draw from Fuller's story is that if King Rex were only less inept, then all would be well in his kingdom. Given his good will, no one need fear him. But the rule of law, it will now be claimed, is not realized if it rests solely on the good will of those in power. It is realized when those in power are effectively constrained to abide by it.

Those in positions of political and legal authority could master the elements of the rule of law, but make it evident to their subjects that they will adhere to the rule of law only if the subjects please them. The subjects must not do things that they disapprove of or challenge their authority in any way. Here the rule of law arguably would not be honored, even if the rulers succeeded in making laws that were effective in guiding the behavior of those subject to them. For this reason, proponents of the rule of law frequently endorse various institutional mechanisms, such as an independent judiciary or entrenched constitutional rights, designed to constrain those in positions of authority to comply with the rule of law. To function well these institutional mechanisms must be supported by informal norms that are, in the main, accepted by legal officials. The nature and details of the needed institutional mechanisms, and the supporting norms, will vary from place to place, but the existence of some such mechanisms, it is widely thought, is necessary to the rule of law.[8]

This aspect of the rule of law requires explanation. The contemplated institutional mechanisms and supporting norms, it could be said, are merely instrumental to the securement of the ideal. They are in no way integral to it. If those in positions of political and legal authority honor Fuller's requirements, but are not constrained to honor them, then the ideal is realized, even if the realization is not secure. What then could explain the more than instrumental connection asserted here between the elements of the rule of law and the mechanisms in question? The clue to an answer can be found by returning to Fuller's claim that the rule of law expresses an internal morality of law. Fuller distinguished rule by law from various modes of social control that rely on manipulation and terror.

> To embark on the enterprise of subjecting human conduct to the governance of rules involves . . . a commitment to the view that man is, or can become, a responsible agent, capable of understanding and following rules, and answerable for his defaults. (Fuller, 1964: 162)

The rule of law expresses respect for persons as responsible agents. Even when the law is substantively unjust, it treats its subjects with respect insofar as it treats them as beings capable of planning their lives and adjusting their behavior in light of its demands. Many writers have concurred with Fuller on this key point. In contrast to other modes of social control, law is, they claim, "inherently respectful of persons as agents; it respects the dignity of voluntary action and rational self-control" (Waldron, 2008: 28).

While these claims are indeed suggestive, they are overstated. To see why they are overstated, consider an admittedly artificial example. Imagine that those in positions of authority decide that the most efficient way to get their subjects to behave as they want them to behave is to issue general rules that conform to the rule of law requirements. Imagine further that it is common knowledge among rulers and subjects alike that this mode of governance has been adopted solely because it was judged to be the most effective method of social control. Here it would be hard to sustain the claim that the authorities, in embarking on the enterprise of subjecting human conduct to the governance of rules, were expressing respect for the dignity of their subjects. So rule by law is not inherently respectful of persons as agents. But the rule of law, as has been stated, is an ideal, one that should not be identified simply with rule by law. As a moral ideal, the rule of law expresses moral demands, and these demands are justified, in part, by the value of treating persons, understood as rational agents, with the kind of respect to which Fuller called attention.

The rule of law thus confers a certain standing on legal subjects. They are to be governed in a manner that treats them as agents capable of being guided by general prospective rules announced beforehand and administered impartially. If they are not governed in this manner, they have a right to protest. Institutional mechanisms of the sort alluded to above are necessary to the exercise of this right. A legal system that did not contain measures designed to constrain those in positions of authority to comply with the rule of law, and did not contain institutional channels whereby legal subjects could challenge departures from the rule of law, would not only, in all likelihood, fail to secure its elements, but also fail to express the respect for responsible agency that is integral to the rule of law understood as an ideal of political morality.

2. Autonomy and Planning

The rule of law has value for imperfect and unjust legal systems, but it is doubtful that it has value under all conditions. A legal system that enforced slavery could realize the rule of law. Slaves could know beforehand what was expected of them, and the rules could be general, consistent, and stable and administered impartially. Institutional mechanisms could be put in place to ensure that the rules satisfied the elements of the rule of law and were applied nonarbitrarily, even on the slaves. But such a legal system would remain evil, and it would be sufficiently hostile to personal freedom that the rule of law might cease to make any meaningful contribution to personal freedom or to express any morally valuable form of respect.

Be this as it may, the moral value of the rule of law is best seen not by looking at the radically unjust state, but at the well-ordered state. Since we are here focusing on the contribution that this ideal makes to personal freedom, let us sketch a picture of the well-ordered freedom-supportive state. This picture will make some controversial assumptions about the nature of personal freedom. It will be assumed that personal freedom is intimately tied to personal autonomy in two key respects. First, the freedom that the freedom-supportive state should promote is, in the main, the freedom that enables people to live autonomous lives. Second, in determining how free people are, we must refer to the contribution that particular freedoms make to their autonomous agency.

An autonomous life is here understood to be one in which a person charts his own course through life, choosing projects and assuming commitments from a wide range of eligible alternatives, and making something out of his life according to his own understanding of what is valuable and worth doing. So understood, autonomy applies to a person's whole life or to substantial stretches of it. It is a personal achievement, not a birthright or a guarantee.

Since autonomy is a personal achievement, the well-ordered freedom-supportive state cannot ensure that its members are autonomous. But it can establish conditions that foster the achievement of the ideal. The conditions that it can effectively establish are the conditions of political freedom. Politically free people may fail to be autonomous, but, if so, their failure is not the failure of their state. Our immediate questions, then, are how to characterize this political freedom and how to understand the rule of law's contribution to it.

The freedom-supportive state establishes conditions that promote the autonomous agency of its members. Planning agency is integral to autonomy, but autonomous agency includes more than planning agency and it is important not to claim too much for planning agency. On the planning account of political freedom, the state promotes autonomous agency by promoting planning agency. But, as mentioned at the outset, the planning account is not a complete theory of political freedom, since it must presuppose a background understanding of entitlements. In a well-ordered state this background understanding will reflect a sound view of legitimate entitlement—a point to which I shall return in a moment. For now, we need to identify the key components of autonomous agency. To be autonomous a person must have internal competences, secure access to a wide range of valuable options, and live in a tractable environment. A little more specifically, an autonomous person needs to meet a threshold with respect to five general conditions: (1) mental capacities, (2) character traits, (3) options, (4) independence, and (5) environment.

Now, obviously, a good deal could be said about each of these conditions and their respective thresholds. For present purposes, a few words on each will have to suffice. The mental capacities include the capacities needed to form complex intentions, to pursue plans and goals effectively, and to endorse or identify with adopted plans and goals. The character traits include the self-awareness and vigor necessary to take control of one's affairs as well as the steadiness needed to sustain commitments to the plans and goals that one endorses. The options condition speaks to the need for persons to have access, and to be aware of the fact that they have access, to a sufficiently wide range of options from which to choose in charting their own course through life. (Specific freedoms to do this or that action add to the range of options, but no specific freedom may be necessary for the range to be adequate.) The independence condition concerns the relations between people. To be autonomous, people must be relatively free from the coercion and manipulation of others. This condition supplements the option condition, since a person can have his independence compromised even if he retains access to a sufficiently wide range of options. Finally, the environment condition refers to factors in one's environment, both physical and social, that impinge on one's ability to plan one's life. Some environments are planning friendly, while others are not.

The freedom-supportive state has a role to play in securing all the conditions of autonomous agency, but with respect to the first two conditions its role is limited. In promoting the development of the requisite mental capacities and character traits, the state promotes both planning agency and autonomy. Yet beyond assuring access to basic education, there is not too much the state can do to effectively promote these competences. The third condition—the option condition—brings us back to legitimate entitlements. To plan one's life one needs to know what resources and opportunities are available to one. The option condition requires that one have access to, and knowledge of, a sufficiently wide range of options. It now can be said that in the well-ordered freedom-supportive state these options will be legitimate options. That is, they will be options the pursuit of which do not require people to violate the legitimate claims of others. That is why the planning account of political freedom is incomplete. It must be supplemented by an account of legitimate entitlement.

The relationship between the option condition and legitimate entitlement is, however, complex. We must refer to an understanding of people's entitlements in order to specify an adequate set of options, but legitimate entitlement is, on the view being advanced here, itself sensitive to the demands of autonomy. A legitimate set of entitlements must be autonomy-supporting. This point will prove important in filling out the demands of the planning account of freedom.

The remaining two conditions—independence and environment—bear most directly on planning agency. Our efforts to plan our lives can be thwarted by the interference of others. And even if other persons do not interfere with our plans, these plans can be obstructed by unforeseen and unpredictable events, both naturally occurring and socially engendered. It is here that the rule of law assumes particular importance. Coercion and manipulation can compromise the independence necessary for autonomy, but subjection to the arbitrary power of others compounds these evils. Philip Pettit has recently called attention to a form of domination that is present when a person is subject to the arbitrary power of another, even when interference with her is neither threatened nor forthcoming (Pettit, 1997; Pettit, 2012). The mere knowledge that one is vulnerable to unchecked interference can thwart one's agency. This kind of domination can exist within civil society, as when a woman is intimidated by her domineering husband or an employee is under the thumb of his overbearing boss. But the greatest source of dominating power is the state. And the rule of law provides a vital safeguard against exposure to it. This is the negative value of the rule of law emphasized by Raz and Rawls.

Relatedly, two dimensions of interference relevant to planning agency can be distinguished. One dimension is that of restriction. Interference can restrict us from pursuing courses of action that we need to undertake to successfully complete our plans. A second dimension is that of disruption. Our plans are disrupted by the prospect, and in particular the uncertain prospect, of interference. For example, if I am unable to predict with any confidence whether my government will confiscate private economic assets in the future, then my plan to start up my own business will be disrupted. I may judge it too risky to go forward with the investment necessary for my plan to succeed. Restriction and disruption are related, since both involve interference; but we can distinguish them by reference to a threshold of expectation. If someone credibly threatens to shoot me if I leave my house, then the expectation of interference will be sufficiently high to count as a restriction on my leaving. By contrast, if no one has threatened me, but it is known that a sniper is loose in the city in which I live and that he has been firing at random passersby, my plan to leave my house may be disrupted. I may judge it too risky to leave, and this will count as a disruption, even if I have no reason to think that the sniper is anywhere near my house.

The distinction between these two dimensions of interference is relevant to our present concerns, since the effects of disruption can be worse than those of restriction with respect to planning agency. From the standpoint of a planning agent, it may be better to live in an environment that imposes greater restriction, but less disruption, than one which poses less restriction, but greater disruption. Hayek provides an example (1960: 143). Military conscription is highly restrictive, but if it is known beforehand that all persons will serve in the military for two years when they turn twenty-one, then this strong restriction may not be especially disruptive. Each person can take it into account in planning his or her life. Compare this with a situation in which only half of the eligible persons will be conscripted into the military, but it is very uncertain who will be selected and when they will be called upon to serve. Here the overall restriction is less severe, but the disruptive effects are likely greater.

The rule of law is consistent with a very restrictive legal order, but it reduces the disruptive effects of the restrictions imposed. In this way, it contributes to an environment that facilitates planning agency. In the maximally freedom-supportive state, restrictions on freedom will be limited to those necessary to secure the legitimate entitlements of all members and these restrictions will be imposed in a way that minimizes their disruptive effects. To limit disruption, the rule of law must be fully honored. Legal measures that restrict freedom must be publicly announced, clear in content, predictable, and relatively stable.

This emphasis on predictability and stability does not fully capture the value of the rule of law to planning agency, however. The rule of law checks predictable, as well as unpredictable, power. Arbitrary power involves subjecting people to the capricious will of others. The rule of law does not eliminate this kind of discriminatory power, but it does constrain it. It will constrain it effectively only if people can contest the application of law to their own case. Waldron calls attention to this "argumentative" dimension of the rule of law.

> Courts, hearings, and arguments are aspects of law which are not optional extras; they are integral parts of how law works and they are indispensable to the package of law's respect for human agency. To say that we should value aspects of governance that promote the clarity and determinacy of rules for the sake of individual freedom, but not the opportunities for argumentation that a free and self-possessed individual is likely to demand, is to truncate what the Rule of Law rests upon: respect for the freedom and dignity of each person as an active center of intelligence. (Waldron, 2008: 60)

Waldron sees a tension between this argumentative dimension of the rule of law and the predictability and stability that have been emphasized here. The more that people can effectively contest the legal rules that apply to them, the less predictable they will be. There is a tension here, but the tension is not as great as Waldron suggests. Recall that a key element of the rule of law, as articulated by Fuller, is that there should be a congruence between the law as promulgated and the law as applied. Without this congruence, the predictability and stability of promulgated law will not serve its guiding function. Courts, hearings, and arguments are integral parts of the institutional mechanisms that constrain those in positions of political and legal authority to honor the requirements of the rule of law.

However, in highlighting the argumentative dimension of the rule of law, Waldron has a deeper point to press. The law in a modern society, he claims, is much less settled and less certain than the rule of law ideal—at least as presented here—suggests. Argumentation about the meaning of law is business as usual in such a society (Waldron, 2008: 57). An account of the rule of law that is "less fixated on predictability and more insistent on the opportunities for argumentation" better fits this legal reality. (Waldron 2008: 58). Two responses can be made to Waldron's complaint. First, it can be countered that law in modern societies is not, in fact, as unsettled and indeterminate as the complaint asserts. As Matthew Kramer points out, "countless decisions by adjudicative and administrative officials are utterly uncontroversial and are therefore largely unnoticed by legal scholars who quite naturally prefer to study more exciting occurrences" (Kramer, 2007: 228). The rule of law virtues of predictability and stability are alive and well in the less exciting day-to-day workings of the legal system. Second, the degree to which the law is open to contestation depends in large measure on the degree to which it satisfies the elements of the rule of law. There are sometimes reasons for the law to be more flexible and less constant than the rule of law ideal demands. If legal officials are given wide discretion, then they may be able to make more equitable decisions, since they will be better able to take account of the particularities that each case presents. Abstract and vague rules are less predictable, but easier to adjust to different circumstances. There is, in short, a trade-off between the predictability of law and the discretion that facilitates more equitable decision-making (Posner 1993). An effect of rules that admit of greater discretion in their application is that they will be more open to the kind of dispute and contestation that Waldron celebrates. Proponents of the rule of law ideal (as here characterized) need not dispute any of this. They can allow that there are costs to increasing the predictability and stability of law, but insist that insofar as we recommend the rule of law by appeal to its contribution to personal freedom, we should be more willing than Waldron to pay these costs. The freedom-supportive state countenances a measure of inequitable treatment for the sake of securing a planning-friendly environment.[9]

So far, the discussion has been focusing on the restrictive and disruptive effects of law on planning agency. But the rule of law has positive as well as negative value, as pointed out in the previous section. Law can positively contribute to a planning-friendly environment in a number of ways, some of which have already been mentioned. First, law provides instruments that enable people to commit themselves to certain courses of action in the future, thereby extending their planning agency across time. By binding one's future self, one can more effectively pursue longer-term projects and goals and one can enable others to do so as well. This type of commitment is possible in the absence of law. People in the state of nature can make promises to one another, for example. But, for familiar reasons, the efficacy of promise-keeping as a general practice depends on legal institutions that support it. The rules of contract law in the modern state best serve planning agency when they satisfy the elements of the rule of law ideal. Second, the legitimate plans of people can be thwarted or obstructed by unforeseen events. Legal systems can provide their members with options to insure against these events or they can establish programs that directly provide the insurance. Insurance schemes do not eliminate the possibility of unforeseen bad luck that frustrates one's plans, but they mitigate its effects and, by doing so, they allow one to plan one's life more confidently, secure in the knowledge that one has brought at least some of what is unforeseen under one's control. Once again, the rule of law ideal must be honored if people are to be able to take full advantage of these legally created options. Third, the rule of law plays an important role in an economic order that enables people to coordinate their activities so as to better achieve their respective plans. The link between the rule of law and economic order was a central theme in Hayek's political and economic thought, and his insights on this issue are worth rehearsing here. As Hayek pointed out, "the various ways in which the knowledge on which people base their plans is communicated to them is the crucial problem for any theory explaining the economic process" (Hayek, 1948: 520). The problem of conveying dispersed information to planning agents is solved by the price system of the market. It could also be solved by centralized economic planning if the planners had access simultaneously to all of the relevant information and if they had perfect foreknowledge of all the changes to that information. But Hayek showed that no planner could have access to that information. And without the necessary information, central economic planning becomes an exercise in arbitrary decision-making, as the planners constantly seek to adjust their plans to the changing and unanticipated circumstances that frustrate it. By doing so, the planners, in turn, disrupt the planning activities of countless individuals who have had to rely on them.

Hayek's argument on this issue is important, but its importance for our present concerns should not be overstated. The market order is part of a planning-friendly environment insofar as it enables people to coordinate their activities efficiently and to convey information to one another that is crucial to their economic pursuits. It is also true that the rule of law ideal, as Hayek stressed, excludes a range of governmental interventions into the market order. But it does not exclude all such governmental intervention. At times Hayek wrote as if he thought that any governmental effort to promote a specific end must rest on an arbitrary judgment that it is more worthwhile than other ends. But such a judgment need not be arbitrary in the sense proscribed by the rule of law ideal. Indeed, political judgments about the relative value of specific ends can be well considered and sound. Moreover, there is a dimension of the market order that disrupts, rather than contributes to, a planning-friendly environment. The "creative destruction" of the market order is necessary to its efficiency, but it also unsettles the plans and expectations of all those who are its victims. Both of these caveats to Hayek's argument raise more general questions about the planning account of political freedom that it is now time to confront.

3. CHALLENGES AND REFINEMENTS

Thus far, the discussion has characterized the rule of law and put forward an account of political freedom that explains the rule of law's contribution to freedom. The account of political freedom, the planning account, is not a complete theory and only a sketch of it has been offered. The planning account as presented here is perhaps better viewed as a sketch of a component of political freedom. Yet even understood this modestly, it invites objections.

A first objection targets the gap between autonomy and planning agency. The former includes the latter, but extends beyond it. Autonomous agents have capacities to act spontaneously that are not well expressed in the idiom of planning agency. The planning account of freedom appears to ignore this dimension of our agency, focusing instead on its more structured and less flexible aspects. This leads to a distorted picture of freedom.

There are a couple of things to say in reply. We can point out, first, that spontaneity, while it can be an aspect of autonomous agency, cannot be the whole of it. Someone who adopts no commitments and pursues no goals would not be autonomous. His life would not be a directed life, but rather a life pulled one way or another by whatever impulse or inclination gripped him at the moment. Different plans and commitments allow for variety and unpremeditated action to different degrees. Nothing said here implies that an autonomous life could not be one that aimed to leave wide space for the kind of spontaneity in action we are now considering. At the limit, we can imagine a person who, somewhat paradoxically, adopts the plan of maximizing the opportunities for spontaneous action in his life.

This brings us to the second response. Those whose plans and commitments are relatively unstructured, allowing great scope for change and variety, will be served, not frustrated, by living in a planning-friendly environment. Subjection to unpredictable and arbitrary interference will not further their efforts to live lives that manifest spontaneity and change. Like those who adopt more regimented ways of life, they too have a freedom-based interest in being able to avoid legal penalties and punishments. The rule of law serves them, in this respect, as much as it serves anyone.

Thus while planning agency is not the whole of autonomous agency, it remains true that by securing a planning-friendly environment the state promotes autonomy quite generally. The planning account of political freedom, moreover, is not committed to any general view about the relative value of structure and spontaneity in the plans and commitments of autonomous agents.

The planning account of political freedom does assume, however, that it is in general good for people to be able to carry out the plans they have adopted. It assumes this insofar as it views planning agency as a good to be promoted. And this assumption can be challenged. If the plans of people were not good, would it really be good for them to carry them out?

Two possibilities need to be distinguished. First, as explained, people form plans against a background understanding of their entitlements. In a well-ordered state the background entitlements are just. Let us call a legitimate plan a plan that does not require the infringement of other people's rightful entitlements for its successful execution. The planning account of political freedom can hold that it is good for people to be successful in carrying out the legitimate plans they have adopted. But if their plans are not legitimate, if their execution involves the violation of other people's rightful claims, then it is not good for people to carry them out.

The issue is more complicated, however, than this quick response suggests. Actual legal systems are imperfect. To varying degrees, the entitlements they recognize and protect depart from those that would be secured in a well-ordered state. Yet the rule of law is surely valuable not only for ideal legal systems, but also for actual imperfect ones. In response, we can say this. Generally, the rule of law is valuable for legal systems that are worth sustaining and improving, as opposed to those that ought to be abolished. The entitlements these legal systems recognize and protect, while not fully just, can inform plans that are worthy of promotion.

Still, legitimate plans can be valueless. This brings us to the second possibility. Suppose that a person, who lives under a well-ordered legal system, forms the plan to visit every convenience store in the society in which he lives. This plan is legitimate, but there is nothing to be said for it. Should we say, then, that only worthwhile plans merit promotion? Perhaps, but perhaps not. People may have a freedom-based claim to pursue worthless plans so long as those plans do not lead them to violate the rightful claims of others. This issue is left open by the planning account of political freedom. On this account, if the state obstructs worthless, but legitimate, plans, then it sets back freedom. That is why I claimed earlier that in the maximally freedom-supportive state, restrictions on freedom will be limited to those necessary to secure the legitimate entitlements of all members and these restrictions will be imposed in a way that minimizes their disruptive effects. Note that this claim is fully consistent with the claim that the maximally freedom-supportive state is not the best state, all things considered. Possibly, the state should promote worthwhile plans, not plans as such. Just as one should not claim too much for the rule of law, one should not claim too much for the freedom it serves.

A final objection raises deeper issues than the two objections just discussed. It invites us to consider one of the most difficult problems in the theory of freedom. Is the freedom of a person solely a function of her objective circumstances—the number of options effectively open to her—or is it also a function of her subjective purposes or states of mind? There are compelling considerations that speak in favor of contrasting answers to this question (compare Steiner [1983] and Carter [1999] with Arneson [1985] and Kramer [2003]).

In presenting the planning account of political freedom, it has been claimed that the subjective plans of agents are relevant not only to their autonomy, but also to the determination of their freedom. If their plans are frustrated, either by obstruction or by disruption, then their freedom is curtailed. If an option is relevant to a person's planning agency, then it assumes a significance *for his freedom* that it would not otherwise have. By contrast, if some option has no bearing at all on his plans—or plans he would take up in the future—then its removal from his option set, while it may diminish his freedom to some extent, does not diminish it to the same extent it would if it were an option relevant to his planning agency.

The planning account thus (partially) endorses the position expressed by Berlin in his classic essay on liberty. The extent of a person's freedom depends on "how important in [his] plan of life, given [his] character and circumstances, [the options open to him] are when compared with each other" (Berlin, 1969: 130). On its face, Berlin's claim is plausible. If my plan of life centers on musical accomplishment, and if I have no aptitude or inclination to participate in rock climbing, then, very plausibly, the obstruction of music-related options for me will set back my freedom to a greater degree than a corresponding obstruction of rock-climbing options. But while this claim is plausible, it is vulnerable to a powerful objection that Berlin himself pressed. This objection calls attention to the awkward consequence that, if my freedom depends on my subjective plans and desires, then I can become freer by adapting my plans and desires to the constraints I confront. At the limit, the prisoner can become free by ceasing to care about the limits imposed by the prison walls that enclose him.

The planning account of political freedom is not vulnerable to the extreme version of this objection. Prisoners, not matter how well adapted to their predicament, cannot be free, since freedom requires that one have access to a range of significant options. But the account remains vulnerable to a less extreme form of the objection. On it, a person's freedom can increase or decrease as his plans change, even as the range of options open to him remains constant. Thus he can make himself freer by adjusting his plans to his circumstances. Of course, people generally adopt and pursue plans because they think that they are valuable or worthwhile, and these judgments of value typically do not change when circumstances make the plans more difficult or impossible to pursue. Moreover, people are often invested in their plans, especially their more comprehensive plans, and it is not easy for them to abandon them and take up new ones. Indeed, these facts about people's plans and their planning agency help to explain why the rule of law is as important to freedom as it is. But even so, it remains true that, on the planning account, if one's plans were obstructed one could, in principle, take up other plans with the consequence that one's overall freedom was not diminished.

Call this consequence the *Adjustment Claim*. It can be accepted while rejecting the claim that adjustment to a constraint can eliminate the constraint. Call this latter claim the *Elimination Claim*. The planning account need not deny that constraints on what we can do remain constraints as our subjective purposes with respect to them change. When the musically inclined person loses the option to participate in rock-climbing events, her freedom is diminished. The account claims merely that the contribution an option makes to a person's freedom is affected by the significance it has for her, given her plans.

The Adjustment Claim is not as problematic as the Elimination Claim, and so distinguishing it from that claim is important. But it is still controversial and some will find it unacceptable. They will think that the planning account objectionably runs together freedom and its value to the agent. The subjective plans of the agent are relevant to assessing the value of his freedom, but not its magnitude. Those who hold this view— call it the *fully objective view*—will deny that there is an intimate connection between freedom and autonomy, insisting instead that planning considerations help us to determine the value of particular freedoms for particular agents.

The fully objective view avoids commitment to the Adjustment Claim. But a related worry remains in place. Valuable freedom—that is, the freedom that serves those that enjoy it—will be subject to adjustment, and it is valuable freedom that the freedom-supportive state promotes.

The distinction between freedom and its value is not as sharp as the fully objective view claims, however. Assessments of freedom need to take into account not only the number, but also the quality, of the options open to people. To see this, contrast two political orders. In the first one, the state ensures that all its members have a wide range of options that are securely protected, but in deciding which options to secure and protect, it takes no account at all of the subjective plans of its members. In the second political order, the state secures and protects an equally wide range of options, but it does so in a way that is responsive to the plans of its members.

The two political orders, a proponent of the fully objective view could insist, do equally well in supporting freedom, even though the value of this freedom to individual people differs dramatically between the two orders. In the first political order, people are free, but they lack the satisfaction that the people in the second order enjoy. The second political order is better than the first, but not because it does better in promoting the freedom of its members (see Pettit, 2012: 34–35).

Yet, on reflection, these claims about the two political orders seem less plausible than the Adjustment Claim. The frustration that people would experience in the first political order is not unrelated to their freedom. Despite having many options, they would be unable to lead their lives as they see fit. If this is right, then freedom and autonomy, while distinct, are nonetheless intimately related to each other.[10] It follows that people can increase their freedom by adapting their plans to their circumstances. But talk of adjustment must be taken with a pinch of salt, for, as mentioned, people typically are committed to their plans. The obstruction or disruption of these plans sets back their freedom, and adjustment is usually experienced as a loss of freedom. Even when people succeed in taking up new plans, they will often rightly view the obstruction of their past plans as a significant setback to their freedom.

This point brings us back to the ambivalence about markets expressed above. As Hayek showed, markets enable large numbers of people to coordinate their actions and efficiently pursue their different plans all without central direction. But markets also unsettle established plans and disrupt valued ways of life. For those who accept the planning account of political freedom, both the positive and negative dimensions of the market order must be given their due.

Markets aside, the primary purpose of this chapter has been to discuss the contribution that the rule of law makes to personal freedom. To do so, a particular characterization of the rule of law has been presented, one that emphasizes its value in constraining the exercise of unpredictable and arbitrary power. The rule of law, so characterized, has been embedded in a more general account of political freedom, one that construes freedom in terms of planning agency. A full elaboration, and defense, of this account of political freedom has not been undertaken. This concluding section has sought merely to clarify its implications and to respond to some of the worries it provokes.[11]

NOTES

1. The phrase "planning agency" is adopted from M. Bratman, who, over the years, has developed a rich theory of it. For a recent summary of his views see Bratman, 2014: 15–25.
2. The rule of law is championed by a wide range of liberal writers including Locke, Mill, Hayek, and Rawls. For its role in republican political thought see Pettit, 1997: 174–176.

3. Marmor (2010, 666) claims, in contrast, that "a remarkable consensus prevails in the literature about what the rule of law actually requires."

4. The aim is not internal to every law. For example, the aim of an ex post facto law is not to guide behavior, but to do something else. On this point see Lyons, 1993: 7.

5. The distinction between duty-imposing and power-conferring rules is a major theme in H. L. A. Hart's legal theory. See Hart (1961).

6. A poorly constructed power-conferring rule exposes its subjects to a nullity, but a nullity is not perspicuously viewed as a sanction. For discussion of the difference between a sanction and a nullity, and the unsuccessful efforts to explain the former in terms of the latter, see Hart, 1961: 33–44. Note that an unpromulgated power-conferring rule would expose no one to unjust punishment.

7. Rawls, 1971: 241. These claims should be read to mean that, if the laws are announced beforehand and if it is in one's power to comply with them, then one need never fear an infringement of one's liberty from the penal authorities. The laws themselves may, of course, restrict liberty.

8. Much disagreement over the rule of law centers on disputes over which institutional mechanisms and associated norms best secure it. These disputes are not disputes over the core idea of the ideal, but rather over the best way to establish it in this or that context.

9. The discretion that enables the legal official to adjust the law intelligently to the particular case also allows him to exercise power arbitrarily.

10. Following Kramer, we can say that autonomy is an ideal that is "distinctively connected with freedom" (Kramer, 2003: 433). Autonomy and freedom remain distinct notions. Freedom can be increased in ways that do not increase autonomy, and vice versa.

11. Work on this chapter was supported by a grant from the John Templeton Foundation. The opinions expressed are those of the author and do not necessarily reflect the views of the John Templeton Foundation.

References

Arneson, R., 1985. Freedom and desire. *Canadian Journal of Philosophy*, 15/3, pp.425–448.

Berlin, I., 1969. Two concepts of liberty. In: *Four essays on liberty*. Oxford: Oxford University Press. pp.118–172.

Bratman, M., 2014. *Shared agency*. Oxford: Oxford University Press.

Carter, I., 1999. *A measure of freedom*. Oxford: Oxford University Press.

Fallon, R., 1997. The Rule of Law as a Concept in Constitutional Discourse. *Columbia Law Review*, 97/1, pp.1–56.

Fuller, L., 1964. *The morality of law*. New Haven: Yale University Press.

Hart, H. L. A., 1961. *The concept of law*. Oxford: Oxford University Press.

Hayek, F. A., 1948. The use of knowledge in society. In: *Individualism and economic order*. Chicago: University of Chicago Press. pp. 77–91.

Hayek, F. A., 1960. *The constitution of liberty*. Chicago: University of Chicago Press.

Kramer, M., 2003. *The quality of freedom*. Oxford: Oxford University Press.

Kramer, M., 2007. *Objectivity and the rule of law*. Cambridge: Cambridge University Press.

Lyons, D., 1993. *Moral aspects of legal theory*. Cambridge: Cambridge University Press.

Marmor, A., 2010. The ideal of the rule of law. In: D. Patterson, ed. *A companion to philosophy of law and legal theory*. Oxford: Blackwell. pp.666–674.

Pettit, P., 1997. *Republicanism*. Oxford: Oxford University Press.

Pettit, P., 2012. *On the people's terms*. Oxford: Oxford University Press.

Posner, R., 1993. Law as logic, rules and science. In: *The problems of jurisprudence*. Cambridge, MA: Harvard University Press. pp.37–70.

Rawls, J., 1971. *A theory of justice*. Cambridge, MA: Harvard University Press.

Raz, J., 1979. The rule of law and its virtue. In: *The authority of law*. Oxford: Oxford University Press. pp.210–232.

Steiner, H., 1983. How free: computing personal liberty. In: A. Phillips-Griffths, ed. *Of liberty*. Cambridge: Cambridge University Press. pp.73–89.

Waldron, J., 2008. The concept and the rule of law. *Georgia Law Review*, 43(1), pp.1–61.

CHAPTER 16

....

FREEDOM, REGULATION, AND PUBLIC POLICY

....

MARK PENNINGTON

1. INTRODUCTION

THE relationship between freedom, regulation, and public policy is a complex and contested one. Different political traditions emphasize alternative conceptions of freedom, and whether regulation enhances freedom is a matter of considerable dispute. These disagreements often reflect different assumptions about the character of social order and the attributes of those working within regulatory institutions. The aim of this chapter is to analyze these disagreements. The first section focuses on two conceptions of freedom and sketches a framework for evaluating the likely relationship between different regulatory regimes and their propensity to promote these freedoms. The subsequent sections analyze in greater depth the terms of debate between those envisaging a greater or lesser role for regulation and public regulation in particular, to secure negative freedom and positive freedom respectively.

2. FREEDOM, REGULATION, AND PUBLIC POLICY

....

2.1. Conceptions of freedom

In their book *A Brief History of Liberty*, David Schmidtz and Jason Brennan modify the Hobbesian account of freedom as the absence of external impediments to define *negative liberty* as the "absence of obstacles wrongfully imposed by other people" (Schmidtz and Brennan, 2010: 9). On this conception, the protection of person and physical property is the bedrock of a free society because the capacity to pursue personal projects depends on a private sphere where people can take decisions without the consent of others and where there are protections against violence, theft, and fraud. These "non-interference" rights are thought capable of securing support from agents who otherwise disagree about the ends to pursue in life and/or the means to achieve such ends. Rights of this kind offer the security to produce, to enter contracts, and to freely associate or disassociate with others. The rules and property rights that define the private sphere can be seen as regulations which *restrict* or *interfere* with absolute individual freedoms. From the perspective of securing negative liberty such restrictions may be justified because they may expand the ability for people to pursue their objectives in comparison to a scenario where no rules are enforced and where agents do not know who has the right to take decisions in a particular domain (Schmidtz, 2001).

In contrast to the negative conception, *positive liberty* is a more expansive notion. On the one hand, it can refer to the capacity of agents to achieve their objectives rather than the mere absence of interference in the private realm. This conception is frequently associated with "modern" or "high" liberal theories which suggest that an emphasis on freedom from interference is of limited value when some agents have little scope to pursue their particular ends. The possession of wealth and the availability of attractive and achievable options may be required if a more complete freedom is to be achieved (for example Sen, 1992; Van Parjis, 1995). For many who emphasize the importance of positive liberty, however, having wealth and the ability to "get what one wants" do not define the contours of freedom. On the contrary, people may be slaves to their own desires and the achievement of "true" freedom may also require that one learn how to control these desires, achieving a capacity for self-governance (Sen, 2002).

Whether one defines positive liberty in terms of wealth or self-governance, this conception of freedom may open the way to a potentially more expansive role for social rules and regulations than its negative counterpart. On some accounts, for example, protecting positive liberty requires regulations that introduce minimum standards on pay and conditions into employment contracts rather than simply leaving people not to be interfered with in their bargaining with potential employers (Green, 1986). Likewise, for the proponents of "libertarian paternalism," achieving freedom may require rules which shape the "choice architecture" that faces people in order that they may overcome their own "weakness of will" (Sen, 2002; Sunstein and Thaler, 2003).

2.2. The relationship between freedom, regulation, and public policy

The conceptions of liberty sketched above recognize a potential role for regulation as a necessary requirement of freedom. Regulation itself may be defined as the promulgation of an authoritative set of rules, accompanied by some mechanism for monitoring and enforcing compliance with these rules (Baldwin, Scott, and Hood, 1998: 3). For many economists and public policy analysts the primary source of regulation is the administrative apparatus of the modern state. Indeed, it would be fair to say that the provision of such regulation has been widely seen as offering a basic rationale for the state. It is important to recognize, however, that the state and its attendant processes of policy making and enforcement are by no means the only source of regulation. As scholars of institutional economics and of the sociolegal tradition have emphasized, regulation can also arise through the rule-making and enforcement activities of private individuals, corporate bodies, and voluntary associations (ibid.). It is therefore now common to differentiate between "top-down" or exogenous forms of regulation and "bottom-up" or endogenous variants. The former refers to a process where rules are defined and enforced by an external, political agency which uses formal legal sanctions that rely upon the state's monopoly of coercive power. In the case of endogenous regulation, by contrast, those directly involved in particular social situations devise the rules that constrain their behavior and adherence to them is secured through multilateral boycott. In other cases, regulatory mechanisms may involve a mix of "top-down" and "bottom-up" elements (Ostrom, 2006).

Many analyses of freedom assume a tension between the different conceptions of liberty outlined earlier and the character of the regulatory regimes they may require. Those defining liberty in "positive" terms have typically envisaged a potentially expansive role for public regulations which "interfere" with the negative freedom of private transactors in order to "guarantee" the positive liberties of those lacking in resources or opportunities. There may not, however, be any *necessary* tension between freedom as non-interference and positive freedom. Whether public intervention is required to enhance positive freedom depends largely on claims about the likely effect of such regulation on the opportunities available to the disadvantaged. If public regulation lessens such opportunities, then a regime emphasizing non-interference rights may be better placed to advance positive freedoms, as well as negative ones. Similarly, to emphasize freedom from interference need not be construed as a position opposed to "regulation" per se but may reflect a belief that the most effective regulations that secure both negative and positive freedom are those arising from a process where private agents and voluntary associations craft the relevant rules rather than have these imposed by an external agency—or where external agencies limit themselves to securing a framework within which people have the greatest scope to craft their own regulatory arrangements.

In view of this analysis many disputes about the freedom-enhancing capacities of regulatory regimes ought to be addressed within a framework that combines social scientific theory and evidence to understand the likely effects of alternative structures. This framework needs to focus on how different institutional configurations cope with human weaknesses of various kinds. To assume away these weaknesses when evaluating the freedom-enhancing potential of institutions is of questionable merit because if people are perfect, or at least perfectible, then beneficial consequences would be expected, irrespective of the arrangements in place. It is, for example, hard to understand the rationale for public regulation in a fully "ideal" society. In such a society people committed to ensuring the negative freedom of others would not require any kind of coercive state apparatus to protect each others' rights. Disputes over the extent of particular private domains could be resolved without the possibility of violence. Similarly, any desired principle of resource distribution thought to maximize positive freedom might be guaranteed by voluntary action. The framework pursued in this chapter is therefore skeptical of the value of overly idealized theories. The desirability of institutional arrangements must depend to a significant degree on feasibility issues that reflect their ability to overcome, or at least to minimize, *compliance problems* as these arise in "real world" situations.

The importance of compliance problems can be brought out by examining their significance in relation to an alternative that might understand freedoms in terms of the presence/absence of the *legal entitlements* present under different regimes. On this view, a person who lives under a benevolent slave master who does not *in practice* interfere with their negative liberties might be "unfree" even if their negative freedoms are not interfered with at a particular point in time owing to the absence of a legal entitlement to non-interference. Likewise, people may do extremely well in securing the necessary means to pursue their ends while living under institutional arrangements that do not provide legal guarantees to any resources whatsoever. From a legalistic perspective, persons living under such arrangements might not be considered to have genuine positive liberties. On the view advanced here, however, legal entitlements, while not insignificant, may be of limited value unless they are backed up by credible institutional mechanisms. Entitlements to negative freedoms or to material resources may be ineffective where those charged with securing such liberties may lack the knowledge or the incentives to actually uphold the entitlements in question.

The compliance problems that may advance or constrain freedoms in the above regard are threefold. The first of these are epistemic. People are limited in their cognitive capacities, so even the most intelligent and educated individuals will tend to be relatively ignorant of the society of which they are a part. When the limits of human rationality are tightly drawn, then institutions must minimize the consequences that will follow from human errors and must enable decision-makers to improve the quality of their decisions over time (Hayek, 1948a; Simon, 1957; Gigenrezer and Selten, 2002). For a regime of regulation to advance human freedom, those charged with devising and enforcing the relevant rules must be capable of learning which of their actions is in fact conducive to achieving the freedom/s at stake.

A second set of compliance problems are motivational. People may be unwilling to act in accordance with a particular entitlement if doing so requires massive personal sacrifice. Incentives matter, so if a regulatory regime is to advance freedom it must not require that people be "saints." John Rawls recognizes this when noting that even under "ideal conditions" people should not be expected to devote themselves to causes where their personal actions can have no significant impact on outcomes (Rawls, 1971: 236–237). People may, for example, be fully committed to observing principles of negative and positive freedom but their personal responses to everyday incentives at the micro-level may produce unintended consequences which reduce the relevant freedoms. Even in a relatively ideal world of "full motivational compliance," public goods or collective action problems may lead to coordination failures,[1] so institutions need to be arranged to deal with these effects. Different regulatory regimes should be compared in terms of their propensity to generate collective action problems.

The third set of compliance problems reflect the scope that different regulatory arrangements afford for those not committed to upholding the freedoms of others to be held to account for transgressions. An evaluation of different regimes must consider the potential they provide to identify and to discipline those who breach the relevant rules.

The analysis that follows focuses on the role that these compliance problems play in the arguments of those who envisage a greater or a lesser role for public policy procedures in regulating the actions of citizens and how these arguments relate to both negative and positive conceptions of freedom.

3. NEGATIVE FREEDOM, REGULATION, AND PUBLIC POLICY

3.1. Public regulation and the protection of the private sphere

Though negative liberty is the more minimal of the conceptions considered here, it demands nonetheless a fundamental role for regulation in protecting the private sphere. That regulation is required to protect negative freedom has been taken by some commentators to demonstrate a *necessary* connection between public/state regulation and private freedoms, such as those exercised in commercial markets (Murphy and Nagel, 2004; Holmes and Sunstein, 2013). According to this view, *all* market transactions occur in the "shadow of the state" because it is the state that is the primary instrument for defining and enforcing property rights. This "legal centralist" thesis is adhered to by many who are skeptical of classical liberal and libertarian theories that see the state as potentially antagonistic to negative freedoms. For the followers of Karl Polanyi in particular the idea of laissez-faire or a purely "free market" system is illusory, because it is typically the state that "creates markets" (Polanyi, 1944). Though they reject the strong form of Polanyi's thesis, which maintains that the very propensity for people to value negative freedoms is an artifice of deliberate government intervention, many classical liberals and libertarians hold nonetheless that the state is necessary to overcome compliance problems by upholding the background rule of law that secures a private domain and allows people to enter into voluntary transactions with other rights holders (Buchanan and Tullock, 1962; Buchanan, 1975; Hayek, 1960; Epstein, 2003).

It is important to recognize, however, that "legal centralism" has not gone without challenge. A minority of scholars maintain that rules protecting negative freedoms can be, and historically often were, secured through "legal polycentrism," *without* recourse to formal state structures. The emergence of a secure private sphere, respect for property, and the rule of law arose historically in contexts where, far from protecting the private domain of their citizens, states frequently engaged in predatory behavior (Benson, 1989). As a consequence, medieval merchant communities developed their own system of contract law, private courts, and arbitration systems—the *lex mercatoria*—to secure property and to facilitate transactions that transcended political boundaries. More recently, Leeson's work (Leeson, 2008) demonstrates how the modern equivalent of the *lex mercatoria* has facilitated a huge expansion in international trade in spite of there being no formal global state structures to enforce contracts. There are currently over one hundred private international arbitration organizations worldwide, and more than 90 percent of international contracts contain arbitration clauses. Agreeing to be bound by the terms of private arbitration sends out a signal that the party is unlikely to renege on a deal—with those who refuse to demonstrate such commitment unlikely to find partners to trade. Arbitration agencies meanwhile compete to provide fair and transparent processes of dispute resolution in order to secure more clients. Advocates of legal polycentrism such as Leeson do not rule out the possibility that involvement of public regulatory bodies might facilitate still more private interaction by offering even greater security of property, but they reject the suggestion that property rights and markets are *always* creations of the state.

A weaker form of the polycentric thesis also recognizes the role that states can play in protecting negative freedoms but contends that, given the centrality of compliance problems, states are only likely to deliver these basic regulatory functions under certain institutional conditions. A significant literature suggests that the emergence of a protected private domain which facilitated modern markets occurred in a context of institutional competition (Rosenberg and Birdsell, 1986; North, 1990; Pipes, 1999). The "political anarchy" between competing states that reigned prior to the Industrial Revolution across Western Europe acted as a laboratory for institutional experimentation, enabling—often by accident rather than by design—new institutions offering greater protection to private rights to emerge and to spread by imitation. It was the absence of such competition that may have prevented the emergence of a more secure private sphere under the highly centralized political structures that characterized Russia and China over the equivalent period. For advocates of legal polycentrism, political decentralization helps to overcome the epistemic limitations of more centralized structures, and competition provides an important check against the possibility of public regulatory bodies turning toward predatory actions. When citizens can "exit" to alternative jurisdictions that better protect them from interference, then public officials may have stronger incentives to comply with negative liberties, limiting both their own predatory impulses and those of private predators as well.

It should now be apparent that while public regulation can play an important role in protecting the private sphere, whether states do in fact perform this role may be a contingent matter. The negative freedoms protected by the advanced liberal democracies may have their origins in historical accidents that enabled states to perform tolerably well in protecting basic liberties. It is, however, questionable what the public policy lessons are for those parts of the world lacking such basic institutional protections. It does not follow that, because states have protected negative freedoms in the advanced democracies, the creation or maintenance of such structures can be replicated in other parts of the world where compliance problems may be overwhelming. As James Scott (2009) has argued, in many developing nations, far from protecting basic liberties, state institutions are often vehicles for purely predatory purposes, and for citizens living under such regimes, "escaping from government" might be preferable to living under a state that uses its regulatory powers to engage in organized predation.

3.2. Negative externalities and public regulation

In addition to protections against violence, theft, or fraud, another justification for public regulation is the existence of negative externalities. For many commentators influenced by A. C. Pigou (1920) and modern welfare economics it is not simply direct "interventions" such as violence that constitute a threat to the private sphere, but also cases where private transactions have unintended effects on other agents—as when pollution generated by industry damages the person or property of those living in the vicinity of a production facility. The existence of such unaccounted externalities in a regime which otherwise respects the non-interference principle is thought to provide a strong prima facie case for government intervention in the form of taxes to discourage environmental pollution or direct regulation of the activity concerned. For followers of Pigou, government intervention is required to overcome the failure of private agents to comply effectively with respect for the private sphere of others (Meade, 1952; Bator, 1958).[2]

For followers of Ronald Coase, however, the case for public regulation is much less clear cut. Many discussions of pollution proceed from the assumption that all environmental damages are inherently "bad" and depict a struggle between "perpetrator" and "victim." The Coasian approach, by contrast, suggests that externalities are "reciprocal" in character (Coase, 1960). Those wishing to pollute or damage the environment may not do so for the sake of "imposing costs" on their "victims" but because their activities may be necessary to generate benefits that people in general also value. For Coase, externality problems typically arise when there are diverse and often competing demands for the use of environmental assets and when there is a need to balance these conflicting interests. Whether someone is a "victim," therefore, is really a question of who possesses the relevant "non-interference" rights and whether they wish to trade such rights for compensation. If the right to non-interference resides with those wishing to be pollution-free, then the relevant owners can seek an injunction against non-consensual acts of pollution, or opt to receive direct compensation from the polluter in exchange for allowing the activity to occur. On the other hand, if the right to non-interference resides with the producer/polluter, then those wishing to clean up the pollution must offer to buy the relevant rights. *So long as transaction costs are zero* and the state enforces property rights, then externalities will be eliminated—or if they arise they can be tackled via tort law. According to this account, the primary role of public policy is to specify who has the relevant non-interference rights; resort to more direct forms of public regulation is, however, wholly unnecessary. Though it was not the view expressed by Coase himself, there is no necessary requirement here for property rights to be assigned via a "top-down" process of specification by the state. Rather, as emphasized by the tradition of legal polycentrism, property rights might also arise through a decentralized process where private dispute resolution assigns and enforces the relevant rights (Ellickson, 1991; Anderson and Hill, 2004).

Seen through a Coasian lens, the existence of any unaccounted costs and benefits in "real world" conditions reflects the fact that transactions costs are *not in fact zero* and that the property rights regime is "incomplete." When property rights are assigned in a context of *positive* transaction costs there is no inherent tendency for externalities to be eliminated. Some transaction costs would exist even in a highly idealized context of full motivational compliance—such as, for example, the costs involved in defining boundaries and communicating with potential trading partners. Other transaction costs, however, reflect compliance problems associated with problems of "non-excludability" that may give rise to "free-riding" behavior (Anderson and Libecap, 2014). In contexts where, for example, pollution is generated by large numbers of highly dispersed decisions which taken on their own are insignificant but in the aggregate can lead to large negative effects, no single polluter may have any incentive to desist from a transgression (ibid.).

Recognizing such problems in enforcing private property rights has led Pigovian-influenced commentators to suggest that the most effective way of addressing externalities is to have a more direct role for public policy measures in controlling the activities of private agents. For followers of Coase, however, this conclusion does not *necessarily* follow because the same frictions that prevent the enforcement of property rights also exist under *any* institutional alternative involving direct government regulation. A comparative institutions approach is required to consider the likely extent of compliance problems under different types of "solution."

While the Coasian approach offers no panacea solutions, its policy preferences are weighted nonetheless toward a greater reliance on private property rights and contractual bargaining. There are two arguments here suggesting that direct government regulation may generate greater compliance problems than when private decision-makers are left to bargain toward their own solutions and where public policy actions are confined to enforcing those bargains.

The first of these arguments is an epistemic claim that, given the cognitive limitations of decision makers, attempts to impose regulatory solutions from the center are unlikely to match the dispersed knowledge of the tradeoffs that would be made by those affected by the externalities in question. Decision makers on the ground, though imperfectly informed, may be more knowledgeable about which forms of regulation may eliminate or reduce external effects at a tolerable cost. In addition, a process of contractual bargaining between property owners may generate more knowledge about the costs and benefits associated with different levels of "regulation." Most environmental goods are not completely indivisible, so their supply can vary across different territorial zones, and this enables them to be packaged as "club goods"—such as, for example, those found in proprietary residential communities (see, for example, Foldvary, 1994). In the latter, individuals and organizations contract into a meta-level organization that regulates the freedoms of those entering the community concerned by specifying controls on the use of land. The advantage of such contractual, decentralized solutions is that they may enable people to discover the costs and benefits associated with different levels of regulation and to retain the freedom to move to those jurisdictions reflecting their own trade-offs over which activities should be subject to "interference" in the private realm. Because they are subject to competition from rival clubs and organizations, the market process is likely to push the suppliers of such contractual regulation closer toward people's preferences for environmental protection (ibid.).

The second argument for property rights is one from incentives. It suggests that while non-excludability problems may make it difficult for rights holders to enforce property claims, addressing externalities via direct public regulation may generate still greater non-excludability issues. In a regime emphasizing contractual bargaining, private actors have scope to "contract around" the external effects of other people's behavior by using the "exit" option and "voting with their feet" to enter those arrangements that minimize undesired interferences. In the case of contractual land use regulation such as that supplied by private residential communities, people may, for example, make relatively easy comparisons in terms of housing costs, amenities, and regulatory provisions across communities when deciding where to reside. They may also have strong incentives to become well informed about their purchasing or locational decisions because these will directly affect the quality of the regulatory environment under which they live.

By contrast, the scope and incentives to avoid publicly generated externalities may be more limited—and especially so when regulation is determined by central government agencies. When individual voters cannot, save by leaving the country, exit from principal–agent relationships with public regulators, they may be forced into a series of collective action problems that may subject them to externalities generated by the political activities of others.[3] Voters in general have few incentives to be well informed about the effects of many public regulations, because in a large-number electorate the chance that their decision to become better informed will affect who wins an election is infinitesimally small (Tullock, 1994). In addition, regulatory policies that concentrate benefits on a relatively small number of actors may attract well-organized lobbies that face lower costs of monitoring and disciplining free-riders. By contrast, measures diffusing benefits across large groups may not bring forth organized support proportionate to the numbers affected, owing to the higher costs of controlling free riding in large-number situations (Olson, 2000). In the case of land use regulation, for example, there is evidence that statutory public regulation is frequently "captured" by homeowner coalitions that block new residential development at the direct expense of the mass of unorganized housing consumers, who face much higher house prices as a result (Pennington, 2000).

Though he continues to be associated with an "interventionist" approach to externalities by both critics and supporters of public regulation, the problem of capture was one that Pigou also recognized. Thus,

It is not sufficient to contrast the imperfect adjustments of unfettered private enter-prise with the best adjustments that economists in their studies can imagine. For we cannot expect that any public authority will attain, or even wholeheartedly seek, that ideal. Such authorities are liable alike to ignorance, to sectional pressure and to per-sonal corruption by private interest. A loud-voice part of their constituents, if organ-ised for votes, may easily outweigh the whole. (Pigou, 1912: 247–248; 1932: 331–332)

The Coasian analysis does not rule out cases where direct public regulation may be required, but it does suggest limiting these to pragmatic judgements about when prop-erty rights solutions and private contracting are impossible or prohibitively costly. Regional- or national-scale air pollution may be examples in this category, and there is some evidence that public regulatory bodies, such as the Environment Protection Agency in the United States, have had success in reducing pollution levels at a tolerably modest cost (Adler, 2012). Problems of international pollution and the issue of anthro-pogenic climate change also appear to be cases where no contractual process of private bargaining is likely to develop, and these too might support the case for public regula-tion as the "least bad" option. It is important, though, to recognize a final option high-lighted by the Coasian approach—that of "doing nothing." It was Coase's sensitivity to the importance of compliance problems that led him to recognize that both "market failures" and "government failures" may be so extensive that the costs of allowing an externality to persist may be less than the costs of trying to enforce private property rights or governmental regulations (Coase, 1960: 18). Which particular externalities match these criteria will always be the subject of political controversy, but any approach acknowledging compliance problems must recognize that losses in negative freedom owing to externalities may sometimes be outweighed by even greater losses from seek-ing to eliminate them.

4. Positive Freedom, Regulation, and Public Policy

If there is debate over how far public policy should regulate private actions to protect negative freedoms, similar questions arise concerning the role that public regulation should or should not play in seeking to promote positive liberties.

4.1. Positive freedom and economic regulation

Many writers in the liberal egalitarian and social democratic traditions have long main-tained that government regulation of the market economy and civil society is essential if the positive freedom of the disadvantaged is to be secured. John Rawls, for example, suggests that the negative freedoms emphasized by classical liberals and libertarians do not meet the requirements of justice because they fail to recognize that distributive shares are determined by factors that are "arbitrary from a moral point of view" (Rawls, 1971: 72). The inheritance of natural advantages such as intelligence, strength, and good health, and social advantages such as the good fortune of being born into an educated and supportive family, are all factors that enable people to lead prosperous lives and thus to have more positive freedoms, but none of these factors can be said to have been "deserved" by the actors concerned.

For Rawls and his followers the "basic structure" of society must ensure the equal value of people's liberties, and this requires that economic inequalities generated by markets be modified to meet the requirements of the "difference principle"—that they work to maximize the material position of representative agents from the least advantaged class. Traditionally, Rawlsians have suggested that this requires welfare-state-style arrangements where there is a "distributive branch of government" to reallocate income. In the latter part of his career, however, Rawls paid increasing attention to a regime type he described as "property-owning democracy" (POD). Arguments in favor of this regime are of particular interest to this chapter because they suggest a more expansive role for the regulatory state that goes well beyond conventional income redistribution schemes.[4]

Rawslian POD reserves a central place for public regulators to engage in wholesale intervention in market processes. Some of the powers it proposes are similar to those endorsed by interpretations of neo-classical welfare economics emphasizing the significance of "market failures" owing to imperfect competition and imperfect or asymmetric information. Other proposed interventions are more far-reaching, including the empowerment of public agencies to break up industries, to favor worker cooperatives, and, where necessary, to alter prices where these are deemed incompatible with a suitably egalitarian distribution. Where the welfare state seeks to ameliorate inequalities that arise from private markets, a POD would intervene more directly in the operation of markets to prevent background inequalities in life chances and resources from arising in the first place (O'Neill and Williamson, 2012).

Where liberal egalitarians and social democrats see a significant role for public regulation in securing positive liberty for all, contemporary classical liberals and libertarians reject these proposals, not because they downplay the value of positive liberty but because they contend that the structures favored by egalitarians are unlikely to function as intended owing to overwhelming compliance problems. Seen in this light, Rawls' analysis of compliance issues is asymmetric in character. On the one hand, he considers the compatibility of POD with "justice as fairness" under "ideal theoretic" conditions of "full motivational compliance," where problems such as regulatory incompetence or capture of the regulatory apparatus by predatory agents are assumed away. On the other hand, however, Rawls rejects classical liberal regime types as incompatible with "justice as fairness" because they *lack* a formal regulatory and redistributive apparatus that *guarantees* the fortunes of the least advantaged. For many classical liberals and libertarians, however, it is not primarily the existence of regulatory or redistributive mechanisms that guarantees a particular conception of freedom or justice, but whether these mechanisms *can work systematically* to guarantee the freedoms in question. With full motivational compliance to Rawlsian principles, a classical liberal minimal state, though lacking a regulatory and redistributive apparatus, *could* ensure that the positive freedoms of all are secured, and that those who have acquired market power *do not* then use it to harm the interests of the least well off. Insofar as this scenario is thought implausible owing to compliance problems such as lack of generosity from private actors or from weak incentives, then consistency requires that one also examine the likely effect of similar or indeed different compliance problems that may arise under more extensive regulatory regimes. On a classical liberal or libertarian view, due consideration of these issues tilts the balance away from the interventionist regimes favored by Rawls and many social democrats—even assuming the desirability of Rawlsian outcomes.[5]

The first issue here is the informational assumptions underlying suggestions that governments should regulate markets not meeting the terms of so-called perfect competition or perfect information. Hayek demonstrated more than sixty years ago that the standard of full information equilibrium is of doubtful value when judging the capacity of a free enterprise system to improve general living standards and hence positive liberties (Hayek, 1948a; Hayek, 1948b). Markets are only likely to approach "perfection" in the neo-classical sense when there is little disagreement and no new knowledge to be spread. In the grain market, for example, where it is hard to differentiate supplies and where techniques are well known, prices are unlikely to be affected significantly by any one actor. Yet when products can be produced in a variety of ways, and where it takes much longer to discover appropriate resource combinations, management techniques, and organizational forms, those creating the most suitable methods may generate significant profits and acquire "market power" before others are able to emulate them (ibid.). Such power is not necessarily evidence of "market failure" but often reflects superior foresight in conditions of uncertainty where knowledge is not "given" in advance, but has to be "produced." Entrepreneurial action is often of the "price-making" variety where firms duel with one another, launch price-cutting campaigns, and fashion new products and new forms of business organization—and it is precisely the inequalities in pricing power emergent from this process that pushes the market *in the direction* of equilibrium by spreading knowledge about the business models to copy and those to avoid. Equilibrium will, however, never be reached, because there will *always* be perturbations generated by new innovations and discoveries that demand further adjustments (ibid.).

Seen through this lens, the alternative to "imperfect" markets is not "perfect competition" but price setting and attempts to regulate entry by government licensing boards. From a Hayekian perspective, however, there is no obvious mechanism for public regulators to differentiate which prices and profits represent undue "market power" from those that reflect better entrepreneurial foresight. In markets, it is the clash of competing ideas and interpretations of the economic environment dispersed across multiple property owners that enables a process of trial-and-error learning. Regulators must themselves operate in a context of uncertainty and imperfect knowledge—but because their decisions are not subject to direct competition from agents with rival interpretations and because they have no equivalent of profit-and-loss accounting, they have the capacity to affect the operation of markets but little measure of whether their decisions are improving the allocation of resources in comparison to alternatives (Boettke, 1997: Boettke, Coyne, and Leeson, 2007). There are therefore grounds to question whether regulatory interventions in markets will *systematically* work to enhance living standards and the positive freedoms they may bring.

Similar obstacles may face proposals to break up industries deemed to exhibit excessive concentration of capital and to favor particular ownership models such as worker cooperatives. If the goal is to enhance positive freedom, then there is little reason to favor small business or worker cooperatives over big business, especially where the latter is able to offer consumers, and especially poorer consumers, a better deal. One of the key drivers of US productivity growth in recent years has, for example, been the retail giant Walmart, whose business model has lowered prices across the retail sector, increasing the purchasing power of low-income people (Basker, 2007). The key issue here is whether public regulators can know enough about which particular ownership structures meet the terms of the difference principle. Classical liberals and libertarians suggest that competition may be a better mechanism to determine the appropriate mix between firms of different sizes and ownership structures than public regulation. Public regulators have no equivalent of the profit-and-loss mechanism that communicates opportunities for mutually advantageous exchanges in markets, so it may be hard for them to judge whether their attempts to regulate the ownership of industry are commensurate with maximizing the material condition of the worst off. In addition, in a context of rising living standards it may be more in tune with respecting the freedom of individual workers to allow them to use their own bargaining power in markets to decide whether or not they prefer working in a conventional business enterprise or prefer workers' cooperatives, rather than have their option set determined by a central regulator (Tomasi, 2012).

In addition to these epistemic problems, the regulatory powers that would be available under a POD may create incentives for those controlling the regulatory apparatus to favor their own interests or those of powerful groups. Business interests may, for example, engage in rent-seeking behavior using regulation as a tool to protect their own position and to restrict competition. Liberal egalitarians and social democrats typically explain problems of regulator capture in terms of "money power" and the effect of large-scale inequalities that enable wealthy special interests to buy political influence at the expense of the least advantaged and of the fair value of their political liberties. According to this view, the disproportionate influence of the advantaged will not be addressed unless underlying power and wealth differentials are undermined by a combination of income redistribution and regulatory interventions, both in the structure of the economy and through measures such as campaign finance reform, which it is hoped will limit the ability of the wealthy to buy political influence.

From a classical liberal or libertarian perspective, however, money power alone does not best explain the problem of unequal power relations within the regulatory state. These may be better accounted for by asymmetric information and differential incentives for collective action. It tends to be easier for relatively small and concentrated producer interests derived from both capital and labor, which can gain disproportionately from a change in the structure of regulation, to acquire information and to overcome the collective action problems involved in lobbying regulators than it is for highly dispersed consumer interests, who may collectively be disadvantaged by such regulation but who face greater transaction costs of association. Such problems are exacerbated because wealth transfers that occur via regulatory controls tend to be much less visible to those negatively affected than is the case with direct income transfers (Tullock, 1994). While predatory cartels can and do form in market economies, these are typically unstable in the absence of coercive legal measures that enforce exclusionary practices. Seen through this lens, the best way of avoiding domination by powerful economic interests is to minimize the scope of the political/regulatory machine that enables wealthy incumbents to secure protection from newcomers.

The debate between social democrats and classical liberals/libertarians over the role of public regulation in promoting positive freedom may only be advanced by an appeal to a combination of social scientific theory and evidence on the effects of different regulatory structures—yet in the absence of any "pure" classical liberal/free market models and anything resembling a Rawlsian POD, the evaluation of such evidence will, to a considerable extent, remain conjectural. On the egalitarian/social democratic side, evidence from Scandinavia demonstrates that "interventionist" social systems need not reduce the capacity of the economy to produce the wealth which enhances the positive freedoms of citizens (see, for example, Lindert, 2004). On the classical liberal/libertarian side of the argument, however, authors note that cross-country comparisons of growth with various indices of economic freedom point toward a strong correlation between prosperity and a low-regulation environment that protects private property rights. While countries such as Sweden and Denmark have high levels of income redistribution, these economies, though far from being paragon "free" economies, often have relatively low levels of direct government regulation in markets—and nowhere near that required by a Rawlsian POD (for example, Bergh, 2014).

4.2. Positive freedom and the regulation of behavioral bias

In addition to arguments about the wealth-related effects of public policy interventions, recent debates have increasingly considered the role that public regulation should or should not play in "shaping" the choice sets available to individual actors. Theorists such as Amartya Sen, Cass Sunstein, and Richard Thaler have questioned the traditional liberal view that the choices people make are a reasonable indicator of the subjective value they attach to the options concerned. According to Sen (2002), for example, we should not always trust the "revealed preferences" of individual agents as reflecting their "true" best interests because, faced with sociocultural belief systems that narrow their options, people may "adapt" preferences to their environments by lowering their expectations. For Sunstein and Thaler (2003), meanwhile, cognitive and psychological biases highlighted by behavioral economists may prevent people from achieving their own stated objectives. At issue here are "weakness of will" and "short-sightedness" about risks, which may lead people to make sub-optimal decisions. In a health-care context, for example, people may be over-optimistic and underestimate the dangers associated with some lifestyle choices such as the consumption of fatty foods or the failure to acquire health insurance.

If the choices people make do not concord with their interests, then, far from restricting freedom, regulations may increase freedom by making it more likely they will realize their own goals. Sen (2002), for example, recommends public education campaigns and more direct social policy interventions to undermine asymmetric relationships in the family where the revealed preferences of women might be thought to reflect adaptation to culturally conditioned gender roles. Sunstein and Thaler (2003), meanwhile, favor interventions such as compulsory enrollment in private or state-run insurance plans, the stricter regulation of choices to enter contracts governing risk and insurance which may have long-term consequences, and measures to make fatty foods less attractive to the consumer.

While few commentators doubt the existence of adaptive preferences and cognitive biases, critics do doubt the capacity of public regulators to intervene in a manner that will *systematically* enhance the rationality of individual decisions. First, there is the distinct possibility that regulators charged with changing other people's behavior will themselves exhibit many of the behavioral biases that are supposed to be in need of attention (Boettke, Caceres, and Martin, 2013). Only where regulators have biases that somehow directly counteract the biases of the citizens whose behavior they regulate might beneficial outcomes be expected—yet the possibility of aligning the biases of citizens and regulators in such a way other than by pure chance seems unlikely. Second, it is possible that regulators may have particular biases of their own, such as, for example, a tendency to overestimate the value of "expert" knowledge. Third, it is far from clear that policy makers and regulators have the epistemic capacity to distinguish between the "real preferences" or "objective interests" of people and those that result from cultural or cognitive biases. In the case of adaptive preferences, for example, regulators need to judge whether a woman's endorsement of asymmetric gender roles reflects her "real" beliefs or those of an oppressive social environment. Women in some parts of the developing world are not, however, passive observers, but vocal advocates of traditional gender divisions, and mistaken attempts to change their practices through direct government regulations may produce significant resistance that may create negative consequences well beyond the particular behavior targeted. In the case of cognitive biases, meanwhile, regulators need to distinguish preferences for, say, fatty food that are "genuine" from those distorted by "weakness of will." Yet detailed knowledge of the reasons people make the choices they do, whether rational or otherwise, may be more likely to reside with those who actually make the choices concerned. Moreover, different behavioral experts have contradictory views on the appropriate response to particular decision-making biases, so it is far from clear why the choice of any one set of regulations should be publicly enforced.

To question the role of public regulation in this context is not to accept the status quo as optimal or desirable, but to suggest that more decentralized attempts to challenge cultural norms and behavioral biases may be better placed to deal with the epistemic burdens involved when it is not clear where peoples' "real interests" lie and when there is uncertainty over the best methods of encouraging behavioral change. In the case of adaptive preferences, for example, the classical liberal tradition has long emphasized a greater role for cross-cultural contact through trade and economic growth as an *indirect* route to exposing people to alternative possibilities and thus to challenge, incrementally, established cultural norms (Bauer, 1971). There is some evidence that economic contacts do a better job in promoting cultural change than deliberate policy interventions (Heath and Mobarak, 2014). Decentralized mechanisms may be better placed to promote beneficial change than centrally imposed solutions that may have the appearance of cultural imperialism. Similarly with respect to cognitive biases, in an environment allowing freedom of association and disassociation, people may join clubs and voluntary associations that may exert different kinds of social and peer group pressure to channel their behavior in various ways. Religious associations and sports clubs have long performed this role, and the various reward programs offered by gyms and health insurers, such as minimum-term memberships and penalty charges for early withdrawal, are all examples of decentralized strategies to cope with "weakness of will" and "short-sightedness." A regulatory framework with minimal public intervention may allow for competition between different strategies to overcome behavioral bias and enable individuals and civil associations to learn which types of regulation aid fulfillment of their goals more effectively than centrally imposed attempts to manipulate the choice architecture.

5. CONCLUSION

This chapter has sought to explore the relationship between freedom, regulation, and public policy. I have suggested that instead of seeing an inherent tension between negative and positive conceptions of freedom and the regulatory mechanisms they require, attention should focus on the effect of alternative structures on different dimensions of freedom as these play out in "real world" conditions where compliance problems are of paramount concern. Though far from exhaustive, the framework outlined here suggests that social scientific work on the behavioral attributes of actors operating under different regulatory regimes should be brought to the forefront of normative debates about the institutional prerequisites of freedom. This requires an interdisciplinary approach where the insights of economics and political science are brought to bear on the ethical analyses of political theorists and philosophers of freedom.

NOTES

1. It is important to distinguish between "assurance problems" and "compliance problems." In the former case people may need to coordinate on a set of regulations—such as "driving on the right"—and there may be a role for public authority in choosing such rules. Once they have been chosen, however, it will be in all or most drivers' interests to adhere to the rules,

making them effectively self-enforcing. Compliance problems, by contrast, refer to situations where it may *not* be in the personal interests of an individual or a group of individuals to adhere to the rules in question and where there may as a consequence be a need for monitoring or enforcement procedures.

2. Many economists adopting this reasoning do so from an aggregative utilitarian perspective that wishes to equalize private and "social costs" rather than one emphasizing the protection of individual negative freedoms, but the basic point about the need to curtail activities which impinge on others is fully compatible with an approach concerned with taking measures to avoid unwanted interference in the private sphere.

3. These problems may be ameliorated somewhat under a system of political federalism that allows for inter-jurisdictional competition (Buchanan, 1975).

4. It is not clear how much Rawls is concerned with "positive" liberty as opposed to the "fair value" of various liberties. In so far as the difference principle is concerned with maximizing the bundle of goods held by the least advantaged, however, this does suggest that the freedoms of the least advantaged are a function of the material resources that different regime types place at their disposal. Rawls seems here to be concerned with the distribution of positive liberty.

5. I have argued elsewhere that consideration of the compliance problems inherent to different principles of justice, as distinct from the political economic regime types often deemed more or less compatible with such principles (in Rawls' case, liberal socialism and property-owning democracy), provides grounds to reject Rawlsian justice (see Pennington, 2014).

References

Adler, J., 2012. Is the common law the free market solution to pollution? *Critical Review*, 24(1), pp.61-85

Anderson, T., and Hill, P., 2004. *The not so wild, wild west: property rights on the frontier.* Stanford, CA: Stanford University Press.

Anderson, T., and Libecap, G., 2014. *Markets and the environment.* Cambridge: Cambridge University Press.

Baldwin, B., Scott, C., and Hood, C., eds., 1998. *A reader on regulation.* Oxford: Oxford University Press,

Basker, E., 2007. The causes and consequences of Walmart's growth. *Journal of Economic Perspectives*, 21(3), pp.177–198.

Bator, F., 1958. The anatomy of market failure. *Quarterly Journal of Economics*, 72(3), pp.351–379.

Bauer, P., 1971. *Dissent on development.* London: Wiedenfield and Nicholson.

Benson, B., 1989. The spontaneous evolution of commercial law. *Southern Economic Journal*, 55(3), pp.644–661.

Bergh, A., 2014. *Sweden and the revival of the capitalist welfare state.* Cheltenham: Edward Elgar.

Boettke, P., 1997. Where did economics go wrong? *Critical Review*, 11(1), pp.11–64.

Boettke, Caceres, Z., and Martin, A., 2013. Error is obvious, coordination is the puzzle. In: R. Franz and R. Leeson, eds. *Hayek and behavioural economics.* Basingstoke: Palgrave Macmillan. pp.90-110

Boettke, P., Coyne, C., and Leeson, P., 2007. Saving government failure theory from itself. *Constitutional Political Economy*, 18(2), pp.127–143.

Buchanan, J., 1975. *The limits of liberty.* Indianapolis: Liberty Fund.

Buchanan, J., and Tullock, G., 1962. *The calculus of consent*. Ann Arbor: University of Michigan Press.

Coase, R., 1960. The problem of social cost. *Journal of Law and Economics*, 3(1), pp.1–44.

Ellickson, R., 1991. *Order without law*. Cambridge, MA: Harvard University Press.

Epstein, R., 2003. *Scepticism and freedom*. Chicago: University of Chicago Press.

Foldvary, F., 1994. *Public goods and private communities*. Cheltenham: Edward Elgar.

Gigenrezer, G., and Selten, R., 2002. *Bounded rationality: the adaptive toolbox*. Cambridge, MA: MIT Press.

Green, T. H., 1986. Liberal legislation and freedom of contract. In: P. Harris and J. Morrow. T. H. Green. Cambridge: Cambridge University Press. pp.192-212.

Hayek, F. A., 1948a. Economics and knowledge. In: F. A. Hayek. *Individualism and economic order*. Chicago: University of Chicago Press. pp.33-56

Hayek, F. A., 1948b. The meaning of competition. In: F. A. Hayek. *Individualism and economic order*. Chicago: University of Chicago Press. pp.92-106

Hayek, F. A., 1960. *The constitution of liberty*. London: Routledge.

Heath, R., and Mobarak, M., 2014. Manufacturing growth and the lives of Bangladeshi women. NBER Working Paper 20383, Washington DC.

Holmes, S., and Sunstein, C., 2013. *The cost of rights*. New York: Norton.

Leeson, P., 2008. How important is state enforcement for trade? *American Law and Economics Review*, 10(1), pp.61–89.

Lindert, P., 2004. *Growing public*. Cambridge: Cambridge University Press.

Meade, J., 1952. External economies and diseconomies in a competitive situation. *Economic Journal*, 62(245), pp.54–67.

Murphy, L., and Nagel, T., 2004. *The myth of ownership*. Oxford: Oxford University Press.

North, D., 1990. *Institutions, institutional change and economic performance*. Cambridge: Cambridge University Press.

Olson, M., 2000. *Power and prosperity*. New York: Basic Books.

O'Neill, M., and Williamson, T., eds., 2012. *Property owning democracy: Rawls and beyond*. Oxford: John Wiley.

Ostrom, E., 2006. *Understanding institutional diversity*. Princeton, NJ: Princeton University Press.

Pennington, M., 2000. *Planning and the political market*. London: Continuum.

Pennington, M., 2014. Realistic idealism and classical liberalism: evaluating free market fairness. *Critical Review*, 26(3–4), pp.375–407.

Pigou, E., 1912. *Wealth and welfare*. London: Macmillan.

Pigou, E., 1920. *The economics of welfare*. 1st ed. London: Macmillan.

Pigou, E., 1932. *The economics of welfare*. 4th ed. London: Macmillan.

Pipes, R., 1999. *Property and freedom*. London: Harvill Press.

Polanyi, K., 1944. *The great transformation*. Boston: Beacon Press.

Rawls, J., 1971. *A theory of justice*. Cambridge, MA: Harvard University Press.

Rosenberg, N., and Birdsell, L., 1986. *How the west grew rich*. New York: Basic Books.

Schmidtz, D., 2001. The institution of property. *Social Philosophy and Policy*, 11(2), pp.42–64.

Schmidtz, D., and Brennan, J., 2010. *A brief history of liberty*. Oxford: Oxford University Press.

Scott, J., 2009. *The art of not being governed*. New Haven, CT: Yale University Press.

Sen, A., 1992. *Inequality re-examined*. Oxford: Oxford University Press.

Sen, A., 2002. *Rationality and freedom*. Cambridge, MA: Belknap.

Simon, H., 1957. *Models of man*. New York: Wiley.

Sunstein, C., and Thaler, R., 2003. Libertarian paternalism. *American Economic Review*, 93(2), pp.175–179.

Tomasi, J., 2012. *Free market fairness*. Princeton, NJ: Princeton University Press.

Tullock, G., 1994. *Rent seeking*. Cheltenham: Edward Elgar.

Van Parjis, P., 1995. *Real freedom for all*. Oxford: Oxford University Press.

CHAPTER 17

....

BOUNDARIES, SUBJECTION TO LAWS, AND AFFECTED INTERESTS

....

CARMEN E. PAVEL

THE legitimacy of organizing our political life in distinct communities demarcated by boundary lines is coming under fire with renewed enthusiasm. Some argue that state borders are but lines in the sand, whose contours have been changed by the shifting winds of historical accident, the arbitrary whim of powerful nations, and wars of conquest and colonialism (Beitz, 2000; Carens, 1987). Because they have cropped up in morally arbitrary ways, existing boundaries do not have significant normative force. Consequently, their attendant political communities are just so many sand castles, vulnerable to caving under incessant practical and philosophical pressure.

One such practical pressure comes from the fact that the effects of the decisions of one country are felt across geographical boundaries, and therefore existing political communities do not track neatly the group at the source of a decision with the group that ultimately endures its effects. Some propose as a way out of this impasse the "all affected interests" principle (Goodin, 2007; Gould, 2006; Held, 2005). Its proponents argue that while democratic theory has provided guidance for *how* groups should make decisions democratically, it has had much less to say on the question of *who* should make decisions democratically. The "all affected interests" principle (AAIP) says that political decisions should be made by those whose interests are likely to be affected by these decisions. AAIP purports to offer normative criteria for drawing boundaries around political communities in less arbitrary and more morally legitimate ways, by ultimately endorsing a global democracy as the only legitimate form of political rule.

Despite its initial attractiveness, this chapter will argue that AAIP should be rejected as a principle for selecting membership in a political community. After a brief overview of the AAIP, I will offer three critical lines of argument. First, the AAIP cannot allocate rights of political participation because it serves a different purpose from the one attributed to it by its defenders. AAIP is not as well fit as an instrument for deciding membership as it is a signaling device for claims of harm that must be evaluated and addressed. Second, what helps Goodin and others justify (nothing less than) the global demos is the indeterminacy of the principle itself, which is a feature that should recommend neither the principle nor the global demos for addressing the problem of political membership. This internal critique spells out why the AAIP is rather unhelpful as a means of distinguishing whose interests are affected and which interests can ground the authority of democratic politics. Third, there is an alternative explanation for why certain people should be included in the political decision-making of a group and others should not, that better captures the reasons communities have for extending the democratic franchise. This explanation draws on the modern notion of democratic self-rule.

I will not take up the many deep questions all of the recent debates raised in connection to the AAIP. My goal is to challenge the interpretation of the principle on terms that its proponents have set, without attending comprehensively to its considerable implications for political theory and practice. Nonetheless, insofar as specific arguments developed within these debates rely explicitly or implicitly on the scaffolding provided by the AAIP, their plausibility will rise and fall with the plausibility of AAIP.

1. The Case for AAIP

Consider Amartya Sen, who says:

> the actions of one country can seriously influence lives elsewhere. This is not only through the deliberate use of forceful means (for example, the occupation of Iraq in 2003), but also through less direct influences of trade and commerce. We do not live in secluded cocoons of our own. And if the institutions and policies in one country, influence lives elsewhere, should not the voices of affected people elsewhere count in some way in determining what is just or unjust in the way a society is organized, typically with profound effects—direct or indirect—on people in other societies? (Sen, 2009: 129–130)

The idea that those who are affected by a political decision should have a say in it has become increasingly popular. The target for revision is the traditional model for representing democratic decision-making, which is captured by Joseph Schumpeter's somewhat redundant definition: any group that makes decisions in a democratic way counts as democratic (Schumpeter, 1962: 244–245). However, as Robert Dahl and Robert Goodin are quick to emphasize, this formal definition is at best incomplete and at worst unhelpful. Suppose that in South Africa only whites were allowed to make decisions democratically. Would that count as a democracy? If one hundred men in one hundred million make decisions for everyone, "would we call the rulers a demos and the system a democracy"?[1] That the answer to this Schumpeterian challenge is obviously *no*, suggests to Goodin that there are standards internal to democratic theory to prefer that the demos be constituted in a certain way.

The answer lies not, Goodin thinks, in sharing a common territory, or a common history, or in having some sort of sentimental attachment to other people who happen to inhabit the same stretch of land. Those factors are all arbitrary from a moral point of view and they cannot by themselves serve as acceptable grounds for constituting the demos. Rather, what matters is that those people's interests become intertwined (Goodin, 2007: 48). Consequently, the reason blacks in South Africa are entitled to be equal members of the political community is that their interests are affected by its decisions. This is why "protecting the people's interests is thus the most plausible candidate for bringing the 'who' and the 'how' of democratic politics into alignment," Goodin says (2007: 50).

Although it seems at first that membership in the demos based on shared territory is a good approximation of whose interests count, it is a misleading one, defenders of the AAIP say. David Held, for instance, points out that lots of people who live outside a given country's territory are affected by that country's policies, often in significant ways, particularly if that country is a powerful one. Pollution crosses borders, so if the Germans build a nuclear plant close to the Danish border, with potentially negative effects for the Danish, this would be a reason for the latter to participate in German economic and environmental policy (Held, 2005: 251). And according to Goodin, Iraqis and pretty much everybody else in the world are affected by U.S. politics, and consequently they should have a vote in U.S. elections (2007: 57). Furthermore, people's life chances are significantly shaped by the decision of states and international organizations, Carol Gould argues, and such effects support "a right of input by these others into the decisions that impact them" (2006: 54).

AAIP proponents defend different version of the principle. For instance, David Owen defends the "all actually affected interests" principle: "All whose interests are actually affected by a decision should be able to participate as equals in the democratic decision-making process" (2012: 133). Goodin ultimately endorses the "all *possibly* affected interests" principle as the most plausible. What he means is that people are *affected* both by a certain decision, but also by the failure of alternative decisions considered.[2] Consequently, at least for Goodin, the AAIP triggers an inflationary, growing spiral of inclusion and he embraces this inflationary tendency wholeheartedly. According to him, the implication of taking AAIP seriously as a criterion for making the demos is that we end up with global demos as *the only acceptable* outcome for political decision-making: "virtually everyone in the world should be entitled to vote on any proposal. A maximally expansive franchise, ignoring boundaries both of space and time, would be the only legitimate way to constitute the demos" (Goodin, 2007: 55). When the franchise balloons dramatically, the scope for legitimate exclusion shrinks accordingly. The radical implications of AAIP may be what makes it attractive to its proponents, but as I will show in the next two sections, as a principle of political membership it suffers from insuperable difficulties.

The various proposals for the AAIP as a means of drawing boundaries can be grouped into two distinct positions: either (i) the AAIP requires communities to be restricted to small, localized demoi, that only make decisions on issues that concern them, or (ii) it requires a global demos. This chapter will argue that (i) has the problems of shifting constituencies and indeterminacy, and (ii) culminates into various undemocratic outcomes. Before giving reasons for this skepticism, I would like to propose a different understanding of the AAIP, as a sort of signaling device for claims of harm.

2. THE INTEREST IN CONTROL
OVER ONE'S LIFE

AAIP captures a familiar intuition that individuals should be in control of the forces that shape their lives. The ability to exercise control over one's life is a moral primitive, an essential interest of independent moral value. This moral primitive does not automatically determine the set of rights of control for protecting specific interests, yet it provides, as T. M. Scanlon has argued, "a basis for arguments in support of the personal rights that secure and protect such control" (1976: 12). This means that an interest in control over one's life does not by itself justify assigning rights for particular forms of control, such as rights of political participation.

Thus we can distinguish between *protecting the interest in control* in a particular area of life, and granting *the right to have a say* over all decisions that affect that area, including over other people's decisions (Scanlon, 1976: 12). Individuals have an interest in whom they marry; however, this interest does not grant each person a right to participate in others' decisions on whether to marry them or not.[3] Liberal societies have decided that the best way to protect the interest in having a say in whom to marry is to grant the right to make one's decisions in choosing marriage partners freely but not in having a right to have a say over how potential partners choose.

Individuals make decisions about whom to marry, socialize with, and bestow economic opportunities upon in ways that profoundly affect other people's interests. In each of these areas, societies grant different forms of control over decisions made by some that affect others, and sometimes no control at all, as in the case of marriage. We can in fact differentiate *at least three different ways* of protecting people's interests that involve different degrees of control over others' decisions. In the case of personal decisions such as marriage, society assigns no say over the decisions of others, consistent with respecting the personal autonomy of all. To protect against financial fraud, the members of a society participate in making the rules that constrain everyone's financial decisions. For example, victims of fraud are often entitled to monetary compensation. A right to compensation is one of the ways in which the society protects the interest each person has in economic security. This interest does not translate into a right to have a say over how others make their decisions, even when those decisions affect one's interests. Finally, in electing a president, all the members of a demos participate in making a political decision. In these examples we go from no say in the decisions of others that affects us (marriage), to some indirect say (regulating financial decisions), to equal participation in the decision (choosing a president).

Systems of rights apportion particular forms of control people can exercise over their lives by distinguishing the different ways that people are affected by the actions of others. Rights thus determine when people are entitled to have a say and when they are not. In some instances, having a say over others' decisions would grant individuals an unacceptable degree of control over other people's lives. The *interest* in having a say over how other people's decisions affect one and the *standing* to make those decisions can come apart. This is as true of politics as it is of other areas of life in which people have large stakes in the outcome. Having the standing to make political decisions is but one way to protect one's interest in control over one's life, but it is not the only way, and it certainly does not follow that every time some people are affected by others' decisions, they gain a standing to make decisions for themselves and others. This is a distinction that those who defend the "all affected interest principle" require but fail to provide.

We could not make sense of our moral life if we did not separate protecting interests from granting the standing to have a say. Religious communities should be able to buy land and hire employees to help run their activities without extending their "demos" to include those affected by the transactions, the potentially interested landowners, and the potential pool of employees respectively. Companies and universities should be able to decide which employees they hire and how to run their internal affairs, without inviting everyone affected as a participant with equal voice. So we have to explain why, contra defenders of AAIP, a qualified version of right to have standing holds, mutatis mutandis, for groups claiming political autonomy within a given territory. And although a full defense of this claim is not possible here, I will suggest some reasons to believe that this right of political participation piggybacks on a well-worn-out principle of democratic politics, namely democratic self-rule, which parallels respect for autonomy in the individual case. But first, I want to argue that we have additional reasons to be suspicious of AAIP as a strictly political principle.

3. PROBLEMS INTERNAL TO THE AAIP

There are additional complaints against the AAIP which are by now familiar. Two major difficulties, the problem of the shifting constituency and the problem of indeterminacy, prove that the principle can provide no guidance for how to reconstitute political communities. First, AAIP produces shifting constituencies. Membership in the democratic community changes with specific decisions. Think of one of Goodin's examples, that of the U.K. referendum on whether to pay reparations to its former colonies (2007: 53–54). Whether the interests of people living in former British colonies are affected depends not just on who makes the decision, but also on *what the decision is about*. Had the decision not been about reparations, but about economic policy, or going to war, the group of people whose interests is affected would be different.

Therefore, one cannot decide who is entitled to vote until the nature of that decision has been revealed. This means that the constituency constantly changes with the policy issue, and no two policies or decisions will have the same constituency. Assuming direct democracy is not always feasible, especially with extremely large groups, making political decisions requires a system of representation. But representation assumes long-term cooperation among individuals who rely on a basis of shared values, who foster institutional continuity, and whose interaction with each other leads to building trust over time. All of these in turn presuppose politically stable consistencies. To allow the political unit to vary constantly is to undermine, as David Miller puts it, the conditions that make democratic governance possible in the first place (2009). The shifting constituency problem leads to a dead end.

Second, AAIP is beset by indeterminacy. Even knowing the nature of specific decisions does not tell us what the decision group should be. Any policy will affect different interests to varying degrees, and is likely to affect some interests more directly or more immediately than others (Näsström, 2011: 124–125). When the European Union adopts tariffs on steel imports, it affects current producers of steel and potential future ones, everyone who works in the steel industry and also those in the mining industry in every country, those who produce machinery for steel plants, those who buy steel products, those who use them to create other products, and so on. But as Sofia Näsström points out, these difficulties convince proponents of AAIP not to discard it but to qualify it (2011: 125). In an effort to make the principle more precise, Goodin proposes that those whose basic interests are most vitally affected by a particular decision have the strongest claim to a say in it. Gould similarly insists that only those whose basic human rights are affected should have a say (2006: 54).

Let us consider basic interests. Those and only those who basic interests are affected can vote on a particular policy. However, focusing on basic interests still falls short of settling the question of political membership. To see why, we can resort to Ian Shapiro's basic interests list. Shapiro has deployed his interpretation of relevant interest to address a different application of AAIP within a bounded democratic community, but his list is equally useful for Goodin's purposes (Shapiro, 2001: 37). Shapiro offers a "comparatively minimal" specification of basic interest: people have interest in nutrition, security, health, education (so they can develop human capital and become competent adults [2001: 85–88]). These are what he calls "the essentials to survive in the world" (Shapiro, 2001: 88). The basic interest version of AAIP says that only people whose basic interests are affected by a decision should have a say in that decision.

With this list we can more accurately diagnose the problem with using AAIP to determine political membership: we cannot know how basic interests are affected and whose interests are affected until we know something about the set of alternative decisions contemplated. Suppose that the policy question for debate is building an electricity dam on the river Huang He in China. The voting population would be constituted by those for whom the project would threaten their "essentials to survive in the world," to adopt Shapiro's language. But who is part of this group depends on many factors, some of which cannot be ascertained beforehand. Whether people's basic interest are significantly affected depends on their proximity to the river, the terms of the relocation, the extent to which people profit from the new electric power generated by the dam, substantive changes in the local economy, and other factors. The "basic interest" view still leaves the decision group underspecified.

Additionally, on the "basic interests" interpretation the principle has counterintuitive implications. If only those whose basic interests are substantially affected have a say in matters of policy, those whose basic interests are not thus affected do not have a say. For some policies, such as space research or recreational drug laws, nobody's basic interest would be affected, meaning that these policy decisions would basically lack constituencies. For other policy questions, groups that should normally be included in decision-making should be excluded under the basic interests view. Policies involving the right to abortion would not affect men's basic interests because such policies would not affect their "essentials to survive in the world"; therefore it would follow that men should not have a say in those policies. But this seems odd. Men may not be entitled to have a say in a particular abortion decision, but they certainly have an important stake in policies that determine whether they are able to have children or not and the conditions under which abortions take place without prejudice to the life and health of future children. The trouble with the basic interest view is that it offers unacceptable reasons for exclusion and thus it produces antidemocratic outcomes.

For less than the global demos, one needs to identify both which interests count, and the appropriate ways in which they are affected. Moreover, we need to worry about the institutional setup required to make this specification of the principle work. We can expect that people will not spontaneously sort themselves out based on the proportion to which their basic interests will be affected by various decisions. Therefore, applying the principle requires, in effect, a central agency (we can call it the Ministry of Public Participation) to determine the proportion to which people's interests are affected depending on the decisions contemplated, in order to determine who has a say and how much of a say that person has in which decision. As a mechanism for distributing rights of political participation, this agency would harness an enormous amount of political power. Concentrating so much power within one institutional center does not seem like a promising vision of democratic life.

Broadly speaking, AAIP is noncommittal with respect to two different ways of thinking about political membership. The first captures the way most scholars working in the tradition of democratic theory have used it. Despite advances in formal political equality in developed democracies, which grants every citizen the same legal protections and privileges, democratic processes can be detrimental to the interests of historically disadvantaged or minority groups. In this case the AAIP as a signaling device recommends tinkering with procedural rules to enhance these groups' democratic representation, to safeguard a space for autonomous decision-making, and to grant them greater bargaining power, all of these changes taking place *within* the geographical boundaries of existing states (Benhabib, 2004; Dovi, 2002; Rehfeld, 2005; Young, 2002).[4]

The inability of AAIP to generate useful criteria for membership in distinct political communities is not a problem if one takes the maximalist view, which says that the only legitimate way to make the demos is to include everyone. Yet abandoning the idea of local demoi comes at a high price. To a certain extent, polities can restrict by fiat the application of their laws, by stipulating the geographical area to which these laws apply. The elected officials of the city of London make decisions regarding its road maintenance, police and fire protection, zoning and public space use, traffic, and transportation. Only London's residents who are also citizens of the United Kingdom participate in electing the city officials, including the mayor, although French and Japanese tourists can also be affected, and sometimes profoundly so, by the city's rules and regulations. Nonetheless, it is wrong to give these tourists a voice in the election of local officials or directly in the administrative and political decisions of the city. Giving outsiders a voice in these local decisions amounts to a kind of moral imposition, undue interference with the autonomy of a group to decide its own fate.

Ian Shapiro is clear on the dangers of arbitrary domination created by overinclusion: "Allowing an equal say in a decision to people with greatly different stakes in the outcome generates pathologies similar to those involving large differences in capacities for exit" (2001: 235). The local demos becomes subject to the whims of people who may well be in the majority, have no commitment to protecting the interest of the minority, and no particular knowledge of local conditions and required trade-offs between different kinds of projects and policies. Outsiders can manipulate the resources of the local group to benefit their own interests and exploit the locals. Different groups can also have different ideas about what political ideals to pursue, and in a global demos, groups that are at a numerical disadvantage have no way to express those values independently. And as Iris Young claims, efforts to suppress or assimilate indigenous groups or culturally distinct groups are so commonplace in current political practice and past history that those efforts are likely to be encouraged by an institutional setup that gives large majorities more power (2002: 251–256). Some essential individual freedoms such as freedom of religion, freedom of association, and cultural freedoms are particularly threatened. Having distinct, autonomous political communities reduces the danger of potential or actual domination of some groups by others.

The ultimate consequence of taking AAIP seriously is that on the more localist version, it would be really difficult to say who should be involved in which decision, and on the maximalist version, everybody would have to decide on the largest and smallest of issues, on those affecting small communities as well as the global polis. The principle would lead to domination, decision fatigue, and a lack of fit between the scope of the applicability of political decisions and the configuration of the group making them.

The more plausible interpretation of what the principle demands is that offered by David Owen, who concludes, after going through several different interpretations of the principle, that ultimately it does not entail that those affected by the decisions of a polity are entitled to membership in that polity. They are at most entitled to an impartial consideration of their interests within a common scheme of rules, and to the consideration of only those interests that others owe to them as an obligation of morality (Owen, 2012: 135, 138). This is in line with an understanding of AAIP not as a decision principle directly applicable to democratic politics, but as a moral primitive in the sense that Scanlon argues for, which helps orient our judgment as one criterion necessary to decide what rights to assign to individuals and groups, but not the only one, and certainly not as a political principle that assigns specific rights of control.

4. THE SUBJECTED INTERESTS PRINCIPLE AS AN ALTERNATIVE

Is the interest in having a say over political decisions best served by being a member of a self-contained demos or of an all-inclusive global demos? This question is hard to answer based on the AAIP alone. The global demos answer relies in part on a misinterpretation of the relevance of the examples that challenge Schumpeter's formal definition of democracy. South Africa and America prior to civil rights reform show that not every group that makes decisions in a democratic way counts as democratic, unless additional conditions are met. For Goodin, those conditions have to do with the fact that the lives of large parts of the population in both countries were affected by the decision of the demos. But relying on AAIP as an explanation of what is wrong with Schumpeter's formal definition proves *too much*. The reason the affected interest view is unsatisfactory for the South Africa example is that many other people's interest are affected, to different degrees, by the decision of its ruling body and institutions. Not just blacks in South Africa, but the people in neighboring countries, as well as people living in countries with which South Africa has close economic and political ties, are affected by its policies and should be included as equal political members with a say in its affairs.

However, there is a more effective answer to this challenge. Schumpeter's formal definition is problematic not because it leaves out people who are affected by the decision of the demos, but because it leaves out people who are subject to the rules and decisions of a political community, yet they do not participate in making them. The excluded are prevented from exercising collective self-rule. Also known as the "all subjected" principle, the principle of democratic self-rule says that people should have a voice in determining the laws and institutions that they are subject to, and the democratic part requires that they have an equal voice (Fraser, 2010: 65; López-Guerra, 2005: 225; Näsström, 2011: 118–122).

There is thus an important difference between being a subject of a system of laws and institutions and having one's interests affected by that system. This is a difference in kind and not just in degree. The idea of a subject of a system of laws and institutions captures a rather mundane distinction between, say, those who live in the United States and are subject to its laws and institutions and those who live in Japan and are therefore not subject to the same laws and institutions, unless they visit for short periods, in which case they are bound by U.S. laws without being subjects. Being a subject therefore seems to require additional elements, such as an ongoing relationship with a community and its institutions, rights and obligations of citizenship, and a normative expectation of compliance with and support for the institutional system one is a subject of.

Some think that what it is to be a subject is explained by the element of coercion involved in upholding a system of laws and institutions.[5] Arash Abizadeh, for example, argues that "*the democratic justification for a regime of border controls is ultimately owed to both members and nonmembers*" (emphasis in original 2008: 44). Since "the coercive exercise of political power must be democratically justified to all those over whom it is exercised," and since both the members of a political community and non-members equally are subjected to the coercive interferences of border controls, the justification of those boundaries is owed to all, members and non-members alike (Abizadeh, 2008: 45). Abizadeh adopts the familiar principle of democratic legitimacy, or a version of it: namely, that political power can only be justifiably exercised over those who are subject to it. Since both outsiders and insiders are subject to coercion, the only legitimate demos is the unbounded demos, or the global demos. Although using a different starting point, Abizadeh embraces Goodin's conclusion that the only justified demos is the demos that includes everyone (Abizadeh, 2008: 46; Abizadeh, 2012: 876–877).

But pace Abizadeh, coercion cannot be enough. Subjection to laws requires a *systematic, pervasive, and ongoing* relationship between the subjected and the political authority. Being subjected to coercion may give at most a claim to outsiders to be treated in certain ways, or to have their interests taken into account in some measure by the community making immigration policy, but to infer from this more modest claim the radical claim that those thus subjected to border coercion must have a say in the making of immigration policy, and perhaps an equal say, is to make an unjustified argumentative leap.

Coercion is exercised in the protection of all kinds of boundaries, and in many, if not most, instances, it cannot be plausibly followed by the requirement that those coerced have a say. A and B may own property together and coercively deny C access to it, but this fact does not give C a joint decision right in deciding what are A and B's property boundaries or how they use it. Any kind of voluntary association in which A and B exclude C, through the use of coercion or other means, does not give C a right to a say. The point is of course not to argue that states are voluntary associations, but to point out that there is a variety of cases in which being subject to coercion in the protection of some boundary does not automatically entitle one to a say.

While being subject to coercion is an important part of being a subject of a system of laws in general, it is not sufficient. It is not merely that whoever lives in the United States is coerced by the laws. The Japanese and Mexicans who may try to cross its borders will be coerced as well in virtue of border regulations and controls, even while treated differently by these regulations. However, system of laws do more than coerce; they solve coordination problems, distribute goods and services, require financial support, and demand compliance. Subjects do their part by following the law, paying taxes, and engaging in cooperative behavior with others. And this is an ongoing, systematic, and pervasive relationship. People are subject to the coercion of a state for most of their lives or significant portions of it; the coercion happens within a system of institutions that regulates and affects many aspects of an individual's choices, life prospects, and well-being. Coercion seems necessary to explain when one is a subject, but it is not sufficient.

There are additional questions about who else besides permanent, exclusive residents are subjects. Long-term guest workers and illegal aliens seem to raise especially stringent challenges to any unproblematic definition of what makes one a subject of a system of laws.[6] Different countries have chosen to treat guest workers and illegal aliens differently, with some awarding them full citizenship, with all the rights and obligations that this status entails, and others refusing to enfranchise them. A functioning political constituency must consider these questions, make decisions about the direction in which the demos expands, and reflect on the internal and external constraints that shape that process.

One might worry that the principle of democratic self-rule is also indeterminate, and it therefore suffers from the same weakness as the AAIP as a means to demarcate the demos. This worry would be unfounded. The demos at the heart of the principle of democratic self-rule contains a stable core, which can redefine its boundaries at the margin, for example by becoming more inclusive over time. By contrast, the localist version of the AAIP, the one plagued by indeterminacy, implies no stable core, because the demos can change completely depending on the issue over which the decision is made. The demos of the democratic self-rule principle is always determinate (even if not always justly determined), while the one called forth by AAIP almost never is.

5. ARBITRARY BORDERS AND DEMOCRATIC SELF-RULE

Those who raise the boundary problem are quick to emphasize that the idea of democratic self-determination presupposes a "self," a demos who is supposed to make decisions in a democratic way. Existing demoi are arbitrarily constituted by historical contingency, unjust wars, and border agreements that reflected the wishes of the powerful. The fact that democratic theory cannot tell how to avoid this arbitrariness is a sign of the incoherence of democratic theory itself, and of its incapacity to solve the most important problem at its core (Abizadeh, 2008: 46–47; Näsström, 2011: 116).

Democratic theory suffers no such dramatic failures. It is true that existing borders are historically arbitrary, but arbitrariness can be consistent with moral acceptability. Domestic partnerships, business collaborations, and religious groups are all constituted in arbitrary ways, meaning that their members and partners are not preselected according to a publicly justifiable rule or heuristic. Such associations come together haphazardly and for a variety of reasons. Yet it makes perfect sense to say that although the constitution of such groups is arbitrary, how members treat each other is not. Still, these are all voluntary associations, and one might argue that it is acceptable for the composition of such groups to be arbitrary, but the issue of membership in contemporary states is different. The latter are far from being voluntary associations of like-minded people. True enough. But the arbitrariness of (most) borders of existing states can be made morally defensible.

Some such arbitrary borders have been drawn as a result of recent injustices, and groups affected by these injustices have legitimate claims to restore them to the status quo ante. The Iraqi invasion of Kuwait was justifiably overturned because it interfered with the rights of the Kuwaiti people to self-determination. The sweeping anti-colonial movements in the middle of the twentieth century that resulted in independence for many states was similarly based on historic claims of groups of people who saw their right to self-determination unjustly interfered with. But other injustices are too deeply buried in the fog of a distant past to serve as a basis of claims to redraw current boundaries. Going back four hundred years to trace rightful claims to national boundaries would greatly disturb social peace for people who have made lives within existing boundaries for generations and have expectations to be able to continue those lives undisrupted.[7] Some "statute of limitations" must surely apply to claims of historical injustice with respect to boundaries that go too far back in time. How far back we should be able to go to undo injustice it is hard to say, but though arbitrary, existing borders have substantive weight for the sake of stability and peace. The arbitrariness of borders might not have been defensible fifty or a hundred years after the injustices that gave rise to them took place, but the passing of time has made it possible for the individuals within those borders to create stable and flourishing communities, and to organize their own lives around the opportunities that those communities have offered.

The value of the principle of democratic self-rule rests on specifying *who else* should be a member once there is a partially constituted demos, but it does not give us grounds for deciding *who should initially be a member*. Very generally, it suggests that *all people* who are subject to a common system of laws and institutions should participate in making the political decisions that govern them, but it does not specify criteria for *which people* should come together to create a common system of laws and institutions. In other words, democratic theory is agnostic about how the demos is constituted on the first go, but has more to say about appropriate requirements to make the demos fully democratic and thus legitimate. And this limitation does not reveal any inconsistency or incoherence at the heart of democratic theory. The fact that democratic theory cannot tell us who is the "self" that is subject to self-government is no more of a failure than contract law's inability to tell us who the contracting parties are. Without offering a way of escaping the historical arbitrariness of the origin of political communities, democratic theory offers an appropriate avenue for making historical contingencies morally acceptable and publicly justified (Benhabib, 2004: 66).

Membership in distinct political communities represents a reasonable way to apportion political control for protecting people's interests and to respect the AAIP in practice. The principle of democratic self-government means that the people inhabiting a political community make the decisions that govern it, even when others' interests are likely to be affected. Among those decisions is the inclusion and exclusion of outsiders. Democratic self-rule draws the line between legitimate and illegitimate exclusion.

While people subject to the laws of a political community should have a say in its political decisions, outsiders do not have a claim to participate in making those decisions.

The principle of democratic self-rule has several advantages over the AAIP. One is specificity. The principle of democratic self-rule can point precisely to the individuals or group of individuals who are subject to a system of rules and institutions and should be candidates for inclusion in the authorizing public. The case of South Africa during apartheid proves it. Another advantage of the principle of democratic self-rule is that it avoids the inflationary spin of AAIP. It better approximates the connection between those who make up the demos and over what issues the demos can rule, without falling into the trap of granting virtually everyone in the world a vote on any proposal, which is an indefensible implication of AAIP on democratic grounds. Finally, the principle of democratic self-rule gives plenty of reasons to reform the existing practice of various political communities while preserving and building on a common-sense account of democratic participation. It accepts as legitimate the practice that local demoi are entitled to decide on matters that are essential to their own members without undue interference from the outside.

The defenders of the AAIP may object that this alternative grants too much to the status quo. After all, borders, a common history, shared sympathies, and identification with a particular political community are all morally arbitrary ways of constituting the demos. It is of course true that many political communities have acquired the membership they did due to highly contingent historical forces, and their borders have been drawn in not just arbitrary but sometimes clearly unjust and illegitimate ways. And while this may give reason to correct the border misalignment to the extent possible, it does not show that borders *in general* are unjustified (Risse, 2008). Borders are justified for marking off places that engender acts of self-constitution by peoples who seek to make for themselves a separate public space and a unique political identity.

The principle of democratic self-government leaves unanswered additional questions about political membership having to do with aliens and asylum seekers, for instance. To settle these questions, additional normative criteria will be required. But as Seyla Benhabib has pointed out, taking these new criteria into account is compatible with exercising self-rule: "[W]hile the demos, as the popular sovereign, must asset control over a specific territorial domain, it can also engage in reflexive acts of self-constitution, whereby the boundaries of the demos can be readjusted" (2004: 48). Confronting the problems raised by migration and displacement requires that political communities therefore reexamine their practices of exclusion, but it does not require that they eliminate them.

Fundamentally for Goodin, the problem with the principle of democratic self-rule is that "[l]ots of rules have extraterritorial effects without having, literally, extraterritorial application" (2007: 49). This is the reason why, in his view, the democratic self-rule principle warrants rejection, as do other ways of justifying bounded political communities. Yet the AAIP is compatible with different ways of granting people control over issues that affect them in order to protect their interests, and in order to do so on problems that extend beyond borders, an alternative approach may be in order. For example, Ben

Saunders shows that the best way to protect interests is to focus on rights, and rights are best respected "by limiting the power of groups to infringe on them, rather than by requiring them to include or enfranchise the rights-holders" (Saunders, 2012: 2). The question of whether to give distinct groups standing, and therefore authority, to make certain decisions within their jurisdiction, and the question of how to manage the effects of those decisions outside the jurisdiction, can be separated in a manner compatible with AAIP, without resorting to the global demos.

6. CONCLUSION

The AAIP invites a fallacy that is spreading among people thinking about international justice. It is becoming commonplace to argue that since people in different parts of the world are affected by remote decisions, they are entitled to a say in them. This chapter has argued that the best way to understand the AAIP is not as a principle that assigns specific rights of political participation, but as a signaling device, a red flag that encourages us to acknowledge, interpret, and find solutions for managing the negative effects of people's actions on each other.

As a moral primitive, the AAIP can provide no practical guidance on how to allocate political membership. But the fact that we do not have clear normative guidelines for constituting political communities is not as troubling as it might seem at first glance. The legitimate concerns having to do with the absence of equal political status, and the problem of negative externalities, that animate the proponents of AAIP can be adequately addressed by the existing principles and tools. The ideals of democratic self-rule and individual rights have been a force both for improving the condition of many historically marginalized groups and for resisting encroachments on the political autonomy of groups from outside. Discarding this hard-won wisdom in the name of reducing the import of historical contingencies creates a philosophical vacuum that cannot be easily filled.

In addition, insisting that the only acceptable demos is the global demos would delegitimize acts of self-constitution for groups of people that would like to create and maintain a distinct community from others. The global demos, far from making people be more in control of their lives, would make them less so. The bigger the size of the demos, the less any one individual will be able to affect its policies and have her own concerns addressed. If the AAIP promises to unburden political communities of the need to make decisions for themselves, by allowing outsiders to participate in those decisions, then it is a principle that we should have great reservations about.

In the end, we need to make peace with some contingency in political life. Suggesting that the obligations that arise out of moral and political associations are morally arbitrary and lack normative force if they are the result of historical accident is making arbitrariness do too much work. Many of our personal and public associations are the result of contingent forces, but their history, however accidental, generates morally relevant facts about our obligations to each other. Just us we cannot decide a priori who should make up cultural or professional groups, but we can say intelligible things about how people within those groups should treat one another, so too there is no principle that says who should be part of a political community at its founding, but liberal-democratic principles have a lot to say about how people should treat each other once they are part of one.

Acknowledgments

I would like to thank David Miller, Ian Shapiro, Annie Stilz, Colin Bird, Jennifer Rubenstein, Loren Lomasky, John Trasher, Chad von Schoelandt, Helen Frowe, Massimo Renzo, Mary Ann Franks, Lorenzo Zucca, Mathew Smith, Daniel Viehoff, Graham Long, Ori Herstein, Ekow Yankah, and the participants at the colloquium in the Department of Philosophy at the University of Arizona and the colloquium at the University of Virginia's Political Philosophy, Policy and Law program for feedback on earlier drafts.

Notes

1. Dahl, quoted by Goodin (2007: 47).
2. Both what the consequences turned out to be, and what they *may have been*, must be taken into account in deciding who is affected and therefore included in the demos. For example, the United Kingdom's decision to send reparations greatly affects the interest of those living in former colonies. But even if the U.K. decides not to send reparations, thus leaving them no better and no worse off than they were before, Goodin claims that the decision not to send reparations should be seen as affecting them *in a broader sense*, because if the decision "had gone the other way, their interest would have been greatly advanced" (2007: 53–54).
3. This example was made famous by Nozick (1977: 269).
4. Rehfeld introduces the concept of "communities of interests" to argue for redesigning constituencies within existing states along non-territorial lines in his book. Iris Young thinks of democratic authority along the lines suggested here, but also expresses considerable sympathy for a position similar to Goodin's in the last part of her book *Inclusion and Democracy*.
5. See, for instance, the exchange between Abizadeh and Miller in *Political Theory* (Abizadeh, 2008; Miller, 2010; Miller, 2009: 218–223).
6. For example, Claudio López-Guerra argues on the basis of the principle of democratic self-determination that permanent nonresidents should be disenfranchised in political communities in which they no longer reside (2005: 216–217).
7. Anna Stilz argues, for instance, that descendants of people who have been moved around as a result of changing borders have a legitimate claim to the new state territory as a condition of the stable exercise of their autonomy, whereas the descendants of those displaced lose a legitimate claim to the territory of the displaced person's state, and acquire claims in the territory of the new state they are a member of (2011: 582–587).

REFERENCES

Abizadeh, Arash, 2008. Democratic theory and border coercion. *Political Theory*, 36(1), pp.37–65.

Abizadeh, Arash, 2012. On the demos and its kin: nationalism, democracy, and the boundary problem. *American Political Science Review*, 106(04), pp.867–882.

Beitz, Charles R., 2000. Rawls's law of peoples. *Ethics* 110(4), pp.669–696.

Benhabib, Seyla, 2004. *The rights of others: aliens, residents, and citizens*. Cambridge, MA: Cambridge University Press.

Carens, Joseph H., 1987. Aliens and citizens: the case for open borders. *The Review of Politics*, 49(2), pp.251–273.

Dovi, Suzanne, 2002. Preferable descriptive representatives: will just any woman, black, or Latino do? *The American Political Science Review*, 96(4), pp.729–743.

Fraser, Nancy, 2010. *Scales of justice: reimagining political space in a globalizing world*. Reprint edition. New York: Columbia University Press.

Goodin, Robert E., 2007. Enfranchising all affected interests, and its alternatives. *Philosophy & Public Affairs*, 35(1), pp.40–68.

Gould, Carol C., 2006. Self-determination beyond sovereignty: relating transnational democracy to local autonomy. *Journal of Social Philosophy*, 37(1), pp.44–60.

Held, David, 2005. Democratic accountability and political effectiveness from a cosmopolitan perspective. In: David Held and Mathias Koenig-Archibugi, eds. *Global governance and public accountability*. Oxford: Blackwell. pp.240–267.

López-Guerra, Claudio, 2005. Should expatriates vote? *Journal of Political Philosophy*, 13(2), pp.216–234.

Miller, David, 2009. Democracy's domain. *Philosophy & Public Affairs*, 37(3), pp.201–228.

Miller, David, 2010. Why immigration controls are not coercive: a reply to Arash Abizadeh. *Political Theory*, 38(1), pp.111–120.

Näsström, Sofia, 2011. The challenge of the all-affected principle. *Political Studies*, 59(1), pp.116–134.

Nozick, Robert, 1977. *Anarchy, state, and utopia*. New York: Basic Books.

Owen, David, 2012. Constituting the polity, constituting the demos: on the place of the all affected interests principle in democratic theory and in resolving the democratic boundary problem. *Ethics & Global Politics*, 5(3), pp.129–152.

Rehfeld, Andrew, 2005. *The concept of constituency: Political representation, democratic legitimacy, and institutional design*. Cambridge MA: Cambridge University Press.

Risse, Mathias, 2008. "Imagine there's no countries": a reply to John Lennon. *HKS Working Paper No. RWP08-020* Harvard Kennedy School.

Saunders, Ben, 2012. Defining the demos. *Politics, Philosophy & Economics*, 11(3), pp.1–22.

Scanlon, Thomas, 1976. Nozick on rights, liberty, and property. *Philosophy & Public Affairs*, 6(1), pp.3–25.

Schumpeter, Joseph A., 1962. *Capitalism, socialism, and democracy*. 3rd ed. New York: Harper Perennial.

Sen, Amartya, 2009. *The idea of justice*. 1st ed. Cambridge, MA: Belknap Press of Harvard University Press.

Shapiro, Ian, 2001. *Democratic justice*. New Haven, CT: Yale University Press.

Stilz, Anna, 2011. Nations, states, and territory. *Ethics*, 121(3), pp.572–601.

Young, Iris Marion, 2002. *Inclusion and democracy*. New York: Oxford University Press.

CHAPTER 18

··

DEMOCRACY AND FREEDOM

··

JASON BRENNAN

FREE countries tend to be democratic; democratic countries tend to be free. Unfree countries tend to be non-democratic, and non-democratic countries tend to be unfree. Why?

There seems to be an intimate connection between democracy and freedom. But the nature of this connection is disputed. Some hold it is merely a positive correlation: the background conditions that tend to cause liberal politics also tend to produce democratic political structures. Some think there is causation: perhaps liberalism causes democracy, democracy causes liberalism, or they are mutually reinforcing.

Many people—including most American laypeople—insist that democracy is not merely positively correlated with liberalism, and is indeed more than a useful instrument for promoting liberty. They believe that democratic politics itself is an important kind of freedom, that democracy is essential to freedom, or that the rights to vote, run for office, and participate are themselves constitutive of what it means to be free.

This chapter outlines possible connections between democracy and freedom. First, it will be shown that there is indeed a robust positive correlation between democracy and various forms of liberal freedom. Second, the chapter will examine and critique an argument purporting to show that exercising equal political power in a democracy directly enhances citizens' autonomy by making them authors of the laws. Third, the chapter will examine and critique the argument that republican democracy is essential to enhancing freedom because it prevents citizens from being dominated. It is argued that we should be skeptical of these latter two positions.

1. DEMOCRACY AND LIBERALISM DEFINED

··

At base, "democracy" refers to a range of ways of allocating political decision-making rights. Democracy is an answer to the question, who rules? As Thomas Christiano (2006) elaborates, the term democracy "refers very generally to a method of group decision making characterized by a kind of equality among the participants at an essential stage of the collective decision making." David Estlund (2008: 38) says democracy is the "actual collective authorization of laws and policies by the people subject to them."

Democracy is defined here as a system of government in which fundamental political power is shared equally by all adult members of society. A regime will be called democratic to the extent it has regular, competitive elections, without electoral fraud or manipulation, and with universal adult suffrage (Economist Intelligence Unit, 2012; Freedom House, 2013).

A country will be counted as liberal to the extent it recognizes and effectively protects basic civil and economic rights. Among civil liberties are included the right to free speech, free assembly, free association, freedom of conscience, right of bodily integrity and freedom from abuse and assault, freedom of lifestyle choice, rights to protest, the right to exit, and freedom of sexual choice. The definition also includes liberal procedural rights in the criminal justice system, including rights against unwarranted search and seizure, the right to a fair and expeditious trial, the right to be presumed innocent until proven guilty, the right to hear and question one's accusers, and habeas corpus. Among economic liberties are included the right to acquire, hold, use, give, and in many cases destroy personal property, to make and enter into contracts, to buy and sell goods and services on terms to which all parties consent, to choose one's occupation, to negotiate the terms under which one will work, to manage one's wealth, to create things for sale, to start, run, and stop businesses, to own private property in the means of production, to develop property for productive purposes, and to take risks with capital.

It is not claimed that by definition democracies recognize and protect citizens' civil or economic liberties. Some might wish to say a country that severely curtails civil liberties should not qualify as democratic, even if it has regular contested elections. However, our goal here is to determine whether a particular way of allocating political decision-rights correlates with liberal freedom. For that purpose, we should avoid loading liberalism into the very definition of democracy.

2. How Free Are Citizens of Democracies?

Liberalism and democracy are not connected on a conceptual level. At least in principle, a non-democratic regime could fully realize liberal freedoms. Similarly, a democracy could run roughshod over its citizens' civil and economic liberties. If there is a connection between liberalism and democracy, this will be an interesting empirical finding.

We cannot measure degrees of freedom or democracy as easily as we can measure GDP, life expectancy, or height. However, each year various institutes, think tanks, and foundations conduct extensive research on the political conditions around the world. For example, Canada's Fraser Institute produces the widely cited annual "Economic

Freedom of the World" index. *The Wall Street Journal*, in conjunction with the Heritage Institute, also produces an annual Index of Economic Freedom. Freedom House and *The Economist* each produce similar ratings of protection for civil liberties, as well as indices that score countries on how well they implement basic democratic electoral procedures. Using such indices, we can examine whether various liberal freedoms and democratic political procedures tend to be correlated.

Freedom House's "political rights" score and *The Economist*'s "electoral process and pluralism" score are both meant to measure the degree to which countries have universal adult suffrage and free, open, competitive, and uncorrupt elections. Countries that fail to have these things—whether they are active monarchies, dictatorships, communist single party states, or whatnot—receive bad scores. Both indices try to avoid conflating political rights with *other* civil or economic liberties. Thus, if there turns out to be any correlation between, say, Freedom House's "political rights" score and various measures of economic or civil liberty, this is an interesting rather than trivial result.

Many countries that Freedom House or *The Economist* describe as authoritarian are democracies *on paper*. They have constitutions that formally guarantee competitive elections, universal suffrage, and fair voting rights. But Freedom House and *The Economist* do not rate a country as democratic unless it actually uses democratic procedures. Similarly, the Fraser Institute and *The Wall Street Journal* do not rate countries as economically free merely because their constitutions "guarantee" the rule of law or substantive due process in protecting property rights. They score countries by what they do, not what their constitutions say they will do.

As figure 18.1 shows, there is a clear and strong positive correlation between democracy and economic freedom. Note that in figure 18.1, a *lower* political rights score counts as *more* democratic. Freedom House scores the freest countries a 1 and the least free countries a 7. Thus, the negative slope of the regression line shows a positive correlation between political rights and economic freedom.

Using different measures gets similar results. If we substitute *The Wall Street Journal*'s rankings for the Fraser Institute's, the correlation increases slightly to 0.4994. If we

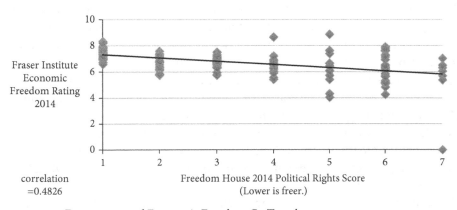

FIGURE 18.1. Democracy and Economic Freedom Go Together

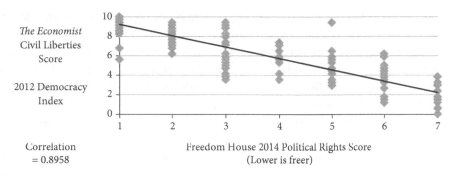

The Economist
Civil Liberties
Score

2012 Democracy
Index

Correlation
= 0.8958

Freedom House 2014 Political Rights Score
(Lower is freer)

FIGURE 18.2. Democracy and Civil Liberties Go Together

substitute *The Economist*'s electoral process and pluralism ratings for Freedom House's political rights scores, the correlation drops slightly to 0.4669. Regardless, the correlations are similar and robust.

As figure 18.2 shows, there is an even stronger positive relationship between democracy and civil liberties. Here, *The Economist*'s measure of civil liberties is graphed against Freedom House's Political Rights score. Once again, for Freedom House, a lower political rights score indicates a country is *more* democratic. Thus, the negative slope represents a positive correlation.

Once again, substituting different rating systems yields similar results. (The correlation holds steady at around 0.9.)

Figure 18.2 might be misleading because it provides a snapshot of conditions at any given year. Sometimes democratic countries elect bad leaders who seize power for themselves. When democracies collapse into authoritarianism, leaders tend to suppress democratic procedures and civil liberties at the same time.[1] Since the protection of political rights and of civil liberties tend to fall in tandem, the correlation seen above might overstate just how much protection democracy offers on behalf of liberal rights. Countries that currently have high political rights scores also have high civil liberties scores, but some such countries are vulnerable to collapse.

In common English, we use the words "liberty" and "freedom" not merely to refer to a range of civil and economic rights, but also to refer to the power or capacity to achieve one's ends. We say that Superman is free to fly while I am not, not because no one *stops* him from flying, but because he has the *power* to fly. For this reason, G. A. Cohen (1995: 58) claims that wealth and positive freedom are intimately connected. Cohen argues that "to have money is to have freedom." The more wealth one has, the more one is able to do, and in that sense, the more freedom one has.

For the sake of argument, let us accept Cohen's argument and ask, do people in democracies tend to have more positive liberty? As figure 18.3 shows, they do.

Once again, substituting different measures of freedom or different GDP/GNI estimates yields similar results.

As seen in figure 18.4, which is reproduced from Gwartney, Lawson, and Hall, 2015: 24, if we confine ourselves to looking at the absolute levels of income held by the

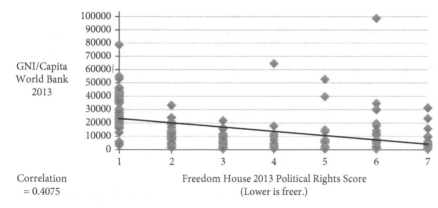

Correlation
= 0.4075

Freedom House 2013 Political Rights Score
(Lower is freer.)

FIGURE 18.3. Democratic Countries Tend to Be Richer

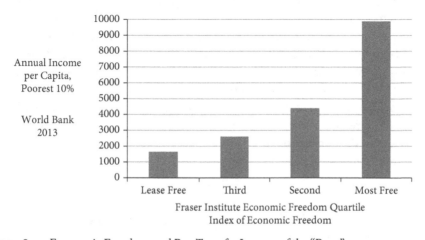

Fraser Institute Economic Freedom Quartile
Index of Economic Freedom

FIGURE 18.4. Economic Freedom and Pre-Transfer Income of the "Poor"

bottom deciles in the most and least democratic countries, we get similar results. Note that the graph below shows absolute, purchasing price parity-adjusted levels of income *before* any welfare payments have been made. Since richer and freer countries tend to have more generous welfare systems, figure 18.4 understates the disparity in the standard between the bottom 10 percent in the economically freer and the less free countries.

Of course, strong correlation does not imply causation. These correlations do not tell us whether democratic politics tends to lead to liberal results, whether liberal politics tends to lead to democracy, whether some third factor tends to produce both, or whether democracy and liberalism tend to be mutually reinforcing. There is an extensive literature debating this question. There are empirical papers supporting each position, as well as papers arguing that democracy and liberalism are in tension, despite their strong correlation.

For instance, Daron Acemoglu and James Robinson (2013) recently argued that regimes fall into two broad types: extractive and inclusive. In extractive regimes, power is concentrated into the hands of the few, and these few in turn use their power to expropriate wealth and dominate the majority. In inclusive regimes, power is widely dispersed. Institutions and laws in inclusive regimes tend to be designed to benefit the majority of citizens. Inclusive regimes tend to enjoy the rule of law, respect for private property, and reduced economic rent seeking. In turn, this leads to greater economic prosperity and respect for civil rights.

Despite these correlations, we should not assume that democracies are liberal because most citizens in democracies are strong advocates of liberalism. As Scott Althaus, Bryan Caplan, and Martin Gilens each conclude (using different surveys and data sets), the modal and median citizens in the United States are much less supportive of economic or civil liberties than more elite, educated, and higher income citizens. For instance, Caplan (2001; 2007: 51) shows that while educated or high IQ voters support free trade, the modal American advocates economic protectionism. Gilens (2012: 106–111) similarly finds that educated, rich voters are more in favor of protecting civil liberties than typical voters, especially poor and uneducated voters. Elites tend to support same-sex marriage, oppose the Patriot Act, oppose torture, and advocate widespread access to birth control and abortion services, while modal and poor American voters tend to have the opposite preferences. Althaus (2003: 11) obtains similar results: the typical and median voter is less in favor of economic or civil liberty than the more knowledgeable voter. The United States is significantly freer than we would expect it to be if politicians just gave the majority of voters exactly what they want. The policies that actually obtain are generally more liberal than what the model, mean, or median voter wants. Gilens (2012: 80) argues this is because presidents and other leaders are much more responsive to the expressed policy preferences of the rich than the poor.

3. DEMOCRACY AND AUTONOMY

Many people believe democracy is more than just a useful instrument for producing liberal freedom. In the United States, most laypeople regard the American War of Independence as a fight for freedom, not because victory was expected to produce any spectacular gains in liberal rights, but simply because it replaced a foreign constitutional monarchy with democratic self-rule. In their view, Americans became free because they became their own lawmakers.

This conception of freedom—that to be free is to be the author of the laws—has a long history. Benjamin Constant (1988: 81) claims that the ancient Greeks and Romans viewed freedom not as a matter of liberal rights, but as authorship of the law:

> the liberty . . . of the ancients . . . consisted in exercising collectively, but directly, several parts of the complete sovereignty; in deliberating, in the public square, over war and peace; . . . But if this was what the ancients called liberty, they admitted as compatible with this collective freedom the complete subjection of the individual to the authority of the community.[2]

Isaiah Berlin (1997: 178) similarly noted that one prominent conception of liberty identifies liberty with autonomous self-control, and, in particular, with "self-government": "[One] sense of the word liberty derives from the wish on the part of the individual to be his own master." On this conception of liberty, what makes a citizen free is not that his government leaves him alone, but that he is a part of that government.

In this vein, Justine Lacroix argues that *exercising* one's equal political rights in a democracy enhances autonomy. She says (2007: 192), "Liberty . . . is rather akin to the concept of autonomy, that is to say that liberty does not mean the absence of law but rather the respect of the laws that men have made and accepted for themselves." She thinks for citizens to be autonomous, it is not enough that one merely possess the right to vote, but must also actively vote. (Indeed, she thinks they should be *forced* to vote.)

Many democratic theorists—from Rousseau onward—believe democracy uniquely enables citizens to realize autonomous self-government. In an idealized democracy, the governed are themselves the authors of the laws that govern them; any constraints imposed by law are constraints they themselves imposed. Thus, the thought is, democracy enables citizens to be fully autonomous. In contrast, in a non-democratic system, citizens will always subject to laws that are not of their own making or choosing. The laws will in some way be imposed upon them.

One problem with trying to link democracy and autonomy on the conceptual level is that, in the real world, what democratic governments do is not entirely a matter of the will of the people. First, it is unclear whether we can attribute to a winning majority a collective will or point of view (Arrow, 1950). Second, as Gilens (2012) has shown, in real-life democracies, some voters count more than others. In the United States, presidents are about six times more responsive to the policy preferences of the rich than the poor. Third, congresspeople, bureaucrats, and administrators do not merely implement the will of the people, but have agendas of their own (Mueller, 2003). In response to worries like these, some democratic theorists claim the problem is just that real-life democracy falls short of the ideal; in an ideal, properly functioning democracy, citizens would be fully autonomous authors of the laws.

But this brings out a deeper problem, a problem that remains even in ideal conditions. Suppose every voter counted the same, and suppose government agents were mere technicians who scrupulously carried out the will of the democratic majority. Even here, while the democratic majority as a collective would have autonomy, it is unclear why this would enhance the autonomy of individual citizens. In an idealized democracy, the answer to the question of "Who rules?" is "*We*—but not you or I." Democracy empowers collectives, not individuals.

For the sake of argument, grant that by voting, a citizen can become the partial author of the laws that govern her. Grant that if she abstains, or if she is denied the right to vote, then she has no partial authorship over the laws, and thus the laws are in some way imposed upon her. Notice, however, that even on this charitable assumption, voting confers autonomy upon a voter only if her side wins. If her side loses, then she is not in part the author of the laws.

However, even if her side wins, and if she is thus a partial author of the law, it remains unclear why we should regard this as conferring upon her any morally significant degree of autonomy. In a properly functioning democracy, each citizen has an equal share of fundamental political power. But this is a small share indeed. There are 210 million eligible voters in the United States, so by law I hold 1/210 millionth of the fundamental political power in the United States. This does not empower me in any significant way. If I were to vote against a hawkish candidate, it is not as though the resulting wars will be fought a 210-millionth degree less aggressively. If I were to vote for open borders, it is not as though the borders would become a 210-millionth more open. Rather, for any one of us in a contemporary democracy, regardless of *whether* one votes or abstains, and regardless *how* one votes, the same political outcomes would happen anyway. We each have some power, but our individual power does not matter.

An individual's vote has an effect on political outcomes only if she changes the outcome of the election. Casting a vote is like playing the lottery—there is some small chance that a single vote will break a tie. But the probability that a voter will break a tie is vanishingly small (Brennan and Lomasky, 1993: 56–57, 119).[3] Individual votes rarely matter. Thus, even if a voter in a winning coalition is in some way causally responsible for the laws, it seems extravagant to call her the autonomous author of the laws, or to claim that the laws that govern her are laws she herself imposed.

Robert Nozick (1974: 290–292) gently mocks the theory that democracy grants individual citizens autonomy with a story called the "Tale of the Slave." Suppose Hagar the Slave has a cruel master, who imposes arbitrary punishments. As the master ages, he becomes kinder. He only punishes Hagar for violating posted rules. When the master dies, he bequeaths all 10,001 of his slaves, including Hagar, to 10,000 of the slaves, excluding Hagar. As a result, 10,000 other slaves collectively own everyone, including Hagar. For Hagar, this just means she now has a 10,000-headed master rather than a one-headed master. Her new 10,000-headed master sometimes asks her for advice about what rules should be imposed upon all 10,001 slaves. As a reward for her advice, they grant her the right to make that decision herself whenever the 10,000 masters are evenly split—5,000 to 5,000—over what to do. Finally, since they have never been evenly split, they just include Hagar's vote with theirs all the time.

At the end of the story, many readers think the slave never stopped being a slave. But by the end of the story, the situation resembles modern democracy. Being an equal member of a rule-making body, especially a large one, does not give one much control. Each slave in the Tale of the Slave can legitimately claim that everyone else makes all the decisions and that the decisions the collective makes would have occurred without her input. Individuals have no power.

In a democracy, the majority of voters, considered as a collective, in some sense rule themselves and everyone else. If majorities frequently change, every citizen might eventually have the opportunity to be part of a winning majority. But it is unclear why we should regard this as empowering individual citizens, or giving them greater real autonomy. Individual citizens have only a vanishingly small chance of making a difference. Even when an individual votes in favor of the winning side, had she reversed her vote, or refused to vote at all, the same political outcomes would have occurred anyway.

4. DEMOCRACY AND NON-DOMINATION

"Neo-republican" political philosophers argue that there is a tight connection between democracy (of a sort) and freedom. Notably, they do so in part because they reject the traditional liberal conception of freedom. They can accept the points made above—that is, that while democracy and liberal freedom are strongly correlated, it is conceptually possible to have one without the other. But, they argue, liberals have a defective conception of freedom. Once we replace this defective conception with a superior one, we will see that freedom and democracy (of the right sort) are tightly bound, and not merely as a matter of empirical correlation.

Republican political theorist Philip Pettit asks, what is problematic about the master-slave relationship? It is not merely that the master might be cruel to the slave, or might interfere with the slave. To see why, imagine you are a slave with an unusually kind and liberal master. The master never issues any orders or interferes with you in any way. However, Pettit says, you remain in some important sense *less* free than non-slaves. While the master does not interfere with you or control you, he retains the right and ability to do so.

Isaiah Berlin, in his famous (1997) essay on different conceptions of liberty, claims that liberals tend to regard freedom as the absence of interference from others. Pettit maintains that this liberal conception of liberty cannot properly explain what is wrong with the master-slave relationship. After all, no one interferes with the slave, but the slave remains unfree. Pettit thinks we thus need a third conception of liberty: liberty as non-domination. Freedom is not the absence of interference; rather, freedom is the absence of *domination.*

One person (call him the dominator) is said to dominate another person (call him the victim) when the dominator has the capacity to interfere with the victim's choices, and the dominator can exercise this capacity at will, with impunity (Pettit, 1996: 581). On this definition of freedom, a person is free only when she is not subject to the arbitrary will of another.

Republicans hold that a properly constituted democracy is essential to realizing freedom as non-domination. Though republicans have a different conception of liberty from liberals, they concur with liberals that unlimited direct democracy would undermine citizens' freedom. Like liberals, they advocate due process of law, checks and balances, separation of powers, and constitutionally protected rights of free speech and assembly (Lovett, 2014). Like liberals, they also recognize that these devices are imperfect. In any democratic government, government agents—from police officers to bureaucrats to senators—will always enjoy some degree of arbitrary power over others.

Republicans hold that to prevent domination and to reduce the degree to which government agents wield this arbitrary power, citizens must be actively engaged with politics. Frank Lovett (2014) says,

> The standard republican remedy . . . is enhanced democracy. . . . Roughly speaking, the idea is that properly-designed democratic institutions should give citizens the effective opportunity to contest the decisions of their representatives. This possibility of contestation will make government agents wielding discretionary authority answerable to a public understanding of the goals or ends they are meant to serve and the means they are permitted to employ. In this way, discretionary power can be rendered non-arbitrary in the sense required for the secure enjoyment of republican liberty.

To "enhance" democracy in this way, republicans hold that we need two major sets of changes. First, there must be *greater public deliberation*. Political decision-makers, such as legislative bodies, courts, or bureaucracies, routinely should present the rationale behind their decisions in public fora, where the public may challenge and debate these reasons. Some republicans argue that some such fora should serve as "courts of appeals," in which citizens can object to or even overturn decisions (Pettit, 2012). Second, there should be greater *inclusion and real political equality*. All citizens must have an equal right to participate in such public contestation. Republicans hold that formal political equality is not enough. Some citizens (in virtue of wealth, family, or prestige) have more de facto influence and power than others. To ensure that all citizens can participate on an equitable basis, there should be limits on campaign financing, advertising, and lobbying. In summary, republicans think that regular, contested, competitive elections are not enough. They think we need deliberative democracy both before and after decisions are made. We need to protect the political sphere from being unduly influenced by money, fame, or other irrelevant factors.

Thus, republicans, unlike liberals, deny that citizens under a benevolent liberal dictator would be free. Republicans advocate what they regard as a distinct and superior conception of liberty, and hold that a robustly participatory and deliberative democratic regime of the right sort is essential to realizing this form of freedom.

Note that many republicans do not merely hold that freedom as non-interference needs to be supplemented with freedom as non-domination. They regard freedom as non-domination as an *alternative*. Thus, many republicans are skeptical of traditional liberal freedoms. They are committed to many traditional liberal rights only insofar as such rights are necessary to ensure equitable deliberative democracy. On this point, Brennan and Lomasky (2006: 240) complain,

> In a Pettit republic, the determinations of democratic majorities bring about far fewer restrictions of individual liberty than is the case in liberal democracies. That is not because political rule is exercised with a lighter hand; just the reverse. Rather, it is because republicans decline to classify most impositions on individual preferences as liberty restricting.

For instance, republicans are comfortable with a remarkable degree of paternalistic intervention into citizens' private lives. The state must consider the *interests* of citizens, but not necessarily their *preferences*, and so, on the republican view, the state may continually impose upon citizens what it deems to be in citizens' best interest (Brennan and Lomasky, 2006: 241). For many republicans, it does not matter if a state continuously and actively interferes with its citizens' lives. So long as citizens are not *dominated*— because they enjoy regular opportunities to deliberate and contest the laws as equals— these citizens count as free.

The original theoretical motivation for republicanism was supposed to be a defect in the traditional liberal conception of freedom as non-interference. Supposedly, liberals cannot adequately explain just what makes slaves unfree. Recall Pettit's point: even if a master never interferes with or controls the slave, the master *could* do so with impunity.

However, to liberals, this seems less like a deep challenge and more like a call for clarification. Perhaps Berlin's essay is misleading—perhaps it is not really true, pace Berlin, that liberals traditionally hold that a person is free if and only if no one interferes with her. Liberals seem to have a ready explanation for why even slaves with kind, liberal masters are nevertheless unfree. The problem is that slaves lack adequately enforced rights against interference. A liberal could just say that a person is free to the extent that her rights against interference are adequately protected from threats. This formulation of the liberal conception of freedom might sound almost the same as freedom as non-domination, but, as Brennan and Lomasky complained above, republicans are happy to license frequent state interference in ways that liberals would count as rights violations. One way of stating Brennan and Lomasky's worry about republicanism, then, is that republican "freedom as non-domination," as far as liberals are concerned, is compatible with the state dominating individuals.

If slavery is legal, the law fails to recognize the slave as a rights-holder, and instead treats her as chattel. If slavery is illegal but the master still enslaves her, then the problem is that no government or agency successfully protects the slave's liberal rights. So, perhaps Berlin's definition of liberal freedom is indeed inadequate, but it remains unclear whether, to explain what makes slaves unfree, we must reject liberalism and accept republicanism.

A further problem with republicanism is that its institutional recommendations may be unrealistic. If so, then the institutional recommendations might protect republican freedom in ideal conditions, but not in realistic conditions. If so, then republicanism would do little to justify real-world democracy.

To see why the republican institutional recommendations might be unrealistic, consider the role of democratic deliberation in their theories. Republicans and deliberative democrats imagine deliberation as being like an idealized philosophical discussion. They imagine deliberators as sincere, open-minded, consistent, and rational speakers, who are committed to finding consensus and who avoid manipulating one another. (Habermas, 2001: 65). They thus expect deliberation to enlighten and ennoble participants, to lead to consensus, and to generate better political policy.

For instance, Hélène Landemore (2012: 97) says, "Deliberation is supposed to . . . Enlarge the pools of ideas and information . . . ., Weed out the good arguments from the bad . . ., [and] Lead to a consensus on the 'better' or more 'reasonable' solution." Bernard Manin, Elly Stein, and Jane Mansbridge (1987: 354) say that democratic deliberation is a process of training and education. Amy Gutmann and Dennis Thompson (1996: 9) claim that even when deliberation fails to produce consensus, it will generally cause citizens to respect one another more.

The problem, though, is that real-world deliberation rarely proceeds the way deliberative democrats want it to proceed, and it (thus?) rarely delivers the results they want it to deliver. Diana Mutz (2006: 5) remarks, "It is one thing to claim that political conversation has the *potential* to produce beneficial outcomes if it meets a whole variety of unrealized criteria, and yet another to argue that political conversations, as they actually occur, produce meaningful benefits for citizens." In a comprehensive survey of the empirical research on democratic deliberation, Tali Mendelberg (2002: 154) concludes that the "empirical evidence for the benefits that deliberative theorists expect" is "thin or non-existent." For instance, deliberation generally tends to exacerbate conflict rather then mediate it (Mendelberg, 2002: 158). Instead of debating the facts, people try to win positions of influence and power over others (Mendelberg, 2002: 159). High-status individuals talk more, are perceived as more accurate and credible, and have more influence, regardless of whether the high-status individuals actually know more (Mendelberg, 2002: 165–167). Deliberators use language in biased and manipulative ways (Mendelberg, 2002: 170–172). Deliberation tends to cause group polarization; it moves people toward more extreme versions of their ideologies rather than toward more moderate versions (Sunstein, 2002). Deliberation often causes deliberators to choose positions inconsistent with their own views, positions which the deliberators "later regret" (Ryfe, 2005: 54). Rather than causing consensus, public deliberation might cause disagreement and the formation of in-groups and out-groups (Hibbing and Theiss-Morse, 2002). It can even lead to violence (Mutz, 2006: 89). And so on.

Further, even if republicans are correct that checks and balances, deliberative fora, courts of appeals, and the like would help reduce domination, it is unclear why this requires *universal* adult suffrage. To illustrate with a simple case, suppose that everyone in the country were allowed to vote and deliberate, except for *me*. While this might make me a "second-class citizen" and might be objectionable on egalitarian grounds, it seems unlikely that this would cause me to be dominated or would reduce my freedom in any meaningful way. If, despite the rule of law, checks and balances, and widespread deliberation, politicians and others can still interfere arbitrarily with my life, granting me the right to vote or deliberate would not suddenly stop them dominating me. As we discussed above, individuals have vanishingly little effective political power.

Now, if were to disenfranchise an entire race or group of citizens with shared interests—for example, all blacks—this probably would expose them to the threat of domination. But it does not follow that widespread disenfranchisement necessarily exposes citizens to domination.

One of the major debates in contemporary democratic theory is whether we should prefer democracy to epistocracy. An epistocracy is a political system in which, as a matter of law, citizens receive political power in proportion to their political knowledge (Estlund, 2008). The primary motivation behind epistocracy is a concern that most citizens in contemporary democracies are ignorant or misinformed about the relevant facts and social scientific theory needed to form sound political preferences (Delli Carpini and Keeter, 1996; Somin, 2013). Epistocrats believe that limiting the political power of the ignorant or misinformed might produce better political outcomes for all; it might better serve the common good. For instance, an epistocrat might advocate that the rights to vote or run for office should be conditional upon passing a test of basic political knowledge (Brennan, 2011), or that the highly educated should have extra votes (Mill, 1861).

While there are many important objections against epistocracy, epistocracy appears to be compatible with republican liberty, if not republican concerns for equality. Consider a form of epistocracy in which suffrage is restricted only to citizens who can pass a test of basic political knowledge. Suppose only the top 50 percent of citizens pass the exam. Will this top half of voters thus dominate the other half? It seems unlikely. An epistocracy could retain the other "enhancements" republicans favor—deliberative fora, citizens' courts of appeal, limits on campaign spending, and so on. If these procedural checks and balances would prevent government officials or special interest groups from dominating citizens when everyone is allowed to participate, it is not clear why they would suddenly fail if ignorant or misinformed citizens were not allowed to vote.

Further, ignorant and misinformed citizens are only contingently excluded. They *can* acquire rights to vote and participate; they just have not. In both a democracy and an epistocracy, "Elected officials serve, if not at the pleasure of citizens, at least in the absence of gross displeasure." (Brennan and Lomasky, 2006: 234). If an epistocracy starts to mistreat ignorant citizens, they could acquire voting rights by studying harder. And if they are not able to study hard enough to acquire such rights, it is unclear why giving them voting rights would protect them. They are, by hypothesis, badly informed. Even if they could vote, they mostly likely do not have the background social scientific knowledge needed to cast their votes in ways that would protect them.

5. CONCLUSION

Constitutional democracy is strongly correlated with liberal freedom. Democracies generally have a high degree of respect for civil liberties, and a moderate degree of respect for economic freedom. Democracy might also be valuable for other reasons— for example, perhaps it is essential or useful for realizing the right kinds of equality, or perhaps democracies tend to make good political decisions.

But most people tend to equate freedom with democracy and democracy with freedom. Here, we should be more skeptical. While democracy empowers or grants law-making autonomy to collectives, it does not follow that it empowers or grants autonomy to the individuals who form part of those collectives. Widespread democratic participation might be a good thing, but describing it as constitutive or essential to personal liberty is a stretch.

NOTES

1. E.g., Bolivia and Venezuela's political rights and civil rights scores have been declining gradually at the same rate for the past ten years.
2. Raaflaub (2003: 222–223) disagrees—he argues that the ancient Greeks were in fact concerned with modern civil rights as well.
3. One might object that individual voters can "change the mandate." But political scientists are almost uniformly skeptical that mandates exist. See, for instance, Dahl, 1990; Noel, 2010; Grossback, Peterson, and Stimson, 2006; Grossback, Peterson, and Stimson, 2007.

REFERENCES

Acemoglu, Daron, and Robinson, James, 2013. *Why nations fail*. New York: Crown Business.

Althaus, Scott, 2003. *Collective preferences in democratic politics: opinion surveys and the will of the people*. New York: Cambridge University Press.

Arrow, Kenneth J., 1950. A difficulty in the concept of social welfare. *Journal of Political Economy*, 50, pp.328–346.

Berlin, Isaiah. 1997. Two concepts of liberty. In: Henry Hardy, ed. *Isaiah Berlin, The Proper Study of Mankind*. New York: Farrar, Straus, Giroux. pp. 191-243

Brennan, Geoffrey, and Lomasky, Loren, 1993. *Democracy and decision*. New York: Cambridge University Press.

Brennan, Geoffrey, and Lomasky, Loren, 2006. Against reviving republicanism. *Politics, Philosophy, and Economics*, 5, pp.221–252.

Brennan, Jason, 2011. The right to a competent electorate. *Philosophical Quarterly*, 61, pp.700–724.

Caplan, Bryan, 2001. What makes people think like economists? Evidence on economic cognition from the "Survey of Americans and Economists on the Economy." *Journal of Law and Economics*, 44, pp.395–426.

Caplan, Bryan, 2007. *The myth of the rational voter*. Princeton: Princeton University Press.

Christiano, Thomas, 2006. Democracy. In: Edward N. Zalta, ed. *Stanford Encyclopedia of Philosophy*. Available at: <http://plato.stanford.edu/entries/democracy/>.

Cohen, Gerald A., 1995. *Self-ownership, freedom, and equality*. New York: Cambridge University Press.

Constant, Benjamin, 1988. The liberty of the ancients compared with that of the moderns. In: *Constant: Political Writings*, trans. Biancamaria Fontana, pp.308-328. New York: Cambridge University Press.

Dahl, R. A., 1990. The myth of the presidential mandate. *Political Science Quarterly*, 105, pp.355–372.

Delli Carpini, Michael X., and Keeter, Scott, 1996. *What Americans know about politics and why it matters*. New Haven: Yale University Press.

Economist Intelligence Unit, 2012. Democracy Index 2012: democracy at a standstill. Available at: <http://pages.eiu.com/rs/eiu2/images/Democracy-Index-2012.pdf>.

Estlund, David, 2008. *Democratic authority*. Princeton: Princeton University Press.

Freedom House, 2013. Freedom in the World 2013. Available at: http://www.freedomhouse. org/report/freedom-world/freedom-world-2013

Gilens, Martin, 2012. *Affluence and influence*. Princeton: Princeton University Press.

Gutmann, Amy, and Thompson, Dennis, 1996. *Democracy and disagreement*. Cambridge, MA: Harvard University Press.

Grossback, L. J., Peterson, D. A. M., and Stimson, J. A., 2006. *Mandate politics*. New York: Cambridge University Press.

Grossback, L. J., Peterson, D. A. M., and Stimson, J. A., 2007. Electoral mandates in American politics. *British Journal of Political Science*, 37, pp.711–730.

Gwartney, James, Lawson, Robert, and Joshua Hall. 2015. *Economic Freedom of the World: 2015 Annual Report*. Toronto: Fraser Institute.

Habermas, Jürgen, 2001. *Moral consciousness and communicative action*. Cambridge, MA: MIT Press.

Hibbing, John R., and Elizabeth Theiss-Morse. 2002. *Stealth Democracy*. New York: Cambridge University Press.

Lacroix, Justine, 2007. A liberal defense of compulsory voting. *Politics*, 27, pp.190–195.

Landemore, Hélène, 2012. *Democratic reason*. Princeton: Princeton University Press.

Lovett, Frank, 2014. Republicanism. In: Edward N. Zalta, ed. *The Stanford Encyclopedia of Philosophy*. Available at: http://plato.stanford.edu/entries/republicanism/.

Manin, Bernand, Stein, Elly, and Mansbridge, Jane, 1987. On legitimacy and political deliberation. *Political Theory*, 15, pp.333–368.

Mendelberg, Tali, 2002. The deliberative citizen: theory and evidence. In: Michael X. Delli Carpini, Leonie Huddy, and Robert Y. Shapiro, eds. *Political decision-making, deliberation, and participation, vol. 6, Research in micropolitics*, pp.151-194. Amsterdam: Elsevier.

Mill, John Stuart, 1861. Considerations on representative government. Available at: <http://www.constitution.org/jsm/rep_gov.htm>.

Mueller, Dennis, 2003. *Public choice III*. New York: Cambridge University Press.

Mutz, Diana, 2006. *Hearing the other side*. New York: Cambridge University Press.

Noel, Hans, 2010. Ten things political scientists know that you don't. *The Forum*, 8(3), article 12.

Nozick, Robert, 1974. *Anarchy, state, and utopia*. New York: Basic Books.

Pettit, Philip, 1996. Freedom as anti-power. *Ethics*, 106, pp.576–604.

Pettit, Philip, 2012. *On the people's terms: a republican theory and model of democracy*. New York: Cambridge University Press.

Raaflaub, Kurt, 2003. *The discovery of freedom in ancient Greece*. Rev. ed. Chicago: University of Chicago Press.

Ryfe, David, 2005. Does deliberative democracy work? *Annual Review of Political Science*, 8, pp.49–71.

Somin, Ilya, 2013 *Democracy and political ignorance*. Stanford: Stanford University Press.

Sunstein, Cass, 2002. "The law of group polarization," *Journal of Political Philosophy*, 10, pp.175–195.

CHAPTER 19

CAN CONSTITUTIONS LIMIT GOVERNMENT?

MICHAEL HUEMER

1. THE NAIVE THEORY OF CONSTITUTIONAL GOVERNMENT

MANY defenders of limited government propose to rely, at least partly, on a written constitution as a bulwark against undue expansion of governmental power. On a naive conception, one can prevent governmental abuse of power simply by carefully writing down, at the time a government is created, the things that the government should and should not do. The government will then lack any powers not granted to it by its founding document.

Few are so naive as to assume that a government will never in fact abuse its power or violate its constitution. American high school students are regularly taught that a remedy for such occasional violations is provided by their country's form of government: the Supreme Court of the United States carefully reviews laws and other official actions of (the rest of) the government and strikes down those that it finds unconstitutional. More generally, Americans are taught (and generally appear to accept) that theirs is a system of "checks and balances," whereby each of the major branches of government—the legislative, executive, and judicial branches—has distinct powers that it can use to ensure the integrity of the other branches, preventing the others from abusing their power. Thus, Congress' power to impeach the president serves as a check against abuses by the executive. The integrity of the judiciary is ensured by the president's power to appoint Supreme Court justices, together with the requirement of congressional approval for these appointments. The presidential veto power can be used to prevent Congress from passing too many laws. And so on. The Constitution, according to this theory, provided for its own protection precisely by setting up this structure of divided government with a balance of powers.[1]

The experience of the United States, however, indicates that this mechanism is unreliable at best. With a written constitution that would seem to impose such strict limits on the power of the central government as would make most libertarians proud, the United States has nonetheless witnessed sweeping expansions of governmental power over the course of its history of a sort surely never contemplated by the framers of that constitution. Why has the U.S. Constitution so spectacularly failed to restrain the federal government? Must all written constitutions prove similarly impotent, or could a constitution be better designed such that it would effectively restrain its government?

This chapter discusses the empirical evidence of the impotence of a written constitution, using the United States as a case study. It then offers several theoretical explanations for the failure of the Constitution to restrain government as intended. It concludes by proposing three broad constitutional provisions that might have greater success in restraining government.

2. The Failure of Constitutional Government: The American Case

It is easy to see that the U.S. Constitution has not restrained government as it was intended to do. The U.S. Constitution is, as legal documents go, short and easily understandable. Of particular interest is Article I, Section 8, which lists the powers granted to Congress, as follows:

> The Congress shall have Power To lay and collect Taxes, Duties, Imposts and Excises, to pay the Debts and provide for the common Defence and general Welfare of the United States; but all Duties, Imposts and Excises shall be uniform throughout the United States;
>
> To borrow money on the credit of the United States;
>
> To regulate Commerce with foreign Nations, and among the several States, and with the Indian Tribes;
>
> To establish an uniform Rule of Naturalization, and uniform Laws on the subject of Bankruptcies throughout the United States;
>
> To coin Money, regulate the Value thereof, and of foreign Coin, and fix the Standard of Weights and Measures;
>
> To provide for the Punishment of counterfeiting the Securities and current Coin of the United States;
>
> To establish Post Offices and Post Roads;
>
> To promote the Progress of Science and useful Arts, by securing for limited Times to Authors and Inventors the exclusive Right to their respective Writings and Discoveries;
>
> To constitute Tribunals inferior to the supreme Court;
>
> To define and punish Piracies and Felonies committed on the high Seas, and Offenses against the Law of Nations;

> To declare War, grant Letters of Marque and Reprisal, and make Rules concerning Captures on Land and Water;
>
> To raise and support Armies, but no Appropriation of Money to that Use shall be for a longer Term than two Years;
>
> To provide and maintain a Navy;
>
> To make Rules for the Government and Regulation of the land and naval Forces;
>
> To provide for calling forth the Militia to execute the Laws of the Union, suppress Insurrections and repel Invasions;
>
> To provide for organizing, arming, and disciplining, the Militia, and for governing such Part of them as may be employed in the Service of the United States, reserving to the States respectively, the Appointment of the Officers, and the Authority of training the Militia according to the discipline prescribed by Congress;
>
> To exercise exclusive Legislation in all Cases whatsoever, over such District (not exceeding ten Miles square) as may, by Cession of particular States, and the acceptance of Congress, become the Seat of the Government of the United States, and to exercise like Authority over all Places purchased by the Consent of the Legislature of the State in which the Same shall be, for the Erection of Forts, Magazines, Arsenals, dock-Yards, and other needful Buildings; And
>
> To make all Laws which shall be necessary and proper for carrying into Execution the foregoing Powers, and all other Powers vested by this Constitution in the Government of the United States, or in any Department or Officer thereof.

That is the entire section, and the entire list of legislative powers. Furthermore, it is undisputed that the Constitution is intended to provide a complete account of the government's powers. This last point is made explicit by the Tenth Amendment:

> *Amendment 10:* The powers not delegated to the United States by the Constitution, nor prohibited by it to the States, are reserved to the States respectively, or to the people.

Thus, to the extent that the Constitution genuinely restrains the government, every act of Congress must fall under one or more of the clauses listed above—everything the Congress does must consist in collecting taxes, or borrowing money, or regulating foreign trade, etc.

In fact, the activities listed in Section 8 comprise only a small fraction of the programs and policies presently undertaken by Congress. No clause in Section 8 authorizes Congress to regulate recreational drugs, private firearms, or highway speed limits; to subsidize agriculture, education, science, or the arts; to establish an FDA, EPA, CIA, FBI, NASA, or departments of Agriculture, Education, Energy, Health and Human Services, Homeland Security, Housing and Urban Development, or the Interior. Nothing authorizes the government to control health care, operate a national retirement program, or maintain national parks. This is just to list a few of the most prominent activities authorized by Congress. If one opens to a random page in the Code of Federal Regulations (a set of books currently over 150,000 pages long), one finds regulations covering such minutiae as the spacing of spark plug gaps, the use of the phrase "all day protection" on antiperspirant labels, and the proper way of signing documents in certain obscure financial transactions.[2] At a rough guess, at least 95 percent of the U.S. government's activities are unconstitutional on their face.

The point here is not to attack all of these programs as socially harmful or otherwise ill-advised. Whether these laws and programs are *good policy* would require lengthy discussion that is beyond the scope of this chapter. The present point is simply that their existence testifies to the impotence of the Constitution as a tool for constraining government.

According to the naive theory described in section 1 above, this situation ought to be impossible, because the Supreme Court should strike down such unconstitutional laws. Of course, there will often be reasonable disagreement about whether a law is constitutional or not. But surely when a law is *obviously* unconstitutional, it will be struck down.

Why has this not happened? Historically, an important turning point came during the Great Depression, under the Franklin D. Roosevelt administration. Roosevelt's "New Deal" social programs were initially struck down by the Supreme Court as unconstitutional.[3] In response, Roosevelt proposed the Judicial Procedures Reform Bill of 1937, which would have allowed President Roosevelt to appoint six new judges to the Supreme Court (his so-called "court packing" plan). His intention was evidently to appoint enough people friendly to his politics to outvote the judges who had been opposing his programs. Shortly after Roosevelt introduced this plan, the Court began, by a narrow margin, to reverse course and approve Roosevelt's policies, whereupon Roosevelt abandoned the court packing plan.[4] Even without the court packing plan, during his twelve years in office, Roosevelt had the chance to legitimately appoint eight of nine Supreme Court justices.

Thus it transpired that, by 1942, the Court was staffed with justices who were determined to approve Roosevelt's policies, whatever the Constitution said. Their style of thinking is illustrated by the case of *Wickard vs. Filburn* (317 U.S. 111), decided in that year. Under the Agricultural Adjustment Act of 1938, the government had imposed limits on the amount of wheat that farmers could grow. Roscoe Filburn was a farmer in Ohio who had exceeded his assigned quota of wheat. Filburn disputed the enforcement of the law against him, arguing in court that the excess wheat he produced was used purely on his own farm and that the federal government thus had no authority to regulate this production.

After a district court ruled in favor of Filburn, the government appealed to the Supreme Court, which overruled the district court and ruled unanimously in favor of the government. Their reasoning: as a result of producing this excess wheat, Filburn would buy less wheat from other sources than he otherwise would have. If many people were to act similarly, this would cause the price of wheat to drop. Furthermore, some wheat is traded between states. There would thus be an effect on interstate commerce. Therefore, in restricting Filburn's production of wheat for consumption on his own farm, Congress was exercising its power "to regulate commerce . . . among the several states," as granted in the third clause of Article I, Section 8 of the Constitution.

This is not a reasonable interpretation of that clause. Whether one considers the framers' intent, or the public meaning at the time the Constitution was ratified, or the public meaning at the time of the ruling, or the broad values and principles implicit in the document as a whole, it is not plausible that Justice Jackson's interpretation faithfully explains the meaning of the commerce clause.[5]

The point here is not that the Agricultural Adjustment Act was bad policy (though it can be argued that it was). The point is that decisions of this kind show the failure of the Constitution to limit government. A court that accepts *Wickard* would allow regulation of almost anything, and the willingness to take such interpretive liberties makes it extremely difficult to craft any language limiting the power of government.

3. A Theory of Constitutional Failure

On a theoretical level, the impotence of the U.S. Constitution is unsurprising. There are a number of explanations for this failure. Though the following problems are probably very common among constitutional governments, they are not inevitable; indeed, part of the aim of section 5 will be to describe how most of these problems could be alleviated.

3.1. Who enforces the Constitution?

Laws typically require enforcement. Ordinary statutes are meant to restrain citizens, and they are enforced by the government against individual citizens. The Constitution, on the other hand, is meant to restrain the government. But there is no one more powerful than the government to enforce the law against the government. Therefore, it looks as though the Constitution must be enforced by the government itself. As Madison wrote, "[Y]ou must first enable the government to control the governed; and in the next place oblige it to control itself" (Hamilton, Madison, and Jay, 1952: 163).

There is a prima facie problem with this proposal. Compare the analogous proposal for ordinary statutes: that statutes should be enforced by individuals against themselves; for example, thieves should arrest and prosecute themselves. This proposal inspires little confidence. In the same way, it would seem overly optimistic to expect the government to enforce a law against itself.

3.2. The branches of government are natural allies

Some would address the preceding problem by pointing out that there are different *branches* of government, and thus that one branch may enforce the Constitution against another branch. This theory was advanced by the original defenders of the U.S. Constitution, following the ideas of Montesquieu (Montesquieu, 1748: 11.4, 11.6;

Hamilton, Madison, and Jay, 1952: numbers 47–51; Jefferson, 1782: 214–215). The theory is missing one crucial element: an account of why it would be in the interests of one branch of government to restrain another from abusing its powers.

If one branch of government tries to expand its own powers by taking over the powers of *another branch*, then we might expect that other branch to act to forestall the expansion. But what is of most concern is the case in which a branch of government tries to expand its powers, not at the expense of another branch of government, but at the expense of *the people*, that is, by assuming new powers not granted by the Constitution to any part of the government. Why should a second branch of government be concerned to prevent this kind of abuse?

In this sort of case, there is no genuine opposition among the branches of government. Indeed, all three branches may increase their power simultaneously. If the legislature takes to regulating matters that it is not constitutionally authorized to regulate, the legislature thereby becomes more powerful. The executive branch, whose job is to enforce those laws, and the judicial branch, which interprets those laws and determines when they have been violated, will both also tend to become larger and more powerful as a result of the greater extent of regulation. Thus, if each branch wants to be more powerful, they are natural allies, not opponents.[6]

3.3. The failure of checks and balances

For the same reason, the lauded "checks and balances" of the American system fail to serve their function. The powers that each branch of government has over the others *could* be used to ensure the faithfulness of those other branches to the Constitution. But there is simply no reason for thinking that they would be so used, rather than being used to undermine the Constitution. For example, the president could use his power to appoint Supreme Court justices to ensure that only judges with a firm commitment to the Constitution will be appointed. Or he could use it to ensure that only judges who will rubber stamp expansionist government policies will be appointed. We have no reason to assume that the former would be more likely than the latter.

3.4. The self-image of government

The job of government, presumably, is to govern—that is, to control the people. Similarly, by popular understanding, the job of "lawmakers" is to make laws. If one hires a group of people with a full-time job of making laws, they will search for laws to make, no matter how many laws there already are. This creates a tendency toward overregulation. In existing governmental systems, the legislature also has the power to repeal laws, but neither the legislators themselves nor the citizens see the central job of a legislator as that of removing laws. Almost everyone sees the central job of a legislator as that of making laws.

In the modern United States, an enormous bureaucracy—consisting of such agencies as the FDA, EPA, Department of Health and Human Services, and so on—has been appointed to assume the burden of making detailed regulations, under authority granted by Congress. This army of bureaucrats, again, sees their job as being to regulate, and they are employed full-time in this task. Thus, they are always on the lookout for new ways to restrict and control the activities of people in the sphere to which their particular agency is devoted.

3.5. The lack of punishment

Statutes are typically enforced through punishments assigned to violators, such as fines and imprisonment. Similarly, it is natural to think that a constitution, to be effective, should be enforced through punishments. If one violates the Constitution, to what punishment will one be subject?

In almost all cases, the actual answer is "none." For example, when President Obama ordered the summary execution, via drone strikes, of certain suspected terrorists (including some U.S. citizens) without due process, he had no cause to fear that he would actually be prosecuted and punished for his action, through either jail time or even a monetary fine, even if his action had been found unconstitutional (al-Awlaki, 2013). At most, the Supreme Court might some day hold such executions unconstitutional, in which case they would simply order presidents in the future to desist. Thus, government officials who are interested in violating the Constitution have little reason not to give it a try, since the court may (as in *Wickard*) find in favor of the government—and even if they find against the government, the officials who violated the Constitution will face no punishment.[7]

3.6. The difficulty of challenge

In the American system, one cannot challenge a law or other government action in court merely because one considers the government action unconstitutional. To have "standing" to challenge an action of the federal government, one generally must be directly harmed or be about to be harmed by that action. The harm must be concrete, demonstrable, and directed at oneself or a limited group to which one belongs; it may not be speculative, nor may it be a harm that one bears equally with the rest of society.[8] In some cases, to obtain standing, one must violate the law and be prosecuted, assuming the risk of punishment in the event that one loses the case. Moreover, those who challenge a government action must take on enormous costs in both time and money.

In *Lujan v. Defenders of Wildlife*, environmental groups sued the Secretary of the Interior, intending to argue that the secretary had misinterpreted the Endangered Species Act in a way that would be harmful to certain endangered species. (Briefly, the issue concerned U.S. funding for certain foreign development projects and the secretary's decision that the Endangered Species Act did not apply to such foreign activities.)

The Supreme Court ultimately ruled that the environmental groups lacked standing to sue, because they could not show that *they themselves* would suffer a concrete harm as a result of the secretary's action. It thus did not matter whether the secretary's decision was legally incorrect, nor did it matter how much the decision might harm the natural environment.

Returning to the case of President Obama's extra-judicial execution program, when Anwar al-Awlaki (a U.S. citizen living in Yemen) was targeted for assassination, his father, Nasser al-Awlaki, sued the government to prevent the assassination, arguing that the killing would violate Anwar's constitutional rights. The court rejected Nasser's suit, partly on the grounds that he did not have standing to file it, since he was not himself the target of assassination. To challenge the government, Anwar would have to have first surrendered to American authorities in Yemen and then sought access to U.S. courts.[9]

These cases illustrate, perhaps contrary to the popular understanding, that the Supreme Court sees its role as solely that of resolving courtroom disputes between specific interested parties—not that of enforcing the Constitution or addressing illegal government actions in general.

3.7. Public ignorance

Some defenders of limited government would rest their faith on the democratic process, arguing that leaders who unduly expand governmental power will be voted out of office. If citizens were concerned to preserve the Constitution, this could equally serve as an enforcement mechanism for the Constitution. Unfortunately, however, public knowledge of the U.S. Constitution is low; for example, most Americans cannot even name the three branches of government (Camia, 2011).

There is a well-known, systematic explanation for the failure of democracy (Caplan, 2007; Huemer, 2013: 209–213). Individual voters have almost no incentive to expend the time and effort to become informed or think rationally about political issues, because each individual knows that his probability of personally affecting the outcome of an election is approximately zero. This explains not only why Americans tend to be ignorant of relevant facts about most public policy issues, but also why they tend to have minimal knowledge of their own government's Constitution. As a result, legislators and presidents suffer very little political cost for unconstitutional behavior.

4. WHERE THE CONSTITUTION DID NOT FAIL

Notwithstanding the above observations, the U.S. Constitution has an enormous influence on the present government. There are three important kinds of constitutional provisions: provisions of institutional structure, procedural provisions, and provisions describing substantive powers and constraints (hereafter: structural, procedural, and substantive provisions).

The *structural* provisions of the Constitution have generally been followed faithfully. For instance, the government of the United States is divided into a legislative, an executive, and a judicial branch. The legislature is divided into a House of Representatives and a Senate. The executive branch includes a president and a vice-president. The judicial branch includes a Supreme Court and a variety of inferior courts. All of this is as stated in the founding document.

Likewise, the Constitution's procedural provisions tend to be well-respected. Laws are passed only when a majority of both houses of Congress vote for them. In the case of a presidential veto, the law passes only if a two-thirds supermajority votes for it in both houses. The Senate does not, for example, claim to have created a law despite the failure of the House of Representatives to vote for it.

It is mainly the *substantive* provisions of the Constitution that have been violated. The government has chosen, as in the *Wickard* case described above, to "interpret" descriptions of its powers in an extremely expansive manner.

What is the explanation for this divergence in the treatment of different kinds of constitutional provisions? Perhaps it is easier to pull off a substantive violation than it is to pull off a structural or procedural violation. To bring off a substantive violation, Congress, for example, need only pass a law, using the same lawmaking procedures described in the Constitution, that does not correspond to any of the Congress's enumerated powers.

But how would Congress bring off a procedural violation? The procedural provisions determine what *counts* as the government, or some branch of the government, making a certain decision. The general acceptance of these procedures is part of what enables the government to function. For a government, or any organization, to function, it is important that, even when the members disagree about what decisions *should* have been made, they can still agree upon what decisions *have in fact* been made by the organization. If some members wish to change the decision-making procedures, they must, to avoid chaos, secure general agreement within the organization that the decision-making procedures have been altered—but to secure that agreement, they would generally have to follow the existing procedures.

A structural violation—eliminating an authorized part of government or introducing an unauthorized part—is also difficult to pull off. The elimination of an existing governmental structure is difficult, since the individuals employed in that structure are unlikely to accept its elimination. For instance, if the president were to declare the Supreme Court disbanded, the justices sitting on the Court would reject the pronouncement. The president could then attempt to have the judges arrested, but it is unclear whether law enforcement personnel would obey the president or the judges. The potential for chaos generally deters the branches of government from moves of this kind.

How could a new part of government be created? A group of people not hitherto part of the government could declare themselves to make up a new part of government, but this is very unlikely to be accepted by the rest of society or the existing government.

Another possibility is that the existing government, using its existing decision-making procedures, could create a new part of government, as when Congress creates regulatory agencies tasked with implementing general mandates given them by Congress. It is not clear, however, that this should be considered a violation of the constitutionally prescribed governmental structure.

5. Toward a More Effective Constitution

5.1. Why pursue an effective constitution?

Having seen how and why the U.S. Constitution has failed, we can now ask whether in principle a constitution could be designed so as to avoid such failures, that is, to genuinely restrain the power of government.

Some would regard what has here been called "the failure of the U.S. Constitution" as a *good* thing. Those who support extensive regulation and social programs may be thankful that the Constitution proved impotent, since otherwise an enormous array of regulations and social programs might never have been adopted (their adoption would have required amendments to the Constitution). But the issue here is not really one of the desirability of economic regulation or social welfare programs. The question is whether government can be constitutionally constrained in general. Even those who disagree with the rigorous constraints laid out in the actual U.S. Constitution will usually agree that *some* constraints are appropriate. One can hold that the list of legislative powers in Article I, Section 8 should have been longer, while agreeing that there should be a limited set of legislative powers. Thus, the question of whether and how a constitution can be designed so as to effectively constrain government should be of interest to readers with a range of political persuasions.

Our earlier analysis suggests that mere changes in the *substantive* provisions of the Constitution—the description of the scope of governmental powers—would be of little use. It is not, for example, that government power expanded beyond its intended limits because the interstate commerce clause was unclearly phrased. Rather, the Supreme Court chose, in essence, to nullify substantive constitutional constraints for political reasons. If that is the case, then it does not matter how clearly the substantive provisions are stated. What we should seek, therefore, are *structural* and *procedural* changes that would address the problems listed in section 3 above.

5.2. Supermajority rules

One simple measure would be to require a supermajority vote—say, a two-thirds majority—to pass any legislation.[10]

Substantive provisions, such as those of Article I, Section 8, *if effective*, would be preferable to the blanket measure of making *all* legislation more difficult to pass, since the substantive constraints could specifically target areas where legislation is undesirable. The supermajority rule here contemplated is a comparatively crude measure, which would result in some desirable legislation failing to pass, while some undesirable legislation passed nonetheless. The one advantage of this measure is that, as a procedural provision, it has a better chance of actually being respected.

Why think that a supermajority rule would do more good than harm? There are three broad reasons. First, legislators tend to be biased in favor of making more laws; when in doubt, they will prefer to legislate rather than leave matters alone. This bias exists partly because legislators conceive their job as that of making laws, and partly because human beings in general tend to be biased in favor of intervention. In the case of almost any problem in almost any area, most people find it difficult to countenance doing nothing; indeed, the idea of simply leaving things alone when there is a problem scarcely occurs to people.

Second, the overwhelming majority of potential laws that one might think of are bad; thus, even if the legislature is fairly reliable (say, 70 percent) at judging whether a law is desirable, there will be many more false positives than false negatives. Consider an analogy: very few medical treatments applied before modern times were beneficial, and most were harmful. Why? Given that doctors aimed to help their patients, how could they so systematically fail to do so? Part of the explanation is that the overwhelming majority of interventions in the human body that one might think of are harmful; if one randomly picks something to alter in the body, the chances are close to 100 percent that the alteration will be harmful. This is why one should typically avoid medical interventions unless one has very accurate and detailed knowledge of the human body, of a sort that no one before modern times possessed. In a similar manner, because the overwhelming majority of coercive interventions in society are harmful, one should impose a high bar for justifying any such intervention.[11]

Third, it is generally worse to make a bad law than it is to merely fail to make a good law. This is because it is morally worse to engage in unjustified coercion than it is to merely fail to engage in coercion that would have been justified. For example, it is worse to imprison an innocent person than to fail to imprison a guilty person. Governmental laws generally involve exercises of force; the population is to be coerced into obedience, with force used to impose punishments on those who violate the law. If the law is unjustified, then this will constitute unjustified coercion. Because of the moral seriousness of unjustified coercion, it is better to err on the side of caution when it comes to passing laws.[12]

The proposed supermajority requirement takes account of these concerns in a way that the conventional simple majority rule does not. If it is best to err on the side of caution when it comes to lawmaking, but most lawmakers are instead biased in favor of making more laws, then it makes sense to impose procedural requirements that make it more difficult to pass laws. By and large, when the case for a particular proposed law is very strong, it will be possible to convince a supermajority to vote for that law. When it is not possible to convince so many legislators to endorse a law, this will usually signal that the case for the law is weaker.[13]

Obviously, these are only general tendencies—in some cases, a large supermajority might favor a law for which the case is objectively weak, while in other cases, a law with a very strong case might remain controversial. So the supermajority requirement hardly solves all problems. The claim in its defense is merely that it constitutes some improvement over the simple majority rule.

5.3. The negative legislature

The legislative power should be vested in two separate bodies: a *positive legislature* and a *negative legislature*. What is meant by a "positive legislature" is simply the ordinary sort of legislature that we are familiar with from every country that has had a legislature at all. Its job would be the making of laws.

The idea of a negative legislature, by contrast, has not yet been tried. The negative legislature would be a body (which may be elected in the same manner as the positive legislature) whose sole power would be the *repeal* of existing laws. It would have no power of *passing* any law.

This proposal is intended to address two major problems raised in section 3. One problem was that legislators tend to be biased in favor of regulation, partly because they view "making laws" as their job description. The negative legislators, in turn, would view "repealing laws" as *their* job description. Thus, just as positive legislators are constantly employed in looking for new rules to make and new restrictions to impose, the negative legislators would be employed full-time in looking for ways of removing unnecessary rules and restrictions.

Another problem was that the idea of "checks and balances" in the current U.S. government is hollow, because the branches of government are not genuinely opposed. By contrast, the positive and negative legislatures would be well and truly opposed to each other, since the sole power of the negative legislature would be to undo precisely what the positive legislature had done.

A number of practical issues might arise with this proposal, of which only a few can be discussed here. The first is whether the negative legislature should have the power of repealing only *part* of a law. For instance, if a bill with 100 sections is passed, should the negative legislature be able to repeal Sections 27 through 38, leaving the rest intact? More extremely, should the negative legislature be able to delete only a single sentence from a law? Call this the power of "partial repeal."

Here is an argument for allowing partial repeal: if partial repeal is *not* allowed, then the positive legislature can attempt to push through measures that they know would normally be rejected by the negative legislature, simply by packaging those measures with other provisions that the negative legislature would be loath to remove. Of course, the negative legislature could repeal the law anyway, and hope for the positive legislature to re-pass only the unobjectionable parts. But this game of chicken could be hazardous to society.

Perhaps more importantly, even without any manipulative intentions on the part of the positive legislature, it may often happen that some parts of a law are desirable while others are objectionable. The negative legislature should not be forced to choose between removing the good parts and accepting the bad parts.

On the other hand, here is an argument against allowing partial repeal: removing only part of a law may in some cases drastically alter the effects of the remaining parts. The negative legislature might therefore use the power of partial repeal to in effect pass its own legislation by judiciously choosing which parts of a law to delete. The negative legislature could even *expand* government power by deleting portions of a law that were designed to restrict the powers of government agents.

On the whole, it seems that partial repeal should be permitted. The potential to use this power to in effect produce new legislation or strengthen existing legislation would likely pose a small problem at most. Probably it would not often be possible to use the power to produce some distinct desired law. Furthermore, the negative legislature, due to its self-conception as a remover of laws, would most likely have less motivation for expanding government power than the positive legislature; it is therefore unlikely that the positive legislature would enact restrictions on government power that the negative legislature opposed.

One might worry that partial repeals could simply render laws unworkable, because some portions of a law depend on other portions to work. But this is just a concern that the negative legislature might be foolish in their altering of laws. The ordinary legislature in existing political systems might be similarly foolish, enacting unworkable laws; there is no reason for expecting the negative legislature to be more foolish than an ordinary legislature.

A second question is whether the negative legislature should be subject to the same sort of supermajority voting requirement as the positive legislature. For example, should a two-thirds majority be required to repeal laws?

Since the supermajority requirement is meant to counter a systematic bias in favor of legislation, but the negative legislature only *removes* legislation, there is no need for a supermajority rule in votes of the negative legislature. A simple majority rule should suffice.

One might wonder whether a *sub*majority voting rule should be adopted—for instance, a rule whereby a law is repealed when at least *one-third* of the negative legislature votes to repeal it. This rule, however, would render more serious the risk of the negative legislature strengthening government power by selective repeal of laws or portions of laws. Suppose, for instance, that one-third of the negative legislature opposes a certain statutory restriction on the power of certain government agents; the remaining two-thirds supports the restriction. In such a case, the minority should not be able to remove the restriction. Thus, a simple majority voting rule seems appropriate for the negative legislature.[14]

5.4. The "Constitutional Court"

In addition to the ordinary court system, there should be a "Constitutional Court" dedicated solely to assessing the constitutionality of actions by the rest of the government. This court should differ from the present U.S. Supreme Court in four main ways.

First, as stated, the Constitutional Court would function solely to assess constitutionality. Because the court would have no other duties, it would have more time to devote to the important task of assessing the constitutionality of government actions. A larger number of government actions would thus be subjected to review. In addition, because assessing constitutionality would be the court's sole function, the court would have a stronger self-image as a defender of the Constitution than the present Supreme Court. With nothing else to do, the Constitutional Court would be constantly on the lookout for unconstitutional actions by the government.

Second, though individual citizens could file lawsuits against the government in the Constitutional Court, this would not be the only way of securing judicial review; rather, the Constitutional Court should have the power to initiate cases of its own accord, to review any governmental action for constitutionality, without the need for outside parties to initiate a civil or criminal case. This addresses the problem raised in section 3 concerning the difficulty and expense of challenging unconstitutional government actions. There would need to be a special prosecutor's office devoted particularly to prosecuting the government—that is, to presenting in the Constitutional Court the case against some government action. The rest of the government would send its own attorney to defend itself, as in the present system.

Third, the Constitutional Court's decisions should be rendered by a jury of citizens, with a distinct jury selected for each case, rather than by a panel of professional judges. The reason is that professional judges tend to identify with the authority of the state, as they are themselves government employees and authority figures; as a result, they have a bias in favor of government power. Avoiding this sort of bias is of crucial import for the job of a constitutional court. A jury of ordinary citizens would be more likely to remain relatively free of pro-government bias. More than one jury could be empaneled at a time, enabling multiple cases to be heard at once, thereby increasing the number of government actions subject to review. In the case of statutes under constitutional challenge, the judge should advise the jury on how the courts are likely to construe the statute; nevertheless, the jury should have the authority to reject a statute as unconstitutional for any reason that they deem convincing, even if this reason entails disagreement with the judge on legal matters.

Why would the jurors in these cases make better decisions than ordinary voters, who commonly lack basic knowledge of current issues and of the political system in general? One reason is that both sides would thoroughly present their cases before the jury, over the course of days or weeks if necessary. There is thus reason to believe that jurors would be much more informed about the issues in the case before them than ordinary voters typically are about current political issues. In addition, as a member of a twelve-person body, each juror would have much more reason to believe that his opinion *mattered* than does a person who is only one among millions of voters. Individuals are much more likely to exercise care in forming their positions when they know that they have a serious chance of actually affecting the outcome.

Fourth, the Constitutional Court would have the responsibility to *pass sentence* on government officials found to have violated the Constitution—that is, to order these officials to be punished. Punishments could include removal from office, monetary fines, and imprisonment. Furthermore, no government official should have the power to pardon other government officials for offenses of which they are convicted in the Constitutional Court. The main purpose of this is the same as that of punishments attached to ordinary statutes—to deter future violations. For example, imagine that President George W. Bush had been sent to prison for his decision to authorize warrantless wiretapping. In that scenario, the Obama administration might have been more chary of authorizing mass data collection by the NSA.

6. Conclusion: The Prospects for Limited Government

Enthusiasts for political freedom support either limited government or anarchy. One key objection often raised to limited government is that no one knows how to design a government that will actually remain limited over the long term. The experience of the United States seems to bear out this fear; the U.S. government has in the past 230 years expanded far beyond the limits imposed by its Constitution, notwithstanding the putative checks and balances built into the system. Two questions naturally arise: why has this expansion taken place? And can a government be designed that would avoid it?

A number of factors contributed to the illicit expansion of government. Most notably, the separation of powers failed to restrain government because the three branches of the U.S. government are not genuinely in opposition. Each branch can use its powers as easily to undermine as to defend the Constitution, legislators and regulators believe their job is to make laws, there are no legal punishments attached to constitutional violations, and challenging unconstitutional government actions is difficult and costly.

An improved political system would include one or more of the following provisions: (1) the procedure for passing any new law should require a two-thirds majority vote; (2) there should be a negative legislature with the sole power of repealing existing laws; (3) there should be a court dedicated to reviewing government actions and assigning punishments to government officials guilty of constitutional violations. In the interests of caution, it would be best to adopt all three of these measures in addition to the sort of substantive constraints embodied in existing constitutions.

This is not to say that limited government is feasible or desirable, all things considered (in comparison, for example, to anarchy); it has not been the aim of this chapter to answer that question. The sole question has been: *given* the goal of establishing a limited government, what is the best way of designing a constitution? Whether the measures proposed here would succeed in restraining government remains to be seen. But there is good reason to believe that they would at least improve the prospects for limited government.[15]

NOTES

1. These optimistic views are commonly presented in American civics textbooks; see Dunn and Slann, 2000: 24; McClenaghan, 1994: 56–59.
2. See, respectively, 40 CFR, Appendix I to subpart V of part 85 (H)(1)(b); 21 CFR 350.50(b)(3); 26 CFR 157.6061.
3. See *Carter v. Carter Coal Co.*, 298 U.S. 238 (1936); *A. L. A. Schechter Poultry Corp. v. United States*, 295 U.S. 495 (1935); *Louisville Joint Stock Land Bank v. Radford*, 295 U.S. 555 (1935).
4. See *NLRB v. Jones & Laughlin Steel Corp.*, 301 U.S. 1 (1937); *West Coast Hotel Co. v. Parrish*, 300 U.S. 379 (1937).
5. Balkin (2011: 164–165) argues that *Wickard* was correctly decided. For discussion of the problems with *Wickard* and related decisions, see Epstein, 2014: 168–179.
6. This criticism was first advanced in the Anti-Federalist Papers (Pole, 1987: 62–63; essay XI by Brutus).
7. Government officials *might* suffer political costs, such as loss of voter support, as a result of violating the Constitution. In practice, however, this is very rare. Of course, *unpopular* government actions incur political costs, but constitutionality appears to make little difference to what is popular or unpopular; see point (g) below in the text, and note the popularity of the unconstitutional policies mentioned in section 2 above.
8. *Lujan v. Defenders of Wildlife*, 504 U.S. 555 (1992), pp. 555–556.
9. *Al-Aulaqi v. Obama*, 727 F. Supp. 2d 1 (2010). After the assassination, Nasser al-Awlaki sued various government officials for killing his son; this case was also dismissed in federal court (*Al-Aulaqi v. Panetta*, 35 F. Supp. 3d 56 [2014]).
10. In the original debate about the U.S. Constitution, George Mason proposed such a super-majority rule for commercial and navigation laws (Pole, 1987: 128). For a modern, qualified defense of supermajority rules, see McGinnis and Rappaport, 2007.
11. Cf. McGinnis and Rappaport, 2007: 1165–1168.
12. For elaboration of the second and third points, see Huemer, 2012.
13. An anonymous reviewer points out that most bills pass the U.S. Congress unanimously (see Rybicki, 2008). Nevertheless, some important bills are controversial and would be affected by a supermajority rule. In this minority of cases, the supermajority requirement would probably be beneficial. Another concern is that legislators may resort to logrolling to gather enough votes for the supermajority. However, logrolling should occur mainly when a bill is initially just short of passing. Since there is no particular reason to expect that more bills would fall just short of a two-thirds majority than would fall just short of a simple majority, the frequency of logrolling is unlikely to be significantly affected.
14. Why not a rule whereby removing a *restriction* on government power requires a two-thirds majority, but removing a law that *expands* government power requires only a one-third minority? This is the sort of substantive provision—requiring judgments about what counts as more or less government power—that the government cannot be trusted to faithfully implement (recall section 4 above).
15. I would like to thank two anonymous reviewers for their helpful comments on the manuscript.

REFERENCES

al-Awlaki, Nasser, 2013. The drone that killed my grandson. *New York Times*, [online] July 18, p.A23. Available at: <http://www.nytimes.com/2013/07/18/opinion/the-drone-that-killed-my-grandson.html?_r=0> [accessed January 13, 2014].

Balkin, Jack, 2011. *Living originalism*. Cambridge, MA: Harvard University Press.

Camia, Catalina, 2011. Survey: Americans don't know Constitution, civics. *USA Today*, [online] Sept. 16. Available at: <http://content.usatoday.com/communities/onpolitics/post/2011/09/constitution-knowledge-sandra-day-oconnor-tea-party-/1#.UtEjz5w9CXo> [accessed January 13, 2014].

Caplan, Bryan, 2007. *The myth of the rational voter*. Princeton, NJ: Princeton University Press.

Dunn, Charles, and Slann, Martin, 2000. *American government in comparative perspective*. 2nd ed. New York: Addison-Wesley.

Epstein, Richard, 2014. *The classical liberal constitution: the uncertain quest for limited government*. Cambridge, MA: Harvard University Press.

Hamilton, Alexander, Madison, James, and Jay, John, 1952. *The federalist*. In Robert Maynard Hutchins, ed. *Great Books of the Western World*, vol. 43. Chicago: Encyclopaedia Britannica. *The Federalist* originally published 1787–88.

Huemer, Michael, 2012. In praise of passivity. *Studia Humana*, 1, pp.12–28.

Huemer, Michael, 2013. *The problem of political authority*. New York: Palgrave Macmillan.

Jefferson, Thomas, 1782. *Notes on the state of Virginia*. Paris.

McClenaghan, William A., 1994. *Magruder's American government*. Needham, MA: Prentice-Hall.

McGinnis, John, and Rappaport, Michael, 2007. Majority and supermajority rules: three views of the Capitol. *Texas Law Review* 85, pp.1115–1183.

Montesquieu, Charles-Louis de Secondat, 1748. *The spirit of the laws*. Paris.

Pole, J. R., ed., 1987. *The American Constitution: for and against*. New York: Hill and Wang.

Rybicki, Elizabeth, 2008. The "clearance process" in the Senate and measures approved in the 110th Congress through June 30, 2008. Congressional Research Service Memo, [online] July 10. Available at: <http://web.archive.org/web/20100615000000*/http://demint.senate.gov/public/_files/2008-07-23_CD_Clearance_Process.pdf>

PART IV

CULTURE,
DIVERSITY,
EXPECTATIONS

CHAPTER 20

....

FREEDOM AND RELIGION

....

RICHARD J. ARNESON

EACH person should be left free to form her own beliefs on matters of religion in conditions of wide freedom of speech and expression.[1] Each person should be free to affiliate with any existing church that is willing to take her on as a member, or form her own church or sect or association directed to religious aims, with willing fellow adherents. Each person should be free to worship, in public and in private, with like-minded others, according to the tenets of her faith. Moreover, each person should be left free to practice the tenets of her religious faith, unless the actions her religion prompts her to take would violate the moral rights of other persons.

Many people in the contemporary world affirm religious freedom as just characterized. In addition, many of us also believe that each person has the right to be free from state interference in matters of religious faith. That means that the government should not sponsor one religion or church, or endorse or support any particular religion or church or religious views. Nor should the government favor religion over nonreligion or the religious over the nonreligious. Nor should citizens seek to bring it about that government does any of these forbidden things (Audi, 1989; but see McConnell, 1990; McConnell, 1992).

In the U.S. Constitution, these two aspects of religious liberty are summarized in the part of the First Amendment that prohibits government from establishing any religion and from hindering its free exercise. Many written constitutions of many countries profess a similar doctrine.

Although freedom of religion has wide appeal around the world in our time, the doctrine is also widely controversial. But even among those who broadly favor religious liberty, deep unresolved puzzles remain as to how it is best understood and how it might best be justified. This chapter examines some of these unresolved puzzles.

A preliminary clarification is needed, although it introduces large issues this chapter will not try to settle. When we discuss *religious* liberty, what exactly are we talking about? What distinguishes the religious from the nonreligious? Many answers that have been given will strike many of us as underinclusive or overinclusive or both (underinclusive in some respects and overinclusive in others). If we say religions profess faith in a Supreme Being, a God of traditional theology, we are narrowly excluding Buddhism and Hinduism and other religious traditions beyond the Judeo-Christian. If we identify religion with "faith in some higher or deeper reality than exists on the surface of every-day life or can be established by scientific inquiry" (Greenawalt, 2006: 134), we would be including speculative philosophical metaphysical doctrines as religious, which seems inapt. Also, some long-standing churches such as the Unitarian, whose doctrinal content is thin to the vanishing point, would be classified as nonreligious. If we identify the religious with "all deep convictions about the purpose and responsibilities of life" (Dworkin, 2013: 107), we obliterate the line between religion and secular moral thought.

For practical purposes it may suffice to start with doctrines and practices that ordinary common sense confidently classifies as religious and then simply identify the religious as anything sufficiently similar to that. We can identify features that often mark what is paradigmatically religious without seeking necessary and sufficient conditions. Here I follow suggestions made by Greenawalt (2006). In seeking a rough idea of the religious, we should have in mind not only types of belief and doctrine but also churches and sects and similar institutional practices. Not all those who propound religious ideas seek to found communities of the like-minded who will band together for ritual, worship, the building or organization, and proselytism, but many do.

The arguments of this chapter deny that qualifying as religion or religious should entitle one to special protection of liberty. Nor should special accommodation be made to the religious to help them carry on in their beliefs and practices. If nothing by way of special treatment should turn on whether an entity is or is not a religion, the sketchiness and vagueness of the idea may not matter so much.

1. RELIGIOUS LIBERTY AND RELIGIOUS ESTABLISHMENT

A political society that protects the liberty of each person to speak freely on religious matters, worship according to one's creed, and organize churches and sects with like-minded others, might yet be nonneutral in its religious policies, by sponsoring or supporting one religion or set of religious beliefs over others (Greenawalt, 2008; Leiter, 2012). State sponsorship of some sectarian doctrine over others might seem unfair to adherents of nonfavored sects.

One attempt to see state establishment as possibly fair proposes that we should not confine our view to some particular political society but should rather look at government sponsorship and favoritism on a world scale. Suppose the world were divided into many independent political societies, some of which establish particular religious doctrines, in such a way that everyone's religious belief will be established in some society to which she has access. Imagine that Judaism is the established faith in Israel, the Sunni Muslim faith in Iraq, evangelical Christianity in the United States, atheism in Sweden, and so on. Might this world regime qualify as fair to all religious adherents? One might hold that establishment would be unfair to adherents of nonestablished views, who receive less favored treatment in their home societies, even if a privileged status is available for them elsewhere. The idea might be that the global establishment scheme is more unfair to individuals, the more burdensome and costly it would be for them to relocate to a society in which their favored doctrine is privileged.

Another possibility is that a state establishment that gives privileges to false beliefs would be bad, but a state establishment that involves state support of true beliefs warranted by the balance of available reasons would be good. As a practical matter, some might doubt that public officials or democratic voters would be reliable at singling out true rather than false beliefs for establishment. Such suspicion of government competence would be compatible with holding that state establishment properly oriented to the right and the good would be unobjectionable.

2. A Puzzle about State Neutrality

Here is one puzzle. Many people are inclined to hold that the truth of a religious claim is irrelevant to its aptness as a basis for morally acceptable public policy. Morally acceptable public policies must be justifiable in terms acceptable to all citizens regardless of their particular religious commitments. David Estlund (2008) states this idea with elegant simplicity: Even if the Roman Catholic pope has a pipeline to God, that would not give the pope the moral right to make Roman Catholicism the established religion and use state power in other ways to favor this particular religious doctrine over others.

Let us suppose that having a "pipeline to God" means that the pope has a true warranted belief that Roman Catholicism is the unique route to salvation and that unless people live and die as Catholics, they lose irrevocably the chance to gain in the afterlife an eternity of bliss. Imposing and maintaining Catholicism as the established religion does not guarantee that those who live under this regime will embrace the true faith and attain salvation. But this course of action would increase everyone's chance of gaining eternal salvation. Given all this, if the pope recognizes even a modest duty of beneficence (to act efficiently to improve people's welfare), he ought to seize state power and impose and maintain Catholicism as the established religion, if he can do so. And the rest of us ought to assist him in this effort. The imperative to respect religious liberty, no matter the weight of reasons that support it, is canceled in these circumstances. The stakes are just too high. This argument does not literally require the claim that outside the Church there is no salvation and that the payoff of salvation for an individual is infinite in value—an extremely high finite value will do.

On the other hand, if the pope has a high subjective confidence that he uniquely has a pipeline to God, but there is no reasoned warrant for this idea, then we ought to band together to prevent him from gaining any power, much less state power or political power of global reach. The greater his subjective confidence, and that of his followers, and the more we suspect he will conscientiously act beneficently by his lights, the more dangerous he is likely to be.

Some respond to the deep and sharp conflicts of opinion among people of diverse theological views by saying we can all have sufficient confidence in our particular salvation beliefs reasonably to guide our own lives by them but insufficient confidence to impose our views by force on others. But this comfortable vision of people disagreeing tooth and nail while peacefully living together in harmony requires the idea of a private reason—a consideration that is a reason for one person, but not for others. But reasons are inescapably public. If there is reason for me to save the whales, there is reason for others in a position to help. If there are agent-relative reasons for me to help my own children, there are agent-relative reasons for anyone to help her own children. If the reasons I have that bear on choice of conduct are genuine reasons, they are in principle shareable—my reasons can be made available to you, and become your reasons. A principled basis for mutual toleration of other people professing views that are anathema from your standpoint is not ready-to-hand plain common sense—just the opposite.

Another possibility is that even if I believe my own religious views are correct and others are in error, I might also believe that it is wrong to force others to act against their beliefs unless they are wrongfully harming others. My moral inhibition against coercing others might be strengthened, the less confidence I have in my current beliefs. These beliefs suffice as reasons for guiding my own conduct, but fall short of what would be required to overturn the moral norm against coercion.

However, one might flip this point on its head. The more confidence I have in the correctness of my beliefs, then if I accept an obligation of beneficence to save others from peril, the more the no-forcing norm looks overrideable. If I am very confident that you will plunge off a bridge to your death unless I force you to sway from your present path, I should help you by forcing you.

Of course, the Roman Catholic Church is not saying *extra ecclesiam nulla salus* these days. But the basic problem remains. Religions claim that enormous benefits will accrue to followers, and only their followers, and religions differ widely in theologies and prescribed rituals and commandments for daily life. Compromise is difficult between adherents of radically opposed theological views. Jesus Christ is either the Redeemer and Son of God, who has shown us the path to salvation we must follow—or he is not. If the end of the world is fast approaching, as many Christians believe is foretold in the Bible, it is silly to worry about worldly issues such as climate change, war, the diffusion of nuclear armaments, and the prospects for economic development of the underdeveloped regions of the Earth. If there is no reason to believe the end of the world is fast approaching, the religious claims to the contrary are very dangerous ideas.

The puzzle is that religious liberty is often partially interpreted as requiring government neutrality on religious matters. The government is to take no stance for or against any religious doctrine. Neutrality here requires that the government should not act to promote one controversial religious doctrine over others, nor favor the adherents of some controversial doctrine over the adherents of other views, nor pursue any policy that could only be justified by a claim that some controversial religious doctrine is superior to others (on the idea of neutrality, see Patten, 2012; also Nussbaum, 2011). But this stance of neutrality makes no sense, especially where huge consequences are at stake. Religions make large empirical, metaphysical, and moral claims that if true are of the utmost importance for all of us. The claims cry out for assessment. If religious claims, claims backed by religious reasons—for example, about divine intentions as revealed in a sacred book—are inapt as a basis for state laws and other public policies, that can only be because the arguments and evidence that can be adduced for these claims do not withstand critical scrutiny. But if the norm of government neutrality in religious matters is rejected, then it would seem that the state should favor better religious doctrines and steer its members away from worse ones, and the question arises: why should the state even tolerate religious creeds and sects that are exceptionally defective from an epistemic standpoint, promulgating claims no reasonable person should accept?

The generic case for wide freedom of speech and expression and for other basic civil liberties provides a sensible reply to the suggestion that in matters of religion the state should act to restrict people's liberty to embrace defective heresies, dangerous falsehoods. Let us assume that it is accepted that there should be wide freedom of speech and expression along with freedom of assembly and freedom of association. These basic civil liberties will encompass the liberty to speak freely on religious matters, proselytize for one's chosen faith, assemble with like-minded others to worship and engage in ceremonies and rituals of one's choosing, and form organizations to promote adherence to one or another particular religious doctrine. We do not need to advance special religious freedom rights to secure these widely accepted freedoms. The religious freedom rights are included in generic civil liberties.

The response to the first puzzle just suggested immediately gives rise to another puzzle. Many us believe that we all owe one another special solicitude for religious liberty. Not all liberties are of equal importance. The government via its traffic safety regulations massively restricts one's freedom to drive cars however one might wish, but this is not deemed oppressive. But religious liberty has special importance. Moreover, religious liberty includes not only liberty of speech, expression, and worship but also liberty to put one's faith into practice, to live according to the dictates of one's chosen faith, at least up to the point at which one's acting on religious belief violates basic moral rights of others. The puzzle is to interpret and assess the claimed special status of religion and religious liberty.

3. A Thumb on the Scale Favoring Religious Concerns?

Freedom of religion, though under threat in some regions, is assigned special protection in the written constitutions of many political societies. The European Convention on Human Rights stipulates that "Freedom to manifest one's religion or beliefs shall be subject only to such limitations as are prescribed by law and necessary in a democratic society in the interests of public safety, for the protection of public order, health or morals, or for the protection of the rights and freedoms of others."

Why single out religion for special protection in this way? The judgment that ordinary religious activities such as proselytizing and church-going merit protection does not require a further judgment that religion merits special protection.

The question "why single religion out for special protection" bites hard for those who hold the background belief that in a democratic society, the majority should rule, and that up to some point, the fact that a law has been enacted by duly established democratic procedures renders it legitimate to enforce the law both on the majority that supported it and on others who do not support it. Is there is a special right to religious freedom that stands in the way of enforcing an otherwise legitimate democratic law on the ground that enforcing it would interfere with religious people's freely practicing their religion? On this issue, see Koppelman, 2013; Greenawalt, 2006; Greenawalt, 2008; and Leiter, 2012.

Examples may help to clarify this concern. Suppose that a democratic political society bans the production, sale, gift, and consumption of hallucinogenic drugs such as LSD and mescaline. These laws might be justified or unjustified; set that question to the side. Consider three claimants who might demand that the law should be rewritten or interpreted by courts to exempt them from the requirement to conform to this law on the ground that it restricts their freedom unjustifiably. That is, the claimants maintain that even if the law is acceptable as applied to most people, it would not be acceptable if imposed on them, because they would be specially burdened by conformity. One claimant objects that her religion requires the use of hallucinogenic drugs in religious ceremonies and rituals that are crucial to the practice of her faith. A second claimant objects that her deepest ethical convictions require her to explore altered states of consciousness, including the altered states induced by LSD or mescaline, to facilitate her attainment of emotional states favorable to treating people as they ought to be treated and to her discovery of the important moral truths. A third claimant objects that her chosen way of life places at its center an activity such as surfing or rock climbing that becomes a sublimely valuable experience when practiced while in an altered state of mind induced by appropriate doses of hallucinogens. If the society in which these claimants live has a political constitution that forbids government to restrict the free exercise of religion or in some similar way gives special legal protection to freedom to carry on religious activities, the first claimant has a presumptive good claim to legal relief, the second a doubtful but possible claim, and the third no claim at all. Why is this fair?

If one examines current writings that touch on this question by constitutional law scholars and interpreters of religious liberty, one finds two broad types of answer. One says that religion is really morally special, and merits special protection. The second response denies that religion is really morally special. On this view, either the appearance that current policies in democratic societies that are especially solicitous of religious liberty is false, or the appearance is correct, in which case the legal policies that cater to religious concerns in a way that would be justifiable only if religion were somehow special ought to be eliminated or reformed.

4. Religion Is Special in That It Should Be Specially Disfavored *and* Favored

The "religion is special" response to the puzzle about why religion should be singled out for special favorable treatment when governments are handing out benefits or restricting people's freedom itself divides into two broad categories. One line of thought suggests that religious beliefs are both specially disfavored and specially favored in the government policies of a morally acceptable democratic constitutional regime, the disfavoring and favoring roughly balancing each other. Compare the belief that God hates heresy and the belief that racial discrimination is wrong. A political society ought to abjure the establishment of religion, as does the U.S. Constitution and as do those of many other societies. This means that the government should not take action that supports one religious belief over others or supports the religious over the nonreligious. Any government action to suppress heresy would be based on some particular religious belief as to what is true religion and what is heresy, and government action on this basis would run afoul of any sensible no-establishment rule. In contrast, there is no bar to government taking action on nonreligious beliefs, such as the belief that it is wrong to discriminate against people on the basis of race, sex, religion, or national origin. Establishment of moral claims by such actions as passing laws forbidding discriminatory conduct is perfectly acceptable in a country that rejects all religious establishment. So religious beliefs are disfavored in a way.

Given this fact, and given its appropriateness, there may be some need for redress or compensation, which takes the form of giving special weight to claims that the enforcement of a law that has a legitimate secular purpose and is not on its face motivated by dislike or hostility to any religious group would nonetheless pinch hard against the religious interests of some people, who should on this ground be exempted from the legal requirement to conform to the law. Call this position *special-accommodation-for-religion-offsets-the-no-establishment-burden* (Greene, 1993).

Objection: The suggestion advanced in this chapter is that the basis for ruling out religious claims as the grounding of laws and public policies is that these views are poorly supported by evidence and argument. We lack reason to believe any of these religious doctrines is true, so we lack reason to put state power behind any of them. But this is not any sort of reason to put a thumb on the scale favoring special protection of religious liberty or favoring religious over nonreligious demands for exemption from requirements to obey otherwise acceptable laws.

The countersuggestion might be that the main reason to favor no-establishment is not that religious doctrines per se have epistemic defects, but rather the judgment that governments are particularly inept at distinguishing better from worse religious doctrines and so should be barred from endorsing any. Reply: The fact that a claim is likely to be controversial is not per se a reason that it cannot figure in a sound justification of state policy. Moreover, even if governments tend to be bad at discriminating better from worse doctrines, that should not inhibit a government that is exceptional in this regard from basing policy on sound judgments.

One possible basis for holding that religion requires special treatment is that religious disputes are specially explosive and likely to cause conflict, reduce people's disposition to cooperate with those deemed outsiders, and threaten civil peace. Also, adherents of religious views held by a small minority of a society's population are specially vulnerable to discrimination and even persecution, even in democracies.

Objection: in many modern democracies with diverse populations, the tendency of religious disputes to cause civil strife is very muted, if discernible at all. Where this is so, this argument for special treatment for religion has slight purchase. But also, if it is true that religious discord does gives rise to persecution, the ground for state action here is to protect people from persecution. This we should do in an even-handed way, whether the persecutors are motivated by religion, racial ideology, national chauvinism, contempt for people who do not espouse liberal opinions, or other motives.

Further objection: If religious disputes threaten social cooperation and civil peace, we might suspect that the tendency of people to embrace simplistic religious dogmas insulated from rational reflection and criticism is the underlying problem. So rather than treat religion with kid gloves, perhaps the government should promote secular education and deliberative institutions and practices and campaign against irrational embrace of religious dogmas, while sustaining full civil liberties including free speech for all. This in effect would be a regime of secular establishment.

5. Religion Is Especially Valuable and Should Be Favored

The second line of thought along the "religion is special" path forthrightly affirms that religious activities and practices are on the whole specially valuable in a way that justifies special favorable legal treatment of religion and special protection specifically of religious liberty.

The claim to the special quality of religion takes various forms.

One version of the claim is that religious dictates present themselves to adherents as absolute categorical imperatives that we must obey come what may (McConnell, 1990; McConnell, 1992). Religious demands are implacable, and so when they put a believer in conflict with man-made law, the demand for compliance is unreasonable, or at least specially burdensome. Or one might hold that duties to a divine being are orders of magnitude more compelling than any secular obligations to behave in one way or another toward other members of society. The secular obligations are apt for compromise and flexibility; the religious obligations, not so.

Objection: These contrasts fade upon examination. Many versions of morality impose duties that are categorical in the sense that we are bound to obey them regardless of our desires or aims. Some moral duties may be exceptionless, and are deemed to hold come what may. Many people in fact treat requirements of secular morality as imposing obligations of conscience that are of overwhelming importance in their lives and present unyielding demands. Moreover, in fact, people who are religious vary in the degree to which they are religious or uphold religious commandments as overpowering their other aims and concerns, brooking no compromise.

Another version of the claim is that religions offer frameworks of belief that endow life with meaning, significance, and purpose. Religions answer persistent and urgent questions about what kinds of beings we are and what is our proper relationship to other humans and to the natural universe. Art and other human enterprises contribute to this quest for meaning, but by history and tradition, religion is the preeminent human enterprise that plays this role (see Nussbaum, 2008; Koppelman, 2006).

Objection: First, it is not obvious that the search for cosmic significance or meaning in life is valuable at all, much less of incomparable value. Perhaps the search for enormous significance in human life reflects illusion or the understandable but unjustified wish of humans to see themselves as central players in a narrative of great importance.

Setting this worry aside, we should resist the idea that religion uniquely or specially or in some quintessentially wondrous way endows our lives with meaning and significance. People find meaning and significance in many ways. Any goal that one regards as worth pursuing can give meaning. Religious doctrines often provide adherents with ways of making sense of frightening and distressing aspects of the human condition, and these consoling religious ideas, such as an eternal afterlife and transmigration of souls, are highly appealing and resonate with our deepest aspirations and fears. But consolation and solace come in many varieties, many of them secular.

Martha Nussbaum associates the special value in religion with the human capacity to search for ultimate meaning in life, a full account of the place of humans in the cosmos and of how we should live and what is valuable. The capacity is one all humans have, and its exercises merit special respect and solicitude. A related view suggested by Andrew Koppelman asserts that finding the true ultimate meaning of human life has objective value, and hence searching for ultimate meaning is instrumentally valuable. Since the state is appropriately barred from pronouncing on the comparative worth of different methods and strategies for the search for ultimate significance, the reasonable state policy is a blanket support for any and all of them.

Objection: The ensemble of ways of searching for ultimate meaning encompasses astrology, searching for ways to interact with outer-space aliens, devoting oneself to a family business, extolling the Mafia, and much else. The proposal under review sweeps too broadly, and would if accepted justify a policy of special protection for a very wide range of activities that no one finds deserving of that status. Moreover, even if the capacity to search for meaning is valuable, it is implausible to think that any exercise of the capacity, good, bad, or ugly, has value. If we focus on more narrowly religious exercises of the capacity, taking religion to be whatever is sufficiently similar to paradigm cases of religion such as Christianity, Judaism, Buddhism, Hinduism, and so on, we are back to the question we started with: what makes religion per se specially valuable?

Brian Leiter (2012) denies that religion should be appraised highly, because our ordinary understanding of religion identifies it as, inter alia, beliefs that are chosen and ratified in epistemically defective ways that fall short of standards of scientific method and moral argument. It seems misleading to define *religion* as a belief system that is epistemically defective. Some religions claim to be rationalist enterprises, and if, for example, we somehow came to decide that Roman Catholicism as defended by St. Thomas Aquinas is a uniquely rational belief system, we would not cease regarding Roman Catholicism as a religion. But Leiter nonetheless might be correct that religious beliefs as a matter of fact are accepted by their defenders, including sophisticated defenders, on the basis of epistemically suspect reasons that pay little heed to standards of rationality we should embrace.

We seem to be encountering a dilemma. Attempts to explain why religion is special and therefore merits special legal deference either fail to distinguish religion from other types of human practice and activity or, if they succeed in identifying what is unique about religion, fail to explain why religion so conceived should be thought specially valuable or meritorious. On either horn of the dilemma, we lack good reason to treat religion as special in a way that justifies deference to it, favoring religion over other interests and concerns of citizens.

6. Conscience Should Receive Deferential Treatment

One strategy of response to the puzzle of understanding why freedom of religion is especially important and merits special legal protection identifies freedom of religion with liberty of conscience and proposes a norm of respect for conscience (see Perry, 2007; also Arneson, 2010; Arneson, 2014).

If conscience is a capacity to form a judgment about what is morally required, prohibited, and permissible, respect for conscience might be thought to manifest itself canonically in willingness to exempt from the requirement to do what is legally required a person whose conscience conflicts with that requirement. Someone who is conscientiously opposed to fighting in wars might be exempted from conscription into military service; someone who is conscientiously opposed to paying income taxes might be excused from the requirement to do so.

One immediate worry is that accommodations of religion that many people support do not involve eschewing the attempt to force people to act against their conscience. Another worry is that accommodations of religion that tend to be provided in current societies are overwhelmingly limited to religious claimants, not a broader category of conscientious objectors.

Moreover, it is far from clear or obvious that the fact that someone conscientiously opposes what law requires him to do is in itself a basis for exempting him from the requirement to obey. We might argue that in a well-functioning, diverse democracy one should conform one's conduct to legal requirements to which one is conscientiously opposed, unless one reasonably believes that the consequence of acting against one's conscience would be serious violation of some people's important moral rights. In a diverse democracy people will tend to disagree on important moral matters. Conscientious judgments on many issues do not tend to converge. In this situation, there might well be many sets of rules such that enforcing any one of them would be better from everyone's moral standpoint than enforcing none. One loses from being required to conform to rules that offend one's beliefs but gains when others do the same. In this scenario, allowing majority rule to override conscientious judgment as the determiner of what we do can be a fair cooperative practice. Given that we benefit from others suppressing conscience and conforming to majority rule, we should reciprocate when majority rule requires us to act against our own conscience. Here we are going against our first-order conscientious judgment, that just considers the issues on their merits and ignores what others are doing, but we are conforming to our second-order judgment that does take account of the behavior of others regarding the deliverances of their first-order conscientious judgments.

The cooperative practice of being willing to go along with others when we think they are morally in error for the sake of securing the greater moral gains of coordination is important. But quite apart from this consideration, there is a further question about the fairness of accommodating dissenting conscience by allowing conscientious objectors to avoid the costs of conforming to law. On the face of it, shifting the burdens of compliance with law in the way that the exemption for conscientious objectors does is unfair to those required to bear the burdens of conforming.

If an exemption to the general requirement imposed on citizens to obey the law is sparingly granted, the negative consequences for others may be slight. Since almost all citizens are still required to obey the law, even with the narrow exemption in place, whatever legitimate purposes the law was enacted to achieve will still be fulfilled. Since very few persons are exempted from the law, the consequences of shifting the burdens of compliance on the remaining citizens will be very slight. Yet a problem is evident. Unless there is justification for singling out some people for exemption on a narrow basis, the scheme is unfair. In actual fact, if we take recent history as our guide, the supposedly broad norm of accommodation to claims of conscience will in practice become a narrow norm of accommodation to claims of the religious. This occurs because the courts and other legal agencies granting exemptions can see that a wide interpretation would trigger a deluge of claims, and this they want to avoid. So we are left with the initial puzzle: why single out religion for special status, in the form of a disposition on the part of democratic governments to grant exemptions from legal requirements to those who can claim that conforming to the requirements would get in the way of the practice of their religious faith?

7. Equal Citizenship?

A perhaps more promising doctrine of religious liberty starts with the idea that the state is obligated to show equal respect and concern to all citizens and refrain from imposing policies that fail to treat all citizens as equal citizens. (For an argument that core liberal ideas require the state to refrain not just from promoting some controversial religious views but more broadly from promoting any controversial views as to what is intrinsically valuable in life, see Quong, 2011.) The claim then is that a generous doctrine of accommodation of religion is required to show equal respect and concern to religious adherents along with other citizens and to avoid imposing policies that treat some as second-class citizens.

Laws and other state directives that single out particular religious doctrines or their adherents for disfavored treatment are plausibly ruled out by equal respect and concern. For example, a law that offers a benefit to all citizens except Lutherans would be treating Lutherans as second-class citizens. So would a law that was crafted to disfavor Lutherans specifically without referring to them by name.

The rub here lies in our interpretation of the requirement to disparage none and treat all as equal citizens. This requirement is said to apply to the state and to individuals insofar as they seek to influence state policies. Assume the requirement, suitably interpreted, is acceptable. Without attempting a full interpretation of the requirement, we should accept these constraints on any plausible construal.

First, the fact that a state policy with its justification conflicts with some moral or empirical belief one holds is false does not in itself qualify the policy as failing to treat one with equal respect or denying that one has the status of equal citizen. For example, if my religion tells me that whites are the superior race and good jobs and positions of authority should be reserved for whites only, a state policy that forbids discrimination on the basis of race in employment and assignment to public office opposes my belief. Religious doctrines take clear and substantive stands on a raft of empirical and moral questions, and many of these doctrines are flatly opposed to scientific consensus and any reasonable moral principles.

Second, that the law benefits some citizens more than others, including me, or benefits some and imposes disadvantages on others, including me, does not automatically indicate that I am being disparaged, treated as less than equal. In a pluralistic democratic society, the majority will routinely ends up favoring some and disfavoring others. If we pass banking regulations, some bank stockholders and bank customers may lose, and others may gain. Even if we hold that government should be neutral as between controversial ways of life and conceptions of the good, this neutrality norm does not plausibly require that each government action must be neutral in its effects, bringing about exactly the same net benefit for all citizens who might be affected. So the sheer fact that an otherwise acceptable law happens to bring about worse consequences for those trying to practice Methodism than for others should not in itself raise red flags of warning that something is amiss. However, whenever law pinches some with extra severity, there is the possibility that an accommodation for those especially burdened may be justified.

8. Accommodation: The Welfare Approach

Law is a blunt instrument of social control. Legal rules will employ fairly coarse-grained distinctions, and rightly so, because in many settings the attempt to make the law more nuanced and more closely in conformity to what is morally right would create a fine-grained rule that is difficult and costly to administer, with predictably worse results as assessed from the standpoint of moral principle. So consider a law that is appropriately coarse-grained. For purposes of illustration, let us just assume that a law that prohibits suicide and assisted suicide is morally acceptable, because most suicides are wrong in virtue of bringing about bad consequences for the person who kills herself or for other affected persons. If someone says "I want to kill myself," you hand the person a loaded gun, with the intention of facilitating the person's killing himself, and the person shoots himself and dies, you should be criminally liable for the death. Nonetheless some suicides are surely permissible and some may even be morally required, and assisting someone to commit suicide reasonably may be morally permissible or required.

The mechanism of enforcement of law can provide needed flexibility for such cases. A citizen who witnesses a legally prohibited assisted suicide may decline to report the incident to the authorities; a policeman who witnesses such an event may decline to make an arrest; if an arrest is made, a prosecuting attorney may decline to prosecute; and if a trial is held, a jury can vote to acquit even if the facts of the case and applicable law indicate a guilty verdict is called for. Such discretion can go awry, but can also improve the degree to which the legal system protects rights and advances the general welfare.

Even a perfectly fine-grained legal rule tuned with exquisite sensitivity to moral requirements might place greater burdens on some citizens asked to conform to the rule. But consider the broad range of cases in which the achievement of a collective good requires costly conformity to rule, and conformity is far more costly for some citizens, who might be excused from this requirement with little or no loss of achievement of the collective good. In such cases the law is more fair if it bends in one way or another to allow those specially burdened the freedom not to comply. This is accommodation of those specially burdened. The law against assisted suicide induces a morally better outcome if it allows physicians to assist the suicide of those who face painful terminal illness or a devastating chronic medical problem that makes continued life a punishment for self and others. Or consider a legal rule that forbids swimming after dark at the sole local swimming hole, in its application to a handicapped, disfigured, strong swimmer who very much values the activity of swimming but unavoidably finds it psychologically very hard to swim at a public beach in daylight. He should be allowed to swim at night. In all cases the metric for assessing an accommodation claim is the degree to which the person seeking accommodation, compared to others, would suffer a welfare loss if it is not granted, balanced against the degree to which either (1) the ends of the law are less fulfilled or (2) the burdens on those expected to conform to law are increased, if the exemption is granted.

So far we have been considering informal accommodation, but sometimes a degree of formality is helpful. Confronted with a legal ban on nude swimming on public beaches and a well-known proclivity of nudist enthusiasts to frolic without clothes on a certain remote beach, the police may announce publicly that they will devote zero resources to enforcing the nudity ban at that particular beach. But there might also be a court-ordered rule or an exemption written into a statute by lawmakers. (These maneuvers make the law more fine-grained and possibly more difficult to administer, but without triggering prohibitive practical difficulties.)

For any accommodation, the question arises: is it fair? It may be unfair to single out one class of persons and not others from exemption. Granting an exemption to some may also increase the burdens of compliance with the law on others, and this can be unfair. The welfare accommodation account just outlined provides a framework, not a formula for resolving these issues. The suggestion then is that religious interests and concerns as such should get no special priority or privilege in the determination of whether any accommodations should be made with respect to the enforcement of any particular law. In the determination as to whether an otherwise acceptable law unduly pinches some who fall within its scope by imposing disproportionate burdens of welfare loss on them, religious interests and nonreligious interests should be treated evenhandedly.

9. Religious Accommodation

The approach to accommodation outlined here can be compared to other approaches to accommodation of religion advanced by legal and political theorists. Attention here is focused on discussions concerned to interpret the religion clauses of the First Amendment of the U.S. Constitution, but readers should keep in mind that our topic is what morality requires, not what the U.S. Constitution or any other country's written constitution is best interpreted as asserting.

At some time in the past the U.S. Supreme Court seemed to be committed to a position that singles out religious freedom as taking special priority. On this view, a citizen can successfully claim entitlement to accommodation in the form of exemption from the requirement to obey an otherwise applicable law if she can show that (a) the law applied to her imposes substantial burden on the free exercise of her religion and (b) no compelling state interest opposes granting her an exemption. If there are few religious claimants, the degree to which the law's purposes are fulfilled would typically be only slightly lessened if exemption is granted, so a compelling state interest opposing the granting of the exemption sought will rarely be identifiable. The manifest problem with this approach is that it puts a heavy thumb on the scale favoring citizens with religious commitments and religious interests over other citizens, and this is unfair.

A hypothetical example of a case in which accommodation to facilitate religious freedom would probably be acceptable according to the approach to accommodation endorsed in this chapter may help to show where lines of controversy emerge. Imagine that there is a public school system in place funded by general tax revenue, and the public school system operates alongside privately funded and operated schools. Suppose the privately funded schools are either exclusive schools attended by the children of wealthy parents or religious schools. The curricula of all private schools are vetted and regulated by the state to ensure all children receive adequate education. The nonwealthy parents who want to provide religious schooling for their children complain that the requirement to pay tuition and fees for religious schools and also to contribute as taxpayers to the public school system poses a special onerous burden on them, which neither

wealthy parents placing their children in nonreligious private schools nor parents sending their children to public schools have to bear. They ask for either state contributions
to tuition payments paid by parents sending their children to religious schools or tax
relief from the full burden of contributing to the public school system (Galston, 2002;
Macedo, 1995). This claim on its face has merit.

One might endorse aid to religious schools or a voucher system to the same effect
without accepting the idea that parents have a right to determine the content of their
children's education. Parents generally have a strong right to raise their children as they
see fit so long as the parents are adequately competent. These parental rights must be
balanced against the independent rights of children. Prominent among these rights is
the right of each child to be educated in ways that expose her to alternative perspectives on the world and that give her the capacity to think critically and independently
about the beliefs instilled into her by others, including her parents. Parents have rights
to indoctrinate their children into their own favored beliefs, but children have rights to
be trained and socialized in ways that equip them to seek the truth by their own lights.
Along the same line, each child has the right to be trained in general-purpose skills that
will help her to flourish in any of a wide variety of plans of life that she might as an adult
choose for herself.

What exactly the child's right to independence requires by way of state assistance is
not obvious and clearly varies with circumstances. One boundary line is evident in the
case of *Wisconsin v. Yoder*. In that case the parents of a religious sect demanded exemption from a state law requiring attendance at school by all children through the age of
sixteen. The parents claimed that attendance at secondary school would reduce the
prospects that the child would eventually maintain allegiance to the religious sect community and would interfere with the religious community's efforts to socialize adolescents into community sect loyalty. The child's right to independence and an open future
should have trumped these considerations and brought about denial by courts of this
demand for religious accommodation. In the same way, a demand by nonreligious farm-
ing parents that their children be excused from secondary-school attendance in order to
increase the children's willingness and ability to work as adults on the family farm does
not add up to a justified claim for exemption from applicable state law.

Some examples that might be construed as religious accommodation cases are better
understood as free speech cases, with the understanding that religious speakers have the
same free speech rights as anyone else. Consider compelled speech in public schools, by
way of such practices as compulsory saluting of the national flag in the classroom and
compulsory recitation of a Pledge of Allegiance affirming loyalty to the nation's basic
political arrangements. Freedom to speak as one wishes on matters of public concern
includes the right not to speak at all, and a fortiori not to speak in favor of views one
rejects. Hence it would be wrong to force or pressure adult citizens to salute the flag or
recite a pledge of allegiance. What about children? Children lack the full free speech
rights of adults, but gradually acquire some rights of freedom of expression as they grow
older. It would be wrong to prevent high-school-age children from having some opportunity to express their views on controversial matters in the school setting, by speech

and also by symbolic means such as wearing pins, medallions, or shirts with slogans printed on them. Some residue of free speech rights attaches even to primary-school youngsters, mainly rights not to be compelled to engage in speech or symbolic acts with speech content against their convictions.

Consider now another range of cases. If state law forbids consumption of LSD, peyote, mescaline, and other hallucinogenic drugs, should an exemption be granted to members of a religious sect whose central church rituals revolve around consumption of some hallucinogenic drugs? (See Marshall, 2000; Galston, 2002.) The example is perhaps clouded by initial doubts that there could be a reasonable justification of any law along these lines in the first place. Let us set this concern to the side, as irrelevant for our purposes. The welfare accommodation approach would not rule out the possibility that accommodation could be justified, but would rule out favoring the religious by granting an exemption to the law for those who need (say) peyote for religious ceremonies while denying an exemption for those who need peyote for serious enhancement of nonreligious activities (such as climbing or surfing). If widening the exemption would be too costly or destructive of the law's purposes, and no nonarbitrary, narrowly crafted exemption can be devised, there should be no exemptions, and certainly not a special exemption just for the religious claimants.

The welfare accommodation approach might prompt the objection that it is fatally tone-deaf to the special nature of claims of conscience and improperly assimilates them to concerns about people's welfare or well-being. The objection would be that it is not that one would be worse off in self-interested terms if one acts against conscience, but that acting against conscience is wrongful behavior, destructive of one's integrity, and the state should make every effort to avoid presenting its citizens with the choice of acting against conscience or being faced with serious criminal penalties for violation of the state's law.

This objection raises issues already discussed in this chapter. Roughly, if the state forbids an act that is permissible or even morally obligatory, this is wrong (sometimes horrendously wrong) and a serious violation of the autonomy of the citizen whose chosen course of action is forbidden. If the state forbids what is anyway wrongful (e.g., theft or murder), and this prohibition conflicts with the individual's conscientious judgment, the affront to autonomy should have no weight on the scales. If the state forbids what would be permissible except for the state's scheme, including prohibition, to advance some legitimate purpose, the issue is more subtle. However, if the state's plan, including coercion, is morally acceptable, the sheer fact that one conscientiously disagrees is not a reason to exempt one from the requirement. Conscientious objection to a law might in some cases reasonably prompt supporters of the law to lessen their degree of confidence in its justification, but sometimes is not always.

We do all have a general interest in living by our own lights and being guided by our own views of what is right and good and appropriate and what strikes our fancy (so coercion always requires a justification). Being confronted with a conflict between the state's commands and one's conscience presents one with a messy and unpleasant situation, which anyone would reasonably prefer to avoid. If a grievous and especially aggravating situation of this sort can be avoided by minor adjustment on the part of others, at small cost to them, this is an accommodation the others ought to extend. This welfarist reading of the generic case for accommodation does not in any obvious way make hash of claims of conscience.

Christopher Eisgruber and Lawrence Sager (2007) propose an interpretation of religious liberty as demanded by the U.S. Constitution that is in some respects close to the welfare accommodation approach this chapter is defending. (Recall that our issue is not what this or that country's constitution asserts, but what morality requires. Thus the concern of this chapter and the issue that Eisgruber and Sager are addressing are different.) Let us imagine that someone might propose that the U.S. Constitution as interpreted by Eisgruber and Sager gets it right so far as the morality of religious liberty is concerned. Whether or not they are right as a matter of constitutional interpretation, what they propose might be right as a claim about political morality—what we owe to one another by way of uses of state power.

Their suggested approach has three components. One is the insistence that religious people, like others, have robust rights of free speech and expression, freedom of association and assembly, and other basic civil liberties. We should agree with them on this point. A second component in their view is that "no members of our political community ought to be devalued on account of the spiritual foundations of their important commitments and projects. Religious faith deserves special constitutional solicitude in this respect, but only because of its vulnerability to hostility and neglect" (Eisgruber and Sager, 2007: 52). The third component is a claim that government should be neutral in its treatment of citizens' religious and nonreligious concerns—that is to say, apart from concern to prevent religious discrimination, "we have no constitutional reason to treat religion as deserving special benefits or as subject to special disabilities" (ibid.).

Regarded as a claim about how a decent society should set its political arrangements, the nondiscrimination or "no devaluation" view is appealing but problematic. A decent society seeks to regulate its affairs according to what is truly just and right. The just state does not aspire to be neutral between correct and incorrect views about what ways of treating people are fair and unfair and what life outcomes for people are advantageous and disadvantageous for them. Nor can the just state be neutral between empirically adequate and empirically inadequate views as to what the actual and likely consequences will be of the policies it might enact. Religions pronounce on these matters. Insofar as religious views dovetail with our best accounts of what is right and good, the laws and public policies of a just state will not conflict with religious views. Insofar as the state succeeds in enacting just policies, and these conflict with religious doctrines, in a clear and obvious sense the state does devalue or disparage these views.

We need to be careful to avoid a sort of Orwellian doublespeak here that pretends that religious people who experience state policies as hostile to their cherished beliefs are simply mistaken or confused (see Smith, 1995, and Smith, 2001, for a sympathetic account of the plight of the religious under a secular constitutional regime). For example, if my religion tells me that whites are the superior race and good jobs and positions of authority should be reserved for whites only, a state policy that forbids discrimination on the basis of race in employment and assignment to public office opposes my belief. If my religion tells me that God created the world in six days, a public-school curriculum that includes a scientifically sound biology class puts the weight of state authority against my religious belief. Religious doctrines take clear and substantive stands on a raft of empirical and moral questions, and many of these doctrines are flatly opposed to scientific consensus and any reasonable moral principles.

Moreover, a society that eschews endorsing particular or generic religious claims and does not eschew endorsing particular moral and scientific claims in effect has embraced a secular establishment. Its treatment of religious and nonreligious claims is asymmetrical and nonneutral. From the religious believer's point of view, not only does the state refrain from endorsing particular religious views that she regards as true and of the greatest importance for our lives, the state also implicitly or explicitly rejects the methods that she considers appropriate for discerning the fundamental truths that we must accept in order to live well. These methods include absorption of divine revelation as recorded in a sacred book authenticated by one's religious tradition, and as plumbed by interpretations of its message, along with introspection and meditation on one's own religious experiences. They are given no credence whatsoever in the public culture of a secular society striving to be just.

10. Conclusion

The argument of this chapter may seem to have come full circle in a disastrous way. Its starting point is that religious liberty is violated by state establishment of religion—the state's endorsing some religious doctrine or favoring adherents of some religious doctrines over others. But we added that religious liberty is not violated if—a big if—the state's laws and other directives enact justice (are justified by correct moral principles), even if just laws make it more burdensome for people to live according to their religious faith. Doesn't this amount to an embrace of an unfair state establishment of secular humanism or atheist morality or the like? Is the suggestion supposed to be that secular ideas are privileged as possibly acceptable justifications for state laws whereas religious doctrines are ruled out as inadmissible? Why would this be fair?

Some respond to this worry by maintaining that state power should be used only in ways that are justifiable from any reasonable citizen's standpoint, be it religious or nonreligious (Rawls, 1996; Weithman, 2010). The trick in carrying out this strategy successfully would be to identify uncontroversial and consensual justifications of policies that meet this constraint without ruling out as inadmissible policies that surely ought to be established and enforced (no slavery, no totalitarian intrusions on privacy, no discrimination on the basis of race or skin color). The suggestion advanced in this chapter is that only secular moral ideas will be suitable bases for state policies—not any and all such ideas, only correct ones, or ones that in our present state of moral knowledge are singled out as most likely to be correct. The suggestion licenses a form of secular establishment. But the claim that only certain secular moral ideas are picked out by the balance of moral reasons properly weighed is just an assumption we have made, not a claim we have tried to support by argument. Reason goes where it goes. So far as the arguments of this chapter go, it could turn out to be the case that some particular religious doctrine—for example, some version of evangelical Christianity or the Sunni Muslim faith—is singled out as correct by the balance of reasons properly weighed (for skeptical arguments against theistic claims see Mackie, 1982). If so, the correct religious liberty doctrine would scrap no-establishment while still embracing religious liberty in the form of toleration (wide civil liberties for all, including adherents of any and all faiths and doctrines). In the same spirit, we should conclude by noting that the acceptability of the welfare accommodation approach to the problem of whether to make special legal provision so that state laws do not prevent people from living according to the dictates of their religious faith depends on arguments, which we have not tried to supply, showing that this approach is supported by decisive moral arguments and required by justice rightly understood.

Note

1. The author thanks two anonymous reviewers for sage comments on a draft of this chapter.

References

Arneson, Richard, 2010. Against freedom of conscience. *San Diego Law Review*, 47, pp.1015–1040.

Arneson, Richard, 2014. Political liberalism, religious liberty, and religious establishment. In: Hanoch Dagan, Shafar Lifshitz, and Yedidia Z. Stern, eds. *The role of religion in human rights discourse*. Jerusalem: Israel Democracy Institute. pp.117–144.

Audi, R., 1989. The separation of church and state and the obligations of citizenship. *Philosophy and Public Affairs*, 18, pp.259–296.

Dworkin, Ronald, 2013. *Religion without God*. Cambridge, MA: Harvard University Press.

Eisgruber, Christopher L., and Sager, Lawrence G., 2007. *Religious freedom and the Constitution*. Cambridge, MA: Harvard University Press.

Estlund, David M., 2008. *Democratic authority: a philosophical framework*. Princeton, NJ: Princeton University Press.

Galston, William A., 2002. Liberal pluralism: the implications of value pluralism for political theory and practice. Cambridge, UK: Cambridge University Press.

Greenawalt, Kent, 2006. *Religion and the Constitution, vol. 1, Free exercise and fairness*. Princeton, NJ and Oxford: Princeton University Press.

Greenawalt, Kent, 2008. *Religion and the Constitution, vol. 2, Establishment and fairness*. Princeton, NJ and Oxford: Princeton University Press.

Greene, Abner S., 1993. The political balance of the religion clauses. *Yale Law Journal*, 102, pp.1611–1644.

Koppelman, Andrew, 2006. Is it fair to give religion special treatment? *University of Illinois Law Review*, 2006, pp.571–604.

Koppelman, Andrew, 2013. *Defending American religious neutrality*. Cambridge, MA: Harvard University Press.

Leiter, Brian, 2012. *Why tolerate religion?* Princeton, NJ: Princeton University Press.

Macedo, S., 1995. Liberal civic education and religious fundamentalism: the case of God v. John Rawls? *Ethics*, 105, pp.468–496.

Mackie, J. L., 1982. *The miracle of theism: arguments for and against the existence of God*. Oxford: Oxford University Press.

Marshall, William P., 2000. What is the matter with equality? An assessment of the equal treatment of religion and nonreligion in First Amendment jurisprudence. *Indiana Law Journal*, 75, pp.193–217.

McConnell, Michael W., 1990. Free exercise revisionism and the Smith decision. *University of Chicago Law Review*, 57, pp.1109–1153.

McConnell, Michael W., 1992. Religious freedom at a crossroads. *University of Chicago Law Review*, 59, pp.115–194.

Nussbaum, Martha, 2008. *Liberty of conscience: in defense of America's tradition of religious liberty*. New York: Basic Books.

Nussbaum, Martha, 2011. Political liberalism and perfectionist liberalism. *Philosophy and Public Affairs*, 39, pp.3–45.

Patten, Allen, 2012. Liberal neutrality: a reinterpretation and defense. *Journal of Political Philosophy*, 20, pp.249–272.

Perry, Michael J., 2007. *Toward a theory of human rights: religion, law, courts*. Cambridge, UK: Cambridge University Press.

Quong, Jonathan, 2011. *Liberalism without perfection*. Oxford: Oxford University Press.

Rawls, John, 1996. *Political liberalism*. New York: Columbia University Press.

Smith, Steven D., 1995. *Foreordained failure: the quest for a constitutional principle of religious freedom*. Oxford: Oxford University Press.

Smith, Steven D., 2001. *Getting over equality: a critical diagnosis of religious freedom in America*. New York: New York University Press.

Weithman, Paul, 2010. *Why political liberalism? On John Rawls's political turn*. Oxford: Oxford University Press.

CHAPTER 21

FREEDOM AND INFLUENCE IN FORMATIVE EDUCATION

KYLA EBELS-DUGGAN

THE task of raising children seems centrally to involve shaping their values or normative outlook. But many hold that imposing our conceptions of the good on others is incompatible with individuals' entitlement to freedom or autonomy. The worry can be seen as a version of the same, broadly Kantian, moral commitment that finds expression in liberal political theory: each person should be free to choose for himself what to regard as good and, within wide parameters, guide his own life by these normative commitments. Children's vulnerability to those primarily responsible for their upbringing arguably makes imposition seem particularly threatening here, even as their need for guidance makes it seem especially necessary. How, then, can conscientious parents both respect their children's claims to freedom and responsibly execute their childrearing task?[1] Call this *the liberal dilemma of childrearing.*

Anxiety about the liberal dilemma grips much of the contemporary philosophical discussion of children, education, and moral formation. A standard solution has developed in response: to avoid undue influence and respect children's claims to freedom we ought to educate in a way that puts each child in a position to choose for herself what to value once her agency is developed enough to do so. Standardly, this is put as the claim that we ought to educate children for autonomy (e.g., Ackerman, 1980; Feinberg, 1992; Macedo, 1995; Callan, 1997; Gutmann, 1999; Brighouse, 2006).

I will argue that, while it is true that parents ought to educate for autonomy, and that this provides a resolution of the liberal dilemma, the resolution does not work as most autonomy advocates imagine. Many think of educating for autonomy as a way of avoiding teaching a particular normative outlook or conception of the good, grasping the second horn of the dilemma. But construed as an alternative to teaching a particular set of value commitments, the aim of putting children in a position to freely choose their own commitments is hopeless (Ebels-Duggan, 2014; Ebels-Duggan, 2015). On a more attractive conception of autonomy, the perceived tension between educating a child into a particular conception of the good and respecting her freedom turns out to be an illusion. Thus, the liberal dilemma is not so much resolved as dissolved. We can, and should, both intentionally shape our children's normative outlooks and educate them in a way that aims to make them autonomous adults.

I begin by showing how the dominant interpretation of the autonomy solution depends on a specific, and implausible, moral psychology. Section I lays out Joel Feinberg's classic statement of this standard view and raises an important question about it. Section II explains how, in order to make the view work, its advocates must contrast values, commitments, and desires that are inculcated into a person through education with those that are authentically his own. But, I argue, this distinction proves impossible to draw. Section III sketches an alternative conception of autonomous commitments as those over which we exercise first personal authority in a particular sense. This account does not support the contrast between one's own commitments on the one hand, and commitments that result from upbringing or education on the other. It thus undermines the supposed opposition between the two poles of the liberal dilemma. While the aim of educating for autonomy, so conceived, rules out certain approaches to childrearing, it does not provide positive guidance about what to teach a child. Section IV argues that childrearing norms capable of providing such guidance are derivative from, rather than independent of, norms that direct the formation of our own substantive normative commitments. This means that the best that each parent can do, from his own point of view, is to make thoughtful judgments about what is right and good, and guide his childrearing by these, just as he guides his other activities by them.

1. Feinberg on Open Futures

In a classic article, Joel Feinberg provides the basis for the most widely favored response to the liberal dilemma of childrearing (Feinberg, 1992). He argues that children have an interest in and right to an "open future." His argument begins with the claim that, as individuals in their own right, children have equal moral status with adults. In particular, they have claim to any right that we normally assign to adults, either in its full-blown form, or as part of a class Feinberg calls "rights in trust." The right to bodily integrity or freedom from violence is an example of the first sort. Autonomy rights are the central case of rights in trust.

An adult's autonomy rights consist in the freedom to guide her own life according to her own value judgments. It is generally wrong to interfere coercively with an adult's attempt to live as she sees fit simply on the grounds that her choices are poor ones. But, due to their underdeveloped agency, children are not yet able to make authoritative value judgments that are due this sort of deference, and so cannot have autonomy rights in a straightforward way. Feinberg thus holds that their autonomy rights must be treated as rights in trust, rights to be preserved for them by the adults responsible for their upbringing until they are able to exercise them. On his view, preserving these rights amounts to leaving options open for a child until she is able to choose among these options for herself. The idea that ensuring children an open future in this sense provides the key to solving the liberal dilemma enjoys near consensus in philosophical discussions of education and childrearing.[2]

Feinberg's interest lies partly in claiming that children's entitlement to an open future justifies state intervention in child-rearing practices that do not achieve this aim. But we can also take him to be offering a potential resolution of the liberal dilemma of child-rearing as it presents itself to conscientious parents. That is, we can read him as giving advice to parents and educators who are concerned both to raise and educate their children well and to respect their right to freedom. If Feinberg is correct, then rather than trying to pass on some single worldview or conception of the good, the good parent aims to put her child in a position to choose his own normative commitments upon maturity. She thereby resolves the liberal dilemma.

But the suggestion that we could secure for a child an open future *rather than* teaching her a particular normative outlook embodies an important confusion. To bring out this confusion, we must consider more closely what it means to have access to options among which one can freely choose. Feinberg's discussion provides at least three possibilities. According to the first, one gives a child access to options by developing her physical powers and her talents.[3] A second, related idea understands access in terms of having knowledge and information rather than being kept in ignorance. Feinberg's advocacy for state intervention in the limited education that some Amish parents would choose for their children can be interpreted along these lines.[4] But Feinberg's leading idea of access seems to be a psychological, or we might even say *existential*, sense. Options are accessible to a person in this third way if they seem "live" to her, if she can actually imagine endorsing or engaging in them, and can take them seriously as possibilities for her own life (cf. Callan, 1997). This existential conception of access to multiple normative views provides the most natural apparent contrast to attempts to teach a child a single, particular conception of the good.[5]

Suppose that we accept this psychological conception of access for the purpose of interpreting the notion of open futures, and look to enact Feinberg's proposed solution to the liberal dilemma. We next need to know which options matter: to which possibilities are children entitled to have existential access?[6] One possible answer is that the conscientious parent would try to *maximize* the options open to her child. Some things that Feinberg says suggest that he endorses this maximization view. For example, he speaks of "the claims of children that they be permitted to reach maturity with *as many open options, opportunities, and advantages as possible*" (Feinberg, 1992: 80, emphasis added).[7] Later he appeals to an ideal of maximization in support of a case for apparently massive government intervention in childrearing: "Ideally, the neutral state . . . would act to let *all influences*, or *the largest and most random possible assortment of influences*, work equally on the child, to open up *all* possibilities to him" (ibid. 85, emphasis added).

The maximization strategy has an important theoretical advantage over alternatives: it does not require specifying a boundary between options that a conscientious parent must leave open and those she can permissibly foreclose. But this advantage comes at the cost of implausible normative upshots. On a moment's reflection, it seems wildly implausible that we harm or wrong a child any time we make living according to some set of normative commitments psychologically inaccessible to him, regardless of the content of that view. Consider, for example, the careful work many parents put into raising their children to regard everyone as entitled to consideration. The aim of these efforts is that their children reach maturity with a settled conviction that it is wrong to harm others without very significant reason. If these parents succeed, their children will not be able to take alternatives—thoroughgoing egoism, for example—seriously as real possibilities for their lives. This and other options will be existentially closed to them. Nor is this merely a regrettable side effect of achieving a goal that could be balanced against the restriction of existentially available options. Closing these possibilities *is* the goal. Nevertheless, teaching children to regard everyone as entitled to consideration strikes me not only as unobjectionable, but as a non-optional and non-controversial element of good parenting.

From here, it is not difficult to multiply examples. Consider the massively funded attempts of profit-seeking corporations to shape children's values, loyalties, and self-conceptions. Suppose that parents aim to shield a child from these influences as much as possible. Moreover, suppose that they do so as part of a conscientious attempt to raise the child in a way that makes the materialist conceptions of the good on which so many such corporations depend existentially unavailable to him. Given the pervasive presence of these influences, foreclosing materialist options will be an uphill battle, but our question is whether it would be wrong to try, or wrong to succeed. I am not sure exactly what Feinberg imagines when he says that children should be exposed to the largest and most random possible assortment of influences, but the maximization view seems unable to treat corporate advertising or the evaluative outlooks that it promotes differently from other influences. But it is implausible to think that allowing for-profit corporations, among others, to influence our children's outlooks is something that we should do for our children's sake and in the interest of making them more free.

Any plausible version of the open futures view will thus reject the maximization strategy and allow that some influences may be blocked and some possibilities closed without any harm or wrong to the child. The responsible parent does not merely expose her child to the largest and most random set of influences, but rather makes considered judgments about which influences are salutary and which are rightly excluded and actively seeks to close certain existential possibilities. But with any retreat from the maximal options position, the advocate of the right to an open future incurs the argumentative burden that that position promised to avoid. He now needs some principled way of drawing the line between those possibilities that a child is entitled to have open and those that we do not wrong her by closing.

A supporter of the open futures view might try appealing to the set of options on which autonomy rights permit adults to act, roughly the limits of liberal tolerance (cf. Clayton, 2006). Given the way that Feinberg's argument unfolds, this would have an appealing logic. The child's right to an open future is supposed to be the manifestation of the same rights that show up as autonomy rights for adults. It may thus seem plausible that conscientious parents will seek to make a normative conception existentially available to their children just in case a liberal state should permit an adult who had that conception to act on it. If this worked, advocates of the autonomy strategy could borrow whatever justification liberal political philosophers provide for setting these boundaries in a particular way. For example, they might rely on Rawls's distinction between reasonable and unreasonable disagreement over comprehensive doctrines (Rawls, 1993). While specifying these limits is no easy task, it would at least be one that Feinberg and other advocates of an open future need not shoulder on their own.

But, even if we assume that liberal political theorists have a defensible principled basis for sorting between reasonable and unreasonable conceptions of the good for their purposes, that line does not fall in the right place for ours. The question of which conceptions of the good a liberal government should allow is distinct from the question of which a good parent would commend to her child. Unsurprisingly, different considerations bear upon how these two questions, respectively, should be settled. In particular, that a certain way of life is a waste of time, or even that it is impermissible, are not reasons for a liberal government to interfere with those who enact it. Political liberals thus favor political protection for acting on a very wide range of normative commitments, including some they themselves (rightly) find objectionable, impermissible, or worthless. But, though they do not support coercive intervention on the part of the government, the triviality or wrongfulness of a way of life are good grounds for discouraging individuals, especially children for whose upbringing we are responsible, from regarding it as a serious option for themselves.

Some examples may help dispel any doubts about this. Suppose that we treat Rawls's grass counter as reasonable for political purposes, meaning that we would not countenance government intervention in his life plan. This should not commit us to thinking that we have reason to encourage anyone to regard emulating him as a live possibility. Or, returning to the example above, we can think that the government should not forbid people from acting on a normative outlook built around particular brand loyalties, while also thinking that parents may, and perhaps must, act to discourage their own children from this sort of self-conception. Morally objectionable outlooks provide the starkest kind of case. It is morally impermissible to be a neo-Nazi, and also morally impermissible to publicly advocate for neo-Nazi views. Liberals nevertheless standardly support the free speech rights of neo-Nazis. Such support should not commit them to thinking that a conscientious parent would raise her child to be existentially open to advocating for neo-Nazi views.

The view under consideration would license inference from the claim that a view should be politically protected to the claim that it would be wrong to discourage a child in your charge from taking up that view. But we seem to have good reason to limit government interference in a wide range of ways of life that parents also have good reason to seek to close for their children. The view under consideration would not allow that this is even a possibility. This is not a cost that anyone should be willing to pay.

2. WHICH DESIRES ARE MY OWN?

Late in his article Feinberg acknowledges that a child's upbringing will inevitably close some options, and seeks to articulate the conditions under which such limits are compatible with children's freedom. Perhaps moved by concerns similar to those above, he offers a quite different way of carving out the possibilities or options made available by an ideal upbringing. Rather than appeal to the limits of liberal tolerance, he suggests that the options that must be kept open are those that the child in question would or will choose when he reaches maturity.[8] One result is that the particular options that we would be wrong to close vary with idiosyncracies of the individual child.

But this suggestion threatens to render the view unhelpfully circular. The claim is that children's upbringing should respect their freedom to act on the decisions that they will make as adults. But the decisions that they will make as adults will surely depend on the upbringing that they receive. So this understanding of the entitlement to an open future does not appear capable of guiding decisions about how to raise and educate a child.

Feinberg himself raises this objection to the view:

> At the early stage the parents cannot even ask in any helpful way what the child will be like, apart from the parental policies under consideration, when he does have relevant preferences, values, and the capacity to consent. That outcome will depend on the character the child will have then, which in part depends, in turn, on how his parents rear him now. (Feinberg, 1992: 94)[9]

To break out of this circle, advocates of the open futures solution to the liberal dilemma need a way to distinguish those desires, proclivities, and commitments properly regarded as a child's own from those inculcated in him through education. Only this would render an education that defers to the child's own values distinct from one that imposes the parents' or educators' conception of the good.

Feinberg believes that he can draw this needed distinction. Granting that the choices that a child will eventually make depend to some extent on how she is raised, he asserts that they will not depend only or wholly on this. Children are malleable, but they are not completely so, and this provides some fixed points that can guide those responsible for their upbringing. So Feinberg attempts to draw a distinction between those desires, values, and proclivities educated into a child and those that are her own by appealing to her innate or presocial tendencies.[10] He is far from alone in making this sort of move.[11] And, on reflection, it seems to be no accident that authors favoring something like the open futures solution converge on the class of innate tendencies. If one seeks a set of tendencies that could contrast with those that result from education or upbringing, it is hard to see where one could look other than to the presocial.

But assigning innate or presocial tendencies, as a class, the normative status that they would need to break the circle is unattractive. In order to do the work, these natural tendencies must serve as the bases for a normative outlook most properly regarded as the child's own, such that she is autonomous when they are allowed to develop and flourish, and attempts to suppress or reform them violate her freedom. Pairing this with the affirmation of a right to an open future commits Feinberg and others to treating tendencies, desires, and character traits that are innate as having presumptive authority to set the course of a person's upbringing. But it is far too simplistic to grant such authority to innate or presocial desires, per se. Suppose a particular child, or people in general, are innately inclined to hoard more than their share of scarce goods, to undervalue the contributions of others, to fear things that do not warrant fear, or to make in-group/out-group distinctions based only on superficial physical characteristics. The mere fact that tendencies such as these precede attempts to raise or educate a child cannot be sufficient to imbue them with authority. To think so would surely amount to a crude naturalistic fallacy.

There are more general reasons to reject this sort of privileging of innate desires and tendencies as well. It is not as if proclivities that arise in us without influence from other people arise without any influence at all. Presumably all of our innate proclivities have some cause, be it genetic, environmental, or some combination. In this way they are not more freely held than those resulting from our education. Yet Feinberg seems committed to the idea that impersonal forces generate commitments that have greater standing to be called my own than do those commitments influenced by the intentional actions of other persons. Put this way, the idea is difficult to accept. Moreover, this standard strategy appears to grant the uneducated desires of children normative precedence over the reflective value judgments of adults. As a guiding principle this looks much more like an abdication of child-rearing responsibility than an attempt to carry out such responsibilities.

We should conclude that the category of innate or presocial desires and proclivities, those values and commitments that a person develops "naturally" in contrast to those she develops in response to the intentional educative efforts of others, is not normatively homogenous. Some members of this set certainly deserve encouragement and nurture. But the conscientious parent will look to reshape or even eradicate others.

On reflection, it may seem so obvious that a good upbringing would not leave all innate proclivities untouched as to raise the worry of uncharitable interpretation. So let us recall how we got here: In response to the liberal dilemma of childrearing, Feinberg claims that the conscientious parent would respect a child's right-in-trust to autonomy. Doing so amounts to aiming to leave or make a range of normative outlooks open to her, in the sense the she will be able to take these seriously as options for her own life. The parent who accepts this view and tries to enact it needs some way of determining which possibilities matter. A simple maximization approach fails. Nor can we appeal to the choices that she will in fact make, since this raises an acute problem of circularity. Natural, innate, or presocial tendencies are brought in in hopes of breaking this circle. Understanding these as distinctively free would give content to an autonomy-respecting education. However, there seems to be no independent motivation for carving out the distinction this way, and we have seen that doing so leads to unattractive normative conclusions.

I claimed above that innate or presocial desires are apparently the natural leading candidate for a class of tendencies that could be contrasted with the outcomes of education as a person's own. That this option proves so unsatisfactory thus calls the very idea of such a contrast into question. The next section will consider a quite different way to identify a person's own autonomous commitments. I will argue that, though autonomy conceived in this more attractive way can provide an answer to the liberal dilemma and some guidance in upbringing, it does not provide an alternative to educating children into a particular conception of the good, as Feinberg and many others hope.

3. AUTONOMY: AN ALTERNATIVE CONCEPTION

Consider the classic Kantian conception of autonomy. Whereas Feinberg regards our innate desires and inclinations as paradigmatic expressions of our agency, Kant, in at least some of his work, treats inclinations as the central threat to our autonomy (Kant, 1998). He does so because he thinks of inclinations as forces occurring in us with respect to which we are passive (Ebels-Duggan, forthcoming). On this way of thinking they are not something that we do, and so not ascribable to us as agents. They are merely part of the circumstances in which we act (cf. Schapiro, 2009). By contrast, when we consider the reasons that support acting a certain way, determine that these reasons are sufficient, and act on this determination, we bring our own activity to bear and so act autonomously.

So Kant understands autonomy as a matter of *first personal authority* over our attitudes (cf. Moran, 2001). Our principles, or maxims, of action count as our own because we determine their content through our own assessment of the reasons supporting them. This supposedly marks a difference between our principles of action on the one hand, and our inclinations or desires on the other. The former are subject to the authority of our judgments while the latter are motivational states that simply happen in or to us. But we need not follow Kant in this way of sorting attitudes in order to embrace his conception of autonomy as first personal authority.

Consider an example. If I were to encounter a poisonous snake while hiking, I would be afraid. But the fear does not seem to be a mere force, some arational part of the causal order. It is, rather, an intelligible, warranted response to the danger of the situation. When all is going well, the fear arises through my attention to and thinking about actual features of my situation and would change in response to changes in my interpretations of these features. Upon realizing that what I took be a poisonous snake is really perfectly harmless, my fear would dissipate, replaced by relief. Fear that is describable in this way is fear over which I have first personal authority.

When my attitudes—not just my judgments but also my desires and emotions—respond in this way to my assessment of the reasons supporting them, I do not experience them as alien forces occurring in me. It then makes sense to attribute them to myself, to regard them not just as happening to me but as something I am doing, free expressions of my own agency. Contrast a phobia: if I am subject to a phobia of snakes, my feeling of fear persists even in the face of my wholly sincere and considered judgment that there is no danger. In this case the fear does incur on me as an alien force, something that happens in me and is not subject to my authority.[12]

First personal authority, so conceived, provides an alternative conception of what it is to hold a desire, value, or commitment freely or autonomously. This approach ascribes an attitude to a person's own free agency if it is responsive to her judgments about or appreciation of the reasons for it.[13] We can then use this conception to interpret the idea that children should be put in a position to choose their normative commitments for themselves: choosing for one's self is exercising first personal authority over one's commitments—that is, forming these in a way that is responsive to one's own attention to and thinking about the reasons that would bear on them.

A full defense of this approach to autonomy is beyond the scope of this chapter, but suppose that we try to understand a child's autonomy rights-in-trust along these lines. Children have a right to be educated in such a way that they are able to exercise first-personal authority over their normative commitments or conception of the good. The conception a child so educated comes to embrace will be responsive to his own appreciation of the reasons and values that support it. He will be able to affirm it from the inside. On this view, children's autonomy rights *do* provide important guidance for parents, but they *do not* stand in tension with attempts to educate children into a particular set of values or conception of the good.

This way of understanding children's autonomy rights provides genuine guidance in child-rearing and education, guidance that is more attractive in content than the alternatives considered above. To see what it would rule out, return to the case of for-profit companies seeking to shape the normative outlooks of the next generation through sophisticated advertising campaigns. Such campaigns need not, and standardly do not, put their audience in a relationship of first personal authority with the desires they aim to generate in order to succeed. The influence at which they aim is strictly causal, not distinctively rational. The purveyors of these campaigns are as happy to circumvent as to engage the agency of those whom they address, and so need not articulate or otherwise display genuine reasons for wanting or valuing the products on offer. Their aim is simply effective production of the desires in question. If they most efficiently accomplish this by associating their products with other things the audience finds attractive—fun, or family, or sex—they will, even if this association has no basis in reality. Desires so produced may well be recalcitrant in the face of agents' judgments that they are not really warranted. If so, they are not autonomous in the sense above, but this need not interfere with the aims of the corporations in question.

The liberal dilemma looks real only if we assimilate the aims of parents who seek to communicate their particular normative commitments to their children to the corporate advertising model. Many theorists exercised by the dilemma grant that parents do have an interest in passing on their particular values and way of life, but also claim that this interest is in tension with, and must be balanced against, their children's interest in and right to autonomy (e.g., Callan, 1997; Gutmann, 1999). The supposed opposition between these two interests would be genuine if, like profit-seeking corporations, parents' interest in shaping their children's outlooks were merely instrumental to some further extrinsic end of their own. Such parents would be concerned only to produce effective normative commitments of a particular content in their children, and happy to use whatever methods most efficiently accomplished this. They would not particularly care about putting children in a position to appreciate the reasons supporting their commitments and so to exercise first personal authority over them.

Like the target of relentless advertising, the child so educated may well end up alienated from her desires, commitments, and values. She does not necessarily arrive at or maintain them through consideration or appreciation of the reasons for them, but, like a phobia, they may nevertheless function effectively in her psychology (cf. Brighouse, 2006). Such an upbringing leaves her divided against herself, unable to determine the content of her own commitments through the exercise of her own judgment. This is an important lack of freedom or autonomy, and children certainly have an interest in avoiding this outcome. Metaphors of balancing interests would apply if parents have an interest in producing it.[14]

However, this picture badly misconstrues the aims and interests of the parents. Parents who seek to raise children in a particular worldview are almost never trying to get their children to choose a way of life as one might buy a product. In stark contrast to profit-driven corporations, they do not view the shaping of their children's normative commitments instrumentally. Nor do they standardly understand the exercise of whatever influence they have as indulging some self-regarding interest or preference. Rather, their intrinsic end is to help their children genuinely appreciate what is genuinely valuable.

The aims of such parents are not in tension with educating for autonomy in the relevant sense. On the contrary, they require it: these parents will accomplish their aims only by putting their children in a position to actively appreciate the reasons for their commitments and so to exercise first personal authority over them. They succeed only if the commitments their children have as a result of their upbringing are also the children's own in the most full-blooded sense. On this way of thinking, neither the contrast between commitments that are a child's own and those educated into him, nor talk of balancing parents' interests in passing on their commitments with children's interests in autonomy, has any application.[15]

The conception of autonomy as first personal authority thus dissolves the liberal dilemma: Conscientious parents educate their children for autonomy, but this comes to something very different from what Feinberg and others imagine. It is an element of, rather than an alternative to, educating them into a particular normative outlook or worldview.

4. Two Derivative Norms

Feinberg looks to answer two questions. First, *which possibilities must we leave open for a child in order to respect her right to an open future?* Second, *which desires, commitments and proclivities count as distinctively her own?* He derives a resolution to the first from the answer to the second: the possibilities that we should look to leave open for a child just are those that her own desires and proclivities pick out. So, on the standard view that he exemplifies, educating for autonomy is supposed to both resolve the liberal dilemma and provide parents with substantial guidance about what to teach their children.

On the account defended here, autonomy cannot play this role. In principle, commitments of any content could be held autonomously, but not all normative outlooks can serve as bases for a good upbringing. Educating for autonomy, as I intend it, is thus necessary but far from sufficient for responsible parenting or education. Since this conception of autonomy does not support a contrast between autonomous commitments and those educated into a person, it does not provide the fixed point that would be needed to specify which range of options we must leave open to respect a child's right to an open future and so break out of Feinberg's circle. We require some independent way of answering the first question, specifying the content of the options to which children are entitled.

It seems that the correct, though perhaps disappointing, view is simply that we should be concerned to leave open a sufficient range of valuable possibilities.[16] If we teach a child to value things not worth valuing, we wrong her, even if we do so in a way that allows her to exercise first personal authority over the commitments in question. And if one's upbringing leaves one unable to appreciate some things that are worth appreciating, then important possibilities are not available. On the other hand, inability to regard options that have no value as genuine possibilities is simply a mark of wisdom or moral maturity. This inability is not something that a good parent will try to avoid, but something he will try to help his children achieve.

If we accept the idea that the possibilities that we should leave or make existentially open to children are just the valuable ones, then discerning what to teach a child depends on having and exercising good normative judgment of our own about which possibilities these are. A commitment to educate our children for autonomy, or to secure for them an open future, does not yet address questions about which commitments to commend to them. The guidance that the idea that certain possibilities must be left open for children provides is wholly derivative from norms that tell us what the valuable possibilities are or how to settle this question for ourselves. This may be disappointing, insofar as it was hoped that the idea of open futures, autonomy, or the freedom to choose one's own commitments could provide some independent direction concerning what to teach children. It cannot.

Consider how this applies to the Amish case. Feinberg contends that a traditional Amish upbringing violates children's rights to an open future. He suggests that this is because Amish parents look to pass on a particular normative outlook, rather than leaving their children free to choose their commitments autonomously. But the Amish parents presumably do look to put their children in a position to appreciate the value of the way of life that they impart, and so to hold these commitments autonomously in the sense that is defended here. Moreover, though they do foreclose a range of possibilities, this does not distinguish the Amish from any other parents. They may readily agree that they should give their children existential access to a range of valuable possibilities. Their disagreement with Feinberg turns wholly on the question of which options fall within such a range, and this disagreement, in turn, derives from differences between their normative outlook and his.

That the options existentially closed by such an upbringing are important and valuable ones seems to be the motivating idea behind the court opinion that Feinberg quotes approvingly:

> The State is . . . attempting to nurture and develop the human potential of its children, whether Amish or non-Amish: to expand their knowledge, broaden their sensibilities, kindle their imagination, foster a spirit of free inquiry, and increase their human understanding and tolerance. It is possible that most Amish children will wish to continue living the rural life of their parents, in which case their training at home will adequately equip them for their future role. Others, however, may wish to become nuclear physicists, ballet dancers, computer programmers, or historians, and for these occupations, formal training will be necessary. (*Wisconsin v. Yoder*, 237–238; quoted in Feinberg, 1992: 86–87)

You probably agree with Feinberg's assessment of the relevant values, and so may also agree with his conclusion that the Amish upbringing is objectionable. But it is important to recognize that the objection could not be narrowly focused on their approach to child-rearing. If there is a problem with the way these parents raise their children, it is not that they aim to communicate a particular set of values. It is, rather, that they aim to communicate the particular normative outlook that they do, *their* normative outlook, one that holds that the Amish way of life is importantly superior to the alternatives listed by the court. Though he might not want to put it this way, Feinberg's view is that the Amish parents should instead teach their children *his* normative outlook, on which the alternatives are at least as worthwhile as a traditional Amish life. Even if he is right about this, this course of action could not seem justified to the Amish parents themselves unless they first experience a wholesale conversion to something like Feinberg's worldview.[17] The point is that the idea of educating children for an open future is not doing, and cannot do, any independent work in guiding parents' thinking about what to teach their children. The best that any parent can do by her own lights is to teach her children the conception of the good that she herself thinks is best.

One might try to resist this, by suggesting that what matters is not which particular normative outlook or way of life a child is encouraged to choose, but rather the attitudes toward alternatives that her upbringing commends. But these second-order attitudes, no less than the first order, are among our particular normative commitments. So direction for which attitudes to communicate to children about second-order matters is also derivative from prior norms guiding our own convictions. In addition to choosing how to live our particular lives, we need to strive for insight about how to regard various alternatives: some possibilities would have been just as good; others would have been just as good, but for the fact that we lack certain talents; still others would have been less worthwhile; and some would not have been permissible to carry out. Raising children well certainly depends on communicating to them the right view on these matters, but again we can say nothing helpful about how to carry this out that is independent of judgments about what these right views are.

There are further second-order judgments of a somewhat different kind. These concern the level of confidence that we should have in our commitments, and the extent to which we should be open to skeptical doubts about them. But here too there is very little that we can say at a general level about how to answer these questions. Some normative commitments warrant unshakable confidence, while others should be endorsed much more tentatively. When we disagree over child-rearing practices, we may be disagreeing about which are which.

We have now identified two norms that can guide us in answering the pressing question of what to teach our children. First, the content of children's education should not unnecessarily close off valuable possibilities for their future way of life. Second, we should teach children to have the right second-order attitudes toward their various first-order normative commitments. But no one could apply these directives without reliance on his own substantive normative convictions. Moreover, their application just amounts to an attempt to pass these substantive convictions, the content of one's own worldview or conception of the good, to those in one's charge. Thus, conscientious parents must strive to get their own views about these matters right, and then do their best to impart these same attitudes to the children for whom they are responsible.

So child-rearing norms capable of providing sufficient guidance are derivative from, not independent of, our particular evaluative outlooks. They provide no alternative to imposing our own normative views on those whom we raise, but direct us to educate our children to the best of our ability, guided by our own conceptions of the good. The account of autonomy given in section III should put to rest the fear that this will, of necessity, unduly limit children's freedom. If we teach our children to value truly valuable things, and do so in a way that allows them to exercise first personal authority over their commitments, then we have raised them in a responsible way and rendered them free to choose their own commitments in the only sense that we should. Of course if we teach them to value the wrong things, or close off options that should have been left open, we wrong them.

Perhaps it is disappointing that no philosophical theory of freedom can eliminate this danger, but it should not be surprising. A commitment to our children's freedom can tell us something about how to raise them, but it cannot substitute for the difficult work of doing our own normative reflection to come to considered judgments about what is worth valuing and loving or how we should live. The ideal parent gets it right about her own first- and second-order normative commitments. She looks to pass on these convictions because she is properly concerned to help her developing child get these essential matters right. The unsurprising upshot is that child-rearing requires a great deal of wisdom and good judgment and there are almost certainly no ideal parents. We are massively vulnerable to those who raise us, and thus child-rearing is a daunting task. Notions of freedom, autonomy, and an open future provide no shortcut for carrying it out.

Notes

1. I am interested in how adults who have significant responsibility for a child's care, upbringing, and education broadly construed should face this apparent tension. I will use "parent" to name the relevant adults, but what I say applies to non-parental guardians who stand in a traditional parenting role. Much also generalizes to other caregivers and educators, though this introduces additional issues about the division of responsibility and authority between parents and non-parents that I do not engage here.

2. See, for example, Ackerman, 1980; Gutmann, 1999; Macedo, 1995. For dissent, see Burtt, 1996; Burtt, 2003; Wolterstorff, Stronks, and Joldersma, 2002; Ebels-Duggan, 2014; Ebels-Duggan, 2015.

3. Feinberg offers an extreme example: if one cut off a child's legs before she was able to walk, one would thereby violate her freedom to choose to walk, even though she is not yet capable of exercising this choice (1992: 77).

4. "To be prepared for anything, including the worst, in this complex and uncertain world would seem to require as much knowledge as a child can absorb throughout his minority" (Feinberg, 1992: 82).

5. It may also be thought to partially ground the value of access in the other two senses: no option will be existentially open as a way of living my life if I do not know about it, or if I lack the requisite skills.

6. Feinberg initially claims that what must be kept open are "basic options" (ibid. 78), but makes no attempt to explain what this phrase picks out. Later, criticizing a legal decision favoring deference to the educational choices of Amish parents, he writes, "An impartial decision would assume only that education should equip the child with the knowledge and skills that will help him choose whichever sort of life best fits his native endowment and matured disposition. It should send him out into the adult world with as many open opportunities as possible, thus maximizing his chances for self-fulfillment" (ibid. 84). There seem to me to be three distinct positions about what neutrality amounts to here: (1) that it is neutral to put a child in a position to pursue a life that fits his native endowment; (2) that it is neutral to put him in a position to pursue a life that fits his matured disposition; and (3) that it is neutral to put him a position that leaves open as many opportunities as possible. I discuss each of these in the text.

7. The context here is specifically regarding a variety of religious views. Feinberg does not explain why the maximization rule should apply to choices about religious commitment in particular. He appears to be leaning on his own prior substantive normative convictions about the nature of religious commitment and its role in a life well lived. We will return to a similar point in the last section, with respect to Feinberg's treatment of the Amish case.

8. At one point, Feinberg claims that the inevitable narrowing of a child's options in upbringing is compatible with respect for his rights "provided it is somehow in accordance with actual or presumptive, explicit or tacit consent" (Feinberg, 1992: 94). This is helpful only if we can understand when the actual or explicit consent of a child would be necessary or sufficient to authorize our actions on the one hand, and what counts as presumptive or tacit consent on the other. It is hard to see a way forward with these questions that does not land us in the same circularity problems discussed in this section.

9. Cf Feinberg, 1992: 95: "In a nutshell: the parents help create some of the interests whose fulfillment will constitute the child's own good. They cannot aim at an independent conception of the child's own good in deciding how to do this, because to some extent, the child's own good (self-fulfillment) depends on which interests the parents decide to create."

10. Feinberg refers to these, variously, as "his own governing values, talents, and propensities" (Feinberg, 1992: 85), "the basic tendencies of the child" (ibid. 96), and "basic tendencies and inclinations, both those that are common to the species and those that are peculiar to the individual" (ibid. 91). Early in the paper he takes as a touchstone for freedom what the child will become if his growth is kept "natural and unforced."

11. This attempt to understand a child's autonomy rights in terms of his natural desires is echoed in several later authors' treatments of this same issue. Many appeal to the idea of "authentic desires," claiming that a child's autonomy comes to enacting these. See, for example, Brighouse, 2006; cf. Clayton, 2006; Ackerman, 1980.

12. The possibility of direct, non-observational knowledge of our own commitments is a mark of autonomy so construed, while lacking this possibility indicates the alienation that is its opposite. I learn that I am subject to the phobia by observing the things that I do, what it is difficult to bring myself to do, or by looking to other evidence like the physical reactions associated with fear. While some of this evidence may be more readily available to me than to others, it is not the sort of evidence that others are in principle barred from having. By contrast, when I exercise first personal authority over my mental states, I can justifiably ascribe them to myself without regard for evidence about myself. As Moran (2001) puts it, the question about my own attitudes is transparent to the question about the world, the contents at which these attitudes are directed. Transparency of this sort is a characteristic feature of first personal authority, and thus of states that, on this conception, count as autonomous.

13. Cf. Moran, 2001; Smith, 2005; Scanlon, 2008; Hieronymi, 2014.

14. This misleading setup of the question as requiring that the interests of parents and children be traded off against each other is surprisingly widespread in the literature concerning the proper role of the liberal state in education. Unsurprisingly, those who construe the problem this way standardly conclude that the state has wide latitude to intervene in parental education decisions. If this really were the shape of the problem, it would be hard to see why the purported interest of parents should be allowed any authority at all.

15. It is also compatible with an approach that does not try to *state* reasons, or give arguments for, the commitments in question. There are other, often better, ways of helping children appreciate reasons. For example, parents and educators may best help a child develop a love for beautiful music by exposing her to this music, and perhaps seeking to direct her attention to what is good about it, rather than simply asserting or trying to argue that it is good. The person who appreciates what is wonderful about Mozart's music has a love for the music that displays the marks of first personal authority. We need not be able to articulate the reasons for our mental states in order to exercise first personal authority over them.

16. We will still have to make choices, because there are more worthwhile things that could be appreciated than there is time to appreciate them in a single life. And while a child's natural proclivities can and should help guide these selections, we must make our own judgments about which of these proclivities are responsive to worthwhile possibilities.

17. This makes the case for government intervention in these child-rearing practices much more fraught than Feinberg's presentation suggests. If we are to coercively override the judgments of these parents, we must do so on the grounds that their normative outlook is seriously misguided, treating important valuable options as if they were not so. It is far from clear that we should empower the government of a pluralistic society to make and coercively enforce that kind of judgment. See Ebels-Duggan, 2013.

REFERENCES

Ackerman, B., 1980. *Social justice in the liberal state.* New Haven, CT: Yale University Press.

Brighouse, H., 2006. *On education.* New York: Routledge.

Burtt, S., 1996. In defense of Yoder: parental authority and the public schools. In: I. Shapiro and R. Hardin, eds. *Political order.* New York: New York University Press. pp.412–437.

Burtt, S., 2003. The proper scope of parental authority: why we don't owe children an "open future." In: S. Macedo and I. M. Young, eds. *Child, family and state.* New York: New York University Press. pp.243–270.

Callan, E., 1997. *Creating citizens.* New York: Oxford University Press.

Clayton, M., 2006. *Justice and legitimacy in upbringing.* New York: Oxford University Press.

Ebels-Duggan, K., 2013. Moral education in the liberal state. *Journal of Practical Ethics,* 1(2), pp.34–63.

Ebels-Duggan, K., 2014. Educating for autonomy: an old-fashioned view. *Social Philosophy and Policy,* 31(1), pp.257–275.

Ebels-Duggan, K., 2015. Autonomy as intellectual virtue. In: H. Brighouse and M. MacPherson, eds. *The aims of higher education.* Chicago: University of Chicago Press. pp.74–90.

Ebels-Duggan, K., forthcoming. Bad debt: the Kantian inheritance of Humean desire. In: Dai Heide and Evan Tiffany, eds. *Kantian Freedom.*

Feinberg, J., 1992. The child's right to an open future. In: *Freedom and fulfillment: philosophical essays.* Princeton, NJ: Princeton University Press, pp.76–97.

Gutmann, A., 1999. *Democratic education.* Princeton, NJ: Princeton University Press.

Hieronymi, P., 2014. Reflection and responsibility. *Philosophy and Public Affairs,* 42(1), pp.3–41.

Kant, I., 1998. *Groundwork of the metaphysics of morals.* New York: Cambridge University Press.

Macedo, S., 1995. Liberal civic education and religious fundamentalism: the case of God v. John Rawls? *Ethics,* 105(3), pp.468–496.

Moran, R., 2001. *Authority and estrangement.* Princeton, NJ: Princeton University Press.

Rawls, J., 1993. *Political liberalism.* New York: Columbia University Press.

Scanlon, T., 2008. *Moral dimensions: permissibility, meaning, blame.* Cambridge, MA: Harvard University Press.

Schapiro, T., 2009. The nature of inclination. *Ethics,* 119(2), pp.229–256.

Smith, A., 2005. Responsibility for attitudes: activity and passivity in the mental life. *Ethics,* 115(2), pp.236–271.

Wolterstorff, N., Stronks, G. G., and Joldersma, C. W., 2002. *Educating for life: reflections on Christian teaching and learning.* Grand Rapids, MI: Baker Academic.

CHAPTER 22

FREEDOM AND THE (POSTHUMOUS) HARM PRINCIPLE

DAVID BOONIN

THE only legitimate reason for limiting a person's freedom, Mill famously declared, is to prevent him from harming others. This edict, which has come to be known as the Harm Principle, strikes many people as quite plausible. Let us suppose that it is true. What would this entail about our freedom with respect to how we treat the dead? Suppose, for example, that Alice wanted to have her ashes scattered near the top of her favorite mountain but that when she died Ted decided to flush them down the toilet instead. Would the Harm Principle forbid us from interfering with Ted's freedom in this case? On the face of it, the answer seems to be yes. In order to be a subject of harm, one must have interests that are capable of being set back. A person has such interests but a pile of ashes does not, and so a person is capable of being harmed while a pile of ashes is not. And if no one would be harmed by Ted's act, then the Harm Principle forbids us from interfering with his freedom to perform it.

But things are not so simple. This is because there is a potentially powerful argument in defense of what I will call the Posthumous Harm Thesis, the claim that it is possible for an act to harm a person even if the act takes place after the person is dead. If the Posthumous Harm Thesis is true, then Ted's act might turn out to harm Alice despite the fact that it takes place after Alice is dead. And if Ted's act turns out to harm Alice, then the Harm Principle will not forbid restricting his freedom to perform it after all. More generally, if the Posthumous Harm Thesis is true, then the Harm Principle will turn out to forbid fewer restrictions on freedom than would otherwise be the case. In order to fully understand the implications of the Harm Principle, then, one must critically engage with the literature on posthumous harm. Doing so is the goal of this chapter.

1. The Posthumous Harm Argument

Although the Posthumous Harm Thesis strikes many people as counterintuitive, the argument in its defense that I want to focus on here is grounded in a kind of intuitive judgment that most people seem inclined to make. Consider the case of Bob. Bob wants his marriage to Carol to be monogamous and he believes that it is, but in fact Carol cheats on him regularly. It seems plausible to most people to say that Bob's life is not going as well as he thinks it is going. Let us suppose that this is true. If Bob's life is not going as well as he thinks it is going, then Carol's acts are making his life go worse than it would otherwise be going. Were it not for those acts, after all, his life would be going in precisely the way he thinks it is going, which is better than it is actually going. And since it also seems plausible to say that if an act makes a person's life go worse than it would otherwise go, then the act harms that person, it seems plausible to say that Bob is being harmed by Carol's acts. So let us suppose for now that this is also true.

If Bob is being harmed by Carol's acts, we need a theory of harm that can account for this fact. The theory cannot be one that requires a harmful act to cause a change in the victim's mental states because the acts that are harming Bob are having no effect on his mental states. What it feels like to live Bob's life is precisely the same regardless of whether Carol is secretly cheating on him. What, then, could account for the presumed fact that Bob is nonetheless being harmed by Carol's acts? There seems to be only one plausible answer. Carol's acts harm Bob because they frustrate a certain desire that Bob has: a desire that he be in a monogamous relationship with Carol. If Bob were truly indifferent between Carol's cheating and not cheating, after all, we would not be inclined to think that her cheating was making his life go worse. We can put this account more formally, where p is a proposition stating that a particular state of affairs obtains at a particular time, in terms of what I will call the Desire Satisfaction Principle: S is in a harmed state at t if at t S desires that p and p is false.

The Desire Satisfaction Principle does not insist that frustrating a person's desires is the only way to harm that person. It merely says that it is one way of doing so. But while it is therefore quite modest in this respect, the principle is nonetheless strong enough to account for the claim that Carol's acts are harming Bob. Carol's acts harm Bob, according to the principle, because they prevent a certain state of affairs from obtaining that Bob wants to obtain: the state of affairs in which he is in a monogamous relationship with Carol. In addition, the Desire Satisfaction Principle seems theoretically plausible independent of its having plausible implications in particular cases like that of Bob and Carol. This is because it seems plausible at a more general level to suppose that at least part of what it is for a person's life to go well is for it to go the way that the person living the life wants it to go. Since the Desire Satisfaction Principle seems to offer the only plausible way to account for the presumed fact that Carol's acts are harming Bob, and since the consideration it appeals to seems to be independently plausible, the principle seems to offer the best explanation of the presumed fact that Carol's acts are harming

Bob. If Carol's acts really are harming Bob, we therefore have reason to accept the Desire Satisfaction Principle.

Let us now suppose that this, too, is true and return to the case of Ted and Alice. While she was alive, Alice had a strong desire that her ashes be scattered near the top of her favorite mountain after she died, a desire not simply to believe that they would be scattered there, but a desire that they actually be scattered there. If the Desire Satisfaction Principle is true, then it seems that Alice is harmed by Ted's act, despite the fact that it takes place after Alice is dead. Ted's act, after all, seems to frustrate Alice's future-oriented desire in the same way that Carol's acts frustrate Bob's present-oriented desire. And if Alice really is harmed by Ted's act, then the Posthumous Harm Thesis is true. It really is possible for an act to harm a person even if the act takes place after the person is dead.

The argument that I have briefly sketched here can be summarized as follows:

> P1: Carol's acts harm Bob
> P2: If Carol's acts harm Bob, then the Desire Satisfaction Principle is true
> P3: If the Desire Satisfaction Principle is true, then Ted's act harms Alice
> C: Ted's act harms Alice

And since the conclusion of this argument entails that the Posthumous Harm Thesis is true, the argument can be taken as a defense of that thesis. For this reason, I will refer to the argument as the Posthumous Harm Argument. If the argument is successful, then many restrictions on freedom that would otherwise run afoul of the Harm Principle might very well turn out to be compatible with it.

2. EVALUATING THE ARGUMENT'S FIRST PREMISE

The Posthumous Harm Argument rests on three premises. Each premise initially seems plausible. But all three have been subject to numerous objections. The goal of the remainder of this chapter is to consider some of the most important of these objections and to point to ways in which they might be overcome. There is not enough space here to discuss all of the objections that have been raised against the argument or to consider the many responses that might be made to attempts to overcome the objections that are discussed here. But we can at least hope to show that the argument is considerably more robust than many people seem to give it credit for and that proponents of the Harm Principle must therefore take it seriously in mapping out the implications of their position.

The first premise of the Posthumous Harm Argument maintains that Carol's acts are harming Bob. The defense of this premise rests entirely on the intuition that Bob's life is going worse than it would be going if Carol were not cheating on him. There are therefore two ways in which a critic of the first premise might respond: deny the intuition or try to explain it away. Some people apparently lack the intuition that Bob's life is going worse because of Carol's cheating. The best response that a defender of the first premise can offer to them appeals to other relevantly similar cases. Suppose, for example, that it is important to Rachel that only her husband sees her when she is undressed, that she believes that she is successfully ensuring that this is the case, but that every night a peeping Tom is in fact watching her as she takes off her clothes, taking pictures of her, and posting them on the internet. Or imagine a more extreme case in which Sarah is raped every night while she is completely unconscious and is never made aware of this fact. Even someone who is not moved by the case of Bob may well agree that things are not going as well for Rachel or Sarah as they think they are.

Finally, and perhaps most forcefully, there is the case of Nozick's experience machine.[1] Imagine a device that can simulate all of the experiences that a person might hope to have over the course of a life so perfectly that the person hooked up to it genuinely believes that the experiences are real. Robert, for example, thinks that he is making all of his dreams come true: developing great friendships, marrying a wonderful man and raising a lovely family of thriving children, succeeding at an important and challenging job, climbing mountains, helping others, and so on. But instead of actually doing any of these things, Robert is in fact spending his entire life hooked up to a machine that is generating the illusion that these things are happening. Even someone who is not moved by the cases of Bob, Rachel, or Sarah may well feel the force of the thought that Robert's life is not going as well as he thinks it is going. If none of these cases have any effect on you, then there may well be no way to convince you to accept the first premise of the Posthumous Harm Argument. But on the assumption that at least one of them does, that case can be used to ground the argument's first premise. We will proceed on the assumption that the case of Bob and Carol is sufficient for this purpose, but any of the other cases can be substituted in what follows and it should make no difference to the merits of the argument.

A critic of the first premise might concede that most people do have the intuition that Carol's acts are harming Bob but maintain that this is due to some feature of the case that makes it difficult for them to evaluate the situation clearly. One version of this kind of debunking response maintains that when you consider a case like that of Bob, your intuitions are confused by the fact that you are trying to adopt two conflicting viewpoints at the same time.[2] What happens, on this account, is that you try to imagine yourself living Bob's life and you then ask yourself how you feel about this prospect. This means that you enter the picture twice: once as a character in a thought experiment and then again as an evaluator having an intuitive reaction to the situation of the character in the thought experiment. You as the character Bob do not know that Carol is cheating on you, but you as the evaluator of the case involving Bob do know that Carol is cheating on Bob. Because at the evaluative level you do know that Carol is cheating on Bob, it is difficult if not impossible for you to accurately imagine what Bob's life is actually like when you are trying to picture yourself living Bob's life. As a result, when you try to imagine what it is like to live Bob's life, what you really end up imagining is living the life of someone who is aware at some level that his wife is cheating on him. You are then inclined to think that Carol's infidelity is making things worse for Bob. But, according to this objection, your inclination to think that things are going worse for Bob arises entirely from the fact that you are illicitly imagining what it is like to be someone who is aware, at least at some level, that his wife is cheating on him and who as a result has, at least at some level, some unpleasant feelings that he would not otherwise have. And if that is correct, then the fact that you initially find yourself inclined to think that things are going badly for Bob, assuming that you do initially think that things are going badly for him, provides no reason for you to continue to think this once you remind yourself that Bob himself has no idea what Carol is up to.

It seems plausible to suppose that at least some people who respond to the case by thinking that Bob's life is not going as well as it would be going if Carol were not cheating on him do so at least in part because they succumb to the confusion that this conflicting perspectives objection identifies. But even if this is so, this provides no reason to reject the claim that Bob's life is not going as well as it would otherwise be going. It simply shows that we need to test the claim by appealing to a case whose results cannot be explained away by appealing to this kind of debunking account. Here is one way to do that. For purposes of illustration, let us assume that you are married, but if that is not the case you should be able to modify the response to make it better fit your own circumstances. Either way, start by thinking back to how things were going for you ten minutes ago. We will assume that you have a clear and vivid memory of just how it felt to be you ten minutes ago and that ten minutes ago you were not believing at some level that your spouse was cheating on you. Next, ask yourself how well you think your life was going ten minutes ago. Now, suppose that you learn that your spouse was, in fact, cheating on you ten minutes ago and ask yourself whether this new information has an effect on your judgment about how well your life was going ten minutes ago. Most people would probably answer this question in the affirmative. Upon learning that their spouse had been cheating on them ten minutes ago, they would conclude that their life had not being going as well ten minutes ago as they had been thinking that it was going.

If this is your response to this case, you should reject the conflicting perspectives objection to the first premise of the Posthumous Harm Argument. This is because rather than trying to imagine that you are Bob right now, that Carol is cheating on Bob, that you as the character in the thought experiment do not know this, and that you as the evaluator of the story in the thought experiment do know this, you can instead simply picture Bob in the way that you have been pictured here: Bob is accurately remembering what his life felt like ten minutes ago, he has just now discovered that Carol was cheating on him ten minutes ago, and he is now considering whether, as a result of this, he should think that his life ten minutes ago was going less well than he thought it was going at the time. If you agree that you would now judge your life ten minutes ago to have been going worse than you thought it was going at the time if you were now to discover that your spouse was cheating on you ten minutes ago, then you should still agree that Bob's life is going worse for him because Carol is cheating on him. And this judgment cannot be undermined by the conflicting perspective objection. When you are asked to assess how things are going for Bob in the original version of the story, you may have difficulty imagining Bob's life without illicitly picturing Bob as someone who is at least dimly aware that Carol is cheating on him. But when you were asked to remember how you felt ten minutes ago, there is no reason to worry that you were mistakenly remembering that ten minutes ago you were on some level believing that your spouse was cheating on you. Since your reaction to that case cannot be contaminated by the problem of conflicting perspectives and since it generates the same conclusion about Bob's life as does the original version of the case, the problem of conflicting perspectives provides no reason to doubt the claim that Carol's acts really are harming Bob.

A second kind of debunking response to the first premise of the Posthumous Harm Argument provides a different reason for you to distrust your initial intuitions in the case of Bob. On this second account, the problem with relying on your initial response to that case is that you cannot help but recognize and be influenced by the fact that Bob might later find out what Carol has been up to.[3] If he does find out that Carol has been cheating on him, this will cause Bob to have unpleasant feelings. Having these unpleasant feelings will make him feel worse than he would otherwise feel. And it is the risk of suffering these negative feelings that Carol's cheating exposes him to, according to this risk-based objection, that accounts for the fact that you find yourself thinking that Bob's life is not going as well as it would be going if Carol were not cheating on him. But if the only reason you think that Carol's cheating on Bob is making Bob's life go worse depends on its increasing the possibility of his life feeling worse to him in this way, then the fact that you think that Bob's life is going worse provides no support for the claim that an act can make a person's life go worse even if it is truly impossible for the act to make the life feel worse. Since in the case of posthumous harm it is literally impossible for what happens to Alice's corpse to make Alice's life feel worse to her, we must be convinced that Bob's life is going worse for him even if we are absolutely certain that he will never find out about Carol's cheating in order for our response to that case to provide a satisfactory foundation for the Posthumous Harm Argument. In order for it to successfully ground the argument, that is, the first premise must be interpreted to mean that Carol's act harms Bob even if there is absolutely no risk of his ever finding out about it. And this risk-based objection seems to give good reason to doubt that our initial response to the case of Bob provides support for so strong a claim.

We can test the merits of this second debunking response by modifying the case so that it is literally impossible for Bob to find out what Carol is up to. Suppose, for example, that Bob has undergone a medical procedure that renders him permanently incapable of believing that Carol is cheating on him. Even if he sees her clearly having sex with another man right in front of his eyes, for example, his brain is irreversibly unable to interpret what he sees as evidence that she is having an affair. She can brag to him about her lover, show him pictures of her trysts with him, do absolutely anything she wants, and he will never be able to interpret what he is seeing or hearing as evidence that she is cheating on him. If the risk-based objection is correct, then this change in the nature of the story should change our intuitions about the case. If the only reason we initially thought that Bob's life was going worse than he thinks it is going is that we thought that it was bad for him to be exposed to the risk of finding out that Carol is cheating on him, then we should no longer think that his life is going worse than he thinks it is going in the version of the story where he is not exposed to that risk.

In this revised version of the case, it does not seem that things are going better for Bob than they were in the initial version. If anything, it seems even worse to have a spouse cheating on you right in front of you while you are incapable of recognizing it than to have a spouse stealthily cheating on you behind your back. Most people will probably have the same reaction. In addition, Nozick's case involving the experience machine seems to be immune to the debunking response that grounds this risk-based objection. When most people think that it would be worse for Robert to spend his life hooked up to the experience machine, it is not because they worry that there is some risk that he will later find out that he had been hooked up to it and be upset by this discovery. They simply think that Robert would be living a better life if he were actually doing the things that he wants to do rather than being deluded into thinking that he was doing them. These considerations suffice to show that our belief that Carol's behavior is making Bob's life go less well than it would otherwise be going does not depend on our belief that Bob might find out what Carol is up to. And if it does not depend on this further belief, then this risk-based objection must also be rejected.

Most people respond to cases like that of Bob and Carol by thinking that Bob's life is not going as well as he thinks it is going. I see no good reason to insist that this is simply because they are not thinking about the case with sufficient clarity and care. Even after extended reflection, then, it still seems reasonable, at least to me, to accept the first premise of the Posthumous Harm Argument.

3. EVALUATING THE ARGUMENT'S SECOND PREMISE

Let us now suppose that the first premise of the Posthumous Harm Argument is correct in maintaining that Carol's acts are harming Bob. The second premise of the argument maintains that if this is so, then the Desire Satisfaction Principle is true. A number of objections have been raised against this claim, too, but the discussion here will be limited to just one so that it can be considered in some detail.[4] So consider the case of Chris:

3.1. Chris

Today is Chris' fiftieth birthday. Ever since he was a young boy, Chris had a strong desire to celebrate his fiftieth birthday by listening to rock music. One week ago, his tastes began to change, and this morning he woke up with a desire to listen to easy listening music instead. We have to decide what music to play at Chris' party today. We want to make the choice that will make things go better for Chris.

The Desire Satisfaction Principle maintains that S is in a harmed state at t if at t, S desires that p and p is false. What does this principle entail about the case of Chris?

The answer depends on whether we restrict the scope of the principle to present-oriented desires or extend it to future-oriented desires as well. Suppose first that we restrict the scope of the principle to present-oriented desires. If right now I desire that I be in Prague right now, for example, then the principle entails that I am in a harmed state right now if it is false that I am in Prague right now. But if right now I desire that I be in Prague a year from now, then this restricted version of the principle does not entail that I am in a harmed state right now if it is false that I will be in Prague a year from now. On this temporally restricted version of the principle, the fact that for most of his life Chris had a strong future-oriented desire to listen to rock music on his fiftieth birthday proves irrelevant. All that matters for determining what would make things go better for him is what his present-oriented desire is. Since his present-oriented desire is to listen to easy listening music, this means that the temporally restricted version of the Desire Satisfaction Principle entails that we would make things go better for Chris by playing easy listening music on his fiftieth birthday rather than rock music. And this clearly seems to be the intuitively correct result.

Suppose instead that we extend the scope of the principle to include future-oriented desires as well. Doing so is necessary in order to use the principle to justify the Posthumous Harm Thesis because the only desires that can be frustrated after a person is dead are the future-oriented desires that she had while she was still living. But it is precisely this unrestricted version of the principle that seems to run into problems in the case of Chris. Since for most of his life up until now Chris had a future-oriented desire to listen to rock music on his fiftieth birthday, the temporally unrestricted version of the Desire Satisfaction Principle seems to entail that we would make things go better for Chris now by playing rock music at his fiftieth birthday party despite the fact that he would now prefer to listen to easy listening music. If we play easy listening music for him now, after all, we will satisfy only one of his desires, the present-oriented desire that he has right now to listen to easy listening music, but we will frustrate a large number of his desires: those future-oriented desires that he had over a long period of time that were desires that he listen to rock music on his fiftieth birthday. If we instead play rock music for him now, we will satisfy that large number of his desires and frustrate only one of his desires, the desire to listen to easy listening music right now. It therefore seems clear that if we include both present-oriented and future-oriented desires in our considerations, we must conclude that things will go better for Chris on the whole if we play rock music for him right now rather than easy listening music, despite the fact that Chris himself would rather listen to easy listening music. This result seems sufficiently implausible to warrant favoring the restricted version of the principle over the unrestricted version, and the restricted version is incompatible with the Posthumous Harm Thesis.

This is a potentially powerful objection. But it ultimately arises from a failure to draw two important distinctions. The first is a distinction between two kinds of future-oriented desires: those whose objects are conditional on the persistence of the desire itself and those whose objects are not.[5] Suppose, for example, that when teenage Chris said that he wanted to listen to rock music on his fiftieth birthday, he had been asked this question: is what you want right now that on your fiftieth birthday you listen to rock music even if at that time you prefer easy listening music to rock music, or is what you want right now that on your fiftieth birthday you listen to rock music on the assumption that at that time you will still prefer rock music to easy listening music? If Chris would have given the latter answer to this question, then his previous desire to listen to rock music on his fiftieth birthday was conditional on the persistence of the desire. If he would have given the former answer, then his previous desire was unconditional in this sense. The second distinction is a distinction between two senses in which a state of affairs might be said to make things go better for Chris. "Better" could mean that it would make his life as a whole go better or it could mean that it would make the rest of his life go better. Having incurred one hundred units of pain yesterday rather than incurring fifty units of pain tomorrow would make Chris' life as a whole go worse, for example, but from the point of view of his life today, having the hundred units of pain behind him rather than having fifty units of pain ahead of him would make the rest of his life go better.

These two distinctions combine to defeat the changing desires objection in the following way. Suppose first that Chris' past future-oriented desires were conditional desires. All he wanted when he was younger was that he listen to rock music on his fiftieth birthday if when he turned fifty he still preferred rock music to easy listening music. If that was all that Chris wanted when he was younger, then the proposition that he wanted to be true on the day that he turned fifty was "I am listening to rock music today if I prefer rock music to easy listening music today." Since on his fiftieth birthday today Chris does not prefer rock music to easy listening music, playing easy listening music for him today will not make false the proposition that for so long he wanted to be true. If his past future-oriented desire to listen to rock music on his fiftieth birthday was a conditional desire, therefore, the temporally unrestricted version of the Desire Satisfaction Principle will not entail, as the changing desires objection claims it entails, that we make things better for Chris by playing rock music on his fiftieth birthday.

Now suppose that Chris' past future-oriented desires were unconditional desires. What really mattered to Chris for so many years was that he listen to rock music on his fiftieth birthday even if by that point he did not like listening to it. What does the temporally unrestricted version of the Desire Satisfaction Principle entail about this version of the case? Here it depends on what we mean by making things better for Chris. Suppose first that we want to make things better for Chris in the sense that we want to make sure that his life from this moment on goes as well as possible. In that case, to the extent that we focus on satisfying his desires, we should ignore all of his past desires, regardless of whether they were conditional or unconditional, and aim to satisfy the desires that he has now or will have in the future. Given that he now desires to listen to easy listening music today, we should therefore play easy listening music on his fiftieth birthday. The changing desires objection will again be mistaken in its claim that the temporally unrestricted version of the Desire Satisfaction Principle entails that we make things better for Chris by playing rock music on his fiftieth birthday.

But suppose instead that by "better," we mean that we want to make sure that Chris' life as a whole goes as well as possible. On this version of the case, where we want to make things better in the whole life sense and where Chris' past future-oriented desires were unconditional—and only on this version of the case—the temporally unrestricted version of the Desire Satisfaction Principle does indeed entail that we make things better for Chris in terms of desire satisfaction by playing rock music on his fiftieth birthday, just as the changing desires objection says it does. But on this version of the case, this seems like the right thing to say. If we really do care about Chris' life as a whole and not just about the rest of it, then we have to care about his past desires and not just his present and future desires, just as we would have to care about his past experiences and not just his present and future experiences on the assumption that they, too, make a difference to how well a person's life goes. If we care about his life as a whole, for example, we should prefer that he incur fifty units of pain tomorrow rather than that he have incurred one hundred units of pain yesterday because this would minimize the total amount of pain that his life as a whole contains, even though it would increase the amount of pain that his life contains from here on out. In the same way, and for the same reason, given that on this understanding of the case what Chris really wanted for so long was to listen to rock music on his fiftieth birthday even if by that point he no longer liked rock music, given that this past desire that he had would be satisfied if we were to play rock music for him today, and given that we want to make his life as a whole go better and not just the rest of his life, we should prefer that he incur a bit of desire frustration today rather than that he have incurred a much greater amount of desire frustration over a period of many years in the past because this would minimize the total amount of desire frustration that his life as a whole contains. And so on this understanding of the case, it really can make sense for us to play rock music for Chris on his fiftieth birthday. Whether his past desires were conditional or unconditional, then, and whether we want to make things better for him in the whole-life or rest-of-life sense, there is no version of the case of Chris on which the temporally unrestricted version of the Desire Satisfaction Principle produces an objectionable result. The changing desires objection should therefore be rejected.

4. Evaluating the Argument's Third Premise

The third premise of the Posthumous Harm Argument maintains that if the Desire Satisfaction Principle is true, then Ted's act harmed Alice. One objection to this claim arises from the fact that harm requires a subject. It is possible for Carol's act of cheating on Bob to be harmful, for example, because at the time of Carol's act there is a subject who can be harmed by it. The subject who can be harmed by the act is Bob. But it does not seem possible for Ted's act of flushing Alice's ashes down the toilet to be harmful because it seems that there is no one who could serve as the subject of harm in that case. Alice is dead at the time of Ted's act and to say that Alice is dead is just to say that there is no Alice, and so no subject to be harmed by Ted's act. But if there is no subject to be harmed by Ted's act and if harm requires a subject, then there is no harm caused by Ted's act. This no subject objection has been pressed by a number of writers.[6]

Most arguments in defense of the possibility of posthumous harm concede that Alice herself is not harmed in a case like this but maintain that there is a subject of harm nonetheless: some part or aspect or interest of Alice that has in some sense survived her death.[7] This concession strikes me as both problematic and unnecessary. The subject of harm in the case of Ted's act can simply be Alice—not dead Alice, the pile of ashes, and not some kind of surviving ghost of Alice, a mysterious post-mortem entity that carries on where Alice left off, but simply Alice herself, the living, breathing human being as she existed prior to her death. That Alice, after all, is the person who had a strong desire to have her ashes scattered near the top of her favorite mountain after she died, and that is the desire that was frustrated by Ted's act of flushing them down the toilet instead. As a result of Ted's act, that is, it is the life of Alice herself that turned out to contain one less satisfied desire than it would otherwise have contained. So it is Alice's life that Ted's act ended up causing to go less well than it would otherwise have gone. This is the distinctive response to the no subject objection that George Pitcher famously offered, and it seems to be considerably more promising than the alternatives.[8]

Pitcher's response to the no subject objection, though, strikes most people as creating more problems than it solves. Ted's act, for example, takes place after Alice is dead, but the subject of the harm brought about by Ted's act is supposed to be Alice while she was still alive. Alice was alive before she was dead, not after, and so it seems that Alice suffers the harm associated with Ted's act before the act that results in the harm takes place. This means that the harmful act occurs after the harmful consequence that the act brings about, which would require some form of backward causation to occur. But backward causation is impossible. And so it seems that Pitcher's response to the no subject objection must be rejected.[9]

This purported problem can be overcome by appealing to the distinction between an act's causing a particular event to occur and an act's being responsible for the fact that a particular proposition is true. An act at t_2 cannot cause an event to occur at t_1. My throwing a rock today cannot cause you to have been struck by a rock yesterday. But an act at t_2 can be responsible for the fact that a particular belief at t_1 is true. My throwing a rock today can make it the case that when you believed yesterday that I would throw a rock today you believed correctly rather than incorrectly. This distinction can rescue Pitcher's response to the no subject objection from the backward causation objection because the Desire Satisfaction Principle does not require Alice to be on the receiving end of a harmful event in order to be harmed, just that she have a frustrated desire, and because what is true of beliefs in this context is also true of desires.

Suppose, for example, that while she was alive, Alice believed that her ashes would be scattered near the top of her favorite mountain after she died. In that case, Ted's subsequent act of flushing her ashes down the toilet would make it the case that while she was alive she had a false belief rather than a true belief. This conclusion does not require any kind of mysterious backward causation. Ted's act does not somehow cause Alice to have had one belief in the past rather than to have had a different belief. It simply renders the status of the belief that she did have in the past false rather than true. But the same reason for thinking it unproblematic that Ted's later act can make Alice's earlier future-oriented belief false rather than true is also a reason for thinking that Ted's later act can make Alice's earlier future-oriented desire frustrated rather than satisfied. If what she desired while she was alive was that the belief be true rather than false, then by rendering the belief false rather than true, Ted's subsequent act of flushing her ashes down the toilet rendered her desire frustrated rather than satisfied. The claim that Alice herself is the subject of harm in the case of Ted's act, therefore, does not require an objectionable form of backward causation.

It may seem, though, that this response to the backward causation objection rests on an objectionable conception of harm. One reason for thinking this arises from the claim that in order for an act to harm a person, it must make things worse for that person than they were before the act took place. As Glannon puts the point in pressing this objection to Pitcher's position, "[w]hen a person is harmed, she is made worse off than she was by the obtaining of some state of affairs that thwarts her interests."[10] This temporal change requirement is clearly satisfied in typical cases of harm. If I punch you in the nose, my act causes you to suffer a sensation of pain that makes you worse off than you were before you were suffering it. And, perhaps more importantly, the temporal change requirement is also satisfied in the case of Bob and Carol. Carol's act of cheating on Bob makes Bob worse off than he was before Carol cheated on him. But according to the response to the backward causation objection developed here, Ted's act of flushing Alice's ashes down the toilet does not really make Alice worse off than she was before Ted's act. Indeed, the response depends on precisely the opposite claim: that things were already worse for Alice while she was still alive in virtue of Ted's subsequent act. If the temporal change requirement imposes a legitimate constraint on whether an act can count as harming someone, then my response to the backward causation objection entails that Ted's act did not harm Alice.

But the temporal change requirement is mistaken. An act can harm a person without making that person worse off than they were before the act occurred. It can do this by making them worse off than they would otherwise have been even if they are not worse off than they were before. Consider the case of Wayne. Wayne was conceived by in vitro fertilization. Prior to Wayne's conception, a lab technician placed the sperm and egg that would shortly give rise to Wayne in a Petri dish and left the room. Before the sperm had a chance to fertilize the egg, an intruder entered the room and poured toxic waste into the Petri dish. The toxic waste damaged the sperm and egg before they came together and, as a result, Wayne was conceived as a blind child when he would otherwise have been conceived with normal vision. Wayne went on to live a good life despite his disability, but he would have lived an even better life if he had not been blind.

It is clear that the intruder's act harmed Wayne. It caused Wayne to be blind when he would otherwise have been sighted. But it is also clear that the intruder's act did not make Wayne worse off than he was before or cause Wayne to go from a better condition to a worse condition. The act caused Wayne to be blind rather than sighted, but since Wayne was blind for his entire life, there was no point at which being blind made him worse off than he was before. The case of Wayne therefore serves as a counterexample to the temporal change requirement. It also identifies a particular way in which an act can harm a person despite the fact that it does not make the person worse off than they were before. Since it is clear that the intruder's act harmed Wayne and that it made things worse for Wayne than they would otherwise have been without making things worse for him than they were before, the case of Wayne provides support for the claim that an act can harm a person by making that person worse off than they would otherwise have been. If this counterfactual condition is correct, then not only is there no reason to think that this response to the backward causation objection depends on a defective account of harm, but there is a positive reason to conclude that it does not. Ted's act of flushing Alice's ashes down the toilet rather than scattering them near the top of her favorite mountain did not make Alice's life go worse than it was going before Ted's act occurred, but it did make Alice's life go worse than it would otherwise have gone. And if making Wayne's life go worse than it would otherwise have gone is enough for the intruder's act to harm Wayne, then making Alice's life go worse than it would otherwise have gone is enough for Ted's act to harm Alice.

5. CONCLUSION

Critics have raised a number of additional objections to all three premises of the Posthumous Harm Argument, but responding to them and to the many concerns that may be raised against the preliminary responses that have been provided to the objections considered here will have to wait for another occasion. In the meantime, this chapter has tried to stablish that the Posthumous Harm Argument is considerably more robust than it may at first appear and that proponents of the Harm Principle must therefore take the Posthumous Harm Thesis seriously when using the principle to help answer the question of when it is legitimate to restrict a person's freedom.

NOTES

1. See Nozick, 1974: 43.
2. See, e.g., Feldman, 2004: 42.
3. See, e.g., Feldman, 2004: 42.
4. See, e.g., Heathwood, 2006: 541–542; Portmore, 2007: 29–33. The example discussed here is based on one in Heathwood, 2006.

5. See Parfit, 1984: 151.
6. See, e.g., Partridge, 1981: 253; Callahan, 1987: 347; Wisnewski, 2009: 55–57.
7. See, e.g., Feinberg, 1984: 83; Serafini, 1989–1990: 332, 330; Sperling, 2008: 36; Belliotti, 2012: 165, 167.
8. See Pitcher, 1984: 184.
9. Proponents of the backward causation objection include Sperling (2008: 21–22) and Taylor (2005: 315; 2012: 14–15).
10. Glannon, 2001: 138–139. Sperling presses the same objection to Pitcher: "Whether someone is harmed by an event is determined by reference to what she was before, and whether her position has improved or regressed" (2008: 22).

REFERENCES

Belliotti, Raymond Angelo, 2012. *Posthumous harm: Why the Dead are Still Vulnerable.* Lanham, MD: Lexington Books.

Callahan, Joan C., 1987. On Harming the Dead. *Ethics,* 97(2), pp.341–352.

Feinberg, Joel, 1984. *Harm to Others.* Oxford: Oxford University Press.

Feldman, Fred, 2004. *Pleasure and the Good Life.* Oxford: Clarendon Press.

Glannon, Walter, 2001. Persons, Lives and Posthumous Harm. *Journal of Social Philosophy,* 32(2), pp.127–142.

Heathwood, Chris, 2006. Desire Satisfactionism and Hedonism. *Philosophical Studies,* 128(3), pp.539–563.

Nozick, Robert, 1974. *Anarchy, State and Utopia.* New York: Basic Books.

Parfit, Derek, 1984. *Reasons and Persons.* Oxford: Clarendon Press.

Partridge, Ernest, 1981. Posthumous Interests and Posthumous Respect. *Ethics,* 91(2), pp.243–264.

Pitcher, George, 1984. The Misfortunes of the Dead. *American Philosophical Quarterly,* 21(2), pp.183–188.

Portmore, Douglas W., 2007. Desire Fulfillment and Posthumous Harm. *American Philosophical Quarterly,* 44(1), pp.27–38.

Serafini, Anthony, 1989–1990. Callahan on Harming the Dead. *Journal of Philosophical Research,* 15, pp.329–339.

Sperling, Daniel, 2008. *Posthumous Interests: Legal and Ethical Implications.* Cambridge: Cambridge University Press.

Taylor, James Stacey, 2005. The Myth of Posthumous Harm. *American Philosophical Quarterly,* 42(4), pp.311–322.

Taylor, James Stacey, 2012. *Death, Posthumous Harm, and Bioethics.* New York: Routledge.

Wisnewski, J. Jeremy, 2009. What we Owe the Dead. *Journal of Applied Philosophy,* 26(1), pp.54–70.

PART V

ECONOMIES AND NORMATIVE TRADE-OFFS

CHAPTER 23

EXPLOITATION
AND FREEDOM

MATT ZWOLINSKI

1. Introduction

A free society is one that allows its citizens wide latitude to live their lives as they see fit. Such a society does not generally attempt to dictate what its citizens shall *believe* in matters of religion, politics, or morals. And, at least in the ideal case, it interferes with individuals' freedom of *action* only insofar as is necessary to protect the like freedom of others.[1] The implications of such freedom are generally thought to include not only considerable scope for so-called "personal" liberties such as freedom of speech and movement, but also some substantial scope for economic liberties in matters such as occupation, trade, and property ownership as well.[2]

Because a free society will restrain itself to prohibiting only a certain *class* of immoral actions—namely, those that wrongfully infringe upon the freedom or rights of others—individuals within such a society will have the legal right to do many things that are morally wrong (Spooner, 1875; Waldron, 1981). Precisely how large this "protected sphere" of individual liberty ought to be is a matter on which there is and no doubt will continue to be considerable disagreement among liberal theorists. But however much they may differ on the details, liberals are genuinely united in holding that there is vital difference between the class of actions that are the proper grounds for *moral sanction* and that which is the proper ground for *legal coercion*. Tolerance of a certain amount of immorality appears to be part of the price of freedom.

There is one particular type of immorality, however, that has proven to be a constant source of worry to advocates of a free society, and a favorite target of its critics. If a free society is one that mostly leaves its citizens alone to run their own lives, it is probable that some people will, through a combination of bad choices and bad luck, find themselves in positions of *vulnerability*, while others will wind up in positions of *power*. Moreover, given the tendencies toward selfishness inherent in human nature, it also seems likely that those who find themselves in power will sometimes use that power to take unfair advantage of the vulnerable. It seems likely, in other words, that a free society will, by virtue of its freedom, be one in which there will be significant opportunities for *exploitation*.

The charge of exploitation is one that is today most commonly associated with Karl Marx's critique of the capitalist economy. But, from a somewhat broader perspective, Marx's critique is merely one instance of a form of argument with a much longer and more pluralistic historical pedigree. There are many ways, and many contexts, in which power can take advantage of vulnerability. And there are likewise many ways to diagnose the nature and extent of this problem, and many prescriptions for addressing it.

The purpose of this chapter is to explore the relationship between exploitation and the free society, with a special emphasis on two of the most important institutions of such a society: the market and the state. Marx's analysis of the relationship between those two institutions is of central importance to anyone seeking to understand the nature of exploitation, and that analysis will be examined in section 3. Before that, however, section 2 will examine a neglected forerunner to Marx's account—the classical liberal theory of exploitation as set forth by nineteenth-century French liberals such as Jean-Baptiste Say and Frédéric Bastiat.

Both the classical liberals and Marx provide us with important insights concerning the nature of exploitation in the state and in the market. But neither group developed a philosophically sophisticated and tenable account of just what exploitation *is*. Section 4, therefore, examines one attempt to do this by analyzing exploitation in terms of *equality*. A concern with equality has played a central role in thinking about exploitative exchange. But as section 5 will show, considerations about *equality* are ultimately subordinate to more basic considerations of *fairness*, and it is in this concept that a philosophically defensible account of exploitation must be grounded.

With a better understanding of exploitation in hand, section 6 turns to the role such an account might play in examining various social norms and legal rules that seek to *minimize* exploitation. It turns out, unfortunately, that the relationship is less direct than might have been hoped. Even a society concerned to minimize exploitation should not necessarily adopt rules to prohibit all exploitative acts. This leaves the liberal concerned with reducing exploitation faced with a difficult problem, which is briefly considered in the concluding section 7.

2. FREEDOM AGAINST PRIVILEGE

From 1665 to 1683, Jean-Baptiste Colbert served as the French minister of finance under Louis XIV. Under his reign, the French state would take an unprecedented role in the management of the French economy (Viner, 1937; Cole, 1964). Colbert saw it as his task to use the power of the state in order to nurture key industries, and thereby to bolster the economic power of the French nation relative to its European neighbors. Politically,

Colbert was an ardent nationalist. And his political nationalism begat one of the purest historical instances of economic *mercantilism*.

Under Colbert, the importation of printed cotton textiles (calicos) from India was prohibited in order to protect the French linen, woolen, and silk industries. In 1694, the manufacture, sale, and even *possession* of buttons made from any material other than silk was prohibited at the behest of the *boutonniers-passementiers*, whose own practice of handmade silk buttons was threatened by changes in fashion and technology. And half-beaver hats were prohibited from 1664 to 1700 in order to drive consumers to *full-beaver* hats—a change welcomed, unsurprisingly, by those who derived their livelihood from the processing and sale of beaver pelts.

But by far the most significant method employed by the mercantilists was the grant of "privilege"—a conferral of monopoly power upon some favored producer which carried with it a variety of special rights including, usually, the exclusive right to manufacture and/or sell certain kinds of goods within a specified geographical area (Cole, 1964: 135). Such monopolies were allegedly necessary in order to protect key industries from foreign competition, to ensure that goods met certain specified standards of quality, to spur employment, and to secure a favorable balance of trade. In reality, though, grants were often made for reasons of a less public-spirited nature. Monopolies were bestowed by the state largely in order to confer an economic benefit upon some favored courtier or to raise revenue for the state (Ibid., 135). Indeed, grants of monopoly swelled to such an extent during the Colbert regime that revenue derived from them came to replace taxation as the state's main source of income, accounting for more than half of all funds received (Rothbard, 1995: 220).

Mercantilist policy would eventually come under fierce criticism, most notably from the pen of Adam Smith, whose *Inquiry into the Nature and Causes of the Wealth of Nations* was an extended critique of the doctrine, but also by French economists such as Jean-Baptiste Say. For Say and his followers in the French *industrialist* school, mercantilist privileges destroyed the natural harmony of interests that existed between producers and consumers in a free economy. In the absence of such privileges, Say held, the only way that individuals can *consume* the resources of others is to *produce*—to take "a product in one state and [deliver] it in another, in which it has a greater utility and a higher value" (Say, 1821: 12). Production is necessary for consumption because unless one offers one's trading partners something more valuable than what one is asking of them—and something that they couldn't get more cheaply on their own in the absence of trade—they can simply say "no." The fact that market exchange is voluntary means that it will only take place when *both* parties believe that they will get more value from what they receive than from what they give up. It means that in the absence of force, fraud, irrationality, or misunderstanding, market exchanges will be mutually beneficial.

Under mercantilism, however, the link between production and consumption is severed. Instead of one's ability to consume being dependent upon one's ability to serve the interests of one's consumers, mercantilism makes the ability to earn wealth dependent on political patronage. As Say noted,

> If one individual, or one class, can call in the aid of authority to ward off the effects of competition, it acquires a privilege to the prejudice and at the cost of the whole community; it can then make sure of profits not altogether due to the productive services rendered, but composed in part of an actual tax upon consumers for its private profit; which tax it commonly shares with the authority that thus unjustly lends its support. (Say, 1880: 146–147)

Say's intellectual followers would go on to develop this insight into one of the most important pre-Marxian theories of class conflict. For these classical liberals, the two great classes into which society was divided were *productive* laborers and *unproductive* social parasites. The class of productive laborers was understood broadly to encompass not only those who exerted physical labor to create tangible goods and services, but anyone who worked to make goods more useful than they would otherwise be—so laborers, yes, but also entrepreneurs, *arbitrageurs*, and even capitalists in their role as managers and overseers of investments. The unproductive classes, in contrast, consisted of those who purportedly consume value but do not produce it, such as "the army, the government, and the state-supported clergy" (Raico, 1992: 395). But of all these groups, it was the government and its agents that were singled out for special scorn. As one of the leading figures of the *industrialist* movement, Charles Comte, wrote:

> We must never lose sight of the fact that a public functionary, in his capacity as functionary, produces absolutely nothing; that, on the contrary, he exists only on the products of the industrious class; and that he can consume nothing that has not been taken from producers. (Comte, 1817: 29–30)

The *industrialists* almost certainly overstated their case on this point. There is no good reason to believe that government is *inherently* unproductive. Governments do, after all, make things like roads, canals, and public services such as defense. And despite the inefficiency with which governments often seem to operate, it seems likely that the utility of the things they produce is at least *sometimes* greater than the utility of the resources they consume.

But behind this overstatement lies an important truth: governments, unlike ordinary market actors, have both the *capacity* to act unproductively over the long run, and a strong *incentive* to do so. This truth rests upon a crucial difference between government and ordinary market actors, namely, that government has the power to *compel* interaction. Government's taxes must be paid, and its regulations complied with, whether you like it or not, on pain of fines or imprisonment. Unlike the grocer, then, who must provide his customers with food that is good enough, and cheap enough, to make purchasing it worth their while, the government can demand citizens' money or obedience without having to offer them anything more valuable in return. Thus, government *can* use the resources at its disposal to produce something of greater value, but it *need not* do so. Unlike the grocer, its livelihood is not dependent on its doing so.

This is true even in democratic governments. It is tempting to think of votes as playing the same role in political exchanges as consent does in market exchanges. Since politicians cannot gain power without the consent of the governed, it would seem, they will only gain power when the bargain they propose to their constituents is one that leaves them better off, on net. But however great an advance democratic government may have been over previous forms, it does not avoid the problem of state exploitation. This is because even if democratic elections involve a kind of consent, this consent is *majoritarian* rather than *individualistic* in nature. As many classical liberals noted, and as modern public choice economics has confirmed, democratic elections allow majorities to harness the power of the state to exploit minorities. Democratic governments impose the will of the majority by force. And this means that minorities in a democracy lack the power to say "no" to proposed exchanges that make them worse off.[3]

Government's coercive power thus puts it in a position to *exploit* its citizens—or, to use the language of the French classical liberals, to *plunder* them.[4] Because of its power of coercion, government can compel its citizens to act in ways that actually *set back* their interests, but that *advance* the interests of the state. Unlike the natural harmony of interests that exists between buyers and sellers in the marketplace, then, there is a sharp *conflict* of interest between citizens and the state, and therefore also between citizens in their capacity as producers, and citizens in their capacity as beneficiaries of state largess.

Exploitation as the French classical liberals conceived of it was thus a form of predatory, parasitic behavior, through which one party gained at another party's expense. And since it was precisely the coercive power of government that made this kind of predation possible, the *solution* offered by the early classical liberals was to remove the possibility of that coercion, or at least to minimize its scope. If institutional incentives made it likely that the state would use its power to establish protectionist tariffs to exploit consumers for the benefit of certain producers, then perhaps the state ought to be stripped of that power altogether. Certain core functions of the state might be indispensable for social harmony, and might be such that no entity other than the state could provide them effectively.[5] But beyond that core, the powers of the state ought to be severely limited. With greater freedom and with the elimination of privilege would come the erosion of power, as the classical liberals saw it, and the erosion of power was the surest way to end the exploitation of man by man.

3. Capitalism, Freedom, and Exploitation

The belief in a harmony of interests among individuals in a free, capitalist market is a hallmark of classical liberal thought (Viner, 1927; Zwolinski and Tomasi, 2016: ch. 7). For the classical liberals, exploitation is something that can only occur *outside* the market—when the requirement of mutual consent is dropped and the power of governmental coercion makes possible the zero-sum transfer of wealth from one party to another.

But, thus stated, the classical liberal theory of exploitation appears to rest on two premises, each of which can be, and has been, called into question. It is not obvious, in the first place, that there really exists a *harmony* rather than a conflict of interests between buyers and sellers in the marketplace. And second, while transactions in a capitalist economy might *appear* free, there is some reason to think that this surface appearance of liberty belies the underlying reality of bondage.

This was the argument made by Karl Marx, who derived from his rejection of classical liberal premises an altogether different theory of the relationship between capitalism, freedom, and exploitation. For Marx, not only is exploitation *possible* in a capitalist economy; it is *inherent* in it. And thus the solution to the problem of exploitation lies not in the expansion of capitalist "freedoms," but their abolition.

The starting point for Marx's argument is the observation that force and violence are endogenous to the capitalist system, not something alien imposed upon it by government. For Marx, the practical and theoretical foundation of the capitalist system is private ownership in the means of production. But unlike Locke, who saw private property as originating in a peaceful process of discovery and labor, Marx saw capitalist property as an institution that both originated in and owed its continued existence to violence. The actual distribution of property rights under capitalism owes at least as much to the *theft* of labor under slavery and feudalism as it does to productive labor itself (Marx, 1977: chs. 26–28). And capitalist legal systems cement that theft through the centralized coercive power of the sate. This means that those who *lack* legally recognized property in a capitalist system are subject to violent interference in their lives from both the owners of capitalist property and the police who enforce their legal claims.

Such individuals must eat, sleep, and clothe themselves. But they are able to do so only by gaining access to property that is owned by others. In order to obtain the money needed to buy the necessities of life, they must produce. And in order to produce, they must sell their labor to the owners of capital. For, lacking any property in the means of production themselves, they have nothing to produce *with* that does not belong to someone else.

Propertyless workers are therefore dependent upon owners of capital for their survival. Of course, the dependency is not entirely one-way. Workers' labor is powerless without capital on which to labor. But so too is capital powerless without someone to labor on it. Even still, Marx saw capitalists as wielding all the power in the relationship. There is a relative abundance of labor compared to capital, and this means that the wage any laborer can demand from capitalists is limited by strong competitive pressure from other laborers. Ultimately, Marx thought, that competitive pressure means that the wage (or price) of labor will be determined in the same way as the price of any other good in a capitalist market: by its cost of production. And since the cost of production of a day's labor is the simply the cost of keeping the laborer *alive* for another day, the wage of labor will be bare subsistence (Marx, 1977: ch. 6).

Workers' wages will therefore be low *despite* the fact that, according to Marx, their labor has the unique power to create more value than it costs to produce. Labor, and labor alone according to Marx, can create *surplus value*. But because of their poor bargaining position relative to capitalists, laborers are not in a position to benefit from any of the surplus value they produce. Instead, that value goes straight into the pockets of the capitalist. The surplus value created by the worker thus becomes the source of capitalist profit and, since it can be reinvested, the source of capital's growth over time.

For Marx, then, exploitation consists of the forced extraction of surplus value from the laborer by capitalists. Importantly, Marx did not think that the activity of exploitation necessarily reflected any kind of ill will on the part of capitalists. Capitalists do not exploit because they are bad people; they exploit because they are compelled to do so by the logic of capitalism. Exploitation is the only possible source of profit under capitalism, and firms that do not generate a profit will fail, and be replaced by others that will. The solution to the problem of exploitation therefore cannot lie in moral suasion—convincing capitalists to be better people, or to pay their workers a better wage. It can only lie in radical, systematic change to the capitalist system as a whole.

Marx's theory of exploitation suffers from a number of well-known problems. For instance, the theory was meant to provide an explanation for the profitability of capitalism as a whole. But even if Marx is right that labor is exploited in some sense, this fact cannot be what *explains* capitalist profit. For if it were really true that exploitation of labor was the only source of profit for capitalists, then one would expect to find industries to be more profitable in proportion as they are more labor-intensive, and one should expect profit to decline in industries as they become more mechanized. But not only are these predictions not realized; they are precisely backward.[6]

On a technical level, the main source of problems for Marx's theory of exploitation is the labor theory of value on which it rests. Marx was not wrong to assume that labor was productive, but it was a mistake to assume that labor is *uniquely* productive, and that labor's productivity is the sole explanation of capitalist profit and economic value. Everything that Marx said about the productive powers of labor could just as easily have been said about any other commodity, and thus Marx's employment of a *labor* theory of value is merely the product of an arbitrary decision on his part. A "corn theory of value" or a "land theory of value" would have been just as defensible, and would have resulted in a theory that was formally indistinguishable from Marx's own.[7]

But the more important mistake behind Marx's theory of exploitation is also more basic. The reason Marx faces a puzzle in explaining capitalist profit in the first place is that he wrongly assumes economic value to be an objective property of the objects of exchange. If value is in the object, and all that capitalist modes of production and trade do is move objects around from person to person, then it makes sense to wonder how capitalism as a whole can *create* any value. When a capitalist purchases eight hours of a worker's labor, he must either pay that worker *more* than his labor is worth, *less*, or the *same*. And this would mean either that neither party gains from the exchange at all, or that one party can necessarily gain only by virtue of the other party's loss.

The correct answer to this challenge, of course, is that economic value is *not* in the object itself, but in a relationship between the object and a human agent. The same object can have different values to different people depending, among other things, on their particular tastes and the amount of the particular resource already available to them. It is not because water is unimportant that its price is so low, but because there is already so much of it available. The market price of water, like that of all other goods, reflects its *marginal, subjective value.*

It is because value is subjective that exchange in a capitalist economy—including the exchange between laborers and capitalists—can be *mutually* beneficial. Capitalists are able to derive profit not because they have stolen value from the laborer, but because they have *created* value in cooperation with the laborer. Both the laborer and the capitalist walk away from their exchange a winner, having traded away something they value less in exchange for something they value more. And the same is true of the exchange between the capitalist and her customers, her suppliers, her landlord, and so on. In a free economy in which potential trading partners have the right to say "no," positive-sum, mutually beneficial, wealth-creating interactions are the norm. On this point, at least, the classical liberal economists were right, and Marx was wrong.

4. Exploitation and Equality

Early classical liberals held, and some contemporary libertarians still do hold, that exploitation is impossible in a free market—that it is an evil made possible only by the coercive power of government. Marx, in contrast, held that capitalist markets are *necessarily* exploitative—that exploitation is an inevitable outcome of capitalist economic institutions, irrespective of the character of the persons who occupy them. Each of these accounts contains some genuine insights into the moral nature of capitalist markets, but both are ultimately too ideologically rigid, and thus unsatisfactory from a theoretical perspective.

A better approach must begin with a more defensible account of exploitation. Today, the dominant philosophical approach is one that conceptualizes exploitation in terms of *unfairness*. Specifically, exploitation is usually thought to consist of *taking unfair advantage* (Wertheimer, 1996; Wertheimer and Zwolinski, 2015).

Stated in these broad terms, this account of exploitation leaves considerable room for interpretation, especially of the key term "unfairness." But this breadth is a virtue, rather than a weakness, for it allows us to incorporate the insights of rival accounts such as the Marxist and classical liberal theories, while discarding their defects. In response to the Marxists, we can concede that capitalist employment relationships *may* be exploitative, but we will add that they will be so only *if and to the extent that* those relationships are unfair. A mining company that takes advantage of its local employment monopoly to pay its workers mere sustenance wages while reaping extremely high profits might be acting exploitatively, even while a software company that pays a premium to attract talented workers is not.

Similarly, in response to the classical liberals, we can grant that government taxes and transfers may be exploitative, but again only if and to the extent that such policies involve a kind of unfairness. The classical liberals were correct to attack legislation that privileges special interests at the expense of the common good. But there is no a priori reason to suppose that *all* legislation must be of this kind. Laws that impose burdens on all for the benefit of all could be fair, and therefore non-exploitative.

On a fairness account of exploitation, then, neither free markets nor government coercion is *necessarily* exploitative. But both have the *potential* to be.

It is tempting to try to analyze the idea of unfairness in terms of a set of necessary and sufficient conditions. But both the history of failure of such attempts and the apparent context-sensitivity of judgments of fairness and unfairness give reason to doubt the viability of such approaches. What reason is there, after all, to suppose that the criteria of fairness for relations between romantic partners will be identical to those for arm's-length transactions in the marketplace? "Fairness" is probably best understood as a shorthand way of referring to a set of loosely related social norms that have evolved in different social contexts to meet different social needs. A plausible account of fairness, and thus a plausible account of exploitation, will therefore be a *pluralistic* one.

For purposes of this discussion, however, the main point of interest is exploitation in the context of debates over political economy. And in this context, there might appear to be a single relevant criterion of fairness on which an account of exploitation might be based: equality. Many have thought that an exchange will be fair, and hence non-exploitative, if and only if that exchange is *equal* in some sense. So, for instance, it might seem that what is really wrong with exploitation in the Marxist sense is that the laborer is not being paid a wage equal to the value his labor produces for his employer. And, similarly, it might seem that the exploitation identified by the classical liberals involves citizens not receiving a good or service from the government that is of equal value to the taxes they are required to pay.

Trying to analyze "fairness" in terms of "equality" might seem to make little progress toward clarity. For, after all, "equality" seems to admit of at least as wide a range of different and incompatible interpretations as "fairness." If a fair exchange is an equal exchange, then in *what respect* is it equal?

Here is one approach. As was explained in the previous section, voluntary cooperative exchanges are generally mutually beneficial. In other words, both parties typically walk away from them better off than they were *ex ante*. After all, if they did not expect to be made better off by the exchange, they could have simply declined to enter into it.

Cooperative exchanges thus create what economists call a "social surplus." To illustrate, suppose your old television is worth $50 to you—not much, because you bought a new one and you don't use the old one any more. On the other hand, I just moved into town and need a new TV, and I'd be happy to pay $100 for one like yours. So we bargain, arrive at a price of $75, and make a deal. You give up something you value at $50 in exchange for $75, and come away $25 richer. I give up something I value at $75 in exchange for something I value at $100 and walk away $25 richer. *All together*, we're $50 richer. This is the social surplus.

This suggests one way of thinking about the idea of equality in the context of fair exchanges. An exchange is *equal*, we might say, and hence fair, if it involves an *equal division of the social surplus*. Exploitative exchanges, in contrast, are those in which one party commands a disproportionately large share of the social surplus, leaving the other party with little or nothing to gain.

As a first pass, this account seems reasonably plausible. It would seem, for instance, to differentiate between the exploitative and non-exploitative cases of capitalist employment we described above. A monopsonist employer, for example, is in a position with significant *bargaining power*. Suppose that employer gains $10 per hour worth of value from an employee's labor. An employer like that could afford to pay its workers $9 per hour and still make a profit. But if potential employees have nowhere else to go, why should it pay that much? Why not pay employees as little as it can get away with—maybe $5 an hour, just barely over the subsistence level of $4? In this case the employment relationship would generate a social surplus of $6. But $5 of that surplus would go into the pocket of the employer, while only $1 goes to the laborer. Might not that lopsided division of the social surplus be precisely what is unfair, and thus exploitative, about this kind of labor?

The same basic analysis can be applied to the classical liberal account of exploitation, though here the matter is complicated somewhat by the fact that government transfers will sometimes be *zero-sum* exchanges that do not create *any* social surplus. If the government takes $100 from Peter and gives it to Paul, society is no richer and no poorer after the transfer than it was before. But even if we cannot analyze this "exchange" in terms of the idea of a social surplus, we can still appeal to the more general idea of "equality of benefit" to explain why it is exploitative and wrong. The problem with this kind of transfer is that it benefits Paul at Peter's expense. If Peter and Paul shared equally in both the benefits and the burdens of the policy, we would be far less inclined to think of the policy as exploitative.

5. EXPLOITATION AND UNFAIRNESS

Thinking about fairness in terms of equality seems to explain many of our intuitive judgments about exploitation. Unfortunately, it cannot explain them all. Consider the following stylized example of exploitation:

> **Drowning:** Adam is in imminent danger of drowning in a lake when Bob rows by on the only boat in sight and offers to rescue him—but only if Adam promises to pay Bob $10,000 upon his return to safety.

In this example, Bob clearly takes advantage of Adam's desperate situation to unfairly benefit himself at Adam's expense. The exchange is an exploitative one.

But notice that while the exchange between Adam and Bob is exploitative, it is also mutually beneficial. Bob obviously benefits from the deal, walking away $10,000 richer in exchange for only a few minutes of his time and a trivial amount of labor. But Adam walks away better off too. Without the exchange, he would have died. Bob's rescue offer gives him back his life, which presumably he values much more highly than the $10,000 he gives up to save it. Both parties come away from the deal with more than they gave up.

Indeed, if we think about the exchange in terms of the social surplus it generates, it seems likely that Adam gains *more* from the exchange than Bob. Most people put a fairly high value on their continued existence. So, suppose Adam values not dying at $1 million. In that case, he gives up something he values at $10,000 in exchange for something he values at $1 million. Bob, in turn, gives up something he values at close to $0 in exchange for something he values at $10,000. The exchange creates a social surplus of $1 million, but fully *99 percent of that surplus* goes to Adam, leaving Bob with a mere 1 percent. If exploitation consists of grabbing the lion's share of the social surplus of an exchange, then we are forced to conclude that drowning-victim Adam is actually exploiting boat-rowing Bob—an unlikely result!

What this example seems to suggest is that we cannot appeal to the concept of equality to explain the concept of fairness. Doing so gets things precisely backward. Equality is not basic. Rather, it is *fairness* that is the more philosophically basic concept, and that explains when and how equality is, or is not, an appropriate measure of fairness. Sometimes an equal division is a fair one. But sometimes it is not.

A big part of what accounts for our intuitive judgment in **Drowning**, probably, is the extremely low cost at which Bob is able to provide Adam with the service he so desperately needs. Saving Adam's life requires almost nothing in the way of time, energy, or risk. It is true that Bob's act produces a great deal of value for Adam, but there does not seem to be much in Bob's action to entitle him to demand a share of that value, let alone an *equal* share.

Things would be different if Bob had gotten to the rescue by a different route. Consider a different example.

> **Salvage:** Dawn lives near a lake, and knows that every spring, tourists come up to the area, underestimate the treacherousness of the lake's waters, and swim out farther than they can handle. After posting several signs in an unsuccessful attempt to ward reckless swimmers off, Dawn decides to buy a boat, quit her day job, and spend her springtime days cruising the lake looking for swimmers to rescue. She does not find them often—sometimes a whole month goes by without a single one. But when she finds swimmers like Claire, she rescues them, and she charges them a hefty fee for her services.

Perhaps you think that Dawn's behavior is morally wrong. Even still, you will probably concede that it is not *as* wrong as Bob's. And part of what makes it less wrong is that Dawn, unlike Bob, has invested a significant amount of resources in her rescue. Dawn does not just stumble upon Claire while she is busy doing something else. She has made a deliberate sacrifice of time and resources precisely so as to put herself in a position to be there when Claire needed her. Because she has made this investment, the high price she charges Claire for a rescue does not result in an unusually large profit for Dawn[8].

Most of it simply goes to covering her costs. To charge any less, then, would involve Dawn's operating her business at a loss. Perhaps if she is independently wealthy and able to sustain it, that would be a morally exemplary thing for her to do. But it would seem to be asking a lot to say that it is what she is morally *required* to do.

Part of what determines whether an economic transaction is unfair, then, is whether the benefits the perpetrator derives from the exchange far exceed her costs. But, as the following example illustrates, this is not the only factor.

> **Painting:** Faith has created, with just a few minutes' work and some cheap paint, a work of art with which Eric has fallen madly in love. Eric asks Faith if the painting is for sale, to which Faith replies that it is, but only for $10,000.

Is this exploitative? Is it unfair? Eric is no doubt unhappy that the selling price is so high. But in demanding a high price for her art, has Faith really treated Eric *wrongly*?

One thing that might lead us to say that Eric is not wronged is the fact that the consequences to him of not being able to purchase the painting are, in the grand scheme of things, not so bad. Whereas in **Drowning** Adam stood to suffer the loss of his life, in **Painting** Eric stands only to suffer some mild disappointment. In game theoretic terms, Eric's BATNA (Best Alternative to a Negotiated Agreement) is pretty good. And we might think that one of the features that unfair exchanges characteristically have is that they involve a sharp disparity in *bargaining power*, such that whether the exchange goes through or not matters a lot more to victim A than it does to perpetrator B. Or, more formally, that

$$\text{Value (BATNA}_B) - \text{Value (BATNA}_A) \geq \text{Disparity Threshold}$$

where "Disparity Threshold" specifies the level at which the difference in power becomes sufficiently great as to render the exchange not genuinely voluntary.[9]

Perhaps, then, it is only when B takes advantage of her greater bargaining power (understood in terms of BATNA differential) to derive disproportionate benefit that the exchange is unfair, and hence exploitative. If B is proposing to sell A a luxury item without which A could easily make do, as in **Painting**, then the difference in bargaining power is not there and thus neither is the potential for exploitation. But even if the difference in bargaining power *is* there, and therefore the exchange is not fully voluntary, it does not automatically follow that it is unfair or exploitative. For an unfair exchange is one in which B *takes advantage* of her bargaining power. And B could very well choose not do to that by, say, setting the price at a level that more closely reflects her actual costs.

Still, while economic concepts such as "BATNA" and "cost of production" can provide some headway in thinking about the difference between fair and unfair exchange, they cannot tell the whole story. This is both because there is more to unfairness than just economics, and because even the economic issues might themselves be conditioned by more fundamental moral principles.

First, an exchange can be unfair in ways that have nothing to do with the economic terms of the exchange. Suppose, to borrow an example from Chris Meyers, that Carole, who is lost along a deserted desert highway, encounters Jason, who is driving the only car she's seen for days, and asks for a ride. Jason responds that he will drive her to safety, but only if she allows him to sodomize her first (Meyers, 2004).

We could, if we wished, attempt to assimilate this case to other more straightforwardly economic ones by thinking about the disutility Carole attaches to allowing herself to be sodomized as different only in quantity, not in kind, from the disutility she experiences in paying a certain amount of money for a ride. But it seems far more natural, and more plausible, to analyze the wrongness of this exchange not in terms of the "excessive cost" it imposes upon Carole, but in terms of the *disrespect* with which Jason treats Carole in making this offer. In making his rescue dependent upon Carole's submitting to a degrading and physically invasive act, Jason has failed to treat Carole with the respect she merits as a human person. That is why the transaction is exploitative.[10]

Even when narrowly economic considerations appear to be paramount, however, their moral force might still depend, and be conditioned by, more fundamental moral principles. Return again to **Painting**. Part of what leads us to conclude that this transaction is not exploitative, I argued, is that Eric would not suffer much harm if he were unable to purchase the painting at the high price demanded by Faith. Because Eric does not really need the painting, Faith simply does not have much *power* over Eric in this situation.

But there is a deeper and more important point here as well: Faith simply does not *owe* it to Eric to sell him the painting at *any* price, low or high. Even if Eric is *obsessively* drawn to the painting and would sink into a deep state of unhappiness without it, Faith is under no moral obligation to part with it. And if she *is* willing to part with it, she has the moral license to set whatever price for it she wishes.

In this respect, **Painting** is fundamentally unlike **Drowning**, since part of what grounds our judgment of exploitation in that latter case seems to be the belief that Bob has a moral obligation to rescue Adam. It would be morally wrong of Bob to let Adam drown, and so it is unfair and exploitative of Bob to make his rescuing Adam *contingent* upon Adam's paying him an exorbitantly high sum. In **Painting**, in contrast, Faith is under no obligation to sell to Eric at all, and so it is not wrong for her to make her sale contingent upon Eric's paying her a very high price. Whether a high price is exploitative or not, then, depends not merely on what B's costs are, nor on what A's needs are. It also depends on what B's *moral duties* are, and specifically on whether she has in this particular case any moral duty that would make it wrong for her to interact with A on certain terms, or to refrain from interacting with him at all.

If, as seems likely, the best account of our moral duties is a pluralistic one, it will also be the case that the best accounts of fairness, and of exploitation, will be pluralistic. Such a pluralism has the marked advantage of allowing us to account for a wide array of judgments about exploitation in diverse contexts. The disadvantage, if there is any, is the loss of the apparent theoretical unity that a more monistic account seems to provide. A pluralistic account of exploitation makes figuring out what is exploitative and what is not a complicated matter. Or, more accurately, it *reflects* the fact that figuring out what is exploitative and what is not is complicated.

6. THE RULES OF THE GAME

But while questions about the fairness or unfairness of individual acts of exchange are complicated, this complexity is multiplied when those acts are considered not in isolation, but as part of a complex system of social norms and public policies. Social groups have a variety of rules and standards with which individuals are expected to comply in their dealings with one another. Those rules and standards are developed, promulgated, and enforced upon members of the social group, sometimes through decentralized, informal mechanisms such as custom and manners, and sometimes through more formal, centralized mechanisms such as statutory law.

The fact that there exist various social norms dealing with exploitation means that individual acts of exploitation cannot be viewed in an entirely acontextual manner, in the way that stylized philosophical thought experiments sometimes encourage us to do. It is necessary, but not sufficient, to consider such acts on their individual merits. It is also important to bear in mind the fact that such acts are *tokens* of a more general *type* of action that is the object of a social norm.

The fact that particular acts are situated in systems of social norms complicates the analysis of such acts, partly by making the morally proper *response* to such acts difficult to determine. When we think about how to respond to a particular act of exploitation out of context, we need only concern ourselves with the character of the act and the agent who performed it. Does the act deserve condemnation? Is the agent worthy of blame? Of punishment? Our answers to these questions, in turn, might depend upon how much harm the action caused, whether the agent knew what he or she was doing, whether there are any kind of mitigating circumstances that might justify or excuse the agent's actions, and so on.

Sorting out the answers to these questions can be difficult enough. But figuring out how our social norms and legal rules ought to respond to *all* actions of this general *type* is far more so. For when we consider types of actions, rather than tokens, it is no longer sufficient to restrict our analysis to the intrinsic character of the actions or the agents who perform them. We must also consider how our responses to those acts will affect *other* acts of the same type in the future, as well as other acts of different but also morally relevant types.

To illustrate, suppose we believe that prostitution is a characteristically exploitative practice. How, then, should we respond to it? Suppose we think about this question in terms of a stylized thought experiment designed to isolate our reaction to a particular act, apart from its context. We observe a man treating a prostitute exploitatively, and we have the option of either pushing a button to stop the act and punish the man, or not. Framed in this way, the case for prohibition and punishment seems strong: the act is wrong, the agent is blameworthy, and prohibition and punishment seem like morally appropriate responses to these facts.

But now consider the same sort of act in a broader context. Prostitution is characteristically exploitative. Should we, then, adopt a *social norm* of prohibition and punishment for acts of this type? Let us stipulate that, on their own merits, *each and every* token of the type is wrong, and all of the agents who perform those act-tokens are morally blameworthy. This is a significant assumption. But significant as it is, it is still not enough to clinch the case for a norm of prohibition and punishment. For in deciding whether such a norm is justified, we must consider how people are likely to *respond* to the existence of the norm—a dynamic consideration lost in the static world of our philosophical thought experiment. Will those who exploit prostitutes respond to the threat of punishment by stopping their exploitative activity? Or will they, instead, continue to exploit but do so in secret, moving the activity of prostitution "underground" away from the eyes of the law? If they do the latter, will this make the exploitation of prostitutes even *worse*, by eliminating whatever social and legal protection prostitutes might have had available to them when their activity was recognized as a legitimate form of economic activity?

In our static, acontextual thought experiments, we get to assume that our actions have the results we desire. If we say we would push the button to protect the innocent and punish the guilty, then the innocent are saved and the guilty are given their due. But in the real world, people have minds of their own, and they use those minds to adapt to the norms and rules of their environment in ways that serve *their* ends, ends that are not necessarily the same as those of the people who designed the norms and rules in the first place. Anticipating such responses and designing norms and rules so as to take them into account can be difficult. But if the goal is to design *better* norms and rules, it is a task that must be faced, for the consequences of abdicating it can be dire.

The upshot for this analysis is that even if capitalist *acts* are exploitative, it does not necessarily follow that social norms or legal rules *prohibiting* such acts will be justified. It is not obviously true that sweatshop labor is exploitative (Zwolinski, 2007). But even if it is, it is still a separate question what should be *done* about it. Sometimes norms that attempt to suppress exploitation make it worse, as perhaps happens in cases involving the criminalization of prostitution. And sometimes norms successfully stamp out exploitation only by channeling people toward other forms of morally objectionable behavior. Workers who are laid off because a sweatshop has closed down in response to new legal restrictions are not *exploited*. But they are *neglected*. From the standpoint of morality as a whole, that is not an obviously superior result. From the standpoint of the victims, it is almost certainly worse.

7. Conclusion

There is a sense, perhaps, in which Marx was right in thinking that exploitation is a permanent feature of a "free," capitalist society. But the reason for this fact is not what Marx thought. It is not that capitalist labor relationships are necessarily exploitative. They have the potential to be so insofar as they are unfair. But so long as we think, as we probably should, that not all capitalist labor relationships are *necessarily* unfair, we need not think that they are necessarily exploitative, either.

The real reason that exploitation might well be a permanent feature of a capitalist society is that there is quite possibly nothing that can be done to get rid of it. Or, at least, nothing that one should be *willing* to do. Social norms and legal rules meant to suppress exploitation can be devised—prohibiting some activities like prostitution, or regulating others like wage labor. But there is no guarantee that these regulations will have the intended effect. Instead of ending exploitation, they might simply drive it out of sight. And even if the regulations produce the hoped-for outcome, they might well produce *other* outcomes as well, of a less appealing sort.

But even putting such concerns aside and assuming that the problem of unintended consequences can be avoided, there remains another problem. We can seek to ameliorate exploitation in the market by entrusting the state with the power to regulate the market for the common good. But in doing so there is a risk of reducing *one* sort of exploitation only by facilitating a *different* sort. As the early classical liberals noted, and as modern public choice economics has confirmed, the state can be a source of exploitation too, and the more power is put into the hands of the state to correct the deficiencies of the market, the more dangerous a source it becomes.[11]

The challenge, then, is to reconcile the insights of the classical liberals such as Say and Bastiat on the one hand, and Marx on the other. It is to design institutions that will effectively protect individuals from private exploitation at the hand of their fellow citizens, without putting them in too much danger of being exploited by the very powers originally established to protect them. This is a difficult and delicate balance to strike. But one thing is virtually certain—no set of institutions will successfully *eliminate* exploitation. A free society must try to minimize exploitation, or to reduce it as much as possible consistent with a proper attention to other relevant moral values. But utopia is not an option.

NOTES

1. See, for example, John Rawls' original formulation of his first principle of justice, which held that "each person is to have an equal right to the most extensive basic liberty compatible with a similar liberty for others" (Rawls, 1971: 60). A little more than a century earlier, Herbert Spencer set forth a rather similar principle in his "law of equal freedom" (Spencer, 1995: 95). For a discussion of Spencer's much-misunderstood liberalism, with special emphasis on his thoughts on our duties to the poor and vulnerable, see Zwolinski, 2015.
2. Rawls, of course, believed that only a very limited set of economic liberties qualified as basic liberties worthy of the highest protection a liberal state could offer. See Rawls (1971). For an argument that economic liberties are worthy of more stringent protection even according to Rawls' own premises, see Tomasi, 2011.

3. This worry about the "tyranny of the majority" was of course famously expressed by both Tocqueville and Mill. In the twentieth century, this insight was developed and refined by public choice economists such as James Buchanan and Gordon Tullock (Buchanan and Tullock, 1962).

4. Discussions of "plunder" were common among nineteenth-century French classical liberals, but especially in the writings of Frederic Bastiat. See Bastiat, 1998.

5. Most of the nineteenth-century classical liberals, including Bastiat, were not anarchists. Instead, they defended a version of the minimal, night watchman state—*l'état gendarme*—the powers of which would be strictly limited to the protection of life, liberty, and estate. The one exception to this generalization is the Belgian-born economist, Gustave de Molinari, who in 1849 set forth the earliest known articulation and defense of what would come to be known as the "anarcho-capitalist" theory of government (Molinari, 1849). Bastiat, Comte, and most other French liberal economists were sharply critical of his proposal. See, for discussion, Hart, 1981a; 1981b; 1982; Zwolinski and Tomasi, 2016: ch. 3.

6. This problem was originally identified by Eugen Böhm-Bawerk (Böhm-Bawerk, 1962). Marx himself was aware of it (Marx, 1977: 290), and after his death his followers even instituted a prize essay contest to try to solve this "problem of the average rate of profit." See Arnold, 1990: ch. 3 for discussion.

7. See Wolff, 2002: 115. For a summary of criticisms of the labor theory of value, see Elster, 1985: ch. 3.

8. Indeed, the fact that Dawn has posted warning signs suggests that she is not even *trying* to earn as high a rate of profit as possible. This fact about Dawn's intention probably also plays a role in our judgment about the permissibility of her charging what she does for her services.

9. I borrow this idea (and the formula) from Mike Munger, for whom this analysis of bargaining power plays a role in the analysis of "euvoluntary exchange." See Munger, 2011.

10. For an account of exploitation that makes considerations of respect for persons central, see Sample, 2003.

11. For the public choice analysis of rent-seeking, see Buchanan, Tollison, and Tullock, 1980; Euzent and Martin, 1984; Tullock, Tollison, and Rowley, 1988.

REFERENCES

Arnold, N. S., 1990. *Marx's radical critique of capitalist society: a reconstruction and critical evaluation*. New York: Oxford University Press.

Bastiat, F., 1998. *The law*. 2nd ed. Translated by D. Russell. Irvington-on-Hudson, NY: Foundation for Economic Education.

Böhm-Bawerk, E., 1962. Unresolved contradiction in the Marxian economic system. In: *Shorter Classics of Eugen Böhm-Bawerk*, vol. 1. Translated by A. Macdonald. South Holland, IL: Libertarian Press. pp.201–302.

Buchanan, J., Tollison, R. D., and Tullock, G., 1980. *Toward a theory of the rent-seeking society*. College Station: Texas A & M University.

Buchanan, J., and Tullock, G., 1962. *The calculus of consent*. Ann Arbor: University of Michigan Press.

Cole, C. W., 1964. *Colbert and a century of French mercantilism*. Hamden: Archon Books.

Comte, C., 1817. De l'organisation sociale considérée dans ses rapports avec les moyens de subsistence des peuples. *Le Censeur Européen*, 1, pp.1–66.

Elster, J., 1985. *Making sense of Marx*: Cambridge, MA: Cambridge University Press.

Euzent, P. J., and Martin, T. L., 1984. Classical roots of the emerging theory of rent seeking: the contribution of Jean-Baptiste Say. *History of Political Economy*, 16(2), pp.255–262.

Hart, D., 1981a. Gustave de Molinari and the anti-statist liberal tradition, part I. *Journal of Libertarian Studies*, 5(3), pp.263–290.

Hart, D., 1981b. Gustave de Molinari and the anti-statist liberal tradition, part II. *Journal of Libertarian Studies*, 5(4), pp.399–434.

Hart, D., 1982. Gustave de Molinari and the anti-statist liberal tradition, part III. *Journal of Libertarian Studies*, 6(1), pp.83–104.

Marx, K., 1977. *Capital*. Vol. 1. New York: International Publishers.

Meyers, C., 2004. Wrongful beneficence: exploitation and third world sweatshops. *Journal of Social Philosophy*, 35(3), pp.319–333. [online] Available at: http://search.ebscohost.com/login.aspx?direct=true&db=phl&AN=PHL2062555&site=ehost-live

Molinari, G. de, 1849. De la production de la sécurité. *Journal des Économistes*, 21(1), pp.277–290.

Munger, M. C., 2011. Euvoluntary or not, exchange is just. *Social Philosophy and Policy*, 28(02), pp.192–211. doi:10.1017/s0265052510000269

Raico, R., 1992. Liberalism, Marxism, and the state. *Cato Journal*, 11(3), pp.391–404.

Rawls, J., 1971. *A theory of justice*. 1st ed. Cambridge, MA: Belknap Press.

Rothbard, M. N., 1995. *An Austrian perspective on the history of economic thought: economic thought before Adam Smith*. Vol. 1. Cheltenham, UK: Edward Elgar Pub.

Sample, R., 2003. *Exploitation: what it is and why it's wrong*. New York: Rowman and Littlefield.

Say, J.-B., 1821. *Letters to Mr. Malthus, and Catechism of political economy*. London: Sherwood, Nelly, and Jones.

Say, J.-B., 1880. *A treatise on political economy, or the production, distribution, and consumption of wealth*. New York: Augustus M. Kelly.

Spencer, H., 1995. *Social statics*. New York: Robert Schalkenbach Foundation.

Spooner, L., 1875. Vices are not crimes: a vindication of moral liberty. *The Collected Works of Lysander Spooner*, vol. 5, pp.1–38. Indianapolis: Liberty Fund.

Tomasi, J., 2011. *Free market fairness*. Princeton, NJ: Princeton University Press.

Tullock, G., Tollison, R. D., and Rowley, C. K., 1988. *The political economy of rent seeking*. Boston: Kluwer.

Viner, J., 1927. Adam Smith and laissez faire. *Journal of Political Economy*, 35(2), pp.198–232.

Viner, J., 1937. *Studies in the theory of international trade*. New York: Harper.

Waldron, J., 1981. A right to do wrong. *Ethics*, 92(1), pp.21–39.

Wertheimer, A., 1996. *Exploitation*. Princeton, NJ: Princeton University Press.

Wertheimer, A., and Zwolinski, M. (2015). Exploitation. *The Stanford Encyclopedia of Philosophy* (Summer 2015 edition), Edward N. Zalta (ed.) [online] Available at: http://plato.stanford.edu/entries/exploitation/

Wolff, J., 2002. *Why read Marx today?* Oxford: Oxford University Press.

Zwolinski, M., 2007. Sweatshops, choice, and exploitation. *Business Ethics Quarterly*, 17(4), pp.689–727.

Zwolinski, M., 2015. Social Darwinism and social justice: Herbert Spencer on our duties to the poor. In: C. Boisen and M. Murray, eds. *Distributive justice debates in social and political thought: perspectives on finding a fair share*. New York: Routledge. pp.56–76.

Zwolinski, M., and Tomasi, J., 2017. *A brief history of libertarianism*. Princeton, NJ: Princeton University Press.

CHAPTER 24

··

VOLUNTARINESS, COERCION, SELF-OWNERSHIP

··

SERENA OLSARETTI

1. INTRODUCTION

CLAIMS of voluntariness and the converse notion of force are invoked as the bases for conclusions about people's rights and responsibilities in a wide range of contexts. Consider a few of them. Whether individuals voluntarily consent to political authority may affect their political obligation. Whether they voluntarily choose to undergo a life-terminating procedure may determine the legitimacy of euthanasia. Whether the economic transactions people enter into are forced may undermine the validity of those transactions' outcomes. Whether the inequalities that arise between persons reflect their voluntary choices may, under certain conditions, render those inequalities just. In these and other cases, whether someone chooses or consents or assents to something voluntarily, or conversely, whether a person's choice is forced, is thought to have normative significance.

Despite the pervasiveness of claims of voluntariness, the notion of voluntariness itself has received less direct attention than have the related notions of freedom, coercion, autonomy, and self-ownership. The aim of this chapter is to bring to light and assess the distinctive role and normative significance of voluntariness for our judgments about people's rights and obligations. In particular, the chapter addresses two main questions about the relevance of voluntariness.

The first is whether voluntariness itself, or only the absence of coercion, has normative significance. This question arises because the latter view—that what matters, specifically, is that people not be coerced by others, where people not being coerced by others identifies only a particular subset of cases of undermined voluntariness—is often defended, or at least implicitly assumed, by political and moral philosophers.

Whether or not this view is correct has important consequences. For example, whether only coerced choices, rather than all forced choices, undermine the legitimacy of the outcomes of those choices affects the moral status of the free market and the justified scope of state regulation of market exchanges, as market exchanges are claimed to not be instances of coerced choices, even if they were forced. After examining the merits of each of the two opposed positions—that all force disrupts the justice of transactions, versus only coercion—this chapter identifies the possibility of defending a third one, on which what is normatively significant is whether someone intentionally contributes to rendering another person's choice forced. The second question this chapter explores concerns the relation between voluntariness and self-ownership. The principle of self-ownership holds that individuals possess over themselves—that is, over their mental and bodily powers—the largest range of private property rights compatible with everyone else's having an equal set of such rights. Defenders of self-ownership champion it as a principle of liberty, and some have carefully analyzed its connection to freedom as non-prevention, arguing for the value of self-ownership rights as protecting a particular distribution of freedom. What defenders of self-ownership have generally not noticed, however, is that the notion of voluntariness is integral to the very concept of self-ownership and that, as a result, different possible conceptions of self-ownership can be formulated, depending on our understanding of what the conditions are for choices to be voluntary. This, too, has important consequences. What emerges is that the concept of self-ownership is indeterminate in a way that has hitherto gone unnoticed. Moreover, any attempt to make it determinate must proceed by formulating an account of voluntariness on the basis of which it can then be claimed that some ways of interfering with people constitute breaches of self-ownership *insofar as* they amount to forcing them to do or choose certain things. Moreover, if being a self-owner amounts to not being forced to surrender what one owns to others, and if it can be argued that the conditions for not being so forced are not present, for example, in free market transactions, then endorsement of self-ownership, far from supporting the free market as its defenders have standardly assumed, in fact calls for its regulation.

The two main questions this chapter addresses highlight the importance of paying attention to the notion of voluntariness and its normative relevance. Moreover, they are closely related. If the principle of self-ownership must make reference to a particular understanding of what counts as choosing voluntarily and being forced to choose, then answers to the first question—over whether only coerced choices or also of other types of forced choices are wrong and unjust—are relevant for developing a satisfactory response to the challenge of the indeterminacy of self-ownership, raised by the second question. The two main questions are discussed in sections 2 and 3 respectively. Before turning to those, section 1 sets the stage by identifying the notion of voluntariness as distinct from related notions such as freedom and autonomy, and a few constraints which a plausible account of voluntariness must meet.

2. THE DISTINCTIVENESS
OF VOLUNTARINESS

The first task in an analysis of the normative significance of voluntariness is to isolate that notion from cognate ones with which it is often conflated. These include, principally, the ideas of freedom, coercion, and autonomy. In several discussions, the idea that someone's choice or action is non-voluntary, or that someone is forced to choose or act,[1] has been treated as if it were reducible to the idea of a person's being free (and/or to her being autonomous, and/or to her being non-coerced). There are at least two different types of discussions in which this occurs.

First, on some views of freedom as positive freedom, a person's choosing voluntarily in some sense is both a necessary and sufficient condition of her being free. Positive freedom views take internal obstacles to the performance of actions to constitute hindrances to freedom; on these views, a person is free to the extent that she is rid of desires that she is alienated from, desires that prevent her from acting as she really wants to act, and to the extent that she acts on desires that she endorses (Berlin, 1969). An agoraphobic who is house-ridden against his better judgment will register, on these views, as unfree to leave his house, independently of whether there are any legal or other external obstacles to his leaving it; and his staying within the confines of his house, insofar as it is driven by his phobia, is not seen as an exercise of his freedom. Since acting out of desires that one is alienated from can be described as a kind of non-voluntary action (or as acting unfreely, or unwillingly), and, conversely, acting out of desires that one endorses can be described as a case of voluntary action (or of acting freely, or willingly), these positive freedom views see voluntariness and freedom as indistinguishable. Along similar lines, voluntariness has been conflated with the notion of autonomy, where the latter is defined as consisting in acting freely in the sense just sketched above. Being forced to act is seen as equivalent to acting unfreely, or on the basis of desires that one regrets having or does not identify with (Dworkin, 1970; Cohen, 1988).

Even defenders of negative freedom, however, have often neglected to identify voluntariness as a notion that is distinct from that of freedom. In some cases—this is the second kind of discussion in which voluntariness and freedom have been treated together, as if the conditions for one guaranteed the other—voluntariness has been encompassed within the idea of negative freedom as a result of the latter's identification with the absence of coercion (Berlin, 1969; Hayek, 1960; Hospers, 1995). On these views, freedom is viewed as the absence of coercion. Coercion, in turn, is defined as the deliberate interference by some person with another person's course of action, interference that subordinates the latter's will to that of the coercer (Hayek, 1960). Since coercion thereby involves what is ordinarily considered to be non-voluntary action, and since coercion is the converse of freedom, a person's being unfree necessarily involves her choosing non-voluntarily, and her choosing voluntarily is at least a necessary condition for her being free.

It is plausible to think that the conflation of voluntariness with the cognate notions of freedom, autonomy, and coercion has led to a neglect of an analysis of the conditions for voluntariness as a notion distinct from these, and of its relation to them. This is regrettable, because arguably each of these notions, on a plausible interpretation of them, picks out a relevant value, and we will be better placed to explicate those values and identify the conditions for their realization by distinguishing between them and by examining their relation. Moreover, as I argue below, the commitment to the value of people's making voluntary choices is more central than has generally been thought to deep-seated convictions about the disvalue of coercion and the value of self-ownership. In this context, the fact that the notion of voluntariness has been less often the object of close study than have those of coercion and of self-ownership appears to be unjustified. An account of voluntariness is in fact needed both to help identify the wrongness or badness of coercion, and to render determinate the value of self-ownership.

These claims, which are elaborated and defended at greater length in the next two sections, presuppose a particular view of the constraints which I think any conception of voluntariness must meet in order to be plausible. Moreover, although they do not presuppose any one particular conception of voluntariness, some other claims that will be made alongside them do. So before proceeding, in the rest of this section something should be said about both the constraints which it would seem that any plausible account of voluntariness must meet, and about the particular conception of voluntariness that will be endorsed (which meets those constraints, and furthermore, reflects other substantive moral commitments). In turn, before saying anything about these issues, a clarification is in order about what is involved in making them.

The formulation and defense of an account of voluntariness is not centrally an exercise in conceptual analysis, although it would be odd to pay no regard to ordinary usage of the concept when identifying the object of our discussion. We start with the assumption that at least some of the uses of the concept refer to something that has normative significance—after all, the familiar claims about the significance of voluntariness with which this chapter started are predicated on at least implicit ordinary understandings of what voluntariness is, and the defensibility of judgments such as these is what prompts our analysis of the notion of voluntariness in the first place—and then we ask whether and, if so, why, what we ordinarily take to be appropriate usages of a concept do identify a value. This is a substantive moral question, and our answer to it—what account of voluntariness we endorse, and what justified constraints such an account meets—will therefore invariably reflect substantive moral convictions. The observations that follow about the constraints which any plausible account of voluntariness must meet, and about what conception of voluntariness is taken to be defensible, are not, then, meant to be value-neutral in the sense of presupposing no substantive moral commitments. Nonetheless, they can be seen to be intuitively plausible and not unduly controversial, in that they can command the allegiance of defenders of a variety of views in political philosophy.[2]

This should be evident with regard to the two main constraints which, it would seem, a defensible conception of voluntariness should meet. These are, first, that the notion of voluntariness must be *explanatory*: it must explain why people act, or choose, as they do, and not only or even primarily what choice situation they face. Moreover, more specifically, the explanation in question must make reference to people's motivations: as the etymology of the term suggests, when we ask whether someone acted voluntarily, or was forced to act as she did, we are interested in what has engaged the person's *will* and moved her to act. The notion of voluntariness must, secondly, also be able to play a certain *justificatory* role; in particular, it must be able to undergird attributions of responsibility, as people's voluntary choices—for example, the choice of entering a contract, that of making a promise, or that of consenting to an interference—can change their and others' entitlements and obligations. That the notion of voluntariness should be capable of playing this role has an immediate important implication: the notion of voluntariness cannot be one that would support too broad a range of judgments of force, since if it did it would then be implausible to hold that force thus understood is an excuse or a justification for not holding someone liable for some stated consequences of his (allegedly forced) choice. This would be implausible, most obviously, because it would be insufficiently sensitive to the interests of those with whom the person who is said to have made a forced choice has transacted: if we thought a sale contract invalid all too easily, and allowed one party to default, we would all too easily allow the other party to be harmed. But, as it has been pointed out, a view of this kind would also be implausible from the point of view of the agent whose choices are in question, as we all have an interest in being bound by some choices that we make in less than ideal conditions; the latter, then, should still count as voluntary in some sense. One extreme illustration of this point is offered by cases like that of Hume's surgeon, or cases of "double-bind": an injured person who needs an operation in order to survive has an interest in being able to give her legitimating consent to the surgery (Scanlon, 1999; see also Wertheimer, 2012), as does a destitute person whose only way out of poverty is selling a kidney (Radin, 1996). In these cases, the fact that someone acts in order to avoid a dire outcome should not justify viewing their choices as non-voluntary in a sense that would justify impugning as void, and/or as impermissible, the contracts these individuals make.

These two features which an account of voluntariness should have—that it should capture the fact that whether people's choices are voluntary must make reference to people's motivations for acting in certain ways, and thereby explain why they act as they do; and that it should be able to serve as the basis of a defensible range of judgments about people's rights and liabilities—seem to pull in different directions. For while the first feature seems to require that whether or not a person acts voluntarily depends on subjective factors—how she perceives the nature of her choice situation is what impacts on her motivation to choose as she does—an account of voluntariness that relied on such subjective factors alone for determining whether a choice is voluntary would be ill suited to play a justificatory role. This is because an account on which choices are deemed voluntary or forced by reference only to subjective factors would support too wide a range of judgments of force: someone would count as forced to choose something whenever she perceives the alternative to be ineligible, either in absolute terms or by comparison to the option she does choose. Worries of this kind have arguably motivated some political philosophers to shy away from a motivational account of force (Cohen, 1988; Nozick, 1974 explicitly rejects a comparative account of voluntariness on these bases).

I have offered an account of voluntariness which I think can meet both these constraints (Olsaretti, 1998; 2004; 2008). On my view, a choice is voluntary if and only if it is not forced, and it is forced if and only if it is made only or primarily because the alternative to it is unacceptable, where the standard for the acceptability of options is an objective standard of well-being, and unacceptable options are those which, by that standard, fall below a certain threshold. A paradigmatic example of an unacceptable option is a hazardous job that threatens frustration of people's basic needs. This account of voluntariness meets the two constraints sketched in virtue of taking both subjective and objective elements as relevant for judgments of voluntariness. Voluntariness is clearly a feature of the choices people make, or the actions they perform, as distinct from freedom, where the latter is understood as the availability of actions one is unprevented from performing (see Olsaretti, 2004: 137–141 for further elaboration of the relation between freedom and voluntariness). Whether a choice is voluntary depends on people's motives, as a person must be motivated by the fact that the alternative to what she chooses is unacceptable for her choice to be forced. At the same time, whether or not a choice is voluntary is not fully subjective, for whether or not an option is unacceptable is determined by reference to non-subjective factors, that is, by an independent, non-subjective standard of well-being, and one on which only some well-being shortfalls—those which would bring the agent below some threshold such as a basic needs threshold—are deemed to be unacceptable. As a result, the account in question would not support too wide a range of claims of force.

Nonetheless, the account does support the conclusion that the patient's contract with Hume's surgeon and the destitute person's with the kidney buyer are forced, where this has some normative consequences for what liabilities people may be seen to acquire as a result of those contracts. This implication of the account may seem unpalatable (Murphy, 2007; Wertheimer, 2012; Scanlon, 1999), and in order to avoid it, it may seem that we have to either relax further the conditions for voluntariness (so that the choices in question would come out as voluntary), or to give up the claim that voluntariness is a necessary condition for responsibility as liability. In response, I think we should do neither thing, and instead endorse a contextual view of the role of voluntariness, on which the conditions for voluntariness are different depending on what the normative significance of voluntariness judgments is supposed to be. We need not, and we should not, expect that there is only one normatively relevant sense in which actions or choices can be voluntary, such that, when the conditions for voluntariness thus understood are satisfied, then any and all of the various consequences that we think voluntary choices can justify are, in fact, justified. Instead, there are various senses in which choices can be voluntary, and they have different normative significance.

To see this, note that whether or not choices are voluntary is thought to affect the moral responsibility, entitlements, and obligations of the persons whose choices are voluntary, those of the persons they transact with, and those of third parties; moreover, with regard to each of these parties, there are different aspects of their normative situation which could be changed as a result of voluntary choices having been made. For example, if Audrey enters a contract with Burt whereby Audrey commits to paying Burt a certain amount in exchange for having Burt carry out a life-saving operation on her, several things may follow from the fact that Audrey's choice is, or is not, a voluntary one. Whether or not Audrey's choice is voluntary may have consequences for her own entitlements and obligations, where these are of various kinds: for whether she has a complaint as a result of Burt's undertaking the operation and whether she would have a complaint if Burt refused to carry it out after all; for whether she has an obligation to pay Burt the remuneration they agreed; and, if moral evaluation is relevant in this case, for whether she is morally praiseworthy or blameworthy for her action. Relatedly, and secondly, whether or not Audrey's choice is voluntary may change various aspects of Burt's normative situation, affecting whether or not it is permissible and obligatory for him to carry out the operation; whether he is praiseworthy or blameworthy for him to exact that particular price for it; whether he is entitled to receive that particular amount of money; whether he is entitled to third parties' abstaining from interfering with his agreement with Audrey and/or to their stepping in to enforce its terms if Audrey departs from them. As this last observation highlights, the voluntariness of Audrey's choice may also have normative significance, thirdly, for third parties (Scanlon, 1982; Freeman, 2001), potentially expanding their liberties (they may, as a result of the voluntariness of Audrey's choice, no longer have an obligation to prevent Burt from undertaking certain incursions on Audrey's body, and/or they may no longer have an obligation to prevent him from exacting payment from her), or augmenting their obligations (they may acquire an obligation to Audrey and/or Burt to enforce the terms of the contract they have entered into).

As this brief sketch of the potential normative consequences of choice suggests, they vary both in terms of *whose* situation, and in terms of *what specific aspects* of a person's normative situation, are affected. Depending on which of these various normative consequences of people's choices is at stake, different conditions may have to be met for the choices that are said to justify them to in fact so justify them, where some of these conditions are ones that determine whether a choice qualifies as voluntary in some of various possible senses in which choices can be voluntary. For example, the sense in which actions must be voluntary for an agent whose choice is in question to be morally praiseworthy is different from that in which her choice must be voluntary for that person to be justifiably required to internalize some of the costs of her choices (see Olsaretti, 2004; Olsaretti, 2008). While for an agent to be morally praiseworthy for her action it seems enough that it is voluntary in the sense that it is intentional and the product of deliberation, more demanding conditions for voluntariness apply when what is at stake is not the moral appraisal of the agent for her choices, but her liabilities. On this view, to say that someone was forced to act as she did is compatible with deeming her morally praiseworthy for acting in that way (see Olsaretti, 2008).

Moreover, and along similar lines, just what costs people may be justifiably held liable for may depend on the agent's choices being voluntary in different senses (Olsaretti, 2009). So, going back to Hume's surgeon, the fact that his patient makes a choice under duress, or non-voluntarily in the sense sketched earlier (for he evidently would only make that choice because the alternative he faces is unacceptable), may mean that he is not liable to pay the surgeon an exorbitant price the surgeon may wish to extract from him; but the fact that the patient's consent is intentional and informed may suffice to authorize the surgeon's operation, and perhaps also to justify holding the patient to compensate the surgeon for some of the costs the surgeon has to incur (Olsaretti, 2013c).

When asking when a choice is voluntary, then, we should first of all ask what the sense of voluntariness at hand is supposed to be relevant for. Our answer to the latter question will influence our answer to the former. These observations in favor of a contextual approach to the analysis of voluntariness parallel similar claims made by others about coercion (Wertheimer, 1987; Berman, 2002). The account of voluntariness sketched earlier, then, does not purport to identify the conditions for voluntariness in all the senses in which we speak of the latter and view it as having normative significance. It is, instead, an account of one sense of voluntariness which is relevant for people's substantive responsibility, that is, for holding them liable for some consequences of their choices, as we do when, for example, we hold them to the terms of a contract they have entered into (for the distinction between moral and substantive responsibility, see Scanlon, 1999). Appeal to this sense of voluntariness, it will now be argued, also helps capture an important aspect of the wrongfulness of coercion and of the value of self-ownership.

3. COERCION AND VOLUNTARINESS

Views of the conditions under which individuals are coerced differ quite substantially—most importantly, they vary in terms of whether they assess the coerciveness of a proposal by reference to a baseline relative to which the proposal worsens the situation of the victim, and in line with whether coercive interference is seen to necessarily involve violations of moral requirements, as with the highwayman's violation of his victim's right to life and of his property rights (for an overview, see Anderson, 2006). Despite these differences, all accounts of coercion support, or are at least compatible with, the claim that individuals who are coerced to act are forced to act in the sense of force identified in the previous section. Whatever else being coerced involves, philosophers agree that it involves having one's will be put under undue pressure, which pressure motivates an agent to act as she does when the coercive proposal succeeds, and the agent is, in fact, coerced (Wertheimer, 1987; Berman, 2002; Frankfurt, 1988; Zimmerman, 1981).

The account of voluntariness I have outlined in the previous section offers a precise understanding of what kind of pressure on the will is involved in cases in which individuals are coerced, and also provides a criterion for deeming that pressure as undue. Being forced to act involves acting only or primarily in order to avoid an objectively unacceptable option, so an agent who is forced is moved by a concern to avoid serious harm to his well-being. This fact is what justifies thinking that the pressure he acts under is undue, and what distinguishes cases of coercion from cases in which, just like with coercion, agents may be similarly irrational to choose otherwise than they do, and may therefore not reasonably be expected to choose otherwise, but in which they nonetheless are not describable as forced, and therefore also not describable as coerced, to choose. These cases include situations in which agents face a range of acceptable options, one or some of which are either objectively or subjectively clearly superior to alternatives. They also include limited choice situations in which, although agents only face one acceptable option, their choice of that option is not motivated by their lacking acceptable alternatives, but rather, by features of that option which, given their preferences, make that option choiceworthy in their eyes. In both these types of cases, the nature of the available options and individuals' preferences are such that there is a sense in which individuals could not choose otherwise than they do: it would be irrational for them to not choose the option which, in either comparative or absolute terms, is worthy of being chosen by them. Yet they would not count as being forced to choose as they do. Nor, if we understand coercion as involving being forced, could they count as having been coerced to choose as they do.

So, in the standard highwayman case, the victim is coerced to surrender his money in that he surrenders it only because the alternative is unacceptable. But a person who is given the options to surrender either £50 in exchange for nothing, or £50 in exchange for a winning lottery ticket the winnings of which will more than compensate her for its price, is not coerced to choose the latter option. Similarly, if someone is put in a situation in which the only decent job she can choose is the job she very much wants—suppose she would be penalized heavily if she chose any other job, but would have chosen this very job even if these penalties on alternatives were not in place—she could not say she was coerced to choose the job she does choose.

Understanding coercion as a type of forcing, then, helps to clearly demarcate cases of coercion, capturing the sense in which the latter involves acting under undue pressure on one's will. Relatedly, it also helps account for an important aspect of the wrongfulness of coercion, which has to do with the latter's connection to unfreedom, and for the fact that coercion undermines responsibility. The last point follows straightforwardly from the remarks, in the previous section, that voluntariness is a necessary condition for holding individuals liable for some outcomes. Recall that substantive, not moral, responsibility is involved here (see Scanlon, 1999; Olsaretti, 2008). The fact that someone's choice to enter a contract was forced can justify not holding that person to the terms of that contract (as in the case of the patient to a surgeon who charges an exorbitant price for his life-saving operation); it can also justify not requiring a person to internalize certain costs of her choices in other types of cases (someone who is forced to expose herself to the risk of driving a motorbike without a helmet and is injured as a result would have a complaint against being denied free medical assistance). If coercion is a type of forcing, then we can account for why it undermines responsibility independently of whatever else coercion may involve.

As for the relation between coercion and unfreedom, the fact that coercion is a type of forcing justifies the view that agents' freedom—more specifically, their freedom of choice, which is none other than their ability to choose voluntarily—is compromised when they are coerced (Zimmerman, 1981). This will be true independently of whether coercion also involves a curtailment of people's negative freedom, something which it typically, although not necessarily, does. Coercion typically involves a curtailment of people's negative freedom, relative to the situation in which the victim was prior to the coercive proposal, in that in many cases an effective way in which to exert undue pressure on people's will is by restricting their option set, often by removing certain conjunctive freedoms (Carter, 1999; Olsaretti, 2004). In the highwayman case, to take that paradigmatic case again, the robber renders the victim unfree to both retain his wallet and remain unharmed (he removes from the victim the conjunctive freedom to do those things). But negative freedom, or freedom of action, is not necessarily impaired when individuals are coerced. This is because individuals can be coerced by coercive proposals which are credible bluffs (Nozick, 1967). But it is also because in some cases the coercer's proposal involves only the withholding of options, rather than the removal of any options that individuals had in the pre-proposal situation, so it does not look as though the victim's negative freedom is decreased. One instance of this is the case of a drug dealer threatening to withhold the daily drug supply from his client unless the latter gives someone a beating (Nozick, 1967). In these cases, although the agent's freedom of action is not curtailed, his freedom of choice is impaired. Viewing coercion as a type of forcing cashes out, then, the respect in which all coercion necessarily involves a loss in people's freedom.

If conceptualizing coercion as a type of forcing, and focusing on that aspect of it, captures several morally salient features of coercion—the fact that it involves undue pressure on the coerced agent's will, the fact that it undermines some responsibility, and the fact that it always involves a loss in freedom—we may be tempted to think that there are no morally salient differences between coercion and other types of forcing, including what are often described as cases of duress, and that there are no reasons to single out coercion as wrongful while condoning other types of forcing. Elsewhere I have argued for that view in the context of a discussion of the justice of market transactions (Olsaretti, 2004). In that context, the question of whether transactions are coerced or forced carries relevance not primarily for the moral evaluation of the character of the individuals who transact with the parties who are forced to choose: we are not in the business, there, of appraising the moral character of the employer who offers a worker the hazardous job the latter cannot refuse. Instead, whether individuals are forced matters in that context for whether they should be held to the terms of the transactions they have partaken in and for whether the outcomes of those transactions respect justice (Olsaretti 2013a). Once we keep in mind this fact—in line with the motivation for endorsing a contextualist approach to voluntariness, outlined at the end of the previous section—the respects in which coercion differs from other types of forcings (for example, the fact that with coercion, unlike with force, there is always someone who intentionally does the coercing) are arguably not salient (see Berman, 2002).

Some political philosophers, however, defend the opposite position, holding that coercion is relevantly different from other types of forcings, and indeed, that only coercion undermines responsibility and disrupts the justice of outcomes (see Barnes, 2012).

According to that view, choices that are not coerced, even if they are forced, can be binding and ground responsibility. Choices made on an unregulated market are a case in point here: even if a destitute worker could be described as forced to accept a hazardous job, his choice is seen as legitimating insofar as he is not coerced. (Libertarians in fact also deny that the worker's choice is forced, and think that the absence of coercion guarantees voluntariness—see Nozick, 1974: ix; but they can press their point that only coercion undermines responsibility even if they grant that some non-coerced choices like this one are forced. Here we are interested only in that point, so we will not discuss disagreement with the claim that the worker's choice is forced.)

A denial of the claim that all types of force are on a par, even with regard to only a particular set of normative consequences of judgments of voluntariness and force, need not lead us to embrace the libertarian position just mentioned. We need not choose between thinking, on the one hand, that there is no morally salient difference between duress and coercion and any other types of forcing, and, on the other, that coercion is uniquely problematic for the legitimacy or justice of the outcomes. A third position seems defensible, one that strikes a middle ground between the other two positions that have been sketched by holding that only some cases of force are wrongful, or especially wrongful, that is, those in which some agent *intentionally and avoidably contributes to another agent's being forced* to choose or to act. We can refer to these as cases of intended forcings. Standard cases of coercion are one instance of intended forcings: here one agent intentionally removes some freedoms from another agent, or renders some options ineligible, so as to place the latter in a situation in which she is forced to choose as the coercer wishes. Another type of intended forcing is what David Zimmerman calls coercive offers: proposals which improve the situation of the person who receives the proposal relative to the pre-proposal baseline, but where the maker of the offer is responsible for the direness of the pre-proposal baseline (Zimmerman, 1981). One such case, as Zimmerman notes, is that in which someone offers to rescue someone stranded in the desert in exchange for a substantial compensation, after she placed him there or prevented the stranded party from availing herself of alternative means of leaving the desert. But cases of intended forcings also include, importantly, a further type of transactions: those in which one party intentionally and avoidably sets the terms of the offer in such a way that the choice made in response to it is a forced one. The employer who offers the stranded proletariat a hazardous job, when he could offer him an independently choiceworthy option, is intentionally contributing to the worker's making a forced choice.

Like the libertarian position, which singles out coercion as uniquely problematic, and unlike the view which holds that all force undermines responsibility, the view in question is relational: only force that is in some sense the result of a relationship undermines substantive responsibility. More specifically, in identifying whether all or only some force undermines substantive responsibility, the view in question sees as normatively significant that someone intentionally interacts with someone else with a view to subordinating the latter's will to his own. (Note that, in line with what was said in section 1, upholding this view is compatible with thinking that, from the point of view of *other normative consequences* of the nature of the interaction, whether coercion was exercised is relevant. For example, we could think that all coercers are blameworthy, while this is not the case of all those who contribute to making someone's choice forced. In this sense, we could say that coercion involves wrongdoing in a way that intentional forcings do not.) But note that, even if we endorsed this view, rather than the view on which voluntariness is a necessary condition for substantive responsibility, an analysis of voluntariness and its normative significance remains crucially important. The latter enables us to identify what constitutes an intended forcing, capture an important aspect of why intended forcings are problematic, and notice that, even if intentionally interacting with others so as to subordinate their will is especially significant, coercion, once again, is not uniquely bad.

4. Self-Ownership and Voluntariness

An analysis of voluntariness is also of crucial importance for our understanding of another notion, that of self-ownership. Self-ownership is partly defined through voluntariness, and any formulation of self-ownership is indeterminate without a particular account of the conditions under which the choices people make are voluntary in the relevant sense, that is, in the sense that is necessary for people's self-ownership to count as being respected. This twofold truth about the relationship between self-ownership and voluntariness has gone unnoticed, yet it has several important implications.

The notion of self-ownership is the idea that individuals possess over themselves—over their bodily and mental resources—property rights; more specifically, defenders of self-ownership defend equal and full self-ownership, that is, the claim that individuals possess over their mental and bodily powers the largest range of private property rights compatible with everyone else's having an equal set of such rights (Cohen, 1995; Otsuka, 2003). The rights in question are said to include rights to use, control, and alienate in any way and under any condition the property holder freely chooses—whether by consuming, destroying, giving away, or exchanging with willing others at any price that can be agreed—the objects over which she has private property rights.

Even from this brief statement of the principle of self-ownership it is readily apparent that integral to the notion of self-ownership is a notion of the voluntariness of choice: under what conditions exchanges and transfers of property rights count as rights-respecting crucially depends on what are deemed to be the appropriate conditions for the property rights holder to be said to *choose* to use, control, and alienate the objects she has property rights over. This should come as no surprise, since conferral to individuals of self-ownership rights is openly defended as a way of endowing persons with the ability to decide for themselves how to expend their energies, and of protecting them from being forced to serve others: a self-owner is someone who has "*a right to decide* what would become of himself and what he would do, and as having a right to reap the benefits of what he did" (Nozick, 1974: 171); she is a person with "moral authority to *decide* how to live their lives" (Vallentyne, 2000: 321). More specifically, self-ownership includes "a very stringent right of control over and use of one's mind and body that bars others from intentionally using one as a means *by forcing one to sacrifice life, limb, or labour*" and "[a] very stringent right to all the income that one can gain from one's mind and body . . . either on one's own or through unregulated and untaxed *voluntary exchanges* with other individuals" (Otsuka, 2003: 15). On this point critics as well as defenders of self-ownership converge: "the polemically crucial right of self-ownership is the right not to (*be forced to*) provide product or service to anyone" (Cohen, 1995: 215).

In all these statements of self-ownership, this notion is explicated in terms of *being able to make free or voluntary choices, or not being forced to choose* how to use one's mind and body. Notions of voluntariness and force are constitutive of that of self-ownership, and this could not be otherwise, given that self-ownership rights include Hohfeldian powers, that is, the ability to change one's moral relation to what one has claims over, such as the power to exchange, donate, and lend one's property. As a result, self-ownership rights, like all private property rights, are not claims against interference as such, but rather, claims against *unconsented to* or *unchosen* interference: if we endorse self-ownership, the right to not be killed, properly described, is the right to not be killed *without one´s consent*, just as the private property right over my computer is the right to not having my computer removed or touched without my consent. So, some notion of what counts as consenting in the relevant sense—or as a voluntary choice to transfer or waive one's claim right against interference—is integral to the concept of self-ownership. Relatedly, we need an account of what counts as consenting (or, in other words, an account of the circumstances under which an action that seems to consist in the exercise of a Hohfeldian power is indeed such), in order to know in any particular case whether someone's self-ownership rights are respected or violated. Your full property rights in yourself, for example, consist, among other things, in your having a power to hire out your labor; in order to know whether a particular transaction in which someone else has come to control and use your labor time and you have come to earn a weekly salary in exchange for that respects your self-ownership rights, we need to know whether that transaction occurred voluntarily. (We would think it a breach of your self-ownership rights if someone conscripted you to work, or made you sign a contract at gunpoint, and then paid that weekly salary into your bank account. For further development of these points, see Olsaretti 2013b.)

The fact that some notion of voluntariness and force are integral to the concept of self-ownership has a number of important consequences.

The first and most obvious one is that, unlike what some defenders of self-ownership have suggested (Otsuka, 2003), they cannot do without an account of voluntariness. They cannot proclaim that, whether or not some transactions are voluntary or forced, what matters on their view is whether they are rights-respecting, since whether or not they are rights-respecting depends on whether they are voluntary. They need an account of voluntariness because in its absence the notion of self-ownership is *indeterminate*, and it is indeterminate in a way that has not been noticed before. (For other charges of indeterminacy, see Waldron, 1988; Fried, 2004.) Since notions of choice or consent are integral to that of self-ownership, we cannot specify when an individual enjoys self-ownership, and when she does not, without assuming, at least tacitly, a standard whereby the individual is deemed to have chosen or consented in the relevant sense. In the absence of an account of what counts as voluntary or forced exchanges, the principle of self-ownership only yields determinate prescriptions in a world in which individuals do not interact with one another: it entails, in these cases, that everyone has a right to withold his mental and bodily resources.[3] But as soon as any interaction occurs among individuals, whether or not any changes in the configuration of property rights that may ensue is just (i.e., self-ownership-rights respecting) depends on our account of when people can be said to have voluntarily chosen, as opposed to being forced, to transfer their rights.

A second consequence of the fact that self-ownership is partly defined through voluntariness is that the account of voluntariness that defenders of self-ownership adopt cannot be a rights-based one: since an account of voluntariness is needed to help spell out what counts as infringements and what count as legitimate exercises of self-ownership rights, it cannot make the voluntariness of choice depend on whether self-ownership rights are infringed in the process. This point is important. It means that rights-based conceptions of voluntariness and of coercion, whatever their intuitive plausibility, are barred from playing the role which we are here suggesting the defender of self-ownership needs a notion of voluntariness to play. An example would be the Nozickian view that whether or not the choice that an agent makes in a limited choice situation is non-voluntary depends on whether those who restricted the agent's options acted within their rights (Nozick, 1974): this view could not be deployed to identify cases in which the choices individuals make are voluntary or forced in a way that justifies concluding that their rights of self-ownership are respected or violated. Similarly, if a defender of self-ownership wished to defend the claim that only coerced choices (rather than all forced choices) were self-ownership-undermining, the account of coercion in question should not be a moralized one that posited rights-infringement to be a condition for choices made in response to pressure to be coerced (Wertheimer, 1987).

This remark leads onto discussion of a third and important consequence of the fact that notions of voluntariness and force are integral to that of self-ownership: different interpretations of self-ownership are possible, depending on what view is adopted regarding what constitute voluntary and forced choices. To see this point starkly, consider the "polemically crucial right" of self-ownership mentioned earlier (Cohen, 1995), that of not being "forced to" sacrifice life, limb, or power, or not to be "forced to assist others." When is it the case that people would be *forced* to assist others, as opposed to *voluntarily* choosing to assist them? Defenders of self-ownership and of its inequality-engendering potential have unanimously assumed that exacting redistributive taxation from a citizen would contravene her self-ownership—that this would be a case in which the citizen is forced to assist others—while demanding that the worker stick to the terms of the hazardous job contract would not—that this would be a case in which the worker is not being forced to sacrifice life, limb, and labor. These claims, it now becomes apparent, in fact rely on a particular understanding of what counts as a voluntary exercise of people's rights over themselves. It is open to critics of these claims to challenge that understanding, and adopt, in its place, an alternative one of what counts as voluntary exercise of rights, and therefore of what respect of self-ownership requires.

This will mean, minimally, that critics of the self-ownership-based defense of inequalities can now deny that their critique of inequalities is premised on a rejection of the principle of self-ownership. They need not abandon self-ownership to oppose its inequality-engendering potential, and can therefore claim to be able to uphold some central claims made in the name of self-ownership, such as the claim that people should not be enslaved or treated paternalistically,[4] while rejecting the inequalities that self-ownership has, until now, been seen to justify. These critics of inequalities can go even further, and argue that the interpretation of self-ownership they adopt, reflecting a different understanding of the conditions under which people choose voluntarily in a sense that ensures that their self-ownership is respected, is a more apt interpretation of the principle of self-ownership. An argument along these lines could proceed by bringing to light the rationale for the adoption of self-ownership rights—such as the commitments to giving people control over themselves, to protect their autonomy, to ensuring that they may not be treated as means only, and to allow each person to "*decide* what would become of himself and what he would do" (Nozick, 1974: 171)—and then showing that the alternative interpretation of self-ownership, on which self-ownership rights are breached not only by coercion but also by intentional forcings and perhaps by other types of force, does more justice to those underlying commitments than the notion of self-ownership which libertarians adopt. (For an argument with a similar structure, but deployed in support of the different conclusion that we should abandon self-ownership, where the latter is assumed to necessarily be libertarian self-ownership, see Cohen, 1995: chapter 10.)

Earlier on in this section it was remarked that the account of voluntariness on which defenders of self-ownership can rely cannot be rights-based. Defenders of self-ownership-generated inequality cannot say what they have often said, namely, that the reason the citizens would count as forced to sacrifice life, limb, and labor, while the worker does not, is that the former's but not the latter's self-ownership rights are curtailed. Arguably, there is no non-rights-based account of voluntariness that is both intuitively plausible—minimally, it should support a prohibition of coercion, even when the latter is not negative-freedom constraining, and of fraud—and that also warrants viewing the citizen, but not also the worker, as forced in the relevant, self-ownership-threatening sense. Whether or not such an account can be defended is crucial for the endeavor to formulate and defend self-ownership-generated inequalities. Defenders of self-ownership, as well as those concerned with the wrongness of coercion, should pay closer attention to voluntariness and force.

Acknowledgments

For comments on this chapter, I am very grateful to Paul Bou-Habib and to two anonymous readers. I owe special thanks to David Schmidtz for his comments and for his unwavering support and patience as volume editor.

NOTES

1. I use these two ideas interchangeably, and view force (which I also refer to as "non-voluntariness") as the converse of voluntariness. I prefer the term "non-voluntary" to "involuntary" as the latter is often associated with behavior or actions that are not intentional, and thus fail to be voluntary in a less demanding sense than the one I use.

2. For example, as far as theories of justice are concerned, the account of voluntariness sketched below could be endorsed by various types of liberal egalitarians, but also by defenders of the principle of sufficiency.

3. Robert Nozick remarks (1974: 52): "Peaceful individuals minding their own business are not violating the rights of others. It does not constitute a violation of someone's rights to refrain from purchasing something for him (that you have not entered specifically into an obligation to buy)." But as soon as individuals interact, what constitutes "minding their own business," and under what conditions individuals count as having entered an obligation to one another, are harder facts to establish and cannot be established without, among other things, an account of what constitutes consenting or choosing to interact or undertake obligations in specified ways.

4. The conception of voluntariness sketched in section 1, which, it is now suggested, could undergird a different conception of self-ownership from the familiar one which libertarian political philosophers adopt, would still ground a condemnation of paternalism, understood as forcing someone to do or not do something, for the sake of that person's well-being. Because, on this conception of voluntariness and force, what a person's *motivation* is, as well as the nature of the options she chooses, is crucial, a person who chooses or does what is objectively good for her, but only because someone has rendered the alternatives unacceptable, is forced to act as she does. Accordingly, such interventions would count as breaches of her self-ownership.

REFERENCES

Anderson, S., 2006. Coercion. *Stanford Encyclopedia of Philosophy*. (Summer 2015 Edition), Edward N. Zalta (ed.), <http://plato.stanford.edu/archives/sum2015/entries/coercion/>

Barnes, G., 2012. Why is coercion unjust? Olsaretti vs. the libertarian. *Analysis*, 72, pp.457–465.

Berlin, I., 1969. *Four essays on liberty*. Oxford: Oxford University Press.

Berman, M., 2002. The normative functions of coercion claims. *Legal Theory*, 8, pp.45–89.

Carter, I., 1999. *A measure of freedom*. Oxford: Oxford University Press.

Cohen, G.A., 1988. *History, labour, and freedom: themes from Marx*. Oxford: Clarendon Press.

Cohen, G.A., 1995. *Self-ownership, freedom, and equality*. Cambridge, UK: Cambridge University Press.

Dworkin, G., 1970. Acting freely. *Nous*, 4, pp.367–383.

Frankfurt, H., 1988. Coercion and moral responsibility. In: H. Frankfurt, *The importance of what we care about*. Cambridge, UK: Cambridge University Press. pp.26–46.

Freeman, S., 2001. Illiberal libertarians: why libertarianism is not a liberal view. *Philosophy & Public Affairs*, 30(2), pp.105–151.

Fried, B., 2004. Left-libertarianism: a review essay. *Philosophy & Public Affairs*, 32(1), pp.66–92.

Hayek, F.A., 1960. *The constitution of liberty*. London: Routledge & Kegan Paul.

Hospers, J., 1995. What libertarianism is. In: T. Machan and D. B. Rasmussen, eds. *Liberty for the twenty-first century: contemporary libertarian thought*. MD: Rowman & Littlefield. pp.5–17.

Murphy, L., 2007. Review of *Liberty, desert and the market*. *Economics and Philosophy*, 23, pp.125–138.

Nozick, R., 1967. Coercion. In: P. Laslett and W. Runciman, eds. *Philosophy, politics, and society*. 4th series. Oxford: Blackwell. pp.101–135.

Nozick, R., 1974. *Anarchy, state and utopia*. Oxford: Blackwell.

Olsaretti, S., 1998. Freedom, force, and choice: against the rights-based definition of voluntariness. *Journal of Political Philosophy*, 6(1), pp.53–78.

Olsaretti, S., 2004. *Liberty, desert and the market: a philosophical study*. Cambridge, UK: Cambridge University Press.

Olsaretti, S., 2008. Debate: the concept of voluntariness—a reply. *Journal of Political Philosophy*, 16(1), pp.112–121.

Olsaretti, S., 2009. Responsibility and the consequences of choice. *Proceedings of the Aristotelian Society*, 109(2), pp.165–188.

Olsaretti, S., 2013a. Libertarianism and coercion: a reply to Barnes. *Analysis*, 73(2), pp.295–299.

Olsaretti, S., 2013b. Rescuing justice and equality from libertarianism. *Economics and Philosophy*, 29, pp.43–63.

Olsaretti, S., 2013c. Scanlon on responsibility and the value of choice. *Journal of Moral Philosophy*, 10(4), pp.465–483.

Otsuka, M., 2003. *Libertarianism without inequality*. Oxford: Oxford University Press.

Radin, M.J., 1996. *Contested commodities*. Cambridge, MA: Harvard University Press.

Scanlon, T.M., 1982. Nozick on rights, liberty, and property. In: J. Paul, ed. *Reading Nozick*. Oxford: Blackwell. pp.107–129.

Scanlon, T.M., 1999. *What we owe to each other*. Cambridge, MA: Harvard University Press.

Vallentyne, P., 2000. Left-libertarianism: a primer. In: P. Vallentyne and H. Steiner, eds. *Left libertarianism and its critics: the contemporary debate*. Basingstoke: Palgrave. pp.1–20.

Waldron, J., 1988. *The right to private property*. Oxford: Clarendon Press.

Wertheimer, A., 1987. *Coercion*. Princeton, NJ: Princeton University Press.

Wertheimer, A., 2012. Voluntary consent: why a value-neutral concept won't work. *Journal of Medicine and Philosophy*, 37, pp.226–254.

Zimmerman, D., 1981. Coercive wage offers. *Philosophy and Public Affairs*, 10, pp.121–145.

CHAPTER 25

THE IMPARTIAL SPECTATOR AND THE MORAL TEACHINGS OF MARKETS

VIRGIL HENRY STORR

1. INTRODUCTION

THE market is an area where buyers and sellers exchange goods and services. It could refer to a particular geographic location (e.g., the local bazaar). It could also refer to a sphere where buyers and sellers exchange a particular good (e.g., the market for oranges) or set of goods (e.g., the market for foodstuffs) or all the goods that are exchanged in a particular community. Conceived of in this way, markets are ubiquitous. It is difficult to imagine a modern society without a quite extensive market and almost impossible to imagine any society without at least a nascent market. Moreover, the scope of the market appears to be continually and unrelentingly expanding, including an increasing number of people in its nexus and touching more and more aspects of our daily lives. It is perhaps not surprising, then, that there has been a great deal of concern about not only the economic features of the market but also its social and moral aspects. What are the institutional prerequisites for well-functioning markets? How does engaging in market activity affect our social relationships? And, the question to be answered here, does engaging in the market have moral consequences, and if so, what are they likely to be?

Market skeptics have persuasively argued that the market is a social arena that is not simply amoral but that has negative moral consequences. We cannot, they insist, interact in the market and come away unchanged. Instead, they argue, the market brings out the worst in us and, might, if we are not careful, even make us morally worse people. Our worst selves, they suggest, are not only given free reign in the market but are rewarded and, thus, encouraged in the market.

Market apologists have offered two basic responses to this kind of charge: (a) that the market is amoral and (b) that the market transforms private vice into public virtue.

The market, most market advocates will insist, is an amoral social arena. Markets, they argue, are neither good nor bad. People bring and live their values out in the market, which can easily and happily accommodate both sinners and saints. To accuse the market of promoting vice or to credit it with promoting virtue are, thus, both seen as out of bounds. Although most market apologists tend to stress the amoral character of the market, many will also point out that the market has the potential to transform private vices into public virtues. The greedy businessman, they explain, acting with regard to his self-interest is compelled (as if by an invisible hand) to satisfy the needs and desires of others, since that is the only way in the market that he can improve his condition. His selfish desire to better his own condition pushes him to serve others by offering more and better goods and services. Stated another way, in the market our passions are held in check by our interests.

Unfortunately, neither response actually addresses the critics' concerns. Neither response actually discusses whether or not the market promotes virtue or vice. The first response—that is, the argument that markets are amoral—denies the charge by pointing out that it is possible to remain virtuous while engaging in market activity. It does not address the market critics' assertion that there are likely to be many more sinners in the market than saints. Instead, it suggests that if there are more sinners than saints in the market, then we must ascribe blame elsewhere. The market is not and, in fact, cannot be at fault. The second response—the argument that the market transforms private vice into public virtue—does not avoid the market critics' assertion that the market promotes viciousness, but embraces and even celebrates it. On this view, the market functions by pitting our vices against one another. If selfishness comes to dominate in the market it is nonetheless possible that society will be materially better off.

This chapter, however, directly discusses the moral teachings of the market, that is, the moral sentiments individuals are likely to acquire and develop as they engage in the market. It begins with a brief discussion of Adam Smith's moral philosophy and, in particular, his use of the impartial spectator, the imaginary figure that each of us constructs to offer us moral guidance as we negotiate our lives.[1] Next, it will be argued that there are good reasons to believe that our impartial spectators might be changed by our dealings in the market. The impartial spectator is a product of our moral imaginations. The people that we interact with and the situations that we experience affect our moral imaginations. To the extent that we interact with people and have experiences that are different in the market from elsewhere, then, the market has the potential to affect our impartial spectators. Next, the lessons that markets do not tend to teach us will be discussed. Rather than celebrating selfishness and greed, it will be argued that the market tends to punish both vices. However, the market, it is conceded, is unlikely to promote the traditional virtues in the form that they are promoted in other contexts. The bravery that must be exhibited by the inventor as he introduces a new product to the market is admittedly quite different from the bravery of the soldier as he charges into enemy lines. Still, it is argued in the next section, the market does promote virtue. The market is a moral teacher. The final section offers concluding remarks.

2. The Impartial Spectator Is the Arbiter of What Is Proper

Adam Smith famously began his *Theory of Moral Sentiments* with the observation that human beings, though in many ways selfish creatures, nonetheless care about the well-being and the opinions of others. "However selfish soever man may be supposed," Smith wrote, "there are evidently some principles in his nature, which interests him in the fortune of others, and render their happiness necessary to him, though he derives nothing from it except the pleasure of seeing it" (Smith, 1976: 9). We feel joy when others, particularly those we care about, are happy and we feel sadness when others, particularly those around us, are sad. Similarly, we desire and receive pleasure or a lessening of our pain when others enter into fellow-feeling with us. We want them to feel joy when we feel joy and we want them to feel compassion or pity when we are sad. As Smith writes, "nothing pleases us more than to observe in other men a fellow-feeling with the emotions of our own breast" (1976: 13).

Our care about the well-being and opinions of others, Smith explains, manifests itself in our capacity for sympathy (i.e., our ability to enter into fellow-feeling with the passions of others) and our desire for mutual sympathy (i.e., the desire for others to enter into fellow-feeling with us). When someone dear to us has experienced good fortune or some great calamity, we imagine ourselves in their place; we think of how we would feel if their condition were our condition; we in essence make their feelings our own. Likewise, when we have experienced good fortune or are suffering under the weight of some great tragedy, we desire and expect those who are close to us and are aware of our circumstances to sympathize with our condition.

Thus, our desire for mutual sympathy and the pleasure that we derive from mutual sympathy determines how we judge the sentiments and conduct of others and of ourselves. If we are able to sympathize with the passions of others we judge those passions to be proper. If we are unable to sympathize with the passions of others we judge them to be improper. As Smith explains, "when the original passions of the person principally concerned are in perfect concord with the sympathetic emotions of the spectator, they necessarily appear to this last just and proper, and suitable to their objects" (1976: 16). To say that we sympathize, then, is to say that we approve.[2] Similarly, to say that others are able to enter into fellow-feeling with us is to say that they approve of our passions and our behavior.

We are not, however, satisfied with the approval of others. We wish to be genuinely worthy of their approval. According to Smith,

> Nature, when she formed man for society, endowed him with an original desire to please, and an original aversion to offend his brethren. . . . But this desire of the approbation, and this aversion to the disapprobation of his brethren, would not

alone have rendered him fit for that society for which he was made. Nature, accordingly, has endowed him, not only with a desire of being approved of, but with a desire of being what ought to be approved of; or of being what he himself approves of in other men. (Smith, 1976: 116)

We do wish to receive praise but we also wish to be worthy of the praise that we receive. Absent this desire to be praiseworthy, Smith explains, we would not be inspired to actually abhor vice but, instead, would be satisfied to conceal our vices (1976: 116).

Because it is possible that we might receive praise without being praiseworthy or that we might fail to receive praise even though we are worthy of praise, Smith insists, we are in need of an "independent" arbiter of our actions. For Smith, the man in the breast, which is our internal representation of the impartial spectator, performs this function.[3] The impartial spectator is an imaginary construction that individuals call upon as they evaluate their own sentiments and conduct. It is in many respects a stand-in for the judgments of our behavior that others in society would render if they were unencumbered by their own particular biases and were fully cognizant of the rationale behind our actions and the circumstances under which we acted (Smith, 1976: 110). As Smith explains,

> though man has . . . been rendered the immediate judge of mankind, he has been rendered so only in the first instance; and an appeal lies from his sentence to a much higher tribunal, to the tribunal of their own consciences, to that of the supposed impartial and well-informed spectator, to that of the man within the breast, the great judge and arbiter of their conduct. The jurisdictions of those two tribunals are founded upon principles which, though in some respects resembling and akin, are, however, in reality different and distinct. The jurisdiction of the man without, is founded altogether in the desire of actual praise, and in the aversion to actual blame. The jurisdiction of the man within, is founded altogether in the desire of praise-worthiness, and in the aversion to blame-worthiness; in the desire of possessing those qualities, and performing those actions, which we love and admire in other people; and in the dread of possessing those qualities, and performing those actions, which we hate and despise in other people. (Smith, 1976: 130)

Though we care about the opinions of others, we care much more about the opinions of the impartial spectator. Above all, we wish to seem proper in his eyes. We seek his approbation and hope to avoid his disapprobation.

According to Smith, to be perfectly virtuous, which for Smith means to be prudent, just, and beneficent, is to always be mindful of the gaze of the impartial spectator (Smith, 1976: 237). As he writes, "the man of real constancy and firmness . . . has never dared to forget for one moment the judgment which the impartial spectator would pass upon his sentiments and conduct" (1976: 146). Similarly, "the prudent man is always both supported and rewarded by the entire approbation of the impartial spectator, and of the representative of the impartial spectator, the man within the breast" (1976: 215). And, as he further explains,

> The man who feels the full distress of the calamity which has befallen him, who feels the whole baseness of the injustice which has been done to him, but who feels still more strongly what the dignity of his own character requires; who does not abandon himself to the guidance of the undisciplined passions which his situation might naturally inspire; but who governs his whole behaviour and conduct according to those restrained and corrected emotions which the great inmate, the great demi-god within the breast prescribes and approves of; is alone the real man of virtue, the only real and proper object of love, respect, and admiration. (Smith, 1976: 245)

For Smith, the perfectly virtuous do not simply ape the behavior that would be pleasing to the man in the breast. Instead, the perfectly virtuous individual actually "adopts" the sentiments of the impartial spectator (1976: 147). As Smith explains, the perfectly virtuous man "almost identifies himself with, he almost becomes himself that impartial spectator, and scarce even feels but as the great arbiter of his conduct directs him to feel" (1976: 147). The impartial spectator, then, performs two critical roles for Smith: (a) he weakens the pull of self-love and (b) he teaches us what it means to be virtuous (1976: 83).

This is, of course, not to say that the impartial spectator would have us prefer others to ourselves. On the contrary, the impartial spectator demands that we be prudent, which is to wisely look after our own well-being. But this does suggest that there ought to be limits to our self-love. We should avoid excesses. And, moreover, we should in all things also act according to the rules of strict justice and proper benevolence. Stated another way, we are pushed by the impartial spectator to care about the impact of our actions on others. For Smith, the impartial spectator and our desire for his appropriation is what enables us to counteract "the strongest impulses of self-love" (1976: 137).

Smith has hinted at how the judgments of the impartial spectator might be altered as we experience new situations and as we meet new people. This suggests that it is, thus, possible that our impartial spectators can be changed as a result of our engaging in market activity.

3. THE IMPARTIAL SPECTATOR CAN BE CHANGED BY THE MARKET

The market, like all other social settings, is an arena where individuals seek the approbation of the impartial spectator. Recall that, for Smith, the impartial spectator encourages us to be prudent—that is, to concern ourselves with our own fortunes, our own reputations, and the other things that promote our own comfort and well-being. Moreover, the impartial spectator not only encourages us to concern ourselves with how our actions affect others, but also offers us guidance as to when our actions are likely to positively or negatively affect others. Thus, it is unlikely if not impossible for individuals to success-fully negotiate the market without the guidance of the impartial spectator.[4] For Smith, then, absent the guidance of the impartial spectator, the profitable businessman who plays by the rules, the conscientious and hard-working employee, and the discerning consumer, all familiar figures in any market, would not exist.

To say that the impartial spectator even offers us counsel during our market dealings, however, does not say anything about whether or not his counsel will be heeded or about whether or not the counsel that he might offer might be systematically altered by our interactions in the market. It could be the case that under the temptation presented by the possibility of earning higher profits we simply disregard the advice of the impartial spectator. Or it could be the case that the market is such a corrupting space that even the impartial spectator comes to be corrupted, promoting vice instead of virtue as being proper and deserving of approbation.

Smith himself appeared to be aware of both concerns. As he writes, "the propriety of our moral sentiments is never so apt to be corrupted, as when the indulgent and par-tial spectator is at hand, while the indifferent and impartial one is at a great distance" (1976: 154). Furthermore, even "when he is at hand, when he is present, the violence and injustice of our own selfish passions are sometimes sufficient to induce the man within the breast to make a report very different from what the real circumstances of the case are capable of authorizing" (1976: 156).

There are also several reasons to believe that the counsel offered us by the impartial spectator might be systematically altered for better or worse by our experiences in the market. First, the impartial spectator is a product of our moral imaginations. As Smith explains,

> Whatever judgment we can form concerning [our own actions] . . . must always bear some secret reference, either to what are, or to what, upon a certain condition, would be, or to what, we imagine, ought to be the judgment of others. We endeavour to examine our own conduct as we imagine any other fair and impartial spectator would examine it. (Smith, 1976: 109)

The impartial spectator is not simply imparted to us from outside of us but is also gener-ated from within us. He is, thus, not purely an exogenous figure without any real connec-tion to the lives that we have lived. Instead, he is endogenously created and developed from within us.

Second, our moral imaginations and so our impartial spectators are affected by our experiences. Although Smith believes that the impartial spectator is a universal fig-ure (i.e., no one is unable to reference him), he does not appear to believe that we are born with fully formed representations of the impartial spectator who is able to give us counsel in every and all circumstances that we might encounter as we go about our daily lives. Instead, the man within the breast becomes increasingly refined through-out our lives. As we encounter new situations, we observe what conduct and sentiments prompt approbation from others and which elicit disapprobation; we imagine how an independent arbiter in possession of the relevant facts would respond to our passions and our behavior in that new context. Thus, the impartial spectator is likely to be altered by our being exposed to new and varied situations. The impartial spectator is both a guide as we experience the world and is affected by our experiences in the world. The situations and circumstances that people are exposed to when they enter the market, to the extent that they are different from the situations and circumstances that they are or will be exposed to outside of the market, can thus shape our impartial spectators.[5]

Third, our moral imaginations, and thus our impartial spectators, are (in part) products of the people that we know.[6] As Smith explains,

> Were it possible that a human creature could grow up to manhood in some solitary place, without any communication with his own species, he could no more think of his own character, of the propriety or demerit of his own sentiments and conduct, of the beauty or deformity of his own mind, than of the beauty or deformity of his own face. . . . Bring him into society, and he is immediately provided with the mirror which he wanted before. It is placed in the countenance and behaviour of those he lives with, which always mark when they enter into, and when they disapprove of his sentiments; and it is here that he first views the propriety and impropriety of his own passions, the beauty and deformity of his own mind. (Smith, 1976: 110)

Arguably, bringing someone into the market performs a role similar to bringing the solitary person into the society. For good or for ill, engaging in the market enlarges our social circles; we interact with more people than we would if we were not engaged in market activity. And those interactions have the potential to be quite meaningful. As I have argued elsewhere (see Storr, 2008; Storr, 2010), the market is a social arena where meaningful conversations beyond bids and asks occur and where meaningful social relationships beyond competition and exchange take place. Although it is possible that the social bonds that we observe in the market were established elsewhere, it is also possible that social bonds that were established inside the market continue to live outside the market. The market brings us into close proximity with individuals who would have otherwise been strangers. In so doing, it enlarges the circle of individuals whose genuine approbation we desire. The impartial spectator is, thus, likely to be transformed by our being brought into association, even close association, with individuals in the market whom we are unlikely to meet elsewhere.

Moreover, individuals have preferences among those with whom they engage in trade that they are willing to pay a premium in order to satisfy. These preferences can have to do with the race, ethnicity, religion, class, and gender of a would-be trading partner, or with their attitudes, characteristics, demeanor, and reputations. Individuals in the market can sometimes gain (profits and approbation) by acting or by actually being a certain way or by failing to act or be a certain way. Our impartial spectators learn and then teach us to moderate our passions and conduct so that we avoid incurring losses by offending our potential trading partners. The man in the breast is, thus, likely to be affected by the preferences of our potential trading partners.

This suggests that the market should be an arena where this kind of moral education takes place. Suggesting that the market can shape which sentiments and conduct we consider proper and deserving of approbation and which we consider improper and deserving of disapprobation, however, says nothing about what kinds of values our impartial spectators will come to promote once we encounter the market.

4. THE MARKET DOES NOT TEACH US TO BE SELFISH, NOR DOES IT TEACH US TO BE BRAVE[7]

Critics have argued that engaging in market activity can be corrupting. Aristotle (1981: I.x), for instance, believed that there was something unnatural about the kind of wealth-getting that occurred in the market. He believed that the sort of activity where individuals tried to gain from one another was "justly censured."[8] Similarly, Marx (1994, 49) worried that the greater the scope for market activity, the more egoistic man would become. In fact, Marx believed that the market could transform man into "a spiritual and physical monster." Mandeville (1988: 325) has also insisted that there is a necessary trade-off between virtue and wealth. Likewise, MacIntyre (2007: 254) worried that "the tradition of virtues is at variance with central features of the modern economic order and more especially its individualism, its acquisitiveness and its elevation of the market to a central social place." And Sandel (2012: 9) has argued that markets crowd out virtue, and that market values can crowd out nonmarket values. As the scope of the market expands, according to this view, our humanity becomes increasingly damaged and distorted. The expansion of the market makes us more selfish and greedy than we would be if the market were held in check.

On the surface, Smith also appears to embrace this view. He repeatedly derides the "natural selfishness and rapacity" of the rich (see, for instance, Smith 1976: 184). And, as he famously wrote, "it is not from the benevolence of the butcher, the brewer, or the baker, that we expect our dinner, but from their regard to their own interest. We address ourselves, not to their humanity but to their self-love, and never talk to them of our own necessities but of their advantages."

It is clear, then, that Smith believes that self-love plays a significant and even a critical role in the market. To suggest that appealing to self-interest rather than to benevolence is a much more fruitful approach to securing our daily meal, however, is a far cry from saying either that there are no virtuous people in the market (whose benevolence you can count on in certain circumstances) or that the market promotes or depends on vice.[9]

First, as has repeatedly been pointed out, self-love is distinct from selfishness.[10] Indeed, though he believed it to be natural, Smith was quite critical of selfishness and did not believe that the impartial spectator would approve of our being selfish. In fact, selfishness was one of our passions that Smith believed ought to be kept in check by our self-command (Smith, 1976: 25). But while selfishness is something to be controlled, self-love is to be promoted. As Smith writes, "every man is, no doubt, by nature, first and principally recommended to his own care; and he is fitter to take care of himself than any other person, it is fit and right that it should be so" (1976: 82).

Additionally, Smith believed that there were limits on how much self-love we might countenance in others.

> In the race for wealth, and honours, and preferments, he may run as hard as he can, and strain every nerve and every muscle, in order to outstrip all his competitors. But if he should justle, or throw down any of them, the indulgence of the spectators is entirely at an end. It is a violation of fair play, which they cannot admit of. This man is to them, in every respect, as good as he: they do not enter into that self-love by which he prefers himself so much to this other, and cannot go along with the motive from which he hurt him. (Smith, 1976: 83)

We are simply unwilling to endorse individuals preferring themselves to the point where they are willing to deal unfairly with others. We can countenance and even celebrate advantages that others might enjoy which we do not, so long as we believe that those advantages were earned.

In recommending that we appeal to the self-interest of others rather than to their benevolence, Smith is not suggesting that the market is incompatible with benevolence or that the market somehow destroys benevolence and promotes selfishness. It is instead a practical claim about the limits of benevolence (e.g., we should not expect it without limits from strangers in or outside of the market). Moreover, to say that the market can funnel even the selfishness and rapacity that is all too common in the rich into socially beneficial directions is not to suggest the market promotes that selfishness and rapacity. Smith is, instead, suggesting that the market checks our selfish passions (i.e., there are real limits placed on our self-love).

Second, the market actually disciplines or punishes bad actors (Smith, 1978: 538). Individuals will tend to avoid trading partners who are dishonest. Since at least Akerlof (1970), economists have been aware that there are costs associated with dishonesty. Akerlof argued that the costs associated with engaging in market activity in a context where dishonesty is rampant (which includes higher transaction costs) could actually drive markets out of existence. Likewise, Adler (1992) concludes that if dishonesty is universal, then markets will fail, but that dishonest suppliers can actually be driven out of the market or forced to be honest if at least some suppliers are honest.

For the market to promote vice it would have to expose us to circumstances where vice received praise and was thought to be praiseworthy (and virtue received disapprobation and was thought to be blameworthy), or where the individuals whom we encountered were relatively more vicious than the individuals whom we tended to encounter in other contexts, or where we were rewarded for immoral behavior. As will be argued below, none of this appears to be the case in the market.

It might, however, be complained that the market does not promote traditional virtues or, rather, that it does not promote the traditional virtues in the form in which they are promoted in other contexts. The market, for instance, might not systematically reward the kind of self-denial that we see in a monastery, or the kind of courage that we observe on a battlefield, or the kind of love that we observe between a mother and child.[11] There is, however, no reason to believe that the market would tend to punish people who exhibited these virtues. For instance, research on the relationship between corporate social responsibility and firm profitability and value is somewhat mixed (see, for instance, Aupperle, Carroll, and Hatfield, 1985; McGuire, Sundgren, and Schneeweis, 1988; Pava and Krausz, 1996; Sen and Bhattacharya, 2001). Enterprises that engage in charity do not seem to do any better or any worse on average than firms that do not. Admitting that the market does not promote these particular virtues in the traditional way, however, is not the same thing as admitting that the market is incompatible with (new forms of) these virtues, and is not at all like admitting that the market can only thrive in the absence of these virtues. Mandeville might very well be correct that the market can survive and even thrive if peopled entirely by knaves and still be wrong that the market cannot make do without them.

That the market does not promote the traditional forms of the traditional virtues does not mean that the market does not promote virtues of any sort.

5. STILL, THE IMPARTIAL SPECTATOR IS CHANGED IN THE MARKET FOR THE BETTER

Several scholars have made the point that markets are moral training grounds where virtues are rewarded and cultivated.[12] Novak, for instance, has argued that "commerce . . . teaches care, discipline, frugality, clear accounting, providential forethought, . . . respect for reckonings . . . fidelity to contracts, honesty in fair dealings, and concern for one's moral reputation" (1984: 179). Similarly, McCloskey has argued that, far from making us more selfish and greedy, markets have actually made us ethically better. As she writes, "capitalism has not corrupted the spirit. On the contrary, had capitalism not enriched the world by a cent nonetheless its bourgeois, antifeudal virtues would have made us better people than in the world we have lost. As a system it has been good for us" (2006: 29). According to McCloskey, the four cardinal virtues (prudence, justice, temperance, and courage), as well as the three transcendent virtues (faith, hope, and love), are not only compatible with life in commercial society but are encouraged in our commercial dealings. And, as I have argued elsewhere, if markets "are given a chance to flourish, we will grow wealthier, healthier, better connected with far flung relatives and friends, better educated, better behaved, more generous, more compassionate, more tolerant, more trusting, and more just. The market will deliver cures for cancer and new, post–crude oil, energy sources. If allowed to flourish, the market will also make us better connected and more virtuous" (Storr 2009: 291).

Our exposure to the market is likely to positively impact our impartial spectators in several ways.[13]

First, recall that the impartial spectator is a product of our experiences. The market places us in circumstances where we have to consistently concern ourselves with the desires and well-being of others—that is, it puts us in a particular relationship with others where their advantage has to be a significant concern. This concern for others that we must exemplify in the market if we wish to be successful extends beyond any narrow concern about what goods and services they might want from us. It extends to how they wish to be treated. It also extends to the kind of trading partner that they wish to deal with. People wish to be treated decently by their trading partners and are willing to pay a premium to exchange with trading partners who treat them well (Adler, 1992). Specifically, people wish to engage with trading partners who are honest, and they are willing to pay a premium to engage with firms that they feel they can trust (Kumar, 1996).[14] Similarly, the returns on promoting worker satisfaction and customer loyalty are positive (Loveman, 1998). There is also a positive relationship between a firm's reputation and its financial performance (Roberts and Dowling, 2002). In the market, there is a feedback mechanism that encourages us to act and to be better than we would in the absence of the market.[15]

Second, recall that the impartial spectator is a product of the people whom we know. We come into contact with a hopefully expanding and potentially quite varied group of others in the market. As the scope of the market and thus the extent of the division of labor expands, the number of people with whom we have to interact as we negotiate our daily lives increases, perhaps quite dramatically.[16]

The market thus enlarges our spheres of sympathy or intimacy—that is, we come to care about the opinions and well-being of more people than we otherwise would as a result of our dealings in the market. As Smith writes, "colleagues in office, partners in trade, call one another brothers and frequently feel towards one another as if they really were so" (1976: 224). And as Hayek explains,

> That interdependence of all men, which is now in everybody's mouth and which tends to make all mankind One World, not only is the effect of the market order but could not have been brought about by any other means. What today connects the life of any European or American with what happens in Australia, Japan or Zaire are repercussions transmitted by the network of market relations. . . . The benefits from the knowledge which others possess, including all the advances of science, reach us through channels provided and directed by the market mechanism. Even the degree to which we can participate in the aesthetic or moral strivings of men in other parts of the world we owe to the economic nexus. (Hayek, 1978: 112)

The farmer in Texas cannot be indifferent to the lot of the textile manufacturer in China. The typical merchant has frequent contact with dozens, if not hundreds, of customers daily and cannot really afford for any of them to think him vicious. The typical merchant also comes to genuinely care about the well-being of those dozens, if not hundreds, he encounters daily in the market.

Paganelli (2010) has argued that the market is a civilizing space because it increases our opportunity to interact with a growing number of strangers. By frequent exposure to strangers, we develop the habit of moderating our passions so that they accord with spectators who know very little about us. In this process of repeatedly moderating our passions, we develop the habit of propriety. The market is, she argues, a moral incubator because of these frequent interactions with strangers. In her opinion, markets allow for the level of social distance between individuals necessary for moral development. Her concern that moral development only takes place in the company of strangers, however, is somewhat exaggerated. If our commercial relations always remained strangers, it is just as likely that we would concern ourselves with their view of us only so far as it could affect our interests as it is that we would genuinely grow more moral as a result of frequent interactions with them. We could, for instance, merely conceal our vices, an effort that would be much easier to accomplish if the strangers we met in the market tended to remain strangers. The social distance of strangers in the market might very well leave them outside our spheres of sympathy, making us indifferent to their views. Paganelli is aware of this concern. As she writes, "while commerce may generate the right distance for moral development for most, it may also generate too little, or too much distance for some" (2010: 437). Since human beings are social creatures, the relationships that we form within the market will also tend to become overlaid with social content (Macneil, 1986; Granovetter, 1985; Storr, 2008), making us even more desirous of mutual sympathy with our commercial friends and making us desire, all the more, to seem virtuous in their eyes. The market is, thus, a moral incubator because of the volume and variety of individuals with whom we are brought into (potential) friendship.[17]

The impartial spectator is thus exercised in a particular way during our market dealings. In the market, we are placed in a context where we have to concern ourselves constantly with how our sentiments and conduct appear to others whom we depend on, not only for their approbation, but also for our livelihoods. In the market, we are also moved to interact in potentially meaningful ways with countless others with whom we would not otherwise be in contact. Again, the more and varied people we interact with, the more cosmopolitan that we are, the more likely our impartial spectators are to be genuinely impartial, the less likely they are to be parochial, and the more closely the man in the breast approximates the truly impartial spectator. The market thus promotes more than a move toward tolerance; it actually promotes a move away from parochialism and partisanship.

Our impartial spectators are constantly advising us as we engage in market life. The circumstances that we find ourselves in, as well as the people with whom we interact, both change our impartial spectators. Although we are more likely to succeed in the market by appealing to our potential trading partners' interests rather than their humanity, we will certainly fail in the market if we do not learn enough about them to discover what their interests in fact are, or if in our dealings with them we offend their humanity. The impartial spectator is changed for the better in the market.

6. CONCLUSION

The critics of the market are correct. We cannot enter the market and emerge unscathed. We are changed, and arguably quite profoundly, by our dealings in the market. But the critics are wrong to claim that the market makes us ethically worse off. The reverse is actually true. The market is a moral space that (a) generates morally defensible and even preferable social outcomes, (b) thrives when peopled with moral actors, and (c) pushes us to be morally better people.

Defending the first two claims, that the market generates morally preferable social outcomes and thrives when peopled with moral actors, is beyond the scope of this effort. It is possible, however, to articulate a defense of these claims. See, for instance, Hirschman (1997), McCloskey (2006), Zak (2008), Storr (2009), and Langrill and Storr (2013) for at least partial defenses along the lines suggested here.

This chapter defends only the third and perhaps most controversial of those claims, that the market makes us morally better people (because it punishes vice and promotes the bourgeois virtues). By placing us in circumstances where we interact with more people who are quite different from each other and from us, by forcing us to interact with them in a way where we have to concern ourselves with their desires and well-being broadly defined, our moral imaginations come to be oriented in a particular direction. If in the market we came to be surrounded by viciousness, then it is possible that our impartial spectators might come to be corrupted. Because we ourselves wish and are prepared to pay a premium to interact with ethically better people, and because others will offer us a premium for being ethically better than our competitors, our impartial spectators, as a result of our market dealings, urge us toward virtuousness.

If true, the argument presented above would mean that market interventions would have not only economic consequences but moral consequences as well. Stated another way, if markets thrive when private property rights are well specified and respected, contracts that were freely entered into are enforced, and the rule of law prevails, then movements away from this ideal environment would not only hamper the market's potential to deliver desired goods and services, but would also diminish its moral potential. This should give us tremendous pause when considering any intervention into the market.

ACKNOWLEDGMENTS

I would like to thank David Schmidtz, Dan Russell, Dan Klein, Brianne Wolf, and the participants of the Center for the Philosophy of Freedom colloquium for useful comments on earlier versions of this chapter. I would also like to thank The University of Arizona Center for the Philosophy of Freedom for generous financial support.

Notes

1. The judgments offered by this figure are those judgments that relevant but impartial others would have regarding our behavior if they were in possession of all of the facts. Arguably, if the relevant others changed, so would the judgments rendered by the impartial spectator. See, for instance, Smith's discussion of what is valued in barbarous lands. The discussion of Smith's moral philosophy offered here is admittedly brief. See Otteson (2002), Hanley (2009), and Forman-Barzilai (2010) for more detailed discussions. See, also, Raphael (2009) for how Smith's conception of the impartial spectator compares to other conceptions of how we develop and employ a moral sense or conscience.

2. Note that Smith uses "sympathy" in a variety of ways in *The Theory of Moral Sentiments*. See Haakonssen (1981: 51) for an elaboration of this point.

3. The terms "the man in the breast" and "the impartial spectator" are used interchangeably throughout this chapter to mean essentially that imaginary construct that we call upon as we make our moral judgments. Arguably, though Smith at times will draw a sharp distinction between the impartial spectator and the man in the breast, with the impartial spectator being a universal construct and the man in the breast being his internal representation, Smith has also used them interchangeably. See Leroch's (2008) effort to disentangle the possible interpretations of the impartial spectator.

4. For Smith, then, the propensity to truck, barter, and exchange, a propensity that Smith thought all human beings possessed, is a necessary but not sufficient condition for successfully negotiating the market. It is the profit motive that leads individuals to concern themselves with the wishes of others and with the variables that would affect the profit motive.

5. Competition, exchange, and profit-seeking all have corollaries outside of the market but take on a different form inside of the market.

6. "Our continual observations upon the conduct of others insensibly lead us to form to ourselves certain general rules concerning what is fit and proper either to be done or to be avoided" (Smith, 1976: 159).

7. This section and the following section take up the same question that Graafland (2009) does but arrive at a different conclusion.

8. See Russell (2009) for a discussion of phronesis and its role in offering guidance as to what passions and conduct we ought to consider moral. It is unclear on this reading why it would not be possible for a merchant or a banker guided by phronesis to live a moral life. Thus, Aristole's anti-market sentiments do not seem to be essential to his system.

9. See, for instance, Smith's critique of Mandeville's view: "It is the great fallacy of Dr. Mandeville's book to represent every passion as wholly vicious" (Smith, 1976: 312). See also Schmidtz (1997) for a useful discussion of this point. As Schmidtz explains, self-interest need not imply that we have no regard for others.

10. See, for instance, Nieli, 1986: 617.

11. As Smith remarked, "Another bad effect of commerce is that it sinks the courage of mankind, and tends to extinguish martial spirit" (1978: 540).

12. This has elsewhere been referred to as the "doux commerce" thesis—the notion that trade dulls our passions (Hirschman, 1997; Smith, 1978: 538; Montesquieu, 1961: 8).

13. Notice that this is a stronger claim than that the market selects for individuals with certain moral sentiments. While I agree with this weaker claim, I argue below that the market not

only selects for individuals with certain moral sentiments (weeding out individuals who are less moral) but also that it improves our moral sentiments. The claim advanced here is also a stronger claim than that the market teaches us to pretend to be virtuous. Again, although I agree with this claim, I argue below that the market actually teaches us to be genuinely virtuous.

14. Similarly, Zak and Knack (2001) have found a positive relationship between trust and economic growth. Ensminger (2004) concludes that there is a positive relationship between the degree of market integration and the commitment to fairness exhibited by a community.

15. Admittedly, this feedback offered by profit and loss is not unambiguous. Losses, for instance, could mean that the product being provided is not socially beneficial or that it is not being advertised effectively. Moreover, the signal that profits and losses are meant to convey could be obscured.

16. Consider, for instance, Smith's discussion of the woolen coat: "the woolen-coat, for example . . . is the produce of the joint labor of a great multitude of workmen" (1981: 22). See also Read's (1958) allegory of the pencil, whose production depends on countless people across the globe. Additionally, see Rivoli's (2005) discussion of how t-shirt manufacturing has become a global trade that connects cotton producers in the southern United States with textile produces in parts of Asia. This is not to suggest that each of these exchanges will result in meaningful social interactions. It does suggest that there is a greater opportunity to connect with an increasing number of people from possibly quite different backgrounds than we would occur if the division of labor were less expansive and markets less developed. There is in fact the opportunity for social contact between the buyer of the woolen and the cashier, the cashier and his supervisor, the supervisor and the shop owner, the shop owner and the supplier, and so on. The key point is that these opportunities for social interaction would not have occurred outside a market context.

17. Of course, distance might result in there being a lesser kind of sympathy than we might expect between two people who are physically or socially closer. But the point to stress is that the market shrinks both physical and social distance, or more precisely, it brings people who are far apart into closer contact than we might expect given their social and physical distance. Thus, as the saying goes, markets make the world "a smaller place." The closer and the more frequent the contact, the more likely it is that people approximate the ideal of (mutual) sympathy. Moreover, market relationships can and frequently do (albeit not always) become more than mere market relationships. Buyers and sellers sometimes do become actual friends, coworkers do socialize outside of work, and family businesses are common features of markets (Storr 2008). The market might not do all the work but, like a primary-school teacher, it can lay a solid foundation.

References

Adler, Moshe, 1992. On being honest and behaving honestly. *Games and Behavior*, 4(1), pp.1–17.

Akerlof, George A., 1970. The market for "lemons": quality uncertainty and the market mechanism. *Quarterly Journal of Economics*, 84(3), pp.175–188.

Aristotle, 1981. *The politics*. London: Penguin Books.

Aupperle, Kenneth E., Carroll, Archie B., and Hatfield, John D., 1985. An empirical examination of the relationship between corporate social responsibility and profitability. *Academy of Management Journal*, 28(2), pp.446–463.

Ensminger, Jean, 2004. Market integration and fairness: evidence from ultimatum, dictator, and public goods experiments in East Africa. In: Joseph Heinrich et al., eds. *Foundations in human sociality*. Oxford: Oxford University Press.

Forman-Barzilai, Fonna, 2010. *Adam Smith and the circles of sympathy: cosmopolitanism and moral theory*. Cambridge, UK: Cambridge University Press.

Graafland, J. J., 2009. Do markets crowd out virtues? An Aristotelian framework. *Journal of Business Ethics*, 91(1), pp.1–19.

Granovetter, Mark, 1985. Economic action and social structure: the problem of embeddedness. *American Journal of Sociology*, 91(3), pp.481–510.

Haakonssen, Knud, 1981. *The science of a legislator: the natural jurisprudence of David Hume and Adam Smith*. Cambridge, UK: Cambridge University Press.

Hanley, Ryan P., 2009. *Adam Smith and the character of virtue*. Cambridge, UK: Cambridge University Press.

Hayek, F. A., 1978. *Law, legislation and liberty, vol. 2, The mirage of social justice*. Chicago: University of Chicago Press.

Hirschman, Albert O., 1997. *The passions and the interests: political arguments for capitalism before its triumph*. Princeton, NJ: Princeton University Press.

Kumar, N., 1996. The power of trust in manufacturer-retailer relationships. *Harvard Business Review*, 74 (November–December), pp.92–106.

Langrill, Ryan, and Storr, Virgil H., 2013. The moral meanings of the market. *Journal of Markets and Morality*, 15(2), pp.347–362.

Leroch, Martin, 2008. Adam Smith's intuition pump: the impartial spectator. *Homo Oeconomicus*, 25(1), pp.1–22.

Loveman, Gary, 1998. Employee satisfaction, customer loyalty, and financial performance: an empirical examination of the service profit chain in retail banking. *Journal of Service Research*, 1(1), pp.18–31.

MacIntyre, Alasdair, 2007. *After virtue*. 3rd ed. South Bend, IN: University of Notre Dame Press.

Macneil, Ian R., 1986. Exchange revisited: individual utility and social solidarity. *Ethics*, 96(3), pp.567–593.

Mandeville, Bernard, 1988. *The fable of the bees: or, private vices, publick benefits*. Vol. 1. Indianapolis: Liberty Fund.

Marx, Karl, 1994. *Selected writings*. Edited by Lawrence H. Simons. Indianapolis: Hackett.

McCloskey, Deirdre N., 2006. *The bourgeois virtues: ethics in the age of commerce*. Chicago: University of Chicago Press.

McGuire, Jean B., Sundgren, Alison, and Schneeweis, Thomas, 1988. Corporate social responsibility and firm financial performance. *Academy of Management Journal*, 31(4), pp.854–872.

Montesquieu, Charles, [1748] 1961. *De l'esprit des lois*. Paris: Garnier.

Nieli, Russell, 1986. Spheres of intimacy and the Adam Smith problem. *Journal of the History of Ideas*, 47(4), pp.611–624.

Novak, Michael, 1984. *Freedom with justice: Catholic social thought and liberal institutions*. New York: Harper and Row.

Otteson, James, 2002. *Marketplace of life*. Cambridge, UK: Cambridge University Press.

Paganelli, Maria P., 2010. The moralizing role of distance in Adam Smith: *The theory of moral sentiments* as possible praise of commerce. *History of Political Economy*, 42(3), pp.425–441.

Pava, Moses, and Krausz, Joshua, 1996. The association between corporate social-responsibility and financial performance: the paradox of social cost. *Journal of Business Ethics*, 15(3), pp.321–357.

Raphael, D. D., 2009. *The impartial spectator: Adam Smith's moral philosophy*. Oxford: Oxford University Press.

Read, Leonard, 1958. I, pencil. *Freeman*, 8(12), pp.32–37.

Rivoli, Pietra, 2005. *The travels of a t-shirt in the global economy: an economist examines the markets, power, and politics of world trade*. Hoboken, NJ: John Wiley & Sons.

Roberts, Peter W., and Dowling, Grahame R., 2002. Corporate reputation and sustained superior financial performance. *Strategic Management Journal*, 23(12), pp.1077–1093.

Russell, Daniel C., 2009. *Practical intelligence and the virtues*. Oxford: Oxford University Press.

Sandel, Michael J., 2012. *What money can't buy: the moral limits of markets*. New York: Farrar, Straus and Giroux.

Schmidtz, David, 1997. Self-interest: what's in it for me? *Social Philosophy and Policy*, 14(1), pp.1077–1093.

Sen, S., and Bhattacharya, C. B., 2001. Does doing good always lead to doing better? Consumer reactions to corporate social responsibility. *Journal of Marketing Research*, 38(2), pp.225–243.

Smith, Adam, 1976. *The theory of moral sentiments*. Indianapolis: Liberty Fund.

Smith, Adam, 1978. *Lectures on jurisprudence*. Indianapolis: Liberty Fund.

Smith, Adam, 1981. *An inquiry into the nature and causes of the wealth of nations*. Vol. 1. Indianapolis: Liberty Fund.

Storr, Virgil H., 2008. The market as a social space: On the meaningful extra-economic conversations that can occur in markets. *Review of Austrian Economics*, 21(2 & 3), pp.135–150.

Storr, Virgil H., 2009. Why the market? Markets as social and moral spaces. *Journal of Markets and Morality*, 12(2), pp.277–296.

Storr, Virgil H., 2010. The social construction of the market. *Society*, 47(3), pp.200–206.

Zak, Paul J., 2008. *Moral markets: the critical role of values in the economy*. Princeton, NJ: Princeton University Press.

Zak, Paul J., and Knack, S., 2001. Trust and growth. *Economic Journal*, 111(470), pp.295–321.

PART VI

BODY AND MIND

CHAPTER 26

DISCIPLINARY SPECIALIZATION AND THINKING FOR YOURSELF

ELIJAH MILLGRAM

PRETTY much all of us take the Enlightenment for granted. And "all of us" means not just this chapter's primary audience, analytic philosophers, but also we academics, we participants in Western market economies, we citizens of Western democratic republics. To be sure, there are cultures that have not assimilated this initially European event, as well as pockets of pre-Enlightenment ways of thinking here at home—New Age spiritualism, "alternative" medicine, palm readers, feng shui, astrology, and so on—but we think of them as belonging to an unassimilated periphery. Here in the center (in mainstream political debate, in the corridors of power, and in the ivory tower), we act like it's a done deal. Just for instance, the triumph of the Enlightenment seems so secure that we no longer pursue mopping-up operations: why even bother denouncing those residual superstitions?[1]

But the very victory of the Enlightenment has been its undoing—and not at the cultural and political periphery, but within the academy, the corporate world, technocratic bureaucracies, and democratic institutions of governance. This chapter will explain how it has happened that a side effect of the Enlightenment's success has made its ideals no longer attainable, and how, slowly but surely, what the Enlightenment took to be its most important achievements have been undone. We are now living in a transitional period, which we might as well call the Great Endarkenment: the verge of the new age of superstition that we will enter if we do not understand and come to terms with the problems to which the Enlightenment has given rise. Preserving both the value and possibility of freedom depends first on characterizing and then on finding workable solutions to them.

1. What Was the Enlightenment's Philosophy of Logic?

What *was* the Enlightenment? Many things, of course, but as it wrapped up, one of its most distinguished theoreticians summarized its central commitment as growing up into independence of judgment. "Enlightenment," Kant announced, "is man's emergence from his self-incurred immaturity" (Kant, 1991: 54; emphasis deleted), and he further explained what he meant by that: immaturity is a matter of letting other people do your thinking for you. The Enlightenment's many rejections—of prerepublican modes of political organization, of inherited theological doctrines and ecclesiastical privilege, of philosophical traditions that seemed to be too tightly entwined with social forms of the past, and of just plain magical thinking—can be seen, in retrospect, as upshots, or even just symptoms, of that central commitment, to thinking for yourself. To anticipate the course of the argument, the commitment to thinking for yourself has turned out to be self-undermining. But first—and now let us redescribe the Enlightenment from perhaps an unusual point of view, that of a philosopher of logic—consider what assumptions could reasonably motivate the demand.

Imagine what it would be like if confirmation theory, as envisioned by logical positivists such as Rudolph Carnap, had worked out: if there were a routinized method for systematically deploying evidence to arrive at conclusions that the evidence supports. (In their program, deductive logic was held up as the model for analytic treatments of inductive inference; the aspiration was to make conclusions about matters of fact mechanically checkable.) If it were possible to say, across the board, what evidence can consist in and how it can be collected (as in the logical positivists' so-called protocol sentences), and if the technique of bringing it to bear were proceduralized, and if the procedure reflected an independently specifiable criterion of correctness, then there would *just* be a right answer and a way to get it: empirical inference correctly done could always be the mere calculation of what is already, prior to the calculation, the correct result. Similarly, imagine what it would be like if a calculation—perhaps the sort of arithmetic exercise envisioned by the early utilitarians—sufficed for making social and individual choices. If the inputs to the procedure determined what choices (of acts, or of rules, or for that matter of social institutions) were correct; if correctness of those practical conclusions, given those inputs, was independent of any deliberation or choices made by any actual human; then, like the operations of deductive logic, all practical conclusions would be mechanically checkable.[2] Call what we're imagining the *procedural utopia*.

Now, often there is a point to doing something for yourself that others could just as well do for you, in something like the way that the cake is a more special gift if you bake it yourself. We sometimes think it is good for children to learn how to do something themselves, and in something like this spirit, Kant took the only significant obstacle to thinking for yourself to be a childish timidity—that is, a moral and ethical failing—and his own prescription for training adults into the "courage" and "resolution" to think for themselves was the freedom to address the reading public, which he called "the public use of reason." One side of his idea has become very familiar: in the so-called marketplace of ideas, the best of them will win out. The inspiring flip side has been neglected: as one's ideas are tested in the marketplace, that is, as they undergo public intellectual scrutiny, one will overcome that timidity and attain intellectual autonomy, and not just *intellectual* autonomy: freedom of expression, of a certain carefully characterized sort, will put you on the road to moral adulthood.

But, regardless of such benefits, you only have the latitude to insist on autonomy when you can endorse two complementary assumptions. The first, of course, is that you *can* think things through for yourself. The second is that you *have* to do it yourself, because we do not live in the procedural utopia. After all, if there were such a transparent test for correctness, if there were a calculation that would *just* get it right, insisting on doing it yourself would be allowable and even praiseworthy on occasion (when doing it your own way is on a par with making the gift by hand, all by yourself), but precious, self-indulgent, and irresponsible when anything important was at stake. Imagine your fully grown child complaining to you that, while she understands that you meant well, you had messed up her life irretrievably by insisting on doing it your way, rather than just following the instructions in the manual. If there *were* such a manual, that sort of complaint would be perfectly in order.[3] Kant's position was a reasonable one to adopt only because—with a handful of exceptions such as deductive logic—there simply is no way to determine what theoretical or practical conclusion to draw, other than to have someone examine the considerations in play and to figure it out.

Psychologism in philosophy of logic holds that the subject matter of logic is the operations of the mind: logic is concerned with what counts as correctly performing a particular mental activity, namely, reasoning; it is not in the first place about what abstract objects (such as propositions) stand in what entailment relations. When John Stuart Mill borrowed Archbishop Whately's definition of "Logic [as] the Science, as well the Art, of reasoning," meant to provide "a right understanding of the mental process . . . [and] a system of rules, fitted for [its] direction" (Mill, 1967–1991: 7:4), he was giving a characterization typical of the psychologistic tradition. The contrary view, almost universally endorsed today, is that the correctness of a conclusion is independent of human mental activity.[4]

However, autonomy, intellectual or otherwise, is a requirement when an investigator or deliberator who has lined up all the considerations he can, and examined whatever entailment relations he can make out, inevitably faces the moment depicted in a famous Sidney Harris cartoon (reproduced in Dennett, 1991: 38) where, in the middle of a blackboard, a step has been drawn in and labeled, "Then a miracle occurs." That is, after all of the preparation, he must *make up his mind* what he believes or is going to do, and, in almost all cases that matter, what he has managed to line up cannot itself *tell* him what that will be. The Enlightenment makes sense only if psychologism is the right approach in philosophy of logic: if the best we can do is to assess how well the mental activity was performed, because part of the process being assessed is that miracle moment.

Deference to the individual's autonomy, both practical and intellectual, is a substitute for a full understanding (the sort of understanding that could be recast as an algorithm) of how effectively to solve theoretical and practical problems.

There are still neo-Carnapian confirmation theorists, and there are still crude Benthamite utilitarians, but the procedural utopia has never been more than a philosophical fantasy. The Enlightenment was right; we *don't* have a mechanical procedure for figuring out what to believe and what to do; we *don't* have an independently applicable criterion that determines what the correct theoretical and practical conclusions are; we neither know how we in fact do it, nor how to do it right. Psychologism *is* the right approach in philosophy of logic. The Enlightenment's implicit view was that, if we put our minds to it, and allowed ourselves such aids as a healthy dose of unfettered criticism, we would not do that bad a job of drawing our conclusions.[5] And for a little while that turned out to be true enough. While it is important to acknowledge the many disappointments, not least in the political arena, nonetheless, astonishingly, individuals were able to take up the responsibilities imposed on them by Enlightenment ideology—until the Enlightenment itself changed the human species form.

2. We Are (Now) Serial Hyperspecializers

Imagine a space alien to have visited our planet, any time during the course of human history prior to the last three hundred years or so, and to have written up field notes on humanity in the logically distinctive register of the natural historian.[6] The alien would have noticed that human beings, like a number of other terrestrial species, manage to occupy several distinct ecological niches, and that they exhibit specialized adaptations to these niches. Some humans, he would have observed, feed themselves by tending animals (in something like the way that some ants tend aphids, he might note); others harvest plants; still others prey on fish; others confine themselves to parenting and alloparenting; yet others do none of these things, but occupy a handful of exotic, hard-for-an-alien-to-describe ecological roles in which they sometimes prey on, sometimes exchange products or services with, the food-producing humans. (We would call these specialized adaptations blacksmiths, priests, warriors, and the like.) Although caste memberships of these kinds might initially have seemed hereditary to the alien, at some point he would have been in a position to record that, perhaps modulo sexual specialization, just about any human, if placed from birth in the correct social location, is able to specialize into any one of the limited number of roles available. However, these creatures would have seemed to the alien to exhibit something very much like imprinting; exposed to that initial social environment, and having become a farmer, or a fisherman, or a wet nurse, they do not subsequently respecialize, and come later to inhabit a different ecological niche.

Now imagine that the alien has returned for a followup study, just about now. He would note that the human beings' adaptive strategy has become startlingly different. From a naturalist's point of view, a species is to be characterized in terms of its implementation of an ecological strategy, and so similarities in appearance notwithstanding, they might as well be a different species.

The new species-wide strategy still involves specialization to ecological niches, but where before these niches were fairly simply defined, and quite limited in number, now they are much more highly articulated, and there are many more—apparently indefinitely many more—of them. Some of the names the alien might list, taken from the creatures' own vocabulary, would perhaps be: web site designer, pastry cook, tactile interpreter, network administrator, registered lobbyist, roastmaster, sommelier, oncologist, radiologist, philosopher of biology . . . And whereas, earlier on, the phenomenon of a human being's moving from one specialized role to another was rare enough to be neglected in a fully adequate natural history, in the meantime it has become common enough to count as a trait without which the form of life cannot be successfully described. People do not do it all that often (and sometimes get through life without doing it at all), but they do retrain, and occasionally switch careers as many as five times.

We will return in a moment to the characterization of the new ecological strategy, and in particular to aspects of it that the alien, standing outside of it, is unlikely to get right. In the meantime, we can name the later strategy. The human beings that the alien observes on his return visit today are *serial hyperspecializers*.[7]

We, who know the history of this transformation from the inside, should occasionally remind ourselves what it looks like from the alien's perspective. And we should also remind ourselves how it happened. It was the exercise of public reason, so important to Kant, which produced the bodies of knowledge and technique built into these hyperarticulated specializations, and which promises to produce indefinitely many more of them: indeed, by the mid-nineteenth century, William Whewell needed to invent a word for the new classes of specialists who were most responsible for this proliferation; he called them "scientists" (Whewell, 1847: 2:560). The phenomenon of people thinking for themselves has dramatically changed what, from the point of view of a natural historian, would in an Aristotelian vocabulary be called the human species form. If you like, there has been an unnoticed extinction event: humanity has vanished, we are their replacement, and that drastic ecological reconfiguration was the work of the Enlightenment.

3. Rethinking Your Assumptions

As it turns out, when you grow up and start thinking for yourself, you do not merely leave older baggage behind; you start finding things out, and that is especially true when you think out loud, addressing the public as, in Kant's phrasing, "a man of learning." And as it further turns out, when it is not just you, but many people finding things out, the way human beings generally live in their social and natural environment changes. Back before the Enlightenment kicked off, a reasonably intelligent, reasonably diligent person could know his way around pretty much everything there was to know, enough to form thoughtful judgments on the basis of that knowledge, and be sufficiently at home in it to make his own contributions, more or less across the board. (We call some of those people "Renaissance men.")

But as the pool of information grew, and more importantly, as the repertoire of skills needed to access and deploy different parts of that pool grew as well, the shared body of knowledge and technique was inevitably divided up into much narrower domains, consigned to the expertise of specialists. Specialists in such a society do not merely memorize information that other specialists or generalists do not. First, they have to develop and master proprietary systems of representation, in order to control their part of the pool of information; the upshot is that, increasingly typically, no one who is not the same sort of specialist can so much as *understand* the information in that part of the pool. Second, specialists internalize standards and guidelines that govern both their thinking about matters of fact and their choices of what to do; these standards and guidelines are also unintelligible to nonspecialists, and consequently, different sorts of specialist have startlingly different priorities and concerns. A slightly exotic example that will turn out to matter presently: specialists of different sorts are adept at—and have internalized standards for—very different forms of argumentation; if you are not the relevant sort of specialist, you cannot tell whether a given argument of the kind they trade in is any good.

Consequently, autonomy is rarely a live option for serial hyperspecializers. To explain how and why, let us step through a series of progressively deeper obstacles to thinking for yourself.

First and most obviously, a serial hyperspecializer is in the business of relying on what he is told by serial hyperspecializers in other specializations; he relies on them both when he must take action outside of his own area of specialization, and when his own specialization invokes outside expertise.[8] Part of thinking for yourself is rethinking the assumptions you are relying on; you are not equipped to rethink your assumptions when they are the deliverances of expertise not your own; thus, much of the time, serial hyperspecializers are not equipped to think for themselves.

Perhaps just a little less obviously, the problem is compounded by a common technique for passing information over disciplinary barriers, namely, dumbing it down. Normally, within one of these highly specialized fields, there is a great deal of nuance worked into both representations of fact and action-guiding assessments; accordingly, extensive specialized training on the part of users of those representations and assessments is almost always presupposed. For instance, within a field, a model may be understood to give usable results only sometimes, results which must be intelligently interpreted. Since outsiders cannot make head or tail of the hedges and qualifications, and cannot be expected to supply the intelligent interpretation on their own, when information and assessments are exported from a specialized discipline, they have the nuance, hedging, and qualifications stripped out.[9] This problem turns up one step earlier than the inability of a would-be autonomous agent to rethink assumptions; quite frequently, for the very reasons he is unable to, those assumptions are already low-quality surrogates for the premises that would be needed as the basis for responsible and intelligent deliberation.

Thus an agent aspiring to think for himself normally starts off not with what he needs to know, but with simplified—often ruthlessly simplified—substitutes. Even if he somehow looked up what he needs to know, he would be unable to understand it: a specialized system of representation can only be mastered through lengthy and intensive training. Even if he in some superficial sense understood it, he would not know what to do with it: the ability competently to deploy information generated by and for specialists depends on acquiring the relevant standards and guidelines, and that too normally presupposes lengthy and extensive training. So such an agent is not in a position to rethink his own views responsibly, which is to say that he is not in a position to think for himself.

4. Objections: Testimony and Public Space

That first lap of argument was straightforward, but it is not too early to get a couple of objections out of the way. First of all, a champion of the idea that we are pretty much all right as we are might allow that perhaps we cannot rethink the pronouncements of other specialists for ourselves, but reply that most of real life is lived within a shared public space, that that public space is not the domain of experts, and that autonomy matters most when it has to do with decisions precisely in the public space.

But we should not just assume that activity within the shared public space is more important than any other part of life. It no doubt gets more media play, but that is because the shared space is a lowest common denominator of our cultural market; Hollywood makes romantic comedies rather than movies about civil engineering, because everyone is expected to experience romance, but very few people are engineers. However, supporting the industrial production of a class of cultural artifacts in this manner does not make an activity more important.

In any case, that objection misunderstands what serial hyperspecialization has inevitably made of the public arena in which we interact with our fellow citizens. Because the machinery that supports even the most generic interactions is now managed by teams of specialists, serial hyperspecializers find themselves confronted, not with a public arena whose workings they understand and can reason intelligently about, but with a user interface. When what serial hyperspecializers count as the generic environment they share has come to take its structure from the many specializations that impinge on it, its inhabitants will not understand how that public space works—even when they are well trained in its user interface. An example: everyone knows how to pay for goods and services; very few people understand what sort of information traces are left by their bank card, what uses are made of them, and how a pattern of purchases can subtly affect the shape of one's life. Another example: helping those less fortunate than yourself is, in our current user interface, typically a matter of making a donation to a charitable organization; as it turns out, you have to be intimately familiar with the workings of NGOs to have any idea whether your contribution is likely to make things better or worse—and sometimes, a further layer of anthropological expertise is needed to figure those workings and their upshots out (Mosse, 2005). A third example: everyone knows how to vote, and the issues and allegiances on which they express their opinions are vigorously debated within the shared public space. But only specialists understand how voting works in our political system; only specialists understand how that public debate is managed. And of course no matter how vivid the voters' opinions are, generally their correctness turns on specialized knowledge that almost no voters will possess or understand.[10]

Next, it is likely to be objected that we are overstating the requirements on autonomy, intellectual and otherwise. After all, one must in any case trust the testimony and practical assessments of others.[11] Thinking for yourself, the objection continues, requires that you can *rely* on your premises, not that you can rethink them. And surely the point of having experts is that we can rely on them.

We are about to turn to the mistake embedded in the objection: that if you can believe what an expert says, that should be enough. However, it is important anyway to register a further aspect of the difficulty being pressed here, namely, that identifying experts on whom you can rely is harder than it looks. Surely thinking for yourself involves at least being able to take responsibility for the choice of experts on whom you rely. But to ascertain who the right experts are, you have to be that sort of expert yourself.

5. DEFEASIBILITY AND LOGICAL ALIENS

The point of helping oneself to the pronouncements of specialists is to deploy them in one's own arguments; anyway, that is the point if one is trying to live up to the Enlightenment ideal of thinking for yourself. Moreover, it is normal to have to integrate the deliverances of different categories of authoritative specialists into a single train of thought, in order to support or dispose of some conclusion which one is considering. To see why this sort of deployment and integration is a nontrivial challenge, let us take as the central case the one in which the specialists' deliverances are supported by arguments.

Now, any argument that is not deductive is *defeasible*, that is, even if the argument is reasonable on the face of it, and would defaultly go through, it can be aborted by any of indefinitely many defeating conditions. Here is a sample entailment that might be used to build nondeductive arguments: because academics compete to place their work in highly ranked journals, the more selective the journal in which it is placed, the better the work. Although this generalization can be used to construct arguments for assessing the quality of academic output, those arguments will not necessarily go through—for instance, if the supply of journal reviewers has been exhausted and is not being replenished, or if the reviewers in a small subspecialty are able to recognize each other, and play tit-for-tat strategies in an iterated prisoners' dilemma. (In fact, these conditions obtain most of the time: an argument that goes through, ceteris paribus, is not to be confused with an argument whose conclusion is *probably* true.) As is standardly the case when an argument is defeasible, there are—obviously—indefinitely many other circumstances in which arguments constructed using this entailment would fail.[12]

Doing a decent job of thinking for yourself requires sensitivity to the defeating conditions of the arguments supporting your views, and if you are not an expert in the subject matter of those arguments, you do not generally control those defeating conditions. Continuing the example, an academic outsider, who is assured that so-and-so publishes in highly ranked journals in his field, who draws the conclusion that so-and-so's work must be of high quality, and who then relies on that work himself, just does not know enough to have the right sort of second thoughts—although every now and again an Alan Sokol will remind people that those second thoughts ought to be pretty pressing.

So the difficulty faced by the Enlightenment ideal goes deeper than the fact that serial hyperspecializers are not normally able to assess the quality of the expert descriptions, assessments, and, for that matter, direct instructions which they have no alternative but to consume, and it goes deeper than the fact that they cannot rethink them on their own. When you are assembling a defeasible argument, you should be confident in your conclusions only to the extent that you control the argument's defeasibility conditions—in a less fancy way of saying it, your confidence should not outrun your ability to catch problems and bugs that crop up in your argument. On the one hand, you do not control the defeasibility conditions of arguments that are conducted in other areas of expertise and that supply you with premises for arguments in your own area of expertise. On the other, you cannot expect experts in other areas to be sensitive to defeaters to their arguments that crop up when they are applied in your own area of expertise. Thus the level of confidence that serial hyperspecializers should have in the conclusions of even moderately demanding arguments is low. When you try thinking for yourself, and you have to deploy the conclusions of specialists in other disciplines, you cannot trust what you come up with.

The problems of cross-disciplinary defeasibility management are amplified and deepened by a further obstacle. Recall that induction into one of the many specializations characteristically involves adopting its proprietary modes of argumentation. Now, there is a dramatic philosophical term of art for someone who has a different logic than you do: he is a *logical alien*. The notion is usually introduced on the way to an argument that there could be no such thing: logical aliens, the received wisdom has it, are inconceivable, and the very notion is incoherent.[13] But once we have serial hyperspecializers clearly in view, because specialists' standards for correct argumentation are not shared, we should be prepared to find that we live in a society of people who are logical aliens with respect to one another. And that is what we *do* find. When philosophers work at imagining logical aliens, they tend to tell stories about visits from outer space, or faraway primitive tribesmen. But if you are an academic employed by a university, and you want to meet a logical alien, you do not need to walk any farther than the other end of the hall—or at most, to an adjacent building on your very own campus.

The psychologism implicit in the Enlightenment's demand that you think for yourself has as an upshot that you can judge whether an argument is any good only when you can, as we now say, wrap your mind around it. Perhaps you do not need to come up with that judgment for yourself. But when you rely on someone, in a manner that we understand to preserve your autonomy, you are delegating the investigation of your question to him, and you accept his conclusion because the way he went on to conduct the investigation was pretty much the way you would have done it—say, if you had had the time, and were where you needed to be to take a look. That is, you accept the results because the investigation is conducted correctly by your own lights.

However, when you delegate part of your deliberation to a logical alien—put less dramatically, to a specialist whose idea of what a good argument is differs from yours—what he comes up with will not normally conform to standards you accept. When an outsider is aware of another discipline's internal standards, he may well, and is even likely to, think they are wrongheaded. (For example: try explaining a transcendental argument to a developmental psychologist or a chemist.) Because you are not delegating to someone who thinks as you do, we no longer have an explanation for how delegation of this sort preserves your autonomy—or, perhaps more carefully, we have not yet elaborated a notion of autonomy that makes room for such an explanation.[14]

Our third version of the threat to autonomy, then, is that as far as any one sort of serial hyperspecializer is concerned, many other serial hyperspecializers are logical aliens. Any serial hyperspecializer is, willy-nilly, the epistemic and practical client of serial hyperspecializers of other types. As we now understand thinking for yourself, when you accept a premise from someone else, you allow it to be reasonably and intelligently arrived at only if you would endorse the reasoning that produced it—that is, if that is the way you would have thought through the question yourself. But because the arguments deployed by experts in other specializations do not conform to standards of argumentation that you have internalized and that make sense to you, you are not in a position to make your willingness to adopt them contingent on this sort of endorsement.

6. We're All in the Same Boat

In the exposition to this point, we adopted the perspective of an individual who is forced to rely on others. It is now time to take a step back and remind ourselves that the members of a society of serial hyperspecializers are symmetrically dependent on one another.

The Enlightenment insistence on thinking for yourself was tied up with the concern that those who did not would have their thinking done for them by other people who *were* thinking for themselves; Jeremy Bentham, typically, thought that you would be taken advantage of by "sinister interests." Back in the day, someone else could have, in principle, done just as good a job of figuring things out as you would have yourself, and the job you would have done might well have been perfectly adequate. However, the problems we have been identifying are problems for *anybody*. Consequently, nowadays, when you let someone else do your thinking for you, while there is still coordination of interests to worry about, the main worry ought to be that, no matter how sincerely the person you are delegating your thinking to has your interests at heart, he is no better equipped than you are to perform the task that you are unable adequately to execute yourself. It is not just that, after a couple of centuries of *Aufklärung*, thinking for yourself, when it comes to just about anything that really matters, is no longer an option: that no matter how resolute or courageous you are, you have to let others do most of your thinking for you. Rather, the most pressing problem is that, when you do, it's the blind leading the blind.

Let us stick with the view from above, and continue to represent the very general pattern of dependencies in terms of arguments. In a society of serial hyperspecializers, an individual starts out most moderately serious trains of thought by accepting premises from specialists in other disciplines; he conducts the train of thought, typically, within his own area of expertise; while he may be the end user, ordinarily his conclusion will be conveyed to a client who is himself a specialist in yet a further discipline. The boundaries between one specialist's stretch of argument and another's are merely artefacts of the intellectual division of labor: in the view from above, all these stretches of argument make up *one* (likely very long) argument. So the question we are really considering is how it is possible to monitor the quality of lengthy and complex arguments that are, so to speak, draped over indefinitely many areas of expertise. Here's a very blunt assessment: we do not have any well-understood way of managing such arguments.

7. Fighting for Freedom

We began by suggesting that the Enlightenment is being undone, and now that we have a clearer rendering of the dynamics of the process, we had better ask ourselves just how urgent a concern it really is. Maybe we should just leave behind the moralistic demand that each of us grow up and think for himself. After all, doesn't it happen often enough that when you ask philosophers to provide an *argument* for being autonomous, you walk away empty-handed—even when they are Kantian moral philosophers, the ones that you would think would have those arguments if anyone did? Maybe there are actually no good reasons to regret the passing of the Enlightenment, in which case, the tone of world-historical drama with which this chapter began was no more than theatrics.

Say that freedom is, inter alia, the ability to do what one decides, and say that liberty is centrally a matter of protecting freedom from governments and other authorities. Surely freedom is valuable primarily because the ability to do as one decides is valuable (although we want to acknowledge the many secondary ways in which it also matters, such as avoiding the humiliation of having obnoxious bosses tell you what to do). But the ability to do as you decide to is valuable in the first place because you can think for yourself, and when you do, having enough confidence in your own conclusions to act on them is not simply unreasonable. If it *were* unreasonable, your best option would be to hope for a Jeeves to whom to entrust the management of a life as lived by Bertram Wooster.[15]

The Great Endarkenment thus directly undercuts our commitment to freedom and to liberty. And it undercuts those commitments indirectly as well. Eternal vigilance, we are told, is the price of liberty; vigilance involves thinking things through for yourself, and if you cannot, the question of what your liberty is *worth* is likely to be moot. It is small consolation that those to whom we lose our liberty are bound to be about as incompetent as we are ourselves.[16] Keeping our freedom, keeping our liberty, and keeping the both of them worth hanging onto mean figuring out what it could be to take realistic and meaningful responsibility for the conclusions of our theoretical and practical arguments—for our assessments, opinions, and choices—within a society of serial hyperspecializers. That is to say, it means arresting and reversing the Great Endarkenment.

However, returning to an earlier stage of our collective intellectual development would be neither possible nor desirable. Although it proved to be self-undermining, this author does not regret the Enlightenment for a moment. Thus our task is to recast its aspirations so as to preserve what was important in them, while rendering them attainable in a society that is ever more specialized.

Many efforts on many different fronts will be necessary, and we had better be thinking them out from scratch; it is clear from the outset that older ways of addressing the challenges posed by older forms of specialization—for instance, education in the classics—are not going fix the problems we have surveyed. We do need to inventory and analyze the devices that we are currently using to cope, however clumsily, with hyperspecialization as we now have it; but we should not imagine that such a survey can be more than preliminary groundclearing. In any case, an intelligent response to a challenge of this order of magnitude begins with understanding and successfully characterizing it. Only once we understand the problem will we be able to devise and verify solutions to it.

Recall the earlier suggestion that the difficulties of the Enlightenment that are well along to undoing its achievements are problems in philosophy of logic. Logic, conceived in the psychologistic manner demanded by the Enlightenment itself, is the theory of reasoning done right (but allow that this sort of theory may amount to a system of directives); philosophy of logic, then, will be the discussion and theorizing meant to eventuate in and frame such a theory. (For instance, the dispute at which we gestured earlier, as to whether logic should be construed psychologistically or antipsychologistically, is squarely within the ambit of philosophy of logic.) Recall that the first of the problems on our list comes under the heading of cross-disciplinary interface management: when an argument traverses multiple specializations, how can information and guidance be moved over those disciplinary barriers? The second was the question of how to manage the defeasibility conditions of an argument, when a stretch of the argument and the intellectual control of its defeaters belong to different areas of expertise. Here we were considering especially the problem of how the different specialists already mobilized when articulating such an argument can cross-check its various stretches for defeaters;

but there is also the broader problem, of how to bring to bear necessary expertise in areas that did not lie on the pathway of the argument.

The third problem has to do with our need to accept the expert pronouncements of specialists that are arrived at on the basis of procedures and in conformity with standards that either we do not understand, or that conflict with the standards and procedures we ourselves endorse. Facing up to it will require a change of approach in philosophy of logic, over and above the turn back to psychologism.

The variations in sensibility across the natural sciences—especially and in particular with respect to what can count as a good argument—are both commonplace and awkward enough to have given rise to a genre of joke: "How do a mathematician, a physicist, and an engineer"—and here is one typical continuation—"prove that all odd numbers are prime?" Disciplinary specialization looks like relativism come home; but what we need to understand is how, if the way physicists solve problems looks to an engineer like a *joke*, and vice versa, the both of them are willing to use each other's solutions as premises in their own arguments. That willingness is of course modulated; sometimes a specialist (or a layperson) will correctly accept expert pronouncements produced to standards that he does not endorse, and sometimes not; what makes the difference, and why? Philosophers of logic have almost always been concerned to delineate what reasoning done correctly is—that is, the *one* thing that counts as reasoning done correctly—and have not been figuring out how to make use of the results of reasoning that does not live up to the standards of argumentation that we accept ourselves.

If the problems at the bottom of the Great Endarkenment are problems in the philosophy of logic, then they are, first of all, problems for philosophers. Here I am going to convey my own view on this point tersely, and through a series of bald assertions.

All cultures have wisdom literatures (or oral traditions that occupy that role); these often take up questions that we regard as typically philosophical: for instance, how a good life is to be lived. The ancient Hebrews left us *Job* and *Ecclesiastes*; we have produced, less impressively, the books lining the shelves of the self-help section of your local bookstore. Philosophy began when one individual, whom we still remember, made a nuisance of himself by asking those with opinions about such matters what their argument was. Thus argumentation has been central to philosophy from its very beginnings, and it does seem to me that there is an Aristotelian way of saying just how it figures into philosophical views and positions, namely, as its material cause: just as clay is the matter out of which ceramics are made, so argument is the material out of which philosophy is crafted. (I should say precisely here that because I have not yet argued for that claim, it remains only potentially philosophy—the form or design of a combination of philosophical ideas.) Indeed, if you look at any philosophical tradition, you will find that it has a view of what it is to conduct argument correctly. Typically, that view is distinctive, and a great deal of the shape of the tradition is to be explained by looking to its view of argumentation. Thus I am often tempted to say that the remainder of philosophy stands to logic, or to philosophy of logic, as applied ethics traditionally conceived stands to straight moral theory: all the rest of philosophy is applied philosophy of logic.

Because of the role of argument within the craft of philosophy, philosophers are almost always explicitly trained in their methods of argumentation to an extent that is at least out of the ordinary in other fields. Moreover, the theory of rationality comes up again and again as a topic of explicit discussion in all walks of philosophy. This is a heritage we can bring to bear on the management of methods of argumentation that vary from specialized discipline to specialized discipline, but which nonetheless must be integrated with one another.

Philosophy of logic is first philosophy. The answers we need to stave off the Great Endarkenment have to do with how serial hyperspecializers can conduct reasoning that traverses multiple areas of specialization; the discipline we must turn to for those answers is philosophy of logic. Philosophy of logic is, and as I have just suggested, not merely as a verbal or classificatory matter, philosophy. So reversing the Great Endarkenment is the job, in the first place, of philosophers. And in the end, if the challenges of the Great Endarkenment are met, and the problems listed here are solved, it will be by philosophers, for a further reason. Philosophers have to solve these problems, because anyone who does solve them will, whether or not he has been trained by the academic discipline that now bears the name, *thereby* count as a philosopher.

Acknowledgments

I would like to thank Sarah Buss, Heather Douglas, Chris Maloney, Maneesh Modi, Adam Morton, and David Schmidtz for helpful conversation. Carla Bagnoli, Teresa Blankmeyer Burke, Sam Fleischacker, Svantje Guinebert, Jamie Hardy, Buket Korkut-Raptis, Jeffrey Seidman, Jim Tabery, and two anonymous reviewers gave me comments on earlier drafts. The Center for the Philosophy of Freedom at the University of Arizona provided support, work space, and valuable feedback over the course of a retreat, and the John Simon Guggenheim Memorial Foundation provided fellowship support. The essay draws material from a review of Steven Hales, ed., *A Companion to Relativism*, in *Notre Dame Philosophical Reviews*, April 2012; an expanded version of the essay appears as the title essay of *The Great Endarkenment* (Oxford: Oxford University Press, 2015).

Notes

1. Certainly there have been attacks on the Enlightenment from within the academy: for instance by Michel Foucault and Alasdair MacIntyre (e.g., Foucault, 1995; Foucault, 1988; MacIntyre, 1988; MacIntyre, 1990). But these are positioned as dissent against an overwhelmingly dominant paradigm.
2. To be sure, that correctness is independent of human mental activity does not entail that cognition cannot be *about* human mental activity.

    Likewise, in those decision procedures, the inputs are in large part facts about preferences, or hedonic responses, or, more generally, facts about the psychologies of agents. For in-period worries about the program, see Neurath (1959).

3. That said, the second assumption is not a component of the views of all Enlightenment figures. Jeremy Bentham, for instance, thought that there was a way to specify the correctness of a choice that was independent, in the relevant sense, of agents' deliberations. His own argumentative practice did not, however, reflect his theoretical views (Millgram, 2017), and perhaps inevitably so.

4. Antipsychologism was one of the McCarthyisms of the previous century's academia, and philosophers are brought up with the article of faith that psychologism is (or rather, was) an unforgivable doctrine; few of them are aware of the nature of the debate from which that condemnation emerged. But see Kusch (1995) and Ringer (1990: 295–298) for the social role of accusations of psychologism in, respectively, German philosophy and German intellectual culture more generally.

5. An example of this cast of mind can be found in Mill's *On Liberty*, in the seventh paragraph of its second chapter (Mill, 1967–1991: 18:231f).

6. For an elegant characterization of that register, see Thompson, 2008: Part 1; for a short overview, see Millgram, 2009b.

7. For further pieces of the story, see Millgram, 2015.

8. For a very helpful description of the phenomenon, see Hardwig, 1985.

9. Following up on that for-instance, it is all too easy to imagine someone, faced with the model he is not competent to use, gruffly insisting: "Just give me a probability!" Indeed, we should expect to find that the function of probabilities, all too often, is to mediate cross-disciplinary communication in just this way.

10. For an introduction to issues pertaining to voter knowledgeability and voters' openness to argument and other forms of persuasion, see Converse, 1964; Zaller, 1992.

11. As I have argued myself; see Millgram, 1997: ch. 7.

12. For a slightly more leisurely introduction to defeasibility, see Millgram, 2015: 131–133; for examples of defeasibility in inference about matters of fact, see Millgram, 2009a: 94–96; for examples of defeasibility in practical inference, see Millgram, 2005: 135, 173; for tit-for-tat strategies, see Axelrod, 1984.

13. E.g., Quine, 1966: 102 or Davidson, 1984: 137; Lear, 1990: 190ff is one of the more interesting rebuttals. Wittgenstein, 1983: 1:§143, 148–152, at any rate on its standard reading, is also meant as such an argument.

14. Could one sustain one's autonomy nevertheless, by adopting a posture of, so to speak, extravocational skepticism? Perhaps one could assign suitably lower probabilities to expert pronouncements, or perhaps one could populate one's view of the world with conditional beliefs, of roughly the form, "If so-and-so really *does* know what he's talking about, then . . ." But recall that those probabilities often serve to mask unmanageable but real complexity. Moreover, the cognitive load involved in keeping track of all those if-clauses will quickly swamp most reasoning—this latter is an allowable consideration within psychologistic philosophy of logic—and sooner or later, but rather sooner, it will be necessary to detach. In any case, one cannot *act* merely conditionally. And finally for now, we know what this looks like in real life. The people who attempt to preserve their autonomy by adopting this sort of skeptical posture end up marginalized cranks. In a functioning economy, not everyone can be living off the grid.

15. As in, for instance, Wodehouse, 1984; for a darker depiction of misguided autonomy, see Laxness, 1997.

16. That is, borrowing the illustration in the previous note, you may go looking for a Jeeves, but if the argument is on track, you are not going to *find* a Jeeves: no one out there can

make the case that if he runs your life for you, he will avoid these obstacles. But that does not mean that you have a particularly strong claim to freedom; once freedom is not worth very much, we cannot treat a protected sphere of choice as the default. For example, we might reasonably decide that a bias toward conservatism is safer than allowing individuals to follow broken arguments to nonstandard conclusions, and accordingly opt to set in stone what is now an occasional practice: that of having personal decisions made by informal committees of acquaintances.

REFERENCES

Axelrod, Robert, 1984. *The evolution of cooperation*. New York: Basic Books.

Converse, Philip, 1964. The nature of belief systems in mass publics. In: David Apter, ed. *Ideology and discontent*. New York: Free Press of Glencoe. pp.206–261.

Davidson, Donald, 1984. *Inquiries into truth and interpretation*. Oxford: Clarendon Press.

Dennett, Daniel, 1991. *Consciousness explained*. Boston: Little, Brown.

Foucault, Michel, 1988. *Madness and civilization*. Translated by Richard Howard. New York: Random House.

Foucault, Michel, 1995. *Discipline and punish*. Translated by Alan Sheridan. New York: Random House.

Hardwig, John, 1985. Epistemic dependence. *Journal of Philosophy,* 82(7), pp.335–349.

Kant, Immanuel, 1991. An answer to the question, "What is Enlightenment?" In: Hans Reiss and H. B. Nisbet, eds. *Kant: Political writings*. Cambridge: Cambridge University Press. pp.54–60.

Kusch, Martin, 1995. *Psychologism*. London: Routledge.

Laxness, Halldór, 1997. *Independent people*. Translated by J. A. Thompson. New York: Vintage.

Lear, Jonathan, 1990. *Love and its place in nature*. New York: Farrar, Straus and Giroux.

MacIntyre, Alasdair, 1988. *Whose justice? Which rationality?* Notre Dame: University of Notre Dame Press.

MacIntyre, Alasdair, 1990. *Three rival versions of moral enquiry*. Notre Dame: University of Notre Dame Press.

Mill, John Stuart, 1967–1991. *Collected works of John Stuart Mill*. Toronto and London: University of Toronto Press/Routledge and Kegan Paul.

Millgram, Elijah, 1997. *Practical induction*. Cambridge, MA: Harvard University Press.

Millgram, Elijah, 2005. *Ethics done right: Practical reasoning as a foundation for moral theory*. Cambridge: Cambridge University Press.

Millgram, Elijah, 2009a. *Hard truths*. Oxford: Wiley-Blackwell.

Millgram, Elijah, 2009b. Review of Michael Thompson, *Life and action. Analysis Reviews,* 69(3), pp.1–7.

Millgram, Elijah, 2015. *The Great Endarkenment*. New York: Oxford University Press.

Millgram, Elijah, 2017. Mill's epiphanies. In: Christopher Macleod and Dale Miller, eds. *A companion to Mill*. Oxford: Wiley-Blackwell.

Mosse, David, 2005. *Cultivating development*. London: Pluto Press.

Neurath, Otto, 1959. Protocol sentences. In: A. J. Ayer, ed. *Logical positivism*. New York: MacMillan. pp.199–208.

Quine, W. V. O., 1966. Carnap and logical truth. In: *The ways of paradox*. New York: Random House. pp.100–125.

Ringer, Fritz, 1990. *The decline of the German mandarins*. Hanover: Wesleyan University Press.

Thompson, Michael, 2008. *Life and action*. Cambridge, MA: Harvard University Press.

Whewell, William, 1847. *The philosophy of the inductive sciences*. London: John W. Parker.

Wittgenstein, Ludwig, 1983. *Remarks on the foundations of mathematics*. Rev. ed. Edited by G. H. von Wright, Rush Rhees, and G. E. M. Anscombe. Cambridge, MA: MIT Press.

Wodehouse, P. G., 1984. *Carry on, Jeeves*. Harmondsworth: Penguin.

Zaller, John, 1992. *The nature and origins of mass opinion*. Cambridge: Cambridge University Press.

CHAPTER 27

FREE WILL AS A PSYCHOLOGICAL ACCOMPLISHMENT

EDDY NAHMIAS

1. FREE WILL AS PSYCHOLOGICAL CAPACITY

IMAGINE writing a philosophy paper or a short story. You imagine a range of options for presenting the argument or the plot, the structure, some sentences. But first, the opening line. You want to get it right. There are better and worse answers to the question: How should I begin? And regarding the rest: How should I proceed? To *ask* these questions requires the capacity to imagine a range of alternatives, and there are better and worse alternatives to imagine. To *answer* these questions requires the capacities to select among those alternatives, and there are better and worse ways to select them. People possess, to varying degrees, the diverse range of psychological capacities needed to write a philosophy paper or a story: capacities to imagine a wider range of relevant options, to shift attention away from less—and towards more—promising options, to select the better options, and to execute these choices—making the imagined future the actual one. Furthermore, different people, in different situations, have better and worse *opportunities* to exercise these capacities—for instance, free time to let the mind wander and put words on paper. We don't know a lot about how these psychological capacities work or what underlying mechanisms explain their functioning (and malfunctioning). But when the sentences flow from your exercising these capacities for imagination, attention, selection, and execution, well, then *you* are the author of your paper or your story. And you deserve some measure of credit for the good ones, culpability for the bad ones.

So it is with free will, or so I will argue. For an agent to have free will is for her to *possess* the psychological capacities to make decisions—to imagine alternatives for action, to select among them, and to control her actions accordingly—such that she is the author of her actions and can deserve credit or blame for them. For an agent to choose freely (or act of her own free will) is for her to have had (reasonable) *opportunity to exercise* these capacities in making her decision and acting. There is a lot packed into these initial definitions, some of which will not be unpacked in this chapter. We will focus, first, on the under-appreciated point that these capacities for free will, like the capacities for writing, are possessed to varying degrees, and that people have better and worse opportunities to exercise them. Free will and free action are graded notions: we have degrees of freedom, and accordingly, degrees of responsibility.

Second, as with the capacities to write, the capacities that underpin free will have both *structural* and *normative* components. To have normative components means that the capacities can function more or less effectively. As with most capacities, such as those involved in biological reproduction, perception, riding a bike, or playing piano, there are criteria for what counts as their proper functioning, better and worse ways for them to be exercised. In the case of free will, as with writing, we cannot fully formalize these normative components. But clearly there are better and worse ways of writing a philosophy paper (ones we aim to teach our students) and better and worse papers (which we aim to assess properly when grading them). Similarly, there are better and worse ways of making decisions (ones we aim to teach our children) and better and worse decisions (which we aim to assess properly when we hold each other or ourselves morally responsible). As discussed below in section 2, there is a long philosophical tradition of treating free will as the set of capacities that, when properly functioning, allow us to make *wise* decisions, ones that contribute to our leading a good or flourishing life. On this view, free will is a psychological accomplishment.

Regarding structural components, capacities are typically composed of a number of other capacities, each of which is enabled by a complex organization of parts or mechanisms; in the case of our psychological capacities, these parts are primarily subserved by neural processes. Free will is often treated too simplistically, for instance, as a special metaphysical causal power or as a faculty to make decisions in light of one's reasons. Other capacities, however, have been under-appreciated—notably, capacities to imagine alternative future courses of action and capacities to control one's attention as one considers these alternatives. As with authoring a story, the ability to imagine various options and consider their merits is a crucial first step in the deliberative process, one that underlies our experience of freedom of choice, of having alternatives for action, such that any alternative's occurrence causally depends on what one decides. Free will is not just about selecting among options, but also about imagining alternatives from which to choose (Sripada, 2016). Free will also includes our abilities to shape our non-deliberative, non-conscious mental activity and to shape our situations so that we act in accord with our goals even without exercising the capacities for conscious decision-making. Similarly, we are still exercising our capacities to write a story when we are lucky enough to have the words flow without our having, at each step, to imagine various options and choose among them.

While these psychological capacities for free will are remarkable, they do not require anything metaphysically mysterious. We are far from fully understanding how they work, but there is no reason to assume that they are non-natural or non-physical—that is, that they require causal powers that cannot be integrated into the mechanisms and laws that organize the physical world.[1] While some have suggested that free will disappears in light of discoveries that we are physical beings governed by the laws of nature (e.g., Harris, 2012), a more plausible view is that the sciences of the mind can help us discover *how* free will works (Nahmias, 2014). Psychology and neuroscience will increasingly illuminate the mechanisms that underlie the capacities essential to free will, as they have with complex human capacities such as perception, language, and memory. These sciences are also discovering that we have *less* free will than we tend to think—that our capacities for decision-making do not always meet the normative criteria we think or hope they do.

Conversely, these sciences can also help us find ways to develop the relevant capacities more fully. Like other psychological capacities, we gain free will as we develop the relevant capacities. As a species, we attained these capacities through a fortuitous evolutionary history. As individuals, we develop these capacities as we mature, and we hope to raise our children to allow these capacities for free will to develop more fully. In the near future, we will increasingly develop methods to alter our psychological capacities more directly, using drugs or neural interventions, potentially enhancing our free will and autonomy. We will have to make hard, hopefully wise, decisions about which of these interventions will contribute to human flourishing (Schaeffer, Kahane, and Savulescu, 2014).

2. A BRIEF HISTORY OF FREE WILL

Debates about free will have been overly obsessed with the question of whether free will is compatible with determinism, the thesis that the state of the universe at any time, in conjunction with the laws of nature, entails the state of the universe at any other time. This is so even though the status of determinism is for physics to discover, presumably with no notice of human psychology, and even though the dominant theory of physics suggests that determinism is false. The recent obsession with determinism was based in part on a definition of free will as the ability to do otherwise; for instance, Peter van Inwagen urges us to focus solely on "the free-will thesis" that "we are sometimes in the following position with respect to a contemplated future act: we simultaneously have both the following abilities: the ability to perform that act and the ability to refrain from performing that act" (2008: 329). A substantial proportion of work on free will in the past fifty years has been devoted to his Consequence Argument (1983) for the conclusion that determinism is incompatible with the ability to do otherwise, and to Harry Frankfurt's argument (1969) that the ability to do otherwise is not necessary for moral responsibility (and perhaps free will).

These debates are fascinating and important. But they skew the discussion away from other important questions, including other potential threats to free will and other crucial components of free will. Increasingly, philosophers define free will as the set of abilities to control one's decisions and actions such that it is justified to hold one morally responsible for them—that is, such that one can deserve to be blamed or praised for them (O'Connor, 2014; McKenna and Coates, 2015). On this view, there is more to free will than the ability to do otherwise. Most theorists recognize this, at least implicitly, whether they are compatibilists about free will and determinism or incompatibilists. Indeed, the disagreements among the competing theorists conceal a great deal of common ground regarding crucial capacities for free will, including cognitive capacities to consciously consider alternatives for action and to make choices based on one's reasons for action.

Consider two *compatibilist* theorists. For Frankfurt an agent with free will possesses "the capacity for reflective self-evaluation" (1971: 12) and is "prepared to endorse or repudiate the motives from which he acts . . . to guide his conduct in accordance with what he really cares about" (1993: 114). Jay Wallace describes similar capacities in terms of "reflective self-control: (1) the power to grasp and apply moral reasons, and (2) the power to control or regulate one's behavior by the light of such reasons" (1993: 157). Now consider two *incompatibilist* theorists. Laura Ekstrom states, "An agent enjoys freedom of action only if the agent's act results from a preference—that is, a desire formed by a process of critical evaluation with respect to one's conception of the good" (2000: 108). And Timothy O'Connor argues that free agents "such as ourselves are conscious, intelligent agents, capable of representing diverse, sophisticated plans of action," adding that he is "unable to conceive an agent's [freely] controlling his own activity without any awareness of what is motivating him" (2000: 121, 88). And the list goes on.[2] Most incompatibilists accept that these capacities for reflective and rational decision-making are both necessary for free will and compatible with determinism. But the debate focuses primarily on whether some additional power or ability, such as agent-causation, is a further necessary condition for free will (see section 5, "Free Will as Forward-Looking").

Furthermore, the way earlier philosophers discussed free will suggests that they were not focused on the ability to do otherwise, but instead on these capacities for reflection, self-knowledge, rationality, and self-control, often with an explicit normative component describing the proper functioning of these capacities. Michael Frede (2012) concludes his detailed history of the origins of the notion of free will by describing the shared features of the range of views he considers, from Aristotle to Stoics to Augustine and many others:

> They all involve the idea that to have a good life one must be able to make the choices one needs to make in order to have such a life. . . . So, to be free, to have a free will, we have to liberate ourselves from these false beliefs and from attachments and aversions which are not grounded in reality. We can do this, moreover, because the world does not systematically force these beliefs, attachments, and aversions on us. (178)

In other words, free will involves the capacities to make good choices, free from influences that distract and detract from such choices. This view of freedom as the set of capacities required to make good choices continues with figures such as Aquinas, Locke, Spinoza (a skeptic about libertarian free will), and Reid, a proponent of agent-causation, who points out that "moral liberty" requires "practical *judgment* or *reason*. . . . [without which] whatever the consequences may be, they cannot be imputed to the agent, who had not the capacity of foreseeing them, or of perceiving any reason for acting otherwise than he did" (1788, IV).

We might use some other term, such as "autonomy," to label the capacities for effective decision-making and self-determination described above, and reserve "free will" as a philosophical term of art to refer to the ability to choose otherwise. But such a move would come at the cost of diverting us away from this historical tradition, from important strands of the contemporary discussion, especially those linking free will to moral responsibility, and from ordinary usage, which takes as paradigmatic of free will humans' uniquely well-developed capacities to deliberate consciously and to make choices without external constraint (e.g., Monroe and Malle, 2010).

In any case, my goal is not to offer an analysis of necessary and sufficient conditions for free will. Rather, my proposal for analyzing free will seeks reflective equilibrium among our ordinary experiences of, and intuitions about, free will, its usage in historical and contemporary discussions, and importantly, its connection with other psychological capacities, setting it up for scientific exploration rather than quarantining it from such exploration. I will, for the most part, assume compatibilism about free will and determinism, rather than arguing that it is the correct view or that it is the intuitive view to most people, as long as they are not misunderstanding determinism to mean that the relevant psychological capacities are bypassed (Murray and Nahmias, 2014). Regardless of whether compatibilism is true, however, the main points of this chapter go through. As suggested above, even incompatibilists think that the psychological capacities described here are crucial features of free will or of an important variety of freedom. We need to analyze these capacities, to study their neuropsychological (structural) components, in part to understand the degree to which humans, and different individuals, possess them, and to consider their normative components, in part to understand how we might improve them and our opportunities to exercise them.

3. Some Neglected Capacities for Free Will

Paradigmatic exercises of free will or free choice include some or all of the following components, each of which requires specific psychological capacities (referred to by number in what follows):

(1) Recognizing that a decision needs to be made.
(2) Imagining various options one might take—i.e., imagining different decisions one might make and the likely future outcomes of those decisions.

(3) Evaluating those options and imagined outcomes in light of one's desires, cares, values, goals, and plans. This process includes a capacity to shift attention towards or away from considerations one evaluates as more or less relevant. (Some of the most important decisions are about which of one's competing desires, values, goals, and plans one evaluates as more important than others.)

(4) Deciding—i.e., selecting an option.

(5) Forming relevant intentions to carry out that decision—i.e., forming proximal intentions (to act now), forming distal intentions (to act at some later time), or developing more general plans of action.

(6) When necessary, exercising willpower (or strength of will) to act in accord with these decisions, intentions, and plans.

A seventh capacity allows us to act freely—in accord with decisions we have made or at least with motivations we would accept if we considered them (Nahmias, 2007)—and to be potentially morally responsible without going through the processes just described:

(7) Habituation and self-binding—i.e., carrying out actions that significantly increase the probability that one will act in accord with prior decisions or plans *without* conscious deliberation or intention-formation at the time of action, including making efforts to alter one's current habits, to regulate one's emotional reactions, and to structure one's environment to avoid competing temptations.

Some of these components are neglected in discussions of free will, perhaps because they are thought to be "passive" rather than "active." Typically, we do not actively (or consciously) control whether and when a problem is posed requiring a decision (item 1) or which specific options come to mind as we deliberate (2), often relevant intentions follow automatically from decisions (5), and often we act without conscious deliberation (7). However, we sometimes engage in these processes in more active ways, consciously considering what decisions must be made, trying to come up with more options to consider, actively shifting attention away from distracting or irrelevant options, and imagining specific action plans in order to prepare oneself to carry them out automatically (e.g., as when athletes or musicians imagine performances ahead of time).[3] In any case, we should not assume that exercising free will only involves "active" (e.g., voluntarily controlled) processes. Conversely, philosophers, especially compatibilists, have focused their attention on the capacities to be reasons-responsive—recognizing and evaluating what reasons one has for various options (3) and accordingly deciding (4) and forming intentions (5) (e.g., Fischer and Ravizza, 1998; Wolf, 1990). Others emphasize that the capacities for evaluation and decision must be properly sensitive to *moral* reasons (e.g., Wallace, 1993; Scanlon, 2008) or to which of our first-order desires we identify with (Frankfurt, 1971).

We should cast a wider net and recognize that all of these capacities are properly considered important components of free will. Each contributes to our capacity to make effective decisions and to act in ways that express the sort of person we want to be, such that we can be held accountable for so acting (Wolf, 2015). Each of these capacities has normative features—criteria, even if controversial, for better and worse functioning. Each can and should be understood as graded—possessed to varying degrees, with varying degrees of opportunity to exercise them. And each has structural features that can be naturalized and understood better with psychological and neurobiological research. Here, however, let us focus attention on the neglected capacity of imagination (2).

Our experiences of choice and free will clearly include the experience of there being multiple options for future action. It is contentious whether some of these experiences include (even implicitly) the content that these options are possible while also holding fixed *all* past and current conditions and laws of nature (Nahmias, Morris, Nadelhoffer, and Turner, 2004; Deery, Davis, and Carey, 2015). But it should not be contentious that, once we recognize that a decision needs to be made (1), we typically imagine various future possibilities (2). As we consider these alternatives, we often begin imagining (consciously representing) the way they might play out, depending on what we do along the way, often letting our minds freely wander further "downstream" into the future and into various "offshoots" of the alternatives that may depend on later decisions.

These capacities to imagine options (and options within options) might seem to exaggerate what we ordinarily do during decision-making. Indeed, we do not exercise these capacities every time we make decisions, nor is doing so required for an action to be free, as is evident when we act automatically but autonomously using the relevant capacities (7). However, consider the planning that you do as you shower, drive, or drift off to sleep, or your deliberations as you prepare and then write a paper, or recent experiences making a difficult decision, for instance, about what to tell a friend seeking advice or which of your competing projects should get priority. We sometimes risk obsessing over a decision—over-imagining and over-evaluating options—and may make efforts to stop and make a decision (4). Nonetheless, our imagination of future options is what explains not only our experience of freedom—of feeling free to actualize some among a range of options we imagine *if* we choose it—but also our *being* free, since we often have the capacity and opportunity to actualize more than one option depending on which we actually choose (Sripada, 2016; Velleman, 1989). Conversely, we are typically unable to choose an option that we have not even considered. Failures of imagination set limits to our freedom.[4]

These capacities for imagination are uniquely well developed in human beings. Few other species have evolved the capacities for "prospection" (or mental time travel), which allow us to represent scenarios far in the future, reason about their probabilities, and vary our representations of them consistent with features we hold fixed, such as the laws of nature or our goals. If other animals, such as apes or corvids, have these capacities, they appear to represent and plan only a short distance into the future (Suddendorf and Corballis, 2007; Gilbert and Wilson, 2007). This capacity appears to be related to and subserved by some of the same neural systems as other representational capacities involved in episodic memory, counterfactual reasoning, and mindreading.[5]

Possessing and exercising these representational capacities, including those involved in imagination, are compatible with the truth of determinism. Indeterminism is not required for it to be possible to imagine alternative future options or for it to be true that each of these options would (likely) occur were we to choose it. All we need here is "epistemic freedom" to veridically believe that nothing prevents us from choosing among incompatible imagined options and that each one would be "made true" by our choosing it (see Velleman, 1989).[6] These capacities are also consistent with naturalism, at least assuming that arguments that conscious mental states must be non-physical are unsound. Assuming these representational capacities are in fact subserved by our remarkably complex brains, then neuropsychological explanations of imagination will offer explanations for much of our experience of free will. And assuming that neural processes involved in imagination and deliberation have appropriate downstream causal effects on our decision-making, then it will be inappropriate to say that these experiences are illusory (Nahmias, 2014).

Why are these capacities for imagination particularly important for free will? First, as Chandra Sripada (2016) convincingly argues, they provide "latitude for self-expression" (see also Seligman, Railton, Baumeister, and Sripada, 2013; Kennett and Matthews, 2009). They allow one to represent one's self in various future situations and evaluate whether each situation best achieves one's goals or even best expresses one's self— whether, for instance, one will be proud of or disappointed with the person one imagines in that situation. Like other animals, humans have the capacity to evaluate some options without consciously considering them, but just as we (presumably) cannot write philosophy papers entirely non-consciously, it seems unlikely that we can evaluate particularly complex options without consciously imagining them first.

Second, barring unlikely neurobiological discoveries suggesting the causal irrelevance of the neural activity that subserves imagination, our imagining options or failing to do so literally opens or closes possibilities for future action. Typically, one cannot successfully carry out complex actions, much less complex plans, unless one has imagined how to do so. Unimagined options are typically not really options. What we imagine is hence a difference-making cause in what we end up doing.

Third, imagination is properly tied to our attributions of responsibility. When we blame other people or ourselves for making poor or immoral decisions, we often say, "You should have known better." The implication is either that you did know better and still chose a worse alternative, perhaps motivated by self-interest or weak exertions of willpower, or that you failed to recognize better options. The latter is a type of failure of imagination. In such cases, it is sometimes true that you possess the capacities to imagine better options and had requisite opportunities (e.g., time) to exercise those capacities, and yet you failed to do so. "Think!" or "Think about how that would make him feel!" we say to our friends or children when they do the wrong thing, often meaning that they should have taken the time to try to imagine the possible (negative) effects of their actions and that nothing prevented them from doing so. Again, concerns clearly arise here about determinism and what counts as a genuine ability or opportunity to exercise capacities differently than one actually does. But our ordinary attributions of responsibility seem to involve inquiry into whether the agent in question possessed the relevant capacities and had a *reasonable* opportunity to exercise them, both of which have plausible analyses consistent with the potential truth of determinism (e.g., Vihvelin, 2013).

If we consciously recognize an option O as a potential action that we have the capacities and opportunity to carry out, and yet we choose not to take it, then we are responsible for choosing not to. If we knew O was a (morally) better option, then we are blameworthy for our choice. Conversely, we can be praiseworthy for imagining the better option, recognizing it as better, and choosing it. However, our control over what options come to mind during deliberation is limited. If we fail to imagine a better option than the one we choose, then it is often difficult to determine whether we "should have (or could have) known better."

Here the role of attention in free will becomes relevant. The idea that we are able to bring to mind particular thoughts *at will* starts to look incoherent if we interpret it to mean that we can represent the content of the thought *before* we represent it or we have to consciously make a non-conscious idea conscious, and such thinking initiates a problematic regress. It is not clear that people think we have such incoherent abilities (contra Harris, 2012). However, we do seem to have some degree of ability (a) to shift our attention towards, for instance, the general question, "Should I think more (or harder) about the consequences of making this choice or about options other than this one?" and (b) to shift our attention away from options that we evaluate as inconsistent with our values and goals, as too risky, as impossible to actualize, as irrelevant, and so on. Developing these capacities for controlling attention as we imagine and evaluate options and their consequences is a significant goal of educating our children, students, and each other. Our capacity for free will improves as we improve our ability to attend to factors that are relevant to our deliberative task and to shift attention away from bad or irrelevant options.

We should be realistic about the extent to which we have *direct* volitional control over our imagination, evaluation, and attention. Instead, we may often control our decisions, to the extent that we do, in more *indirect* ways. These indirect methods, some of which are involved in habituation (7), are another under-explored aspect of our capacities for free will. One habit we may try to inculcate in ourselves and others is to regularly ask the question about whether to try to think more, but also to know when to stop asking it. We also have capacities to habituate, or re-habituate ourselves, so that we manage to act in accord with answers we would offer to these questions *without* having to consider them.

4. Degrees of Freedom and Developing Free Will

For some theories of free will, it is an awkward question when and how children acquire free will, and when and how our ancestors evolved to acquire it, especially within a naturalistic worldview without sharp boundaries based on new metaphysical entities, such as non-physical minds or new types of causation. On naturalistic views, we can examine the structural components of capacities for free will to find some answers to these questions. This view is, however, consistent with threshold distinctions. Animals or infants with no capacity to imagine multiple future options do not possess free will. However, once the relevant capacities are in place, different species and different individuals can possess them to varying degrees. In contrast, existing discussions of free will seem to suggest that one either has it or does not, perhaps because the focus on determinism leads some incompatibilists to conclude we have no free will at all and others (libertarians and compatibilists) to argue that humans can have free will without much consideration of the degrees of freedom we have.[7] Once we understand free will as a set of cognitive capacities, we can better consider what causes breakdowns in free will, including the usual suspects of addiction, compulsions, insanity, and other disorders of motivation or rationality, but also cases less often examined in which people's capacities for imagination or memory may be diminished (Kennett and Matthews, 2009).

In addition to individuals' possessing the capacities for free will to varying degrees, individuals have varying opportunities to exercise these capacities. Opportunities to exercise one's capacities for imagining future options can be limited by external constraints imposed by one's culture (note 4 of this chapter). They can also be limited by situational factors we do not recognize and would not want to influence us if we knew about them (Nahmias, 2007). For instance, in bystander intervention experiments, the presence of passive bystanders prevents some subjects from recognizing the situation as one in which their help is required (see Ross and Nisbett, 1991). Lack of time and energy clearly impose limits on our opportunities to imagine options or properly evaluate them or to exercise self-control. To the degree that we can minimize these limitations, however, we can increase people's opportunities to exercise their free will.

Finally, we have varying degrees of freedom, and potential for developing free will, because of the normative components of the relevant capacities. Our students may have the structural capacities to write philosophy papers and ample opportunity to exercise them, but they have varying abilities to write *good* papers. Determining the normative criteria for possessing effective capacities for, and admirable exercises of, free will is at least as difficult as answering many other normative questions. However, here are three suggestions.

First, there are two "internal" criteria for effectively exercising free will. One is imagining options that will advance one's goals, values, and interests, as one understands them. People succeed in exercising free will to the extent that they imagine new and more effective ways of acting to achieve their own goals and to act in accord with their values. Indeed, people feel more free when they imagine better options and effectively select one, more so than when they simply imagine more options or remain uncertain about which to select (Lau, Hiemisch, and Baumeister, 2015; Nahmias, Morris, Nadelhoffer, and Turner, 2004). A second criterion involves managing to actualize what one has imagined as the best future course of action, primarily by forming effective intentions and plans (5) (Bratman, 1987), exercising self-control as necessary (6), and habituating oneself to act accordingly (7). Both of these internal criteria involve making one's imagined future match the actual future, but neither requires that the goals or values one succeeds in carrying out actually are good, morally or pragmatically.

The third criterion for accomplishing free will is more "external." It involves imagining, evaluating, and actualizing options that advance the goals, values, and interests that one *should* have. Here, the view Frede attributed to historical figures comes to the fore, since it suggests that free will includes the capacity to make choices that will contribute to a good or flourishing life (cf. Wolf, 1990). Again, it takes imagination and creativity to recognize options *better* than existing ones, including for our own life and our culture, and options that are better than our more "default" behaviors (e.g., to be self-interested or to act on immediate motivations rather than on other-directed or long-term interests). To the extent that we can imagine new options, including better goals or values and better ways of achieving existing goals, we gain freedom.

There is a seemingly paradoxical feature of this view. Those individuals who possess to lesser degrees the capacities for free will, or who have worse opportunities to exercise them, will often be the individuals who make bad choices, ones that negatively impact their own and others' lives. If so, the people who make choices we are most inclined to blame, or most resent, are often those who, on this view, are less responsible for those choices. This is a feature we should learn to live with. Once we better understand the limitations on free will, we should accordingly cultivate both forgiveness towards, and a desire to help develop, the capacities and opportunities of those who make bad choices due to these limitations. This response is more humanistic and pragmatic than the one suggested by those who argue that we all lack free will entirely, so that no one genuinely deserves any blame or retributive punishment, a view which suggests we should treat wrongdoers on a disease model that enforces rehabilitation when possible, and quarantine when not (e.g., Harris, 2012; Pereboom, 2014).

It may also turn out that all of us possess the relevant capacities and opportunities to a lesser degree than we tend to think. For instance, we may have limited capacities to prospectively imagine and evaluate options rationally, more often rationalizing our existing motivations and prior decisions. And we may be influenced by unnoticed situational factors or unconscious biases significantly more than we think. If so, then empirical investigation will help us recognize these limitations and may offer ways to overcome them.

5. FREE WILL AS FORWARD-LOOKING

The views developed in this chapter suggest that free will involves a set of skills or knowledge. The capacities for imagining possibilities for action and their potential outcomes allow us to know what we *could* do. The capacities for evaluating these options allow us the potential to know what we *should* do. And the capacities involved in self-control and habituation involve *knowing how* to do what we decide or plan to do.

Agents have free will to the extent that they *possess* these capacities for imagination, decision-making, and self-control. They "have what it takes" to act of their own free will and to be responsible for what they do. Such agents do not always have the *opportunity* to exercise these capacities when they act. They may be constrained by external pressures or persons or compelled by internal pressures in such a way that they have no (or less) reasonable opportunity to exercise their capacities for free will. Without such opportunities, they are typically not responsible (or less responsible) for that action. Finally, agents may or may not actually exercise their capacities for free will even when they do have the opportunity to. If they do, they will typically be responsible (and blameworthy for bad choices, unless they could not be expected to have known relevant obligations or information). If they do *not* exercise their capacities for choice and control even though they had the opportunity, then they are also typically responsible, in this case for their failure of imagination, attention, or effort ("You should have known better" or "You should have tried harder"). Hence, if agents are not *exempt* because they lack the relevant capacities for free will or if agents are not *excused* because they lack the relevant opportunity to exercise these capacities, then they are responsible for what they do. They deserve credit or blame for their actions; they are an appropriate target of gratitude or resentment; it may be fair to reward or punish them (Strawson, 1962).[8]

Those used to the traditional philosophical debates about free will may still be wondering how the capacities for free will described here help answer the long-standing worries about determinism or more recent worries about naturalism. This chapter has not focused on answering arguments that free will is incompatible with determinism or naturalism. Some evidence suggests that the default or intuitive view is neither incompatibilist nor non-naturalist (Murray and Nahmias, 2014; Nahmias, Shepard, and Reuter, 2014), in which case, compatibilists should not play defense so much. Rather, we should offer the most viable positive account of how our capacities for imagination, decision-making, and self-control work and how they explain our experiences of and beliefs about free will, and whether they support our practices of moral and legal responsibility. We can then consider whether they require indeterminism or more "metaphysically robust" powers.

In this chapter we have focused on the forward-looking features of free will, especially our psychological capacity to imagine future possibilities that do not yet exist, as well as capacities to shift our attention towards possibilities that cohere with our goals and values and to habituate ourselves to act accordingly. Once we focus on these capacities, we can ask whether they could exist and have the appropriate causal relations with future behavior if it turned out that determinism or naturalism were true.

Responding to the "bottom-up" problem of naturalism is relatively easy. It is a mistake to think that our forward-looking capacities are causally irrelevant, or bypassed, if they are subserved by neural processes. Instead, naturalism simply suggests that we will eventually understand *how* free will works in the brain, not that we will or should come to see it as an illusion *because* it works in the brain. Assuming that the eventual neurobiological theory of our conscious representational capacities does not eliminate their causal role in decision-making and action, there is no reason to think naturalism threatens free will (Nahmias, 2014). That "my brain did it" does not compete with *my* having done, and recognizing this allows us to see that naturalism does not entail *bypassing* of our conscious selves or of our capacity to shape our future lives based on what we imagine them to be.

The "backwards-looking" problem of determinism is more difficult to brush aside. One worry is that determinism would entail that we can never do otherwise, never have an opportunity to exercise our capacities for choice differently than we actually do. Though it will not satisfy many incompatibilists, this worry is best addressed by arguing that the ability to do otherwise, holding fixed *all* conditions and laws, is not the best analysis of the capacities and opportunities required for free and responsible agency (e.g., Vihvelin, 2013).

Another worry is that determinism would entail that we are not the *causal source* of our decisions because they have prior causes ultimately beyond our control (this worry does not dissipate even if some causal relations are indeterministic). Again, by focusing on the forward-looking causal effects of our capacity to actualize one, among several, imagined future options, we can recognize that determinism does not entail bypassing of these causal effects, which will diffuse some of the more intuitive threats from determinism (Murray and Nahmias, 2014). Furthermore, determinism does not entail that there are any *particular* variables beyond our control (e.g., in the distant past) that cause our decisions; instead, our deliberations are the nexus of an ever-expanding set of prior causes, such that, among those causes, our exercising our capacities for free will will often be the causal difference-maker, or most significant causal explanation, for our actions. Even if determinism is true, no variable better explains some of our decisions than the variables involved in our imagining and evaluating future options (Deery and Nahmias, 2017).

Even if one imagines that some further condition for free will would somehow provide a more satisfying response to these alleged threats from naturalism or determinism, the capacities for free will discussed in this chapter are a psychological accomplishment. We can imagine and write our own stories in impressive ways that open up real options unavailable to creatures lacking these capacities.[9]

NOTES

1. Whether free will requires that some of those laws are indeterministic is another question, but indeterminism is possible even if physicalism is true (as quantum physics shows), and such indeterminism might influence neural processes during human decision-making (see Kane, 1996). Conversely, some problems allegedly posed by determinism remain even assuming a non-naturalist metaphysics (e.g., the impossibility of self-creation; Strawson, 1986).
2. For instance, compatibilists Fischer and Ravizza (1998), Nelkin (2011), Wolf (1990), "agnostic" Mele (2006), libertarian Kane (1996), and skeptics about free will, Double (1991) and G. Strawson (1986).
3. I am not claiming that any of the processes involved in 1–6 always occur with conscious awareness. We may be able to non-consciously evaluate options or form plans. It is an empirical question whether such processes can occur as effectively without conscious

awareness as with it, but there is some evidence that conscious awareness is required for at least some complex mental processes and behaviors (Baumeister et al., 2011; Levy, 2014).

4. While free will is often treated as an internal feature of agents (as in the trope that the prisoner in chains is unfree yet still has free will to choose how to react to imprisonment), this view neglects the importance of imagination to free will. Our circumstances can limit our opportunities for imagining options: we do not control which alternatives pop into consciousness as we consider what to do and we are not able to choose unimagined alternatives. For instance, regardless of their capacities, most women during most of history have been raised such that they lacked the opportunity to imagine many options for future action open to men. Such constraints, though not literal chains, limited women's opportunities to exercise their capacities for free will, such that these external constraints imposed internal constraints.

5. These capacities are subserved by the "default network" in the brain, active when people are not carrying out other tasks and are instead mind-wandering or imagining (Raichle and Snyder, 2007). It is possible that our capacities for imagination are dependent on, and evolved as side effects from, our capacities for "mindreading" (prediction and explanation of others' behavior based on their mental states), which requires the ability to represent information not directly perceived but inferred from observable behavior. Human mind-reading capacities may have evolved as part of a feedback loop of selection pressures for increasingly subtle deception and detection of deception within complex cooperative relationships (including reciprocal altruism). If so, then our ancestors ("Adam and Eve") gained free will from the fruit of knowledge of other minds and from the sins of subtly manipulating each others' minds and avoiding such manipulation.

6. However, our experience of imagining alternative options, while we hold fixed other conditions, might help to explain our experience of choice as indeterministic (see Deery, 2015).

7. Note that compatibilism is just a claim about the possibility of free will in a deterministic universe, not the thesis that humans actually have it. Yet historically, all compatibilists have suggested that humans have free will and have focused little attention on other potential threats to free will (e.g., epiphenomenalism or limitations on our capacities for rational decision-making) or the degree to which such threats may be actual for humans. "Cagey compatibilism" is my name for the view that says determinism is irrelevant to free will but that other theses and potential scientific findings are relevant to free will and could suggest we have less than we think.

8. We should say "may be" fair because there are moral questions about when and what types of punishment are fair that go beyond questions of free will. Compatibilists are sometimes expected to establish that we can have the sort of free will that justifies retributive punishment, but there may be independent reasons to reject the fairness of some forms of retribution.

9. For helpful comments on this chapter, I thank Chandra Sripada, Andrea Scarantino, Oisin Deery, Adina Roskies, and participants at a workshop at the Center for the Philosophy of Freedom at the University of Arizona.

References

Baumeister, R. F., Masicampo, E. J., and Vohs, K. D., 2011. Do conscious thoughts cause behavior? *Annual Review of Psychology*, 62, pp.331–361.

Bratman, M., 1987. *Intentions, plans, and practical reason.* Cambridge, MA: Harvard University Press.

Deery, O., 2015. Why people believe in indeterminist free will. *Philosophical Studies*, 172(8), pp.2033–2054.

Deery, O., Davis, T., and Carey, J., 2015. The free-will intuitions scale and the question of natural compatibilism. *Philosophical Psychology*, 28(6), pp.808–814.

Deery, O., and Nahmias, E., 2017. Defeating manipulation arguments: interventionist causation and compatibilist sourcehood. *Philosophical Studies*, 174, pp. 1255–1276.

Double, R., 1991. *The non-reality of free will.* New York: Oxford University Press.

Ekstrom, L., 2000. *Free will: a philosophical study.* Boulder: Westview Press.

Fischer, J. M., and Ravizza, M., 1998. *Responsibility and control: a theory of moral responsibility.* Cambridge: Cambridge University Press.

Frankfurt, H., 1969. Alternate possibilities and moral responsibility. In: *The importance of what we care about.* 1988. Cambridge: Cambridge University Press. pp.1–10.

Frankfurt, H., 1971. Freedom of the will and the concept of a person. In *The importance of what we care about.* 1988. Cambridge: Cambridge University Press. pp.11–25.

Frankfurt, H., 1993. On the necessity of ideals. In *Necessity, volition, and love.* 1999. Cambridge: Cambridge University Press. pp.108–116.

Frede, M., 2012. *A free will: origins of the notion in ancient thought.* Berkeley: University of California Press.

Harris, S., 2012. *Free will.* New York: Free Press.

Gilbert, D., and Wilson, T., 2007. Prospection: experiencing the future. *Science*, 317(5843), pp.1351–1354.

Kane, R., 1996. *The significance of free will.* New York: Oxford University Press.

Kennett, J., and Matthews, S., 2009. Mental time travel, agency and responsibility. In: M. Bortolotti, ed. *Psychiatry as cognitive neuroscience: philosophical perspectives.* New York: Oxford University Press. pp.327–350.

Lau, S. Hiemisch, A., and Baumeister, R., 2015. The experience of freedom in decisions: questioning philosophical beliefs in favor of psychological determinants. *Consciousness and Cognition*, 33, pp.30–46.

Levy, N., 2014. *Consciousness and moral responsibility.* New York: Oxford University Press.

McKenna, M., and Coates, D. J., 2015. Compatibilism. In: E. Zalta, ed. *Stanford encyclopedia of philosophy.* (Fall 2014 Edition). http://plato.stanford.edu/archives/fall2014/entries/compatibilism/.

Mele, A., 2006. *Free will and luck.* New York: Oxford University Press.

Monroe, A., and Malle, B., 2010. From uncaused will to conscious choice: The need to study, not speculate about people's folk concept of free will. *Review of Philosophy and Psychology*, 1(2), pp.211–224.

Murray, D., and Nahmias, E., 2014. Explaining away incompatibilist intuitions. *Philosophy and Phenomenological Research*, 88(2), pp.434–467.

Nahmias, E., 2007. Autonomous agency and social psychology. In: M. Marraffa, M. Caro, and F. Ferretti, eds. *Cartographies of the mind.* Dortrecht: Springer. pp.169–185.

Nahmias, E., 2014. Is free will an illusion? Confronting challenges from the modern mind sciences. In: W. Sinnott-Armstrong, ed. *Moral psychology, vol. 4: Free will and moral responsibility.* Cambridge, MA: MIT Press. pp.1–25.

Nahmias, E., Morris, S., Nadelhoffer T., and Turner, J., 2004. The phenomenology of free will. *Journal of Consciousness Studies*, 11(7–8), pp.162–179.

Nahmias, E., Shepard, J., and Reuter, S., 2014. It's OK if "my brain made me do it": people's intuitions about free will and neuroscientific prediction. *Cognition*, 133(2), pp.502–513.

Nelkin, D., 2011. *Making sense of freedom and responsibility*. New York: Oxford University Press.

O'Connor, T., 2000. *Persons and causes: the metaphysics of free will*. New York: Oxford University Press.

O'Connor, T., 2014. Free will. In: E. Zalta, ed. *Stanford encyclopedia of philosophy*. (Fall 2014 Edition). http://plato.stanford.edu/archives/fall2014/entries/freewill/.

Pereboom, D., 2014. *Free will, agency, and meaning in life*. New York: Oxford University Press.

Raichle, M. E., and Snyder, A. Z., 2007. A default mode of brain function: a brief history of an evolving idea. *Neuroimage*, 37(4), pp.1083–1090.

Reid, T., 1788. Essays on the active powers of man. In T. Nadelhoffer, E. Nahmias, and S. Nichols, eds. *Moral Psychology: Historical and Contemporary Readings*. New York: Wiley-Blackwell. pp.236–245.

Ross, L., and Nisbett, R., 1991. *The person and the situation: perspectives of social psychology*. New York: McGraw-Hill.

Scanlon, T. M., 2008. *Moral dimensions: permissibility, meaning, blame*. Cambridge, MA: Harvard University Press.

Schaeffer, G. A., Kahane, G., and Savulescu, J., 2014. Autonomy and enhancement. *Neuroethics*, 7(2), pp.123–136.

Seligman, M., Railton, P., Baumeister, R., and Sripada, C., 2013. Navigating into the future or driven by the past. *Perspectives on Psychological Science*, 8(2), pp.119–141.

Sripada, C., 2016. Free will and the construction of options. *Philosophical Studies*. doi: 10.1007/s11098-016-0643-1

Strawson, G., 1986. *Freedom and belief*. Oxford: Clarendon Press.

Strawson, P., 1962. Freedom and resentment. *Proceedings of the British Academy*, 48, pp.1–25.

Suddendorf, T., and Corballis, M., 2007. The evolution of foresight: what is mental time travel, and is it unique to humans? *Behavioral & Brain Sciences*, 30(3), pp.299–313.

van Inwagen, P., 1983. *An essay on free will*. Oxford: Oxford University Press.

van Inwagen, P., 2008. How to think about the problem of free will. *Journal of Ethics*, 12(3/4), pp.327–341.

Velleman, D., 1989. Epistemic freedom. *Pacific Philosophical Quarterly*, 70(1), pp.73–97.

Vihvelin, K., 2013. *Causes, laws, and free will: why determinism doesn't matter*. New York: Oxford University Press.

Wallace, J., 1993. *Responsibility and the moral sentiments*. Cambridge, MA: Harvard University Press.

Wolf, S., 1990. *Freedom within reason*. New York: Oxford University Press.

Wolf, S., 2015. Responsibility, moral and otherwise. *Inquiry*, 58, pp.127–142.

CHAPTER 28

PRISONERS OF MISBELIEF

The Epistemic Conditions of Freedom

ALLEN BUCHANAN

THIS chapter will show that those who value freedom—and those who theorize it—should pay more attention to its epistemic conditions. More specifically, they should attend more to the fact that misbeliefs (false or unjustified beliefs) can make our actions unfree. Even on a relatively thin conception of freedom, according to which it is the absence of interference with one's doing what one wants (or even more narrowly, interference by other agents), misbelief can make us seriously unfree in several ways.

Although the chapter will focus on making the case that misbelief can seriously undercut freedom, its broader aim is to show that the same considerations that make freedom important behoove us to be more critical about our beliefs. So even if the conception of freedom deployed in this chapter is subject to criticism, or even if the best way to capture the damage done by misbelief is not best expressed in terms of its making us unfree, this broader aim will have nonetheless been achieved.

Oscar Wilde once quipped that many a young man has made a proposal of marriage in lighting conditions under which he would not venture to purchase a cheap necktie. Similarly, all of us tend to ingest beliefs—and become shaped or misshaped by them—in the most casual fashion. This chapter seeks to show that anyone who wants to avoid being a puppet controlled by others, and who is committed to leading a life of integrity, self-direction, and self-knowledge, ought to be much more concerned about the problem of misbelief than people generally and moral theorists typically are. For cognitively flawed but belief-driven creatures like us, who get most of our beliefs secondhand through the "testimony" of others, such concern is mandatory, both morally and prudentially. Furthermore, as I shall show, when our misbeliefs make us unfree, it is by virtue of our exercise of what for many of us is one of our most valued capacities, our practical reason. To avoid having our basic moral commitments, our own welfare, and our own practical reason subverted, we need to develop, as individuals and collectively, sound strategies for avoiding at least the most typically dangerous misbeliefs.

1. The Epistemic Conditions of Freedom

Perhaps the thinnest—that is, most austere—yet still plausible conception of freedom is this: one is free in the absence of interference with one's doing what one wants to do. Although this conception is thicker than a conception according to which it is only interference by other agents that makes us unfree, it is thicker than some more "positive" conceptions, including the notion that one is free just in case one is able to do what one wants to do. Interference undercuts freedom when it makes one unable to do what one wants to do, but there are many things that can render one *unable* to do what one wants and not all cases of inability are due to *interference*, as will shortly be seen. For now, we will only observe that there are good reasons not to think that every sort of inability to do what one wants makes one unfree. For one thing, if one is unable to do what one wants because one lacks the money necessary to implement one's plans, it is more conducive to a clear moral assessment of one's situation to say so (and then ask whether one's lack of money is an injustice) than to say that one is unfree. For another, and more importantly, if we define freedom as the ability to do what one wants to do, then it follows that we are all massively unfree—and unfree in so many disparate ways, most of which are utterly inconsequential—that the term "freedom" is sapped of the power that it usually conveys. For example, to say that all humans are unfree because none of them can run a mile in one minute or produce bark rather than skin seems odd and rather unhelpful.

Be that as it may, to accomplish the aims of this chapter we need not pretend to settle the dispute between advocates of thinner vs. thicker conceptions of freedom. Instead, we will assume *arguendo* a relatively thin notion, according to which one is free if nothing interferes with one's doing what one wants, on the understanding that not every sort of inability counts as an interference. The nub of the distinction between inability and interference is that interference is one particular way that inability can come about: an interference is something that disrupts a process by which one comes to act. If it can be shown that misbelief makes us unfree on the thin conception, then *a fortiori* we will have shown that it does so on the thick conception according to which one is unfree whenever one is unable to do what one wants, regardless of whether inability is the result of interference or of something else.

Before proceeding, it should be noted that philosophers of freedom have long understood that misbeliefs can lead to unfreedom in an *indirect* manner. In particular, the classical liberals or libertarians among them have emphasized that over-optimistic beliefs about the ability of government to improve human well-being (and about the dominant motivations of government officials) have contributed to the emergence of political arrangements that impair freedom. The concern here, however, is with more direct connections between misbelief and freedom—connections that have generally been neglected in theorizing freedom.

1.1. How misbeliefs about what one is doing can make one unfree

If freedom is absence of interference with one's doing what one wants, then misbeliefs can make one unfree when they involve a fundamental misunderstanding of what one is doing when one acts. For example, if I kill you because I believe I am Alexander the Great and you are a charging war elephant whose driver is resisting my invasion of northwest India, my action is not free. My egregiously false, indeed delusional, beliefs interfere with my doing what I want to do in this sense: they result in my acting in ways that cannot achieve my aim because they lead me to have an aim that is unsatisfiable. My false belief produces an action (trying to kill you) that is massively inappropriate, given what I am trying to do (stop a charging war elephant). The action I perform cannot possibly realize my intention, not just because my intention is unrealizable but because my action cannot even come close to realizing that intention were it realizable (even if I were being charged by a war elephant, my killing you wouldn't help). The gap between what I want to do and my action that the false belief produces is much too great to make even an approximation of success possible.

The consequences for the agent herself of acting on the basis of wildly delusional beliefs can clearly be as bad as or worse than the consequences of other agents interfering with one's doing what one wants to do. In the example just given, my proximate want (here we could just as well say "desire" or "intention") is to stop a charging war elephant, but of course I will not be able to do that because there is no elephant there to be stopped. More importantly, my acting on the false belief that you are a charging war elephant will prevent me from doing something I want to do, namely, avoid killing an innocent person. And if you are in fact my friend, my delusional beliefs will interfere with my achieving something more specific: avoiding hurting you. Finally, my delusion will also interfere with my achieving something else I presumably want to do, namely, determine how to act in a reasonably rational (or at least in a not grossly irrational) way. It is appropriate to talk of interference in all of these instances because the false beliefs disrupt or derail the processes involving the coordination of judgment and volition that are involved in my doing what I want to do, when I exercise my capacity for practical rationality in determining what to do.

Although, for reasons already given, it is questionable to define freedom as the ability to do what one wants (and hence to say that one is unfree whenever one is unable to do what one wants), all the points to be made in what follows could be framed using that definition. For those who prefer to define freedom as the ability to do what one wants, the main thesis can be reframed as follows: misbeliefs can make one unfree when they make one unable to do what one wants by interfering with one's doing it—that is, disrupting the process that connects willing and acting. Later we will qualify this claim, noting that not all interferences are serious enough to qualify as interferences that make us unfree.

1.2. How false beliefs about the circumstances in which one acts can impair freedom

Consider another, less extreme example. If I back out of my driveway and inadvertently smash a kitten who has been sleeping under the fender atop my right front tire, my action is not free in this sense: I wanted to traverse the driveway safely, but my misbelief that all was clear interfered with my doing so.[1] I did not do what I wanted (and intended) to do, because of my misbelief. My misbelief resulted in my coming to act in a way that I would not have acted, given what I want to do, had I possessed true beliefs about the consequences of my acting.[2]

Acknowledging that misbeliefs can make us unfree does not commit one to a broader "positive" conception of freedom, because not everything that prevents one from doing what one wants counts as *interference* with one's doing what one wants. My lack of money renders me unable to satisfy my desire to purchase my own private island in the Caribbean, but it does not interfere with my satisfying that desire in this sense: it does not disrupt or derail the process by which I come to act, at least if that process is minimally rational. The role that the belief that I have insufficient funds plays in that process is not that of a disruptor; rather, in determining what to do, I *should* take the fact that I have very limited funds into account. To fail to take it into account would be a major error, one that would render my course of action deeply irrational.

In contrast, the belief that you are a charging war elephant *should not* play a role in the processes by which I come to act, and the fact that it does play a role causes the process to derail, severing the proper connection between my willing and doing.

My false belief that all is clear as I back out of the driveway interferes with my realizing my desire to back out safely, just as my belief that you are a charging war elephant interferes with my satisfying my desire to avoid killing an innocent person. In both the charging war elephant case and the smashed kitten case, a false belief throws a spanner in a process of coming to act, with the result that I do not achieve what I want. It renders me unable to do what I want, but in a special way: by means of disrupting or subverting the connection between willing and acting, via false beliefs. The false beliefs in both cases should not figure, but do figure in my determining what to do. Accordingly, we can speak of the misbeliefs as interfering with my doing what I want to do.

So, even if we adopt a narrow conception of freedom as absence of interference with one's getting what one wants and reject the "positive freedom" idea that one is unfree whenever one is unable to realize one's desires, freedom still has epistemic conditions. More specifically, misbeliefs can deprive us of freedom in at least two ways: by causing us grossly to misunderstand what we are doing (the charging war elephant case) or by causing us to make a serious mistake (given our priorities) as to the circumstances of our acting (the smashed kitten case). We get the same result if we define freedom as the ability to do what one wants: misbelief can make us unable to do what we want in its own distinctive way, by disrupting the process that connects willing and acting. Note that "disruption" here is a normative notion: misbelief can cause the process that connects willing and acting to proceed as it ought not to do.

1.3. How false beliefs about effective means can impair freedom

Suppose that I want to drive to a shop I have seen advertised because it has an item on sale that I very much want. I falsely believe that the shop is in Paris, Texas (which is only a few miles away), when it fact it is in Paris, France. This false belief disrupts—or one might say derails—the process by which I come to attempt to secure the item I desire. It causes me to choose an utterly inappropriate means of getting the item I want, namely, driving to Paris, Texas instead of going to Paris, France. Even worse, had I known that the shop was in Paris, France, I would have decided that the item I sought wasn't worth the cost of getting it. So, if freedom is the absence of interference with doing what one wants to do, it is this misbelief, which leads me to opt for an entirely inappropriate means of getting what I want, that makes my action unfree.

Consider now another case where I have a false belief that leads me to opt for an inappropriate means for achieving what I desire. I want to remove a screw from a piece of machinery and falsely believe that using a screwdriver with a one-quarter-inch flat head is the best means of doing so, when in fact a three-eighths-inch flat head is the best tool for the job. The one-quarter-inch flat head works well enough, but not quite optimally. This is a case of a false belief interfering with my doing what I want to do, namely, use the best screwdriver for the job; but it seems implausible to say it renders me unfree. From the standpoint of freedom, my reaching for the one-quarter-inch screwdriver and reaching for the three-eighths-inch screwdriver seem indistinguishable.

So here we appear to have a counterexample—either to the claim that freedom is absence of interference with doing what one wants to do or to the claim that freedom is undercut when false beliefs interfere with one's doing what one wants to do. Because, as previously explained, the claim that freedom is absence of interference with what one wants to do has its attractions, it would seem that the proper response to our intuitions in the screwdriver case is to say that in the case of false beliefs, at least, not just any sort of interference deserves to be called instances of unfreedom, but only what might be called significant disruptions of the processes by which motivation, implicit background beliefs, judgment, and intention coordinate to determine action. To put the same point differently: a false belief makes one unfree only if it produces a major discrepancy between what one wills and what one does. In normative terms, false belief makes one unfree only if it leads one to take into account something that it is seriously irrational to take into account or fail to take into account something that it is seriously irrational not to take into account in determining how to act. The screwdriver case does not fit this characterization, but the war elephant, smashed kitten, and wrong Paris cases do.

In other words, what makes it implausible to say that the screwdriver example is a case of unfreedom is precisely what differentiates it from all the preceding examples: in the screwdriver case, unlike the other cases, the false belief does not result in a *significant* disruption of the complex process by which I come to act—that is, a disruption that creates a major discrepancy between my will and my action, thereby making my action subject to the charge of being irrational. In spite of my false belief, I am still able to unscrew the screw.

So, it would seem that whether a false belief renders one unfree depends on the extent—or perhaps more accurately, the normative seriousness—of the discrepancy that the belief causes between what one wills to do and what one does. In the war elephant case, the smashed kitty case, and the wrong Paris case, there is a great discrepancy: from the standpoint of how one should come to act, things have gone seriously wrong. Not so in the screwdriver case.

In saying that misbelief can make us unfree when it sufficiently disrupts the connection between willing and acting, the term "willing" emphasizes how misbelief can disrupt the process by which one comes to act *when one is exercising one's capacity for practical rationality*. Only beings that have that capacity can be unfree due to their misbeliefs. In other words, the interference that misbeliefs produce is parasitic on our practical rationality. The interference occurs when we exercise our capacity for practical rationality in determining how to act, but when this particular exercise is corrupted by virtue of the content of the beliefs on which it operates. In the cases described above, we are the agents of our own unfreedom in this sense: We use our practical rationality to determine how to act, but our misbeliefs cause us to exercise our practical rationality in a way that makes it subject to serious criticism from the standpoint of practical rationality. If it were true that I was Alexander and you were a charging war elephant, then given my ends (as Alexander), killing you would be rational. Yet because of the content of the beliefs upon which my practical rationality operates, I act in a profoundly irrational way. I do not take into account the facts I should take into account and I take into account what is not the case. If all were clear in the driveway, then my putting the car into reverse and gently stepping on the gas would be a rational means toward my end of exiting the driveway safely. But it is not, because I am mistaken in my belief that all is clear. The threat to freedom that misbeliefs pose is due to our rationality. In that sense we are not only prisoners of misbelief; as agents—beings capable of practical rationality—we are also our own jailers.

Some philosophers of freedom who would describe themselves as classical liberals or libertarians might endorse an even thinner conception of freedom according to which one is free only if *no other agent* interferes with one's doing what one wants to do. They would conclude that none of the cases discussed so far are instances of unfreedom.

Now one can see the value of a strategic emphasis, in the context of doing political philosophy, of focusing *first* on that subset of interferences that are due to the actions of other agents, just as one can see the plausibility of Republican theories as a way of according priority, in the project of designing political institutions, to avoiding domination. But it would be just as incorrect to say that the only thing that counts as freedom (or the only important freedom) is absence of interference by other agents as it would be to say that the only thing (or the only important thing) to take into account in the design of political institutions is the avoidance of domination. Absent a sound argument to show that taking into account other values besides the avoidance of domination is infeasible or unavoidably likely to backfire in some serious way, there is no reason for an exclusive focus only on domination if the goal is to design good political institutions. Similarly, there is no reason to hold that from the standpoint of freedom, only interferences by other agents matter.

Nevertheless, even if it were true that freedom, or the most important kind of freedom, was absence of interference by other agents with one's doing what one wants, it would still be the case that freedom has epistemic conditions—and that misbeliefs can make us unfree. I may interfere with your doing what you want by fostering a false belief in you about what are the effective or necessary means toward your doing what you want—if that belief produces a sufficiently serious discrepancy between what you will and what you do. For example, suppose that you want to get a particular job. You mistakenly think that I am giving you sound advice for how to comport yourself in the interview. I tell you that the interviewer loves football and that you should spend a good deal of time in the interview talking about the latest big game. In fact, I know that he loathes football and takes a dim view of people who talk about sports or other leisure activities in interviews. I deliberately interfere with your getting what you want (a successful interview and beyond that a job) by planting a false belief that will, as it were, radically de-couple what you will from what you do. It is true both that I interfered with your getting what you want and that the false belief did so. I interfered with your getting what you want by planting a belief that not only interfered with your acting so as to get what you want, but also did so in such a way as to lead you to choose an utterly counterproductive means for achieving what you desired. The false belief I planted in you resulted in a gross discrepancy between your will and your action and thereby made your action unfree.

To take a more sinister but all too familiar sort of case: propagandists for unjust wars and genocides routinely foster false beliefs about the threats that other groups pose (inventing the threats out of whole cloth or grossly exaggerating them), and these misbeliefs interfere with people's doing some rather important things most of us want to do, including avoiding killing innocent people and avoiding subjecting ourselves to serious risks when we are in fact not in danger. Like the misbeliefs in the war elephant, smashed kitten, wrong Paris, and interview examples, these misbeliefs interfere with one's doing what one wants in this sense: they disrupt the process one normally goes through—and *should* go through—in determining to act, with the consequence that one does not do what one wants to do. The disruptions are significant enough to make us unfree, given that they lead people to do things that are inconsistent with some of their most basic priorities. In that sense, the discrepancy the false beliefs create between what they do and their most stable and strongest priorities is great, and the disruption the false belief causes can rightly be called significant.

1.4. How misbeliefs can make us unfree by limiting our awareness of options

In the preceding two sections respectively it has been argued that misbelief can make one unfree in three distinct ways: by leading one radically to misconceive what one is doing (the war elephant case), by leading one seriously to misunderstand the circumstances in which one is acting (the smashed kitten case), and by causing one to choose an utterly inappropriate means toward doing what one wants to do (the wrong Paris and interview cases). In all three types of cases, misbelief disrupts the process by which action originates, producing a significant discrepancy between the agent's will and what he does, and thereby rendering the resulting action unfree, even if it still qualifies as an action as opposed to a mere movement whose proximate origins are outside us. There is also a fourth, more subtle epistemic condition for freedom: misbelief can interfere with one's doing what one wants to do by causing one to overlook options which, if taken, would enable one to do what one wants (or avoid doing what one wants to avoid doing).

Suppose that, due to low self-esteem fostered by unduly pessimistic parental expectations, a student falsely believes that she is "not college material," and as a result of having this belief does not apply to college. Suppose also that the student would have been admitted to college, had she applied, and would have had a successful college career. Her false belief resulted in her considering a truncated set of options and that interfered with her doing what she wanted to do. If she wanted to choose the best alternative for what do after high school that she was capable of or if she wanted to go about deciding what to do in a reasonable and thorough manner, then her misbelief about her own capabilities interfered with her doing what she wanted and hence made her choice unfree. It also resulted in her doing something she did not want to do, namely, make a decision without considering all the important feasible options. Further, given what was at stake in the decision, we can say that here, too, false belief created a normatively significant discrepancy between what the agent wills and what she does. Because of a misbelief, she failed to consider an option she should have considered and failure to consider it rendered the decision seriously irrational, given what was at stake.

1.5. How shared misbeliefs can impair collective freedom

Sometimes misbeliefs, if shared by sufficient numbers of people who are in a position to influence the direction of policy, can produce mistakenly pessimistic views about the possibilities for progressive social change, and this too can result in a failure to consider all the relevant options. Alternatively, it may merely lead people to dismiss as unfeasible options that are in fact quite viable. In either case, the misbelief can interfere with our doing what we want to do and with our avoiding doing what we want not to do. As examples of misbeliefs that fit this description consider (1) the Just World Hypothesis (a common cognitive bias) and (2) the false empirical assumptions about the inevitability of life-or-death international conflict that were central to the nationalist version of Social Darwinist ideology.

The Just World View is the belief that in general people get what they deserve—for example, that the industrious prosper and the idle do not (Hafer and Olson, 1998; Lerner, 1980). When combined with the cognitive error known as confirmation bias (which will lead one to overlook or discount apparent injustices, if one already holds the Just World View), the Just World View can result in the belief that major social reforms are not needed, especially if one also believes that attempts to achieve major social reforms are risky. In brief, one may believe that injustices are the exception, not the norm, and that proposals for major social reforms are misguided and even dangerous. If this belief is widely shared, genuine possibilities for progressive change will be overlooked entirely or, if acknowledged at all, rejected as too risky or costly. Such misbeliefs, if widely held, can interfere with *our* doing what we want to do, just as they can interfere with an individual's doing what she wants to do. More specifically, assuming that we want to take justice properly into account in collective decision-making and, more generally, want to improve social conditions, shared misbeliefs that underestimate the extent of injustice can interfere with our acting together to do what we want to do and hence make or collective actions unfree.

Consider a less extreme example. Suppose that many people are unaware of the extent of institutionalized racism and specific racial policies (like exclusion of blacks from many of the benefits of the New Deal and the G.I. Bill) in recent U.S. history (Katznelson, 2013). As a result, they underestimate the extent of the continuing negative effects of racism in the United States. Their false beliefs about the extent of the legacy of racism result in their making mistaken judgments about what the priorities should be for U.S. domestic policy. Moreover, if one fails to appreciate how extensive the destructive legacy of institutionalized racism is, one may also fail to appreciate how often it is not the case that people get what they deserve, and this may reinforce whatever tendency one has to espouse the Just World View. That in turn may lead one to think that the rectification of racial injustices generally should be a relatively minor focus of public policy deliberations. Such misbeliefs, if widespread, not only interfere with individual voters doing what they want to do (deciding how to vote in a way that reflects the proper priorities for domestic policy); they also interfere with collective decisions regarding policy priorities. In such cases, our freedom as individuals as well as our collective freedom is undercut by false beliefs.

Theorists of ideology have often focused on this kind of unfreedom. They have proceeded on the assumption that the major question that a theory of ideology should answer is this: why do the numerous people who are victims of an unjust social order put up with it; why do they not rise up and crush the relatively small number of their oppressors? The answer cannot simply be that they are coerced, because the coercive resources of the majority would not be sufficient to maintain their domination if the oppressed refused to cooperate in oppressing their fellows. Rather, it must be that their servitude is due in significant part to their mistaken belief that the social order is not unjust, or at least that the exercise of political power is legitimate. On one especially plausible definition of ideological beliefs, their distinctive character is that they are beliefs that people come to have through processes of belief formation that are epistemically defective, that function to support unjustly unequal social arrangements, and that are pervasive *because* they perform this function (Rosen, 1996: 47). For example, many of the people who are the worst victims of an unjust social order may be enculturated into the belief that their disadvantages are God's will or the result of their own failures, when in fact they have other causes, rooted in the unjust ways in which the social structure shapes people's life prospects. If such beliefs are sufficiently widespread and resilient, the collective action needed to overturn or reform the unjust social arrangements will not be forthcoming. Ideology theory has often emphasized the ways in which ideological beliefs impair freedom, but the contemporary philosophical friends of freedom, especially those of the libertarian variety, have paid little attention to ideology and have not viewed it as a component of a philosophy of freedom.[3]

As a second example of shared misbeliefs making us collectively unfree—and doing so with disastrous consequences—consider how adherence to Social Darwinism appears to have encouraged some leaders to go to war in the twentieth century and led large segments of the population to support their leaders' decisions. Some of the most widely held versions of this ideology included the view that lethally violent conflict among nations was inevitable—indeed, that world history was an arena in which nations fought for dominance and where losing the battle for dominance meant literal extinction or at least servitude.

If this belief is widespread among leaders and the publics whose support is needed to make their decisions effective, it may become a self-fulfilling prophecy. The belief in the inevitability of violent conflict encourages the strategy of the first strike, or in Hobbesian terms, adherence to the Principle of Anticipation. Indeed, it is not even necessary that all or most leaders believe in the extreme nationalist version of Social Darwinism; it is enough that some believe that some others do. Under these conditions, preventive war becomes rational and, to the extent that it is rational, more likely to occur.

Social scientists have shown that leaders who accepted Social Darwinism's factual claims about the nature of interactions were biased toward "preventive" aggression and that they typically attempted to justify striking first on grounds of "necessity" (Jervis, 1976; Kershaw, 2007). The alleged necessity here is rational necessity. Given the requisite premises about the inevitability of violent conflict among nations and the assumptions about how disastrous losing will be, it is rational for each nation to attempt to strike first, even if the result is egregiously sub-optimal for all. To put the same point differently: false beliefs can turn situations where there are genuine opportunities for mutually beneficial cooperation into insoluble collective action problems; and failure to solve the collective action problems can interfere with our doing what we want to do and from avoiding doing what we want not to do.

Further, if enough people believe that violent conflict is inevitable and opportunities for enduring peaceful relations are negligible, then there will be an asymmetry between the risks of false positives and false negatives regarding the other's hostile intentions: a mistaken belief that the other is hostile will have less bad consequences than a mistaken belief that he is not hostile. Under these conditions, rationality may require striking first.

In both of these examples, there is a grim irony: misbeliefs make us unfree by leading us to underestimate the extent of our freedom. Our belief that we are unfree robs us of our freedom, because it interferes with our identifying or taking seriously options for action which, if taken, would enable us to do what we want to do and avoid what we want to avoid. We are prisoners of our own beliefs and we construct our prison through the exercise of our practical rationality.

2. THE SOURCES OF MISBELIEF

So far, this chapter has shown how misbeliefs can make us unfree regardless of whether freedom is understood as the absence of interference with one's doing what one wants or as the ability to do what we want, provided that the interference significantly disrupts the connection between willing and acting. A philosophical theory of freedom, so far as it addresses the problem of protecting and encouraging freedom, should build upon the best available scientific work concerning the sources of misbeliefs that impair freedom in order to develop a feasible conception of the free individual and the free society. We will now sketch the chief sources of freedom-impairing misbeliefs and then consider the idea that existing philosophies of freedom lack the resources to respond adequately to the risks they pose. In other words, current philosophical theories of freedom are deficient both in their characterization of the virtues of the free individual and the institutional virtues of the free society.

2.1. Normal cognitive biases and limitations

One important source of misbeliefs, including misbeliefs that can make us unfree, is normal cognitive biases: errors of judgment or reasoning that are universal or at least very widely distributed among the population of cognitively normal human beings. The following are examples of normal cognitive biases that have been studied extensively in the empirical psychological literature (Sunstein, 2003).

(1) The availability bias: If a particular event can be easily brought to mind or an image of a particular event is repeatedly encountered, one will tend to overestimate the incidence of that type of event.

(2) The representativeness bias: If one's stereotype of As is that they are Bs, then when confronted with an A one will tend to overestimate the probability that it is a B rather than a C, D, etc. (overlooking base rates for the frequency of As, Bs, Cs, etc.).

(3) Natural kinds essentialist determinism: From a very early age, children tend to divide human beings into groups that are thought of as having distinct essences of a deterministic sort: if individual i is a member of group G, then, due to the essence of Gs, i will behave in such and such a way. Under specific social conditions, the disposition toward this sort of natural kinds essentialist determinism can develop into racism or into ethno-national hatred (Hirschfeld, 1998).

(4) Negative generic overgeneralization: If one believes that one member of a group has committed a dangerous or destructive act, one will tend to assume that all members of that group engage in such acts or will do so if given the opportunity. ((4) may be related to, indeed grounded in, (3), but has been characterized as a distinct cognitive error.)

(5) Confirmation bias: If one believes some hypothesis to be true, one will tend to be alert to apparent confirming evidence and will tend to ignore or discount disconfirming evidence.

(6) Conformity bias: Especially with respect to groups with which one identifies or whose approval one desires, one will tend to revise one's beliefs to conform to those that predominate in the group, without good evidence for the need to do so.

All of these normal cognitive biases, as well as a number of others, can foster misbeliefs that, depending on the contingent circumstances, can interfere with one's doing what one wants and can do so in such a manner as to create a significant discrepancy between what one wills and what one does. All, therefore, can foster misbeliefs that make one unfree. In addition, the human mind has various limitations—we are only able to attend to a rather small number of items at a time, and the speed with which we can process complex information is often inadequate, given the time frame within which we need to judge and act. All of these normal cognitive limitations can, under certain circumstances, result in misbeliefs, including misbeliefs that can undercut freedom.

2.2. Epistemically defective social practices and institutions

There are at least two ways in which institutions and less formal social practices can produce widespread misbeliefs: by encouraging misplaced epistemic trust and, more directly, by facilitating the propagation of misbeliefs. Misplaced epistemic trust occurs when people mistakenly identify others as reliable sources of true beliefs or overestimate the breadth or depth of the expertise of those who are experts or mistakenly believe that those who are experts will sincerely express their expert opinions. Every society has institutions or less formal social practices that foster epistemic norms that encourage people to view certain individuals as experts, as sources of relatively epistemically superior "testimony" (in the broadest sense of that term).

Modern societies have developed complex credentialing processes to facilitate the identification of certain kinds of experts (licensed physicians and other medical personnel, certified public accountants, etc.). Credentials serve as heuristics: when they work well they enable "novices" reliably to identify "experts" on the basis of the latter's membership in a credentialed group, rather than having to try to ascertain in a case-by-case manner whether each claimant to expertise actually possesses it.

However, credentialing can be more or less reliable as a solution to the novice/expert problem: the difficulty that those who lack knowledge in a particular domain have in identifying those who do. During the eugenics movement of the late nineteenth and early to mid-twentieth centuries, people who possessed what were regarded at the time as suitable credentials held and promulgated false beliefs about the hereditary basis of common social problems such as poverty and drunkenness. In addition, there appears to have been a lack of clarity on the part of the public and perhaps of the supposed experts themselves as to where the boundaries of their expertise lay, because these individuals were widely trusted not just with respect to their "testimony" about the facts of heredity, but also with respect to their recommendations for social policies and also their moral judgments. The dissemination of the web of flawed beliefs that characterized eugenics, according to prevailing epistemic norms regarding expertise, produced disastrous results, including direct interference with the reproductive freedoms of those deemed to be carrying dangerous genes (Buchanan, 2007).

Whether people succeed in forming true beliefs depends not only on whether their society provides resources for reliably solving the novice/expert problem but also upon whether people successfully solve the prior threshold problem of ascertaining when they need to consult experts. The epistemic institutions and informal social practices of a society can be flawed, then, because they provide inadequate guidance for solving either the novice/expert problem, the threshold problem, or both. Indeed, the character of prevailing epistemic norms may exacerbate the threshold problem, either by encouraging individuals to overestimate their own cognitive competence and thereby fail to consult experts when they should, or conversely by fostering excessive epistemic deference to supposed experts, thereby leading people to denigrate their own cognitive abilities. One of the largest seismic shifts in views about the proper domain of expertise regarding how human beings ought to live was the Protestant Reformation. Many Christians came to doubt that the Catholic hierarchy's claims of expertise were fully warranted and came to trust their own judgment instead.

2.3. Apparently descriptive concepts that include normative distortions

A third major source of misbeliefs—including beliefs which if acted on can foster and sustain serious injustices—is the uncritical use of concepts which appear to be purely descriptive and morally neutral, but which in fact contain deeply problematic assumptions about how things are or ought to be. Consider, for example, the concept of marriage with which opponents of same-sex marriage operate. According to this concept, marriage is a union of a man and a woman. If one accepts that this concept of marriage is the only genuine one—or to put it differently, if one buys the assertion that any union that is not between a man and a woman is not really marriage—then one may be disposed to reject the idea of same-sex marriage out of hand as being a misuse of the term "marriage" and an instance of conceptual confusion. But of course, when opponents of same-sex marriage say that marriage is a union between a man and a woman, they are not merely making a claim about the proper use of the term "marriage." If that were all there was to it, then the proper reply to them would be to point out that the meanings of terms change. Instead, they are assuming that marriage is valuable and that to extend the term "marriage" to same-sex unions would be to debase the term by using it to cover unions that are unnatural, unwholesome, or at the very least morally inferior to unions between men and women. In other words, they are smuggling in a problematic normative conception of marriage under the guise of a factual claim about what marriage is or a conceptual claim about what "marriage" means (and assuming that there is only one proper meaning for the term). Unless this sleight of hand is exposed, this sort of normative essentialist use of an apparently purely descriptive term can foster misbeliefs, including the mistaken belief that to bar same-sex couples from marriage to one another is not a case of discrimination.

Other instances of misbelief fostered by covertly normative but seemingly descriptive terms are familiar from feminist philosophy. Consider, for example, the term "promiscuous" as it has traditionally been used. When women had sex outside of marriage or when they had multiple sexual partners, they were liable to be labeled promiscuous, even though the same behavior when engaged in by men was not regarded as promiscuous (and in some cases was even considered to be evidence of a form of excellence). Such gender-biased understandings of terms for sexual conduct can lead to false (and inconsistent) beliefs about the wrongness of individuals' behavior and even about their character, and also can reinforce mistaken beliefs about normal female sexuality.

2.4. Self-interested promulgation of false beliefs

We are all too familiar with the fact that some people—indeed all of us at one time or another—have an interest in instilling false beliefs in others. We are also all aware that some individuals act on such interests and deliberately and deftly spread extremely dangerous misbeliefs. To my knowledge, however, the genuinely scientific study of the deliberate promulgation of misbeliefs is not at present as developed as the study of normal cognitive biases. This is not surprising because, in general, normal cognitive biases may be more easily studied in experiments than the much more complex interactions between normal cognitive biases and the actions of deliberate purveyors of misbelief, especially when these interactions are mediated by social practices and institutions.

Nevertheless, we may know enough from common-sense reflection and from qualitative work by historians and sociologists to be able to venture a hypothesis: successful deliberate promulgators of misbeliefs typically utilize a folk psychology of normal cognitive errors and a folk social epistemology. They exploit both normal cognitive biases and epistemically defective social practices and institutions, often artfully fostering a synergistic relationship between them. For example, propagandists for genocide appear to exploit the generic overgeneralization error and the predisposition toward natural kinds essentialist determinism when they manufacture or exaggerate the risks that the targeted group poses; and they do so by co-opting institutions that influence belief, including the press, the educational system, the medical profession, the scientific establishment, and in some cases the churches.

It is well known that the Nazis, who developed the most systematic techniques of genocide, first used various social institutions and the norms of epistemic trust they included to nurture hostility toward the Jews in order to build public support for a policy of mass killing. Then they segregated those to be killed from the general population in concentration camps, stripped them of individual belongings, shaved their heads, forced them to wear uniforms, and subjected them to deprivations and brutality that predictably led to a breakdown of the most basic forms of cooperation within the group. Such treatment was well designed from the standpoint of exploiting the generic overgeneralization error and the predisposition to natural kinds essentialist determinism: it encouraged the perception that the members of the targeted group were indistinguishable from one another, radically different from the group in whose name they were persecuted, and lacking in the rudiments of morality even in their treatment of one another. When people are filthy, crowded together, and fighting for scraps of food it becomes easier to foster the perception that they are beings of a different and morally inferior kind, especially if this belief is endorsed by government officials, doctors, and scientists under conditions in which state control of the media precludes dissent from it.

3. CONCLUSION

Existing philosophical theories of the nature of freedom and the circumstances in which it can flourish are insufficiently attentive to freedom's epistemic conditions, underinformed by relevant work in social epistemology and in the empirical study of normal cognitive biases, and too narrowly focused on only some of the institution and social practices that shape beliefs. Philosophers who theorize freedom should explore the possibility that new political action may be required to nurture and sustain favorable epistemic conditions, even in societies that have already followed the basic liberal prescription for progress: heavy reliance on markets and democratic constitutionalism. Significant countermeasures against freedom-undercutting misbeliefs will almost certainly require new policies and new institutional arrangements. Taking the epistemic conditions of freedom seriously may well require a considerable revision of liberal political philosophies.

NOTES

1. This example is due to Al Mele, via personal communication with Michael McKenna. McKenna suggests that my action may be free under one description ("my pulling out of the driveway") but unfree under another ("smashing a kitten while pulling out of my driveway").

2. Of course, this is all compatible with my action of backing out being free in another sense: it was not coerced, it was not compelled by a drug-induced hallucination, nor by a seizure that caused me to lose control of my arms and legs.

3. This is an accurate description if limited to contemporary Anglophone liberal theory. Contemporary German political philosophers, most notably those influenced by the Frankfurt school of critical theory, have been much more attentive to the problems that ideology poses for freedom.

REFERENCES

Buchanan, A., 2007. Institutions, beliefs, and ethics: eugenics as a case study. *Journal of Political Philosophy*, 15(March), pp.22–45.

Hafer, C. L., and Olson, J. M., 1998. Individual differences in the belief in a just world and responses to personal misfortune. In: L. Montada and M. Lerner, eds. *Responses to victimizations and belief in a just world*. New York: Springer. pp. 65-86.

Hirschfeld, L. A., 1998. *Race in the making: cognition, culture, and the child's construction of human kinds*. Cambridge, MA: MIT Press.

Jervis, R., 1976. *Perception and misperception in international politics*. Princeton, NJ: Princeton University Press.

Katznelson, I., 2013. *Fear itself: the New Deal and the origins of our time*. New York: W.W. Norton & Company.

Kershaw, I., 2007. *Fateful choices: ten decisions that changed the world, 1940–1941*. New York: Penguin.

Lerner, M. J., 1980. *The belief in a just world*. New York: Springer.

Rosen, M., 1996. *On voluntary servitude*. Cambridge, MA: Harvard University Press.

Sunstein, C., 2003. Hazardous heuristics. *The University of Chicago Law Review*, 70(April), pp.751–782.

Index